Understanding Contemporary
LATIN AMERICA

UNDERSTANDING
Introductions to the States and Regions of the Contemporary World

Understanding Contemporary Africa, 6th edition
edited by Peter J. Schraeder

Understanding Contemporary Asia Pacific, 2nd edition
edited by Katherine Palmer Kaup

Understanding the Contemporary Caribbean, 2nd edition
edited by Richard S. Hillman and Thomas J. D'Agostino

Understanding Contemporary China, 5th edition
edited by Robert E. Gamer and Stanley W. Toops

Understanding Contemporary India, 3rd edition
edited by Neil DeVotta and Sumit Ganguly

Understanding Contemporary Latin America, 5th edition
edited by Henry (Chip) Carey

Understanding the Contemporary Middle East, 5th edition
edited by Jillian Schwedler

Understanding Contemporary Russia, 2nd edition
edited by Michael L. Bressler

FIFTH EDITION

Understanding Contemporary

LATIN AMERICA

edited by
Henry (Chip) Carey

LYNNE
RIENNER
PUBLISHERS

BOULDER
LONDON

Published in the United States of America in 2022 by
Lynne Rienner Publishers, Inc.
1800 30th Street, Suite 314, Boulder, Colorado 80301
www.rienner.com

and in the United Kingdom by
Lynne Rienner Publishers, Inc.
Gray's Inn House, 127 Clerkenwell Road, London EC1 5DB
www.eurospanbookstore.com/rienner

Library of Congress Cataloging-in-Publication Data
Names: Carey, Henry F., 1953– editor.
Title: Understanding contemporary Latin America / edited by Henry (Chip)
    Carey.
Description: Fifth edition. | Boulder, Colorado : Lynne Rienner Publishers,
    Inc., 2022. | Series: Understanding | Includes bibliographical
    references and index. | Summary: "An unparalleled introduction to the
    complexities of Latin America today"— Provided by publisher.
Identifiers: LCCN 2021038685 | ISBN 9781626379770 (paperback)
Subjects: LCSH: Latin America
Classification: LCC F1408 .U43 2022 | DDC 980—dc23
LC record available at https://lccn.loc.gov/2021038685

British Cataloguing in Publication Data
A Cataloguing in Publication record for this book
is available from the British Library.

Printed and bound in the United States of America

The paper used in this publication meets the requirements
of the American National Standard for Permanence of
Paper for Printed Library Materials Z39.48-1992.

5 4 3 2 1

Contents

List of Illustrations   ix

1 Introducing Latin America   1
   Henry (Chip) Carey and Stacey M. Mitchell
   Structure of the Book   *6*

2 A Geographic Preface   *Marie Price*   11
   Physical Setting   *14*
   Human Geography of Latin America   *26*

3 The Historical Context   *René De La Pedraja*   39
   The Conquest   *39*
   The Colonial Period   *42*
   Portuguese Brazil   *47*
   The Bourbon Era   *50*
   Independence   *51*
   The Nations of Latin America After Independence   *60*
   The Economy of Latin America, 1820s–1914   *64*
   Politics in Latin America, 1820s–1910s   *69*
   Border Wars in South America   *72*
   Destruction of the Indian Nations   *75*
   Revolutionary Nationalism: The Mexican Revolution   *77*
   The Economy of Latin America, 1914–1990s   *79*
   The Cuban Revolution and Resurgence of
      Revolutionary Nationalism   *81*

The Bureaucratic-Authoritarian Regimes *86*
The Spread of Electoral Democracy *90*

4 **Politics**   *Shelley A. McConnell*   91
Authoritarian Rule *93*
Transitions to Democracy *98*
The Turn to the Left *102*
Citizen Inclusion and Empowerment *109*
Challenges to Democracy *112*
Conclusion *119*

5 **Crime and Security**   *Mark Ungar*   121
The Causes of Crime *122*
State Responses *125*
Persistent and Widespread Crime: Two Cases *136*
Current Policy Responses *138*
Conclusion *142*

6 **Economies**   *Scott G. McKinney*   143
Pre-Columbian Economic Life *144*
The Colonial Period *146*
Independent Latin America *150*
Import Substitution Industrialization *156*
The Oil Shock and the Debt Crisis *166*
Latin America as an Emerging Market *173*
Latin America in the Twenty-First Century *177*
Legacies of the Past and Challenges of the Present *182*

7 **International Relations**   *Cleveland Fraser*   185
Organizing Concepts *190*
Historical Legacies *197*
The Cold War Era *201*
Dependency and Debt *204*
The 1980s *206*
The Post–Cold War Era *209*
The Chimera of US Partnership *216*
Contemporary Topics *219*

8 **Environmental Challenges**
Jacquelyn Chase and Susan E. Place   227
Pre-Columbian Cultures and
    Latin America's Environments *228*

Environmental and Demographic Change
  in the Colonial Era *230*
Independence and the First Neoliberal Era *233*
Globalization and the Environment *234*
Population: Distribution, Fertility, and Mortality *242*
Urbanization in Latin America *249*
Conclusion *256*

9 **Social, Political, and Cultural Identities**
  Kevin A. Yelvington   257
Defining Key Analytic and Theoretical Concepts *259*
Colonial Social Formations and
  the Foundations of Identity Politics *268*
Identity Politics in Independent Latin America *272*
Late Twentieth-Century Developments *276*
The Twenty-First Century: Neoliberal Multiculturalism
  and the Identity Politics of Recognition *284*
Conclusion *294*

10 **The Roles of Women** *Susan Tiano and Michael Shea*   297
Production, Reproduction, and
  Gender Roles and Identities *300*
Women in Latin American History *304*
Women in the Formal Labor Force *311*
Women in Latin American Politics *326*
Conclusion *335*

11 **Education** *Fernando M. Reimers*   337
The First Wave of Globalization: Colonization *338*
The Second Wave of Globalization:
  The Age of Revolutions *339*
The Third Wave of Globalization:
  A World Order Based on Human Rights *344*
The Fourth Wave of Globalization:
  The 1990s to the Present *347*
New Challenges to Education in Latin America:
  Populism and Covid-19 *363*

12 **Religion** *Hannah Stewart-Gambino*   367
The Colonial Role of the Catholic Church *368*
The Role of the Catholic Church in
  Liberal-Conservative Battles *369*

The Modern Catholic Church   *372*
Pope Francis: First Latin American, Jesuit, and
   Non-European Since the Eighth Century   *377*
The Rise of Evangelical Protestantism   *378*
Secularization   *381*
Charismatic Catholics   *384*
Major Spiritist Religions   *386*
Conclusion   *389*

13 The Arts   David H. Bost,
Angélica Lozano-Alonso, and David Marcus   391
The Colonial Heritage   *391*
Poetry and Drama   *397*
The Nineteenth and Twentieth Centuries   *399*
Brazil and the Wider Caribbean   *417*
Popular Culture   *418*
Music   *421*
A Cavalcade of Styles   *433*

14 Looking Forward
Henry (Chip) Carey and Kathleen Barrett   435
The Covid Pandemic   *439*
Environmental Disruption   *442*
Racial and Ethnic Conflict   *444*
Gender Issues   *444*
Corruption   *445*
Largest Challenges   *450*

List of Acronyms   453
Basic Political Data   455
List of Nonindependent Territories   463
References   465
The Contributors   497
Index   499
About the Book   529

Illustrations

Maps

2.1	Latin America: Countries and Capitals	12
2.2	Climates and Vegetation	14
3.1	Eighteenth-Century Colonial Latin America	43
3.2	Early Independence Movements	55
3.3	Later Independence Movements	56
7.1	Boundary Disputes Since Independence	186

Tables

5.1	National and Youth Homicide Rates, Select Countries, 2019	123
6.1	Growth in Manufacturing During the World War II Era, 1938–1945	155
6.2	Capital Flows to the Western Hemisphere, 1977–1994	167
6.3	Impacts of the Debt Crisis on Select Economic Indicators, 1970–1990	169
6.4	Rising Commodity Prices and Economic Growth, 2001–2019	181
8.1	Population of Select Mexican Border Cities, 2005, 2010, and 2019	255
9.1	Ethnogenesis and the Development of Group Categories in Eighteenth-Century New Spain	271
9.2	Afro-Descendant and Indigenous Populations and Percentages	289

9.3   Poverty Rates by Ethnic Group in
       Select Countries, 2003–2011   292
9.4   Inequality by Skin Color Group   293
10.1   Desire and Sexual Identity   303
10.2   Labor Force Participation Rates for
       Working-Age Women and Men, 1960–2020   312
10.3   Female/Male Education Attainment   322
10.4   Changing Values in Latin America   325
11.1   Population Who Completed Some Basic Education,
       Various World Regions, 1870–2010   343
14.1   Governance Indicators, 2019   448
14.2   Ranking and Score on the Human Development
       Index and Select Indicators, 2019   449

Figures

11.1   Increase in Attendance and Completion Rates
       in School, 2000–2018   350
11.2   Attendance Rate by Education Level, 2018   351
11.3   Large Gaps in Upper Secondary Education
       Completion by Wealth, 2014–2018   353

Photographs

Andean agriculture   15
Cowboys in the llanos   18
The ancient Mayan city of Tikal   28
Grand Plaza of Independence, Quito, Ecuador   61
Zocalo Square, Mexico City   64
Bolivians train gun on Paraguayan airplane   74
Feminist protesters demonstrate in Santiago, Chile   101
Evo Morales, former president of Bolivia   107
Student protester in front of anti-Sandinista
    mural in Nicaragua   113
Poll worker records vote totals during Guyana's 2015
    national election   118
Mobile community policing   135
Agricultural terraces   146
Panama City, Panama   174
UN Security Council Chambers   193
Organization of American States, Washington, DC   203
Small family size is the norm in advertisement
    for a pharmacy in Goiânia, Brazil   243

Central pivot agriculture, Goiás, Brazil 250
Trash collector, Goiânia, Brazil 254
Luís Suárez playing for Liverpool 265
Patrice Evra playing for Manchester United 265
Marie Soto and Ixil women celebrate the guilty verdict of
  Ríos Montt for genocide 281
The Pelourinho, a historic neighborhood in
  Salvador, Bahia, Brazil 294
Violeta Barrios de Chamorro receives the
  presidential sash from Daniel Ortega 298
Mariela Castro addressing the Latin American plenary
  of the International Conference on LGBT Human Rights 299
President Michelle Bachelet of Chile 334
Public-private partnership, Alianza Educativa in Colombia 352
Rural school in Mexico 355
Twenty-fifth anniversary of the founding of
  the University of Guadalajara 362
Offerings for Iemanjá, goddess of the ocean 387
An orisha in concrete for ritual purposes 389
The Codex Mendoza 392
Chilean poet and educator Gabriela Mistral 406
Oscar Hijuelos, first Hispanic to win a Pulitzer Prize 415
Heitor Villa-Lobos, Brazil's most prominent
  classical composer 427
Mestre Ferradura conducting Capoeira de Rua 429
Carlos Santana, performing at the Cow Palace,
  San Francisco 433

1

Introducing Latin America

Henry (Chip) Carey and
Stacey M. Mitchell

Latin America is a region that defies easy generalization.
It mixes civilizations from colonizing powers and Indigenous and enslaved peoples with globalized economic, cultural, and political influences to produce one of the most diverse and fascinating areas on the planet.

Two decades into the twenty-first century, the region reflects the dramatic changes of the post–Cold War shift to market-driven economies. Many of Latin America's economies are now functioning better than the debt-driven, state models of the Cold War era. Yet, growing inequality and political delegitimation continue to bedevil many countries attempting new political and economic policies, as they find themselves unable to devise satisfactory replacements for the semisuccessful neoliberal policies of the past. Expectations of Latin America leaving the ranks of the "peripheral world" have not materialized. Massive slums, poverty, corruption, racism, organized crime, gang violence, and state-sanctioned murder continue to plague it.

Latin America has a population of some 600 million. Over a third of that number live in Brazil, and more than a sixth in Mexico. In this book, we are examining Mexico and the countries of Central and South America.

Outsiders unfamiliar with Latin American culture and politics may think first of football (*fútbol* in Spanish, soccer in North America) when they think of the region. Another common perception comes from music and dance: reggaeton, reggae, bachata, salsa, and cumbia. Music represents the richness and mutual symbiosis of the interrelationships of Latin American life, as well as the major influence of the United States, even if in this case it is hip-hop and imported Caribbean and Latin American musical forms that evolved from and then returned to Latin America. So, the next time you hear Shakira sing Colombian cumbia—she was born outside the Colombian Caribbean region in Barranquilla—you are probably listening to an eclectic salad of multiple influences, not only tropical music, but also classical forms and African forms from Brazil and Argentina.

Those living outside Latin America have varying impressions of the continent. Some in North America draw inferences about all Latinos, even when Latino immigrants and their communities are diverse politically, racially, religiously, and in their multiple identities. Some may think of the three world famous Mexican film directors who have achieved success with mainstream Hollywood movies: Alejandro González Iñárritu (*Birdman* and *The Revenant*), Alfonso Cuarón (*Roma, Gravity,* and *Y Tu Mamá También*), and Guillermo del Toro (*Pan's Labyrinth* and *The Shape of Water*). Robert Rodriguez, a US citizen, born to Mexican parents in San Antonio, Texas, has also had a huge impact filming Latino themes for markets outside Latin America, as well as inside it, including *El Mariachi* and two sequels: *Desperado* and *Once upon a Time in Mexico;* together they make up the *Mexico Trilogy.* Rodriguez is a best friend, co-investor, and collaborator of US director Quentin Tarantino. Others would cite the world-class slums, perhaps only rivaled in South and Southeast Asia in size, Brazil's *favelas.*

The metaphor of complex interdependence in music and movies helps our understanding of Latin America and its cultures, including its cuisines. Tacos al pastor are a taco of spit-grilled sliced pork heavily marinated in a combination of cumin, cloves, Guajillo chili peppers, achiote paste, pineapple, and vinegar, and commonly served atop a corn tortilla with a garnish of cilantro, onion, and fresh salsa. It is perhaps Mexico's, and the world's, favorite taco. The history of its origin is almost as deep, and unique, as its flavors. It all starts in the Ottoman Empire with the beginnings of globalization.

In 1869, following the seizure of Egyptian land by British and French colonial powers and a decade of construction by enslaved laborers, the Suez Canal opened. It connected the Mediterranean and Red seas, offering a path of transit between Europe, Africa, and Asia quicker than any before it. The ease of transportation brought on by the Suez Canal enabled the rapid and unprecedented expansion of colonial power by European nations over millions in Africa, Asia, and the Middle East. A primary method of projecting this power was via global commodity markets, which, when dominated by large sellers, contributed to the collapse of small manufacturers.

Mount Lebanon, a historic mountain range in the Levant region of the Middle East, was transformed by these changes. Silk producers in the area could no longer sustain a livelihood in the post-Suez globalized market and, despite their long-standing ties to the region, sought to emigrate. From the 1870s to the 1930s, an estimated 340,000 people emigrated from the Levant westward to the Americas. About 120,000 migrated to the United States and 220,000 to locations throughout Latin America (Khater 2017).

Some of these early migrants moved to Puebla, Mexico, a community just southwest of Mexico City. They, like all immigrants, brought with them customs and practices that they soon introduced to their new home. Among these were shawarma, a traditional Levantine method of cooking meat (usually lamb) on a vertical spit and the equally delicious parent of modern-day al pastor. Vendors, as the story goes, began selling the roasted Middle Eastern lamb on pita bread (*pan árabe* in Spanish) in Puebla, and before long the vertical-broiler method of cooking was applied to pork. Tacos al pastor, thus, were born.

Today, tacos al pastor are a hallmark of Mexican cuisine. Their popularity extends far beyond the country of their birth. Like the processes that made it, they are now enjoyed around the world—perhaps one of the most delicious representations of globalization. The story of tacos al pastor is one of transnationalization, and a story common to the development of food, goods, and technologies all over the world (Khater 2017).

Not all aspects of globalization are positive. With the increase of human contact through travel, migration, and commerce, societies are vulnerable to disease and other environmental factors (or negative externalities, like carbon dioxide emissions). One example of this is the Covid-19 crisis. The most catastrophic initial experience of the coronavirus pandemic in Latin America was in the coastal city of Guayaquil, Ecuador, where there were not enough coffins and burial sites in April 2020, leaving hundreds of rotting bodies on the streets. Moreover, many countries have done poorly because of the continent's crowded housing and working conditions, particularly for those who work in the informal economy, who do not eat if they cannot work on a given day.

What did not help the situation was the prevalence of populism and demagoguery in Latin America (as elsewhere), which allowed policies to be formulated based on emotion and the political interest of the ruler, not rational decisionmaking using scientific expertise. Rulers like Nicolás Maduro of Venezuela, Daniel Ortega of Nicaragua, Andrés Manuel López Obrador of Mexico, and Jair Bolsonaro of Brazil all initially denied or played down the severity of the virus and took no careful measures after the lockdowns. This disregard was followed by failed attempts to expand testing, enforce social distancing and masking, use contact tracing, or require social isolation.

With their high levels of poverty and inequality (ECLAC 2019, Isacson 2020a), Latin American countries were more vulnerable to the pandemic than were wealthier nations. An estimated one-fifth of people in Latin America and the Caribbean had at least one of the health conditions that make someone more susceptible to severe symptoms from Covid-19, as well as being at higher risk of infection. In many countries, more than half of employees work in the informal sector. Working in street and market sales, gardening, and construction generally means earning barely enough to survive. Social distancing at work and home and on buses was nearly impossible. A high percentage of people wore masks in public because they realized that their very lives, and those of whom they contacted, depended on that often homemade protection.

Some countries, like El Salvador in mid-2020, instituted urban patrols to arrest those who were not masked. Brazil and Mexico reopened their economies too quickly, before the virus had been suppressed and before proper testing and tracing infrastructures had been put in place. They faced a surging exponential growth in infections as a result. Countries with more demagogic leaders who politicized public health decisions faced much higher rates of community spread and deaths among their populations. Overall, the vaccination rates in the region were lagging behind the rates in most developed countries. As of September 2021, of the world's then 4.8 million Covid deaths recorded, Brazil had the second highest rate of cumulative deaths, with more than 600,000, compared to more than 700,000 in the United States. Mexico had the fourth highest total deaths in the world (280,000) behind India, and Peru had the sixth in the world at 200,000. Relative to their countries' population, Peru has the worst total in the world, as well as the highest rate in the world of excess deaths regardless of cause of death. The vaccination rates in Latin America lag behind the rates in most developed countries, mostly due to other countries' unwillingness to share their vaccines (Worldometer 2021). The lack of rapid response in Brazil and Mexico, evidenced by the slow pace at which testing was implemented, created near-crisis conditions for the countries. Consequently, Mexico was forced to expand its hospital system in order to receive more patients, hiring thousands of medical professionals.

Another issue related to globalization is that of racial injustice, particularly that involving the official use of force against persons of color. The outrage that followed the murder of George Floyd by a police officer in Minneapolis, Minnesota, was not confined to the United States.

The subsequent Black Lives Matter protests that occurred in the United States spread both countrywide and globally. A similar incident occurred in São Paulo, Brazil. A video surfaced in early July 2020 on a major national television program depicting a military police officer subduing a Black female bar owner in her sixties by standing on her neck, while also breaking her ribs and leg. The governor of the state of São Paulo was outraged and fired the two officers involved. However, in Brazil there was no overwhelming response, as police violence remains a major subtext with strong racial undertones. Brazil's record of police killings of civilians under custody is quite dismal, with an average of seventeen occurring daily in Brazil in 2019 and 6,000 deaths in police actions occurring in 2018 (Ahmed 2019). Seventy-five percent of the victims were Black, a striking overrepresentation given the fact that they compose only about 55 percent of the country's population (Torres 2020).

However, dominant depictions of Brazil held by Brazilians, like the nationalisms of many Latin American countries, promote the image of a post-racial society. The official discourse for many years has been of Brazil as a racial democracy, which ignores much of the economic and social discrimination that actually persists. Protests in Brazil until recently have not raised issues of racial confrontation. Instead, inequalities are often attributed to class differences. Racial injustice is muted. "No one in Brazil is racist" is a common refrain, even though police brutality, especially in the north, where the population of Afro-Brazilians is large, has often occurred in secret and with impunity.

Latin America offers students an opportunity for comparative analysis, not merely between states within the region, but also with other areas of the world. When trying to explain variation in democratic development, for instance, there are a number of focal points for comparison among Latin American countries, including economic growth, colonial rule, multiethnicity, political culture, and institutions of clientelism, all of which can be controlled for—and eliminated—as the actual causes of the variation in democratic development. Controlling for the similarities among these countries allows students to isolate whatever causal factors truly impact democratic development. Factors to consider may include the former colonial power (e.g., Britain versus Spain), the particular model of economic development used (import substitution or neoliberal), or even the particular leadership style of a president like Pinochet of Chile or Lula da Silva of Brazil.

Another interesting and insightful comparison could be made between the southern United States and the countries of Central and South America. They share a colonial past that has had substantial implications for their social and political development, particularly regarding governmental treatment of groups with minority status, African Americans in the case of the United States and Indigenous persons in the case of Latin American countries. Moreover, the southern states in the United States and the countries of Latin America were for centuries agriculturally based economies, almost entirely dependent on forced or enslaved labor. Compared to Africa and Asia, the states of North and South America gained independence from colonial rule far earlier, in the eighteenth and nineteenth centuries. This is not to say that independence from colonial rule was synonymous with the emergence of democracy, an observation that applies equally to the United States and Central and South America. And perhaps further research could focus on why, compared to many other countries, those of Latin America have emerged as a leader in the expansion of human rights and achieving justice, reconciliation, and accountability for past governmental misdeeds.

In many ways, the countries of South America benefited from a long period of liberalization under dictatorships. Central America, by contrast, had long guerrilla insurgencies of the left (El Salvador and Guatemala) and the right (Nicaragua). South American countries increased the rule of law before and especially after the military left power. In countries with higher standards of living, the middle class led public participation in opposition to corrupt and authoritarian regimes, such as in Paraguay, Chile, Uruguay, Bolivia, and Argentina. Chile, which endured authoritarian rule under Pinochet in the 1970s and 1980s, still experienced some limited political liberalization, as well as economic growth under the neoliberal market-based policies pursued by the Pinochet regime.

Structure of the Book

In Chapter 2, Marie Price discusses the vast diversity of the region, which encompasses a wide assortment of landforms (from steep mountain ranges to deserts to vast jungles to one of the longest rivers in the world), as well as animal species, cultures, and peoples. It is a complex region, one that, as Price asserts, does not lend itself well to generalizations. At the same time, she contends that "unity in diversity" exists, exemplified by shared experiences with colonial rule, tropical climate and geography, slavery, and dependence on primary goods like agricultural products or minerals for economic survival. Price demonstrates how the geography and climate of the region influenced (and continues to influence) its development both economically and politically.

Chapter 3, by René De La Pedraja, examines the impact that conquest and colonization of the region had on the twin legacies of political and economic development. Students will gain an appreciation of varied legacies of colonial rule across the countries of Latin America.

In Chapter 4, Shelley McConnell traces the progress of democratic development in the region from the colonial era to the present. McConnell highlights the legacy of colonial rule with regard to the emergence of long periods of dictatorial rule, vast inequalities from wealth consolidation in the upper classes, and a relationship of dependency on Europe and the United States, both economically and militarily. At the same time, she illustrates how the spread of democracy has progressed in Latin America over the past few decades and in some cases has possibly consolidated.

In Chapter 5, Mark Ungar explains that the primary targets of crime in Latin America remain the more vulnerable segments of society: children, the poor, women, and the elderly. Ungar focuses much of his chapter on narcotrafficking and its detrimental impact on the well-being of citizens in the countries involved. Ungar associates the causes of crime in Latin America to inequality, social and economic marginalization, high rates of urbanization, and ready access to firearms—the latter a result of decades of civil wars that brought an influx of weapons into the region.

Turning to economic issues, in Chapter 6, Scott McKinney explains the twists and turns that Latin American countries have experienced in their attempts to develop their economies. At the time of independence, McKinney writes, in the former Spanish colonies, "there was a small elite of creoles, a small middle class, and a large poor class that included most of the mestizos, mulattos, Africans, and Indigenous peoples." The combined effects of wealth consolidation in the hands of the few and a focus on mineral extraction and agriculture made Latin American economies extremely vulnerable to external impacts. McKinney discusses the various policies these countries have used over the years to address this vulnerability, as well as the varying results of their efforts.

In Chapter 7, Cleveland Fraser addresses the relationship of the Latin American countries with the rest of the world and with each other. Fraser outlines the theoretical concepts of international relations and their application to interstate relations within the Latin American region and without, both historically and at present. Like other authors in this text, he emphasizes the point that the past experiences of Latin American countries, including colonialism and US hegemony, continue to influence how they confront global and domestic issues of economic growth, climate change, regional security, migration, crime, and domestic instability.

In Chapter 8, Jacquelyn Chase and Susan E. Place examine the interrelationship between the people of Latin America and the environment. They demonstrate that, from the pre-Columbian period to the present day, the environment increasingly has become overexploited and misused to the detriment of societies within the region and beyond. Likewise, production for a global market and higher rates of urbanization in the region have contributed to a sharp increase in pollution. As McConnell discusses in Chapter 4, Chase and Place note that the expansion of agribusiness and oil and mineral production for the global market has not come without opposition, but that the impact of environmental degradation continues to be most acutely felt by the poor.

In Chapter 9, Kevin Yelvington examines the foundations of group identities and their continued importance in contemporary Latin America. Discourses of "racial" and cultural mixing that typify Latin American nationalisms have had the effect of denying structures of racism that exclude many Indigenous people and Afro-descendants. As Yelvington explains, the current scene is characterized by limited rights being ceded to identity-based movements and groups by the state and ruling sectors as long as they do not present serious challenges to established political and economic regimes by threatening a more widespread redistribution of wealth and power. Yelvington's approach is from the perspective of historical political economy, placing economic structures and relationships centrally as causal forces and tracking their development over time, starting in the colonial period and understanding its enduring legacies.

In Chapter 10, Susan Tiano and Michael Shea demonstrate that women in Latin America are regularly challenging traditional gender-related norms and values. More broadly, exploring the role of women in Latin America across the decades, they highlight the crucial part that women from all walks of life have played in the course of political, social, and economic development.

In Chapter 11, Fernando Reimers looks at education in Latin American countries through the lens of the four waves of globalization that had an impact on who should have access to education and what education's purpose is. Reimer associates the first wave with the European colonization of the region; the second wave with an expansion of the ideas of the Enlightenment; the third wave with the post–World War II period and the creation of the United Nations; and the fourth wave with the post–Cold War era. One consistent factor through all of these waves has been the expansion of educational opportunities. Now, however, Reimer is concerned that the Covid-19 pandemic "will undo much of the progress made in closing gaps in access and learning in the past decade, if not more."

In Chapter 12, Hannah Stewart-Gambino focuses on the important role that the Catholic Church has had and continues to have in the countries of Latin America, often assuming a large role in politics. She characterizes the successful inroads made in recent years by Evangelical churches as creating "an increasingly vibrant religious marketplace." At the same time, Catholicism, while weakened from its once powerful stance as a political and social force, has not left the region. Rather it has weathered Marxism, the rise of Protestantism, brutal dictatorial military regimes, and more to act as an egalitarian institution that seeks to combat economic disenfranchisement and promote human and environmental rights, best exemplified by the work of Latin America's first pope, Jorge Mario Bergoglio, better known as Pope Francis. Students may ask, Will Catholicism, as deeply rooted as it is, one day be replaced as the region's dominant religion by the evangelical Protestant Christian churches?

In Chapter 13, David Bost, Angélica Lozano-Alonso, and David Marcus address the mélange of influences that have had a strong impact on Latin American literature, music, and the arts from the precolonial and colonial periods to the present. As the authors suggest, Latin American literature—from the accounts of the early explorers to contemporary "magical realism"—as well as film, music, and art, reflect and contribute to our understanding of the impact of politics and economics on society.

In the concluding Chapter 14, we (Henry F. Carey and Kathleen Barrett) address the prospects for future growth for the countries of Latin America. Our chapter ties together all of the various themes addressed by the contributors and suggests that the emergence of these countries as global forces remains linked to their pursuit of democracy and equitable economic and social progress.

Note

A thank-you to Rayan Semery-Palumbo, a DPhil candidate at Oxford University, for his contribution of the section above on tacos al pastor.

2

A Geographic Preface

Marie Price

Latin America has been considered a major world region for well over a century. The boundaries of the region are relatively unproblematic. It begins at the Rio Grande (called the Río Bravo in Mexico), includes the Caribbean, and ends at the southern tip of South America. Its shared history of Iberian colonization gives it its social and historical identity. And, as much of Latin America lies within the tropics, its verdant forests, exotic wildlife, and balmy weather distinguish it from the temperate and subarctic climates of North America (see Map 2.1).

The imprint of 300-plus years of Iberian rule is still evident. Roughly two-thirds of the nearly 650 million people who live in the region speak Spanish; most of the rest speak Portuguese. Catholicism is the dominant religion, although as Hannah Stewart-Gambino explains in Chapter 12, African religious practices have a long history and Protestant faiths have made recent inroads.

The Spanish and Portuguese colonizers never referred to the region as Latin America. Various labels, such as "Ibero-America," "the Indies," and "the Americas," have all been used, but "Latin America" was invented by French politicians in the 1860s in an effort to suggest a "Latin" link with the Western Hemisphere. This is what stuck, perhaps because it is vague enough to be inclusive of different colonial histories, but specific enough to distinguish it from Anglo-America or North America (Price and Cooper 2007). During the latter half of the nineteenth century the idea of a "Latin America" gained support among intellectuals in the former Spanish colonies who were grappling with a way to build political and ideological unity among the new republics.

11

Map 2.1   Latin America: Countries and Capitals

They too stressed a distinct "Latin" identity separate from the "Anglo" North (Ardao 1980).

Like all world regions, Latin America is diverse, and generalizations are inherently problematic. Considering the disparate levels of economic development among Latin American countries, as well as their diverse ethnic compositions, it would be easy to emphasize division over commonality. The geographic perspective clearly illustrates unity in diversity. There is little dispute, for example, that the region's human geography was completely reworked with the arrival of Europeans. The population of Indigenous peoples declined by as much as 90 percent during the course of the conquest, but Indigenous peoples remain numerous in many parts of Latin America. Large numbers of enslaved Africans were also added to the cultural mix, and today African culture is notable throughout the Caribbean, Brazil, coastal Venezuela, and Colombia. From the late nineteenth century onward, other immigrant groups arrived, from Italy, Japan, Germany, and India, adding to the cultural complexity of the region. Much of the region is tropical, but there are also grasslands and forest as well as mountains and shields (large upland areas of exposed crystalline rock). The area boasts an impressive array of natural resources, including the planet's largest rainforest, the biggest river by volume, and substantial reserves of natural gas, oil, tin, copper, and lithium.

Since Christopher Columbus's journey more than five centuries ago, Latin America has provided the world with many valuable commodities. The early Spanish Empire concentrated on extracting precious metals, principally silver and gold, from Mexico and the Andes. The Portuguese became prominent producers of sugar products, gold, and eventually coffee. By the late nineteenth and early twentieth centuries, natural resource exports to Europe and North America fueled the region's growing economies. Most countries tended to specialize in one or two commodities: wool and wheat in Argentina, coffee and sugar in Brazil, coffee and bananas in Costa Rica, tin and silver in Bolivia, and oil in Mexico and Venezuela. Although the national economies of Latin America have diversified significantly since the 1950s, they continue to be major producers of primary goods for North America, Europe, and East Asia.

We now turn to the basic demographic and cultural patterns of the region, and will use the concept of the Columbian Exchange as a way to understand the ecological and cultural impact of the New World's encounter with the Old World. Whereas Iberian colonization, imports of African slaves, and later migrations of immigrants from Europe and Asia produced a multiethnic and multiracial society within Latin America, recent decades of emigration out of Latin America and the Caribbean to North America, Europe, and Japan have created complex transnational networks that have diffused Latino culture into other world regions. Recently nearly 5 million Venezuelan refugees have migrated to other South American states. Though every modern Latin American state has a unique and diverse Indigenous and migrant profile, these migratory flows have created commonalities among all of them.

Physical Setting

The movement of tectonic plates explains much of Latin America's basic topography. As the South and North American plates slowly drifted westward, the Nazca, Cocos, and Pacific plates were subducted below them. The submerged plates have folded and uplifted the mainland's surface, creating the geologically young western mountains, such as the Sierra Madre Occidental in Mexico, the highlands of Central America, and the Andes (see Map 2.2).

Map 2.2   Climates and Vegetation

The Andes, the most dramatic of these highland areas, run the length of the South American continent for 5,000 miles, with some thirty peaks reaching over 20,000 feet. Created by the collision of oceanic and continental plates, the Andes are a series of folded and faulted sedimentary rocks with intrusions of volcanic and crystalline rock. Consequently, many rich veins of precious metals and minerals are found there. From Colombia to Chile, mines fueled the early wealth of these Andean territories. Yet the movement of plates also unleashes environmental hazards, such as the 8.8-magnitude earthquake in 2010 that seriously debilitated Chile.

The Andes are typically divided into the northern, central, and southern components. In Colombia, the northern Andes actually split into three distinct mountain ranges before merging near the border with Ecuador. High-altitude plateaus and snow-covered peaks distinguish the central Andes of Ecuador, Peru, and Bolivia, where the Andes reach their greatest width. Between Peru and Bolivia is a treeless high plateau called the altiplano. Averaging 12,000 feet in elevation, it has limited grazing potential but important mineral resources.

The southern Andes are shared by Chile and Argentina. Deep oceanic trenches along the Pacific Coast, such as the Humboldt trench along the coast of Chile and Peru, produce surprisingly cool ocean temperatures for a tropical zone. Much of the contiguous highland region was an

Andean agriculture: Potato and wheat harvest in the Andes of Peru, where Amerindian people first domesticated the potato. Credit: Rob Crandall

important zone of settlement for native peoples, who exploited the diverse ecological niches of the mountains and domesticated a tremendous variety of native crops such as potatoes, hot and sweet peppers, and quinoa (Borsdorf and Stadel 2015).

The Mexican plateau is a massive upland area ringed by the Sierra Madres and tilted so that the highest elevations are in the south—about 8,000 feet near Mexico City and just 4,000 feet at Ciudad Juárez. The southern end of the plateau, known as the Mesa Central, supports Mexico's highest population density, in the cities of Mexico City, Puebla, and Guadalajara. The Mesa Central was historically Mexico's breadbasket, but water shortages due to urbanization and rapid population growth threaten the region's productivity (Ezcurra et al. 1999). During the colonial era the Mexican plateau contained rich seams of silver, the focus of economic activity at that time. Today the Mexican economy is driven more by petroleum and gas production along the Gulf Coast and less by the metals of the plateau.

The Caribbean plate contains most of Central America, the islands of the West Indies, and part of Colombia. As the Caribbean plate moves slowly to the east, it triggers volcanic activity and earthquakes in both the Central American highlands and the islands of the Caribbean. The Central American highlands are composed of a chain of some forty volcanoes that hug the Pacific Coast, stretching from Guatemala to Costa Rica and producing a handsome landscape of rolling green hills, elevated basins with lakes, and conical peaks. The legacy of these volcanoes is fertile soil that yields a variety of domestic and export crops. Most of Central America's 48 million people are concentrated in this zone, in either the capital cities or the surrounding rural villages.

The hazards associated with the movement of the Caribbean plate were plainly evident on January 12, 2010, when a 7.0-magnitude earthquake leveled many of the buildings and severely damaged the infrastructure of the Haitian capital of Port-au-Prince, a metropolitan area of over 2 million people. The tragic event affected nearly 3 million Haitians and resulted in the deathS of over 200,000, making it one of the worst natural disasters in the region's history.

Shields are another important landform of the region. These large rocky outcroppings vary in elevation from 600 to 5,000 feet and are remnants of the ancient landmass of Gondwanaland, which began breaking apart 250 million years ago. Most shields are not noted for their agricultural potential because they lack volcanic and sedimentary soils. The Guiana and Patagonia shields are lightly settled and have limited agricultural potential. The Brazilian shield is the largest and most important in terms of natural resources and settlement. It covers much of Brazil, but in the southeastern portion of the country a series of mountains protrude from the shield. Between these mountains are elevated basins with fertile soils, excellent for agriculture. This is where many Brazilians live, in Brazil's largest cities São Paulo and Rio de Janeiro.

Historically the most important areas of settlement in tropical Latin America were not along the region's major rivers but across its upland plateaus and intermontane basins. In these areas the combination of soils, benign climates, and sufficient rainfall produced Latin America's most productive agricultural areas and its densest settlements. Examples of four such areas are the Brazilian shield, the Mexican plateau, the Central American highlands, and the Andes.

Major River Basins

In contrast to the western highlands, humid lowlands characterize the Atlantic side of Latin America. Across these lowlands meander some of the great rivers of the world, including the Amazon, Plata, and Orinoco. The Amazon, draining some 2.4 million square miles, is the largest river in the world by volume and area and the second longest in length—20 percent of all freshwater discharged into the oceans comes from the Amazon.

More than 60 inches of rain fall each year in the Amazon Basin, and many places receive more than 80 inches. It is home to the largest tropical rainforest in the world and a treasure for genetic diversity. The Brazilian government has plans to build up to thirty new dams in its portion of the Amazon to meet the country's growing energy demands. The most contested of these projects is the Belo Monte Dam on the Xingu River, a tributary of the Amazon. Completed in 2019, it is the world's fourth largest hydroelectric generator.

The Plata Basin begins in the tropics and discharges its water in the mid-latitudes near the city of Buenos Aires. This basin has three major rivers—the Paraná, the Paraguay, and the Uruguay—that drain an area from central Bolivia and southern Brazil to northern Argentina. On the Paraná River is Latin America's largest hydroelectric project, the Itaipu Dam, which produces all of Paraguay's electricity and much of the energy used by industry in southern Brazil. The other great river of the region is the Orinoco of Venezuela and Colombia. Although just one-sixth the size of the Amazon watershed, the Orinoco's discharge roughly equals that of the Mississippi River in the United States.

Within these watersheds are vast lowlands at elevations of less than 600 feet. From north to south they are the *llanos,* the Amazon lowlands, the Pantanal, the Chaco, and the *pampas.* With the exception of the

Cowboys in the llanos: The llanos, or plains, of Venezuela are home to cattle ranches and cowboys. Credit: Rob Crandall

pampas, which is a major center of grain and livestock production, most of these lowlands were sparsely settled and long thought of as static frontiers (open lands unsuitable for permanent settlement).

Areas such as the Chaco and the Amazon have experienced a marked increase in resource extraction in the past thirty years, especially due to the booming soybean market (Hecht 2005). Since the 1970s, the Amazon Basin has witnessed a dramatic increase in population, with over 34 million people settling there and bringing about accelerated levels of timber and mineral extraction as well as ranching and soybean production.

The Mexican and Central American river basins cannot match the scale of the South American ones, but they are important nonetheless. Mexico's Río Bravo (called the Rio Grande in the United States) delimits the boundary between Mexico and Texas. With headwaters in the Sierra Madre Occidental, the Río Bravo and its tributaries carry the snowmelt from the mountains through arid northern Mexico. Dams have been built on some of the watershed's major tributaries to produce electricity and to supply water to cities, towns, and farms. The rise of industrialized border cities, such as Ciudad Juárez, has contributed to the degradation of this watershed.

In tropical Latin America, the daily high temperatures are 70 to 80 degrees Fahrenheit and the daily lows are 60 to 70 degrees. Moreover, the average monthly temperatures in localities such as Managua, Port-au-Prince, and Manaus change little. Precipitation patterns, however, do vary and create distinct wet and dry seasons. In Managua, Nicaragua, January and February are dry months, and June through October are the wettest months. The city of Manaus on the Amazon, however, experiences the reverse. June through August are relatively dry, and the long rainy season extends from October to April.

The tropical lowlands of Latin America are usually classified as tropical humid climates that are covered in either forest or savannah (grassland with few trees), depending on the amount of rainfall. The largest remaining tropical forest is in the Amazon Basin, but much of the perimeter of this forest zone has been converted into pasture or farms. In contrast, much of the tropical forest in the Caribbean and in Central America was removed long ago for agriculture and human settlement, although the conservation area called the Mesoamerican Biological Corridor, spanning seven states and parts of southern Mexico, is important on the Caribbean side of Central America.

There are also major deserts in Latin America. The region's desert climates—which receive less than 10 inches of precipitation a year—are found along the Pacific Coast of Peru and northern Chile, Patagonia, northern Mexico, and northeastern Brazil in an area called the Bahia, or *sertão*. Lima, Peru (a city of 10 million), is in the tropics but averages only 1.5 inches of rainfall per year due to the hyperaridity of the Peruvian coast. The vulnerability of this megacity was driven home in March 2017 when mudslides severely damaged the main water treatment facility in the city, cutting off water to several million people for three to six days. There are parts of the Atacama Desert in northern Chile that have never recorded rainfall, giving this desert the distinction of being the world's driest. Such an inhospitable climate, however, hosts a rich assortment of phosphates, copper, and lithium; resources from the Atacama still buttress the Chilean economy.

Not all of Latin America is tropical. In the Southern Cone states, mid-latitude climates with hot summers and cold winters prevail. Of course, the mid-latitude temperature shifts in the Southern Hemisphere are the inverse of those in the Northern Hemisphere (cold Julys and warm Januarys). In the mountain ranges, complex climate patterns result, so that elevation becomes more critical than latitude.

The *tierra templada* (temperate lands), at 3,000–6,000 feet elevation in the tropics, have been described as having an eternal springtime climate of warm days and pleasant nights. The *tierra fría* (colder lands) of the tropics are found at 6,000–12,000 feet. These tropical highlands support agriculture such as wheat, tubers, and even maize, but the daytime highs are cool and the lows can reach freezing. These normal climate patterns and the human ecological systems they support are periodically disrupted by weather events that can dramatically impact Latin America. Three of these that deserve attention are hurricanes, El Niño, and global warming.

Several hurricanes form each season, and the worst ones can devastate communities and agriculture in the Caribbean, Central America, Mexico, and North America (South America is outside of the hurricane belt). Beginning in July, westward-moving low-pressure disturbances form off the coast of West Africa, picking up moisture and speed as they move across the Atlantic. The air masses are usually no more than 100 miles across but occasionally achieve hurricane status with wind velocities of more than 74 miles per hour. Typically, six to twelve hurricanes move through the region, causing limited damage. There are exceptions, however, and most longtime residents of northern Latin America have experienced the full force of at least one major hurricane in their lifetime.

Back-to-back hurricanes (Irma and Maria) in September 2017 devastated the northeastern Caribbean. Irma, a Category 5 storm with sustained winds of 175 miles per hour, hit Puerto Rico, Hispaniola, Cuba, and the Bahamas before striking the Florida Keys. Days later, Hurricane Maria, another Category 5 hurricane, slammed into Dominica, inflicting damage to nearly every structure on the island. By the time it hit Puerto Rico, it had slowed to a Category 4 hurricane with sustained winds of 155 miles per hour, but it was still the strongest hurricane to directly hit the island in eighty years. The storm destroyed homes, bridges, roads, and crops, and knocked out electricity across the entire island of 3 million-plus. Then in 2020, during the height of the Covid-19 pandemic, two Category 4 hurricanes, Eta and Iota, made landfall in Central America in a two-week period. Honduras was especially hard-hit with deaths caused by landslides and flooding, but infrastructure, crops, and homes were affected throughout Central America.

The most studied weather phenomenon in Latin America is El Niño (a reference to the Christ child). It is a warm Pacific current that usually arrives off the coast of Ecuador and Peru in December. Every decade or so, an abnormally large current arrives that produces torrential rains, signaling the arrival of an El Niño year. The 2015–2016 El Niño was a major event for Latin America. In the Plata Basin, heavy rains in December and January caused the worst flooding in fifty years and displaced more than 200,000 people.

El Niño has another, less discussed aspect. While parts of South America experienced record rainfall in 2015–2016, northern Brazil and Guatemala, Honduras, Nicaragua, and El Salvador were affected by one of the worst droughts in decades. In addition to crop and livestock losses, some 3.5 million rural people in Central America faced food shortages.

Modern tracking equipment has improved hurricane forecasting and reduced the number of fatalities, but experts fear that storms of such magnitude may become a more regular occurrence as a result of climate change. A growing body of evidence suggests that global warming will have immediate and long-term implications for the region. Of greatest immediate concern is how a changing climate will influence agricultural productivity, water availability, changes in the composition and productivity of ecosystems, and the incidence of vector-borne diseases such as malaria and dengue fever.

Changes attributed to global warming are already apparent in high-elevation regions. Tropical mountain systems are projected to experience increased temperatures of 2 to 6 degrees Fahrenheit (1 to 3 degrees Celsius) as well as less rainfall. Research has documented the dramatic retreat of Andean glaciers; some no longer exist, such as Chacaltaya in Bolivia, and others have been drastically reduced. Many Andean villages, as well as metropolitan areas such as La Paz, get much of their water from glacial runoff, but as average temperatures increase in the highlands and glaciers recede, localized concerns about future water supplies will accelerate (IPCC 2014).

One of the long-term effects of global warming is sea-level rise. This is a major concern for low-lying coastal areas and the Caribbean. The scientific consensus is that global warming could promote a sea-level rise of 3 to 10 feet (1 to 3 meters) in the twenty-first century. In terms of land loss due to inundation, the Bahamas would be the most impacted country—losing over 30 percent of its land with a 10-foot sea-level rise. Mainland states such as Guyana, Suriname, French Guiana, and Belize are also extremely vulnerable to sea level rise (IPCC 2014).

Environmental Issues

Given Latin America's immense size and relatively low population density, it has not experienced the same levels of environmental degradation witnessed in other parts of the world, such as East Asia. The worst environmental problems are found in cities, their surrounding rivers and coasts, and zones of intense farming (Roberts and Thanos 2003). Vast areas of Latin America remain relatively untouched, supporting an incredible diversity of plant and animal life. National parks throughout

Latin America offer some protection to unique communities of plants and animals. A growing environmental social movement in countries such as Costa Rica, Brazil, and Guyana has provided popular support for environmentally friendly initiatives. According to World Bank estimates, about one-fifth of the Latin American territories are in some form of protected status. It can be argued that Latin America entered the twenty-first century with a real opportunity to avoid many of the environmental missteps seen in other regions of the world, but economic pressures brought about by global market forces are driving governments to exploit their natural resources (minerals, fossil fuels, forests, and soils) aggressively (Bebbington and Bury 2014).

Managing the region's immense natural resources and balancing the economic benefits of extraction with the ecological soundness of conservation are huge challenges. Of the many environmental challenges facing the region, three of the most pernicious are deforestation, degradation of arable lands, and urban environmental pollution.

Due to international interest in tropical forests, deforestation is probably the environmental issue most often associated with the region. The Amazon Basin and portions of the eastern lowlands of Central America and Mexico still maintain important stands of tropical forest. Other areas, such as the Atlantic coastal forest of Brazil and the Pacific forests of Central America, have nearly disappeared because of agricultural use, settlement, and ranching. Likewise, extensive forest clearing for sugar plantations in the Lesser Antilles has nearly eliminated all of the tropical forest over the past two centuries. The coniferous forests of northern Mexico are also being cut down, in part because of the boom in commercial logging stimulated by the North American Free Trade Agreement (NAFTA).

In terms of biological diversity, however, the loss of tropical rainforest is the most critical. Tropical rainforests account for only 6 percent of Earth's landmass, but at least 50 percent of the world's species are found there. Moreover, the Amazon contains the largest undisturbed stretches of rainforest in the world. Over the past four decades, the region's tropical forests were seen as agricultural frontiers that governments opened up in an attempt to appease landless peasants and reward political cronies. The forests fell as colonists created farms and large cattle ranches (Hecht and Cockburn 1989). Forest clearing also occurred due to the search for gold in Brazil, Venezuela, Costa Rica, and Guyana and the production of coca leaf for cocaine in Peru, Bolivia, and Colombia (Young 1996) as well as from logging concessions.

Soil erosion and fertility decline occur in all agricultural areas. Certain soil types in Latin America are particularly vulnerable to erosion, most notably the volcanic soils and the reddish oxisols found in the humid lowlands. The productivity of the volcanic highlands of Central America, for example, has declined over the decades, due to the ease with which these soils erode and the failure to apply soil conservation measures in many localities. The oxisols of the tropical lowlands, by contrast, can quickly erode into a baked claypan surface when the natural vegetative cover is removed, making permanent agriculture nearly impossible. Ironically, the consolidation of large, modern farms in the valleys tends to push subsistence farmers into marginal areas on steep slopes. On these hillside farms, gullies and landslides are a constant threat to rural livelihoods.

The reality of poverty forcing people to degrade their environment is evident in many rural places in Latin America. Nowhere is this connection clearer than in Haiti. The inhabitants of this densely settled country are largely dependent on commercial and subsistence agriculture, which has resulted in serious problems with soil erosion and declining yields. In addition, the majority of Haitians rely on charcoal (made from trees) for their cooking fuel, which places additional strain on the island's vegetation. The deterioration of the resource base is evident from the air: aerial photos reveal a sharp boundary between a denuded Haiti and a forested Dominican Republic. The difference between the two countries is explained, in part, by the lack of affordable fuel alternatives. Whereas many Dominicans can afford to buy liquid or gas cooking fuel, many Haitians cannot.

Because the vast majority of Latin Americans live in cities, it has become increasingly clear that the environmental quality of urban settings has been a focus for local activism. While Jacquelyn Chase and Susan Place discuss urban environmental issues at some length in Chapter 8, it is important to recognize here that many of Latin America's environmentalists worry more about ways to make urban environments cleaner rather than about the future of distant tropical forests. In Rio de Janeiro and São Paulo alone, hundreds of local environmental organizations have pushed for cleaner air, better water, and more green space (Christen et al. 1998).

Despite serious urban environmental issues, people in Latin American cities tend to have better access to water, sewers, and electricity than their counterparts in Asia and Africa. Moreover, the density of urban settlement encourages the widespread use of mass transportation—both public and private bus and van routes make getting around most cities fairly easy. The largest cities, such as São Paulo, Mexico City, Buenos Aires, and Caracas, have subway systems. Increasingly, cost-effective high-speed bus systems, as found in Curitiba and Bogotá, are gaining popularity. Yet the inevitable environmental problems that come with primate (dominant or major) cities that grew rapidly and have widespread poverty cannot be overstated. Improvements to sewer systems, waste disposal, and water treatment plants are expensive. Chronic air pollution has caused debilitating health effects, most notably in Santiago and Mexico City. The money to clean up cities is always in short supply, especially with problems of foreign debt, currency devaluation, and inflation. And because many urban dwellers tend to reside in unplanned squatter settlements, retroactively servicing these communities with utilities is difficult and costly.

A Bounty of Natural Resources

Historically, Latin America's abundant natural resources were its wealth. In the colonial period, silver, gold, and sugar generated fortunes for a privileged few. In the latter half of the nineteenth century, a series of export booms introduced commodities such as bananas, coffee, cacao, grains, tin, rubber, copper, wool, and petroleum to an expanding world market. One of the legacies of this export-led development was the tendency to specialize in one or two major commodities, a pattern that continued well into the mid-twentieth century. For example, in the 1950s, Costa Rica earned 90 percent of its export earnings from bananas and coffee, El Salvador earned over 90 percent from coffee and cotton, 85 percent of Chilean exports came from copper, and half of Uruguay's export earnings came from wood (Wilkie 1997). Even Brazil, the region's largest country, generated 60 percent of its export earnings from coffee in 1955. While Brazil continues to rank as the world's leader in coffee exports, the country's economy has experienced tremendous growth and diversification during the past decade. As a result, coffee remains a significant, though minor, export commodity.

The trend throughout Latin America has been to diversify and mechanize resource extraction, especially in agriculture and mining. Nowhere is this more evident than in the Plata Basin, which includes southern Brazil, Uruguay, northern Argentina, Paraguay, and eastern Bolivia. Soybeans, used for oil and animal feed, transformed these lowlands beginning in the 1980s. Brazil is now the second largest producer of soy in the world (following the United States) and the world's largest exporter. Argentina is the third largest, and production is still increasing: between the late 1990s and 2010, soy production tripled. Added to this crop are acres of rice, cotton, and orange groves; the more traditional plantings of wheat and sugar; and livestock. In northern Mexico, water supplied from dams along the Sierra Madre Occidental has turned the valleys in Sinaloa into an intensive production zone for fruits and vegetables bound for the United States. An explosion of so-called non-traditional agricultural exports is reshaping activities in rural areas—from melons and shrimp in Honduras, to flowers and ferns in Costa Rica and Colombia, to grapes, berries and plums in Chile.

In each of these cases, the agricultural sector is capital-intensive and dynamic. By using machinery, high-yielding hybrids, chemical fertilizers, and pesticides, many corporate farms have become extremely productive and profitable. What these operations fail to do is employ many rural people, which is especially problematic in countries where one-third of the population depend on agriculture for their livelihood. Interestingly, a few traditional Amerindian foods, such as quinoa, are gaining consumers thanks to a growing appetite for organic and healthful foods. Peru, Bolivia, and Ecuador have experienced a recent boom in quinoa production and exports, with much of the crop being grown on small and medium-sized farms.

Mining and fossil fuels continue to shape the economies of several countries in the region. Many commodity prices reached record levels in the past decade, boosting foreign exchange earnings, but prices began to fall in 2013 and have yet to fully recover. Oil-rich Mexico, Ecuador, and now Brazil are able to meet their own fuel needs and to earn vital state revenues from oil exports. Venezuela, one of the countries most dependent on oil revenues, saw its production decline by 80 percent from 2015 to 2020 as the country fell into spiraling political and economic turmoil. Venezuela has the world's largest known oil reserves, but the country currently lacks the technology, capital, and the skilled labor to turn its oil industry around.

Besides oil, Latin America's other important exports are silver, zinc, copper, iron ore, bauxite, gold, and lithium. Chile is the world leader in copper production, far surpassing the next two largest producers, Peru and the United States. Mexico and Peru were the top silver producers in 2015, but Chile and Bolivia were also top-ten producers. Peru was also Latin America's top gold producer, followed by Mexico. Half the world's known reserves of lithium are high in the Andes where Bolivia, Argentina, and Chile meet. This soft silver-white metal is an essential element in lightweight batteries, like those that power cell phones, computer laptops, electric cars, and photovoltaic cells. So far Chile is the leader in extracting and exporting this metal, followed by Argentina. Bolivia, which may have the largest reserves, is still engaged in artisan production techniques and has yet to become a major producer of lithium.

Human Geography of Latin America

Today, 650 million people live in Latin America. This is a striking figure when one considers that in 1950, Latin America was home to 150 million people, which equaled the population of the United States at that time. Now, Latin America's population is double that of the United States. Like the rest of the developing world, Latin America experienced dramatic population growth in the 1960s and 1970s. It outpaced the United States because infant mortality rates declined and life expectancy soared. In 1950, Brazilian life expectancy was only forty-three years; by the 1980s it was sixty-three years; and by 2020 it was seventy-six years. Today, the average life expectancy for the entire region is seventy-six years, compared to seventy-nine for the United States. Four countries account for two-thirds of the region's population: Brazil, with 212 million; Mexico, 128 million; Colombia, 49 million; and Argentina, 45 million (Population Reference Bureau 2020).

During the 1980s, population growth rates suddenly began to slow. The region is still growing, but at a slower pace of 1 percent annually. In the 1960s, a typical Latin American woman had six or seven children. By the 1980s, the average woman had three children, and today the average is two children. A number of factors explain this, including more urban families, which tend to be smaller than rural ones; increased participation of women in the work force; higher education levels of women; and state support of family planning and better access to birth control (Population Reference Bureau 2020).

The distribution of population away from rural areas and into cities is the other major demographic change for the region. A staggering 79 percent of Latin Americans live in cities, which is a rate comparable to Europe and North America. This makes Latin America the most urbanized region within the developing world. The cities in the region are noted for high levels of urban primacy, a condition in which a country has a primary city that is three to four times larger than any other city in the country. Examples of primary cities are Lima, Caracas, Guatemala City, Havana, Santo Domingo, Buenos Aires, Mexico City, and Santiago. In Brazil and Ecuador, two cities dominate all others in the country in terms of size and economic importance: Guayaquil and Quito in Ecuador and São Paulo and Rio de Janeiro in Brazil are examples of dual primacy. Primacy is often viewed as a liability, because too many national resources are concentrated into one urban center. In order to appreciate the magnitude of population growth and the dominance of cities, it is important to address the demographic consequences of Iberian conquest in the Americas.

Conquest and Settlement

The Iberian colonial experience imposed a political and cultural coherence on Latin America that makes it a distinguishable region today. Yet this was not an uncontested transplanting of Iberia across the Atlantic. As a result of the papal-decreed Treaty of Tordesillas in 1493, Spain received the majority of the Americas, and Portugal received a small portion of eastern South America that eventually became Brazil. Through the course of colonization, Spain shifted its attention to the mainland colonies, centered on Mexico and Peru. This left the Caribbean and the Guianas vulnerable to other European powers, most notably England, France, and the Netherlands, and each of these countries established colonies.

Nevertheless, Spain was able to conquer and administer an enormous territory in less than a hundred years. The prevailing strategy was one of forced assimilation, in which Iberian religion, language, and political organization were imposed on the surviving fragments of native society. In some areas, such as southern Mexico, Guatemala, Bolivia, and Peru, native cultures have shown remarkable resilience, as evidenced by the survival of native languages—Maya, Quechua, Aymara, and Guaraní. Later, other European, African, and Asian peoples, arriving as both forced and voluntary migrants, were added to the region's cultural mix. Yet perhaps the single most important factor in the dominance of Iberian culture in Latin America was the demographic collapse of native populations in the first 150 years of settlement.

Native Population Decline

It is hard to grasp the enormity of human and cultural loss due to this cataclysmic encounter between Europe and the Americas. Throughout the region, archaeological sites are poignant reminders of the complexity of precontact (i.e., pre–European arrival) civilizations (Mann 2006). Dozens of stone temples, such as Tikal, attest to how Mayan and Aztec civilizations flourished in the tropical forests and upland plateaus of Mexico and Central America.

In the Andes, farmers still use stone terraces built by the Incas; earthen platforms for village sites and raised fields for agriculture are still being discovered and mapped. Ceremonial centers, such as Cuzco (the center of the great Incan Empire), and hundreds of miles of Incan roads are evidence of the complexity of Amerindian networks. The Spanish, too, were impressed by the sophistication and wealth they saw around them, especially in the incomparable Tenochtitlán, where Mexico City sits today. Tenochtitlán was the political and ceremonial center

The ancient Mayan city of Tikal was abandoned over a thousand years ago. Today tourists from around the world visit this Guatemalan treasure to marvel at the many stone temples. Credit: Rob Crandall

of the Aztecs, supporting a complex metropolitan area with some 300,000 residents. By comparison, the largest city in Spain at the time was considerably smaller.

The most telling figures of the impact of Iberian expansion are demographic. It is widely believed that precontact America (the Western Hemisphere) had 54 million inhabitants; in comparison, Western Europe in 1500 had a population of 42 million. Of the 54 million people, about 50 million lived in Latin America and the Caribbean (Denevan 1992). There were two major population centers: one in central Mexico, with 14 million people, and the other in the central Andes (highland Peru and Bolivia), with nearly 12 million. Nearly all of the estimated 3 million Indigenous peoples who inhabited the islands of the Caribbean were gone within fifty years of contact with Europeans. Even the vast Amazon Basin was not uninhabited, as is often portrayed, but home to over 5 million Amerindians. By 1650, after 150 years of colonization, the Indigenous population was one-tenth its precontact size. The relentless elimination of 90 percent of the Indigenous population was largely caused by epidemics of influenza and smallpox; however, warfare, forced labor, and starvation due to a collapse of food production systems also contributed to the death rate.

The tragedy of conquest did not end in 1650, the population low point for Indigenous peoples, but continued throughout the colonial period and, to a much lesser extent, continues today. Even after the Indigenous population began its slow recovery in the central Andes and central Mexico, there were small tribal bands in southern Chile (the Mapuche) and Patagonia (Araucania) who experienced the ravages of disease three centuries after Columbus landed. Even now, the isolation of some Amazonian tribes has made them vulnerable to disease.

At present, Mexico, Guatemala, Ecuador, Peru, and Bolivia have the largest Indigenous populations. Not surprisingly, these are the areas that had the densest native populations at contact. Indigenous survival occurs in isolated settings where the workings of national and global economies are slow to penetrate.

In many cases, Indian survival comes down to one key resource—land. Indigenous peoples who are able to maintain a territorial home, formally through land title or informally through long-term occupancy, are more likely to preserve a distinct ethnic identity. Because of this close association between identity and territory, native peoples are increasingly insisting on a recognized space in their countries. Indigenous groups such as the Miskito of Honduras and the Guna of Panama have asserted local authority over their lands and have limited autonomy (Herlihy and Tappan 2019).

The Columbian Exchange

Historian Alfred Crosby (1972) likens the contact period between Europe, Africa, and Asia (Old World) and the Americas (New World) to an immense biological swap, which he calls the Columbian Exchange. According to Crosby, Europeans benefited greatly from this exchange, and native peoples suffered terribly from it, most notably through the introduction of disease. The human ecology of both sides of the Atlantic, however, was forever changed through the introduction of new diseases, peoples, plants, and animals. Take, for example, the introduction of Old World crops. The Spanish, naturally, brought their staples of wheat, olives, and grapes to plant in the Americas. Wheat did surprisingly well in the highland tropics and became a widely consumed grain over time. Grapes and olive trees did not fare so well; eventually, grapes were produced commercially in the temperate zones of South America. The Spanish grew to appreciate the domestication skills of native agriculturalists who had developed valuable starch crops such as corn, potatoes, and bitter manioc as well as exotic condiments such as hot peppers, tomatoes, pineapple, cacao, and avocados.

Tropical crops transferred from Asia and Africa reconfigured the economic potential of Latin America. Sugarcane became the dominant cash crop of the Caribbean and the Atlantic tropical lowlands of South America. With labor-intensive sugar production came the importation of millions of African slaves. Domesticated varieties of rice, yams, sorghum, millet, and plantains were brought from Africa in slave ships and became dietary staples throughout the region (Carney and Rosomoff 2009). Coffee, a later transfer from East Africa, emerged as one of the leading export crops throughout Central America, Colombia, Venezuela, and Brazil in the nineteenth century. And pasture grasses introduced from Africa as well as some varieties of cattle enhanced the forage available and the varieties of livestock.

The movement of Old World animals across the Atlantic had a profound impact on the Americas. Initially, these animals hastened Indigenous decline by introducing animal-borne diseases and by producing feral offspring that consumed everything in their path. Over time, native survivors appreciated the utility of Old World animals. Draft animals were adopted, and so too was the plow, which facilitated the preparation of soil for planting. Wool became an important fiber for Indigenous communities in the uplands. And slowly, pork, chicken, and eggs added protein and diversity to the staple diets of corn, potatoes, and cassava. With the major exception of disease, many transfers of plants and animals ultimately benefited both sides of the Atlantic. Still, it is clear that the ecological and material basis for life in Latin America was completely reworked through this exchange process initiated by Columbus.

Re-Peopling the Americas

The dramatic and relatively rapid decline of native peoples simplified colonization in some ways. Spain and Portugal were able to refashion Latin America into a European likeness. And as rival European nations vied for power in the Caribbean in the mid-sixteenth century, the islands they fought over were nearly uninhabited. Yet instead of creating a tropical neo-Europe, a complex ethnic blend evolved. Beginning with the first years of contact, unions between European men and native women began the process of racial mixing that became a defining feature of the region over time. The Iberian courts officially discouraged racial mixing, but not much could be done about it. Spain became obsessed with the matter of race and of maintaining racial purity in its colonies, which had a far larger native population than the Portuguese colony of Brazil. Yet after generations of intermarriage, four broad categories resulted: blanco (European ancestry), mestizo (mixed ancestry), indio

(Amerindian ancestry), and negro (African ancestry). The blancos are still well represented among the elites, yet the vast majority of the people are of mixed racial ancestry.

For the Caribbean islands and the Atlantic Coast of South America, the scarcity of Indigenous labor hastened the development of the transatlantic slave trade. Beginning in the sixteenth century and lasting until the nineteenth, at least 10 million Africans landed in the Americas and an estimated 2 million perished en route. Nearly two-thirds of all enslaved Africans were first sent to the islands of the Caribbean and Brazil, creating a neo-Africa in the Americas (Curtin 1969). In absolute numbers, more Africans landed in Latin America than Europeans in the first three centuries after contact. Yet because Africans were brought in as slaves, their survival rates and life expectancy were much lower than those of Europeans, which undermined their overall demographic impact (Sánchez-Albornoz 1974).

Of course, Africans resisted enslavement. Communities of runaway slaves—called maroons in English, *palenques* in Spanish, and *quilombos* in Portuguese—offer important examples of African resistance and cultural diffusion throughout Latin America. Hidden settlements of escaped slaves existed wherever slavery was practiced. While many of these settlements were short-lived, others have endured and allowed for the survival of African traditions, especially farming practices, house designs, community organization, and language.

Whereas other maroon societies gradually blended into local populations, to this day the Suriname maroons, the largest maroon population in the Western Hemisphere, maintain a distinct identity. These runaways fled the Dutch coastal plantations in the seventeenth and eighteenth centuries, forming settlements along rivers amid the interior rainforest. Six distinct maroon tribes formed, ranging in size from a few hundred to 20,000 people. Clear connections to West African cultural traditions persist, including religious practices, crafts, patterns of social organization, agricultural systems, and even dress. Living relatively undisturbed for 200 years, these rainforest inhabitants fashioned a rich ritual life for themselves, involving oracles, spirit possession, and shamans (Price 1996).

More recently, pressures to modernize and extract resources have placed the maroons in direct conflict with the state and private investors. The maroons in Suriname have been directly affected by the construction of dams, gold-mining operations, and logging concessions. From 1986 until 1992, a civil war raged between the maroons and the Creole-run military, in which hundreds of maroons were killed and villages were destroyed. Although peace was brokered in 1992, the maroons continue to fight for legal recognition of ancestral claims to land and resources.

When much of Latin America gained its independence in the early nineteenth century, the new leaders of the region sought to develop their territories through immigration. Firmly believing in the dictum "to govern is to populate," many countries set up immigration offices in Europe to attract hardworking peasants to till the land and "whiten" the mestizo population. Argentina, Chile, Uruguay, southern Brazil, and Cuba were the most successful in attracting European immigrants from the 1870s until the Great Depression of the 1930s. During this period, some 8 million Europeans arrived (more than during the entire colonial period), with Italians, Portuguese, Spaniards, and Germans being the most numerous. Some of this immigration was state-sponsored, such as the nearly 1 million laborers (including entire families) brought to the coffee estates surrounding São Paulo at the turn of the century. Still others paid their own passage, intending to settle permanently and prosper in the growing commercial centers of Buenos Aires, São Paulo, Montevideo, and Santiago.

Less known are the Asian immigrants who arrived during this same period. Although considerably fewer in number, they established an important presence in the large cities of Brazil, Peru, and Paraguay, as well as throughout Guyana, Suriname, and Trinidad. Beginning in the mid-nineteenth century, most of the Chinese and Japanese who settled in Latin America were contracted laborers brought in to work on the coffee estates in southern Brazil and the sugar estates and guano (waste from seafowl used as fertilizer) mines of Peru. The Japanese in Brazil are the most studied Asian immigrant group. Between 1908 and 1978, a quarter million Japanese immigrated to Brazil; today the country is home to 1.3 million people of Japanese descent. Initially, most Japanese were landless laborers, yet by the 1940s they had accumulated enough capital so that three-quarters of the migrants had their own land in the peripheral areas of São Paulo and Paraná states. Increasingly, second- and third-generation Japanese have taken professional and commercial jobs in Brazilian cities; many of them have married outside their ethnic group and are losing their fluency in Japanese. South America's economic turmoil in the 1990s resulted in many ethnic Japanese emigrating to Japan in search of better opportunities. Nearly a quarter of a million ethnic Japanese left South America in the 1990s (mostly from Brazil and Peru) and now reside in Japan (Kent 2006).

In the Caribbean, owners of sugar estates who feared labor shortages with the abolition of slavery in the nineteenth century sought indentured labor from South and Southeast Asia. Because Guyana and Trinidad were British colonies, most of the contract labor came from India. Today, half of Guyana's population and 40 percent of Trinidad's claim South Asian ancestry. Hindu temples are found in the cities and villages, and many families speak Hindi in their homes. In Suriname, a former Dutch colony, more than one-third of the population is South Asian, and 16 percent are Javanese (from Indonesia).

Emigration and Transnational Networks
Movement within Latin America and between Latin America and North America has had a significant impact on Latino settlement patterns. Within Latin America, shifting economic and political realities have shaped immigrants' destinations. Venezuela's oil wealth, especially during the 1960s and 1970s, attracted between 1 and 2 million Colombian immigrants, who worked as domestic or agricultural laborers. Argentina has long been a destination for Bolivian and Paraguayan laborers. And sugar plantations in the Dominican Republic have relied on Haitian labor, just as farmers in the United States have depended on Mexican laborers. Political turmoil has also sparked waves of international migrants and refugees, such as the Cuban flight from Fidel Castro in the 1960s, the Chilean exodus during General Augusto Pinochet's reign in the 1970s, and the civil war in El Salvador in the 1980s. Today the largest exodus in the region is from Venezuela, where an estimated 5 million people have left the economic shortages and political turmoil of the country in the past decade. The vast majority of these displaced people are settling in Colombia, Peru, Ecuador, and Chile according to the United Nations. This makes Venezuela the most serious humanitarian crisis in the Americas.

Violence in northern Central America, the "Triangle" countries of El Salvador, Guatemala, and Honduras, is again driving people toward Mexico and the United States. In 2014, 2016, and 2021 there were spikes in the numbers of unaccompanied minors from these states crossing into the United States and turning themselves over to authorities as they sought to reunite with family in the United States and to find refuge from gang-driven violence that has produced some of the highest homicide rates in the world. Although some of these youth were able to seek asylum status, many were returned to Central America.

Most Hispanics (also called Latinos or Latinx) in the United States have ancestral ties with peoples from Latin America and the Caribbean. Presently, Mexico is the country of origin for most documented Hispanic immigrants to the United States; two-thirds of the 58 million Hispanics in the United States claim Mexican ancestry, including approximately 12 million who were born in Mexico. Mexican labor migration to the United States dates back to the late 1800s, when relatively unskilled labor was recruited to work in agriculture, mining, and railroads. Although Mexicans continue to have the greatest presence among Latinos in the United States, the number of migrants from El Salvador, Guatemala, Honduras, Nicaragua, Colombia, Ecuador, and Brazil grew steadily in the 1990s and 2000s.

Migrant flows from Mexico, in contrast, have declined sharply since 2010. As the United States–Mexico border becomes harder and more costly to cross, and deportations become more likely, potential migrants are seeking new destinations or staying in their countries of origin. Mexico's net migration rate is near zero, which means the number of people arriving in the country is canceling out the number leaving.

Today, Latin America is both a region of emigration and a region that supports an intensification of migration within the region—especially with the large Venezuelan exodus. Both skilled and unskilled workers from Latin America are an important source of labor in North America, Europe, and Japan. Many of these immigrants send monthly remittances to their home countries to sustain family members. In 2020, the World Bank estimated that immigrants sent over $96 billion to Latin America; much of this money came from workers in the United States. Through remittances and technological advances that make communication faster and cheaper, immigrants maintain close contact with their home countries in ways that earlier generations could not. Scholars have labeled this ability to straddle livelihoods between two countries as transnationalism. A cultural and an economic outcome of globalization, transnationalism highlights the social and economic links that form between home and host countries (Jackiewicz and Bosco 2016). Declining economic opportunities or insecurity within Latin America have forced many individuals to emigrate in order to sustain their families. In the process, a new human geography is being created, one that extends well beyond regional boundaries.

Language

Roughly two-thirds of Latin Americans are Spanish speakers, and one-third speak Portuguese. These colonial languages were so prevalent by the nineteenth century that they were the unquestioned languages of government and instruction for the newly independent Latin American republics. In fact, until recently many countries actively discouraged, even repressed, native languages. It took a constitutional amendment in

Bolivia in the 1990s to legalize native-language instruction in primary schools and to recognize the country's multiethnic heritage (more than half the population is Amerindian; and Quechua, Aymara, and Guaraní are widely spoken).

Because Spanish and Portuguese dominate, there is a tendency to overlook the persistence of native languages. In the central Andes of Peru, Bolivia, and southern Ecuador, over 10–12 million people still speak Quechua and Aymara. In Paraguay and lowland Bolivia, there are 4 million Guaraní speakers; in southern Mexico and Guatemala, at least 6 million speak Mayan languages. Small groups of native-language speakers are found scattered throughout the sparsely settled interior of South America and the more isolated forests of Central America, but many of these languages have fewer than 10,000 speakers. And due to a long history of immigration, the United States has over 40 million native Spanish speakers, which is a larger number than the total populations of most Latin American countries.

Due to the more complex colonial history of the Caribbean, other languages are spoken there. Roughly 11 million people speak French (Haiti, French Guiana, and the islands of Martinique and Guadeloupe); 7 million speak English (Jamaica, Belize, Guyana, Trinidad, and other smaller islands of the Lesser Antilles); and there are about half a million Dutch speakers (Suriname and several small islands). Yet these figures tell only part of the story. Typically, colloquial variants of the official language exist that can be difficult for a nonnative speaker to understand. In some cases, completely new languages emerge; in the Dutch islands of Aruba, Bonaire, and Curaçao, Papiamento (a trading language that blends Dutch, Spanish, Portuguese, English, and African languages) is the lingua franca, with usage of Dutch declining. Similarly, Patois (French Creole) in Haiti has constitutional status as a distinct language. In practice, French is used in higher education, government, and the courts in Haiti, but Patois (with clear African influences) is the language of the street, the home, and oral tradition.

Religion

Like language, the Roman Catholic faith appears to have been imposed on the region without challenge. As Hannah Stewart-Gambino shows in Chapter 12, most countries report between 70 percent and 90 percent of their population as Catholic. Every major city has dozens of churches, and even the smallest hamlet maintains a graceful church on its central square. In countries like El Salvador and Uruguay, a sizable portion of the population attend Protestant evangelical churches, but the Catholic core of this region is still intact. The leader of the Catholic Church, Pope Francis, was born in Argentina, making him the first pope from the Americas.

Yet exactly what native peoples absorbed of the Christian faith is unclear. Throughout Latin America, syncretic religions—the blending of different belief systems—enabled animist practices to be folded into Christian worship. These blends took hold and endured, in part, because the Christian saints were easy surrogates for pre-Christian gods and because the Catholic Church tolerated local variations in worship as long as the process of conversion was under way. One of the most celebrated religious icons in Mexico is Guadalupe, a dark-skinned virgin seen by an Indian shepherd boy. Thought to intercede on behalf of the poor, Guadalupe has become the patron saint of Mexico.

Syncretic religious practices also evolved and endured among Africans in the Americas. Millions of Brazilians practice the African-based religions of Umbanda, Macumba, and Candomblé along with Catholicism. In many parts of southern Brazil, Umbanda is as popular with people of European ancestry as with Afro-Brazilians. Typically, people become familiar with Umbanda after falling victim to a magician's spell by having some object of black magic buried outside their home. In order to regain control of their life, they need the help of a priest or priestess. In the Caribbean, Afro-religious traditions have evolved into unique forms that have clear ties to West Africa. The most widely practiced are Vodou in Haiti, Santería in Cuba, and Obeah in Jamaica.

Race and Inequality

There is much to admire about race relations in the Americas. The complex racial and ethnic mix that was created in Latin America fostered tolerance for diversity. Nevertheless, as Kevin Yelvington shows in Chapter 9, Amerindians and people of African ancestry are disproportionately represented among the poor of the region. More than ever, racial discrimination is a major political issue in Brazil. Reports of organized killings of street children, most of them Afro-Brazilian, make headlines. For decades, Brazil espoused its vision of a color-blind racial democracy that refused to address racism. Evidence from northeastern Brazil, where Afro-Brazilians are the majority, shows death rates approaching those of some of the world's poorest countries. Throughout Brazil, Afro-Brazilians suffer higher rates of homelessness, landlessness, illiteracy, and unemployment. The past few years have seen dramatic changes in Brazilian society as affirmative-action measures have been implemented to open opportunities for Afro-Brazilians. President Luiz Inácio Lula da Silva's government also launched a major poverty reduction program called Bolsa Familia that reduced extreme poverty and income inequality.

Similarly, in areas of Latin America where Indigenous cultures are strong, one also finds low socioeconomic indicators. In most countries, mapping areas where native languages are widely spoken invariably corresponds with areas of persistent poverty. In Mexico, the Indigenous south lags behind the booming north and Mexico City. Prejudice is embedded in the language; to call someone an "indio" is an insult in Mexico. In Bolivia, women who dress in the native style of full pleated skirts and bowler hats are called cholas. This descriptive term, referring to the rural mestizo population, has negative connotations of backwardness and even cowardice. No one of high social standing, regardless of skin color, would ever be called a chola or cholo. But native people are mobilizing. The presidencies of Alejandro Toledo in Peru (2001–2006) and Evo Morales in Bolivia (2006–present), both of Amerindian heritage, offer signs of greater inclusion.

It is difficult to separate status divisions based on class from those based on race. From the days of conquest, being European meant an immediate elevation in status over the Indigenous, African, and mestizo populations. Class awareness is strong. Race does not necessarily determine one's economic standing, but it certainly influences it. These class differences express themselves in the landscape. In the large cities and their handsome suburbs, country clubs and trendy shopping centers are found. High-rise luxury apartment buildings with beautiful terraces offer all the modern amenities, including maid quarters. The elite and the middle class even show a preference for decentralized suburban living and dependence on automobiles, much like North Americans. Yet near these same residences are shantytowns where urban squatters build their own homes, create their own economy, and eke out a living.

Geography of the Possible

Latin America was the first region in the developing world to be fully colonized by Europe. In the process, perhaps 90 percent of the Indigenous population died due to disease, cruelty, and forced resettlement. The slow demographic recovery of Indigenous peoples and the continual arrival of Europeans and Africans resulted in an unprecedented level of racial and cultural mixing. It took nearly 400 years for the population of Latin America to reach 50 million again, its precontact level. During this long period, European culture, technology, and political systems were transplanted and modified. Indigenous peoples integrated livestock and wheat into their agricultural practices, but held true to their preference for native corn, potatoes, and cassava. In short, a syncretic process unfolded in which many Indigenous customs were preserved beneath the veneer of Iberian ones. Over time, a blending of Indigenous, Iberian, and African influences gave distinction to this part of the world. The music, literature, and artistry of Latin America are widely acknowledged.

Compared with Asia or Europe, Latin America is relatively lightly populated, yet still rich in natural resources. However, as population continues to grow along with economic expectations, there is considerable concern that much of this natural endowment could be squandered for short-term gains. In the midst of a boom in natural resource extraction, popular concern for the state of the environment is mixed. Latin Americans are more likely to mobilize around issues of clean water and air in urban environments than biological diversity in remote forest settings. But the creation and maintenance of large national parks and a growing tourism and ecotourism industry are likely to garner support for conservation.

In Latin America, the trend toward modernization began in the 1950s, and the pace of change has been rapid. Unlike people in other developing areas, the vast majority of Latin Americans live in cities. This shift started early and reflects a cultural bias toward urban living with roots in the colonial past. Not everyone who came to the city found employment; thus, the dynamics of the informal sector were set in place. Even though population growth rates have declined, the overall makeup of the population is young. Serious challenges lie ahead in educating and finding employment for the cohort under the age of fifteen. Those who cannot find work often consider emigrating to other parts of Latin America, North America, Europe, or elsewhere to seek better economic opportunities, contributing to the so-called brain drain that adversely impacts societies struggling to promote socioeconomic development.

Latin America is one of the world regions that North Americans are most likely to visit. The trend, of course, is to visit the northern fringe of this region. Tourism is robust along Mexico's border and coastal resorts. Unfortunately, there is a tendency to visit one area in the region and generalize for all of it. Although it is historically sound to think of Latin America as a major world region, extreme variations in the physical environment, levels of social and economic development, and the influence of Indigenous society exist. Therefore, underlying the unifying factors, these differences add much to the texture and complexity of Latin America, making it one of the world's most ecologically and culturally rich regions.

3

The Historical Context

René De La Pedraja

The conquest and colonization of the Americas in the
sixteenth and seventeenth centuries created the conditions for the exploitation of the vast territories described by Marie Price in Chapter 2, as well as
leaving a legacy of weak civilian institutions compared with the dominant
colonial ones, the military, and the Catholic Church. European imperialist
expansion resulted in the defeat and subjugation of the Indigenous peoples
of Latin America, the first non-European area to be conquered, colonized,
and Westernized. It was not until the early nineteenth century that challenges to European domination unleashed revolutionary forces, culminating in the Spanish colonies' independence in the early decades and in later
decades in Brazil, the largest overall colony liberated from Portugal. This
chapter focuses on how Europe imposed itself on the New World and how
independence was achieved, and surveys the nineteenth and twentieth centuries of the independence period.

The Conquest

Spanish colonization began after Christopher Columbus arrived in the
Caribbean in 1492. Ineffective resistance in the islands allowed Spaniards
to exploit conquered native peoples as veritable slaves, initially through
the brutal system of *repartimiento* (from the Spanish verb *repartir,* "to
distribute"), in which native peoples were seized and enslaved. In 1503,
the Spanish crown adopted the legal system of *encomienda* (from the
verb *encomendar,* "to entrust"), replacing the earlier system and oblig-
ing the conquerors to Christianize the natives and treat them justly. This

"civilizing" reform degenerated rapidly, and captured native peoples remained in a state of virtual slavery.

European diseases ravaged Indigenous Caribbean populations, leading to slave-hunting expeditions on the coasts of Florida, Venezuela, Central America, and the Yucatán. These expeditions continued the search for mineral wealth as small gold deposits in the Caribbean became exhausted. Spaniards began occupying northeastern Venezuela in 1510 after the discovery of pearls off the island of Cubagua and expanded into the interior in search of El Dorado (the legendary city of great wealth).

Hernán Cortés set out from Cuba in 1519 to pursue reports of a rich kingdom in the central Mexican highlands. Cortés and his force conquered the vast Aztec Empire—whose population of 20 million was defended by at least 100,000 warriors—by forming alliances with tribes who sought to end Aztec rule, based where Mexico City is located, and by deceiving its king, Montezuma, the powerful Aztec leader. By 1521, central Mexico was under Spanish control.

Indian laborers then leveled the Aztec capital, Tenochtitlán, and built Mexico City on the same site, which became Latin America's wealthiest and largest colonial city. From that central location, Spanish expeditions fanned out to subdue pockets of native resistance. The march into Central America brought Spanish rule to Guatemala, El Salvador, and Honduras by 1525. The Yucatán Peninsula was successfully defended by the Mayan city-states until 1527, when Francisco de Montejo and his son began the conquest that they completed in 1546.

Vasco Núñez de Balboa crossed what later became known as Panama, becoming the first European to view the Pacific Ocean in 1513. Panama City was established in 1519. From this strategic location, Spanish explorers moved into surrounding regions. The Indigenous peoples of Costa Rica's highlands repulsed sporadic Spanish expeditions until the 1570s, when the Spaniards were able to complete the conquest of the Pacific Coast and Central American highlands. Only on Central America's Atlantic Coast did Spanish rule fail to take hold, because it was unattractive to the Spaniards due to a combination of sparse Indigenous populations, the lack of any immediately valuable resources, and the sweltering tropical climate.

Rumors of a rich kingdom to the south led Ferdinand Magellan to discover the straits at the extreme southern tip of South America in 1520. Attempting to find what lay between that point and Panama far to the north, Francisco Pizarro took two exploring expeditions south from Panama along the Pacific Coast of Colombia in the mid-1520s.

Pizarro returned to the Peruvian coast in 1532 with roughly 200 explorers and discovered the Incan Empire, the largest in the Americas. Rather than conducting a frontal attack, Pizarro entrapped the unsuspecting Incan emperor at Cajamarca in 1533. The huge Incan armies could not be assembled in time to stop the advancing Spaniards. The capital, Cuzco, was captured easily, and the entire Incan Empire—which stretched from what is now Quito, Ecuador, to Santiago, Chile—came under Spanish control. In 1535, Pizarro established the Spanish capital in Lima, which became—after Mexico City—colonial Latin America's second most important urban center.

Expeditions fanned out from Peru in the hope of finding precious metals and large numbers of Indigenous peoples for free labor. To occupy the southernmost parts of the Incan Empire, Pizarro sent Pedro de Valdivia, who established Santiago, as the capital of Chile, in 1541. South of Santiago, the Araucanians mastered European warfare methods and resisted Spanish control. The region contained gold, and miners and settlers continued to clash with Indigenous peoples in almost continuous warfare until the late nineteenth century.

A Spanish expedition landed on Colombia's Caribbean coast, and Gonzalo Jiménez de Quesada took this force up the Magdalena River into the highland native kingdom of the Chibchas. After defeating the Chibchas, Jiménez de Quesada established the capital at Bogotá in 1537. To the east, Spanish colonizers converged from the original pearl fisheries on Venezuela's Caribbean coast and the trading routes on the west toward the central region in Caracas, founded in 1567. In Río de la Plata, a Spanish expedition had established Buenos Aires in 1536, but the hostility of the seminomadic native peoples forced starving colonists to relocate to Asunción, Paraguay, where the Guaraní developed a uniquely harmonious relationship with the settlers. Not until 1580 did the Spanish colonists feel strong enough to reestablish Buenos Aires as a permanent settlement.

Spanish explorers continued to push into distant areas. Indigenous civilizations were advanced in aspects of astronomy and mathematics but lacked basic elements of technology—particularly the wheel and iron. Hundreds of Spaniards could easily defeat thousands of Indigenous persons using steel swords, firearms, and cannons. Horses terrorized natives unfamiliar with them. Even though the conquerors were only slightly better than armed civilians, with few professional soldiers, the Spaniards' knowledge of tactics and strategy surpassed the Indigenous peoples' sometimes rudimentary conception of warfare. European diseases were the most terrifying weapon of all, decimating millions.

The native peoples' plight gave enemies of the Spanish crown ample reason to be extremely critical of the conquest and colonization of the Americas. For example, La Leyenda Negra (the Black Legend) attributed great cruelty, evil, and exploitation to the Spaniards. Ironically, the Black Legend was based partly on information from missionaries such as Bartolomé de las Casas (1474–1566), who attempted to end the abuse and enslavement of the natives. Later, leaders of the Latin American independence movements used the Black Legend—a mixture of fact and myth—to justify revolution against the crown.

Despite formal conquests ending by 1580, the task of incorporating frontier regions advanced. The Spanish Empire continued to grow, reaching its greatest extension in the eighteenth century.

The Colonial Period

The conquerors named colonies, for example New Spain and New Granada, in affirming their desire to reproduce Spanish civilization in the New World. Map 3.1 illustrates the colonial divisions. Spanish monarchs treated the colonies as personal possessions, creating structures for government, church, and economy that essentially transplanted European institutions into the Western Hemisphere. Social classes and cultural values, particularly Latin American ones, emerged gradually—often with unexpected consequences.

Spain duplicated its institutions and culture fairly closely in areas with scant numbers of natives, such as along the Río de la Plata, and areas where the Indigenous population rapidly disappeared, such as in the Caribbean islands. Spanish became the sole language, and Hispanic practices rapidly took root. The process of transmitting Hispanic structures and customs took longer and was seldom completed in areas of dense native populations, particularly central Mexico and the Peruvian highlands. Where natives survived the ravages of war, disease, and exploitation, they aptly selected those Spanish objects or traits most suitable for daily life. Native peoples quickly adopted practical materials like iron, the wheel, and wool clothing, as well as the corresponding nomenclature. They came to accept selected Spanish items, customs, and terminology as integral parts of their timeless traditions. They readily accepted some new foods (particularly chicken, eggs, and sugar), but refused to accept the wheat that the Spaniards so insistently imposed on them.

The Spanish *encomienda* succeeded because the authorities based it on existing pre-Hispanic structures. Outwardly converted to Roman Catholicism, the natives preserved many of their spiritist beliefs.

3.1 Eighteenth-Century Colonial Latin America

Despite repeated orders to use only Spanish in official documents, native Mexicans finally adopted the language of the conquerors for paperwork in the 1770s. As native rebellions became infrequent after the sixteenth century, the Spanish crown no longer saw natives as a threat to Spanish rule and tolerated their failure to adopt the new customs and official practices. Consequently, Mexican and Peruvian Indigenous populations had significant control over how they would coalesce with the Spanish world.

The Spanish government tried to prevent the rise of any group or rival institution that might challenge royal authority. This absolutist monarchy relentlessly sought to enforce its monopoly over political power in the conquered territories. First, the royal government removed from power the men who had carried out the conquest of the New World under the sweeping authorizations that the crown itself had granted. Asserting royal power in the Caribbean and marginal areas like Panama proved easier than on the mainland, where the conquerors were well entrenched. The opposition became so violent that in Peru, the Pizarro family led an insurrection against Spain. The crown's obsession with absolute power triumphed in both Peru and Mexico, largely because the government did not revoke the economic privileges of the original conquerors.

Throughout the colonial period, the Spanish government remained reluctant to share political power with the wealthy upper class. An unwieldy separation arose between political power and economic wealth, making colonial government ineffective and cumbersome as government officials—who generally needed funds—tried to impose official policies on wealthy upper classes. This pattern of conflict between economic and political power continues to plague Latin American countries today. Spain left Spanish America a legacy not of open government and consensus building, but of secrecy and absolutism.

The highest-ranking colonial official was the Spanish viceroy appointed by the crown, who, because of slow communication with Spain, enjoyed powers almost comparable to those of the king. Mexico City's viceroy had jurisdiction over North America, and Lima's viceroy had jurisdiction over South America. The distances were too vast for the viceroys, so in the sixteenth century, Spain appointed captain generals to rule over strategic regions such as Santiago, Caracas, and Havana. The captain generals, who were also *peninsulares* (Spaniards), were soldiers whose military practices reinforced the authoritarian nature of colonial institutions. Peru's decline and increased foreign threats convinced Spain to create two new viceroyalties in the eighteenth century, one for Buenos Aires and another for Bogotá.

The colonial government was subject to much abuse and corruption. Moreover, *peninsulares* looked down on *criollos* (creoles; Europeans born in the Americas). Special privileges, called *fueros,* were granted to *peninsulares,* clergy, the military, and government officials. Although abolished in Spain in 1820, *fueros* were continued in Latin America beyond independence. Membership in the *cabildo* (town council) usually remained the only form of political participation available to upper-class *criollos.* Additionally, the centralizing tendencies of the eighteenth century reduced the modest authority of municipal bodies and aroused *criollo* resentment.

The viceroys and captain generals formed the executive branch of government and possessed sweeping legislative and judicial powers. Spanish America's highest courts were the *audiencias,* whose *oidores* (judges) were usually crown appointed *peninsulares.* Effectively, the *audiencia* formed the main council of the viceroy or captain general while functioning as the highest appeals court in Spanish America (appeals later could be taken to Spain). Although most legislation came directly from the king's councils in Spain, the *audiencia* issued local laws and decrees using Roman legal principles, simplifying the application of laws at the personal level. Roman law became one more vehicle to reinforce absolutism and impose authoritarian principles.

Confusion among the three government branches is one of the most problematic legacies of the colonial period. The same officials, whether viceroys or judges, often performed legislative, executive, and judicial functions. By the twentieth century, Latin America was able to define the authority of the executive branch and, to a lesser degree, the judiciary. The failure to develop viable, independent legislatures has often undermined attempts to practice democracy and reinforced authoritarian tendencies (this is further discussed in Chapter 4).

In pursuit of a divide-and-rule policy, Spain created overlapping territorial jurisdictions for viceroys, captain generals, and *audiencias,* and for the parallel Catholic Church structure. Spain successfully prevented any high royal or church official in the New World from challenging the authority of the crown, but at the cost of increased inefficiency. Officials were more concerned with defending their power than with conducting government business. Following independence, the vague lines separating colonial jurisdictions led to conflicting territorial claims and border wars. These conflicts continued, including a long-standing border dispute between Ecuador and Peru that was not peacefully settled until 1999. Tensions between Venezuela and Colombia persist, occasionally erupting for political reasons, as evidenced in July 2010 when Colombian president Álvaro Uribe accused Venezuelan president Hugo Chávez of providing refuge to members of opposition groups, such as the Revolutionary Armed Forces of Colombia (FARC) and the National Liberation Army (ELN). Venezuela and Guyana continue to argue over the Essequibo region, dating back to the late nineteenth century.

Spain justified its authority over the Catholic Church on the grounds that civil and ecclesiastical officials needed to unite to accomplish the vast undertaking of the conquest of the New World. The Catholic Church was powerless without the crown's approval, and the authority extended to matters of religious belief or dogma. Whatever doctrine the pope proclaimed was valid for the New World only if the Spanish crown approved. Even after almost all of Latin America had been converted to Roman Catholicism, the government continued to preserve its authority over the church for the blatantly political reason of allowing no rival power base to emerge (further explored in Chapter 12).

Initially, converting the large native populations to Catholicism was carried out with missionary zeal. The priests learned native languages and established missions in remote areas. However, by the 1560s, few natives remained to be converted. Unable to enter local politics, the clergy devoted itself to profitably managing wealth.

The Catholic Church soon owned the largest percentage of land in Latin America and received a vast income from the properties. The money reserves accumulated, and the church's institutions became the financial lenders of the colonial period. Land was almost the universal collateral, so the failure to repay loans meant the church added foreclosed property to its enormous holdings.

The clergy's spiritual decay caused the Spanish government, in part out of religious conviction but also to avoid questioning its authority, to attempt to revitalize the Catholic Church. Supported by Spain, the Jesuits (of the Roman Catholic Society of Jesus) entered Latin America in 1572. Although the Jesuits encouraged scholarship and independent thinking in their schools, the Inquisition (a special Spanish law court designed to identify heretics and "allow" them to repent or be executed—at times by torture) severely limited intellectual activities. The Inquisition began its Latin American operations in 1569 in Lima and Mexico City and gradually opened branches in other major cities. The Inquisition was a governmental body of clergy whose most valuable contribution was detecting and punishing sexual crimes by priests and other religious personnel. Because natives were considered minors and not fully responsible for their actions, they were exempt from the Inquisition's jurisdiction, although some Mexican natives occasionally became victims. The Inquisition reinforced the tendency toward absolutism. Spain accepted the Inquisition because, as an institution independent of the bishops and viceroys, it provided another check on government and church in the New World.

Throughout colonial Latin America, both the Catholic Church and the Spanish government constructed extensive institutional structures supported by the New World's material resources. The Spanish crown expected the new institutions to be self-supporting and, from the start, demanded a major share of the wealth coming out of the New World. To extract the largest amount of wealth from the New World as easily as possible, the Spaniards established a colonial economy whose foundations were exploiting local labor and mining precious metals—activities that often occurred simultaneously (analyzed further in Chapter 6).

The seventeenth-century decline of Spain's empire gave Europeans the opportunity to establish bases in many deserted Spanish Caribbean islands, starting with the British island of Barbados in 1627 and the Dutch island of Curaçao in 1634. Seduced by tales of great wealth and aware of Spanish weakness, a British force tried capturing the entire West Indies, only to fail in its attack on Santo Domingo. This same expedition captured Jamaica from Spain in 1655, which became the staging base for subsequent British penetration into Spanish America. France also began to occupy West Indian islands and by 1665 gained control of western Santo Domingo, now called Haiti.

The islands occupied by the Dutch, French, and British were excellent ports for an extensive smuggling trade with Spanish America. By the second half of the seventeenth century, the non-Spanish Caribbean had turned to plantation agriculture as the main source of its wealth. Examination of parallel events in Portuguese Brazil illuminates how the plantation system spread to the Caribbean.

Portuguese Brazil

During the period when Spain conquered the West Indies, Mexico, and Central America, Portugal was barely present on the Brazilian coast. Pedro Cabral, leading a Portuguese fleet to India in 1500, was blown off-course and landed on Brazil's coast, which the king of Portugal claimed as a resupply base. Not until 1532 did Portugal establish the first permanent settlement at São Vicente (near present-day Santos on the Atlantic Coast). The two key elements of the Spanish American economy—precious metals and abundant Indigenous labor—appeared to be lacking in Brazil. Therefore the Portuguese, more driven by profit and commercial concerns than were the Spanish, invested in the lucrative spice trade between Europe and the Indian Ocean rather than the Brazilian wilderness.

The reddish dyes drawn from brazilwood trees were in demand in Europe. This attracted the French, who poached the forests that the Portuguese crown considered its own private reserve. To repel both the French and expansionist Spanish expeditions, the Portuguese government sent the first royal governor to San Salvador in 1549. The Portuguese expelled the French from Rio de Janeiro. In the early seventeenth century, the French attempted to reestablish settlements on Brazil's north coast, only to have the Portuguese push them into present-day French Guiana.

As excessive logging made brazilwoods scarce, expeditions called *bandeiras* set out for Brazil's interior in search of precious metals and slaves. Initially, the *bandeiras* (whose members were called *bandeirantes*) found no precious metals and few slaves among the widely scattered native villages. Brazil found its economic salvation on the coast, not in the interior.

Sugarcane grew well in the hot, humid lands along Brazil's coastline. Spanish America neglected the tropical lowland's agricultural potential for the sake of mining, and sugar prices remained high in Europe. Portugal could draw on its experience with sugarcane plantations in the Atlantic islands of Madeira and Cape Verde to introduce a proven and profitable economic model into Brazil. To supply the European demand for tropical crops—particularly sugar—Portugal imported large numbers of slaves from Africa annually to work in Brazil's sugar plantations. Sugar and slaves were inseparably linked during the colonial period, and profits from sugar exports sustained Portuguese colonization in Brazil.

Slaves and sugar made Brazil very wealthy, and many Portuguese migrated to the new country in the hope of finding fortunes. Portuguese merchants enjoyed a monopoly over Brazilian trade; the Portuguese government taxed European imports and sugar passing through Portugal. The Portuguese government's commercial empire in Asia was collapsing in the early seventeenth century; therefore, it needed increasing revenues from Brazil. Brazil replaced Asia as the source of most of Portugal's wealth.

The Dutch, who had attempted to take over Brazil in the mid-seventeenth century, abandoned the struggle because of armed local resistance. Instead, they introduced plantation agriculture in the Caribbean as a more profitable alternative to hostile Brazil. Other European powers followed this example. British Jamaica and French Haiti became the world's principal sugar producers. Production outpaced European demand, however. As sugar prices dropped, Brazil's sugar mills entered a prolonged depression after 1680. Planters struggled to meet loan payments as production costs rose—particularly the higher prices of imported slaves. Brazil stagnated, and Portugal's income and revenue decreased because of the colony's economic problems.

By 1700, the *bandeiras* had found gold deposits in the region of Minas Gerais (the general mines). Mineral exports—mainly gold and, after 1729, diamonds—drove Brazil's economy as sugar sank to second place. As the slave trade shifted to providing Africans for mining, plantation owners had more difficulty supplying their slave force.

Immigrants flocked from Portugal and other parts of Brazil to participate in the gold rushes; the demand for food and goods in the new mining cities provided a powerful stimulus to agriculture and commerce. To supply meat and leather, ranches pushed farther into the interior, thereby broadening the areas under effective Portuguese colonization. The gold fields were located primarily in Brazil's southern half. Additionally, the Portuguese crown shifted the capital in 1763 from Salvador in the north to Rio de Janeiro in the south.

The reliance on mineral wealth made Brazil resemble Spanish America. A crucial difference was that without a large Indigenous labor force, the Brazilians had used African slaves and, to a lesser degree, mestizos (offspring of Europeans and Indians) to work the gold deposits. By the eighteenth century, mestizos had become the largest racial element in the interior, whereas mulattos (offspring of Blacks and Europeans) had become the majority racial element in coastal sugar regions. Because of the constant arrival of new African slaves, many mulattos eventually acquired their freedom (explored further in Chapter 9).

Brazil faced hardships as gold output fell after 1750. Attempting to salvage the Portuguese Empire from economic collapse, the Marquis of Pombal—a virtual dictator because the king had lost all interest in ruling—undertook major initiatives from 1750 to 1777. The imperial bureaucracy—although never as extensive as that of Spain—continued to suffer from corruption, inefficiency, over-centralization, and conflicting jurisdictions. To increase trade between Portugal and Brazil, Pombal unsuccessfully attempted to improve the system of annual fleets (similar to Spain's). He abolished the annual fleets in 1765, allowing individual Portuguese vessels to sail freely anytime between Brazil and Portugal. Similar to the Caracas Company in Spanish America, Portuguese monopoly companies failed and were abolished by 1779.

With gold exports declining, both Brazil and Portugal attempted to grow crops and manufacture products that previously had been imported. Pombal encouraged expanding agricultural production to include new crops such as rice, wheat, and coffee. This combination of using import substitution and developing new crops restored Brazil to prosperity, although it was still dependent on the constant inflow of African slaves.

In the second half of the eighteenth century, no serious challenge to Portuguese rule in Brazil appeared. Pombal had expelled the Jesuits and confiscated their properties in 1759 to eliminate possible rival power bases. Unlike more religious areas in Spanish America, where the expulsion of the Jesuits had undermined royal authority, in Brazil, planters and merchants eagerly purchased most Jesuit lands at bargain prices. Rather than sell the lands to peasants, the Portuguese government reinforced overconcentrating the wealth into less than 1 percent of Brazil's population.

Brazil, without a single university or printing press, appeared content to remain Portuguese; the few failed conspiracies did not disrupt the colonial peace. Tiradentes (Joaquim José da Silva Xavier) in 1788–1789 was the first conspirator, but all of these individuals were from only lower and middle classes. Without upper-class support, no challenge to Portuguese rule would succeed. After the slaves revolted in the 1791 Haitian Revolution, planters dared not suggest political change for fear of provoking a similar uprising among Brazilian slaves.

The Bourbon Era

The real danger of collapse made reforms in Spanish America considerably more extensive than those of Brazil in the eighteenth century. When the Hapsburg dynasty's last Spanish king died heirless, European powers fought the War of Spanish Succession to determine which royal family would occupy Spain's throne. Spain selected a Bourbon (the royal family who also ruled France under Louis XIV), hoping to avoid French invasions. Spanish America was exposed to repeated British naval attacks during the rest of the Bourbon period (1700–1808).

Fear of British attacks gave a military urgency to reform Spanish America, a strategic concern less prevalent in more economically driven reforms under Portuguese Brazil. The economic dimension was present in Spanish America because the model based on exploiting Amerindian and mestizo labor and exporting precious metals was bankrupt. The Bourbon reformers faced the double task of creating effective defense forces for the Spanish Empire's distant frontiers and finding new sources of economic wealth to support the vastly enlarged military establishment.

Prior to making any changes, Bourbon reformers needed to establish an effective government structure to execute their orders, particularly new institutions and taxes. Spain's institutions were largely unmodified since their creation in the early sixteenth century. The Bourbons in the eighteenth century attempted to replace the original institutions with new dynamic agencies full of *peninsulares* and with the minimum possible participation by *criollos*. The old bureaucracy proved resistant, and the Bourbons could often do little more than add another bureaucratic layer to these decrepit institutions.

Beginning in 1763, the combination of newly formed royal monopolies and the presence of new intendants disrupted the existing power relationships. The new intendants, independent of the viceroys and the captain generals, began collecting taxes in 1763, thereby antagonizing both elite groups and the masses. Rather than binding Spain closer to Spanish America, the intendants further strained the imperial relationship.

The intendants, viceroys, and *audiencia* judges continued to mix judicial, legislative, and executive functions. Accountable only to Spain, each was independent and easily displayed despotic power excesses. Secrecy remained the rule; only a few privileged insiders had access to information within the bureaucracy, and officials kept the public ignorant of deliberations and many decisions. The Bourbon reforms reinforced authoritarianism and expectations that policies should flow from rulers rather than the people.

Although local elites embraced the principle of keeping the masses out of government, the Bourbon challenge to the elites engendered a struggle to preserve their influence. Concurrently, the military began functioning independently and feeling superior to the rest of society. Ironically, the Bourbons trained the officers and soldiers who later gained distinction in fighting against Spain during the wars of independence (Chapter 5 analyzes the role of the military in Latin America).

By 1800 it was clear that no further reforms were possible from the Bourbons, who desperately attempted to retain their eroding power over Spanish America. The elites were reluctant to defy established Spanish authorities because of the rigid class structure and fears of unleashing a popular uprising. When the monarchy was clearly endangering the established order, the resulting stress allowed local elites to escape— from both the stifling Spanish commercial system and the domineering royal bureaucracy.

Independence
Early Rebellions
Although the independence period formally began in 1808, in reality, earlier colonial revolts and British attacks formed the opening acts of the struggle for independence. In the late eighteenth century, two revolts of a magnitude previously unknown threatened to overthrow the colonial order completely.

The first occurred in the Peruvian and Bolivian highlands, where natives and mestizos rebelled in November 1780 to overthrow corrupt officials and abolish the new Bourbon taxes. The uprising's leader was a mestizo merchant who was descended from the last Incan emperor, taking the name Túpac Amaru II. Attempting to rally the native masses behind him, Túpac Amaru II declared himself king but never declared independence from Spain. This unclear position undermined his support among Spanish Americans and many mestizos. The fighting degenerated into a racial extermination war against the white *criollos,* who joined with the Spanish forces to crush this bloody insurrection by the end of 1781.

Conversely, the Colombian rebellion was relatively bloodless and lacked the racial overtones that had generated so much hatred. As in Peru, Colombia's revolt was caused by popular opposition to the Bourbon tax policies, but the native population was considerably smaller than Peru's; most rebels were mestizos and *criollos* who called themselves *comuneros.* During mass rallies in March 1781, the townspeople chose leaders to call for repeal of the new taxes. The movement spread quickly, and soon a huge crowd marched on the capital city of Bogotá.

The Spanish government kept almost all of its forces near the coast, especially in the fortress city of Cartagena, to defend against foreign attack; thus the military could not quell the revolt. Consequently, on June 4, 1781, the *audiencia* in Bogotá granted the demand of the *comuneros* to repeal the taxes. The crowds dispersed, and except with one rebel leader, who was later captured and executed, the movement was over.

In Colombia, the revolt taught the upper class how easily Spanish rule could be overthrown. In Peru, the lesson learned was that any change in government released bitter class and racial hatred. While the Colombian upper class remained open-minded about exploring new political alternatives if the opportunity arose, the Peruvian upper class was obsessed with its very survival, thus resisting any attempt to change the nation's political status. These contrasting attitudes later played major roles in shaping events during South America's independence struggle.

External Influences

By 1800, Latin America's economic significance to much of Europe had diminished. Nevertheless, the British maintained their designs of conquering the region's mineral wealth. The French Revolution's outbreak in 1789 ended Spain's alliance with the French Bourbons, who were overthrown, and Spain joined England in a coalition that attempted to destroy revolutionary France. Fear of French armies compelled the Spanish government to switch sides and return to a French alliance in 1796. To safeguard Spain's frontiers, the government, again, was willing to expose Spanish America to British attacks.

British warships began to raid many coastal ports. Old plans to capture Panama and other strategic points resurfaced. A British expedition captured the ill-defended island of Trinidad near Venezuela's coast in 1797, but failed against the determined opposition of new militias in San Juan, Puerto Rico. The most significant British attack came in 1806, when a British force captured Buenos Aires after royal officials fled in panic. The *criollos* were shocked by the disgraceful performance of royal officials; the local militias decided to avenge the dishonor by secretly organizing the expulsion of British troops, who surrendered when surprised by the unexpected *criollo* attack. A second expedition came too late to save the garrison, but it attempted to recapture Buenos Aires in 1807. Determined resistance by well-prepared militias persuaded British commanders to abandon the attack.

The British continental offensive barely dented Spanish America's outer defenses, whose protection depended on the dedication and discipline of the new militia units, not inefficient institutions of a corrupt empire. Military power had passed imperceptibly into the hands of the *criollos* under the Bourbons. Thus, the transfer of political power to the *criollos* who already dominated the economy could not be far away. Unsurprisingly, Buenos Aires was the first region to throw off Spanish rule permanently.

News of events in other parts of the world filtered in, despite attempts by the Inquisition and Spanish government to keep subversive ideas out of the region. After 1783, US ships engaged in smuggling brought news of US independence and ideas about a constitutional republic. The 1789 French Revolution seemingly offered another compelling example for Latin America. The upper classes quickly tempered their revolutionary enthusiasm when slaves in the French colony of Saint-Domingue rebelled and eventually established Haiti, the first Black republic in the Western Hemisphere, in 1804. Latin America's landholders and miners would not rush into independence for fear of triggering social revolts, but no attachment to the old colonial order would deter them from exploiting an opportunity to gain control over regional political structures.

The decay of Spanish institutions was pervasive and reached up to the king and royal family, who foolishly ignored all warnings of a trap and became prisoners of the French. Napoleon Bonaparte attempted to place his brother on the Spanish throne, but Spain's people rejected the new French ruler and began popular uprisings on May 2, 1808. Meanwhile, throughout Spain, many regional juntas, or governing boards, appeared to rule in the name of the captive Spanish king, Ferdinand VII.

Loyalty to the crown, the last cement bonding the Spanish Empire together, dissolved as competing groups attempted to fill the power vacuum left by the royal family's capture. French armies continued advancing through Spain, until only the Cádizian junta was left to defy Napoleon. Spanish America watched these events closely, and in the summer of 1810 the elites in Bogotá, Caracas, Buenos Aires, and Santiago decided to overthrow royal officials and establish governing juntas of Spanish Americans. Elsewhere, particularly Havana and Mexico City, elites tried establishing their own juntas but failed because of fear of unleashing revolts by the Black slaves in Cuba or the native and mestizo masses in Mexico.

The Wars Against Spain

The independence of Spanish America began without bloodshed, but the struggle soon turned into constant warfare, devastating large areas for over a decade. Maps 3.2 and 3.3 illustrate the independence movements. To ease the transition, juntas did not declare independence immediately, instead maintaining the fiction that they ruled in the name of the captive Ferdinand VII. Even this concession failed to calm diehard royalists, who soon started revolts against the juntas.

Caracas proclaimed itself a republic in 1811 but was recaptured by royalist forces the next year. Simón Bolívar attempted to reestablish the republic, but a brutal royalist campaign ended Venezuelan independence in 1814. In Bogotá, Buenos Aires, and Santiago, internal quarrels and civil wars divided the *criollos,* who wasted the opportunity to drive the *peninsulares* from their last strongholds in Peru, Bolivia, and Uruguay.

Mexico experienced a different type of independence struggle. Mexico City's elite missed the opportunity to establish their own junta, passing the initiative to provincial groups. On September 16, 1810, Spanish American priest Miguel Hidalgo—a key plotter—sounded the church bells, urging his parishioners to join the rebellion, which spread rapidly throughout nearby provinces. At the last moment, Hidalgo turned his huge forces away from Mexico City and toward Guadalajara. The failure to capture the capital gave Spain's government time to regroup and to regain the support of upper-class Mexicans, who panicked when Hidalgo's forces engaged in wholesale slaughter of all whites, whether *criollos* or *peninsulares.*

Hidalgo was soon defeated, captured, and executed, but mestizo priest José María Morelos continued the insurrection. Defeated in formal battles, the Mexicans adopted guerrilla warfare against the Spanish armies. The capture and execution of Morelos in 1815 did not end the

Map 3.2   Early Independence Movements

insurrection, and Mexican guerrillas continued to harass the increasingly exhausted Spanish troops. The efforts of the royal government to collect more taxes to pay for the large counterinsurgency army increased resentment of Spanish rule. The Spanish government's control over Mexico rested on disintegrating foundations.

Ferdinand VII regained the Spanish throne with Napoleon's 1814 defeat and released large numbers of Spanish veterans for the reconquest campaign. Spanish battalions contributed to defeating Hidalgo,

Map 3.3   Later Independence Movements

but counterinsurgency campaigns did not seem as glamorous to the Spanish government as pursuing a grand strategy against South America's independent countries. An expedition sailed from Spain to the Caribbean to crush the last Venezuelan patriot strongholds and reoccupy Colombia. Afterward, this force joined Spanish forces in Peru to make a final push down the Andes to press forces in Buenos Aires from the north, which then would be struck from the sea by a second force sailing directly from Spain. Pablo Morillo, imagining himself to be another Cortés, led a Spanish expedition that first subdued Venezuelan resistance and then sailed to

Colombia and landed off the coast of Cartagena in 1815. In supreme irony, the Spaniards, who spent entire fortunes building this fortress city, had to lay siege to Cartagena, which surrendered only because its defenders were starving. The Colombians, who were too divided, could provide no significant resistance, and Morillo soon reestablished Spanish rule in Bogotá and throughout Colombia. Meanwhile, Spanish forces in Peru reconquered Chile in 1814. Of all the original independent areas, only Buenos Aires remained under patriot control by 1816.

Before Spain could complete reconquest of Buenos Aires, Bolívar returned from Venezuelan exile and raised a patriot army in the Orinoco River plains. Morillo postponed his plans to march against Buenos Aires until he could destroy Bolívar's forces. In Venezuela, Colombia, and Chile, Ferdinand VII and Morillo refused any power-sharing arrangement with the *criollos* and retaliated economically and politically against all who participated in the independent regimes.

Both Bolívar in Venezuela and José de San Martín in Argentina saw the chance to end Spanish rule permanently through brilliant military moves. Bolívar left some troops in Venezuela to distract Spanish forces while he marched his main army westward into the Colombian Andes. His flanking march surprised and, after several engagements, defeated the Spanish army in the August 1819 Battle of Boyacá.

All of Colombia fell under patriot control, and Bolívar led a more difficult expedition that was completed only after his troops defeated the Spaniards in the June 1821 Battle of Carabobo. Bolívar sent another force south to expel the Spaniards from Ecuador, which joined the union of Colombia and Venezuela proclaimed in 1821. Panama, the best transit point for moving troops from the Caribbean to the Pacific Coast, also joined the new country.

The South American areas still under Spanish control continued to shrink because of Bolívar's actions and because of a separate campaign conducted by Argentine San Martín, who adopted a new strategy to protect Argentina from an expected Spanish invasion. Previous attempts to march north directly into Peru failed. Instead, San Martín decided to march across the Andes to surprise the Spaniards in Chile before sailing to attack the defended Peruvian coast.

San Martín crossed the Andes and defeated the Spaniards in several battles, the last of which, in Maipú in 1818, ended Spanish rule in Chile. He formed a navy with British sailors and ships, which took the army to Peru and captured Lima in 1821. The Spanish troops withdrew into the interior highlands, and Bolívar assumed the task of destroying the last South American Spanish forces. Bolívar arrived with a considerable force comprising the resources of Colombia, Venezuela, and Ecuador. In December 1824, after extensive fighting, the patriot forces defeated the last Spanish army at Ayacucho and ended Spanish rule throughout South America.

Mexican independence occurred in a rather sudden but almost inevitable manner. In 1820, Ferdinand VII gathered a second expedition in Cádiz to attack Buenos Aires. A mutiny forced the king to relinquish power to a liberal Spanish government. By then, unceasing guerrilla war had thoroughly demoralized the Spanish forces in Mexico, and the Mexican population saw the liberal government in Spain coming to power as an excuse to stop paying war taxes.

Mexico's royal government was disintegrating, but, unlike 1810, this time Agustín de Iturbide, the *criollo* Mexican army commander, would achieve independence. The rebels fighting against Spanish rule were brought into the movement, and, without firing a shot, Iturbide proclaimed Mexico's independence on September 28, 1821. Only the Spanish garrison in the main fortress of Veracruz refused to accept Mexican control until 1823.

Central America, which traditionally enjoyed close Mexican links, was sufficiently impressed to break its Spanish ties and join the new Mexican Empire in 1821. Thus, all of mainland Spanish America—from Mexico to Argentina and including Chile, Peru, Colombia, Central America, and Venezuela—had gained permanent independence from Spain. The Spanish Empire was reduced to Cuba and Puerto Rico in the Caribbean and the Philippines in the western Pacific, which it retained until 1898.

Brazilian Independence

Brazil, with large slave masses toiling in the gold mines and sugar plantations, was the least-likely candidate for independence. If Cuba—with Spanish America's largest slave population—remained under Spanish dominance, then fear of slave rebellions promised to keep Brazil under Portuguese rule. However, actions in Europe unleashed a chain of events culminating in Brazil's independence from Portugal. Although Napoleon was unable to capture the royal family, as so happened in Spain, the Portuguese government had to flee to Brazil in November 1807, days before French armies approached Lisbon, the Portuguese capital.

British warships escorted the Portuguese royal family to Brazil until they were safely established in Rio de Janeiro, which effectively became the Portuguese Empire's capital. This was the only time in history that a Latin American government ruled over colonies, the Portuguese territories in Asia and Africa. The British wanted favors in return, and Portuguese ruler Dom João complied by opening Brazilian ports to direct British trade.

Dom João was so happy in Rio de Janeiro that he refused to return to Portugal, even after Napoleon's decisive 1815 defeat. Furthermore, he formally ended Brazil's colonial status when proclaiming the country to be a "coequal kingdom" with the same rank as Portugal.

The printing press finally came to Brazil, and, for the first time, the king established institutions such as academies, universities, and a national bank. The Brazilian elite were delighted to have their king nearby and shared enthusiastically in the prosperity and feeling of progress that existed during the 1810s.

An 1820 revolt brought a new government to power in Portugal, demanding that Dom João return to Lisbon. In order to preserve the Portuguese Empire's political unity, the king agreed. Dom João left his son, Dom Pedro, behind with instructions to declare Brazil independent if necessary. When Dom João arrived in Portugal, the government was outraged that he had left his son behind. Lisbon insisted on Dom Pedro's prompt return and began to strip Brazil of many privileges Dom João had granted, determined to reduce Brazil to colonial status. However, the Brazilian elite were not about to surrender their newly gained influence.

With the Brazilian elite's full support, on January 9, 1822, Dom Pedro refused to obey the order to return to Portugal. Events flowed with an air of inevitability until Brazil's September 7, 1822, independence proclamation. The Brazilian elite rallied behind Dom Pedro, and only some isolated Portuguese garrisons briefly resisted the Brazilian Empire's proclamation.

Troops from poverty-stricken Portugal deserted almost as soon as they landed, making any Portuguese reconquest of Brazil pointless. In contrast to the experience of Spanish America, Brazil achieved independence with almost no bloodshed, thus escaping both the destruction of war and the legacy of a large military establishment. Although Spanish America disintegrated into many rival nations, Brazil—under a unifying, traditional monarchy—remained a single country, despite repeated revolts. The Brazilian monarchy inherited the existing government structure and retained the overwhelming majority of officials in their posts. Brazil enjoyed distinct advantages in the challenging task of creating a new government and seemingly escaped the worst ravages of its Spanish American neighbors.

The Nations of Latin America After Independence

After independence, emerging Latin American countries faced many common problems. This section examines the most important issues affecting most and sometimes all the individual countries. It follows a roughly chronological presentation to help readers progress from the events after independence to the situation at the end of the twentieth century. For the former Spanish Empire's territories, the biggest and most pressing question was to define the number and size of the new independent republics.

The Political Fragmentation of Spanish America

Although Brazil in the 1840s faced serious regional revolts that threatened to split it into separate republics, the centralizing force of the monarchy kept Brazil's empire together as one political unit. Lacking a similar unifying institution, Spanish America disintegrated into many states whose exact outlines were unclear at independence. Argentina (independent since 1810) and Chile (after 1815) without much difficulty became distinct countries, but the rest of Spanish America drifted through an agonizing experimentation period.

Mexico possessed all the elements of a separate country and for a few years appeared destined to include Central America. The Central Americans joined Mexico's empire under Agustín Iturbide in 1821, but when a revolt overthrew the emperor and established a republic, they created a separate union in 1823. Mexico, already in decline and turmoil, hardly attempted to maintain its rule over Central America, but managed to retain the Chipas region next to Guatemala. The Central American union attempted to rule from Guatemala City, the colonial period's traditional government seat, but when a revolt transferred the capital to San Salvador, disintegration became inevitable. Costa Rica, Honduras, and Nicaragua withdrew in 1838, and Guatemala left the next year. All subsequent attempts to restore the Central American union failed; the unworkable mini republics alternated between chaotic periods and dictatorships.

In South America, the disintegration never reached Central American extremes. Simón Bolívar in 1821 had united present-day Colombia and Venezuela to create the larger Gran Colombia, realizing it was needed to repel Spanish attempts to reconquer the region. As soon as he expelled the Spaniards from Panama and Ecuador, they decided to join Gran Colombia to obtain protection from foreign threats. When Peru attempted in 1828 to annex Ecuador, Gran Colombian armies defeated and repulsed Peruvian invaders. Despite the advantages of a large strong country, only

Bolívar's personal prestige kept the union together. After his 1830 death, separatist demands drove Ecuador and Venezuela to withdraw from Gran Colombia, but Panama remained with Colombia until 1903.

The elite in Gran Colombia's capital, Bogotá, wanted a large country but declined to forcibly impose their will on the outlying regions. When the elite in Peru's capital, Lima, hesitated to include Bolivia, they took advantage of the opportunity to proclaim independence as a separate country in 1825 once the last Spanish forces had been defeated. Bolivian Andrés Santa Cruz, who had ruled Peru in the name of Simón Bolívar in the mid-1820s, made one last attempt to reunify the two countries, achieving a confederation in 1836. Disgruntled Peruvians resented the rule of Santa Cruz, who had never been a member of Lima's elite, and they persuaded Chile to invade Peru and expel Santa Cruz, whose confederation ended in 1839. Peru and Bolivia (at that time with an outlet to the sea) have remained separate countries.

Like Bolivia, Paraguay remained under Spanish control after Argentina's independence from Spain in 1810. Paraguay deposed Spanish officials in 1811, and Argentina reluctantly accepted its existence as a separate country. Uruguay across from Buenos Aires remained under Spanish rule until 1814, but its independence was short-lived; in 1816 the Portuguese monarchy, in an act of aggression, invaded and annexed Uruguay to Brazil. When the Uruguayans revolted against Brazilian rule, Argentina supported the rebels and was at war with Brazil in 1825. The

Grand Plaza of Independence, Quito, Ecuador. Credit: https://www.shutterstock.com/image -photo/panorama-plaza-grande-de-independencia-quito-1188275614

war ended by 1828, when British mediation secured the restoration of Uruguay as an independent buffer state between Argentina and Brazil.

New countries of the former Spanish Empire appeared as distinct entities during the 1820s and 1830s. In South America, Brazil passed intact from the colonial to the independence period, Argentina and Chile emerged as the two most important Spanish countries in South America, while Paraguay and Uruguay became buffer states between Argentina and Brazil. The rugged Andes Mountains made large political union difficult, and soon five separate countries—Bolivia, Peru, Ecuador, Colombia, and Venezuela—carved out their respective spaces in that rugged topography. Mexico City preserved the colonial pattern of ruling over Mexico but failed to extend its authority over a Central America fragmented into mini republics like Guatemala, El Salvador, Honduras, Nicaragua, and Costa Rica.

Foreign Invasions of Spanish America

After independence, inhabitants' desire to reduce the size of government and eliminate taxes meant reducing the army and navy's strength. One of the reasons behind independence was the demand to abolish Spain's taxes to maintain large forces and fortifications. Elites assumed that Western European countries and the United States posed no threat and believed that the often abject poverty of the new independent states dissuaded any would-be invaders. Imperial Brazil's centralized government commanded respect from European powers, but the Spanish American countries usually inspired pity. Spanish America's military combined the two worst situations: too large to facilitate consolidating civilian rule yet too weak to resist foreign attacks.

Even before independence, Britain made numerous attempts to annex Spanish American territories, while the United States pressured the Spanish Empire's northern frontiers. When US forces occupied Spanish Florida in 1819, a weak Spain was forced to recognize that territory's loss and accept the forty-second parallel as Mexico's northernmost boundary in a transcontinental treaty.

The United States preferred negotiation over war with the disintegrating Spanish Empire, whose past glories still commanded some respect. Spanish Santo Domingo's inhabitants, seeing how easily the United States drove Spain from Florida, deposed the royal authorities and proclaimed independence in 1821. They ignored the risks of jettisoning the protective imperial mantle and watched helplessly when a few months later, numerous Haitian troops—veterans of the long wars against France—overran the former Spanish colony. Santo Domingo finally gained independence in 1844 as the Dominican Republic.

Spain could not reconcile itself to the loss of its colonies, and therefore attempted to recover Spanish America. An expedition sailed from Cuba attempting to reconquer Mexico in 1829, but poor organization and leadership required minimal Mexican resistance to force its surrender. Because the Spanish navy surpassed the combined naval forces of the new countries, Spanish fleets sometimes demonstrated naval power, with the mundane goal of securing trade or other economic benefits. Spain returned to the Dominican Republic in 1861 at the request of the local inhabitants, who, having gained independence from Haiti in 1844, feared another Haitian invasion. Despite minimal resistance to Spanish rule, the costly occupation and scarce revenue of this poor region convinced the Spanish government to withdraw from the Dominican Republic in 1865. Spain was involved in a dispute with Peru and Chile in 1865–1866, during which the Spanish navy bombarded Callao (the port of Lima) and Valparaíso in Chile. This was the last demonstration of Spanish power in South America. Afterward, Spain abandoned all ideas of conquest and struggled to preserve its rule over Cuba and Puerto Rico, its last two colonies.

Britain followed US moves against the northern frontier of Spanish America, taking advantage of the weak new republics to acquire territories for the British Empire. Since Britain possessed the world's largest navy and was Spain's principal rival during the colonial period, the modesty of its territorial ambitions was remarkable. Britain thought that, at least for Latin America, commercial domination through trade and finances was a more profitable alternative than expensive direct colonial rule. Nevertheless, settlers and merchants pushed British authority in the Caribbean into the coasts of Nicaragua and Guatemala and the Essequibo region in eastern Venezuela; all were marginal and unoccupied regions of the former Spanish Empire. A direct challenge occurred when British forces drove Argentine authorities from the Malvinas (Falkland Islands) in 1833.

Spanish America's most disastrous invasion was the Mexican War, from May 1846 to February 1848. Aware of the danger to its exposed northern frontier, the Mexican government invited Americans to settle in the region, only to have them revolt and proclaim an independent Republic of Texas in 1836. Many settlers in that Mexican province were part of an effort to create a slave state, as part of the ongoing US conflict over slavery's extension in the territories. When the United States annexed Texas in 1845, a war with Mexico was inevitable because of the ill-defined boundary between the republic and Mexico (Oakes 2017). Well-trained and well-armed US troops drove deep into northern Mexico from Texas, while in the west the US through its navy captured California (Mexico had abolished its navy in 1830). A US expedition landed in

Zocalo Square, Mexico City. Credit: https://www.shutterstock.com/image-photo/zocalo-square-mexico-city-black-white-551591611

Veracruz, marched into the highlands, and captured Mexico City against difficult odds. The Mexican army's performance was miserable, while leadership was so wretched that the country's survival was in doubt. In the 1848 Treaty of Guadalupe-Hidalgo, Mexico lost half of its surface area to the United States and faced reshaping a new identity after the humiliation of a crushing defeat. Mexico had to cede territory that would become California, Nevada, Arizona, New Mexico, Utah, and parts of Oklahoma, Wyoming, and Colorado.

In 1868, Mexico faced another foreign occupation, this time from France. This resembled a foreign invasion, but because of its intimate connection with internal Mexican politics, it is discussed later in the chapter. The militarily weak Latin America suffered many more troop landings, bombardments, blockades, raids, and displays of force by foreign powers.

The Economy of Latin America, 1820s–1914

Between independence in the 1820s and World War I, Latin America's economy experienced two stages. During the first, lasting until the 1870s, most countries attempted to prolong the colonial economy, while in the second stage many shifted their primary focus to producing raw materials and foodstuffs for the industrializing areas of North America and Western Europe.

The First Economic Stage, 1820–1870

Following independence, the first order of business for most of Spanish America was repairing the damage of the struggle against Spain. War had disrupted trade, agriculture, and mining, while the expense of financing the struggle against Spain left few resources for large public works. To fund their normal operating budgets, the new governments borrowed from the London market in the 1820s, and the repayment of these loans soon turned into a crushing foreign debt, a problem Latin America suffered until the rise of cocaine exports in the 1980s. Brazil's peaceful independence spared the country a destructive struggle, but for most of Spanish America, particularly Venezuela, Mexico, and Peru, the ravages of war made it difficult to revive the economy.

The new governments, unable to act on their own, believed welcoming foreign investment and opening ports to foreign trade would suffice to stimulate economic growth. It was easy to repeal the colonial prohibitions on trading with foreign countries, but the flood of cheap European textiles drained Latin America of its gold and silver. The balance of payments became an acute problem, artisan production collapsed, and Latin America abandoned any chance of beginning even the most rudimentary industrialization. Foreign investment proved elusive; attempts to revive mining of precious metals proved disappointing to British investors. Afterward, British capital concentrated on commerce, such as shipping, insurance, ports, and warehouses. Soon, British merchants in Latin America's principal cities displaced Spanish-born merchants who, under the colonial system, monopolized the lucrative overseas trade. Retail trade remained under Spanish merchants, creating a network of corner stores (*bodegas*) throughout Spanish America.

Countries lacking abundant mestizos or Indians had introduced African slaves and the cultivation of export crops to resolve paying for expensive imports. Only Cuba and Brazil adopted the slave plantation model. At first, slavery did not seem to block the introduction of new technology. Cuba inaugurated in 1838 the first railroad of Latin America— and Spain. Most planters did not hesitate to start exploiting slaves rather than improve technology and managerial organization. The slave model did not block innovations such as the telegraph, but there was no rush to adopt new technology. Brazilian planters began to construct the railroads vital for the export of coffee in the 1860s.

From 1800, Britain embarked on a crusade to end the slave trade from Africa and then slavery itself. By 1850, the slave trade was illegal throughout Latin America. However, it was still so lucrative that smugglers brought African slaves to Brazil and Cuba as late as the 1860s. Without an abundant supply of cheap African slaves, the plantations struggled to survive.

Slavery ended in Cuba in 1886 and in Brazil in 1888, but decades before, Latin Americans realized that the slave plantations were no longer an alternative to the traditional exploitation of mestizos and Indians. Latin America's economy continued to decline, reaching its lowest per capita figures in the 1860s. Coincidentally, the advancing industrialization of North Atlantic countries offered modest opportunities for Latin America to reverse the downward spiral.

The Second Economic Stage, 1870s–1914

After 1870 the industrial revolution intensified, spreading throughout Western Europe and engulfing the United States and finally Japan. Of the industrializing countries, only the United States possessed abundant natural resources, but it could profit from Latin America's cheap raw materials. Other industrializing countries needed to import large amounts of foodstuffs and raw materials to fuel their expansion. These global powers, whether as an alternative or as a complement to their colonial empires in Africa and Asia, turned to Latin America to establish additional low-cost suppliers.

Inspection visits convinced Europeans that mining and agriculture were profitable activities. Thus, foreign investment, primarily British, flowed into Latin America after 1870. Improved transportation was urgently needed, because new mineral exports were bulkier than the traditional gold and silver, while many agricultural exports, such as wheat and beef, came from regions farther from the seacoast than the traditional sugar exports. Transportation meant the steam engine for railroads and steamships. In the 1880s, British investment allowed Brazil to begin constructing railroad lines to link the interior with the nearest port city. To bring wheat from the interior to the Buenos Aires port, Argentina constructed an extensive railroad network. Mexico completed its first line in 1873, linking Veracruz on the coast and Mexico City in the interior. US railroads assumed the task of laying track, and by 1910, when several lines joined Mexico with the US border, Mexico enjoyed an extensive if not well-integrated railroad network. However, Latin America's railroad coverage remained uneven. Cuba, whose dense network reached into almost every corner of the island, and Argentina, with the longest network, were at one extreme, while the small and medium-sized countries, such as Bolivia, Colombia, and the Central American countries, held railroad lines that failed to connect their principal regions.

Once the steamship was perfected by the 1880s, fast transportation of goods from Latin America on regular schedules became standard practice and allowed the continent to become a reliable supplier for

Europe (steamship services to the United States lagged in frequency and sometimes availability). European firms owned and operated the steamships, and similar to the railroads, countries or areas without valuable exports had poor and irregular steamship services. To gain some control over their export trade, Chile and Brazil established locally owned steamship companies in the last quarter of the nineteenth century. Peru established its own steamship company in 1906. Otherwise, Europeans controlled Latin America's shipping and had a near monopoly over the insurance, banking, and financial sectors. Consequently, foreign hands controlled almost all the profit-earning steps in the process of bringing Latin American products to the North Atlantic economies.

Regular steamship service also helped provide labor to many parts of Latin America. Large numbers of immigrants traveled safely aboard the steamships rather than being packed into the hulls of cramped sailing vessels for long voyages. Modest-sized steamships provided such a reliable flow of immigrants that some became seasonal workers who came for harvest season and then returned to Europe. Brazil showed how European immigrants could replace slaves in the coffee plantations and also develop areas and activities previously neglected under slavery. Foreign immigration had the greatest visible impact on Chile and Argentina, whose populations acquired the European appearance and customs prevalent until the present. Immigration fueled the expansion of exports of primary goods across much of Latin America.

However, not all of Latin America experienced expansion of exports after the 1870s. Within individual countries, areas such as northern Brazil (except during the brief rubber boom) remained stagnant or in decline. Other countries slowly developed sufficient production capabilities. For example, the expansion of Colombian coffee exports did not begin until the 1910s. Some countries like Ecuador lacked export expansion before World War I.

Contrary to foreign control of trade, transportation, banks, and related services, local elites usually controlled agriculture and mining. Chilean nitrates were locally controlled, but the Chilean and Peruvian copper and Peruvian silver mines were foreign owned. Most new Mexican mines were foreign-owned, and Mexico's petroleum deposits belonged to either British or US corporations. The sometimes overreaching grasp of foreigners for Latin American mineral resources persuaded Argentina to unexpectedly establish the world's first state-owned petroleum company (later known as Yacimientos Petrolíferos Fiscales) in 1910. This isolated action had Latin American implications evident only decades later.

Foreigners preferred to invest in mining, where capital and new technologies gave them considerable advantages, rather than in traditional plantations. Agriculture was generally locally owned, partly because most foreigners did not want to deal with the large rural labor force. Thus, coffee in Brazil and Colombia, wheat and beef in Argentina, and hemp in Yucatán remained under local ownership. Significant exceptions existed. US firms owned the majority of sugar mills in Cuba and the Dominican Republic, as well as Peru's largest sugar mill. Notably, the US company United Fruit grew bananas at plantations in Central America and Colombia and created the US tropical fruit market.

Expanding exports of raw materials and foodstuffs brought political stability to most of Latin America and unforeseen favorable consequences for economic growth. Because Latin American governments received over 90 percent of their revenues from customs duties, increased trade meant increased treasury funds. Some countries, such as Brazil in 1890, adopted the first protectionist tariffs, although the goal was to increase revenue. Exporting-country governments could afford to maintain standing armies and large police forces and even expensive navies. The enlarged military prevented internal uprisings and helped restore business confidence in stable countries. Military contracts became valuable to local producers, while the introduction of electricity in the 1880s provided a convenient alternative to steam engines and manual labor. After 1900, modest factories began producing textiles, beer, and cement. Foreign investors realized that profits were possible by investing in factories and public utilities in countries like Brazil, Mexico, and Peru.

Latin American cities grew during export expansion and held a larger percentage of the population than ever before, although at least 70 percent still lived in rural areas. In countries without export expansion, the rural population was as high as 90 percent. In 1900, Rio de Janeiro, with over 600,000 inhabitants, was the second largest city in Latin America, followed by Mexico City with 380,000 and Santiago, Chile, and Havana, Cuba. Latin America's largest city was Argentina's capital, Buenos Aires, with 750,000 residents. Buenos Aires architecture resembled that of Paris and seemed the least Latin American of all the region's cities. European Argentina best exemplified the success of the export expansion model and ranked among the world's ten richest nations. Although the results of export expansion throughout Latin America were uneven, it appeared in the years before World War I that at least Argentina had managed to catch up with the North Atlantic industrialized nations. Countries like Chile and Mexico were making important strides in economic growth, and other countries were expected to follow this path out of the poverty of the past and into the prosperity of the twentieth century.

Politics in Latin America, 1820s–1910s

The consequence of Latin American independence was almost constant political turmoil. Civil wars, coups, conspiracies, and regional and national revolts appeared endless, yet as countries experimented with constitutions and republican practices, glimmers of stability emerged by the end of the 1800s. The slow and costly experimentation divided Latin America's political history into two main periods: a chaotic stage of near despair from the 1820s to the 1870s, and a stable stage of political evolution from the 1870s to the 1910s.

Liberals Versus Conservatives, 1820s–1870s

New Latin American countries copied foreign structures of government. Republican institutions replaced royalist bodies, and the new republics boasted of presidents, congresses, diplomats, and constitutions. However, defining the exact functions and duties of the new institutions provoked disagreements and led to the formation of the two rival parties—Liberal and Conservative. Even monarchical Brazil experienced the Liberal versus Conservative division. In Brazil, as in Spanish America, actual differences between the parties were greater in theory than in practice.

Liberals wanted to transform Latin America into copies of Western Europe and the United States, a proposition doomed to failure because Latin American Liberals lacked the resources of their wealthier North Atlantic counterparts. Conservatives wanted to preserve the old royalist colonial system, but their efforts were no less unreal than the Liberals' attempts at a modern future. Conservatives preferred strong centralized governments, while Liberals welcomed federalism to give regions a greater voice in governance. Once Liberals and Conservatives were in office, their policies blurred until the differences disappeared, best seen in monarchical Brazil's Liberals being separated from Conservatives only by policy toward the Roman Catholic Church.

Without clear-cut ideological distinctions between Liberals and Conservatives beyond religious policy, politics became a struggle over the spoils of office. Political instability became the rule, and each coup or civil war was inevitably followed by more conspiracies and plots. Mexico, which changed presidents almost yearly between 1823 and 1860, was the worst example, but in cases like Colombia, where the central government was rarely overthrown, the country was plagued with constant revolts and plots.

Because the Brazilian monarchy was successful in putting down revolts and restoring order, many Mexican Conservatives concluded that Mexico needed a monarchy. However, Liberals under Benito Juárez violently disagreed and insisted on imposing their agenda to modernize

Mexico. Liberals defeated Conservatives, who sought foreign support, in the Three Years' War (1857–1860). France, on the pretext of nonpayment of foreign debt, in 1862 established a protectorate in Mexico under the nominal rule of the Archduke Ferdinand Maximilian of the Austrian Hapsburgs. After French troops routed the Mexican Liberals, Maximilian was crowned Mexican emperor in 1863, and in an attempt to gain popular support for his rule, he engaged in a modest set of reforms. Under Juárez's leadership, guerrilla warfare continued to wear down the French forces, whose control never extended beyond the main cities. When the United States threatened to intervene in 1865, France agreed to withdraw its forces, and the popular Liberals regained control of Mexico. The Liberals resumed their reformist program and attained modest results.

During the struggle between Liberals and Conservatives, some regional strongmen, or *caudillos,* appeared. The most infamous was Antonio López de Santa Ana, who held the Mexican presidency frequently from 1832 to 1855. Santa Ana's theatrics increased Mexico's political instability, and his incompetence was responsible for Mexico's territorial losses to the United States.

Two other *caudillos* had more positive contributions. José Antonio Páez, seeking personal power, took Venezuela out of Gran Colombia in 1830 and then remained its ruler until the late 1840s. Páez supported the Conservatives, as Juan Manuel Rosas did in Buenos Aries from 1829 to 1852. Rosas defended the interests of large ranchers and Buenos Aires merchants, becoming popular by leading the resistance to the French and British naval blockades against Argentina of the 1840s. Rosas, like a typical *caudillo,* stayed in power through a network of personal relationships rather than institutional arrangements. The issue of federalism versus centralism had divided Argentina into warring regions since independence, but Rosas avoided the rivalry by building a personal network of support among the local *caudillo*s of each province. In exchange for subsidies and access to foreign trade through the port of Buenos Aires, the independent provincial *caudillos* agreed to recognize Rosas as the nominal head of a paper Argentine Confederation, although he never claimed the vacant presidency. Rosas brought peace, but Argentina needed stable arrangements to stay unified.

The only Latin American country to develop effective government institutions after independence was Chile, because of Diego Portales. A wealthy merchant who joined the Conservative Party, he held Liberal views that he did not publicly proclaim because he felt that Chile was not ready for them. A coup against the Liberals brought Portales to power in 1829, but he refused to become president, instead proceeding to structure the Chilean government along impersonal administrative lines from a cabinet position. As a merchant, he encouraged opening Chile to foreign trade yet also believed that the government should stimulate mining, shipping, and agriculture by measures like subsidies and tariff protection. Once he completed reorganizing the governing structure, he returned to private business but was recalled to the cabinet to deal with the growing threat from the Peruvian-Bolivian Confederation of Andrés Santa Cruz. When Portales was assassinated in 1837, he had established the impersonal structure of government so effectively that Chile defeated Santa Cruz and enjoyed economic prosperity. Chile achieved political stability and maintained an efficient governing system throughout the nineteenth century.

Reforms and Stability, 1870s–1910s

As other countries struggled to catch up, Chile surged ahead to improve its governing institutions. Diego Portales's system relied too heavily on an almost independent presidency to maintain order, but the Chilean congress assumed a significantly greater role in the last quarter of the century. A revolt overthrew President José Manuel Balmaceda in 1891 when he tried to rule without seeking legislative power. Afterward, the principle of congressional control over the budget and most official matters became firmly established. Chile entered the twentieth century with a strong and independent legislature, which reinforced the efficiency of Portales's impersonal government structures.

Although other Latin American countries wanted to imitate Chile's success, the pressure to impose order and stability came from the North Atlantic economies. The intensification of industrialization in Europe and the United States after 1870 increased demand for raw materials and foodstuffs that Latin America could provide. The North Atlantic economy was willing to provide trade, loans, and investment to Latin American countries with stable conditions for the production and export of goods. To consolidate strong governments, Latin America (except Chile) turned to either elite control or dictators.

Elites in Argentina and Brazil closely tied to exports gained control of the government and created a structure supporting their interests. In Brazil, despite the fall of the monarchy and the proclamation of the republic in 1889, changes in government structure proved mostly cosmetic; consequently, the new republic perpetuated the generalized corruption and electoral defects of the monarchy. Because the republican government took care of the Brazilian exporting elite's needs, particularly the coffee planters, Brazil largely ignored the gross incompetence and massive corruption rampant throughout the government.

In Argentina, the new government structures are more effective than Brazil's but not as effective as Chile's. To safeguard the flow of wheat and beef to Europe, Argentine elites constructed an outwardly modern government structure during the last decades of the nineteenth century and politically unified the country. To defuse a situation that already resulted in mini revolts among the lower class, in 1912 the Argentine elites struck a bargain with the middle class through the Sáenz Peña electoral reforms, allowing adult males to vote. Elites gained an ally against the lower class, and a 1919 new middle-class government crushed a general strike by workers. The elites neutralized the lower class but lost direct control over the government to politicians elected by middle-class voters. Nevertheless, Argentina maintained political stability and avoided violent destructive upheavals similar to the Mexican Revolution.

During its first five decades of independence, Mexico suffered more from endemic political turmoil than any other Latin American country. Both the elite and masses desired peace and order. After President Benito Juárez died in office in 1872, the Mexican Liberals seemingly ran out of ideas, opening the door for General Porfirio Díaz, who supposedly was a Liberal, to take power in 1876. Until 1911, Díaz ruled Mexico with a firm hand and promoted its institutional development. Under Diaz's authoritarian rule, the Mexican economy reversed its decline and grew. With increased revenues from exports, Díaz, with a well-trained army and police force, consolidated the central government's authority throughout Mexico. Foreign investment poured into Mexico, whose elite enjoyed unprecedented prosperity. The lower class was brutally repressed and exploited, while the small and slowly expanding middle class had little stake in the authoritarian regime. Although the material and institutional progress under Díaz was undeniable, permanent repression seemed inappropriate to sustain Mexico's economic prosperity and political stability.

Border Wars in South America

By the 1830s, South American countries had their present identities, although demarcation of their boundaries was incomplete. Boundaries were a secondary concern after economic decline until the mid-nineteenth century. Economic growth in the 1860s revived interest in natural resources that could generate profitable exports. However, the possibility of a border war and its outcome depended on how well each country had prepared its military.

The first and most tragic war broke out in Paraguay, whose dictator, Francisco López, saw his small, landlocked country outstripped by the expansion of two bordering giants, Argentina and Brazil. Attempting to stop the inevitable, López went to war against Brazil in 1864 to end its influence in Uruguay. Unsatisfied with the unequal conflict against Brazil, López also invaded Argentina. The resulting Paraguayan War, or War of the Triple Alliance (1864–1870), pitted Argentina, Brazil, and Uruguay against Paraguay, whose highly disciplined army prolonged the struggle until 1870, when López died in battle. Paraguay lost nearly 20 percent of its population and sizable territories to Brazil and Argentina.

While Paraguay's attempt to catch up with wealthier neighbors ended in disaster, Chile, in the War of the Pacific (1879–1883), successfully increased its already substantial economic lead over Peru and Bolivia. Nitrate became a valuable export, and Chile exploited not only its own fields, but also those in the maritime district of Bolivia. Soon, Chilean firms controlled most of Bolivia's nitrate fields; Bolivia decided, in violation of a treaty agreement, to tax the Chilean investors. Chile sent troops in 1879 to capture the nitrate fields, but the struggle was against Peru, which entered the war to try to stop Chilean expansion.

Chilean warships crippled the Peruvian navy and ravaged the coast. The well-organized Chilean army, equipped with superior German weapons, landed near Lima and captured the capital in 1881. The war became more savage when Chileans began marching up into the Andes and encountered guerrilla resistance. By then, the Chileans had achieved all their goals, and negotiations ended the war in 1883. Chile gained the nitrate provinces of both Peru and Bolivia and left the latter country without an outlet to the sea. Chile's triumph in the War of the Pacific apparently confirmed the superiority of export expansion as the best way to bring material prosperity, military victories, and international prestige to a country.

Bolivia learned nothing from the War of the Pacific and repeated the same mistakes during the rubber boom in the Amazon. Bolivia lacked resources to support sufficient forces in the region, and thus attempted to tax the Brazilian rubber tappers, who revolted and established the independent Republic of Acre in 1902 as the first step toward eventual annexation to Brazil. When Bolivia attempted to reconquer the lost territory, Brazil mobilized troops near the Bolivian border and prepared to invade. Confronted with overwhelming force, Bolivia decided to seek a negotiated settlement. Bolivia lost most of the large Acre territory to Brazil but retained other areas of the Amazon jungle.

Bolivians train gun on Paraguayan airplane on May 24, 1934. The Chaco War was fought over the Chaco Boreal wilderness region and lasted from 1932 to 1935. Credit: https://www.shutterstock .com/image-photo/bolivians-train-antiair -gun-on-paraguayan-249572707

Two wars broke out in 1932 during the Great Depression. Bolivia attempted to extend its frontier to the Paraguay River, but the Paraguayan army, reconstituted after the War of the Triple Alliance, defeated the invasion. Paraguay surprisingly went on the offensive and advanced far into the Chaco region of Bolivia. During the Chaco War (1932–1935), Bolivia barely kept the Paraguayan army out of the petroleum fields. With the peace treaty, Bolivia lost large areas to Paraguay.

Peru, also in 1932, seized the Colombian territory of Leticia in the Amazon. Colombia mobilized a large force to expel the Peruvians, who after several engagements, decided to withdraw. Colombia was the only country that did not convert the military advantage into territorial gains, instead satisfied with returning to the boundaries before the Peruvian invasion.

Peru, because its troops escaped without serious losses, proceeded to settle old grievances with Ecuador. Ecuador had been encroaching on Peruvian territory, and in 1941, Peru launched a counteroffensive. Ecuador, small and weak, paid dearly for declaring independence from Gran Colombia in 1830 and could only watch as Peru overran large areas of Amazon territory. Pressure from the United States and Latin

American countries prevented the Peruvian offensive from occupying all disputed border positions in 1941. Wars erupted in 1981 and again in 1995 in unmarked zones until a 1998 treaty clearly defined the border between the two countries.

Destruction of the Indian Nations

Throughout Latin America, many Indians remained outside government control. These Indians, frequently seminomadic, lived in outlying regions never conquered by the pre-Hispanic Indian kingdoms or the Spanish Empire. Because they occupied lands in strategic regions, the failure of the Latin American governments to exercise effective authority could mean invasion by neighbors or foreign countries. Resources in many Indian lands attracted settlers to these remote regions, especially after 1870, when Latin America began expanding its exports. Revenue generated by the export boom improved the effectiveness of Latin American governments, whose rulers could use a better transportation system and improved military to destroy the remaining Indian nations.

The most destructive offensive against the Indian nations occurred in Brazil. Successive waves of Brazilians marched into the interior and into the Amazon Basin to capture and enslave Indians, because subduing Indians was a private endeavor. Brazilians, in minor skirmishes and, rarely, formal battles, conducted slave-hunting raids, a practice dating back to the sixteenth century. Brazilian Indians died in droves, through enslavement and European diseases, and they gradually surrendered to a population of mixed bloods, or mestizos. The Brazilian Empire, convinced by flagrant abuses, abolished Indian slavery in 1831. This proved ineffective, as Brazilian colonists devised ingenious ways to exploit the labor of the vanishing Indians of the Amazon throughout the nineteenth century. Unchecked private ambition had brought the Amazon Basin under Brazilian control at the cost of the almost wholesale extermination of its Indian population.

Contrary to Brazil, Spanish American countries followed a more lenient policy toward Indian nations and forbade Indian slavery. Since the days of the Spanish Empire, conversion and settlement rather than enslavement and exploitation were the accepted policies toward Indian nations, many of which refused peaceful contacts and continued to raid settlements. Through a network of missions and outposts, the Spanish Empire hoped to convert Indians to Roman Catholicism by occasional patrols, shiny gifts, and cash payments, and bring them into a sedentary life, or at least gain peace on the frontiers. By the mid-nineteenth century, Spanish American governments had tired of the expense of peaceful conversion. Brazil's example, with its low costs and large benefits, was too tempting an alternative for Spanish America to resist.

When Porfirio Díaz came to power in 1876, he was determined to end all Indian resistance. Treaties with the United States gave both militaries the right of "hot pursuit" across borders, effectively ending safe havens for the Indians. Díaz sent his enlarged army to defeat and imprison large numbers of Indians, particularly the Yaquis. Mexican authorities followed the Brazilian example of sending Indian captives to work as slaves in the hemp plantations of Yucatán. Indian removal opened lands for investors who wanted to develop the mineral wealth of the north. By the 1890s, Indian resistance in the north had ended, and the Díaz regime turned its attention to quash the Maya chieftains in Yucatán. A massive expedition with modern rifles and artillery captured the last Indian areas of Yucatán in 1901, and the central government exercised full control over Mexico.

Most other Spanish American countries faced the challenge of extending their authority over hostile Indian nations, but only Argentina and Chile mounted military campaigns comparable to those in Mexico. In the 1860s, the Chilean government relied on a string of forts to protect the southern border, but the Indians learned how to bypass fortified places to attack the undefended settlements to the north. The government pushed forts farther south in the 1870s, and after the War of the Pacific success, Chile sent its army to quash all Indian resistance. In 1889, repeating rifles and field pieces slaughtered large numbers of Araucanians, while the survivors became cheap laborers in the large-landed estates of the north. What the Spanish Empire failed to accomplish, the Chilean army achieved in a decade, and Chile never again suffered Indian raids.

Since the establishment of Buenos Aires, colonists and nomadic Indians often clashed, but the vast distances in the grasslands kept violence below that experienced in Chile. However, as the export economy expanded south into the *pampas,* or grass plains, in the early nineteenth century, the Indians, who were a nuisance, became a serious obstacle to cattle-raising. In 1833, the dictator Juan Manuel Rosas led an expedition against the Indians. To defend the newly conquered territories, he established a network of forts and signed treaties with frontier Indians. As in Chile, the Indians learned how to bypass the forts and attack the undefended settlements. The expensive frontier forts drained the budget, and when the expansion of wheat exports made the *pampas* valuable land, Argentina decided to eliminate the Indian threat. General Julio

Roca conducted an extermination campaign in 1879–1880 through the southern *pampas* and into the Rio Negro Valley to the south. Indians not killed became captives in Buenos Aires for cheap labor, and immigrants established settlements in former Indian hunting grounds. Indian raids never threatened the highly productive *pampas* again, while Argentina, just like Chile, extended its political control to the southernmost tip of South America.

Revolutionary Nationalism: The Mexican Revolution

In dictator-run countries, elites faced finding successors for aging strongmen, and informal agreements among elite members ensured a transition to a new ruler. Only in Mexico did the elite fail to agree on a successor to Porfirio Díaz, a split that provided the opportunity for the Mexican Revolution. While the elite wavered, the masses rushed to take matters into their own hands. For the first time in its independent history, Latin America experienced real popular participation in the political process.

Porfirio Díaz manipulated the elections to ensure his overwhelming victory every four years, but mishandled the situation in 1910. Rival candidate Francisco Madero, from the safety of the United States, urged Mexicans in November 1910 to overthrow the dictator. Southern peasants and northern seasonal laborers answered Madero's appeal, revolted, and began to seize control from Mexico's government forces. Not wishing to postpone the inevitable, Díaz resigned from office on May 25, 1911, and left for Europe. In new elections, Madero became president later that year.

Madero attempted to introduce an open political system capable of giving the elite middle class support against the lower class, but the latter, who did the real fighting, demanded land reforms and limits on foreign control. Ultraconservative groups feared losing their former privileges, and Madero lacked the political skills to control the situation. A bloody army uprising in February 1913 overthrew Madero, who days later was executed under circumstances that suggested the complicity of his successor, General Victoriano Huerta. Outrage at the murder persuaded many rebel leaders, such as Emiliano Zapata in the south and Pancho Villa in the north, to reject Huerta's government and recognize the authority of Venustiano Carranza, a duly elected governor. The United States supported the rebels and seized the port of Veracruz in April 1914 to stop the flow of arms and revenue to the Huerta regime. The spontaneous resistance of local Mexican citizens to the US occupation of Veracruz shocked US officials. Huerta's position crumbled, and he resigned and fled the country in July 1914.

A civil war among rebel leaders ensued until Carranza, thanks to his alliance with General Álvaro Obregón, emerged victorious as Mexico's ruler. Carranza convoked a convention to draft a new constitution, whose provisions limited the privileges of the Roman Catholic Church and foreign corporations. The 1917 constitution gave labor many rights and proclaimed state ownership of all mineral deposits, including petroleum. The constitution was not socialistic, as it respected private property and provided favorable conditions for private Mexican businesses. Once Carranza became president under the constitution's four-year term, he conveniently ignored most of its reformist clauses. When Carranza tried to bypass the constitution's "no reelection" provision by placing a puppet in the presidency, Obregón came out of retirement in Sonora and mobilized the army in 1920 against Carranza, who was killed while trying to flee to Veracruz.

"No reelection" became a permanent slogan of Mexican politics, but Obregón knew that the country required new policies to remain stable. He attempted to carry out some of the reforms in the 1917 constitution and distributed land to favored peasants. The destructive revolutionary upheavals since 1910 cost Mexico over a million lives, and it could not rely just on an alliance of the elite and middle class and had to satisfy at least some demands insisted on by the lower classes. The land distribution program declined after Obregón but made the greatest gains during the presidency of General Lázaro Cárdenas (1936–1940). By then, Mexico had a peculiar single-party political system. Other political groups and parties could exist, but the government's control over the electoral machinery always made the official party (known as the Institutional Revolutionary Party [PRI] after 1946) victorious in elections until 2000.

Revolutionary nationalism provided stability to Mexico after 1920 because the government did not have to challenge the elite directly. The upper class escaped new taxes, and whenever land confiscations took place, the former owners received compensation and sometimes restitution for their properties. The Mexican government nationalized the foreign-owned oil industry on March 18, 1938. The Mexican government financed its reform program from oil revenues without having to tax the upper class, whose members benefited most from the subsidies and other official incentives to develop new industrial firms in Mexico. Despite the relatively favorable outcome, the high cost in lives and property damage and the risk of unforeseen harmful results made the elites elsewhere in Latin America reject the Mexican version of revolutionary nationalism. Not until the mid-twentieth century did popular movements have the opportunity to adopt revolutionary nationalism as the answer to the region's mounting problems.

The Economy of Latin America, 1914–1990s

World War I alerted Latin America to the dangers of producing only raw materials and foodstuffs for export, yet most countries soon forgot the wartime shortages of imported manufactures and attempted to prolong export expansion into the 1920s. New industries appeared after World War I, and many existing factories expanded their production to tap into the growing domestic market in large countries such as Argentina and Brazil and medium-sized countries like Chile and Colombia. Because the prices of most Latin American exports had been declining since the late nineteenth century, Latin America's capacity to import new products of modern industry were likewise declining, but this disturbing trend went largely unheeded.

The Import Substitution Stage, 1930s–1960s

Latin America's long-delayed industrialization meant that when the Great Depression struck in 1929, changes in the economy and politics were abrupt, rapid, and extensive. Governments throughout Latin America fell from power through either revolts or elections. During the 1930s, governments of the major Latin American countries strongly promoted establishing factories as the best way to replace the expensive imported manufactured goods. Tariff protection, subsidies, privileges, loans, and even direct state ownership became widespread means to launch Latin America into industrialization. The countries attempted to compensate for the neglect of the previous decades with a rushed effort that resulted in many failures, considerable waste, and inferior products. This frantic attempt to shift to manufacturing became known as import substitution industrialization.

Enterprises existing before 1830 and members of the upper class were best placed to profit from the official encouragements, but the drive to industrialize also gave many the opportunity to acquire wealth and prestige as part of the new industrialist class. Disputes arose between the rising industrialists and the old landholding class, but the overwhelming acceptance of the profit motive and a common interest to control the lower class prevented any deep divisions among these elite groups, who were soon joined by extensive intermarriage. To absorb the new industrialists and their corporate structures, both the upper and middle classes expanded in numbers and percentages of the total population.

While the accountants, clerks, and other white-collar personnel could be counted on to defend the interests of the industrialists, the new industrial working class posed a challenge to elite control. In the 1930s, workers in most factories formed labor unions, whose leaders sometimes became powerful figures able to block the political system. The fear of labor militancy was a major reason why some class-conscious Latin Americans opposed industrialization in the first place. The political systems of Latin America struggled to bring the labor unions into the emerging political and economic structures. First and most successful was Mexico, whose revolutionary nationalism proved effective in controlling not only the peasants but also workers and miners. Although strikes occurred in Mexico, the government found corruption, gangsterism, and favoritism more than adequate to keep industrial workers under control.

While import substitution industrialization continued during the 1940s and 1950s, the heavy capital costs of expanding industrial output while maintaining control over the workers often proved unmanageable for the more open political systems in Argentina, Brazil, and Chile. In Chile, the division between labor and business continued to worsen and polarized a political system heading toward confrontation in the 1970s. Two countries revived the old formula of strongmen, first Brazil with Getulio Vargas (1930–1945 and 1951–1954), then Argentina with Juan Perón (1946–1955). The new dictators did not repress labor but instead brought labor leaders into government coalitions. Vargas neutralized the independent labor movement largely because the overabundance of cheap Brazilian labor made unionization difficult. In Argentina, Perón had to satisfy the militant demands of the unions. Yet neither Perón nor Vargas created arrangements to bring organized labor into the political systems, and so after they fell from power, Argentina and Brazil entered a period of turmoil and uncertainty.

Opening to World Markets, 1970s–1990s

Except for Mexico, Latin America had not solved the political problems caused by import substitution. Import substitution ended by the late 1960s, yet Latin America still spent large sums to pay for imported goods, whose local manufacture was not justified because of the limited purchasing power of the numerous impoverished masses. Population growth intensified, and Latin America faced massive unemployment. Only the Mexican government with its oil income had available funds to finance new industries, but these were insufficient to generate full employment. Since the 1960s, increasing numbers of Mexicans had been crossing illegally into the United States seeking to find temporary or permanent employment.

Starting in the 1970s, Latin American countries attempted to enter a new stage characterized by opening to the world economy. Trade barriers and tariffs went down, and the local factories experienced direct competition with foreign products. To help ease the acute shortage of capital, governments encouraged foreign corporations to establish local plants. Once established, these foreign-owned factories made a larger variety and quality of goods available to the public than possible under import substitution's more limited production. A privatization campaign promoted the sale of many state-owned firms to increase efficiency in production.

The bureaucratic-authoritarian regimes pioneered opening countries to the world economy because they knew they lacked the funds to continue financing industrialization. They could also withstand the political backlash from the closing of firms unable to compete with foreign imports. Opening to the world market proved traumatic. Many firms went bankrupt and unemployment increased. Some strong domestic companies increased their exports. Often, opening markets meant open season on the remaining unexploited raw materials of Latin America, such as forests and wildlife. Besides environmental damage, foreign companies frequently came to exploit the original staple of Latin America, cheap labor.

As the bureaucratic-authoritarian regimes gave way in the late 1980s to open political systems, pressure intensified to limit the adverse effects of opening Latin American economies. The sale of state-owned enterprises slowed in the early 1990s, while governments adopted minimal measures to protect the environment and workers. However, the movement toward opening to world trade and investment continued, as did the goal of tearing down all trade barriers within the Western Hemisphere. Mexico led when, in 1993, it entered the North American Free Trade Agreement, which included Canada and the United States. Chile wanted to join NAFTA, and an optimistic United States targeted 2005 for the completion of a free trade zone extending from Alaska to Argentina.

The Cuban Revolution and Resurgence of Revolutionary Nationalism

As Latin America exhausted the possibilities of import substitution industrialization by the 1960s, rising unemployment and a widening income gap between social classes placed considerable strain on the political systems. Popular movements in some countries broke the barriers of elite dominance and took control of the government. Popular participation rarely took the form of conventional electoral politics and instead usually expressed itself through extreme nationalism with leftist and even Marxist tendencies. These popular movements aroused bitter hostility from both the United States and local elites. The second wave of revolutionary nationalism drew inspiration from the Mexican Revolution. Nonetheless, each of the revolutionary regimes differed from the Mexican example and had its own distinctive characteristics.

Guatemala, 1944–1954

The massive loss of life and property during Mexico's violent turmoil during the period 1910–1920 guaranteed that no Latin American country was willing to copy that precedent. However, Guatemala was the link between the earlier upheaval and the second phase of revolutionary nationalism. Many Guatemalan reformers admired Mexico for nationalizing its petroleum resources in 1938. Positive US influences were also present in Guatemala, which received inspiration from the reformist impulses of Franklin D. Roosevelt's New Deal. Guatemala's first order of business in 1944 was to overthrow the local dictator Jorge Ubico. The popular Juan José Arévalo was elected president in 1945 and embarked upon a realistic program of reform, whose modest accomplishments aroused US hostility.

Guatemala's tragedy was timing: its democratic and populist revolutionary nationalism came too late after the New Deal of the 1930s and too early for the anticommunist Alliance for Progress of the 1960s. Arévalo was well aware of the limits of his power and by the end of his term had entered into a working arrangement with United Fruit, the powerful banana company. In 1951, no such moderation hindered Arévalo's successor, Jacobo Árbenz, who confiscated the majority of United Fruit's plantations. During the Cold War, the United States was determined to destroy the Árbenz regime. Árbenz refused to realize how vulnerable his government was. The Central Intelligence Agency (CIA) had been preparing an operation to overthrow Árbenz, and in June 1954 it launched an invasion and convinced the Guatemalan army to depose Árbenz, who had won free and open elections. After the CIA coup, a wave of reprisals and executions ended Guatemala's peaceful experiment with revolutionary nationalism. United Fruit recovered its lands, and the country sank into repression and endemic guerrilla warfare until 1996.

The Cuban Revolution, 1959–1975

The utter disdain of the United States for democratic institutions in Guatemala radicalized Latin American rebels, who adopted extreme leftist views of Marxist orientation and sought to take power through violent insurrection rather than by elections. The most spectacular success came in Cuba, where the charismatic rebel leader Fidel Castro organized a revolutionary movement that defeated and overthrew the local dictator Fulgencio Batista in January 1959. Castro moved fast, and before the United States or the Cuban elite could react, he gained full control of Cuba. By late 1960 he had nationalized the majority of private properties, both foreign and Cuban. The United States tried too late to control Castro; the CIA-organized Bay of Pigs invasion ended in an embarrassing April 1961 fiasco. A humiliated United States prepared to invade Cuba, and as a preliminary step attempted to weaken the regime by economic sanctions, such as a trade embargo, which continues today. Before the United States could attack, the Cuban missile crisis of October 1962 brought the Soviet Union directly into the clash. The Soviet Union agreed to remove its nuclear weapons from Cuba only when the United States pledged not to invade.

Cuba revived revolutionary nationalism for Latin America, but attempts to export the Cuban experience failed miserably. The United States launched the Alliance for Progress in 1960 to show that alternatives existed to Cuban communism and spent large amounts creating new economic and political opportunities. In the midst of Cold War hysteria, the United States was determined to prevent "another Cuba" in the Western Hemisphere and did not hesitate to intervene with troops, as in the Dominican Republic in 1965, even when no danger existed. Direct US military intervention proved largely superfluous, because local elites realized the danger that revolutionary nationalism posed for their privileges. The panic-stricken elites, with substantial US assistance, bolstered the capabilities of the local military, and troops crushed any guerrilla movements that attempted to repeat the Cuban model. The goal of preventing a "second Cuba" was successful until the late 1960s, with varieties of revolutionary nationalism appearing in Peru, then Chile.

The Peruvian Military Experiment, 1968–1975

In most Latin American countries, military expansion converted the army into the single most important political actor. Only in Peru did the army adopt revolutionary nationalism. Popular outrage at the civilian government's excessive privileges granted to US oil company Exxon convinced the Peruvian military to take power in a bloodless coup in October 1968. More by coincidence than intention, Juan Velasco Alvarado's new government stumbled upon revolutionary nationalism. The Velasco government promptly expropriated the entire petroleum sector (whose deposits were only a small fraction of Mexico's) and nationalized most US properties in Peru. Although the revolutionary military promised compensation, the United States immediately brought pressure by blocking loans from international agencies and other economic reprisals. To maintain its popular support, the revolutionary regime nationalized most of the Peruvian elite's large landholdings and distributed the land to the peasants in the form of cooperatives. The military rulers failed to mobilize peasant support but aroused the intense hatred of Peru's elite. Caught between the crossfire of the United States and the local elite, Velasco's revolutionary regime attempted to survive by securing private foreign loans. When prices of Peruvian exports dropped in 1975, the military lost the resources to continue the experiment in revolutionary nationalism. By then, Velasco was ill, and a moderate general took over the government. Under Peruvian elite influence, the conservative generals suspended the revolutionary program and began to dismantle most of Velasco's accomplishments. Peru sank into economic difficulties, and in 1980 a new guerrilla insurrection began.

The Chilean Democratic Experiment, 1970–1973

In Chile, the experiment in revolutionary nationalism began with free and open elections. Chileans were dissatisfied with growing unemployment and the spread of shantytowns. Chileans had lost faith in the promises of the Alliance for Progress and, in protest, cast their votes for Salvador Allende, the socialist candidate for president. Two other major candidates ran, so Allende won with only 37 percent of the total vote, 1 percent more than the runner-up. Allende believed that US respect for elections and Chile's long-standing democratic tradition ensured the completion of his six-year term. However, the CIA and Chilean conspirators were busy plotting his downfall even before he took office.

Allende's greatest accomplishment was the nationalization of US-owned copper mines. He then carried out a moderate reform program to nationalize larger businesses (whether foreign or Chilean) but left small and medium-sized firms in private hands. He also embarked upon agrarian reform to reduce the excessive concentration of land in a few hands. Landowners were furious, while peasants were angry at the slow pace and began to take land on their own; soon, open warfare broke out in rural areas. Labor unions seized firms by force in cities. A parliamentarian at heart, Allende constantly negotiated deals to calm tempers. Congressional elections increased popular support for his government when long-neglected groups for the first time participated directly in the governing process.

Allende was a US pawn in the Cold War, and in Chile the "second Cuba" had to be prevented at any cost. The United States went beyond blocking loans and economic aid to Chile and tried everything possible to turn the people against Allende. The Soviet Union, facing difficulties of its own and already overcommitted in Cuba, was hesitant to help Chile, and soon the country suffered food shortages and rampant inflation. The CIA and the Chilean military conspired to overthrow Allende. On September 11, 1973, the Chilean military under Augusto Pinochet struck. Allende refused to flee and tried to organize a desperate defense with a few followers at the presidential palace in the hope of rallying support against the coup. After air bombardment, troops overran the palace and Allende died, apparently from suicide. Violent repression ensued as the military rounded up tens of thousands of suspects and executed at least 5,000 Chileans. The most savage military coup in Latin America's history ended Chile's democratic experiment with revolutionary nationalism and inaugurated the most repressive of the bureaucratic-authoritarian regimes of the region.

The Nicaraguan Revolution, 1979–1990

By the late 1990s, neither the United States nor local elites were willing to tolerate any more revolutionary nationalism, whether democratic or not. Only extreme desperation brought Nicaragua to make the last experiment with revolutionary nationalism in the twentieth century. Since 1934, Nicaragua had suffered under the repressive Somoza dynasty, and the last dictator, Anastasio Somoza Jr., was the worst. The United States rejected all pleas to withdraw its support from the hated dictator. An opposition movement slowly emerged under the banner of the Sandinistas. The revolts became more frequent and in 1979 a large-scale insurrection began. In response, the dictator bombed and destroyed cities in a desperate attempt to save his regime. Support from Latin American countries in the form of weapons, supplies, and money allowed the Sandinistas to overthrow the dictator in July 1979.

Like in Cuba, rebel forces defeated the army of the dictator. Daniel Ortega's Sandinista government felt confident about embarking upon substantial reforms while accepting the existence of a large private sector. As the Cold War waned, the US government saw Nicaragua as a Soviet puppet and did everything possible to destroy the regime through economic sanctions. The United States became so obsessed with Nicaragua that the CIA organized a rebel force (*contras*) in Costa Rica and Honduras to launch raids and to prepare an invasion to overthrow the Sandinistas. These military efforts against Nicaragua were a costly failure but served the secondary purpose of diverting scarce resources away from critical areas of the economy. US economic sanctions, including a trade embargo, began to strain the population, and Nicaragua could not sustain the unequal struggle against the United States. The opposition candidates financed and supported by the United States defeated the Sandinistas in the 1990 elections. The only positive note was the peaceful power transfer that took place.

Long before the Sandinistas left office in 1990, revolutionary nationalism ceased being an option for most countries. Nevertheless, Latin America's panic-stricken elites were still not convinced that the danger of a "second Cuba" had passed and sought safety in the region's most repressive and failed political experiment, the bureaucratic-authoritarian regimes.

The Bureaucratic-Authoritarian Regimes

To counter the guerrilla threat, Latin American countries requested help from the United States, in the form of arms and training, to increase the size and efficiency of their military forces. Generals and admirals found themselves controlling large budgets and commanding many soldiers in successful campaigns against urban and rural rebels. The military became each country's largest and most effective organization, while civilian institutions languished in a sea of corruption, favoritism, confusion, and inefficiency. As import substitution reached its limits in the 1960s, the question arose of whether the armed forces could transfer their success in guerrilla warfare to the difficult struggle of reviving economic expansion.

Only in Peru did the military embrace revolutionary nationalism to challenge the local elite; in the other countries, the military strongly defended the elite. Bureaucratic-authoritarian regimes eliminated popular participation and ruled through a combination of military officers and well-educated civilians or technocrats. The military closed legislative bodies, outlawed political parties, and repressed labor unions. These regimes promoted the extension of free market principles and cultivated strong ties with foreign corporations in an attempt to attract investment into Latin America. Apart from Peru, the bureaucratic-authoritarian regimes were rather similar. A discussion of the three main regimes—Argentina, Brazil, and Chile—suffices to reveal the main characteristics of the bureaucratic-authoritarian experiments.

Brazil, 1964–1974

Brazil, the first bureaucratic-authoritarian regime, became the example for the rest of Latin America's military. Unfounded fears that the weak presidency of João Goulart might adopt revolutionary nationalism brought the Brazilian military to power in a bloodless coup in early April 1964. The military at first cooperated with politicians and promised new elections, but once the generals consolidated their grip on the country, they discarded the traditional political leaders. The generals' intention to stay in power a long time was clearly stated when they abolished congress and political parties.

The military strove to apply free market principles, but in practice the policy consisted of favoring foreign corporations and most segments of Brazil's elite while keeping wages low through constant repression of the labor movement. As consumers' purchasing power declined because of falling wages, Brazil exported surplus products from its factories. Remarkably, some years the annual growth rate reached 10 percent, and economists enthusiastically talked about the "Brazilian miracle."

But success proved more apparent than real, because foreign borrowing financed most of the expansion, and the military regime could not repay the loans. Labor unrest and sporadic guerrilla raids persuaded the military regime to adopt a harsh repression policy between 1968 and 1974. Consistent use of torture, mass arrests, and secret executions turned the middle class and some of the upper class against the military regime. Cheap imports and foreign corporations ruined the businesses of many elites, who became bitter enemies of military rule. Without popular input, high officials, whether military or civilian, antagonized many social groups.

By the mid-1970s, the military had authorized the formation of two political parties, one government and the other opposition, but the official party could win elections only in rural provinces, where bosses controlled the local political machines. Not even the contradictory electoral coalition of the most backward regions of Brazil, with the very efficient military, could suspend the end of Brazil's experiment with a bureaucratic-authoritarian government. In a series of slow and partial moves, the Brazilian military strategically withdrew, ceding control to civilians first in the cities and then in the provinces. The last step came in 1985 when José Sarney, one of the old politicians, took office after winning elections. The dismal performance of the Sarney presidency and his civilian successors helped restore the tarnished image of the Brazilian military, whose bureaucratic-authoritarian experiment was not as disastrous and tragic as that of Argentina.

Argentina, 1966–1983
Brazil's apparent initial success convinced Argentina's military to establish a bureaucratic-authoritarian regime. The June 1966 coup wanted to

eliminate any possibility of a revolutionary nationalistic alternative and was also an attempt to prevent former dictator Juan Perón's return to power. An initial wave of repression started the bureaucratic-authoritarian regime, but widespread violent opposition made impossible a permanent transformation of Argentina.

The military concluded that crushing the opposition was a prerequisite for establishing a real bureaucratic-authoritarian regime. The military gained time by allowing the elderly Juan Perón to return to office in 1973. He died less than a year later, and his wife, Isabel, his vice president, replaced him. The Isabel administration was incompetent, but the military allowed her to retain the presidency until March 1976 to discredit the Peronists as a valid alternative.

Back in power, the military launched a ferocious campaign to exterminate terrorist groups and other suspected opponents of the bureaucratic-authoritarian regime. The Argentine military kidnapped suspects and then tortured and secretly killed them. Not until the late 1980s were some of the mass graves discovered. Violations of human rights were rampant throughout the bureaucratic-authoritarian regimes, and only Chile equaled Argentina's bloody record of abuses and extrajudicial executions.

The Argentine military opened the country to foreign corporations and world trade in the hope of restoring economic prosperity. As in Brazil, Argentina's foreign debt ballooned out of control, and inflation accelerated. Wage freezes angered labor unions and the middle classes, anti-government demonstrations increased in size and frequency, and members of the elite who had suffered from the opening of the economy to world competition joined the opposition.

An incident over the British-held Falklands/Malvinas in the South Atlantic gave the military government the opportunity to restore its shattered prestige through a swift occupation of the islands in April 1982. An inept military campaign gave the British the opportunity to recapture the islands in June; this humiliating defeat doomed the bureaucratic-authoritarian regime. Unable to govern a country or fight a war, the military had no choice but to call for elections and concede power to the winner, civilian Raúl Alfonsín, in 1983. By then, Brazil's transition to a civilian government was well under way, leaving Chile as the last of the large countries still trying to preserve its bureaucratic-authoritarian regime.

Chile, 1973–1990

The September 1973 coup ended the revolutionary nationalist experiment of Salvador Allende and imposed on Chile a brutal bureaucratic-authoritarian regime. The military under Augusto Pinochet seized power and arrested tens of thousands of suspects, many of whom stayed for years in the only concentration camps Latin America has ever known. The military promptly killed over 5,000 people in the bloodiest coup in Latin American history. Unlike in other Latin American countries, where generals took turns occupying the presidency, in Chile, one general, Pinochet, emerged as the undisputed leader, with powers exceeding those of traditional dictators.

The Pinochet regime followed the traditional formula of opening up Chile to foreign economies and keeping wages down. The bloody repression of labor unions and the killing or imprisonment of many of its leaders made possible the implementation of low wages. Massive borrowing from abroad brought capital into the economy. The civilian economists seemingly achieved some success, and as the Brazilian "economic miracle" faded in the mid-1970s the "Chilean economic miracle" captivated world attention. The upper class and most of the middle class concluded that military dictatorship was Chile's inevitable price to attain economic prosperity.

Many Chilean firms went bankrupt after the opening of foreign trade, and when the flow of foreign loans abruptly ended in 1982, the Chilean economy collapsed. Unemployment rose sharply, and in 1983, for the first time, massive protests erupted and continued to increase in frequency and size during successive years as the economic situation worsened. Civilian groups who originally supported the dictatorship became Pinochet's opponents, who eventually lost the backing even of conservatives. In a desperate gamble to restore his crumbling authority, Pinochet convoked a referendum in October 1988 to ratify him as president for ten more years. In the military regime's first free election, the dictator suffered a resounding rejection. Opposition groups coalesced behind Patricio Aylwin, who defeated Pinochet's handpicked candidate.

The new civilian president Aylwin took office in March 1990, but Chile's military was massively influential. Pinochet remained the head of the armed forces, and the civilian government could not remove him from office. Only gradually did the new civilian government loosen the military's grip over congress and the judiciary. The succeeding civilian presidencies proved sufficiently competent in both economic and political arenas to remove the possibility of Chile's return to a bureaucratic-authoritarian regime.

Chile was under a dictatorship for seventeen years. Successive Chilean governments attempted to hold Pinochet's government accountable for its violent human rights violations, including mass executions, torture, exile, imprisonment without trial, and even raids on shanty-towns, where men were rounded up and stripped naked in the rain while women and children watched. In 1990 and 1991, a truth and reconciliation commission reported cases of deaths and disappearances. However, though worried that their pain would be forgotten or normalized, people in locations around Chile who suffered enormously were too scared to testify, but in January 2010, President Michelle Bachelet, herself a victim of the dictatorship, inaugurated a memorial museum in Santiago housing a huge collection of archives recording the abuses of the Pinochet government (Dorfman 2018).

The Spread of Electoral Democracy

By 1990, Latin America's bureaucratic-authoritarian experiment was over, and almost every country strove to increase popular participation and move toward an open political system. Because Latin America has such deep traditions of authoritarianism and strong presidential power, the test for the newly elected governments has been not how well they ruled, but rather how well they met people's economic and social expectations without unduly antagonizing local elites. Chile has been modestly successful reconciling the elite and modest economic growth with benefits for other social classes. However, even countries with a longer tradition of electoral democracy, particularly Venezuela, experienced coup attempts.

4

Politics

Shelley A. McConnell

Latin America's colonial inheritance runs deep, based on three centuries of rule by Spain and Portugal. The conquest in the 1500s was a process in which millions of Indigenous inhabitants were killed by war and disease, and later more died performing grueling labor under colonial governments. Some Indigenous groups experienced cultural displacement akin to ethnocide in a violent and tragic remaking of their world. Although colonizers from Europe called the Americas the "New World," it would be more accurate to say Latin America was an old world that was radically transformed—socially, economically, politically, and environmentally—by the conquest and subsequent exchange of goods and ideas with Europe (Miller 2007).

Most of Latin America would become independent in the 1820s through violent independence wars against Spain, and later Brazil would peacefully separate from Portugal. They adopted presidential constitutions patterned on the United States rather than the parliamentary system used in the United Kingdom, though Haiti and Peru have since developed semi-presidential systems. In addition to the executive, legislative, and judicial branches of government, several countries later established a separate electoral branch. The countries retained the civil law systems inherited from Spain and Portugal, modifying them but never adopting the common law practices used in the United States, United Kingdom, and English-speaking Caribbean countries.

Modern Latin American political culture exhibits patriarchal, hierarchic, and patrimonial tendencies that are often ascribed to Iberian cultural origins (Wiarda and Kline 1985). A colonial legacy of weak rule of law encouraged political violence in the form of rebellions, revolutions, military coups, and strong-arm tactics by political strongmen, known as *caudillos*. Poverty, which may be seen as a form of ongoing structural violence, can be traced back to racist colonial maldistribution of land and economic opportunities. Social hierarchies based on race, ethnicity, class, and gender became entrenched such that centuries later inequality and exclusion still make it difficult to build democracy.

Hard on the heels of Latin America's independence from Spain and Portugal, in 1823 the United States unilaterally issued the Monroe Doctrine, warning European powers not to intervene in the Western Hemisphere. It implicitly asserted a US sphere of influence in the Americas, particularly in the Caribbean Basin, which was deemed to be geostrategically vital to US security. A period of US expansionism followed in which the US population pushed westward, displacing American Indians from their ancestral lands and seizing territory from Mexico. American leaders tried to justify US aggression through an ideology of Manifest Destiny that falsely depicted the Anglo-Saxon race as superior and its domination of Latin America as inevitable.

At the end of the 1800s the US economy grew to be the largest in the world, tripling in size (Williams 2012). US victory in the Spanish-American War in 1901 resulted in Spain relinquishing control of Cuba and ceding Puerto Rico to the United States. The United States made Cuba a de facto protectorate by forcing the island nation to adopt the Platt Amendment, which granted the United States control over Cuba's foreign policy as well as use of Guantanamo Bay as a US naval base. US investments in Latin America grew rapidly such that most countries in the region became economically dependent on the United States in what was best understood as a new form of imperialism centered on economic domination.

In 1904, President Theodore Roosevelt's so-called corollary to the Monroe Doctrine made Latin America's subordinate status plain by asserting a US right to intervene militarily in Latin American countries for the collection of debts, and indeed whenever the United States concluded that a country's governance was inadequate. The US Marines were sent to occupy Haiti, the Dominican Republic, and Nicaragua for lengthy periods. President Franklin D. Roosevelt instituted the Good Neighbor Policy in 1933, but this US promise not to intervene in Latin America's internal affairs soon proved hollow.

In short, although Latin America won formal political independence from its Spanish and Portuguese colonizers, the new republics entered into a global system dominated by British and later American capital and military might. As a consequence Latin America remained dependent on foreign powers. Internally, too, independence changed less than one might suppose. It benefited elites of European parentage but left those of mixed race, Amerindians, African slaves, and their descendants trapped in the same exploitative labor systems as before. The roots of the problem lay in the region's agro-export economies centered on commodities that experienced periodic booms and busts. In colonial times these commodities had been silver, cochineal, guano, cacao, sugar, and coffee, and after independence they would include cotton, rubber, and bananas, but Latin America's structural vulnerability to world markets remained unchanged (Topik, Marichal, and Zephyr 2006). This economic dependency, coupled with racist and classist social stratification, would produce profound inequalities that were maintained by authoritarian political institutions. The struggles to achieve full political autonomy, democracy, and a decent standard of living for Latin Americans would remain at the heart of the region's political dynamics into the twenty-first century.

Authoritarian Rule

The countries of Latin America have historically swung back and forth between limited democracy and authoritarian rule (Pastor 1989). With each swing of the pendulum in a democratic direction the breadth of the electorate increased. Whereas once only propertied white men had the vote, voting rights were incrementally extended so that modern Latin America now adheres to the democratic norm of universal suffrage without regard to race, class, or sex. Elites were reluctant to share power, but the end of slavery, increased literacy, the development of industry, and consequent urbanization changed social dynamics and enabled citizens to demand more rights.

Democracies posit that power lies with the people, who may govern directly or authorize representatives to act on their behalf. Elites who control the state machinery are accountable to the public, and like other citizens they are subject to the law. Modern liberal democratic regimes feature citizen participation, guarantees of civil liberties, and competition among differing ideas and between parties and candidates seeking to win elections. Citizens enjoy universal suffrage and also may choose to participate in politics between elections by joining interest groups and social movements to pressure the government for change. Democracy includes more than free and fair elections, featuring such things as the rule of law, independent judiciaries, and meaningful opportunities for citizens to exercise their political rights (Diamond 2008). There is disagreement concerning whether to include social and economic rights as essential to the definition of democracy, but a landmark study of democratic regimes between 1950 and 1990 showed that democracies that do not provide their citizens with a decent standard of living do not last long (Przeworski et al. 2000).

Although Latin America's long-term trajectory in favor of democracy has been encouraging, in the twentieth century progress toward democracy was regularly interrupted by military coups. From the mid-1960s until the end of the 1970s most countries in the region had authoritarian regimes, and in Central America these endured into the 1990s. This means that many adults in Latin America today recall a time when their civil liberties were highly restricted; there was no freedom of speech, freedom of assembly, or freedom of the press, and voting was either nonexistent or confined to local and state elections. During that period, many countries were governed by the military as an institution, but a few had personalist dictatorships (e.g., the Somoza dynasty in Nicaragua) or rule by a dominant political party (Mexico).

Only Venezuela and Costa Rica could have been described as liberal democracies, at least in the minimalist sense that they consistently held free and fair elections for national office and constitutionally endorsed civil rights and liberties. Even in these countries social and economic inequalities were so deep that formal equality under the law did little to remedy the plight of the poor. Colombia had an elected government, but the state was virtually absent in much of the territory held by Marxist guerrilla groups, the largest of which was the Revolutionary Armed Forces of Colombia, founded in 1964. The remaining countries established authoritarian regimes, and all except Peru were politically right-wing and enacted deeply conservative policies that sought to preserve social-class hierarchies premised on economic and social inequality.

Some political culture scholars were not surprised by the collapse of the nascent democracies that had sprouted in Latin America in the wake of World War II and the Allied victory over fascism. They suggested that because the Catholic Church was hierarchical and patriarchic, with a single leader called the pope whose word was deemed infallible, countries with Catholic cultures were more prone to authoritarian rule and unlikely to be democratic. A far more persuasive explanation lies in US policy (Diamond 2008). During the Cold War, which began just after World War II in 1947 and endured until the dissolution of the Soviet Union in 1991, US foreign policy prioritized anticommunist security concerns over democratic governance. A pattern of heavy-handed US intervention in Latin America prevailed, intending to combat communism and advance US private sector interests (Williams 2012).

In 1954, the US Central Intelligence Agency helped Guatemalan rebels to overthrow the democratically elected government of their country because its progressive president, Jacobo Arbenz, had enacted an agrarian reform that nationalized land belonging to the United Fruit Company to distribute it to landless peasants. The United States similarly organized Cuban exiles to overthrow the communist regime of Fidel Castro, which had come to power via revolution in 1959. However, this "Bay of Pigs" invasion failed, and as a defense against US hostility Cuba invited the Soviet Union to place missiles in Cuba that could carry nuclear warheads and threaten much of the US population. US detection of those missiles precipitated the Cuban missile crisis in 1962, thirteen tense days during which the United States and Soviet Union came as close to nuclear war as they ever would. War was averted when the Soviet Union withdrew the missiles in exchange for a US pledge not to invade communist Cuba. Nonetheless, the United States instituted limits on trade, tourism, and financial interactions with Cuba in another failed effort to topple the communist regime. Meanwhile Cuba received substantial Soviet economic support that enabled the island to present a communist development model as an alternative to US dependency. Citizens received free education, healthcare, and other social services that many other Latin Americans lacked. However, the government owned most businesses, national leaders were not elected, and the regime strictly limited civil rights and liberties.

In 1965, President Johnson committed tens of thousands of US troops to an invasion and occupation of the Dominican Republic to prevent a progressive government from coming to power. In 1973 the United States supported a military coup against Chile's elected socialist president Salvador Allende, resulting in a sixteen-year dictatorship by General Augusto Pinochet. In the 1980s, the Reagan administration sponsored an armed counterrevolutionary war against the Sandinista National Liberation Front (FSLN) government in Nicaragua, a socialist revolutionary regime that sought to reduce inequality. The policy financed US proxy forces called counterrevolutionaries, or *contras* in Spanish, to wage so-called low-intensity warfare in an effort to overthrow the Sandinistas. The United States also instituted another trade and financial embargo, badly damaging Nicaragua's social and economic development. In El Salvador and Guatemala the Reagan administration channeled funds to military governments to suppress socialist revolutionary movements and preserve the power of landed elites. This record of US intervention in support of right-wing autocrats and military regimes understandably made Latin Americans skeptical about claims of the United States to support democracy.

In Central America, US support for anticommunist dictatorships permitted a classical form of military rule to prosper in which the military governed directly or with a puppet president providing a facade of democratic governance. Power lay in an alliance between military officers and landed oligarchs who dominated economies based on large estates engaged in monocrop agriculture. Because of their opposition to communism these regimes often enjoyed the support of traditional bishops in the Catholic Church, though other clergy subscribed to a progressive philosophy of liberation theology that advocated for greater social equality.

The Central American dictatorships ran highly underdeveloped economies dedicated to producing agricultural commodities and only the most rudimentary manufactured goods. These countries were generally dependent on the United States as their primary export destination and main source of imports, foreign direct investment, and government aid. Although Costa Rica became democratic in 1948, abolishing its military and spending its budget on social improvements, it was the exception that proved the rule. Elsewhere in Central America, in the absence of any means to obtain change through voting, regime opponents took up arms. In the 1970s, inspired by the Cuban revolution and its achievements in social and economic equality, socialist revolutionary movements spread through El Salvador, Nicaragua, and Guatemala and the region descended into civil war.

In South America, too, radicals had turned to revolution as the only means to force elites to share wealth and power. In response, military regimes seized control of governments through a series of coups in the 1960s and 1970s. They suppressed socialist guerrilla movements relatively quickly, but instead of returning power to civilians as they had so often done before, this time the military remained in government (Isacson 2020d). Portions of the public supported these authoritarian regimes based on their performance in providing security and economic development, but perceptions of government legitimacy were eroded by revelations from human rights organizations, which were aided in some countries by Catholic clergy. Human rights groups documented reports of kidnapping, torture, extrajudicial killings, military assaults on rural villages, and murders committed by paramilitary death squads linked to the military, police, and right-wing governing parties. By contrast, judiciaries and the media often stood silent in the face of government repression or even cooperated with it (Wright 2007).

Latin America's military regimes also presided over an important shift in the region's economic development strategy from import substitution industrialization to export-led growth. In the 1930s, Latin America had adopted import substitution industrialization, putting in place tariffs to protect domestic businesses from foreign competition and fostering industrial production. This had contributed to growth and the development of domestic markets and a small middle class. However, as South America shifted from light industry to the production of more complex goods, it needed capital investment from local elites, the government, and foreign investors. Military governments therefore shifted to a neoliberal development strategy of production for export. They drew in foreign investors by lowering corporate taxes and banning labor strikes to depress wages. This helped to control inflation, as citizens had little money to spend, but it also hurt the working class.

With citizens unable to hold military governments accountable, Latin American governments borrowed heavily from US commercial banks to achieve sufficient capital investment to sustain high growth rates. Between 1975 and 1982, $60 billion was loaned to Latin America, nearly quadrupling the region's foreign debt, with 60 percent of the money flowing to the region's two largest economies, Mexico and Brazil (Green and Branford 2013). The sheer size of the debt, combined with increases in interest rates, spelled disaster. In 1982, Mexico and then Brazil announced they were unable to service their debt, meaning they could not make the interest payments plus repay the portion of the principle due on certain foreign loans. A cascade of smaller countries then defaulted on their loans as well, precipitating what became known as the Latin American debt crisis (Vanden and Prevost 2002). The crisis debunked the claim that authoritarian leaders insulated from public demands would necessarily govern the economy better than elected civilians. Shortly thereafter, one by one, Latin American countries underwent transitions to elected civilian governments, and the military went back to the barracks.

To prevent their own financial collapse, international lenders renegotiated the terms of Latin America's loans, rescheduling the debt to permit repayment over a longer period of time. However, the damage to Latin American economies was deep, and growth rates slowed so dramatically they had trouble keeping pace with population expansion. The 1980s would become known in Latin America as the "lost decade" because no real progress on development was made, in part because there was a net outflow of capital from Latin America. Later, in the 2000s, some highly indebted small countries obtained outright debt forgiveness, but the region as a whole remains deeply in debt and vulnerable to changes in interest rates that are beyond its control.

The International Monetary Fund (IMF) and its most important backer, the United States, required that Latin American governments implement structural adjustment measures to restore their international creditworthiness. Latin American countries were forced to shrink public employment, cut government subsidies on goods and services like cooking gas and bus fares, reform pension systems to reduce payments on which elderly citizens survived, privatize state-owned utilities, ratchet up the value-added tax (collected much like a sales tax), reduce regulation of markets, and liberalize trade. These measures hurt some domestic businesses and the poor, removing social safety nets and making life highly uncertain by contributing to unemployment (Stiglitz 2002). Latin American acceptance of such neoliberal reforms and consequent US support for the elected governments made it appear that for once there was agreement on what constituted good governance, and some observers began to refer to this policy mix as the Washington Consensus. In fact, consensus was absent and the reforms were undertaken of necessity. The overall effects of these policies were that although Latin American economies would begin to grow again in the 1990s, the gains were not well distributed, such that poverty remained much the same and inequality worsened.

Transitions to Democracy

As the Soviet Union weakened, leading to the 1989 fall of the Berlin Wall and transitions to democracy in the former Soviet satellite countries of Poland, Hungary, and Czechoslovakia, the United States grew less concerned about communism in Latin America. The 1990s would be an exceptional political window of time during which the United States supported democratic development, albeit in a liberal form that emphasized elections and formal rights rather than citizen empowerment. By the end of the century every Latin American country except Cuba had an elected national government. Beginning in the Dominican Republic and Ecuador in the late 1970s, then sweeping through Brazil, Argentina, Uruguay, Chile, and up to the Andean countries in the 1980s, Latin America adopted democratic governance in a fashion that lent credence to the notion of "snowballing," in which democracy is believed to spread most quickly from one country to the next where there are cultural similarities and common political histories (Huntington 1991). By the 1990s the trend had reached Central America, where previously only

Costa Rica had been democratic. The capstone to the democratization trend came in 2000 when Mexico's so-called perfect dictatorship of the Institutionalized Revolutionary Party (PRI) was broken by electoral reforms that resulted in the election of the pro-business National Action Party (PAN), ending seventy-one straight years of PRI control of Mexico's powerful presidency.

Latin American militaries had their own reasons for leaving government. They were inherently uncomfortable with governance because policy debates within the officer corps introduced division and disrupted the unity of command (Huntington 1991). Moreover, officers who had trained for national defense did not find professional satisfaction in carrying out the mundane tasks of governance such as paving the streets and running schools and hospitals. Ultimately military governments would give up the reins of power, either via agreements negotiated with moderate civilian leaders, accession to reformist pressures from their publics, or, as in Argentina, where the military had lost a war intended to establish its control of the Falkland Islands, by a collapse of military authority.

Whatever their path to democracy, authoritarian rulers would exit only after issuing themselves an amnesty for the crimes they had committed, and after ensuring that they would retain control over the military as an institution, sometimes even appointing the minister of defense. New civilian governments faced a daunting task to eliminate the remnants of military privileges and influence in governmental affairs. Much progress has been made, but in some countries the military still views itself as the guardian of the constitution and stands poised for intervention. Military subordination to civilian rule remains tenuous in many countries and untested in others.

When it came to their human rights records, outgoing military governments constructed a false narrative that asserted they had acted with restraint, using force only as necessary to eliminate communist revolutionary groups that threatened national security. The military claimed that those who were jailed had committed crimes and merited their punishment while those who were missing had gone into exile voluntarily (Jelin 2003). The truth was very different. Many new democratic governments held truth commissions at which thousands of victims testified about flagrant human rights violations committed by the military, police, and paramilitary death squads (Hayner 2011). Highly trained forensic teams unearthed secret detention centers and mass graves in Argentina, Chile, Guatemala, and El Salvador. It soon became clear that the repression had been widespread and systematic rather than just a series of isolated incidents by a few overzealous officers. In Argentina, for example, more than 10,000 disappearances were documented and the real number of missing persons presumed dead is perhaps as high as 30,000 (CONADEP 1984).

In response to these atrocities, Latin America began a process of transitional justice that is still ongoing, using a combination of truth commissions, trials, public acknowledgment of past wrongs, compensation to survivors, and memorialization through museums and public artworks. The civilian governments sought to foster some degree of reconciliation in societies where conservative citizens who still lauded the military governments lived alongside the victims of military repression. Captured in the title of the Argentine truth commission report *Nunca Más* (CONADEP 1984) was the hope that transitional justice measures could ensure that such horrific human rights abuses would "Never Again" take place.

During the Pinochet dictatorship in Chile from 1973 to 1990, more than 3,000 people were "disappeared" or subjected to extrajudicial killing by state security forces, and the fate of a third of them remains unknown. Under democracy, Chilean governments have attempted to investigate the Pinochet regime's record of political murder through three national truth commissions, in 1990, 2003, and 2010. Prosecutions resulted in over 2,500 convictions. As of April 2019, however, another 1,340 cases remained in progress, of which 76 percent were only in the preliminary phases of investigation. Although at least four cases of enforced disappearances have reportedly occurred since the advent of democracy in 1990, these cases are under criminal investigation and it is clear that impunity no longer exists for human rights violators (Convention on Enforced Disappearances 2019).

By contrast, most countries have had difficulty prosecuting human rights abusers. Peru experienced widespread violence and human rights violations committed both by the state security forces and the Marxist guerrilla groups they fought to suppress. The most prominent of these was the Maoist Sendero Luminoso (Shining Path), founded in 1970, but smaller armed groups like the Tupac Amaru Revolutionary Movement were also active in the 1980s and early 1990s. Peru's General Directorate for the Search for Disappeared Persons believes that at least 20,349 persons were disappeared in those two decades, predominantly adult men, although shockingly 10 percent were minors. A law enacted in June 2016 enabled prosecutions and encouraged identification of clandestine burial sites, identification of victims, and the return of their remains. Nonetheless, as of April 2019, just 403 cases of disappearances had been investigated, and 75 were under investigation, with just 10

Feminist protesters demonstrate in Santiago, Chile, calling for democracy during the military dictatorship of Augusto Pinochet. Credit: Photograph by Kena Lorenzini, donated to the Museum of Memory and Human Rights with permission for republication, https://commons .wikimedia.org/wiki/File:Feministas_en_lucha_anti_Pinochet_(de_Kena_Lorenzini).jpg

convictions. This poor record arose in part because the Peruvian armed forces have refused to testify and share information that is essential to effective prosecution. Pervasive official corruption under the presidencies of Alan García and Pedro Pablo Kuczynski also contributed to the slow pace of transitional justice.

To its credit, Peru has provided financial reparations to 18,352 family members of victims totaling $21 million and has dedicated another $82 million to collective reparations for groups and communities. More recently the Peruvian government has begun human rights training of justice officials, members of the armed forces, the police, and other security personnel in the hope that institutional reforms and inculcation of respect for human rights norms will prevent violations in the future even if punishment for past atrocities is still lacking (Government of Peru 2019).

Over the course of the 1990s, countries in the Western Hemisphere worked together through the Organization of American States (OAS) to establish norms in support of democratic development (Mace and Haslam 2007). In 1990, the OAS General Assembly approved Resolution 1080, which pledged that in the event of a military coup the foreign ministers would meet to take diplomatic action. Soon thereafter the OAS members agreed not to recognize governments that came to power by means other than elections. In 2001 they signed the Inter-American

Democratic Charter, which defined the essential elements of democracy and created a mechanism for expelling undemocratic countries from the OAS. Two affiliated bodies, the Inter-American Commission on Human Rights and the Inter-American Court on Human Rights, conducted investigations, ruled torture a violation of international law, and found that the amnesties forced on incoming democratic governments had no legal standing. Regrettably, after the terrorist attacks on the United States in September 2001, security concerns once again eclipsed US support for Latin American democracy, just as they had during the Cold War.

The Turn to the Left

Public disappointment in the performance of elected governments in the 1980s and 1990s gave rise to a new generation of nationalist leftist leaders who began to articulate resistance to neoliberalism, often characterizing it as a form of US intervention (Levitsky and Roberts 2011). They advocated for a modified form of socialism that accepted the need for capitalism and elections, but placed limits on markets in an effort to protect the interests of the working class. Symbolized most clearly by the 1998 election of Venezuelan president Hugo Chávez, this resistance to neoliberalism would spread to Bolivia and result in the election of union leader Evo Morales in 2005; to Nicaragua, which reelected revolutionary leader Daniel Ortega in 2006; and to Ecuador, which elected progressive economist Rafael Correa in 2007. The goal of these leaders was what Chávez termed "twenty-first-century socialism," which could be distinguished from the classical communism found in Cuba by the continued election of government leaders and their willingness to base the economy on modified market economics rather than state ownership of business enterprises. Chávez and other leaders of Latin America's "turn to the left" favored nationalization of key resources such as oil and natural gas, centered on renegotiation of contracts with foreign companies to keep more of the profits in the country. Although some private property in Venezuela was seized outright, Latin America's new "resource nationalism" was a far cry from full state ownership of the means of production (Weitzman 2012).

The progressive turn in Latin American politics coincided fortuitously with rapid growth in China, whose demand for commodities drove up the prices of Latin American exports between 2002 and 2014 (Hearn and León-Maríquez 2011). As national incomes rose, progressive leaders were able to engage in social spending on the poor, and that had an important effect in lowering poverty and inequality. In 2002, following decades of neoliberal development, over one-third of Latin Americans still lived in poverty, and nearly 80 million people lived in extreme poverty (Karl 2003). Between 2002 and 2017, however, with governments increasing social spending to 53 percent of the budget on average, the poverty numbers decreased continually through 2015 (CEPAL 2019). In 2018, data showed that 30 percent lived in poverty and 66 million lived in extreme poverty. The lowest strata of middle-income earners are highly vulnerable to being plunged into poverty by unemployment, but even when they are added into the calculations, Latin America saw substantial improvements. In 2002 a whopping 71 percent of Latin Americans lived in poverty or the lowest middle-income strata, but that number fell in 2018 to 56 percent of the population. Importantly, the 2.3% increase in poverty between 2014 and 2018 was mostly due to problems in Venezuela and Brazil, while the remaining countries saw poverty continue to fall. What drove the poverty rate down was mainly earnings as governments intervened to expand employment. However, the improvements were also due to public spending, social safety nets, and an influx of foreign remittances, especially to Central America (CEPAL 2019).

Equality also improved, though less than was initially believed. In 2002, one-quarter of the region's national income flowed to just 5 percent of the population, and the richest 10 percent held 40 percent of the region's wealth (Karl 2003). As countries moved away from neoliberal policies, the Gini coefficient, in measuring income inequality for fifteen Latin American countries, fell from 54 in 2002 to 47 in 2018 (with 0 representing perfect equality and 100 perfect inequality) (CEPAL 2019). Assessment of this improvement was nonetheless tempered by looking at better measures of inequality that took into account tax information and net wealth, and that still showed a tremendous concentration of wealth in the hands of the wealthiest 1 percent of the population. Even so, the general picture was one of substantially lower poverty and slightly lower inequality.

Importantly, the gains were not due simply to higher commodity prices but also to how the windfall profits from those booms were spent. This shows that good governance matters even in countries whose peripheral insertion in the international economy leaves them exposed to substantial variations in export prices. Moreover, the discourse used in discussing underdevelopment had shifted. Whereas the Washington Consensus had demanded a smaller role for states in managing the economy, by 2018 international development agencies envisioned the development of welfare states in Latin America as their central goal (CEPAL 2019). The contrast could not have been more stark.

The leaders of the new left who were generating these economic reforms tended to be political outsiders who drew on public disappointment with established political parties. Like the populists of the 1930s, they made promises to provide prosperity and social services. However, rather than connecting to their constituents through political parties and affiliated unions, these modern neopopulists used mass media to communicate directly with the public (Roberts 2007). Some, including Chávez, developed a personality cult. They wielded charismatic authority, meaning they were regarded by their followers as extraordinarily gifted leaders able to discern the correct political path to follow. Their critique of neoliberalism was shared by moderate progressive presidents such as Ricardo Lagos in Chile, Luiz Ignácio Lula da Silva in Brazil, and Nestor Kirchner in Argentina, whose center-left governments were reformist in nature. Key differences between "hardline" and "softline" leftist leaders lay in the extent to which they were willing to limit private property rights in the public interest, and to manipulate politics to stay in office beyond two terms.

In Colombia, by contrast, voters in 2002 chose right-winger Álvaro Uribe, who launched an all-out military campaign against the Marxist rebels who had occupied much of the country for decades. Ignoring concerns of human rights abuses, and with the largest aid package that the United States had ever given a Latin American country, the armed forces dealt the guerrillas repeated military defeats, capitalizing on the fact that key leaders in the FARC had died or resigned. Now holding a more favorable strategic position at the bargaining table, Uribe's center-right successor, Juan Manuel Santos, was able to negotiate a peace accord that ended fifty-two years of war and earned him the Nobel Peace Prize. Colombians were divided, however, with a slim majority concluding that the accords were too lenient toward former guerrillas, who would not be required to serve jail sentences despite having committed numerous serious crimes. The accords were rejected in a public referendum, and with the election of another hard-right government Colombia's peace process was left in limbo. A revised accord would be implemented, but absent broad support the economic and political reintegration of former Marxist guerrillas and right-wing paramilitary forces moved slowly (Isacson 2020c).

In El Salvador, which had also endured a lengthy civil war against a socialist guerrilla army in the 1980s, first the conservatives won election in the 1990s and then the former guerrillas' party won the presidency, but neither could prevent soaring crime rates or generate social equality. Growing political disenchantment with established parties on both sides of the political spectrum produced legislative elections in 2018 in which a stunning 58 percent of voters did not go to the polls despite the fact that voting was obligatory, and another 10 percent either defaced their ballot or left it blank (Diamond 2018). This is evidence of what democratization scholars term *desencanto,* or disenchantment with democracy, which can erode public support not only for a given government but also for all established parties, inviting voters to opt for political outsiders, and if that doesn't work then to support a return to authoritarian rule.

The broad picture of regime change is that although transitions to democracy often went more smoothly than expected, consolidation of democracy has been more difficult. All democracies face challenges, and they are often resilient in formulating solutions precisely because they are able to bring in new leadership with fresh ideas. In Latin America, however, the quality of democracy has varied substantially, deepening in some countries but merely persisting in others. Some countries are little more than electoral democracies, holding periodic free and fair elections but providing few opportunities for meaningful political participation between elections.

A frank assessment suggests that democracy is now failing outright in a handful of countries, and is deeply challenged in others. One example is Haiti, an exceptionally poor country, which in 2010 was struck by a devastating earthquake that leveled portions of the capital city. Haiti has been unable to stabilize democratic institutions despite three decades of assistance from the United Nations and Organization of American States. Nicaragua, which became democratic for the first time in 1990, swiftly regressed to authoritarianism, as is often the case for such first attempts at democratic governance. The dominance of the Sandinista National Liberation Front party became institutionalized in ways that eroded competition for power. President Daniel Ortega obtained a Supreme Court decision allowing him to run for the presidency without term limits. In 2011, after achieving a substantial reduction in poverty rates, Ortega won a third term in elections that were criticized by international observers, and that delivered the FSLN a landslide majority in the legislature such that the party could unilaterally change the constitution. The legislature gave Ortega enhanced decree powers, and the security forces were placed more directly under his control. At the local level, money once provided to municipal governments was rechanneled to neighborhood action councils affiliated with the president's party. By 2016 Ortega had engineered a fourth term and succeeded in having his wife become vice president to cement a familial authoritarian regime that was reminiscent of the Somoza family dictatorship that Ortega had helped overthrow in Nicaragua's 1979 revolution (Thaler 2018).

The instability of democratic regimes was not confined to poor countries with little democratic experience. Venezuela, a country with substantial oil wealth that had remained nominally democratic during Latin America's mid-twentieth-century period of military dictatorship, also slipped into authoritarian practices. After staving off a recall referendum in 2004 and winning elections again in 2006, President Chávez proceeded to dismantle checks and balances, packing the courts and electoral management body. Vertical accountability that is typically provided by the media and civic watchdog groups also declined. Citizens who tried to hold the government accountable found themselves threatened with arrest. Opposition media could not count on getting their broadcast licenses renewed, and journalists investigating government corruption put their very lives at risk (International Crisis Group 2007). Chávez used oil diplomacy, selling oil cheaply to friendly countries in Latin America and the Caribbean, to underwrite the Bolivarian Alliance for the Americas (ALBA). This alliance sought to integrate member states not just economically but also politically and socially so that they could act more effectively to offset US dominance in the hemisphere.

After the 2014 death of President Chávez from cancer, his less charismatic successor, Nicolas Maduro, faced social unrest as declining oil prices produced an economic crisis. In a textbook illustration of the precarious existence of commodity-dependent economies, the country rapidly fell into worse poverty, suffered food shortages, and saw expanding street protests marked by violence. By 2017 an immigration crisis had developed in neighboring Brazil as hundreds of thousands of Venezuelans fled across the border. Maduro responded to criticism with increasingly authoritarian measures, and in 2018 held elections that the OAS denounced as undemocratic, such that many countries did not recognize his second term as legitimate. In 2019 the economy shrank 28 percent, the sixth year in a row of contraction driven by falling oil prices. Hyperinflation exceeding 9,000 percent left the local currency almost worthless (CEPAL 2020). The following year the Fragile States Index ranked Venezuela as the twenty-eighth most fragile state in the world. Among Western Hemisphere nations only the small Caribbean island country of Haiti fared worse (Fund for Peace 2020).

In Bolivia, too, President Evo Morales's receipt of a court decision outlawing term limits might suggest that democracy is at risk. A radical leader, Morales was first elected in 2005 but won reelection twice and held the presidency for fourteen years. He is Indigenous of Aymara descent, and entered politics as a union activist protesting US pressure to curtail the growth of coca. The plant has cultural significance and medicinal uses among Amerindians but is also the base ingredient for cocaine and therefore its cultivation is opposed by the United States. Morales was elected because he rejected US interference and neoliberal economics, and because he advocated for an inclusive state in which Indigenous Bolivians would finally exercise full citizenship.

Morales was able to transform Bolivia, reducing poverty by almost half and tripling the gross domestic product (GDP). Even though Morales was mostly a charismatic populist, he was also divisive and arrogant, sometimes making homophobic or sexist comments. Following Bolivia's 2019 elections, suspiciously, the vote counting stopped for twenty-four hours; when it resumed, Morales was suddenly in the lead. Morales had to flee Bolivia after protesters, the United States, and the OAS all accused him of trying to steal the presidential election. Others, including some US-based academics, took a different view, noting that Morales fled only after the country's military chief publicly suggested that he resign. In the months after his departure, Bolivia was divided, sometimes violently, with enduring disagreement over whether a coup had been perpetuated by Morales or by his opponents, or both (Anderson 2020). A military-backed government took over until an election

Evo Morales, former president of Bolivia and Indigenous leader, who was forced into exile by threats from the military after the OAS concluded that his 2019 reelection bid was rigged. Other foreign election observers did not agree. Credit: Jorgeuzo, https://commons.wikimedia .org/wiki/File:Evo_Morales_in_2006.jpg

could be held in October 2020, nearly a year later, after two postponements due to Covid-19 precautions. The candidate of Morales's party, the former economy minister Luis Arce, won a first-round victory. The United States recognized his government as legitimate despite Arce's history as the architect of nationalization of the Bolivian oil and natural gas industries. In a change of tone from Morales's divisiveness, Arce campaigned to unite Bolivia and govern on behalf of all its citizens.

Enduring inequality makes socialist governing principles appealing to poor voters, but in the twenty-first century antipoverty programming has been implemented by some center-left and even right-wing governments as well. Some success in reducing poverty was achieved through conditional cash transfer programs, which attempted to break the cycle of poverty by paying very poor families a stipend to keep their children in school and get them vaccinations and health checkups. At least eight Latin American countries adopted such cash transfer programs in one form or another, ranging from radical Nicaragua to right-wing Colombia. In Brazil, the center-left Workers Party government expanded the program and poverty fell substantially, but the country had difficulty sustaining its cash transfer programs when economic growth slowed in 2014. President Dilma Rousseff moved funds to continue the program, as her male predecessors had done, but corrupt members of the legislature seized the opportunity to accuse her of covering up budget deficits in order to win reelection. In 2016 they impeached her and removed her from office.

Two years later Brazilians elected an openly sexist right-wing populist president, Jair Bolsonaro, who was frequently compared to US president Donald Trump. Espousing a pro-military, pro-business ideology, Bolsonaro intended to cancel Brazil's flagship cash transfer program, the Bolsa Familia. Surprisingly, amid declining support in 2020, he reversed course. Indeed Latin American governments generally have shown willingness to engage in targeted spending on the poor as opposed to the failed trickle-down strategies that had been favored by authoritarian regimes or the painful structural adjustment policies that new democracies had pursued in the 1990s. However, cash transfer programs are costly, complicated to implement, and vulnerable to becoming politicized when governing parties imply benefits will cease unless voters reelect incumbents.

The divide between the far-left, center-left, and right-wing regimes in Latin America was an expression of different political values among their peoples, and more authentic than the externally enforced and surface-level ideological conformity of the Washington Consensus. In this sense it was a welcome development for democracy. At the same time, some populist presidents concentrated power in their own hands and diminished institutional accountability to the people. New-left leaders offered a needed critique of neoliberalism and some effective antipoverty reforms, but they did not alter the region's historical dependence on mineral and agricultural commodities, and in some countries they deeply damaged mechanisms for upholding the rule of law and restraining presidential power.

Citizen Inclusion and Empowerment

Perhaps the most meaningful change to modern Latin American politics has been the increased empowerment of citizens, especially women, Indigenous people, and the poor. Though democracy is weakening in some countries, it will be hard for the genie of citizen empowerment to be put back in the bottle. Citizens communicate their policy preferences not only in the act of joining political parties, voting for candidates, and advocating for inclusion of specific planks in their party's campaign platform, but also by participation between elections and outside of the party system, for example by joining nongovernmental organizations (NGOs) and social movements engaged in issue advocacy. Although many are pressing for a better standard of living, secular and postmaterialist values are also evident, for example in Latin America's environmental and gay rights movements.

Women's roles in politics have been transformed in the twenty-first century. Previously, in a *machista* cultural context that stressed pride in maleness, women were relegated to a secondary social status (Green and Branford 2013). Constrained by Catholic notions about their appropriate behavior, unmarried upper-class women were tightly chaperoned. Lower-class women struggled under a double-day in which they worked outside the home but remained responsible for childcare and homemaking. Women also bore the brunt of underdevelopment, not only because they were paid less than men and had fewer job opportunities but also because their responsibilities as mothers and housewives were the ones most affected by the absence of basic services such as healthcare and clean water. Women tended to enter the informal economy rather than the formal sector, where a steady wage could be earned, because as itinerant street sellers they could keep their children with them as they sold fruits and vegetables at open-air markets, or newspapers to drivers idling at stoplights.

Many women first became politicized under the military dictatorships (Jaquette and Wolchik 1998). Searching for their missing husbands, sons, and daughters, women joined human rights groups such as the Mothers of the Plaza de Mayo in Argentina, demanding to know where their missing relatives were. Poor women deprived of their disappeared husbands' incomes pooled their meager resources to set up soup kitchens and cooperative childcare groups that enabled some members to pursue paid work outside the home and others to become activists in human rights organizations (Oxhorn 1995).

Once democracy was established, new opportunities arose for women leaders as candidates for political office and appointed ministers of state. Most countries created gender quotas to encourage women to run for elected office, and in countries such as Nicaragua, Argentina, and Costa Rica, women have been elected to the legislature in substantial numbers (Arocena and Bowman 2014). Unlike the United States, many Latin American countries have also elected women to the presidency.

Indigenous people also gained political inclusion beginning in the late twentieth century through social movements and participation in electoral politics at local and national levels. Interestingly, their empowerment has not come about through federalism. Mexico, Brazil, Argentina, and Venezuela have federal systems that allocate some degree of power downward to mid-level and municipal governments. However, federalism has often reinforced the privileged position of rural elites rather than empowering regional ethnic groups. Most Latin American countries are unitary systems that centralize power in the national government and thereby make it difficult for geographically concentrated Indigenous groups to control local political decisionmaking.

Nonetheless, democracy opened new spaces for political organization through nongovernmental organizations, social movements, and political parties, and Indigenous peoples proved adept at using those spaces to claim their rights as citizens (van Cott 2004). In 1992, on the 500th anniversary of Columbus's "discovery" of the Americas, which had of course already been discovered by native inhabitants, Indigenous peoples marched in massive protests against their marginalization. Two years later, responding to the launch of the North American Free Trade Agreement, the Zapatista revolt began in the state of Chiapas, Mexico. Indigenous peoples demanded equal rights, honest elections, and access to land. In Ecuador, a large Indigenous organization, the Confederation of Indigenous Nationalities of Ecuador, disrupted governance by taking to the streets and unseating several presidents, and it continues to mobilize in support of bilingual education and in opposition to oil-centered economic development that threatens the fragile ecosystems on which Indigenous peoples rely. A smaller Ecuadorian Indigenous group, the Pachakutik National Unity Movement, evolved into a political party that won seats in the national congress as well as mayoral and city council races. In the twenty-first century, Indigenous politicians reached the highest political office, winning the presidency of Peru in 2001 and that of Boliva in 2005.

Amerindians have helped design innovative policy changes. In Bolivia they took a leading role in the 2009 creation of a pluri-nationalist constitution that acknowledged cultural rights. In Guatemala, Maya citizens have participated in transitional justice initiatives, including testifying before the international truth commission that was established as part of a United Nations peace process that ended the country's thirty-six-year civil war. Their demands for reparations and full implementation of the peace accords have not prevailed, but they won recognition of the genocide that military rulers had perpetrated against the Maya people in the early 1980s (Rothenberg 2012).

Other groups voicing demands to democratic governments include the Landless Workers Movement in Brazil, which is one of the largest nongovernmental organizations in the world. In Argentina the children of the disappeared, now adults, have organized to obtain justice for their murdered parents, and grandmothers of babies who were illegally put up for adoption by the military government continue searching for their grandchildren. Elsewhere advocacy groups have lobbied for prison reform, better policing and personal security, environmental protection, labor rights, gay marriage, and access to information, as well as protection for children facing adversity (Cleary 2007).

The mushrooming number of civil society organizations in the wake of transitions to democracy has placed myriad demands on governments that are often ill-equipped to meet those demands. Civil society organizations have been accused of destabilizing governments, and even leading "civil society coups" to unseat presidents (Encarnación 2002). In Venezuela and Nicaragua, undemocratic governments have accused NGOs that receive international donations of being agents of foreign governments, arresting their leaders and outlawing protests. In particular, militaries are uncomfortable with the push-and-pull of open governance, which can appear disorderly. In addition, the weakening of political party systems is sometimes erroneously blamed on civil society activism, although NGOs do not seek political office or have a direct claim to representing citizens in the same sense that elected officials do. Despite these tensions, for the most part governments have adapted to citizen participation, and wider inclusion is now understood as part and parcel of a democratic political culture.

Challenges to Democracy

The state of democracy in Latin America overall has improved in the past three decades, but the region's democracies are often low-quality, subscribing to a liberal democratic model that emphasizes elections and civil liberties rather than provision of a decent quality of life. Now those democracies are facing serious challenges in relation to violence, corruption, and weak formal political institutions.

Nicaragua provides an example of a country that has slipped into authoritarian rule and where the state and governing party inflict violence on citizens. Since April 2018 there has been a major crackdown by the Ortega government on political dissent, leaving at least 300 dead, over 2,000 injured, and hundreds arbitrarily arrested and prosecuted. Protests originated against proposals to adjust social security programming and taxation but evolved into a broader critique of the authoritarian regime that had been implemented through co-optation of the country's court system. According to the United Nations High Commissioner for Human Rights, police arbitrarily arrested, and pro-government groups kidnapped, hundreds of people as part of a policy to eradicate opposition voices. In July 2018, new counterterrorism laws were enacted that directly target protesters, and over 130 people were accused of terrorism. By 2020 the government had proposed laws that called for life imprisonment for critics of the government (Amnesty International 2020). Over 102,000 Nicaraguans had fled the country in search of safety. In June 2021, with elections approaching in November, the government arrested six opposition presidential candidates, holding them indefinitely without access to their attorneys. By September 2021, Ortega ordered the arrest of one of his former vice presidents, Sergio Ramírez, one of the most famous novelists in Central America. The regime of the Ortega family, whose vice president is Ortega's wife, Rosario Murillo, stripped one of the two main opposition alliances of its right to participate in the election and arrested key figures in independent media. International observers concluded that conditions for holding meaningful elections did not exist, and countries in Europe joined Canada and the United States in sharply criticizing the consolidation of authoritarian rule (Human Rights Watch 2021).

Violence has been wielded in Mexico not only by government authorities but also by armed cartels seeking to control the illicit drug transshipment routes into the United States. These gangs commit murder with impunity, leaving towns along the Mexican side of the United States–Mexico border living in fear. Women have been murdered at high rates and their dead bodies displayed in ways that show gender is

Student protester in front of anti-Sandinista mural in Nicaragua shoots noisemaking firecrackers in Leon in June 2018.

an element in the gangs' target selection. Human beings are increasingly being trafficked together with drugs and guns. In 2018, crime-related homicides in Mexico hit an all-time high of 33,341 dead. Democracy is beset. In 2018, 130 electoral candidates and other politicians were killed during the national election process (Council on Foreign Relations 2021). Ironically, government efforts to battle drug cartels resulted in their splintering into smaller organized crime networks that are harder to track. These crime rings control select markets and smaller geographical spaces, dominating regional and subregional economies in ways that municipal governments do not have the resources to resist (International Crisis Group 2020).

Spreading violence has, in the past, helped persuade middle-class Latin Americans to endorse military coups, but it seems unlikely that Latin America will undergo another rash of these. In Ecuador, which experienced light-handed military governance in the 1970s with fewer human rights violations, public trust in the military remains high, measured in 2017 at 66 percent, but the regional average was far lower, at 46 percent. Meanwhile the percentage of the Latin Americans adhering to the idea that democracy is the best form of government was 69 percent, a solid majority (Corporación Latinobarómetro 2017). Nonetheless, the following year Brazil elected Jair Bolsonaro as president in part because of his willingness to entrust military officers with the most power they have had since the military dictatorship ended in the 1980s. Active and former military officers in May 2020 held nine of the twenty-two cabinet positions, which allowed the military broad authority over issues like fiscal policy, development in the Amazon, and the response to the Covid-19 pandemic. And when in 2021 President Bolsonaro unexpectedly fired the general he had appointed as defense minister, the heads of the army, navy, and air force all resigned in protest. Their public rebuke of a civilian president's cabinet choice showed they expected to control that post. Military subordination to civilian authority is not absolute.

Though they still favor democracy over authoritarian rule, only about one-third of Latin Americans report being satisfied with democracy, and there are many reasons why. As a general cause of democratic decay, corruption of all branches of government is a historical problem that has only worsened. Guatemalan political parties have received an estimated 50 percent of their funding from organized crime and corruption. An estimated 33 percent of Guatemalan lawmakers are under investigation for corruption even though their jobs give them immunity from prosecution. Monopoly control of television channels results in limited exposure of these democratic depredations (Goldman 2019).

Democracies ranging from Costa Rica to Peru have prosecuted former presidents for corruption, and some of these former leaders have ended up in jail. In Brazil, however, powerful judges and politicians protect each other's interests and obstruct judicial investigation of corruption cases. Brazilian president Bolsonaro is under investigation for corruption, which involves his wife and sons. It is alleged that his family took part in a scheme known as *rachadinha,* which is common in the lower rungs of politics in Brazil. It involves siphoning taxpayer money by keeping ghost employees on the payroll or hiring people who agree to kick back a share of their salary to the boss. Bolsonaro is also being investigated by the Supreme Court for obstruction of justice. However, in 2020 the corruption scandals lost public attention amid the Covid-19 pandemic (Londoño, Andreoni, and Casado 2020).

The Covid-19 pandemic has presented an unprecedented challenge to Latin American governments. It immediately exposed shortcomings in the primary healthcare systems across the region, and within a year of the first case appearing in February 2020 over 600,000 Latin Americans had died of the disease (Gonzáles et al. 2021). As in the United States, people of color and the poor were more apt to die, exposing ongoing social and economic inequalities. Governments took markedly differing public health approaches to the pandemic. In Nicaragua, a very poor country ill-equipped with respirators, the authoritarian government misrepresented the breadth of the crisis, reporting in February 2021 that only 171 Nicaraguans had died of Covid-19. Civil society groups collaborating with nurses and doctors to collect information placed the total nearer 3,000 and independent news media put it at 6,000, arguing that the government was intentionally attributing Covid-19 deaths to other causes. Brazil's pro-business Bolsonaro government initially denied the seriousness of the disease and seemed inclined to let the virus run its course in the hope of achieving herd immunity. The president dismissed basic precautions such as social distancing, and later suggested proven vaccines were unsafe and did not work. A year into the pandemic Brazil had one of the highest infection rates in the world and 260,000 Brazilians had died (Gonzáles et al. 2021).

Freedom of expression and the press are signature characteristics of democracy, but in Latin America political violence has infiltrated politics and threatens those who report on corruption and governmental policy failures. Latin American governments have developed a wide variety of methods to repress investigative reporting, including tax harassment of newspaper and television companies, threats of prosecution, violence, and even murder of investigative journalists. Although a handful of countries have abolished *desacato* (contempt) laws that prohibit the media and others from criticizing public officials, many others have not or still prohibit "offenses against honor" that silence critics in much the same way. Social media and polarized sources of news information are increasingly divisive, and accusations of "fake news" abound.

New technologies similar to the data-mining used in the 2016 US elections now exacerbate tensions in Latin American elections as well. Firms that engage in information operations training, influence, and "psyops," such as Iota Global, have targeted Latin America's military, political, and election markets (see Iota Global website). Another global firm operating in Latin America is Cambridge Analytica, whose investors included Donald Trump's chief fundraisers in the 2016 elections. That company breached Facebook's data on 87 million users. It contributed to Donald Trump's election and the "leave" vote in the United Kingdom's referendum on whether to remain in the European Union. In 2018 it worked for conservative political interests in Brazil, targeting alienated working-class voters in a joint venture with a São Paulo–based marketing firm, Ponte Estratégia, to help elect right-wing populist politicians including President Jair Bolsonaro (Ituasso 2019).

These examples demonstrate that worldwide forces from the pandemic to cyber warfare will continue to affect politics in Latin America, but the main threats to democracy in Latin America may be the weaknesses of its democratic institutions. In presidential systems, a balance of power between the executive, legislative, and judicial branches is expected to prevent any one branch from dominating, but in Latin America that balance was never struck. With their history of *caudillo* strongmen and military rule, Latin American countries developed "hyper-presidential" constitutions that awarded the lion's share of power to the executive branch. Presidents appoint their own cabinets and control the appointment of many civil service positions, allowing them to staff government agencies with their supporters. They play an important role in developing the national budget, can declare states of emergency, and have wide powers of decree. They are perceived as the supreme authority, *el jefe maximo,* underscored by their title as commander-in-chief of the military.

Two opposite yet equally troubling trends have emerged with respect to the executive branch. First, many presidents have left office before their term was scheduled to conclude (Llanos and Marsteintredet 2010). In some instances, as in the impeachment of President Fernando Color de Mello in Brazil, presidential removal seemed to reinforce the rule of law. In others, such as the Ecuadorian congress's removal of President Abdalá Bucaram on the dubious grounds that he was mentally incompetent (in fact he was merely eccentric and corrupt), it seemed political motivations predominated and politicians only paid lip service to the democratic process. When the Paraguayan legislature brought impeachment charges against President Fernando Lugo in 2012 he was given just twenty-four hours to prepare a defense and two hours to present it before the senate removed him from office. Where such ousted presidents were political opportunists rather than committed to liberal democratic principles, opponents sometimes argued that democracy was served by presidential removal, but the rule of law most certainly was not. Democracies embody the rule of law rather than individuals, meaning that power lies in the office held rather than the individual holding it, and that the law is applied equally to everyone regardless of their opinions, political position, or social status. Latin American countries' willingness to investigate and prosecute allegedly corrupt public officials is both new and commendable, but sometimes it is done with ulterior motives that muddy the waters of justice.

Also concerning has been the return of *continuismo,* a practice wherein presidents hold on to power beyond their stipulated term of office by manipulating electoral rules or the constitution (McConnell 2010). This had been a common problem in prior periods when Latin America had experimented with democracy, so much so that when writing new constitutions and electoral laws as part of their transitions to democracy in the 1980s and 1990s, most Latin American countries limited the president to serving only a single term. With time, however, those rules changed and country after country opted to permit reelection to a second term, often including immediate reelection so that a president who was governing well could be retained. Even that was not enough for some ambitious men. In the 1990s, Presidents Carlos Menem of Argentina and Alberto Fujimori of Peru each obtained a onetime option to run for reelection to a third term. In 2010 Colombia's Constitutional Court rejected a similar bid by popular two-term president Álvaro Uribe. In 2009 Venezuelans passed a referendum ending term limits altogether, not only for the president but also for governors and mayors, and Nicaragua's President Ortega engineered a Supreme Court decision to achieve the same ends. Bolivian voters rejected a 2016 referendum to eliminate presidential term limits, but in 2018 President Evo Morales, already in his third term, petitioned the Constitutional Court, which ruled that term limits were unconstitutional.

This pattern indicates that over time those in high office tend to become accustomed to holding power and privilege, and eventually reluctant to lose their jobs. As a result they are tempted to rig elections to deprive the people of the power to elect someone else. Importantly, most Latin American democracies have not chosen to follow these examples, and some presidents who were very popular (e.g., Michelle Bachelet in Chile) adhered to established term limits and stepped down on schedule.

As in all presidential systems, Latin American legislators are also expected to practice oversight on the executive branch to ensure that the implementation of policy by the various cabinet agencies is in keeping with the law. Unfortunately, Latin American legislatures are intermittently effective in this task. The term "delegative democracy" was invented to describe Latin American democratic regimes that have a president whose power is not effectively restrained through the horizontal accountability of institutional checks and balances (O'Donnell 1998).

Political parties are internally underdeveloped, often little more than a vehicle for the political ambitions of one politician, and rise and fall in popularity with that individual, often simply disbanding after a single election (Levitt 2012). Moreover, the proportional representation electoral rules in Latin America generate multiparty systems that are in some cases highly fragmented. With so many parties winning seats in

Poll worker records vote totals during Guyana's 2015 national election. The election was monitored by the Carter Center, which praised the integrity of the country's balloting. The Carter Center has been involved in election monitoring since the 1992 elections in Guyana and is credited with helping improve the country's voter registration, balloting, and counting administration. Credit: Shelley A. McConnell

the legislature, the president's party rarely wins a majority, making it difficult to pass laws to fulfill the president's campaign promises. Often, political parties with widely differing ideologies must join together as a coalition government to pass legislation, and disagreements within the coalition about policy issues can lead those coalitions to break apart. An extreme case is Brazil, which practices an open-list proportional representation system with no minimal percentage of the vote that parties must win in order to obtain a seat. As a consequence, the candidates running for the legislature compete against not only opposition parties but also other candidates within their own party, and if elected they show little party loyalty and quite regularly switch party affiliation (O'Neil, Fields, and Share 2015).

The judiciary runs a distant third in terms of political power, rarely balancing either the president or the legislature. High courts can be important to protect human rights and civil liberties and to adjudicate disputes between the other branches of state, but in Latin America they are hampered in this because they have not achieved adequate separation from the presidency. Magistrates on the high court are not typically given lifetime appointments, so presidents use their powers of appointment to manipulate the composition of the court, stacking it with justices who are their political partisans. Where they have legislative majorities, presidents may even impeach members of the high court, removing those who do not cooperate with presidential directives (Pérez-Liñán and Castagnola 2009). Although judicial reforms during the democratic period have made some headway in strengthening the professionalism of judges and court staff, judicial corruption remains an issue, and a lack of resources has produced severe backlogs of cases.

Weak institutions such as these are especially problematic because Latin America's high inequality levels make its politics more divisive. Simply put, democracy cannot thrive amid extreme inequality. When democratic institutions are corrupt and favor elites over the majority, citizens may come to prefer an authoritarian alternative. In Latin America, the lack of access to decent primary and secondary education, as well as university-level education, along with poor health services, can easily cause citizens to question the legitimacy of the political system. Responses have varied from the election of undemocratic strongmen to street protests of the sort seen in 2019 in many Latin American cities (Carey 2019). Other citizens have simply chosen to leave, voting with their feet as they migrate to Europe and the United States in search of a better life. Among these 396,579 individuals who were apprehended in 2019 by US border authorities as they attempted to enter the United States between ports of entry on the US southwest border without proper documentation were a record 76,020 unaccompanied minors (US Customs and Border Patrol 2019).

Conclusion

Although Iberian colonialism and US hegemony helped Latin America to develop an authoritarian political culture centered on strongman leaders, Latin America today is politically reinventing itself. It is now a largely democratic region with countries that have stable borders and a middle level of development. It is also politically vibrant, conducting experiments in popular empowerment and implementing antipoverty policies that are models for the developing world. Democratic politics today are much more inclusive than in the past, and democracy is undergirded by changes in values and public expectations of governments. Through the OAS and other international institutions, Latin America has done more to institutionalize norms of democracy than any other world region except for Europe. Nonetheless, the quality of democracy is decidedly thin, and a handful of countries have slid backward into authoritarian rule, while Cuba has yet to become democratic.

Violence is still present at serious levels in the form of drug traf-ficking, gangs, and organized crime, but though human security is not fully achieved there has been progress. The civil wars of the 1970s and 1980s that wracked Central America have ended, most boundary dis-putes have been settled through negotiation, justice is being sought in former state terror regimes, and Colombia has reached a tentative peace agreement with the FARC. Economically, Latin America has not escaped commodity dependence and still relies on raw minerals and agro-exports for development, but it has diversified its trading partners. Moreover, some countries have industrialized, and a combination of economic growth and increased social spending has begun to reduce poverty. The United States still has a substantial power advantage, both economically and militarily, but Latin American countries no longer feel obliged to defer to US interests and have opposed the United States on issues where there is substantial regional consensus.

Peace, democracy, and soft-balancing against US power are not the stuff of headlines, but when set against the region's past political record it is clear that Latin America has made meaningful progress toward securing civil liberties, human rights, social equality, and political autonomy. Less certain is whether that progress can be sustained amid continuing economic inequality as citizens realize that democratic gov-ernance is not a panacea for their countries' ills.

5

Crime and Security

Mark Ungar

The biggest threat to the progress brought by Latin American democracy over the past thirty years has been its biggest failure: citizen security. The region's murder rate is 23 homicides per 100,000, more than three times the global average. Five of the world's ten deadliest countries are in Latin America, as are forty-three of its fifty most violent cities. The Northern Triangle—comprising Guatemala, El Salvador, and Honduras—is the deadliest place on Earth. Although the Andean countries are emerging from protracted campaigns against narcotrafficking syndicates, the drug war that Mexico has been fighting since 2006 has killed 41,034 people, on top of the 151,000 homicide victims from organized crime. In 2019 alone, there were 11,813 combat-related deaths, and 35,588 homicides (see https://ucdp.uu.se). Rates of other violent crimes, from assault to rape, are also high.

By eroding basic security, this persistent criminal violence also erodes the region's democracy. Despite decades of harsh military rule, large majorities of Latin Americans—83 percent in El Salvador to 55 percent in Chile—believe that the military should combat crime. Such support is rooted in a lack of confidence in democracies' rules and institutions. In Latinobarómetro's latest survey of eighteen countries, nearly half of Latin Americans—44.6 percent on average—believe their police are involved in criminal activities. Among those countries, slightly more—46.5 percent on average—have "some" confidence in the police. This demonstrates citizens' reluctance to cooperate with security officials by providing them information they need to prevent and solve crimes. This lack of trust triggers a vicious cycle making police agencies less effective.

Amid democracy's great political and economic advances, why has crime risen to such high rates in nearly every Latin American country? This chapter first examines the causes of crime in the region, and then why governments have been unable to address them, using two case studies as examples. It concludes by examining how policy has been improving through an assessment of past failures.

The Causes of Crime

The causes of crime are wide and deeply rooted in Latin America. Poverty, racism, a lack of education, and other conditions are chronic causes around the world. But the region's contemporary political socioeconomic development has led to a focus on specific patterns.

Inequality

Latin America is the world's most unequal region. It has the highest regional Gini coefficient, which is the main measure of income inequality, in which 0 represents perfect equality and 100 perfect inequality. The world average since 2000 has been approximately 42. The only two regions above that average are Latin America, averaging just under 50, and sub-Saharan Africa, averaging just over 45 (United Nations 2019). Of the thirty most unequal countries since 2015, sixteen are in the Latin American and Caribbean region. According to United Nations reports, countries with more inequality have higher probabilities of high homicide rates than countries with less inequality. Based on 2,000 municipalities in Mexico, one study determined that an increment of 1 percent in the Gini coefficient translates into an increase of over ten drug-related homicides per 100,000 people (Enamorado et al. 2014). How does inequality generate crime? Many argue that resentment of those left out of prosperity causes more property crimes. One scholar concludes that uneven economic growth generates more internal demand for narcotics and large "secondary markets" of stolen goods that lead groups to use violence as they compete to acquire and sell them (Bergman 2018), in turn fomenting the kinds of organized criminality discussed here.

Marginalization

A corollary to inequality is marginalization. In Latin America, groups suffering from higher levels of poverty and unemployment, with less access to services, include Indigenous people, Afro-Latin Americans, and women. Such bias has been linked with elevated levels of crime involving youth, who are Latin America's largest single group of violent crime perpetrators and victims. Even before the pandemic in 2019, the gap between national and youth homicide rates was markedly high throughout the region, as seen in Table 5.1.

Urbanization

In Latin America there was one of the most notable transitions from a rural to an urban society in the past five decades. Many of the largest cities have grown in an uncontrolled manner. Accompanying services like education or health failed to keep up, generating marginalized and densely populated areas, such as Brazil's *favelas,* Venezuela's *barrios,* and Argentina's *villas.* Gangs and drug trafficking gained strength in many of these areas, thus increasingly the likelihood of criminal violence. In urban Latin America, in fact, nearly 80 percent of murders occur in just 2 percent of the streets. Homicides tend to be highly concentrated in areas of concentrated disadvantage and socioeconomic marginalization. This pattern can be traced to regional urbanization. Urbanization in Latin America usually accompanies economic growth, with jobs and infrastructure in expanding cities attracting new residents. If this economic potential fails to materialize or begins to reverse, cities will struggle to support swelling populations. Latin America shows the impacts of this more clearly than other regions, with an urbanization rate of 75.3 percent, comparable to that of wealthier North America

Table 5.1   National and Youth Homicide Rates, Select Countries, 2019 (sources in parentheses)

	National Homicide Rate per 100,000 Population	Youth Homicide Rate per 100,000 Population (except as noted)
Brazil	19.3 (Monitor da Violencia, O Globo)	Youth: 23.3 (Statista)
Colombia	25.4 (Presidencia de la Republica)	Youth: 38.4% of all murdered men were ages 20–29 (Instituto Nacional de Medicina Legal y Ciencias Forenses)
El Salvador	36.0 (Policía Nacional Civil)	Half of all those murdered were ages 18–30 (Infosegura)
Guatemala	21.5 (Ministerio de Gobernación)	Under 25 years of age: 43.0 (https://infosegura.org/seccion/guatemala/)
Honduras	41.2 (Secretaria de Seguridad)	Ages 15–19: 68.6; 20–24: 142.3; 25–29: 170 (IUDPAS, Boletin Especial sobre homicidos en Honduras, 2019)
Mexico	27.0 (Secretariado Ejecutivo del Sistema Nacional de Seguridad Pública)	21% of all those murdered were between ages 15 and 24 (https://www.inegi.org.mx/si)
Venezuela	60.3 (Observatorio Venezolano de Violencia)	Youth: 60.3 (Observatorio Venezolano de Violencia)

(77.2 percent) and Europe (74.8 percent) and nearly twice the rates of Africa (37.9 percent) and Asia (36.7 percent) (Cerrutti and Bertoncello 2003). Some studies show how heavy Indigenous migration to the cities aggravates youth tensions. Such urban pressures can also be seen in ownership instability, with an estimated 65 percent of Latin America's urban properties considered "extralegal," or lacking valid property rights that would allow residents to use them as collateral for loans—a key foundation for leaving the informal market, where criminality is higher.

Firearms

The huge number and easy accessibility of firearms in Latin America is widely attributed to be a cause of crime. Firearms are used in at least 73 percent of Latin American homicides—above the global average of 54 percent (UNODC 2020). Latin America had 16.21 gun deaths per 100,000 compared to 3.85 for the United States. Firearms cause 500 deaths and 2,000 injuries daily (Amnesty International 2018), meaning that half of Earth's gun deaths happen in Latin America. Uncontrolled weapons trafficking in Central America, where over 85 percent of murders are committed with guns, added to the large pools of weapons remaining from decades of civil war. In Guatemala, officials estimate three to four illegal arms for every registered one—which would be between 1.5 and 2 million illegal arms. Gun use in nonlethal forms of crime has drastically increased as well. National reports show that rising insecurity and mistrust of state authorities appear linked to increased gun acquisition for self-defense. Most studies correlate increased gun availability with increased crime. For example, in the year following the 2004 expiration of the US ban on assault weapons, Mexico's homicide rate increased for the first time in a decade—with the largest jump in areas closest to the US border and no evidence of a concurrent increase in nonfirearm homicides or other violent crimes (Chicoine 2017).

Impunity

On average there are 24 verdicts for every 100 victims of violent crime. Chronic delays in the criminal justice system violate due process rights and increase impunity. Such impunity deepens citizen anger over large sectors of the population being exempt from the law, from corrupt elites (illustrated by scandals engulfing the political class in countries like Brazil and Guatemala) to petty criminals released by judges. Specifically, impunity increases crime by reducing its risks. A comprehensive study rated countries on an 80-point scale, with an average of 49.1. Five of the eight countries ranking worst were in Latin America—Mexico second

(75.7), Colombia third (75.6), Nicaragua sixth (69.5), Honduras seventh (64.1), and El Salvador eighth (64.1). As a response, citizens often take justice into their own hands. Vigilantism kills thousands of people in Latin America yearly. Most victims are suspected criminals, with many attackers tacitly backed by state officials. Vigilante groups include "auto-defense" groups in central Mexico's Tierra Caliente zone, and "community justice" committees in Bolivia that lynch suspected thieves.

State Responses

Another cause of crime is the state, whose policies are inconsistent and abusive, and plagued by inefficiency and corruption. To tackle the security crisis, governments have responded with a range of reforms since the region began to democratize in the 1980s. But most of them have not had the expected impact.

Initial changes demilitarized the police forces, long centered on military doctrine and repressive tactics, and in most cases controlled by the military itself. Many countries also eliminated or simplified the militarized hierarchies of their police to improve administration and facilitate promotion between the lower level and higher ranks. In countries like Bolivia, where Indigenous people fill the lower ranks and European descendants dominate the higher positions, such divisions reinforced societal stratifications that undermined police effectiveness and police-society relations.

Legal changes were next, building on the human rights movement that helped usher in democracy. Such reforms included mechanisms for police accountability, such as internal affairs offices and national ombudsmen. Significantly, the criminal justice system has been transformed in nearly every country through an overhaul of the penal and process code to strengthen due process of law with new investigative and sentencing courts; a shift of investigative control from police to prosecutors; and replacing judge-based written procedures with oral and adversarial jury processes, which are much fairer to criminal defendants.

An even more transformative change has been community-oriented policing. Originally started in Western democracies in the 1960s, community-oriented policing represents a paradigm shift in policing from a responsive, physical approach to one centered on prevention and citizen engagement. It puts citizens at the center of their security by empowering them to shape the approach, implementation, and evaluation of security though a range of programs from joint committees with police officers to centers for vulnerable groups like youth. All community-oriented policing programs center on the basic idea that citizens need to be incorporated in the formulation, implementation, and evaluation of policing policy and practice. For Latin America, where harsh policing and state power reach back to the colonial era, the community-oriented policing paradigm has been both revolutionary and highly political.

These promising approaches need consistent support to succeed. But contemporary Latin America has failed to build the strong foundations in four major security areas: police capacity, government policy, criminal justice, and understanding the evolving nature of crime.

Police Capacity

Throughout Latin America, police officers lack the training, time, and support to do their job. This inadequacy begins in the academies, which often fail to screen recruits thoroughly or, in the case of postconflict countries like Guatemala, rush training to fill a badly depleted force. In many countries, officers receive only three months of training. Academies also reinforce socioeconomic tensions, because marginalized groups attend overcrowded and dilapidated schools that have few books, computers, or other resources.

Once on the force, police must contend with their poor preparation and highly dysfunctional management. Inadequate budgets deprive them of basic equipment. In many parts of the region, officers complain that they must buy their own uniforms and that the budget for gasoline runs out mid-year. Salaries are atrocious—in several Mexican states, police earn less than $162 a month. There are usually not enough officers to adequately patrol assigned areas due to unannounced changes in shifts and high rates of absenteeism. Special operations often deprive areas of needed personnel, since they require unplanned and temporary schedule changes. Police commissioners struggle to manage disgruntled corps amid inadequate authority and continually changing directives. Officers at all levels are usually rotated every two years, which helps minimize corruption by cutting off links with local criminals, but prevents the knowledge and trust that are key to effective long-term policing. Finally, police are given few opportunities to develop trust-building relationships with the communities they patrol. Many street officers are often just given a gun, which they may not be able to use effectively, and assigned to stand on a corner. While such an approach is poor policing, officers often prefer it to the alternative. They do not feel safe in dangerous areas and do not want to get entangled with powerful groups or become scapegoats in any complaint from citizens. The internal affairs and social services within the police are rarely adequate to help individual officers face these dangers.

Despite new internal affairs offices applying more stringent controls and accountability mechanisms, corruption and abuse remain rampant among police forces throughout Latin America. Police violence includes beatings, unlawful arrests, other rights violations, and organized killings. In 2016, for example, there were allegations of a "death squadron" comprising almost a hundred Peruvian National Police members who, between 2009 and 2016, participated in over twenty-four extrajudicial killings. Allegedly they paid informants to convince criminals to commit kidnappings and assaults so that the police could later "catch them in the act" and claim credit; many criminals were killed in the process.

Government Policy

Presidents are often considered one of the biggest impediments to democracy in Latin America; however, their power over security policy allows circumvention of bureaucratic, judicial, and legislative delays and can thus facilitate democracy. Such dominance obscures an underlying weakness of criminal policy throughout the region, which is in part due to politicization. Crime, since the mid-1990s a top public concern, has become the most common response in the annual Latinobarómetro survey (20,212 people in eighteen countries) to the question, "What do you consider to be the most important problem in your country?" In 2002, 7 percent said crime was the biggest problem; by 2014 the number jumped to nearly 32 percent. Resulting fear spurred the biggest protests in Latin America since its transition to democracy in the 1980s, with record crowds—from Mexico City to Buenos Aires—protesting state inaction. In 2020, police brutality led to weeks of citizen protests in Bogotá, Colombia's capital. The Black Lives Matter movement in the United States inspired additional protests. Many of them focused on violence against Black people, as in Brazil, and others on Indigenous minorities, as in Mexico, Bolivia, Chile, and Ecuador. With fear of crime remaining high among the population, tough anti-crime policy has become part of nearly every electoral campaign, such as in Brazil's 2018 election. Even progressive candidates—like Costa Rican president Laura Chinchilla or Chilean president Michele Bachelet—respond to this pressure (Dammert 2005).

After elections, winning candidates quickly discover the difficulty of reforming entrenched agencies. Seeing an affront to their professionalism and autonomy, police can and do stymie efforts to weaken their authority or change their practice. Presidents, facing such obstruction amid the ticking clock of their terms of office, often forgo institutional reform in favor of short-term action. Civil strife often adds to executive pressure, making security a matter of governmental survival as well as success. Increasingly, the police are needed to control agitation that often culminates in government-threatening protests. In all six collapses of democratic regimes in Latin America since 2000, security forces played a pivotal role by participating in, aggravating, or failing to curb unrest. In 2006, the police were central to the near breakup of Bolivia as several eastern department (provinces) moved toward secession.

Even when steadfastly supporting the police, executives' approach is rarely consistent, linear, or clear. As crime resists different policies, presidents quickly rotate through security ministers and police chiefs. Those officials often have little time or ability to initiate new policies, and therefore are reluctant to make enemies within the security sector. Such coordination is complicated further by frequent changes in government and party control. For example, Mexican president Felipe Calderón overhauled the national security system, creating a powerful public security secretariat and a revamped approach called the "new police model," even though his predecessor was from the same political party. Legislatures are supposed to monitor the implementation of such policies, but throughout Latin America they are either too fragmented or beholden to the executive to oversee or question such policies. Legislative security committees rarely have more than a few staff members, and the kinds of public hearings that question police action are often attacked for being weak on crime.

The fickleness of appointments, conventional thinking, and interests of foreign donors makes institutional reform more difficult. For example, the United States began to draw down funding of anti-narcotic and judicial reforms after Bolivia elected a leftist government in 2005. Foreign governments and international organizations funding security reforms often promote changing approaches whose translation into policy is unclear or counterproductive. For example, parallel support for strengthening human rights and stopping narcotrafficking can clash when anti-drug operations cause violence in rural communities or against criminal defendants.

The overall direction of policing policy has caused the biggest policy clash. As crime continued to rise, the first and biggest reforms that Latin America adopted—new penal process codes and community policing—were attacked as being soft on crime by depriving the police of their power while giving too many rights to accused criminals. By the mid-1990s, popular support grew for giving the police greater legal and detention power, tapping into both long-standing police laws and "zero tolerance" policing credited for historic drops in crime in the United States. Zero tolerance emerged out of the "broken windows" theory, which posited that when deteriorating physical or social conditions are not checked, they allow crime to take root. If a building's broken window is not repaired, it signals that the owner does not monitor or care about the property, which discourages commerce and recreation while allowing panhandling or loitering and leading to more serious crimes like assault or drug trafficking. When it was first implemented in the New York subways by erasing graffiti and detaining fare breakers, it led to increased ridership and revenue. But such policies are effective only when accompanied by social services and accountability. Many people detained under this policy have drug addictions or mental illness; therefore they often return to the streets unless they are given long-term help. This policy needs to be checked by the media and the courts, since it easily leads to police violence. Criticism that this application of zero tolerance was a form of racial profiling was illustrated by reactions to New York's stop-and-frisk policy.

In Latin America, such policies are often stripped of the oversight and constitutional protections available in other countries, turning zero tolerance into an "iron fist" (*mano dura*). This policy opened the door for increased abuse because of Latin America's lack of media, accountability mechanisms, and tradition of unfettered police power. It was supported by many laws in Latin America that legalized high levels of police discretion—for example, detentions based on subjective criteria such as vague suspicion of criminal activity. Central American laws allow police to detain people who do not look like they "belong" in the neighborhoods they are in. For example, Chile's 1998 penal code allowed arrests based on physical appearance. After a long-standing Venezuelan law allowing police to detain "vagabonds" was finally struck down, police replaced it with increased arrests to "check" identification cards or criminal records. Throughout Latin America, community-oriented policing and the *mano dura* coexist in uneasy tension with the policies of prevention and rights that preceded it. El Salvador, for example, once enacted *mano dura* and *mano amiga* ("friendly hand") programs in the same year—which blunted the impact of both.

Latin America's absence of computer statistics, the modern era's other revolutionary police reform, also weakened the impact of "broken windows." The aim is to use computers to gather and analyze crime data, by type and geography, to quickly and effectively deploy human and material resources in response to criminal patterns ranging from a spate of neighborhood robberies to transnational money laundering. Without this, or the cohesive management needed to sustain it, Latin American police could not accurately gauge the impact of zero tolerance or other policies. In Venezuela, a pilot computer project in the capital began to bring down crime, but was derailed by a lack of personnel, administration, information, and security—officers were even killed in front of neighborhood stations. Most countries do not have adequately detailed and updated crime databases. In Mexico, federal officials estimate that 30 percent of states do not report sufficient information to the national database, while state officials who send information acknowledge that these are only general estimates. This lack of reliable and comprehensive information prevents the independent analysis of crime data that is key to effective crime policy.

One of the most globally common and popular anticrime approaches is formation of new forces, from intelligence centers to specialized elite squads. Such expansion can, for example, minimize corruption through agencies like the highly vetted organized security units of Mexico. Appealing to iron-fist demands, militarization is a particularly popular but virulent strain of proliferation. Militarization takes on many other forms in democratic Latin America, including adoption of military tactics by police; special operations and raids, such as against gangs; use of elite soldiers in border areas, as with Guatemala's Kaibiles; military occupations in high-crime areas; formation of joint military-police drug units, as in Mexico and the Andes; and formation of military police, as in Honduras. Once established, agencies find ways to justify their own growth and power, thus undermining accountability and coordination using increasingly more aggressive operations and political networking. The range of policies involved complicates coordination. As a growing Latin American middle class creates consumer markets and transshipment points for narcotics, drug policy must encompass consumption, distribution, addiction, and other issues with often-clashing approaches among state agencies.

Militarization of drug control led to low-intensity warfare in Mexico, reaching a crescendo under President Felipe Calderón (2013–2019). Certain crime families ran private armies to respond to police actions, while maintaining sophisticated transshipment operations across land, sea, and air into the United States. Calderón was accused of taking a $1 billion bribe (by a witness in New York City's criminal trial of Joaquín "El Chapo" Guzmán). Calderón's defense minister, General Salvador Cienfuegos, was arrested and indicted in Los Angeles in October 2020 for drug trafficking. Known as the Godfather (*El Padrino*), Cienfuegos was responsible for the fierce, armed counteroffensives against Mexico's drug cartels that killed thousands of noncombatant civilians in disproportionate attacks, as collateral damage, or in extrajudicial executions. General Cienfuegos took bribes from the H-2 cartel, which smuggled drugs to the United States mainly by sea, and redirected military operations away from H-2 operations. Security agency proliferation has increased exponentially in Latin America through decentralization, regional governance's biggest single modern transformation. Transferring authority for security to provinces and cities makes sense, since they more ably respond to local concerns and conditions. But security decentralization has been poorly implemented, leading provincial and municipal forces to amplify the poor management, accountability, and policies of their national progenitors. For example, Venezuela formed 105 new agencies after a 1989 decentralization law (a 363 percent increase), leading to worsening coordination that contributed to a 200 percent increase in national crime rates. The impacts were strongest in the cities. A large metropolitan area requires a unified crime policy, but many such areas in Latin America have up to fifteen different police agencies under different governmental and crime policies. Elevated levels of personnel turnover, corruption, and patronage further diminish local capacity. The median tenure of security chiefs in Mexico's municipal police is just two years (Sabet 2012: 75). Decentralization increases exposure to crime in poorer regions with less police funding. After police dismantled urban Central American gangs, they reformed in smaller municipalities that have a harder time handling them. Mexican drug cartels broke up into small groups that—lacking the directives, controls, or funding of cartel leaders—turned toward crimes like armed robbery and extortion. Decentralization also opens up opportunities for organized crime. In the region's many large "brown spaces" of weak state presence (O'Donnell 1993), from Petén in Guatemala to Pará in Brazil, criminal syndicates infiltrate or cooperate with their family, landowning, and extractive entities. As decentralization increases state fragmentation, it creates conditions that facilitate crime.

The presence of the *maras* in Mexico and the Northern Triangle—Guatemala, El Salvador, and Honduras—has compounded insecurity in that region. El Salvador's "reformist" president Nayib Bukele (elected in 2019) allegedly agreed to a truce with the transnational organized crime syndicate MS-19, in return for an agreement to improve prison conditions and the eventual release of its leaders. His other policies likewise eroded the rule of law. He used the military to pressure the country's National Assembly in February 2020, and later that spring forced gang members in Salvadoran prisons to sit close together in torturous positions, despite the Covid-19 pandemic. Furthermore, he attacked media outlets that attempted to uncover his opaque dealings with the underworld; in September 2020 the newspaper *El Faro* published reports of secret pacts, which he denied. Mexico's leaders periodically attempted to negotiate with gangs, selectively choosing some drug networks for talks and others for war. This approach is rooted in the government's belated recognition of the limited impact of military approaches and the fact that these organizations kill those who cooperate with judicial or police authorities.

Such extensive decentralization has led to a revival of centralization. Venezuela created its national police force in 2009. In 2006, Mexico began trying to consolidate the thousands of municipal police into state police in a proposal called *Mando Único*. Launched officially by President Enrique Peña Nieto in 2014, it aims to replace the country's 1,800 municipal police units—many of which were plagued by corruption, inefficiency, and assassinations—with thirty-two centralized state departments.

Criminal Justice

Latin America's criminal justice systems are ill-equipped to handle crime and insecurity and therefore they worsen. Police who respond to crime scenes and launch investigations take the first steps in the criminal justice process. But police officers throughout Latin America lack the needed training, equipment, funding, citizen trust, and interagency coordination. Often when police collect evidence, there are no chemical, vehicular, DNA, or other laboratories to test it. Once an investigation begins, prosecutors from the attorney general's office direct the process to the trial stage. But nearly every Latin American attorney general's office lacks detectives, funds, specialized prosecutors, political backing (such as in conflicts with the police), physical protection for those working on high-profile cases, and local offices who can acquire citizen trust and information. In Guatemala, the attorney general's office has no presence in over 40 percent of the country, contributing to just 10 percent of crimes being tried. Complications multiply in complex and organized crime investigations, like money laundering, which require far more expertise. Together, deficiencies among police and prosecutors lead to extensive delays during which evidence fades and witnesses become scarce. Police reports that are actually completed are often riddled with missing and inconsistent information. On average, under 5 percent of Latin American homicides lead to conviction as a result of poor investigations.

Even as prosecutorial power is being fortified in Latin America through laws such as allowing for wiretapping or warrantless searches, actual prosecution is impeded by the lack of support, information, specialists, and protocols. Such conditions also fuel instability among judges, who preside over trials, the third stage of criminal justice.

Judges receiving insufficient police reports are obliged to return the suspects to prosecutors, or release detainees. Such actions, combined with stronger due process protections in Latin America's new penal codes, fuel public perception that courts have become too lenient on criminals. For instance, Ecuador's police claim that one of the biggest problems they face is implementation of the new penal process code, which permits detainees of police operations to be released immediately by judicial authorities (Policía Nacional de Ecuador 2006). Courts throughout Latin America also lack sufficient resources, efficiency, autonomy, and authority. Even in countries where judicial councils were created to ensure that nominations are based on objective criteria, judicial selection is often politicized and negotiated among political parties. Changing rules over dismissal and reappointment curtail judicial independence. Such uncertainty is strongest in the realm of security. Many judges say they face the least independence in criminal cases, due to enormous political pressure to be tough on criminals. Despite countries like Brazil having a wide range of alternatives to incarceration, which are proven to be more effective at reducing crime, judges still overwhelmingly chose to imprison nonviolent offenders. Judges often lean toward a wide interpretation of "police power," which has long been a lightning rod in Latin America because the high levels of repression by security forces throughout history were often legitimized by compliant courts. While the advent of democracy allowed the courts to better hold the police in check, it has also led them to legitimize repressive laws enacted by democratic regimes, such as anti-*mara* statutes prohibiting "illicit association," which allows for widespread police detention.

Prison is the final stage of the criminal justice process. Throughout Latin America, penitentiary systems are incubators of crime rather than centers of rehabilitation. Nearly every prison in the region has exceeded its capacity for prisoners. Overcrowding ranges from 102 percent capacity in Argentina to over 320 percent in El Salvador, resulting in unsafe and unsanitary conditions, and extreme levels of violence. In January 2017, nearly sixty prisoners died in Brazil's Amazonas state during clashes among rival narcotrafficking gangs. Even with penitentiary institutes, basic standards are lacking. In Peru, despite the reforms promoted by the national penitentiary institute, just 23 percent of inmates have access to potable water, 18 percent to medical services, and just over half to adequate food. Prisoners themselves are in charge of security in many prisons, with drugs and other contraband freely flowing across prison walls. Guards and other personnel are often complicit in these activities. When the staff of Bolivia's Palmasola prison were fired for corruption, their replacements took up the same practices. As one of the weakest links in the already weak chain of criminal justice, prisons only deepen Latin America's security crisis.

The criminal code in Brazil dictates that those with a university education, generally wealthier and white, are guaranteed private cells isolated from the general prison population until their trial is complete. This protects them from spending pretrial detention in overcrowded, gang-controlled jails, and can sometimes mean awaiting their trial from home. Yet more than half of Brazil's prison population is eventually released without a conviction. These inequalities have become even more pronounced during Covid-19 in prisons known for overcrowded conditions. Brazil has instituted a near-total shutdown of the country's state and federal prisons to outsiders, including lawyers, reducing prisoners' access to a legal defense. Peru's government temporarily stopped sending people to prison, partly because of the contagion but also because of prison riots. In Argentina, many prisoners were allowed to complete their sentences under home surveillance (Gardiner 2020).

Understanding the Evolving Nature of Crime

The region also struggles to curb criminality due to the evolving nature of criminality. The realm between neighborhood delinquency and transnational cartels contains an increasingly diverse set of criminal groups, including rural militias, neighborhood watches, residential guards, "social cleansing" groups, errant community policing programs, youth gangs, corner-store money lenders, and the violent Central American gangs known as *maras*. Many entities engaged in criminal activity are legal, such as the huge private security sector: Latin America has over 3.8 million private armed guards, dwarfing its 2.6 million police officers (though with much overlap). Because a majority of firms do not register, this sector is really much larger. Guatemala is estimated to have between 80,000 and 200,000 private guards. According to Mexico's National Council of Private Security, over 80 percent of that country's private firms operate outside of local, state, and federal regulations (another example of decentralization's drawbacks) (Oliver 2011).

Scholarship explains such complex criminality by specifying its main dimensions. First is structural, stressing the organized and hierarchal nature of organized crime groups (Abadinsky 2010), rooted in centralized control and strict discipline. Second is the complexity of their crime: the simplest level are predatory "craft" crimes, which are quick activities like carjacking and extortion that do not require extensive planning or organization. More complex are "market" crimes, like nar-

Mobile community policing.
Credit: Mark Ungar

cotrafficking, that involve greater frequency, volume, and cooperation. This dimension includes supply lines, which range from short (such as selling drugs on a corner) to long (such as intercontinental shipping). Third, and facilitating complexity, is criminals' ability to infiltrate and influence state institutions (traditionally defined as racketeering) to shape laws, alter regulations, or get officials to do that work for them. Fourth is social embeddedness, or boosting infiltration, which is a group's integration into a society and economy. Since many organized crime groups provide security, jobs, and other services, such integration is key to their ability to withstand state attacks, classically illustrated by Al Capone's reinforcing of social, economic, and political networks in Chicago. Finally is trafficking of goods, which can be broken down into many categories. One is legality of goods, ranging from absolute (never legal, such as contract killings) to relative (legal under restricted circumstances, such as firearms) to commercial (legitimate but marketed illegally to avoid regulations, such as cigarettes).

Criminals' rapid expansion and diversification have shattered categories used to identify and distinguish among them. Globally, growing markets and decentralized states create unprecedented opportunities to share physical, financial, operational, and electronic resources. From low-income *barrios* to high-end markets, these groups collaborate to produce, transport, and sell an increasingly diverse array of legal and illegal products: narcotics, pharmaceuticals, firearms, and property (such as real estate, ranches, auto shops, tourist resorts); money (from currency exchange to gambling); humans (through emigration, prostitution); and natural resources (timber, minerals, palm oil, and endangered species). With technological leaps in communications and finance, as seen with Bitcoin and malware, these networks are better able to integrate supply lines while both fusing and concealing their simultaneous roles as vigilantes, law enforcers, service providers, and criminals. Such cooperation eases illicit networks' entrance into the regular economy, such as investment of contraband profits in legal goods and services like tourism and ranching. Such lucrative activity ensnares state security officials, who, disgruntled with their own agencies, can benefit by providing protection to criminal groups. In high-crime neighborhoods, officers can leverage their legal and physical powers such as by overlooking gang leaders' abuses or harassing activists. Such collaboration plagues every corner of Latin America. Neighborhood social-work groups become vigilantes funded by hiding narcotics, while land cleared by loggers becomes airstrips for cocaine cartels. Cocaine cultivation in the Andes has grown in nature reserves protected by local officials, while social service groups in Venezuela have used violence and drug trafficking to maintain local order. Venezuela allegedly collaborates with the "Cartel of the Suns" and FARC guerrillas from Colombia in assisting drug transshipment to the United States and elsewhere. Criminal *coyotes* who accompany migrants to the United States have taken advantage of the refugee crisis to charge exorbitant fees and to force those fleeing to smuggle drugs.

Persistent and Widespread Crime: Two Cases
Firearms
Every aspect of crime in Latin America, from corruption to narcotrafficking, demonstrates the fear and damage that it spreads. Some crimes reveal how the dimensions discussed here coalesce, making it difficult for governments to tackle the problem. One example is firearms, which fuel violence in regions like Central America's Northern Triangle, where 85 percent of homicides are committed with firearms, more than the global average of around 42 percent. Many of those firearms travel through channels that the state is unable to control, adding to the stockpile of weapons remaining from the decades of civil war that ended in the 1990s. Such channels include social media sales; the "ant" trade of individuals importing weapons and firearm parts hidden in legal imports such as cars and microwaves; and sales by local workshops and private security firms. Firearms easily cross the region's borders. According to military officials, there are more than 100 blind crossing passes on Guatemala's border and 50 on El Salvador's. The state also profits from arms trafficking. Each year an estimated 25,000 military firearms—including grenades and rocket launchers—end up in the hands of criminal groups like the *maras* and the Sinaloa cartel. In Guatemala, Ministry of Agriculture staff work with organized crime to cut down trees and drive them to the United States, returning with weapons purchased in border

states like Texas. Private security firms provide over 40 percent of illegal arms, selling them to Mexico's biggest criminal groups, such as the Sinoloa cartel and the Knights Templar. Even state agencies created explicitly to curb firearms are limited in basic tasks like registration, licensing, and inspections. In Guatemala, where up to 1.6 million firearms are in circulation, the arms control agency lacks the capacity to suspend licenses. According to El Salvador's arms registry, over 70 percent of licenses in that country have expired. Ballistics testing is a key component of any criminal justice process, particularly in Latin America, where a weapon is used on average up to three times per month, higher than the average of once every six months in the United States. Guatemala's national forensics institute has a skeletal staff of eighteen specialists and an average backlog of 4,000 firearms. Throughout the region, poor cooperation among the police, prosecutors, and military obstructs investigations, to the point where military officials block investigators from entering army bases.

Environmental Crime

Increasing rates of destructive environmental crimes, such as large-scale deforestation, mining, pollution, incursions of protected areas, and illegal road-building, are another security challenge for Latin America. Latin America has responded in the past decade by establishing environmental police units, prosecutors, and courts that provide the on-the-ground enforcement needed to collect evidence and make arrests necessary to halt rampant ecological crime. Nearly half of the region's countries have such units, and more recently created ones, such as those formed by Peru in 2014, are granted increased jurisdictional authority. Environmental ministries support these agencies by providing regulations and policy development, while nongovernmental organizations boost citizen involvement.

Even with political and popular backing, these enforcers face an uphill battle. One reason is the complexity of the crimes they fight. Deforestation is not just cutting down trees; it involves crimes ranging from fraudulent land and permit acquisition to unlawful activities at all stages of forest management and in the production chain of forest goods, from planning to harvest and transport (Tacconi 2007: 3). Another obstacle is corruption: state officials support many of these crimes. In Brazil, 2010's Operation Jurupari exposed a vast network of deforestation over an area larger than Spain, with $500 million of destruction and involving officials from congress to international businesses. The "Panama Papers" corruption scandal revealed a database of 11,300 transactions involving offshore, often laundered or embezzled funds, to escape tax liability. Jürgen Mossack and Ramón Fonseca's Panama-based law firm facilitated the transactions by depositing them in offshore accounts around the world. National officials, public figures, and even kings participated in and benefited from the fraud. Finally, there is a lack of coordination and support at the local level, where municipal officials and citizen leaders are vulnerable to threats, assassinations, and broken agreements. The number of environmental activists killed globally has nearly quadrupled over the past decades, jumping from 50 in 2002 to 212 in 2019. Of the six countries with the highest rates, four are Latin American: Brazil, Colombia, Honduras, and Peru (Colombia was the deadliest in 2019 with sixty-four killings).

Current Policy Responses

The ongoing citizen security crisis in Latin America, with its clear threat to the region's democracies, has resulted in a broad reassessment of security policy and a consensus that even the best-designed responses have been hindered by contradictory approaches, lack of political backing for new laws, inadequate support for the police officers, neglect of interagency cooperation, and, perhaps most harmful, a failure to incorporate citizens. Consequently, current policy responses are working to address those weaknesses.

A first emphasis has been on more integrated, longer, and more advanced training for police officers. In Peru, the average time of instruction between 1990 and 2000 was eleven months; after 2012 it increased to between fifteen and twenty-eight months. Curricula in academies throughout the region have been expanded into areas like constitutional rights and quantitative analysis. There has been particular emphasis on intelligence, with training giving police the ability to more comprehensively gather and apply information through a process known as SARA—scanning, analysis, response, and assessment—in real time.

Many countries are addressing the long-standing weaknesses in their criminal justice investigations. One way is through joint training of police officers, prosecutors, and judges in new laws, with a focus on collaboration in writing and reviewing police reports. Countries are also establishing more comprehensive databases, such as Plataforma México and the Unified Criminal Information System (Sistema Único de Información Criminal), which unites all information relevant to criminal activity, such as stolen-car license numbers, fired police officers' names, private security business owners, and arms warehouse locations (García Luna 2011). Attempts are also under way to humanize and control prisons. The Dominican Republic has pioneered a new penitentiary system centered on rehabilitation and inmate rights.

Honduras, having Latin America's highest homicide rate since 2012, and in some years the world's highest, exemplifies how these strategies can work even in dire situations. With over two-thirds of the population living in poverty, Honduras transited up to 60 percent of cocaine destined for the United States by drug cartels pushed out of Colombia and Mexico. Additionally, the *maras* terrorize neighborhoods through murder and extortion. Corruption permeates the government, from local police (who run about 40 percent of extortion networks) to the president's cabinet and family. Organized crime syndicates control territory throughout the country, dominating the northern coast and border areas, even infiltrating the national anti-narcotrafficking agency established to fight them. The 70,000-guard private sector, dwarfing the 12,000-officer police force, is a major channel for criminal activity, from arms imports to timber exports. The criminal justice system struggles to control crime. The attorney general's office, plagued by corruption and budget shortfalls, was particularly weak. Comayagua, a city of 400,000, reported nearly 400 murders between 2010 and 2012, but only thirty-four investigations were completed, and only three led to a trial and conviction. In 2012, Comayagua experienced the most deadly prison fire in Latin America, with 360 burned to death in a facility built in response to two prison fires a decade earlier that killed nearly 200 people. Honduras thus embodies the extent of the security crisis in Latin America.

Successive Honduran administrations addressed this crisis with a tough response. In 2003, less than five years after the police were removed from military control, the government adopted an iron fist centered on draconian laws, constitutionally questionable detention powers, and the formation of militarized police units, reforming the penal code and restructuring the police force five times. The impact was minimal until a comprehensive reform began in 2014 centered on three main strategies. First was a head-on attack against police corruption. Backed by the Ministry of Security, a purge commission evaluated over 9,000 officers at all levels, leading to the firing or phasing-out of nearly 4,000—three times more than from all previous commissions combined. To fight crime, two specialized agencies were formed: the Office of Police Investigation (Dirección Policial de Investigación) and the Technical Criminal Investigation Agency (Agencia Técnica de Investigación Criminal). Through better cooperation and investigation—including mobile investigation units with the ability to preserve and test crime scene evidence—these two agencies are beginning to dismantle rather than just slow down organized crime networks. They use a computerized statistical approach to systematically gather information on crime networks in order to understand their patterns and arrest all their participants, rather than making quick arrests that would allow their practices to be resumed or replaced. A new police statistics system is assisting by converting criminal data into criminal policy. Perhaps the most transformative change has been the transition of the entire police to a community policing model. At a new police academy formed in 2014, the Instituto Técnico Policial, over 12,000 of the country's 26,000 police officers have been trained with a community-oriented policing curriculum while already-serving officers were retrained under a systemwide community-oriented policing structure.

When provided with the political and financial backing it needs, community policing above all has been the most promising and effective approach throughout Latin America. Such progress requires several mutually supportive approaches. First, elected officials must break the false divide between community policing and tough policing. Instead of allowing community-oriented policing to be dismissed as "social work" or as a dilution of police authority, officials need to show that it is essential for the information and support needed to prevent and solve crimes. Second, community-oriented policing needs to be integrated into actual policing, such as by giving officers promotion incentives and time to work collaboratively with citizens, for example by starting a sporting league. Community-oriented policing must be central instead of complementary to policing.

A third focus should be incorporating prevention into all aspects of security policy. In several Argentine provinces, prosecutors work with schools to identify and help at-risk youth. El Salvador's Municipal Arms-Free Project aims to encourage people to give up their firearms. Elsewhere, centers have been created for men after release from prison or deportation from the United States, when the tendency to reoffend is highest. Finally, community policing must be centered on communities, by giving them the skills, time, and authority to develop and evaluate policy—instead of being handed a police-formulated agenda. In Central America, the group Youth Against Violence (Jóvenes Contra la Violencia) brings young people together to develop strategies. In La Paz, Bolivia's capital, where community policing started with no agenda to maximize citizen ideas, citizens raised issues long ignored by the police, such as illegal dumping and alcohol sales.

Community policing has already been the basis of effective large-scale security policy. Colombia's three biggest cities—Bogotá, Medellín, and Cali—halted high levels of violent crime through civic education, security schools, police training, business partnerships, and other programs like the Youth Power Program (Programa Fuerza Joven) in Medellín. Through these and other policies to integrate public, private, and community resources, these cities were able to reduce crime rates consecutively over many years—no small feat in a country still in the throes of an internal war. In Nicaragua, community participation was incorporated into the national police when it was formed in the 1980s, and is credited for helping to avoid its neighbors' high rates of crime (but also used against citizens during the regime's violent repression of pro-democracy protests in 2018).

Other countries of the region have replicated many of community policing's component programs, such as social crime prevention committees, comprising police officers, community leaders, civil society groups, local businesses, and parents. In Panama, the police's "vigilant neighbors" program draws on community resources and social capital to identify and prevent sources of insecurity. In Montevideo, the capital of Uruguay, a municipal reorganization to empower neighborhood groups boosted community policing. Chile has been at the forefront of institutional change to support community-oriented policing with quadrant plans to divide police jurisdictions into small areas in order to maximize police-community relations. This plan was supported by the Tactical Analysis System (Sistema Táctico de Análisis del Delito) to address specific manifestations of crime—a fusion of preventative and proactive policing. A more controversial application of community-oriented policing, infused with a *mano dura,* has been the "pacifying" police units in the high-crime hilltop *favelas* of Brazil's Rio de Janeiro. Established in 2008, these units combined social services with a campaign to retake territory occupied for decades by drug traffickers and organized crime groups, as well as *milicias,* armed entities composed primarily of military police officers who coerce residents to pay for both legal and illegal services. Though these units have committed abuses, these units have benefited hundreds of thousands of residents through education and employment programs, often with support of local neighborhood businesses (de Paula 2015).

In some cases, community-oriented policing is the driving force behind a complete overhaul. In Argentina, Buenos Aires province's powerful police used their political connections to cover up widespread corruption and abuse until a backlash led to one of Latin America's biggest community-oriented policing restructurings. A 2004 reform package was introduced as a "new paradigm" based on citizen empowerment and a radically different police structure. First, the official and subofficial hierarchies were fused and the number of ranks compressed from seventeen to nine. More radical, the police's entire structure was upended when operative control was transferred to its newly created local communal police and security districts. Civilians were brought directly into this new structure through work with state agencies like the Secretariat of Community Participation. A computerized statistical system and several specialized academies were established, while accountability was strengthened with an internal affairs office empowered to receive and investigate citizen complaints as well as to investigate officer finances, and using a GPS system to monitor police cars. Based on such investigations, a record number of officers were expelled for acts such as extortion, physical coercion, and bribes.

Conclusion

The advent of democracy in Latin America brought unprecedented advances in human rights, freedoms, and economic development. But it also brought a citizen security crisis marked by record murder rates, expanding organized crime, and daily insecurity for most citizens. Forged in the long struggle against authoritarianism, most countries faced this crisis by turning to the benefits of their hard-won democracies, such as community activism, fairer criminal justice, and accountable state institutions. Latin American societies realized that only by drawing on their strengths could the underlying causes of violence—from poverty and inequality to corruption and impunity—be overcome. But as those long-term reforms failed to bring short-term relief, governments increasingly relied on quick fixes, such as the formation of military police and overincarceration, rooted in the region's historical dependence on physical repression. The current deterioration of democracy, from Central America to Brazil, is both a result of and a fuel for such approaches. The citizen security crisis, in short, embodies the current crossroads of Latin American democracy, with many hard choices ahead.

6

Economies

Scott G. McKinney

Previous chapters have treated geographical, historical, political, and military patterns in Latin America. In this chapter I analyze economic life in the region beginning before the conquest, during three centuries of Iberian colonialism, and since independence. I consider economic structures of demand and production; problems of poverty, inflation, and external debt; the tension between free market allocation of resources and government intervention; as well as the twenty-first-century commodity boom and the arrival of Covid-19.

Latin American countries are as heterogeneous economically as they are in all other dimensions. That diversity is epitomized by its largest country. Brazil has had deep and long-lasting inequality of income and wealth, as well as many other social injustices that limit economic mobility. A small minority owns much of the country's land. Landless farmers, as well as the lawyers and priests who work with them, have been murdered for trying to protect their lands from exploitation and expropriation for minerals, timber, and other resources.

Illiteracy and discrimination afflict the Afro-Brazilians and Indigenous peoples. Women also face widespread discrimination in employment. Forced labor is practiced in rural areas, dragging the unsuspecting into conditions not very different from slavery. Half of urban residents live in informal settlements, known as *favelas,* and at least a quarter of the population has inadequate housing (Borgen Project 2019). Neoliberal economic policies have hampered attempts to reduce deep poverty and improve equality of opportunity. How does Brazil, despite half a century of strong economic growth and economic transformation starting in the 1960s, still find itself trapped by the economic legacies of earlier times?

Pre-Columbian Economic Life

Economic life began in the Americas with the arrival of humans searching for sustenance. After crossing the Bering Strait during the ice age of about 23,000–20,000 years ago (Kehoe 2017: 15) and migrating southward, humans arrived in present-day Chile by 12,850 B.C.E. (Moseley 2001: 90). As they dispersed over the two continents and adapted to the environment, they improved their tools and experienced a Neolithic revolution similar to those taking place on the continents they left behind. Remains at Monte Verde in present-day Chile suggest a life based on gathering edible plants and hunting mastodon (Smith 2009). The Painted Rock Cave, overlooking the Amazon River in Brazil, contains evidence of a campsite dated to 10,000 B.C.E. that supported a life of fishing and hunting as well as gathering nuts and fruits (Smith 2009).

The Neolithic revolution—the development of farming—took place between 8000 and 5000 B.C.E. in Mesoamerica with the development of maize (corn), in the Andes with the development of the potato and quinoa (Messer 2010), and possibly earlier in coastal Ecuador with the development of cultivated squash (Mann 2006: 17–18). On the coast of present-day Peru, cultures specialized in coastal fishing and inland irrigation-based agriculture. One of the earliest cities found in this region, Caral, used irrigation to cultivate sweet potatoes, squash, beans, cotton, and gourds (Moseley 2001: 113). The people of Aspero, a nearby fishing settlement dated to 3055 B.C.E., used the cotton from Caral to weave fishing nets, and used the gourds as floats. In exchange, the people of Caral received a steady diet of seafood that the people of Aspero harvested from the rich waters of the Peru (or Humboldt) Current. Here along the Peruvian coast, civilization had a maritime foundation (Moseley 2001), in contrast to other major civilizations developing in river valleys around the world at this time. Associated with this was long-distance sea trade (Moseley 2001: 48–50). Despite the development of farming and the sophisticated process of adaptation, the success of cultures was always subject to sudden or long-term changes in the environment. Along the western coast of South America, intense episodes of the warm El Niño current could reduce the fishing and result in levels of rainfall that destroyed irrigation systems and weakened cultures.

In the Andean highlands, cultures adopted a diversified agropastoral life that included both farming and herding. Around 5000 B.C.E., people on the *puna,* in the high elevations of the Andes, moved from hunting vicuña and guanaco to herding alpaca and llama and raising quinoa, one of the staple grains of the region (Mithen 2004: 267). To take advantage of the diversity of ecosystems that exist in close proximity in this rugged terrain with large variation in altitude, communities controlled vertical archipelagos of land that gave them access to the different crops grown at different altitudes. As a result, though there was a small amount of trade, there was not a large-scale development of markets and money in the region, since each group produced the variety of goods that it needed (Moseley 2001: 44–48).

The Olmec civilization of the Gulf Coast of Mexico, famous for its fine stone carving and colossal carved heads, arose as early as 1800 B.C.E. The economic foundations of this civilization were maize farming and fishing (Coe and Koontz 2008: 59–70). By 1000 B.C.E., the Maya were beginning to settle south of the Olmecs in the Yucatán, present-day Belize and Guatemala, growing maize and other crops. They expanded their ability to produce food and support growing populations by terracing hillsides and reclaiming swampland. By 300–800 C.E., the Maya were building large cities that may have had populations of in excess of 40,000.

New evidence from the Amazon region suggests that this ecosystem was able to support populations much more substantial than previously thought (Mann 2008). By 2500 B.C.E., there were "raised fields, channel-like canals, tall settlement mounds, fish weirs, circular pools and long, raised causeways" in the western Amazon near the border of present-day Bolivia and Brazil (Mann 2000: 786). It is likely that this is the area where peanuts, rubber, tobacco, cacao, and manioc were developed. To maintain the land's fertility once the forest was cleared away, the soil was mixed with charcoal in order to create the fertile *terra preta* (black earth). Across the Amazon region on the Xingu River, from the thirteenth to the eighteenth century, a culture with carefully laid-out communities supported a population of 50,000 (Mann 2006: 306–311).

The cultures that adapted to the various environments of the Andean region were absorbed over a short period of time by the Incas. They began a process of expansion around 1438 and, over a hundred years, pushed the boundaries of their empire to the northern frontiers of present-day Ecuador and southward into Chile and Argentina. They built an impressive system of roads to move their army; stored food in granaries to deal with shortages; and kept track of it all with a system of knots called *quipus* (Mann 2006). In 1491, just before Christopher Columbus arrived in the Americas, the Inca Empire was the largest in the world, and by some estimates the population of the Americas was greater than that of Europe (Mann 2006: 94).

In the Valley of Mexico, the Aztecs were moving in among Toltec people by the beginning of the fourteenth century, and by 1344–1345 they had founded two cities in the middle of a lake at the site of present-day Mexico City. The lake was used for agriculture with the construction of floating islands (Coe and Koontz 2008: 190–191). The Aztecs used dams

Agricultural terraces laid out prior to the Iberian conquest. Credit: Scott McKinney

and terracing in the surrounding region to increase agricultural production. Early in the fifteenth century, they joined with two other kingdoms in a triple alliance and began a process of conquest that took them from the Gulf Coast to the Pacific Coast and to present-day Guatemala by 1502. It is estimated that by the time the Spanish arrived in 1519, the Aztec capital, Tenochtitlán, had a population of 200,000–300,000 (Coe and Koontz 2008: 186–200).

For more than 19,000 years, the people who inhabited the Americas developed in relative isolation from the peoples in Europe, Asia, Africa, and Australia. There may have been some contact, but it was not of a magnitude sufficient to transform these two separate spheres. The two spheres went through similar processes of adaptation to their environments and of social development, but they had different animals, developed different plants, suffered from different diseases, and made different uses of gold and silver.

The Colonial Period

These two worlds came into contact when large numbers of Europeans followed Columbus to the Americas, resulting in a massive exchange of plants, animals, diseases, and culture known as the Columbian Exchange.

Horses, wheat, smallpox, and the wheel came to the Americas, while maize, manioc, potatoes, and possibly syphilis went to Europe, Africa, and Asia. At the same time, the focus of economic activity in the Americas shifted in a fundamental way. It had been a process of adaptation to the local environment to produce a broad spectrum of products needed for survival; suddenly, a process of extracting specific products that had high value in Europe was superimposed on this Indigenous foundation. While Spanish *conquistadores* were interested in individual wealth, the crowns of Spain and Portugal sought to enhance national power.

The theory of mercantilism guided European economic policies during this period. The interests of the crowns in unifying their nations and building powerful states merged with the interests of a rising mercantile class in acquiring the protection and support of the state for their trading activities. The goal of mercantilism was to acquire wealth in the form of gold and silver to be shared between the state and the mercantile class. Wealth was useful to keep in reserve for the unforeseen, to fund government and the military. Exploitation of land, mineral resources, and fish stocks was encouraged; exports were encouraged and imports discouraged; wages were kept low. Government policies regulating trade and protecting economic activity, a strong navy, and a large merchant marine were all viewed as necessary to maintain the mercantilist system (Allen 1987).

As the Spaniards spread out from the Caribbean in the process described by René De La Pedraja in Chapter 3, they found mineral deposits and fertile land at the same time that they were decimating the population with diseases to which the Indigenous peoples had no resistance. In general, the Europeans at this stage were more interested in enrichment through mining and trade than in settling down to farm the land. Nonetheless, the *conquistadores* were given large land grants called *encomiendas,* putting in place an extremely concentrated pattern of landownership that influences Latin America to the present day.

Silver was discovered in the 1540s in Mexico, and in 1545 the Spaniards learned from the Indigenous people about the silver in Potosí, in present-day Bolivia. According to Spanish law, the crown owned the mineral resources, and miners extracting silver or gold owed the Spanish crown royalties, called the *quinto real* (royal fifth). This tax was a disincentive to mining, and, as the quality of the ores declined and profits fell, the crown reduced this to a tenth, the *diezmo* (Brown 1996b). One of the challenges the Spanish faced was finding labor to do the mining. It is estimated that before the Spanish arrived, the population of Peru was 9 million, and that it was reduced by disease to 1.3 million by

1570 (Brown 1996a: 359). Conquerors interested in large-scale projects in mining or agriculture had to find ways of assembling a large labor force, sometimes bringing in enslaved Africans and other times encouraging European immigration. To provide labor for the mine at Potosí, Viceroy Toledo of Peru (1569–1581) resettled the Indigenous population into villages called *reducciones*, which were required to contribute a portion of the available labor, the *mita*, for work in the mines. By 1600, however, the mining was done more by wage labor than by the *mita* (Bakewell and Brown 1996: 61).

Mining activity had linkages to a broader local economy. However much the Spanish crown attempted to control production in its colonies, gradually a complex colonial economic life began to develop. The mercury needed for the process of extracting silver from the ore at Potosí came from Huancavelica, Peru; food to support the miners came from Chile; and draft animals came from Argentina (Cardoso and Helwege 1992: 27). Mexico City became a major trading center, involved in trading cacao from South America, textiles from Asia, and silver and mercury from Peru. Small shops produced a wide variety of goods including furniture, glass, and paper (MacLachlan 1996: 3). *Obrajes* (textile manufactories) became major industries in both Mexico and the highlands of Ecuador (Schodt 1987: 24).

The positive impact that a booming sector such as silver mining has on the broader economy may be weakened by what is called Dutch Disease (Cardoso and Helwege 1992: 33). One negative effect of the boom is a production effect, the tendency for the booming sector to attract labor and capital from the other productive sectors of the economy (Corden 1984: 360–361). In his classic book on the exploitation of Latin America, *Open Veins of Latin America,* Eduardo Galeano describes the eighteenth-century gold rush in Brazil: "The gold explosion not only increased the importation of slaves, but absorbed a good part of the black labor from the sugar and tobacco plantations elsewhere in Brazil, leaving them without hands. The miners were contemptuous of farming, and in 1700 and 1713, in the full flush of prosperity, hunger stalked the region: millionaires had to eat cats, dogs, rats, ants and birds of prey" (1973: 66).

The second negative effect is the consumption effect, the tendency for a region with a sudden increase in income to produce nontradable goods and services such as buildings and restaurant meals and to import tradable goods and services such as manufactured and agricultural products. The combined result of the production and consumption effects is that the domestic manufacturing and agriculture tend to decline. It has been argued that Dutch Disease not only kept Latin America from moving beyond its original role as a provider of natural resources for Europe and North America, but also did the same for Spain (Forsyth and Nicholas 1983).

In order to maintain a successful mercantilist strategy, Spain not only had to be able to find gold and silver, but additionally had to be able to transport it safely to Europe and then produce the manufactures to send to the New World in return for the precious metals. Spain failed on the latter two counts. The ability of the Spanish armada to protect Spanish vessels from piracy declined over time, accelerated by the defeat of the Spanish armada in 1588. Rather than do the manufacturing itself, Spain flooded Europe with its gold and silver to buy manufactured products for the American colonies. In the process of doing this it provided the money needed to launch the system of capitalism that replaced the feudal order (Weatherford 1988: 15).

On the other side of the continent, the Portuguese began to settle Brazil, but in the early stages they found little in the way of gold or silver. The coastline was divided into twelve captaincies, putting in place a distribution of land characterized by inequality and a society dominated by the large landowners. The major economic activity was growing sugarcane and producing sugar. The Indigenous population declined from about 2.4 million in 1500 to half that level by 1808, and so labor had to be supplemented by the importation of Africans, who may have numbered 4 million to 5 million by 1810. Not until the eighteenth century were gold and diamonds discovered in Minas Gerais (Russell-Wood 1996).

Life in the Spanish colonies was shaken up by the succession of a new royal family to the Spanish throne in 1700. As the Bourbons attempted to squeeze more income out of the colonies, tensions rose among both the creoles and the Indigenous peoples. The eighteenth century saw numerous rebellions in the highlands of Peru (Brown 1996a). The wealthy in Mexico were also dissatisfied with the reforms, and growing concentration of land in commercial haciendas put small farmers at risk and created conditions supportive of revolution (MacLachlan 1996: 6).

Independence movements swept Latin America in the early 1800s, but the colonial period left behind some substantial legacies that the independent Latin American nations have had to struggle with ever since. The economies remained dependent on the export of minerals and agricultural products. They inherited the Iberian legal tradition that mineral rights belong to the crown or the state. Last, the way in which the crowns of Spain and Portugal granted land to the leaders of the conquest resulted in a distribution of land and income that was extremely unequal. There was a small elite of creoles, a small middle class, and a large poor class that included most of the mestizos, mulattos, Africans, and Indigenous peoples. Independence from Spain simply replaced the peninsular elite with the creole elite.

Independent Latin America

The newly independent countries of Latin America faced difficult economic challenges. Many of the countries started out with both a heavy burden of debt and extensive damages from the wars of independence. With the exception of Brazil, which did not have to fight for independence, all Latin American countries defaulted on their debt in the first decade of independence (Cardoso and Helwege 1992: 111).

The newly empowered Latin American elites were influenced by the European philosophy of liberalism, which emphasized the idea of liberty under the law: individuals could follow their own interests and desires, constrained only by the liberty of others. In the context of the economy, this philosophy was interpreted as an argument for a market system. All individuals would have equal access to markets and their interaction would lead, as if guided by an "invisible hand," to greater social welfare (Dahrendorf 1987). Liberals in Latin America used these arguments to reduce the power of the Catholic Church, taking its lands so they could be used to grow export crops. Indigenous peoples were also deprived of their land, making land and the labor on it simultaneously available to the new export economy. Liberalism in Latin America included a substantial role for the state, and governments in the region encouraged the liberal system, with "modest export taxes, public investment in social infrastructure, and promotion of foreign investment" (Bulmer-Thomas 1994: 49). Improvements in transportation and industrialization in Europe and North America pulled the Latin American economies into the world trading system. British demand for raw materials, British sales of manufactured goods, British financing, and British shipping all kept the system moving.

Countries entered the global economy by exporting specific products—a chance event referred to as the "commodity lottery" (Bulmer-Thomas 1994: 14–18). The export that a country draws in the lottery is influenced by various natural characteristics as well as historical accidents and entrepreneurial choices. Climate is one important characteristic: countries in the tropical zone will export bananas, sugar, coffee, cacao, and cotton, goods that are not grown in Europe and North America. Countries in the temperate zone of South America will export wheat, wool, beef, fruits, and vegetables that are similar to those found in Europe and North America.

Topographical and geological characteristics are also important. Areas with mountains, such as the western coast of the Americas, southern Venezuela, and central Brazil, will tend to have mineral deposits in concentrations that allow for profitable extraction (Bakewell and Brown 1996: 59). Gold and silver and copper and tin will often be important exports for the countries with this type of geography. On the flanks of the mountains, there will often be petroleum deposits. Along the western coast of South America the early oil production was to be found along the Pacific Coast, whereas more recent development has been on the east side of the Andes, often in the Amazon Basin. Rich reserves are also found offshore, in Lake Maracaibo of Venezuela, in the Gulf of Mexico, and most recently off the coast of Brazil. A third factor is the prevailing wind, heading west in the tropics—giving Latin America the Amazon rainforest on the east side of the Andes and a desert on the Peruvian coast—and heading east in temperate regions—creating forests in southern Chile and a desert in southern Argentina. One final factor that needs to be mentioned is ocean currents, in particular the Peru (or Humboldt) Current, which flows north along the western coast of South America. This cold, upwelling current, rich in nutrients, supports large populations of fish, spurring the early development of civilization along the Peruvian coast and present-day fishing in both Peru and Chile.

The export a country draws in the lottery influences the process of economic development (Bulmer-Thomas 1994: 14–18). Two economic factors that influence the relationship between export growth and economic development are production linkages and the distribution of income. Exports have different types and extents of linkages to the domestic economy. A mine may be an enclave with few local linkages: excavated by foreign engineers with foreign capital equipment, the product shipped abroad to be refined and sold. A small amount of local labor may be employed, but if they are paid relatively low wages, the impact that this mine has on the rest of the domestic economy will be minimal. Some economic activities may have backward linkages; shrimp farming, for example, depends on fishermen who net the shrimp larvae along the beach, laboratories where these larvae are grown to the size appropriate to place in shrimp ponds. At this stage shrimp food is needed and, when the shrimp are full-sized and ready for market, powerful pumps are required to empty the ponds. Other activities may have forward linkages, such as those of petroleum, which can be refined and turned into plastics and then plastic products, or can be used to generate power used in manufacturing. The greater the linkages of an export, the more its growth will encourage economic development.

Once the product is produced and exported, there is the question of who receives the income. This is important in terms of income distribution, investment, and the multiplier effects of domestic demand. First, there are differences in how much of the income returns to the producing country as opposed to flowing to owners abroad. One economic historian reports that the Peruvian subsidiary of Standard Oil of New Jersey paid all the local costs of petroleum production with its local sales of petroleum products, so that none of the revenue from exporting the petroleum returned to Peru (Thorp 1991: 31–32). At the opposite extreme, a locally owned company could return 100 percent of export revenues to the producing country.

The distribution of ownership within the country also plays a role in the process of economic diversification and development. Coffee was produced on large plantations in Brazil so that the flow of income was concentrated and the resulting income distribution very unequal. In Colombia the coffee farms tended to be smaller and family-run, using family labor to produce a high-quality bean. A national organization, the Federación Nacional de Cafeteros Colombianos, had warehouses for coffee and had been able to keep foreign coffee buyers from dominating the market. The result was that the revenues from coffee were more broadly distributed in Colombia than in Brazil, and demand for local products was correspondingly greater (Thorp 1991: 1–11).

The income that does return is shared among capitalists, labor, and the state. Capitalists may spend their earnings abroad or domestically, invest the earnings in the same activity that generated them or diversify into a different economic activity, or put the money in a bank where it can be loaned out to others. Laborers will tend to use a larger proportion of their income for consumption than capitalists will; thus, the distribution of income between capitalists and laborers will influence the balance between the increases in productivity that investment can bring and the expansionary multiplier effect of consumption.

For example, in Peru during the 1890s a substantial portion of the revenues from the coastal agricultural enterprises, sugar and cotton, and from mining, was paid to labor and therefore generated demand for local goods. Linkages to local foundries further expanded the economy. Capitalists had funds to invest and, with the encouragement of rising local demand, invested in local manufacturing, textiles, banks, insurance companies, electricity generation, tramways, and mining. However, by the turn of the century, foreign families had bought up the sugar estates and moved toward more capital-intensive production, reducing total wages and the local demand that resulted from them. Foreign companies moved into the mining sector, falling international transportation costs put the local foundries out of business, and an appreciating currency encouraged exporters to plough their profits back into the export sector rather than diversifying into other sectors (Thorp 1991: 23–34). This example suggests the variety of factors that influence the extent to which an export boom can set in motion a process of economic diversification and development.

The third major recipient of export revenues is the state, either through taxation of private sector earnings, or as the owner of natural resources, or, in some cases, as the developer of those natural resources. Here the issue is whether the state's revenues are used productively, spent domestically or abroad, for infrastructure and capital equipment or for consumption and monuments. Ecuador, for example, has been the beneficiary of a number of booms since it became independent. The foundations for the most recent boom—the petroleum boom—were laid in 1967. A military government took power that year and fashioned a development plan with a goal of promoting "new reforms necessary to expand the potential for national development" (Schodt 1987: 116). Between 1972 and 1979 the role of the state in the economy was substantially expanded: private firms such as Ecuatoriana Airlines were nationalized and new firms such as the Ecuadorian State Petroleum Company were created. The value added by public enterprises rose from 2 to 12 percent of gross domestic product over the period 1972–1983 (Schodt 1987: 112–117). In contrast to the earlier cacao and banana booms, in the case of petroleum the resource was owned by the government. Therefore the revenues flowed directly into its coffers, enhancing its power vis-à-vis the private sector. These cases illustrate the power of the commodity lottery and the variety of ways that an export affects the broader economy through its linkages and income flows.

Dependence on one or two major exports in a volatile global economy tended to subject economies to cycles of boom and bust. Rising demand and prices for a product encourage greater production and increase the country's income. The busts that follow these booms arrive for various reasons. The guano boom in Peru came to an end as the guano—bird droppings that were excellent agricultural fertilizer—was exhausted. Cacao and coffee booms in Central America, the Caribbean, Ecuador, and Venezuela were brought to a halt by the exhaustion of fertile lands (Bulmer-Thomas 1994). Disease can destroy production: Ecuador's cacao plantations were attacked by fungus beginning in 1916 and, two decades later, Ecuadorian production was insignificant (Schodt 1987: 40–41). Competition from new producers can bring down the price of the product: as Brazilian and

West African cacao flooded the world market, the price of cacao fell 60 percent from 1920 to 1921 (Schodt 1987: 40).

The period 1870–1914 is sometimes called the Golden Age of commodity exports. As time went on, Latin American exports shifted from minerals to agricultural output, and the major markets expanded from Britain to include Europe and the United States. Nonetheless, as new exports replaced old, diversification rarely took place. For many countries, one product generated more than 50 percent of export revenues: circa 1913 tin was the source of 72 percent of Bolivia's export revenues; nitrates 71 percent of Chile's; sugar 72 percent of Cuba's; cacao 64 percent of Ecuador's; bananas over 50 percent of export revenues in Panama, Costa Rica, and Honduras; and coffee over 50 percent in El Salvador, Guatemala, Haiti, Nicaragua, and Venezuela (Bulmer-Thomas 1994: 57–60). However, only Argentina, Chile, Cuba, and Uruguay achieved rates of export growth rapid enough to raise real income per capita by 1 percent per year (Bulmer-Thomas 1994: 57–68).

However, even in countries with impressive records of export growth, the benefits of the liberal model of economic development sometimes failed to extend to a sufficient percentage of the population to maintain political stability. As Shelley McConnell explains in Chapter 4, in Mexico the years of the *Porfiriato* (1876–1911) were a period of liberal progress. The Porfirio Díaz government worked to modernize and unify the country, creating a national bank, and building railroads and a telegraph system. The railroads brought formerly isolated regions into the national market and commercial agriculture began to displace communal Indigenous landholdings so that peasants were forced to become sharecroppers or wage laborers. The scarcity of domestic investment led the government to encourage foreign investment, and foreigners responded by buying land, building the railroads, and running the mines. Industrialization began to take place and, as a result, a working class and a middle class developed (Tenenbaum 1996: 12–14). In contrast to the period 1850–1870, when exports were declining, exports grew 4.4 percent annually between 1870 and 1890 and 5.2 percent annually from 1890 to 1910 (Bulmer-Thomas 1994: 65).

Many people were hurt by these economic changes, however, and many were excluded from the political process. The middle class was interested in a more open, democratic system. Workers began striking against foreign owners in 1906; in 1909, Emiliano Zapata began leading peasants in retaking their ancestral lands. Amid calls for social justice and political change, Francisco Madero, a moderate leader from the northern landowning class, called for revolution in 1910, replacing Porfirio Díaz. In

1917 a convention wrote a new constitution that guaranteed social protection for workers, agrarian reform for peasants, and limitations on foreign ownership (Gentleman 1996: 14–16). This case illustrates the tensions created by economic change and the political consequences of failing to share the benefits of that change with the entire population.

With the coming of World War I, Britain's influence in Latin America continued to decline and that of the United States continued to rise. US private investment in Latin America increased substantially. However, the money was used "to increase further the supply of already dangerously surplus agricultural commodities" (Thorp 1998: 108). The prices of these commodities began to fall in 1927 as the world headed toward the Great Depression, and fell more than 50 percent over the period 1928–1932 (Thorp 1998: 104). Unfortunately for Latin America, the interest rates on its debt stayed high and its markets were gradually reduced by rising protectionism in the United States and United Kingdom. Default on the debts followed quickly. Countries responded in various ways to the depression. For example, Colombia, Guatemala, and Brazil began public works projects. Others, such as Ecuador, used new lands to carry out agricultural expansion, and some, such as Peru, simply waited for commodity prices to turn around.

World War II opened a number of opportunities for Latin American countries, and the United States moved aggressively to gain access to raw materials in the region. The war reduced Latin America's access to imports from Europe, Japan, and the United States, opening space for some industrialization in the region. Hence, as illustrated in Table 6.1, industrial production grew by more than 30 percent for some countries over the period 1938–1945 (Thorp 1998).

Table 6.1   Growth in Manufacturing During the World War II Era, 1938–1945 (percentage change in inflation-adjusted value)

	Growth
Argentina	31
Brazil	44
Chile	84
Colombia	62
Cuba	38
El Salvador	33
Mexico	77
Nicaragua	86
Venezuela	41

Source: Thorp 1998: tab. 4.4.

This relatively quick succession of challenges to the liberal system following on the heels of the Golden Age of commodity exports set the stage for a new economic philosophy. The failure of nineteenth-century liberalism to set in motion a self-sustaining process of development led to a search for an alternative, and the industrialization that took place during the war suggested what that alternative might look like.

Import Substitution Industrialization

Import substitution industrialization, derived from dependency theory, became the dominant economic policy of the post–World War II period. Dependency theory suggested that Latin American countries were a periphery that depended on the economic activity in the center, which is to say the higher-income, technologically advanced manufacturing countries (Palma 1987). The system of production linkages in the center is dense, but the center requires raw materials from the periphery as well as a market for its manufactures. The system of linkages in the periphery is less dense and oriented toward the center. To use automobile production as an example, automobile assembly in the United States might use many parts manufactured within the country, while automobile assembly in Ecuador might use mostly parts imported from abroad. If automobile production in the United States were to grow, there would be a multiplier effect within the US economy as many more inputs would be required from domestic producers, but the impact in Latin America might be only a small increase in demand for raw materials. If automobile production in Ecuador were to grow, a good portion of the multiplier effect would be felt in the United States, Europe, Japan, or South Korea, where a majority of the inputs were produced. Thus, because of the greater density of linkages in the countries of the center, these countries are more capable of self-sustaining economic development, whereas the weaker linkages in the countries of the periphery leave them dependent on the demands—overwhelmingly for raw materials—of the center.

Sometimes the concept of declining terms of trade is included in the analysis. This is the idea that over the long run the ratio of commodity prices to the prices of manufactured goods tends to decline, so that the periphery's standard of living will tend to fall (Cardoso and Helwege 1992: 85–88). Historical evidence does not provide strong support for this tendency; nonetheless the concept remains influential (Bulmer-Thomas 1994: 78–82).

Another consideration in the analysis that motivated the shift from nineteenth-century liberalism to import substitution industrialization was the extreme income inequality that continued to characterize Latin American societies. These nations had begun their independent periods with an unequal distribution of land and wealth, and the processes unleashed in the intervening years had not reduced that inequality. Not only was this seen as a problem in moral and political terms, but it was also seen as an obstacle to the process of economic development. If income was concentrated at the top of the distribution, then the lower income groups would not constitute a market for local production; in this case, the benefits of exports would not initiate a self-sustaining process of economic growth (Bulmer-Thomas 1994: 277).

Import substitution industrialization was the policy response that evolved out of this analysis. It involved using government policy to encourage the development of an industrial sector, and so it is also called state-led industrialization. It was argued that reallocating the country's energy toward sectors with high rates of technological progress and rising labor productivity would result in economic development (Eatwell 1987).

The policy was implemented by protecting the young manufacturing sector with tariffs and quotas, by supporting the importation of capital equipment and inputs through overvalued exchange rates, and by encouraging investment with tax incentives, subsidies, and low interest rates. Local production, often accused of being of low quality and inefficient, survived behind walls of protection that raised the price of competing imports in the period 1957–1959 by an average of 143 percent in Brazil and 139 percent in Argentina (Sheahan 1987: 84–87).

The process of import substitution industrialization began with the production of consumer goods and then was encouraged to deepen through establishment of linkages to other local production. Automobile production was a classic place to start. It could begin simply as the assembly of parts imported from abroad, but over time could gradually use more locally produced parts such as tires, window glass, seats, and exhaust systems. The strategy was relatively successful in the 1950s, 1960s, and 1970s. Industrial production grew at annual rates of 5.2 percent during 1960–1965, 6.3 percent during 1965–1970, and 5.8 percent during 1970–1977, faster than in the industrialized countries (but not as fast as in East Asia). Manufacturing output as a percentage of GDP rose from 20.8 percent to 26.5 percent, essentially catching up to the industrialized countries and surpassing every other region by 1977 (Sheahan 1987: 84–85).

The policy has been criticized for creating capital-intensive manufacturing that provided few (though high-paying) jobs. As a result, the goal of improving income distribution was not achieved (Sheahan 1987: 83). Tariff and quota protection created a situation in which multinational corporations (MNCs) could sell in a Latin American country only if they produced there. Thus, much of the industrialization was carried out by MNCs, subverting the goal of strengthening domestic linkages. The emphasis of producing domestically for the domestic market limited the growth of production to the growth of the national economy, since universally applied import substitution industrialization limited each country's ability to export to other Latin American countries (Sheahan 1987: 83). Eventually, as the global situation changed and international trade became more important, import substitution industrialization was criticized for supporting the growth of an inefficient sector that could not compete internationally (Eatwell 1987).

Argentina and Brazil were among the earliest countries to implement import substitution industrialization. A comparison of their experiences provides an interesting insight into the consequences of the division of export income among capitalists, labor, and the state. Argentina began the process under President Juan Perón just after World War II ended, its coffers full of foreign exchange and its economy close to full employment (Sheahan 1987: 179). Perón, interested in building a manufacturing sector and strengthening his political base among the urban working class, used government policy to transfer about half of the agricultural sector's income to the industrial sector. Real wages of urban workers increased 62 percent from 1946 to 1949. As urban incomes rose, domestic consumption of Argentina's exports—beef and wheat products—also increased. As a consequence, Argentina's exports fell 19 percent from 1946–1949 to 1950–1954, resulting in trade deficits (import expenditures greater than export revenues, often financed by borrowing) and shortages of foreign exchange (the currencies used in international trade, such as the US dollar). Perón was deposed by the military in 1955, but the conflict between agriculture and manufacturing in Argentina continues to this day (Sheahan 1987: 179–188). The ripples of Perón's policies could be seen in the first decade of the twenty-first century, when President Cristina Fernández placed heavy taxes on farm output to pay for her government's programs.

Brazil was much less extreme in its attempt to redistribute income. An estimate from 1966 suggests that only about 21 percent of the agricultural sector's income was transferred to the manufacturing sector, and a greater part of the benefits went to capitalists rather than labor. While output per worker rose 6.6 percent annually from 1949 to 1959, real wages (wages adjusted for inflation) in manufacturing rose only 2.4

percent annually. Brazil's export levels were protected by the smaller increase in domestic incomes: Brazilian exports rose 14 percent over the period that Argentina's fell 19 percent. Rapid growth in the economy, however, led to some of the same problems that Argentina encountered, trade deficits and foreign exchange shortages (Sheahan 1987: 179–188). Nonetheless, the contrast between the experiences of Argentina and Brazil highlights the challenges that Latin American countries often face: how to develop a manufacturing sector without doing too much damage to the export sector; how to raise the standard of living without creating trade deficits.

Brazil had a number of advantages that enabled it to move beyond classic dependence and establish a new relationship with the center, termed dependent development (Evans 1979). First, despite the fact that Britain dominated the import-export business and shipping, the coffee plantations were owned by the local elites, who had profits to invest. Second, the Brazilian military had a long-running commitment to achieve national security by producing critical products in Brazil. Third, Brazil is the largest economy in Latin America and has always been willing to use foreigners' interest in its market as leverage to achieve its development goals.

While the British built and operated the railroads, it was sometimes done with Brazilian capital. Once the railroads were in place to haul coffee to the ports, they were available to haul inputs for Brazilian industry and consumer products to a broader market. Industrialization began in food and textiles early in the twentieth century. By the 1970s, the process had deepened to include transportation and electrical equipment, metal fabrication, and chemicals (Evans 1979). Manufactured exports began to play a larger role and coffee played a smaller one as investment by US multinational corporations was added to domestic investment. In order to counterbalance foreign capital, Getulio Vargas built the foundations for an activist state—the *Estado Novo*—during his first period as president (1933–1946). Vargas convinced the United States that if it did not help Brazil build a steel plant, Germany would do so. So a steel company was founded in 1941 with US help and the Companhía do Vale do Río Doce (CVRD) was established in 1942 to mine iron ore. State entrepreneurship in shipping, airlines, port management, and petroleum increased the influence of the government in investment and production (Evans 1979).

Brazil's relationship to the center had changed. It was no longer about the exchange of commodities for manufactures, but about being part of "an integrated system of industrial production whose ownership continued to remain in substantial measure in the center" (Evans 1979: 74). Nonetheless, the poor were still excluded from the benefits of the system as the Brazilian state, foreign capital, and the local elite divided up the benefits. In hindsight, we can see that the process led to the creation of a powerful economic machine and a number of important firms—CVRD, Petrobras, Embraer, and others—which, whether presently private or public, represent a shift of ownership and control away from the center identified by dependency theory. We can see here Brazil taking the first steps toward becoming what is now called an emerging market economy.

While Argentina, Brazil, and most other Latin American countries pursued some variant of import substitution industrialization, Cuba pursued an alternative path of economic and social change. On New Year's Day of 1959, the corrupt and unpopular government led by Fulgencio Batista relinquished power. Fidel Castro, head of a guerrilla army that had been fighting the government for three years, was able to consolidate power quickly and soon moved toward a communist model for remaking the nation (Liss 1996). Before the revolution, Cuba had a close relationship with the United States. Cuba exported sugar to the United States while importing most of its food from the United States. The island was also strongly influenced by US corporate ownership and tourism (Sheahan 1987: 239). However, as the Castro regime implemented a series of revolutionary reforms, Cuba's relations with the United States quickly deteriorated. The new government initiated land reform and, in the process, nationalized a number of US-owned estates, leading the US Congress to retaliate by eliminating Cuba's sugar export quota. Cuba turned to the Soviet Union as a market for its sugar and received Soviet petroleum in return. US companies in Cuba would not refine the Soviet oil and so those facilities were nationalized. The United States imposed a trade embargo on Cuba in the early 1960s, causing Cuba to suddenly have to find other markets for its products and other sources for its imports (Sheahan 1987: 253).

The task of reconceiving a society and an economy cut off from its historical roots was a daunting one. However that history is viewed, the path forward was replete with trial and error. Cuba attempted to reduce its dependence on sugar exports by growing other crops and industrializing. Large private sugar estates, many of them owned by US companies, were replaced by state farms, which were notoriously inefficient because of larger-than-necessary labor forces and rampant absenteeism, declining productivity, and extreme waste.

Though Cuba is discussed in the companion volume *Understanding the Contemporary Caribbean,* we look to Cuba here as an influential model for the countries in this book. Cuba tried to attend to the basic needs of its people without emphasizing consumption (Liss 1996). In its first four years, the regime put great effort into increasing literacy and making primary education available to everybody. It also concentrated on improving health; for example, Cuba's infant mortality was the lowest in Latin America in 1984, half the level of Argentina (Sheahan 1987: 26). A study done in 1977 suggests that Cuba had the most equal income distribution in Latin America (Sheahan 1987: 243, tab. 2.1). Cuba has continued to maintain a reputation of providing high-quality, low-cost healthcare, sharing its expertise with other countries in the region.

Basic consumer goods were rationed and their prices were kept low so that people's incomes were sufficient to buy the things they needed. While an effective egalitarian strategy, it resulted in a great deal of time spent waiting in lines, low incentives to work, and high levels of absenteeism. Ernesto "Che" Guevara introduced the concept of the "new man" who would respond to moral incentives instead of material ones, but by the 1970s this strategy was deemphasized in favor of motivation through differences in pay, greater availability of consumer goods as incentives for work, and greater reliance on prices to reduce time wasted in lines (Sheahan 1987: 243–257; Liss 1996).

However checkered the economic record, Cuba had enjoyed twenty-five years of 4 percent annual economic growth by the mid-1980s. However, 85 percent of Cuba's trade was with socialist countries, and the socialist experiment in Eastern Europe and the Soviet Union was drawing to a close. In March 1990, in response to reductions in Soviet subsidies, oil shipments, and trade, Cuba declared the "special period in peacetime." Foreign investment was encouraged; the government had to allow for self-employment, and it chose to allow use of the US dollar in addition to the peso. Nonetheless, output in the industrial sector fell substantially in the early 1990s, the sugar harvest hit a sixty-year low in 1994–1995, and unemployment soared (Córdova 1996).

In the twenty-first century, Cuba has turned to Venezuela and China as trading partners. Venezuela has entered into a number of agreements with Cuba, exchanging petroleum for technical assistance and medicine. In April 2005 the countries agreed to increase the number of Cuban healthcare workers in Venezuela to 30,000, establish 1,000 free medical centers, train 50,000 Venezuelan medical personnel, and provide surgery in Cuba for up to 100,000 Venezuelans (Erikson 2005).

The perceived communist threat of the Cuban Revolution heralded an era in which several types of military governments came to power in Latin America. The broad spectrum of approaches to economic development that I have described is reflected in the approaches that these military governments took. At one end of the spectrum was the Brazilian military coup d'état against President João Goulart in 1964. A number of repressive military leaders followed a policy of modernization based on foreign capital and exports. The period of strong economic performance from the time the military came to power in 1964 to the eve of the debt crisis in 1980—particularly from 1968 to 1974—is often referred to as the "Brazilian miracle." Industrial value added as a percentage of GDP rose from 35 percent in 1964 to 45 percent in 1982. Export growth grew at greater than 8 percent annually during nine of the seventeen years, and GDP growth did the same. As a result, GDP per capita rose from $1,557 in inflation-adjusted dollars in 1964 to $3,539 in 1980 (World Bank 2009).

In 1968 on the other side of the continent, a military government of a leftist stripe deposed Peru's president Fernando Belaúnde Terry. The military government was led by General Juan Velasco Alvarado, one of a group of military reformers who had been educated at the Center for Higher Military Studies, where they had acquired a sense of social responsibility and "whose views had a strong 'developmental' content" (Thorp 1991: 67). The strategy that this government implemented contrasts in interesting ways with the Brazilian model. It involved building a process of economic growth and development based on the linkages and multiplier effects of commodity exports as opposed to the more traditional import substitution industrialization approach of the Brazilian military. Linkages to raw materials processing were to increase industrial sector jobs, while changes in the ownership of enterprises that would shift control and profits to labor were expected to redistribute income and increase the multiplier effect of commodity exports.

It was a good time to be implementing a development strategy based on primary product exports: from 1962 to 1970, Peru's ores and metals exports had increased 84 percent (World Bank 2009). What the military did not take into account was the difficulty of encouraging foreign and local capital to invest in the military's vision at the same time they were nationalizing some enterprises and shifting ownership of other enterprises to the workers. The military government's first step was to nationalize the petroleum sector and turn operation of the existing oil fields over to PetroPerú, a state enterprise. There was a great deal of optimism that there were substantial fields to be found and that Peru could become a significant oil exporter, but this did not turn out to be the case (Thorp 1991: 70).

The government was interested in increasing the country's mining production and exports and it tried to work with foreign companies to encourage them to invest in new mines. They were successful with one large mining company, but as the government expropriated International Telephone and Telegraph, Chase Manhattan Bank, and other foreign firms, the other mining companies chose not to invest given the uncertainty about the government's intentions. As a result, the government nationalized many mining company holdings. Mineroperú, another state enterprise, took over production and the exporting of the output.

As a result of the private sector's hesitation, a great deal of production and investment shifted to the government (Thorp 1991: 73). The government began to borrow at a time when international lending was flowing easily. From 1970 to 1975, while exports fell 7 percent and ore and metal exports fell 17 percent, debt service (repayment of the debt) rose 17 percent. By 1975 international lending to Peru dried up and, as the trade balance went from positive to negative, debt service became a serious burden (Thorp 1991: 76–77).

The Velasco regime attempted to redistribute income within the country in bold ways. Private firms in the industrial sector were turned into industrial communities, with ownership and profits gradually transferred to the workers. Velasco's economic plan was an innovative approach to using a strong natural resource base, strengthened linkages, and redistributed income to transform an economy. However, international and domestic capitalists were not willing to participate in a strategy where their property was being expropriated. Velasco was replaced in 1975 by another general, who dismantled the reforms and held elections in 1980 in which Belaúnde, deposed in 1968, was reelected (Peloso 1996: 372).

In the case of Peru, the period of military leadership was no miracle. In contrast to Brazil, where GDP per capita started at $1,753 in 1968 and more than doubled to $3,539 in 1980, in Peru GDP per capita only increased from $1,997 in 1968 to $2,256 in 1980 (World Bank 2009).

Elsewhere, Chile experimented with two radically different models of economic development in quick succession. The country went from gradual reform in the 1960s to a brief experiment with socialism in the early 1970s and, subsequently, to a long-term, military-implemented policy of free market economics. The government of Salvador Allende (1970–1973), in addition to representing an attempt to implement a Marxist economic system in the Americas, is an example of economic populism. Economic populism has been described as a strategy that "emphasizes growth and income redistribution and de-emphasizes the risks of inflation and deficit finance, external constraints, and the reactions of economic agents to aggressive non-market policies" (Dornbusch

and Edwards 1991: 9). Dissatisfaction with poor macroeconomic performance and unequal income distribution can tempt governments to encourage economic expansion by spending, increasing wages, and altering property rights to land, natural resources, and profits. The policies implemented
tend to ignore constraints in productive capacity, government and export
revenues, foreign exchange reserves, and the advisability of expanding the
money supply (Dornbusch and Edwards 1991: 9–10).

The populist experience tends to go through four phases. In the first
phase, wages are increased, output increases, and unemployment falls,
while inflation is kept in check by price controls, and shortages are alle-
viated by imports. In the second phase, economic disequilibrium begins
to manifest itself: there are shortages in some sectors, trade deficits and
government budget deficits appear, inflationary pressures begin to over-
power price controls, and goods with controlled prices begin to move
into black markets, but real wages continue to rise. The disequilibria
begin to dominate the scene in the third phase, where there is declining
investment and capital flight; real wages begin to fall and economic output may do the same. The populist experiment has failed and, in the
fourth phase, a new government comes into power, more orthodox economic policies are implemented, and a slow recovery begins (Dornbusch
and Edwards 1991: 11–12).

The need for change in Chile, for a different structure of economic
relations with the rest of the world and for an improvement in the distribution of land and income, was evident to many by the 1960s. President Eduardo Frei, elected in 1964, began a process of reform that
attempted to address these needs (Sheahan 1987: 206–211). When they
became dissatisfied with Frei's gradual reforms, Chileans elected Salvador Allende president in 1970. He campaigned on the promise to lead
them down the "Chilean road to socialism." His view was that the Chilean
economy suffered from too much economic concentration and too great
a dependence on copper exports. In industry, 3 percent of firms produced
more than 50 percent of value added; in agriculture, 2 percent of farms
owned 55 percent of land; in mining, three US companies controlled
"large mining," which produced 60 percent of Chilean exports in 1970;
copper production represented 75 percent of exports; and the richest 10
percent received 40 percent of the income. Allende's structural reforms
included nationalization of all mining; state control of large industrial
enterprises, banks, and the wholesale sector; and accelerated agrarian
reform (Larrain and Meller 1991: 179–181).

Economic expansion and income redistribution were achieved by
increasing minimum wages and public sector salaries, implementing

price controls, and increasing public investment in health and education. Real wages rose 23 percent in 1971, at a time when total output was rising 9 percent, so that labor's share of GDP rose from 52 percent to 62 percent. Government expenditures rose 80 percent in Allende's first year and the money supply increased by 119 percent (Sheahan 1987: 214–215; Larrain and Meller 1991: 195–198).

The Chilean economy began to move into the second phase, where disequilibria begin to appear. The rising income of the working class resulted in a greater demand for food, which had to be satisfied by an increase in food imports. In combination with a decline in the world price of copper, this resulted in a trade deficit. As a result of rising demand and price controls, food began to move from the legal market into the black market. The sense of impending economic chaos led to political polarization, with truckers calling frequent strikes and labor conflicts becoming a serious problem. Workers seized some factories, owners shut the workers out of others, and the government took over the factories, putting more strain on the government budget (Sheahan 1987: 216–218).

The Chilean economy moved into the third phase in 1972 and 1973. Private sector profits and investment fell. Meanwhile, government expenditures and deficits expanded as public sector wages and social security payments increased and subsidies to nationalized firms rose. To cover deficits, the government increased the money supply and inflation hit 261 percent in 1972 and 605 percent in 1973. Real GDP began to decline and real wages followed (Larrain and Meller 1991: 200–205). On September 11, 1973, General Augusto Pinochet took power and began a completely different economic experiment.

The episodes discussed in this section—the import substitution industrialization of Argentina and Brazil, the Cuban Revolution, Velasco's policies in Peru, Allende's populism in Chile—were all efforts to change the economic structure that had developed over the period that liberalism was the dominant economic philosophy. Latin Americans found the dependence on raw material exports, the income inequality, and the economic injustice all intensely objectionable, and they looked for ways to restructure the economy. The results of these efforts varied: they achieved mixed success in stimulating economic growth without reducing inequality in Brazil, and reducing inequality without stimulating economic growth in Cuba, but the Chilean case led to crisis and violent political change. The issues in any attempt to change economic structure result from a country's choice between building on the existing economic foundation or creating a new foundation. Economic change may include groups such as foreign capitalists and local capitalists or it may attempt to move forward without them. These are interesting and important questions, but by 1973 time to answer them was running out; global economic events during the 1970s were about to narrow the range of policy choices.

The Oil Shock and the Debt Crisis

In 1973, an era of cheap and plentiful energy came to an end. Energy prices began to rise early in the year, and, in October, in response to US and European support for Israel, the Organization of Petroleum Exporting Countries (OPEC) imposed an embargo. The effect was to reduce world oil supplies by more than 2 million barrels per day (US Energy Information Administration 1998). The average price of petroleum in the United States rose from $3.39 per barrel in 1972 to $6.87 in 1974 and to $31.77 by 1981 (US Energy Information Administration 2010).

As the price of petroleum rose, the global flow of income changed its pattern substantially, with consumers of petroleum spending much more and exporters receiving much more. Large oil producers that did not have pressing demands on their income deposited these petrodollars in banks, which then loaned them out, or recycled them, to borrowers. As it happened, there were two willing groups of borrowers in Latin America. Petroleum producers with a great deal of poverty and the desire to accelerate the process of economic development, such as Mexico and Ecuador, were willing to spend borrowed money as well as the additional revenues coming from their exports. Conversely, petroleum importers needed to borrow to cover the higher cost of their petroleum imports. GDP growth rates for Latin America averaged out to a healthy 5.8 percent for the period, but inflation rose from 4.7 percent per year in 1970 to 18.8 percent in 1980. In addition, over the decade a dangerous vulnerability developed: external debt in Latin America and the Caribbean rose from 20 percent of gross national income (GNI) in 1970 to 44 percent in 1982 (World Bank 2009).

The events that would expose Latin America's vulnerabilities were unfolding in the United States, where inflation reached 11 percent by 1979. The US Federal Reserve Bank applied a monetarist solution to the problem: if too much money in the economic system results in inflation, then inflation can be brought under control by controlling the money supply. As a result of the bank's policy, the interest rate in the United States increased from 9 percent in 1978 to 19 percent in 1981, bringing economic growth in the United States to a halt during 1979–1982. This affected Latin American economies in three ways. First, the weakened US economy led to a gradual reduction in the price of petroleum, which reduced export revenues for the oil producers. Second, the absence of growth in the US economy brought export growth in Latin America screeching to a halt; it fell from 10.9 percent growth in 1979 to 1.2 percent in 1982. Third, the increase in interest rates meant that Latin American debt service payments more than doubled from 1978 to 1982 (World Bank 2009).

On August 13, 1982, Mexico announced that it could not continue servicing its international debt; the debt crisis had begun. International lenders and investors were unsettled by Mexico's action, and, as illustrated in Table 6.2, total net capital flows to Latin America reversed from $26.3 billion of inflows annually during 1977–1982 to $16.6 billion of outflows annually during 1983–1989, because few new loans were available and the debt had to be repaid. A resurgence in investor confidence in the early 1990s contributed to a dramatic increase in capital inflows to the region, averaging more than $40 billion annually during 1990–1994.

Some important economic dynamics come into play when a country makes the transition from receiving capital to repaying it. The capital that flows in is received in the form of dollars rather than in the local currency; these dollars can be used to import more than the country is exporting, a trade deficit. Usually this inflow of dollars will drive up demand for the local currency and raise its value, called appreciation. This makes imports cheaper, thus increasing their volume. It also makes the country's exports more expensive on the world market, thus decreasing the volume of exports and creating the trade deficit.

When debts are due, countries need to create a balance-of-trade surplus, exporting more than they import to earn the dollars needed to repay dollar-denominated loans. This is generally accomplished by reducing the value of the currency, called depreciation: imports become more expensive and decline while exports become less expensive and increase. This has the potential to be beneficial for the economy, stimulating both the exports and the import-competing sectors, resulting in an

Table 6.2 Capital Flows to the Western Hemisphere, 1977–1994 (annual averages in billions of dollars)

	1977–1982	1983–1989	1990–1994
Total net capital inflows	26.3	−16.6	40.1
Net foreign direct investment	5.3	4.4	11.9
Net portfolio investment	1.6	−1.2	26.6
Other (including bank lending)	19.4	−19.8	1.6

Source: Folkerts-Landau and Ito 1995: tab. 1.1.

increase in output, jobs, and income. One distinct disadvantage is that the costs of imports rise, accelerating the process of inflation. Another is that the economic transition taking place is wrenching and standards of living may fall because the country goes from living beyond its means (by borrowing) to living well within its means (to repay the debt). We can see the impact this transition had on people's lives in the data in Table 6.3. First, GDP per capita, which rose by 37 percent during the 1970s, fell 10 percent from 1980 to 1983 and did not reach the 1980 level again for fifteen years. Second, of that lower level of production, more of it was exported to repay the debt: the trade balance moved from a deficit of 1.7 percent of GDP in 1981 to a surplus of 4.8 percent of GDP in 1984, a reduction in the portion of GDP available for domestic use of 6.5 percent. Third, the very poor were hurt particularly hard as government budgets were reduced, social services cut, and subsidies slashed. The process of eliminating these subsidies was painful economically as the standard of living of the poor fell; it was painful politically as people marched and rioted, occasionally deposed leaders, and often suffered from police and military repression. For all these reasons, the 1980s have been referred to as the "lost decade."

As a result of the substantial size of the debt and its impact in terms of falling standards of living, rising poverty, and rising malnutrition, attempts to alleviate the impacts of the debt crisis went beyond the standard responses. In many countries, the urban poor organized neighborhood soup kitchens and ate together. At the other end of the spectrum, banks that had made loans in Latin America began to sell these loans at a discount in the secondary market, where they were bought by investors who were willing to accept greater risk for the possibility of a higher rate of return. In some cases the buyers were interested in a debt swap: they would turn around and sell the debt to the government that had issued it, receiving local currency from the government that could then be used to buy state enterprises, such as telephone companies, airlines, mines, or petroleum companies, that were being privatized. Another group of buyers in the secondary market were international environmental groups interested in debt-for-nature swaps: the debt would be turned over to the government and the government would reciprocate by using local currency to buy the land and support the protection of a national park or nature reserve (Cardoso and Helwege 1992: 125–133).

The severity of the economic crisis seemed to call for a change in economic philosophy in Latin America. Import substitution industrialization, already subject to criticism, was largely abandoned as the challenges of the debt crisis mounted. Critics blamed this model for creat-

Table 6.3   Impacts of the Debt Crisis on Select Economic Indicators
in Latin America, 1970–1990

	External Debt (% of GNI)	GDP Growth (annual %)	GDP per Capita (constant dollars)	Trade Balance (% of GDP)
1970	20.0	6.2	2,680.30	−0.5
1971	19.9	6.2	2,777.00	−1.3
1972	21.2	6.6	2,887.90	−0.9
1973	18.9	7.8	3,028.40	−0.2
1974	18.7	6.3	3,153.40	−1.8
1975	21.2	3.5	3,185.60	−2.4
1976	23.7	5.1	3,268.60	−0.9
1977	28.4	4.8	3,344.70	−0.6
1978	31.1	3.5	3,381.70	−1.1
1979	31.9	7.1	3,541.30	−1.0
1980	33.0	6.3	3,680.80	−1.6
1981	35.2	0.5	3,616.10	−1.7
1982	43.7	−1.4	3,489.90	0.7
1983	54.0	−2.5	3,329.00	4.3
1984	57.5	3.7	3,381.40	4.8
1985	57.0	2.6	3,397.70	4.5
1986	57.6	4.1	3,465.50	2.5
1987	58.5	3.4	3,512.50	2.6
1988	50.8	0.5	3,463.30	2.3
1989	43.8	0.9	3,430.30	2.9
1990	40.2	0.3	3,381.10	2.2

Source: World Bank 2009.

ing an inefficient industrial sector because, first, it was protected by tariffs; second, the protection varied from industry to industry and resulted in an inefficient allocation of resources, and third, it divided Latin America into small markets where economies of scale (lower costs of production resulting from producing more output) could not be achieved. Import substitution industrialization also required substantial government intervention, leading to excessive government spending, deficits, and international debt, the cause of the crisis in the first place. In addition, much of the industrialization that took place was controlled by MNCs, and, unless its economy was the size of Brazil's, a country was unlikely to have the leverage necessary to deepen the industrialization process (Cardoso and Helwege 1992: 93–99).

As a result of the military coup in 1973, Chile experimented with one alternative to import substitution industrialization even before the debt crisis began. The military's initial goals were to stabilize the economic and political situation. In search of an economic policy that could control Chile's raging inflation, Chile's military government turned to a group of civilian economists trained at the University of Chicago who became known as the "Chicago Boys." As a result, Chile became an early implementer of monetarism and neoliberalism, the economic philosophies that would replace import substitution industrialization and dominate policy in Latin America for the 1980s and 1990s. While the debt crisis hit Chile as hard as it hit any country, it was neoliberalism that was suggested by the International Monetary Fund, World Bank, and US government as the solution to the crisis. Because these three institutions happen to be located within just blocks of one another in the US capital, the policy also became known as the Washington Consensus.

Monetarism argues that inflation is caused by too much money being introduced into the economic system. Since the root cause of the increase in money supply is often that the government has a budget deficit and prints money to cover that deficit, the neoliberal prescription is to balance the government budget. Since conservatives believe that the private sector is efficient and dynamic, in general they recommend that the budget be balanced by reducing expenditures rather than by increasing taxes. One way to decrease expenditures in the long run and increase revenues in the short run is to sell state-owned enterprises to private sector investors, simultaneously eliminating the need to cover their losses and turning operations over to the efficient private sector. Thus, privatization was an integral part of the neoliberal agenda in Latin America.

The other major strand of neoliberal philosophy is the belief that markets do a better job than the government in allocating resources efficiently and thus maximizing society's well-being. The neoliberal agenda therefore includes the deregulation of banking so that competition among banks will increase saving and allocate the loans efficiently. Related to this is liberalizing the flow of capital in and out of the country, allowing foreign capital to flow in and increase the level of investment in the country. Finally, neoliberalism prescribes trade liberalization, reducing or eliminating tariffs and quotas so that a country can export based on its comparative advantage (lower relative costs of production resulting from natural advantages) and import what the economy needs.

One way in which trade liberalization took place in Latin America was in the form of regional trade integration: groups of countries that agreed to reduce restrictions on trade among themselves. In addition to allowing countries in the group to trade on the basis of their comparative advantage, the agreements allowed firms to achieve economies of scale by selling to a larger market, and to strengthen backward and forward production linkages within the region.

As discussed by Cleveland Fraser in Chapter 7, many regional trade groups were actually initiated before the Washington Consensus. The treaty forming the Central American Common Market was signed in 1961. The Andean Pact was signed in 1969, creating the Community of Andean Nations. On the other hand, Mercosur (Southern Common Market), the largest group in Latin America, was created in 1986 as an agreement between Argentina and Brazil and in 1991 was expanded to include Paraguay and Uruguay (Franko 2007: 255–272). A study by the UN Economic Commission for Latin America and the Caribbean (ECLAC) shows that the proportion of trade that Latin American countries had with countries within their trade grouping rose considerably from 1985 to 2002 (CEPAL 2005).

As the advantages of these trade groups became more convincing, more countries joined and more agreements were negotiated among the groups. At the same time, free trade agreements (FTAs) with countries outside the region became important, particularly those with the United States. Mexico joined Canada and the United States in the North American Free Trade Agreement in 1994, and the United States continues to negotiate FTAs with other countries in the region (Franko 2007: 264–277).

One alternative to the neoliberal strategy just described was heterodoxy, which flowed out of economic thinking that put greater emphasis on protecting the poor from the consequences of economic crisis, and had greater faith in the effectiveness of government intervention. Inflation was understood as resulting from lack of excess productive capacity to satisfy rising aggregate demand, rising input costs, and, eventually, an inertial process in which one period's inflation led to continued inflation in the next period.

In Peru, Alan García, elected president in 1985, implemented a heterodox policy. García's policy team did not see neoliberal policy as an effective strategy for Peru (Thorp 1991: 121). They introduced a new currency to stop the inertial component of inflation. Wages were raised to help the poor and increase aggregate demand. Instead of attempting to control all prices, they limited controls to a set of prices that were critical to allow for private sector profits: the exchange rate, the interest rate, public utility prices, and food prices (Edwards 1995: 122). García also made a name for himself as a bold new leader by declaring that Peru would allocate only 10 percent of its export revenues to debt service, allowing the remainder to be used for imported inputs, including food and other necessities.

As in the case of Allende's program in Chile in 1970–1973 and other heterodox policies implemented in the 1980s, the initial period of García's economic policy was a great success. Wages and salaries increased 30 to 35 percent over the first eighteen months, and GDP rose

2.8 percent in 1985, 10.0 percent in 1986, and 8.0 percent in 1987 (Thorp 1991: 129). Inflation fell from 163 percent in 1985 to 78 percent and 86 percent the next two years (World Bank 2009). By 1987, however, price distortions developed in the economy as uncontrolled prices began to rise while controlled prices could not. Meanwhile, the government budget deficit, the trade deficit, and the money supply began to rise. The government began introducing policy packages called *paquetazos,* which included large devaluations. The combination of devaluations and rapid monetary expansion fed the inflationary process.

An interesting twist in García's policy was the process of *concertación.* This process tried to take advantage of the concentration of ownership in the industrial sector, where family-based economic groups each tended to own a diversified portfolio of businesses, properties, and banks. A weakness of many attempts to transform economies is the failure to maintain the support of the private sector. With this in mind, García backed away from policies of expropriation and instead attempted to coordinate economic decisions with the private sector through discussions with the leaders of the major economic groups, known as the "Twelve Apostles." Initially there was a great deal of goodwill and interest on the part of the private sector, but this was squandered through poor communication in 1987 and then completely destroyed with the announcement of a state takeover of the banking system. With this opportunity lost and the difficulties of the debt crisis continuing, García's heterodox experiment failed and the economy quickly worsened (Thorp 1991: 121–141). GDP fell 24 percent from 1987 to 1990 and inflation reached an astounding 7,482 percent by 1990 (World Bank 2009).

Despite these failures, as the lost decade of the 1980s came to an end, Latin America was perceived as having weathered the crisis. Although GDP per capita was not to reach its 1980 level again until 1995, international debt as a percentage of GNI fell to 44 percent in 1989, approximately where it had been in 1982, after having risen above 60 percent in 1986 and 1987. It fell to 33 percent by 1997 before it began to rise again. Commercial banks in the United States and Europe, after a period of denial, began writing off the bad debts they had accumulated before 1982 (Thorp 1998: 226).

A new generation of leaders came to power who, whatever their background, were more likely to implement neoliberal policies than heterodox ones. Fernando Henrique Cardoso of Brazil (1995–2003), Carlos Menem of Argentina (1989–1999), and Alberto Fujimori of Peru (1990–2000) are prime examples. The 1990s was a period of greater trade and more freely flowing international capital, which, as it turned out, presented its own challenges.

Latin America as an Emerging Market

An economic downturn in the United States and changes in regulations that made US mutual fund investment abroad much more accessible turned the attention of US investors toward Latin America and Asia at the beginning of the 1990s. These areas became known as emerging market economies, new areas in which to invest where returns were higher than in the United States and the risks were lower than they had been in the past. The Washington Consensus had liberalized capital flows and spurred privatization, creating investment opportunities. In 1999 foreign direct investment (FDI) was nine times the 1990 level while workers' remittances were 2.6 times their 1990 level. In 2000, investment in stocks and bonds was 3.8 times its 1991 level (1990 data on portfolio investment are not available; World Bank 2009). Capital inflows—FDI, portfolio investment, and loans—represent great potential for developing economies. First, the inflows provide foreign currency that can be used to import goods and services that might otherwise not be available. Second, they offer the ability to invest in productive activities that can increase the output of the country, creating jobs and raising incomes. Overall, the 1990s were a much better decade for Latin America and the Caribbean than the 1980s: GDP per capita rose by 18 percent from 1990 to 2000, compared to an 8 percent decline from 1980 to 1990; inflation fell from 23.8 percent in 1990 to 6.6 percent in 2000. However, it was not all smooth sailing.

The volatility of capital flows in Latin America in the 1990s raised problems in some countries. Although at first Argentina benefited greatly from capital flows, it eventually suffered from overindulging in them. In response to the disastrous experience of the 1980s—the failure of the heterodox Austral Plan that culminated in the 3,080 percent inflation of 1989—President Menem's minister of economy, Domingo Cavallo, established a currency board in 1991. The exchange rate was fixed at 1 new peso to 1 US dollar by guaranteeing convertibility; a person could turn in a peso to the currency board and receive a dollar at any time. As a result, the peso money supply was determined by the quantity of dollars held by the currency board, so that the government could no longer print money to cover its deficits. The theoretical advantage of this system was that the rate of inflation in Argentina would converge quickly to that in the United States; indeed, it fell to 4.2 percent by 1994. The disadvantages of the system were, one, that sudden dollar outflows occurring for any reason whatsoever would result in a decrease in the money supply and a credit freeze where few loans were available; and two, that if the government could not balance its budget, it would be forced to borrow, since it could no longer print money.

Panama City, Panama. Credit: Scott McKinney

The convertibility system was first put to the test at the end of 1994, when Mexico suffered the peso crisis and Latin America suffered the "tequila effect," the name given to the negative spillovers of Mexico's peso crisis. Soon to join Canada and the United States in NAFTA, Mexico was the largest recipient of capital flows to emerging markets in the early 1990s. The capital inflows pushed up the value of the Mexican currency, hurting the competitiveness of its exports and resulting in a large trade deficit. They also allowed the Mexican government to borrow to cover its budget deficit. Mexico entered NAFTA on January 1, 1994, beginning a tumultuous year for a country that was looking forward to enjoying its new position in the world. On the very same day, the Zapatista revolt broke out in southern Mexico, where landless peasants took over a number of towns. This marginalized group of people was not sharing in the benefits of economic growth and had been denied the hope of land redistribution by legal changes that Mexico had made in preparation for entry into NAFTA.

In addition, it was an election year and later that year the governing party's candidate was assassinated. Most significant for Mexico's economic fortunes, portfolio investment fell from $28 billion in 1993 to $7 billion in 1994. The Mexican government did not want to devalue its currency, so it covered its trade deficit out of foreign exchange reserves, which grew dangerously low as the year dragged on. Once the governing party's replacement candidate won the election, the government attempted an orderly devaluation of the Mexican peso. Unfortunately, it lost control of the process to market forces that drove the exchange rate from 3.4 pesos per US dollar in 1994 to 6.4 pesos in 1995.

Investors' reaction to this devaluation, the tequila effect, caused portfolio investment in Latin America and the Caribbean to fall from $71 billion in 1994 to $9 billion in 1995. Economic growth in Latin America declined from 4.7 percent in 1994 to 0.6 percent in 1995; the economy contracted 2.8 percent in Argentina and 6.2 percent in Mexico. While it was a difficult year for Argentina, the country surprised everybody by sticking with convertibility despite the credit freeze that occurred as Argentines pulled their wealth out of the country. This consistency in economic policy had a payoff: global confidence in the Argentine economy strengthened and capital flowed back in (World Bank 2009).

The global economy had not seen the end of the adverse consequences of free-flowing capital, however. In the summer of 1997, the real estate bubble that had been inflated in Thailand burst: portfolio investment in Thailand and East Asia declined, devaluing exchange rates and arresting GDP growth. The same pattern followed in Russia in 1998 and in Brazil in 1999. These crises had significant effects in Latin America. The Asian crisis of 1997 cut world economic growth from 3.7 percent in 1997 to 2.3 percent in 1998, reducing the world price of petroleum in the process and hurting the economies of petroleum exporters such as Ecuador, Colombia, and Venezuela. GDP growth rates in Latin America fell substantially in 1998 and turned negative in 1999.

In Ecuador, the smallest and most vulnerable of these countries, the banking sector—liberalized by the neoliberal agenda—collapsed. As the government increased the money supply in order to bail out the banks, inflation accelerated and the exchange rate rose along with it. The only exit that policymakers could imagine from this crisis was dollarization, where the central bank bought up the local currency with its foreign exchange reserves and thus replaced the sucre with the US dollar (Beckerman 2002: 51–59). As in the case of Argentina's convertibility, the deceleration of inflation was dramatic: by 2004, inflation was 2.7 percent (World Bank 2009).

In Brazil, the reduction in portfolio investment from $18 billion in 1997 to $4 billion in 1998 resulted in a devaluation. Argentina, Brazil's major trading partner, was trapped in convertibility and could not devalue; it was suddenly at a great competitive disadvantage in trade. Brazil's GDP growth fell from 3.4 percent to zero, but Argentina's fell from 3.9 percent to a negative 3.4 percent. As Argentina's external debt rose from 29 percent of GNI in 1994 to 55 percent in 2001 and foreign lenders finally grew leery of the economic situation, Argentina had to abandon convertibility and allow the exchange rate to be determined by the market. The peso quickly depreciated to a third of its previous value. As one would expect, once the shock of the devaluation wore off, economic growth rates were strong from 2003 to 2008, driven by a 57 percent increase in exports from 2001 to 2008 (World Bank 2009).

Volatility in global financial flows has not been the only weakness of neoliberal policies. There has also been the sense that the poorest members of Latin American societies have not been helped, and this has led to a populist reaction. As McConnell explains in Chapter 4, Hugo Chávez was elected president of Venezuela in 1998 with the over-whelming support of the poor, whom he repaid with a massive effort to redistribute income within the society. He restructured social programs around *misiones* (missions) that focus on specific problems such as illiteracy or poor health in lower-income neighborhoods (Rodríguez 2008: 250). Social spending per capita rose over 300 percent during Chávez's presidency, while increases in the minimum wage increased the income of the poorest substantially (Álvarez Herrera 2008: 158–159). The portion of the population living on less than $2 per day fell from 24 percent in 1998 to 10 percent in 2006; the Gini Index, an indicator of economic inequality, improved from 50—relatively high inequality—to 43—one of the lowest levels of inequality in the region, over that period (World Bank 2021b).

In attempting to redistribute income to the poor, Chávez challenged the power of the elite as well as the powerful state petroleum company, Petróleos de Venezuela Sociedad Anónima (PDVSA). The importance of this company is indicated by the fact that petroleum exports have often accounted for 80 to 90 percent of export revenues (Whalen 2007: 59). The conflict between Chávez and PDVSA led to strikes, firings of critical personnel, mismanagement, and underinvestment (Whalen 2007: 9). Venezuela's petroleum production and exports, its major source of revenue, fell, and the government financed its activities by printing money, with rising inflation the inevitable result. It is easy to interpret this as another example of economic populism that will ultimately fail, but it is important to keep in mind the way in which dissatisfaction with the economic results of neoliberalism can bring populist governments into power, as it has in Bolivia, Ecuador, and elsewhere.

As the twentieth century came to a close, the influence of the Washington Consensus on Latin American economic policy was beginning to wane. While the value of careful management of government budgets, debt, and monetary policy seemed to be widely accepted, there were three important criticisms leveled against the neoliberal agenda. First, financial liberalization without the necessary experience and regulation could create weak banking systems prone to crisis. Second, freely flowing capital could be a great temptation to government borrowing, and its sheer magnitude could easily overwhelm Latin American economies, even the larger ones. Third, it was not clear that improvements in the standard of living for the poor and reductions in inequality were occurring quickly enough to fend off the appeal of populist leaders.

Latin America in the Twenty-First Century

Latin America's experience in the new century as well as the region's prospects for the future derive from the interaction between legacies of the past and the major forces that dominate the period. First, the rise of the emerging market economies such as Brazil, Mexico, China, and others as major players on the global economic stage changes the dynamic of world economic relations in a way that may open opportunities for Latin America as a whole. Second, the commodity boom that lasted from 2003 to 2014 had substantial positive impacts on economic activity throughout the region. Third, the growth of large Latin American corporations—the *translatinas*—is raising the global profile of the region and changing the pattern of investment flows as Latin American corporations invest in other Latin American countries. These changes are transforming the economic dynamics of the region in significant ways, but the question of whether they will change the economic structure and the nature of economic development in the region remains unanswered. The fundamental tensions emphasized throughout this chapter remain for Latin America: between the seductive power of commodity exports as the basis for economic growth, on the one hand, and the desire to change the structure of the economy, on the other; between the desire to improve the lot of the poor and the need to maintain the support of powerful economic groups both within the country and internationally.

Brazil is the largest country in Latin America, with an economy that has grown from representing about 30 percent of Latin America's GDP in 1960 to about 40 percent in this century. Over the half-century from 1960 to 2011, its standard of living rose from 10 percent below the Latin American average to 24 percent above it. Its size, rising standard of living, and rich resource endowment, combined with sixteen years (1995–2011) of highly respected leadership, transformed Brazil into an important world power. Brazil's popular former president Luiz Inácio Lula da Silva provided a strong counterpoint to the redistributive populism of Chávez and other populists. He came to the presidency in 2003 with impeccable leftist credentials: a trade union leader, jailed and tortured by the military regime in the 1970s, who ran for president as the Workers Party candidate. The Workers Party manifesto declared that "social development is considered a vital component, rather than a residual outcome, of economic growth" (Baer 2008: 152). It argued that fundamental reform was necessary, but that "rapid economic growth and international competitiveness" were also necessary to achieve social development (Baer 2008: 152–153).

Understandably, international financial markets were quite worried at the prospect of Lula's election, fearing major changes in policy and an unfriendly climate for foreign investment. By the end of his second term in office, however, his record was quite different from that expectation and his presidency was a success in economic terms. Lula continued the cautious fiscal and monetary policies of his predecessor. The payoffs for these policies were continued international confidence in Brazil, an appreciating currency, declining inflation, and a GDP growth rate sufficient to raise GDP per capita by 30 percent (World Bank 2021b).

Lula attempted to improve the lot of the poor with two programs: *Fome Zero,* a program to reduce hunger; and a minimum income guarantee. After a disorganized initial effort, the *Bolsa Familia* program was created to achieve the first goal. By 2006, it provided cash transfers to 11.2 million families on the condition that the children attend school and use healthcare and social services (Baer 2008: 163–164). In pursuit of the second goal, the government raised the minimum wage, reformed the tax system, and restructured the social security system.

In terms of the tension between improving the lot of the poor and maintaining the support of the powerful, Lula's presidency seemed to provide a case where income redistribution was successfully implemented in a context of economic stability and growth. World Bank data show that the percentage of the population living on less than $3.20 per day fell from 22 percent in 2002 to 10 percent in 2011 (World Bank 2021b), resulting in less income inequality.

The *translatinas*—concentrated in Brazil, Chile, and Mexico—are investing in other Latin American countries and beyond. Brazil's particular pattern of development has created some major firms of international importance. A number of the largest firms either started as government enterprises or received a great deal of government and military support. Vale was the world's largest iron ore producer by 2008, a major producer of nickel, copper, and bauxite, and also involved in the manufacturing of steel and aluminum. It was established by the government in the 1940s as the Companhia do Vale do Rio Doce and privatized in 1997. Since then, it has expanded through investment and acquisitions so that only half of its production is now in Brazil. Embraer is the world's largest producer of regional aircraft. It was started by the Brazilian air force and also privatized in the 1990s. It exports 95 percent of its production and is Brazil's leading exporter of manufactured products (Schneider 2009: 165–169). Petrobras, the state petroleum company, was created by the government in 1953 to carry out all petroleum exploration and most of the refining, and it remains a state enterprise. It transformed Brazil from a country that satisfied only 20 percent of its petroleum needs with domestic production to being self-sufficient by 2007. The company has expanded into petrochemicals and invested in natural gas production in Bolivia (Baer 2008).

However, in 2009 Chile became the largest of the Latin American investors in absolute terms, investing in chemicals, agriculture, and commerce in Peru and Brazil, with its FDI representing a remarkable 5 percent of its GDP. Mexico is a major investor abroad, often buying US companies, and Venezuela's petroleum company PDVSA has invested heavily in petroleum and natural gas in Bolivia (Alatorre et al. 2009: 58–63). Nonetheless, the largest business groups in Latin America are relatively small compared to those in other regions. There are also differences in types of production: large Asian firms tend to be concentrated in higher-technology manufacturing such as automobiles and computers, while large Latin American firms are concentrated in raw material production and processing, with the higher-technology manufacturing generally having been left to MNCs from outside the region (Schneider 2009: 173–180).

We can evaluate the impact these large firms have on Latin America's economic development using the Bulmer-Thomas (1994) framework of linkages and income flows. Baer characterizes firms such as Vale and Petrobras as dynamic, expanding in their original areas of production and then in complementary areas such as fertilizers and shipping, petrochemicals, and aluminum production (2008: 224). This is a good example of economic diversification that results when domestic companies reinvest their profits. In many cases, the new activities create production linkages that strengthen the domestic economy and lessen its dependence on the center. The aggregate demand from the investment process, the productive potential created by the investment, and the strengthening of domestic linkages are all ways in which commodity production and exports are transformed into economic development.

The World Bank finds that commodity-led development has been successful for countries such as Australia, the United States, Finland, and Sweden, countries where commodity production was accompanied by high levels of investment in education and in research and development of new processes and products. However, one analyst argues that the level of investment in Brazil and other Latin American countries is not sufficient "to leverage commodity exports into longer-term development" (Schneider 2009: 179–180).

The question of how to leverage commodity exports into long-term development is an important one now that Latin America is being shaped by the rapid growth of the Chinese economy. China is the largest of the emerging market economies, and the rapid growth of an economy that represents such a large proportion of the world's population is a force to contend with. By the first decade of the twenty-first century, it overtook Germany as the second largest exporter in the world (World Bank 2021b) and Japan as the world's second largest economy (Barbosa 2010). China's growth is based on the export of industrial goods to the center, and the production of those industrial goods affects Latin America in three important ways. First, the production of the industrial goods requires great amounts of commodity inputs, and so China must turn to sources such as Africa and Latin America for these inputs (Ellis 2009: 10). Not only does China buy these commodities, but it also has the ability to invest in their production and in the infrastructure necessary to export them to China (Ellis 2009: 3). Over the 1998–2008 period China was not a major investor in Latin America, but it was the fastest-growing one. The United States was still the dominant investor in the region (37 percent) and the *translatinas* the next (10 percent). By 2009, however, four of the fourteen largest acquisitions in the commodity sector were by Chinese companies and 18 percent of the new investment in manufacturing was Chinese (Alatorre et al. 2009: 40, 45).

Second, the increasing incomes of the Chinese population generate a growing demand for food, a major Latin American export (Ellis 2009: 12). Third, Latin America represents a market for China's manufactured goods at a time when growth in China's traditional markets has slowed (Ellis 2009: 4). As a result, the overall impact of China's growth on Latin American economies is to undercut its manufacturing sector and encourage commodity production. China has invested heavily in infrastructure projects, with special interest in railroads. It has bought local companies or created joint ventures to gain diverse transportation options on the Atlantic and Pacific Coasts as well as transit in between. However, the strong Brazil-China relationship under the Workers Party governments of Lula and Roussef changed after 2019, when Brazil's newly elected president, conservative Jair Bolsonaro, regarded China less favorably as he sought favor with fellow populist Donald Trump, who was generally hostile to China (Berg and Aragao 2020).

The demands of the growing Chinese economy unleashed a commodity boom in Latin America that lasted a decade. China's demand for commodities drove up their prices; Latin America's export revenues grew by 70 percent from 2002 to 2018. As shown in Table 6.4, in the years from 2001 to 2013 the price of petroleum almost quadrupled. A broader indicator of the commodity boom is the rise in the terms of trade, which is the ratio of export prices to import prices. The ten-year increase in the terms of trade has ranged from 21 percent in Mexico to 34 percent in Brazil, 64 percent in Argentina, 137 percent in Chile, and 448 percent in petroleum-dependent Venezuela. As in the past, there are benefits: the growth of Latin America's GDP over the ten years from 2004 to 2013 averaged 3.9 percent per year and the standard of living (GDP per capita) increased by 30 percent. During the ten years of the previous commodity boom (1970–1980) the standard of living rose by more: 42 percent. However, at the end of the more recent boom inflation was only 3.4 percent as opposed to the 1980 level of 17.9 percent, and debt service as a percentage of export revenues was only 16 percent as compared to the 1980 level of 40 percent (World Bank 2021b). As a consequence of the improved macroeconomic management of the more recent commodity boom, when the boom ended it was followed only by stagnation rather than debt crisis and a lost decade.

Another major change during the new century, not necessarily related to the commodity boom, has been the decline in income inequality. Latin America has long been known for being the region of the world with the

Table 6.4   Rising Commodity Prices and Economic Growth, 2001–2019

	GDP Growth (% rate of increase)	GDP per Capita (US$)	Debt Service (%)	Inflation (%)	Petroleum Prices ($ per barrel)
2001	0.9	7,479	32.6	4.4	26.0
2002	0.3	7,400	28.5	3.8	26.2
2003	1.6	7,417	28.8	3.8	31.1
2004	6.3	7,787	24.6	4.3	41.5
2005	4.3	8,017	21.6	4.7	56.6
2006	5.3	8,337	21.5	4.3	66.1
2007	5.5	8,692	16.4	5.0	72.3
2008	3.9	8,928	13.7	8.3	99.7
2009	−1.9	8,660	16.5	2.6	62.0
2010	5.9	9,066	13.0	3.5	79.5
2011	4.4	9,357	13.5	5.0	94.9
2012	2.8	9,513	15.7	3.9	94.1
2013	2.8	9,673	16.3	2.6	98.0
2014	1.0	9,668	16.1	3.4	93.2
2015	0.1	9,578	20.7	1.7	48.7
2016	−0.3	9,452	27.4	1.7	43.3
2017	1.8	9,528	24.3	2.3	50.8
2018	1.6	9,588	21.9	2.4	65.2
2019	0.8	9,579	27.8	3.1	57.0

Sources: World Bank 2021b; US Energy Information Administration, https://www.eia.gov/dnav/pet/hist/rwtcA.htm.

most unequal income distribution (Franko 2007: 396). Income inequality is measured by the Gini coefficient, which ranges from 0, indicating perfect equality, to 100, indicating absolute inequality. For purposes of comparison, in 2000 the United States had a coefficient of 41 and Canada 33, indicating that Canada had a more equitable income distribution than that of the United States. On the other hand, that same year the Gini coefficients for Latin America ranged from 43 in Uruguay and 47 in Costa Rica to 59 in Brazil and 62 in Bolivia. Over the next eighteen years, however, the Gini coefficient dropped by an average of almost 8 points in a sample of nine Latin American countries; this is dramatic, because in general, inequality changes slowly. Uruguay's Gini coefficient only moved from 43 to 40 and Costa Rica's actually worsened, but Argentina improved by 10 points and Ecuador by 11, and Bolivia dropped from 62 to 42, very close to the level of inequality in the United States.

This transformation was the result of a combination of economic changes. Most of the improvement reflected a change in the distribution of labor income—in other words, wages and salaries as opposed to interest income, dividends, rents, and profits. The inequality of labor income was diminishing because there was more demand for low-wage labor during the commodity boom and a greater supply of educated high-wage labor resulting from improvements in educational systems (World Bank 2014b: 28–35; World Bank 2014a: 43). Another important factor was the spread of redistributive government programs, often conditional cash transfers that reduced poverty by making cash transfers to the poor and encouraging investment among the poor by making the transfers conditional on medical care and school attendance for the children (Armendáriz and Larraín 2017: 138–139).

Legacies of the Past and Challenges of the Present

The transformation of Latin America's commodity riches into economic development will require developing and refining policies that can continue reductions in poverty and income inequality. This has never been easy in Latin America. As the data show, there are great risks to being dependent on commodity exports (World Bank 2009). Nonetheless, while there remain differences in policy approaches in the region—the populism of Chávez, Morales, and Correa contrasting with the more cautious policies of others—a great deal of progress has occurred. The development of comprehensive economic policies designed to ameliorate poverty without resorting to populist rhetoric, the strategy of using the commodity boom to reduce international debt, and the relatively low level of inflation in the region are signs of a maturing policy environment that may help to free the region from the legacies of economic dependence and inequality. For these policies to have a lasting effect, however, more attention must be paid to education, healthcare, infrastructure, and investment.

The state origins of many of the *translatinas,* some now privatized and some still state enterprises, suggests that Latin America's mix of public sector and private sector activity—quite different from the US model—can flourish. The growth of significant Latin American corporations, bringing with them economic diversification, a strengthening of regional linkages, and the assertion of Latin American control over economic activity, tends to reduce economic dependence. There are many assets available—natural resources, dynamic corporations, a more diverse pattern of trade, and better policymaking—with which to face the complex challenges that remain.

The challenges are substantial. The tragedy that has befallen Venezuela is a cautionary tale. Venezuela has assets, the world's most extensive petroleum reserves, and thus benefited most from the commodity boom. The poverty rate dropped dramatically as a result of Chávez's populist policies, but as this was occurring Venezuela's oil production was falling and its international debt was rising.

Chávez's successor, Nicolás Maduro, has faced a number of serious challenges. First, as shown in Table 6.4, the price of petroleum plunged in 2014. Second, the United States was responding to Maduro's increasingly authoritarian politics with embargoes that reduced Venezuela's ability to borrow money and to export petroleum (Weisbrot and Sachs 2019: 300). The combination caused the economy to contract by 80 percent, resulting in a humanitarian disaster. The health system has collapsed, malnutrition and disease are widespread, and 5 million Venezuelans have emigrated (Oroxom and Glassman 2018).

Underdevelopment, the violence associated with the drug trade, and corruption in Central America and Haiti have resulted in rising migration throughout the region. As with Haitians migrating to Brazil and Argentina, the number of Central American migrants to the United States has significantly increased. In 2019, Guatemalans were the largest migrant group trying to cross the southwestern US-Mexican border (WOLA 2020a). The Trump administration greatly reduced entry of migrants into the United States, as detailed in Chapter 7 by Cleveland Fraser. However, historically, harsh measures to discourage migration have been successful in reducing migration only in the short term. Efforts to control migration backfire if root causes are not tackled. With the continuation of the Covid-19 pandemic, which is causing an increase in poverty, inequality, corruption, authoritarian tendencies, and insecurity, we can expect an unprecedented increase in migration levels (WOLA 2020c).

The global pandemic was a completely unpredictable event, a public health tragedy that countries had to face with very little information to guide them. However, it quickly became clear, even if populist leaders like Brazil's president Bolsonaro would not admit it, that this was the most severe public health and economic crisis in a century. Containing the virus was the key to economic revitalization, as was the case in the Spanish influenza pandemic of a century before. However, the difficulties for Latin America are great, because it is highly urbanized and has large populations living in informal housing and working in the informal sector. Social distancing is extremely difficult, if not impossible, in informal neighborhoods without access to water and sewage service. Workers in the informal sector cannot eat if they do not work, and so a large informal sector accelerates the spread of the virus. Latin America's resilience in the face of the Covid-19 pandemic has been compromised by the neoliberal policies of the 1980s and 1990s, policies that reduced investment in infrastructure and health systems. Governments do not have the funds needed for medicines and equipment, while households are suffering from increasing unemployment and poverty, and lack of food and healthcare (Franz 2020).

Latin America's GDP fell by 7 percent in 2020, according to the IMF (Werner, Komatsuzaki, and Pizzinelli 2021). The magnitude of the reduction varies from country to country, depending on the impact of the Covid-19 pandemic and the country's economic specialization. The Andean countries, exporters of fuels and minerals, have been hurt by lower international prices. Agricultural producers have fared better, as world demand for food has held up. Travel and tourism have been hit particularly hard. In the first five months of 2020, this sector lost $320 billion in exports, with more than 120 million jobs at risk. For those developing countries where tourism represents more than 20 percent of GDP, this represents an emergency. Decreased revenues from tourism threaten natural and cultural heritage, causing habitat deterioration in protected areas as well as the closing of World Heritage sites (Lederer 2020). Latin American governments, hit by falling tax revenues and greater social needs, have borrowed heavily and built up a debt burden that will be difficult to manage in the years to come. The path forward will be difficult, but Latin Americans are accustomed to hardship and consequently resilient. However great the challenges the region faces, it does so with resources that will continue to be valuable to the global economy and a wealth of experience of how to use policy to support economic development; the question is whether the region's governments listen to that experience or ignore it.

7

International Relations

Cleveland Fraser

Latin American international relations have often been overshadowed or have been affected by perilous global issues and dramatic events in other parts of the world. Disturbances in the Middle East and South Asia, debate over the future direction of the European Union, and the rise of China usually dominate headlines. However, significant expressions of continuity and change in international relations primarily involving Latin American countries, both within and beyond the region, also find continual coverage in the international sections of newspapers, in major magazines, and on the internet. Latin American response to the Covid-19 pandemic is but one salient and sobering instance.

Examples of underlying hostility among Latin American countries include Peru's refusal to sell natural gas to Chile for over a century, and Bolivia not selling to Chile until 2007 with the decision of Indigenous leader and president Evo Morales (2006–2019). This is partly explained by the fact that both were defeated by Chile in a war fought in the 1880s. Colombia's "encroachment" into Ecuador in 2008 to clean out suspected sanctuaries for drug smugglers and anti-government guerrillas precipitated a significant diplomatic crisis in the Andean region. Tensions flare up intermittently between Venezuela and Colombia. However, after precipitous economic decline and intense political repression in Venezuela, Colombia and Peru absorbed about 2 million people who fled to these two countries as migrants and refugees. Guyana and Venezuela, Chile and Peru, Argentina and Brazil, Nicaragua and Costa Rica all have long-standing boundary disputes. Map 7.1 illustrates the origins of territorial disputes since independence (for an enlightening discussion of this topic, see Domínguez et al. 2003).

Map 7.1   Boundary Disputes Since Independence

The 1982 war in the Falkland Islands (Islas Malvinas) demonstrated the involvement of a European state, the United Kingdom, in armed conflict with Argentina. US involvement in Caribbean and Central American affairs, and in those of other countries in the region, has been another constant in Latin American international relations. US military interventions in attempted coups or armed insurrections in the Dominican Republic (1916–1922, 1965), Venezuela (2002, 2019), Guatemala (1954), Honduras (2009), Haiti (1915–1934, 1986, 1994, 2004, and

2010), and Grenada (1983) are prominent examples. President Trump's willingness to consider a "military option" in Venezuela was perceived as a significant risk and reckless foreign policy by countries in the region (Goodman 2018). Interestingly, two US citizens were arrested in 2020 in an apparent plot to invade Venezuela and inspire a rebellion (Herrero, Falola, and Horton 2020).

Profound changes in Latin America's orientation toward both the wider world and the United States have also occurred. Indeed, it is worth remembering that movement in the Western Hemisphere toward more open political and economic systems was predated by fifteen years of momentous changes in the former Soviet Union and Eastern Europe, with democratic regime change in Peru and Ecuador in the late 1970s. And just as these seismic political and economic tremors shaped the way we look at the world, they also influenced Latin Americans' perceptions of themselves. Certainly, reverberations of September 11, 2001, altered orientations and policies related to issues of security and international terrorism, and demonstrated that the international environment is extremely complex and challenging. The Great Recession in 2009 and 2010 energized Latin American states to experiment with solutions emphasizing greater cooperation to advance economic recovery and foster greater political unity. Furthermore, Latin American countries are currently experiencing severe economic and public health challenges due to the Covid-19 pandemic. Indeed, Brazil and Mexico trail only the United States in the number of Covid-related deaths. And as vaccines become more widely available, procuring and administering them could be challenging financially and logistically.

There are opportunities as well as challenges. With the signing of the North American Free Trade Agreement, and the renegotiated United States–Mexico–Canada Agreement (USMCA), Mexico signaled its interest in greater economic integration with its neighbors. And who would have believed that three Latin American countries (Chile, Mexico, and Peru), along with Canada and the United States, would participate as full members at annual Asia Pacific Economic Cooperation (APEC) summits?

In today's world, domestic political decisions can have external consequences, and the reverse is also true—the international environment can have important effects on political conditions within a specific country. The concept of intermestic politics has been developed to more accurately reflect these realities (Spanier and Uslaner 1978). Colombia, for example, had struggled to end a decades-long guerrilla insurgency and to destroy production and distribution networks of narcotraffickers. In fact, the domestic concerns of the Colombian government led to an international crisis as Ecuador and Venezuela threatened military retaliation against Colombia's decision to send troops across its border with Ecuador. After torturous rounds of negotiations (and a failed referendum) between the government and the Revolutionary Armed Forces of Colombia–People's Army (FARC-EP), an agreement was finally reached in 2016.

Mexico has had to deal with a rebellion in the southern state of Chiapas, where a group known as the Zapatista National Liberation Army (EZLN) has called for democratic reform, social justice, and greater autonomy from the Mexican state. The Zapatistas have been quite successful in mobilizing international support for their cause, which has complicated the Mexican government's effort to resolve this domestic issue. Moreover, the militarization of Mexico's campaign to eradicate growing violence in northern and central Mexico due to the activities of well-organized and well-armed drug cartels is a domestic response to societal demands for greater security and protection, but the campaign's effects have literally bled across the Mexican-US border. Furthermore, the cartel Jalisto Nueva Generación has launched a war threat to President Andrés Manuel López Obrador (2018–2024). This cartel constitutes the most dangerous drug organization in Mexico, and also has played a key role in the opioid epidemic in the United States.

A 2009 coup in Honduras is yet another instance of domestic political activities (in this case, constitutional reform) having international reverberations, because the Honduran military's actions drew condemnation from the United Nations, the Organization of American States, the United States, and the European Union. Ousted president Manuel Zelaya (2006–2009) conducted negotiations with his opponents from exile in Costa Rica for his restoration to office. After secretly returning to Honduras, Zelaya was granted sanctuary in the Brazilian embassy. In the wake of elections in November 2009, a deal was struck that permitted Zelaya to leave his Brazilian sanctuary for exile in the Dominican Republic, and Porfirio Lobo Sosa (2010–2014) was inaugurated as Zelaya's successor.

Additionally, international institutions have regulated domestic politics, just as the latter have influenced international relations. The Inter-American Court of Human Rights (IACHR), based in San José, Costa Rica, has issued contentious court rulings since 1988. Although member states do not uniformly consider the American Convention of Human Rights to be supreme to domestic law and court decisions, over time the IACHR's rulings have become increasingly accepted as binding in many countries. This is the result of domestic constitutional courts accepting supranational jurisdiction of the IACHR, partly encouraged by the democratic transitions in most states of the region.

An instructive instance of an IACHR decision influencing domestic politics relates to a 2017 holding that the provisions of the American Convention of Human Rights extended the same rights enjoyed by heterosexual couples to those of the same sex. The request had been made by Costa Rica a year earlier, and in 2018 the Costa Rican Constitutional Court also ruled in favor of marriage equality. As one might expect, this issue, as well as the Court's decision, were controversial. Indeed, public opinion polling indicated that over half the population opposed this idea. In the run-up to Costa Rica's 2018 presidential contest, the electoral landscape was changed nearly overnight, as its political fulcrum revolved around supporting a candidate who either favored or opposed this single issue. Fabricio Alvarado Muñoz, an Evangelical Christian, legislator, and singer, ran on a platform strongly opposing same-sex marriage, and his popularity among the public rose from less than 1 percent to 45 percent in a matter of weeks. Indeed, in the first round of voting he actually garnered 25 percent of the vote, more than his opponent, Carlos Alvarado Quesada, who stood at around 22 percent. In second-round voting, however, Alvarado Muñoz was defeated by a margin of 20 percentage points (*BBC News* 2018). Ultimately Costa Rica legalized same-sex marriage in 2020 (Kennon 2020).

Most IACHR cases have concerned violent human rights violations. Some countries have advanced far in accepting Court holdings on how to prosecute war crimes, such as in Colombia, where the rulings have formulated the basis of the negotiated peace process that has sought to end over six decades of civil war with several Marxist guerrilla forces. The Court's authority has often also been bolstered by strong networks of international lawyers advocating human rights. Colombia's commitment to democracy, despite six decades of civil war, has supported a neoconstitutionalist approach, which emphasizes the superiority of human rights and deference to supranational decisions, as well as emphasizing principles of democracy and human rights.

In contrast, not all domestic courts respect the notion of the superiority of international human rights law when it conflicts with domestic law. The leftist government of Venezuela is an example. Interestingly, it was one of the only two democracies in Latin America that were the first (along with Costa Rica) to join the Court's jurisdiction. While originally affording the IACHR extensive authority, Venezuela under the revolutionary Hugo Chávez government, which came to power in 1998, initially continued to pay reparations to victims whose freedoms, according to the Court, had been violated. Initially, the Chávez regime had favored human rights, instituting new protections in its new "Bolivarian" constitution.

However, after the IACHR held that Venezuela had violated judicial independence by removing three judges who had ruled against the government, the Venezuelan Supreme Court ruled that the IACHR had violated the country's constitution—a holding that violated the country's treaty with the IACHR. A similar decision in a subsequent case was also repudiated by the Supreme Court because the regime regarded the IACHR as an imperialist tool.

While one can assume that calculations of Latin American courts and electorates are centered on domestic concerns, their decisions have implications for foreign policy. In the first decade of the twenty-first century, a trend known as the "Pink Tide" swept into power leaders who were more to the left on the political spectrum and who therefore were more likely to advocate or follow policies that did not match those of the United States. Voters in Bolivia, Brazil, Ecuador, Nicaragua, and Venezuela, for instance, selected individuals who were vocal proponents of alternative solutions for the region's problems. Of all of these cases, Venezuela is especially interesting. A country with relatively long-standing democratic practices, Venezuela has had to cope with challenges to its constitutional order. Its former president, Hugo Chávez, led a failed coup attempt in 1992, was elected in 1998, reelected in 2001, became the target of an abortive effort to oust him in April 2002, survived a recall referendum in August 2004, and was reelected again in 2007 and 2013. Chávez gained international attention in his quest to offset the power of the United States and to vault Venezuela into a position of regional leadership and influence.

Global economic crises have raised questions about how Latin American nations should deal with issues of trade, investment, debt, and inflation. These challenges have several important implications for Latin American international relations. The failure of governments to control economic and political turmoil creates conditions that might lead to the reversal of a trend toward more open markets and political systems. These types of political and economic problems also tend to limit the capacity of Latin American countries to pursue their foreign policy objectives. Finally, they might also induce governments to embark on dangerous foreign policy adventures to deflect domestic attention from hard times at home or, alternatively, to withdraw from active participation in international affairs.

Organizing Concepts

Latin America is usually depicted as a subsystem in the international system. The elemental characteristics explored by Marie Price in Chapter

2—including geographic contiguity and regularized patterns of political, economic, and social interaction—have resulted in general recognition among the countries themselves that they constitute a distinctive area in the international environment. This regional system has also typically been divided into subsystems (Atkins 1999: 25–57). Although analysts may define each element slightly differently, I identify four regional subsystems in Latin America: Mexico and Central America, the Caribbean, the Andean countries, and the Southern Cone.

In this context, I seek to address several questions. What is Latin America's role in the international system? More specifically, where has Latin America been, and where might it be going? Are there identifiable continuities in Latin American relations with the wider world? How have changes in the post–Cold War and post-9/11 world affected Latin America? A number of analytic perspectives may be employed to describe and explain Latin America's position in international relations. In my view, seven merit further elucidation.

Realism views international relations as a struggle among nations for power and influence (Morgenthau and Thompson 1985; Waltz 1979). Governments formulate their national interests in terms of *power*, usually defined as economic or military capability. Moreover, nations are assumed to be unitary actors; that is, foreign policy results from decisions made by top-level leadership. The role of popular opinion in formulating external policy is assumed to be minimal, because the public is deemed to be, at best, ill-informed and little interested in foreign affairs and, at worst, susceptible to the "conventional wisdom" of the moment. Given the emphasis among nations on expanding their power and influence, the most salient international issues are those dealing with politico-military affairs. Such issues, typically referred to as "high politics," tend to dominate the international agenda. Issues such as developing the economy, fostering social justice, and protecting the environment constitute "low politics" and are considered secondary to the overarching goal of national security.

International politics is viewed by realists as a serious game that involves winners and losers. In this zero-sum environment, an adversary's gain, by definition, diminishes one's own capacity for action. Whereas power politics does not foreclose reliance on instruments of diplomacy designed to foster cooperation, the threat of force is also a fairly common diplomatic weapon in the realist's arsenal, as are alliances and collective security arrangements. Hence, a central diplomatic objective of realism is to balance and check power and to acquire and protect spheres of influence.

From this perspective, Latin America can be viewed as a venue for great-power rivalry; as such, realism may serve as a framework for understanding Latin America in the nineteenth and early twentieth centuries. It may also provide greater insights into actions of the United States in Central America and the wider Caribbean. Latin America has of course been characterized in the United States as "our own backyard." And in a stratified, hierarchical series of international systems and subsystems, the foreign policy latitude of smaller, weaker powers is constrained by the activities and interests of larger regional and global powers. An alternative paradigm, liberalism, assumes the possibility of positive-sum relationships, where rival states can mutually benefit, even if gains are unequal (Moravcsik 1997). Realism, liberalism, and their variants adopt a dualist approach to explaining state behavior, meaning they assume a degree of objectivity exists in which relationships can be accurately demonstrated by data using the scientific method.

Another means of assessing Latin American foreign and domestic policy relates to the concepts of the logic of consequences, and the logic of appropriateness. In the case of the former, leaders through a rational process pursue policies with an eye toward their impact on state power/ security vis-à-vis other countries. For example, the assumptions of liberalism and neoliberalism serve as useful tools to explain policymaking behavior of many Latin American countries in the post–Cold War era. In the case of liberalism, as the global "third wave" of democratization took hold between the mid-1970s and 1990, the region witnessed the rise of a Latin American civil society that pressed for justice, accountability, and an opening of the political arena. Latin American civil society organizations succeeded in undermining the legitimacy of authoritarian systems and became an inspiring model for the rest of the world. Simultaneously, democratization became entwined with economic development, as countries began to open their economies and embrace neoliberal principles of free and fair trade. The subsequent creation of regional trading blocs as a means to improve economic advancement also fits within the neoliberal framework.

The logic of appropriateness assumes that global economic and political institutions represent the interests and prerogatives of some groups at the expense of others. Whether we are talking about international institutions grounded in the neoliberal tradition, such as the International Monetary Fund (IMF) and the World Trade Organization (WTO), or those power structures that reinforce male perspectives centered on notions of "just war," like the United Nations Security Council, this approach examines the various trajectories of economic and political development in Latin American countries, and critically assesses the influence of those institutions that are controlled by elites in the global North.

Constructivism is in many ways viewed as a response to liberalism and realism. Although its focus is on social position, ideas, and norms, it does not deny the importance of material factors; rather, anarchy is what states make of it. That is, rather than "anarchy" in the international system being an empirical reality, it can be viewed as a social construction that can be perceived and managed in various ways (Wendt 1999). From a constructivist point of view, identities are not static, but can change. In seeking to describe and explain the pursuit of justice and the process of democratization in many Latin American countries, constructivists would suggest that trials and truth and reconciliation commissions, rather than upsetting political stability, challenge historical hegemonic normative systems—premised as they are on the exclusion of persons on the basis of political ideology, ethnicity, and so forth.

The schools of thought described thus far would generally agree that change is a top-down process, influenced in varying degrees by the interests of powerful countries, multilateral institutions, or legal regimes. This is certainly true when it comes to international intervention in conflicts in Latin America in the post–Cold War era. Peace missions in Haiti and Guatemala, for instance, were conducted by the United Nations mostly with an eye for reestablishing stability and creating institution-building activities, with very little agency given to those most directly affected by the conflicts.

Policy analysis adopts a more pragmatic perspective that encourages input from international as well as domestic actors such as individuals and nongovernmental organizations in institutional reform and growth, a

UN Security Council Chambers. Credit: https://commons.wikimedia.org/wiki/File:UN_security_council_2006_(cropped).jpg

goal exemplified by the Local Works program within the US Agency for International Development. Today many Latin American countries, particularly those in South America, look to regional institutions to improve cooperation and regional progress. The notion of intertwining aspects of sovereignty to achieve absolute gains and the spillover from regional trading blocs has brought many of these countries together politically as well as economically. Following the controversial presidential elections in Venezuela in 2018, Brazil, Costa Rica, Argentina, and Ecuador, among several others, roundly criticized Nicolás Maduro's supposed victory, choosing instead to support his opponent, Juan Guaidó. While it cannot be said that these countries agree on all occasions, the fact that they came together to criticize a nondemocratic process clearly indicates that a substantial norm shift has taken place.

One of the most powerful prisms for viewing Latin American international relations has been that of dependency theory, which is based on economic and political relationships between developing and developed countries. There are many variations of this complex theory. For example, Andre Gunder Frank argues that underdeveloped nations are "satellites" of developed metropolitan centers (Gunder Frank 1967). Immanuel Wallerstein envisions a capitalist international economy divided into "core" states that extract cheap labor and resources from "peripheral" ones (see Cockcroft, Gunder Frank, and Johnson 1972). Fernando Henrique Cardoso, former president of Brazil (1994–2002) and a sociologist by training, was also a forceful proponent of this perspective on Latin American political economy (Cardoso and Faletto 1979).

Some dependency theorists, such as Argentine economist Raul Prebisch, offered empirical evidence that the structure of the international trade and monetary systems had disadvantaged Latin American nations. They showed how raw materials and semiprocessed goods on which many countries relied for generating foreign exchange fluctuated in price or actually declined relative to the prices of industrial products the region required for development, and that the rules and norms governing international trade sustained these unequal "terms of trade." With reference to international monetary and investment flows, many of these theorists contend that Latin American nations are dependent on the decisions of multinational corporations, the IMF, international banks, and governments in North America, Europe, and Asia. Therefore, it is easy to understand why they criticized neoliberal modernization and development approaches as ethnocentrically derived from US and Western European models. Basically, the argument holds that Latin America has been constrained in its ability to participate in world affairs because of external manipulation and exploitation by Western capitalist countries in general, and the United States in particular.

In a more extreme version of dependency theory, it was argued that in its quest for markets, capital, and labor, the West had knowingly "stacked the deck" in its favor and deprived nations of the resources necessary for industrialization, diversification, and a rising standard of living (dos Santos 1970). The operation of MNCs was cited as a manifestation of this concerted effort. MNCs were portrayed as international "vampires," draining the economic lifeblood out of their "hosts" by siphoning off profits, depleting resources, and dominating domestic markets. And under certain circumstances they influenced US foreign policy interests, exemplified by US intervention in Guatemala in 1954 and Chile in 1973. There were also nefarious political implications. These dependency theorists claimed that the operation of this asymmetrical relationship created and maintained client political and economic elites who identified more with the West than they did with their own countries. This in turn created a propensity for governments to favor capitalist development and to accede to the norms and principles embodied in the international monetary and trading regimes. It also offered an explanation for developmental failures based on external rather than internal causes.

Dependency theorists emphasize the one-way effects of dependence. Other observers of international relations (Keohane and Nye 1977), however, have recognized that mutual dependence, or interdependence, exists in many relationships. It is almost a cliché to say that the world is rapidly shrinking. Through the internet, one can access the homepage of the Zapatistas in Mexico or communicate with friends in Uruguay. Latin America is also just a few digits away via cell phone. It is only a few hours by airplane to virtually any point in Latin America. Many readers have probably worn Brazilian shoes, have eaten Chilean fruit, or have savored Colombian or Guatemalan coffee at breakfast. Some of the most popular beers in the United States are brewed and bottled in Mexico. Many items of clothing sold in US stores are made in Central America and the Caribbean.

Therefore, some observers have maintained that contemporary Latin American relations can also be placed in the context of an increasingly interdependent and globalized world, for understanding international relations, both generally and in Latin America. What are some of the basic characteristics and assumptions of interdependence? First, in this approach it is argued that although the primary actors in Latin America and the world are still sovereign nation-states, other governmental and nongovernmental actors are increasingly playing greater roles in shaping foreign policy and international relations. For example, as Hannah Stewart-Gambino shows in Chapter 12, the Catholic Church not only influences political life in each country, but also transcends boundaries. Globe-girding corporations have also reduced the power and influence of nations. Political parties, especially those affiliated with international movements such as Christian democracy or socialism, have ties that bind them to both the region and the greater world. And of course the ability of drug cartels and terrorist organizations to operate across national frontiers also poses profound challenges to national sovereignty and security. This view also stresses that changes in the distribution of power in the international system have provided opportunities for smaller powers to define their interests more broadly and to emphasize issues other than those of national security.

In an interdependent globalized world, economic issues have high salience, especially development, debt, and integration. Other concerns— social justice, immigration, human rights, and ecological preservation— have also risen to the fore. And of course the global Covid-19 pandemic has raised issues of public health and safety. In terms of diplomatic strategies, greater weight is placed on soft power such as bargaining and compromise, persuasion, and using regional and international institutions as venues for discussing issues and resolving disputes (Nye 2004). Recall that realism assumes that countries with greater hard power (economic and military capabilities) will tend to have greater success in achieving their foreign policy objectives. The interdependence approach suggests an answer to the question, "If bigger is better, why don't great powers 'win' all of the time?" Under these conditions, less powerful states and nongovernmental actors may be able to mobilize and use different types of power resources effectively, such as persuasion or terror, to offset or neutralize the advantages of larger states. From an interdependence point of view, bigger is not necessarily better—or even best (Nye 2004).

Increasingly important in Latin America is the practice of public diplomacy to both communicate and listen more carefully to other countries to promote cooperation. Listening, therefore, is the first step in public diplomacy, as opposed to mere advocacy. To do so, it is important to move beyond the narrow conception of zero-sum outcomes, as realism would hold. Nation-branding and place-branding focus more on the business side of reaching out to foreign publics to promote the image of a country for tourism or other industries. Latin American diplomats are just getting started using Twitter and other digital social media tools to reach domestic and foreign publics, including diasporas (Aguirre and Erlandsen 2018; Cull 2019).

Historical Legacies

When describing and explaining Latin America's interaction with states outside of the region it is helpful to frame this historical interaction using the paradigms of international relations: realism/neorealism, liberalism/neoliberalism, constructivism, policy analysis (Carey 2021), dependency, and interdependence. Bear in mind that these paradigms are ideal types, and that most policy toward the Latin American countries in Central and South America can be explained by these approaches, either singly or in combination.

René De La Pedraja illustrates in Chapter 3 how most Spanish colonial possessions in Latin America gained their independence in the first two decades of the nineteenth century. Their attempts to free themselves from colonial control were in part "insulated" by the 1823 Monroe Doctrine, which asserted that the time for colonization in the Western Hemisphere had passed and that the United States would view any attempt by a European power to interfere in the area with grave concern. Of course, the United States was hardly in a position to enforce such a sweeping edict. Nevertheless, because the doctrine also served the national interests of the United Kingdom, with its powerful navy, it did provide a sort of deterrent to foreign adventures and the doctrine evolved as a basis on which the United States carved out its own sphere of influence in the Western Hemisphere.

Nearly all countries in Latin America struggled to foster internal unity and external security. During the first half-century of independence, a number of countries in the region sought to establish hierarchy and extend influence. In Central America, Mexico aspired to the role of regional hegemon. In response, the five Central American provinces attempted in 1823 to amalgamate into the United Provinces of Central America. It was not to be. As the result of internal squabbling, this attempt to offset Mexico's power and authority disintegrated in 1838. Each of the five remaining states was left to deal with Mexico and later the United States in its own way. The Andean region also disintegrated, in 1830, as the Bolivarian vision of an integrated Gran Colombia (encompassing Ecuador, Colombia, and Venezuela) faltered in the wake of economic malaise and political turmoil.

In the Southern Cone, the system was also hierarchical, as Brazil, Argentina, and Chile competed for regional influence. Other, smaller states were often drawn into this struggle for power. Indeed, boundary issues sparked conflicts throughout the nineteenth century. To cite two principal examples, in the War of the Triple Alliance (1864–1870), Brazil, Argentina, and Uruguay combined to crush Paraguay, which lost approximately half its territory and all but 28,000 of its male inhabitants (Kolinski

1965: 198). Brazil and Argentina gained control over territory and resources that could (and would) be used in their rivalry for regional influence. Both Paraguay and Uruguay served as buffers between the two great powers in the region. Less than a decade later, Peru and Bolivia were defeated by Chile in a dispute involving access to minerals and fertilizer. In the War of the Pacific (1879–1884), Bolivia lost its only outlet to the Pacific Ocean (Sater 2009).

The nineteenth century was also an era of increasing economic dependence. The United Kingdom in particular provided much of the investment capital and technology necessary for rapid economic development. In many countries, British firms constructed rail, telegraph, and telephone systems, invested in resource extraction, and established the manufacturing base. Especially in the century's later decades—as worldwide demand for commodities such as rubber, petroleum, coffee, sugar, beef, and wheat increased—countries such as Argentina, Brazil, Chile, Mexico, and Venezuela enjoyed economic "boom" times. But this came at a price. Although Latin American economies grew, they were fueled primarily by foreign rather than domestic investments and by a reliance on exporting single crops or commodities to markets in Europe and, increasingly, the United States.

There was another interesting consequence of increased dependence during this period. Some countries, especially in the Southern Cone, lacked the population required to sustain increased demand for skilled and unskilled labor. Therefore, they encouraged migration from Western and Southern Europe and, to a lesser extent, Asia (Endoh 2009). The ethnic and class implications of these policies are analyzed by Kevin Yelvington in Chapter 9. The new immigrants to Argentina and Uruguay, for example, influenced not only domestic political alignments, but also the general foreign policy orientation of these countries toward Europe, the United States, and beyond.

Latin America was not immune to foreign influence of another sort. In spite of the Monroe Doctrine, European powers periodically sought to expand their influence in the Western Hemisphere. One of the most notable examples was an unsuccessful French attempt in the 1860s to establish a monarchy in Mexico, with Prince Maximillian of Austria on the throne. Nevertheless, of all the external actors seeking to expand their power and influence in the region, none exerted such a profound and lasting effect as the United States. In 1904, President Theodore Roosevelt enunciated a corollary to the Monroe Doctrine that held that the United States reserved the right to intervene in the internal affairs of Latin American countries in the event of their misbehavior, especially related to the collection of customs duties.

Roosevelt's view of Latin America was portrayed at the time as "speaking softly but carrying a big stick."

The United States established its own sphere of influence through its acquisition of Puerto Rico and Cuba from Spain in the wake of the latter's defeat in the 1898 Spanish-Cuban-American War. Appended to the new Cuban constitution (1901) was the Platt Amendment, which, among other provisions, explicitly gave Cuba's consent to the stipulation that the United States reserved the right to intervene in Cuba's internal affairs if the US government deemed intervention was required. In 1903, the United States had a hand in accelerating the separation of Panama from Colombia, which had balked at a planned trans-isthmian canal project proposed by the United States and France.

In a precursor to more recent events, Haiti was occupied by US Marines in 1914 to stabilize the political situation and to "clean up" the society. US troops remained until 1930. Nicaragua was also a venue for US troops (1912–1925, 1926–1933) as was the Dominican Republic, which was occupied from 1916 until 1930. The Mexican Revolution, which spanned the first two decades of the twentieth century, provided more immediate examples of US activism. US forces occupied the port of Veracruz in 1914, and US troops spent the better part of a year in futile pursuit of General Francisco "Pancho" Villa in northern Mexico. He was considered to be an outlaw who had crossed the border and attacked towns in New Mexico and become a destabilizing force in the region.

This is not to say that conflict was the dominant pattern of interaction in US–Latin American relations. Diplomatic instruments were also used to foster greater inter-American cooperation and understanding. The United States was largely responsible for reinitiating what would become known as Pan-Americanism, based on the Bolivarian ideal (for an interesting perspective on this concept, see Harrison 1997). Beginning in 1889 with the first inter-American conference in Washington, D.C., the United States and Latin America sought to establish more frequent and institutionalized bases for communication. This and subsequent conferences spawned a number of regional institutions designed to address issues ranging from regional security and conflict resolution to the concerns of children, women, and Indigenous peoples. Nevertheless, it must be noted that the United States viewed this process as a salutary means of expanding its commercial interests in the area, especially in the wider Caribbean. "Dollar diplomacy," coupled with overt military intervention, dramatically expanded US ascendancy in the Western Hemisphere. Concomitantly, European influence and power dramatically declined.

The first three decades of the twentieth century marked ferment and change in Latin America, similar in many ways to most other parts of the world. Latin American societies had been transformed by immigration and accelerating industrialization and trade. One salient implication of this social and economic metamorphosis was the rise of a more complex class structure. Working- and middle-class sectors agitated increasingly for greater participation in political and economic decisionmaking. Between 1910 and 1920, Mexico underwent a profound political, economic, and social revolution, motivated in part by a desire to reduce its dependence on foreign investment and influence. Farther south, in the early 1930s, economic depression precipitated the rise of various forms of authoritarian regimes and economic experiments. Socialism and communism vied for adherents among various segments of Latin American society. Fascism appeared to be an attractive political option to some, especially in those countries (e.g., Argentina) with populations swollen by recent arrivals from Spain, Portugal, Italy, and Germany. Intraregional conflicts over territory were also evident. In 1932, a simmering dispute between Paraguay and Bolivia over the Chaco Boreal flared into a war that lasted three years and claimed 85,000 lives (Garner 1966: 107).

The 1920s and 1930s spanned an era of regional attempts to establish a more equitable framework for the conduct of international relations. For instance, Latin America was initially enthusiastic about participating in the newly established League of Nations. And Latin American jurists and diplomats were in the forefront of reaffirming international legal principles associated with the sovereign equality of states and of nonintervention. One prime example, the Estrada Doctrine (1930), enunciated by Mexico's foreign minister, Genaro Estrada, held that if a particular government controlled its population and territory, it deserved to be accorded diplomatic recognition. No normative evaluation or criteria should be applied (Jessup 1931). This and other contributions to international law reflected historical memories in Mexico in particular, and in Latin America more generally, of external intervention and economic dependence.

The Good Neighbor Policy of Franklin D. Roosevelt (1933–1945) marked a shift in US policy away from the interventionism and power politics of previous administrations. Accordingly, the United States abrogated the Platt Amendment in 1934 and did not overtly retaliate when Mexico nationalized its primarily US-owned oil industry in 1938. One of the questions posed by students of inter-American relations is whether the era of the Good Neighbor was an aberration or the beginning of a movement toward a more cooperative and less conflictual relationship between mature partners.

With the outbreak of World War II in 1939, Latin American nations were compelled to define their objectives in the context of global conflict.

Many—such as Brazil, the Central American countries, and Mexico—supported the Allied cause, led by the United States, the United Kingdom, and the Soviet Union. Some, most notably Argentina, sympathized with Germany, Italy, and Japan. The war disrupted markets, exacerbated problems of growth and development, and set into motion a new set of international forces that dramatically altered Latin American external relations.

Latin America's international role in the pre-1945 period was constrained by the relative lack of economic and military resources necessary to project influence on a global scale. Europe remained the fulcrum around which international relations revolved; Latin America was a secondary arena for European rivalry. In one sense, this insularity from the wider world provided opportunities for aspirants to regional and subregional hegemony to extend their influence, on many occasions by force. Latin America's international role was also limited by other factors. The capacity for international action of Mexico, the Central American states, and such Caribbean states as Cuba, the Dominican Republic, and Haiti was severely limited by US activism and interventionism in their internal affairs. Within the region as a whole, US interventionism increased the sensitivity of Latin American states toward external meddling in their internal affairs. Additionally, the disruption of markets and investment by two world wars and a prolonged economic depression tended both to reduce the propensity of Latin American nations to take a leading role in international affairs, and to heighten the region's awareness of its economic dependency and vulnerability.

The Cold War Era

With the end of World War II, Latin America faced a twofold challenge. First, the United States had emerged from the conflict as one of the world's two superpowers. Economically predominant and militarily preeminent, it was busily attempting to establish a liberal world order based on free trade, stable currencies, and collective security. Second, the United States and the Western world were becoming increasingly aware that their wartime ally, the Soviet Union, did not share the same vision of the postwar world. In fact, the Soviet Union seemed intent on establishing its own sphere of influence in Eastern Europe and expanding its global reach. Thus, with the movement toward confrontation between the Soviet Union and the United States, the international system was transformed into a bipolar one. The implications for Latin American countries were largely negative: a highly conflict-prone, zero-sum international system dominated by the high politics of the emerging

Cold War. Latin America's international role would be defined in terms of its importance as an anticommunist bastion in the US sphere of influence. As one might suspect, this was not generally a period of intense foreign policy activism on the part of Latin American states.

In the years following World War II, two important regional institutions were established. The first was a collective security arrangement signed in Rio de Janeiro in 1947. Known formally as the Inter-American Treaty of Reciprocal Assistance and less formally as the Rio Pact, it declared that any attack by an outside power would be viewed by the signatories as an attack on them all. In 1948, the ninth Inter-American Conference, held in Bogotá, Colombia, marked the creation of a forum for discussion among the nations of the hemisphere, the Organization of American States. This body was intended to foster cooperation and communication among member states, especially in the areas of crisis management, election monitoring, and human rights (Long 2020). As time went on, the OAS became increasingly perceived by Latin Americans as an instrument of US control in its struggle to contain communist influence in the region. For example, the OAS was the forum used to denounce a reformist government in Guatemala as communist and to legitimate its overthrow in 1954. The OAS was also used to isolate Fidel Castro after he began receiving assistance from the Soviet Union in the early 1960s (Shaw 2004).

The 1950s and 1960s underscored difficulties associated with fostering economic growth and political stability. Latin American nations such as Argentina, Mexico, and Brazil enjoyed some success in sustaining economic growth through import substitution industrialization, a strategy intended to reduce dependence on foreign markets and investment through the creation of an industrial base capable of both satisfying domestic demand for consumer durables and other manufactured goods, and providing a strong base for exports. This orientation created incentives to formalize closer economic linkages among Latin American countries themselves. The United States, too, had an interest in ensuring that Latin American countries were improving the quality of life for their citizens. Under the Alliance for Progress, the John F. Kennedy administration (1961–1963) hoped to achieve the twofold goal of strengthening Central and South America against the threat of communism through accelerated capitalist development, and of opening markets for US producers (Taffet 2007).

The 1960s were also a period of ideological and political conflict. Ideologically, the 1959 victory of Fidel Castro in Cuba offered an alternative revolutionary model of development for Latin America. Hence

*Organization of American States, Washington, D.C. Credit: https://commons.wikimedia.org
/wiki/File:Organization_american_states_building.jpg*

the Cuban government was perceived as having an active interest in fostering socialism throughout the hemisphere. It is clear, however, that only
certain elements of the revolutionary movement sought to accelerate the
diffusion of the new Cuban model to other Latin American countries.
Venezuela, which was in the process of institutionalizing a transition to
democratic government, was a target of Cuban-inspired insurgents. Rev-
olutionaries such as the Argentine Ernesto "Che" Guevara (who fought
with Castro) took this one step further by seeking to replicate the success
of the Cuban experience in Africa and Bolivia. Guevara's attempt to
export revolution ended in dismal failure with his death in 1967 at the
hands of US-trained Bolivian counterinsurgency forces (Harris 2007).

Of course, Cuba's role in the Cold War competition between the
two ideological camps was manifested most strongly during the Cuban
missile crisis in October 1962, wherein the Soviet Union had trans-
ported and begun deploying missiles capable of hitting targets in the
United States. This was a surprise to the Kennedy administration, which
decided to impose a naval blockade to ensure that Russian cargo ships
laden with other missiles and military equipment would not reach their
destination. The world held its breath as both sides seemed to be on the
brink of nuclear annihilation. Fortunately, the crisis was averted through
a negotiated settlement whereby the Soviet Union would remove the
missiles, and the United States would commit not to use military force
to overturn the Castro regime. In a move not publicized at the time, the

United States promised to remove missiles based in Turkey that the Soviet Union viewed as threatening to its homeland. Recent scholarship has revealed Fidel Castro's important role in the crisis, and just how close the world came to destroying itself (Dobbs 2009; Plokhy 2021).

The perceived communist threat in the hemisphere marked the demise of a period of political reformism, as Latin American militaries, concerned about communism and economic growth, replaced civilians with generals. Additionally, the abortive attempt to replace the Cuban government through the Bay of Pigs invasion (1961), military intervention in the Dominican Republic (1965), and the 1973 overthrow of Salvador Allende (1970–1973) in Chile can be seen in terms of the legacies of the Cuban Revolution and as manifestations of realpolitik (power politics) on the part of the United States.

The rise of bureaucratic authoritarian systems intent on protecting the state from subversion led to increased levels of domestic tension and international friction (O'Donnell 1979). First, military authoritarian governments, seeking to ensure political stability and economic advance, tended to cooperate with one another (and the United States) on such issues as counterinsurgency and anti-terrorism. Militaries also collaborated in providing a societal justification for establishing national security states. Second, the ferocity and alacrity with which many regimes rooted out suspected subversives and communists focused both domestic and international attention on the issues of human rights and refugees (McSherry 2005). Nongovernmental organizations, such as Amnesty International and Americas Watch, in addition to the administration of US president Jimmy Carter (1977–1981), began to pressure Latin American governments to end impunity and abuse of their citizens.

Dependency and Debt

Along with dependency theory, there are several other theories of international political economy that can be applied to describe the developmental challenges faced by Latin America. Neoliberalism emerged in the twentieth century with the argument that international economic policy, mediated through the IMF, World Bank, regional financial institutions such as the Inter-American Development Bank, and bilateral aid, should be conditioned by requiring conformity to liberal principles of free markets, privatization, and balanced fiscal budgets. While most neoliberal policies were required of Latin American countries at the end of their military or civilian dictatorships, the most radical implementation of neoliberalism came during the Pinochet dictatorship that ruled Chile from 1973 to 1988. The "Chicago Boys," University of Chicago–trained economists who combined neoliberalism with monetarism (low interest rates to tame inflation as a top priority), (re)privatized most companies nationalized during the years of the democratically elected Marxist presidency of Salvador Allende (1970–1973), and followed monetary policy designed to tamp down hyperinflation produced by the Allende government (French-Davis 2010).

With the first oil price shock in the early 1970s, nations producing oil or other commodities possessed a great advantage. It was an era of global inflation, but it was also an era of developmental opportunity. This was especially true for those countries fortunate enough to possess underground lakes of oil, or vast reserves of copper or tin, and even for those that were efficient producers of bananas or other primary resources and commodities. The high price of oil also created pressure for countries to finance their energy bills. What was the solution to this dilemma? For many, it was to borrow from Western banks. The international balance of economic power seemed to be shifting from North America, Europe, and Japan to the oil-producing cartel known as OPEC. Arab countries, such as Saudi Arabia and Kuwait, were receiving large infusions of cash and could not spend it fast enough. There was a limit to the number of airports, ports, hotels, and luxury cars that governments and individuals could build or buy. Thus they began to deposit the surplus into US and European banks. This recycling of "petrodollars" created an incentive among bankers to lend the money to earn interest and positively affect the bottom line.

From the perspective of both parties, the solution was obvious. Latin American countries needed investment capital to accelerate their development and, presumably, to reduce disparities in wealth and income. International bankers needed new opportunities to maximize profits. And at the time, governments seemed to be good credit risks. They controlled commodities that seemed to be continually rising in price, so there was no question that borrowers would be able to pay back their loans. Moreover, governments would not go bankrupt. Thus, during this period, Mexico, Brazil, Venezuela, Argentina, and others borrowed millions of dollars. Another round of oil price increases in the late 1970s induced another round of borrowing.

The increased sensitivity of the developed world to the demands of the less developed world provided an impetus for calls for a dialogue to be conducted under United Nations auspices between the North and South regarding a new international economic order. Mexico and Venezuela were in the forefront of this dialogue, calling for reforms to the trade and monetary regimes and for greater restrictions on the operation of MNCs (for a perspective on this topic from outside Latin America, see Marklund 2020). Although negotiations met with mixed success from the point of view of the Latin American states, one enduring legacy of the process was an increased assertiveness and activism on the part of resource-rich countries. In this era of expanding mutual dependence, the range of foreign policy maneuvers was expanding, as were the economic and diplomatic capabilities of those countries aspiring to regional—and indeed, global—leadership.

As Scott McKinney illustrates in Chapter 6, the boom went bust in the early 1980s as international economic conditions conspired to send the global economy into recession. Increasingly, many Latin American countries were forced to turn to the IMF for assistance. The IMF insisted, however, that before it would make loans to cover shortfalls, a certain set of reforms, called structural adjustment programs, had to be implemented. Many countries viewed the programs as undue interference in their sovereign authority to determine their own economic and political destinies. Structural adjustment programs usually involved currency devaluations to stimulate exports and reduce demand for imported goods. Cuts in government spending to balance budgets and reduce inflation were additional requirements. As one might expect, such spending reductions sometimes adversely affected subsidies for food, energy, transportation, housing, and healthcare. Thus, the burden of economic stabilization was placed not only on Latin American governments, but also on the people. In many instances, these burdens were painful and politically unsettling. These programs, in addition to an upswing in the global economy, eased the crisis. Many Latin Americans lament the 1980s as the "lost decade" of economic growth and development (Fraga 2004).

The 1980s

Latin America was at the forefront of a surprising trend in international politics in the 1980s: the movement away from authoritarian political rule and state-directed economic development, and toward democratic politics and free market economics. The trend began with Uruguay, Peru, Argentina, and Brazil and accelerated until almost every country in the hemisphere became "democratic." This process took different forms in different countries. In some, the military gave up power in an incremental fashion, as in Brazil during the process of *apertura democrática* (democratic opening). In others, longtime leaders were removed or voted out of office. A 1989 coup against Paraguay's seven-time president, Alfredo Stroessner (1954–1989), is a good example of the former, and the Chilean electorate's emphatic "no" in a 1988 referendum on General Augusto Pinochet's (1973–1989) continuation in power illustrates the latter. In Central America, civil unrest and violence characterized the process. In Nicaragua, the Sandinista National Liberation Front (FSLN) seized power in 1979 after ousting Anastasio Somoza Debayle (1967–1979), the last in a line of dynastic dictators. In El Salvador, the Farabundo Martí National Liberation Front (FMLN) struggled to depose a government controlled by the armed forces and supported by the United States.

In both cases, the international system intruded on the internal politics of the area. The Reagan administration (1981–1989) viewed both conflicts as inspired by outside forces. According to this analysis, the FMLN was aided and abetted by the Soviets, who were funneling arms and supplies through Cuba and Nicaragua. The Sandinistas were perceived as instruments of Soviet influence in the Western Hemisphere. And from the perspective of the international system, it appeared that the Soviets were "on the march." They had made gains in the Horn of Africa, were engaged in Afghanistan, and had supported—with the assistance of Cuban proxies—the ascent to power of Afro-Marxist leaders and groups in Angola and Mozambique. Their military strength, particularly in the area of strategic nuclear weaponry, seemed to equal or perhaps even surpass that of the United States.

As enunciated by the Reagan Doctrine, the United States undertook to "roll back" communism by supporting groups and individuals supposedly struggling for freedom against tyranny. In the context of Central America, this meant increasing support in the form of arms and matériel for groups of Nicaraguan exiles in Honduras and Costa Rica. These *contras* began operations in 1982 and carried on a low-level guerrilla campaign in Nicaragua for the next eight years. The United States spent millions of dollars over a ten-year period to aid the Salvadoran government in its bloody struggle against leftist insurgents. The trouble in Central America and the Caribbean galvanized Latin America in opposition to yet another instance of external intervention into the region's affairs and energized the search for Latin American solutions to Latin American problems. In 1983, Mexico, Venezuela, Colombia, and Panama met on the island of Contadora to begin discussing a regional plan to end hostilities in Central America. This group was expanded in July 1985 to include a support group consisting of Argentina, Brazil, and Uruguay.

Central America was not the only arena for conflict in the early 1980s. A long-simmering dispute between Argentina and the United Kingdom over control of the Falkland Islands (Islas Malvinas) flared into war. Asserting that the United Kingdom had no right to control these specks of land off the coast of Argentina, the Argentine government sent troops in March 1982 to reassert sovereign control over the islands. The military government had taken this action in part to deflect attention from the worsening economic and social conditions in Argentina itself. The junta miscalculated, perhaps from a sexist viewpoint. Prime Minister Margaret Thatcher (1979–1990), the "Iron Lady," sent the United Kingdom's most elite military units in a naval armada to sail south thousands of miles. After a fruitless round of shuttle diplomacy by US secretary of state Alexander Haig, the battle was joined. Combat began and the United Kingdom was almost defeated, as Argentina's French-produced Exocet missiles sank or damaged a number of British warships. Ultimately, the fighting shifted to the islands themselves and Argentina's quick defeat prevented profound logistical challenges from overtaking British forces had combat continued more than a few weeks. By June 1982, victory for the United Kingdom was ensured (Hastings and Jenkins 1984). The Falkland Islands War illustrated to Latin America that the United States could not be counted on to support one of its own in a conflict with a European power.

The Reagan administration's anticommunist orientation again manifested itself in the Caribbean with the October 1983 intervention in Grenada. Twenty-five thousand US troops were dispatched to protect American lives and US property and to rescue a group of American students attending an offshore medical school who were trapped by events. The administration feared the leftist government was becoming too closely aligned with Fidel Castro, who was assisting in the construction of an airport capable of accommodating military aircraft. When a more radical faction seized power and ultimately purged the previous leadership, the United States, at the invitation of a group of Caribbean nations, intervened. The message seemed clear: the United States would take action against instability in the region, especially if it appeared to be communist-inspired. The invasion was denounced by many countries in Latin America as yet another example of wrongful US interventionism and power politics.

The drug trade and the activities of powerful cartels of narcotraffickers constituted a new threat to the internal and external security of a host of Latin American countries—especially the Andean nations of Bolivia, Peru, Ecuador, and Colombia. Mexico, Panama, and Jamaica also fit into this group. The drug trade provided an incentive for individuals, cartels, and governments to generate revenue. Trade in narcotics such as cocaine and marijuana had profound impacts on the domestic political climates of many countries. In Colombia, powerful cartels based in Cali and Medellín in effect declared war on the government, assassinating judges, prosecutors, and legislators who attempted to thwart their efforts. In Peru, drugs and ideology formed the basis of guerrilla terror, as a Maoist group known as Sendero Luminoso (Shining Path) sought to create a climate of fear and instability among the people and, more important, to provoke the government into taking action that went against its pledge to respect human rights and democratic freedoms. The drug trade also influenced foreign policy issues. For example, much debate occurred between Latin American countries and the United States regarding the importance of eliminating supply or whether the United States had to do more to cut demand for controlled substances. Sensitivities were raised regarding the dispatch of US drug enforcement agents and military advisers to aid in the struggle.

Finally, drugs also led to another instance of US intervention in Central America: the December 1989 invasion of Panama. The ostensible justification for this operation was to take General Manuel Noriega into custody. It was alleged that Noriega, the leader of Panama (1983–1989), had personally been involved in drug trafficking as well as having sanctioned the laundering of drug profits through Panamanian banks. Moreover, Noriega—reputed to have been on the payroll of the US Central Intelligence Agency—had overturned the will of the people by negating national election results that would have transferred power to moderate, reformist civilians. From the Latin American perspective, Noriega's capture was an outrageous violation of national sovereignty as well as of human rights. It went against earlier attempts to forge closer ties with Panama and the region as a whole through the 1977 signing of the Panama Canal treaties, which established Panamanian sovereignty over the waterway as of 2000.

The Post–Cold War Era

Stunning changes in global politics and economics gave rise to new sets of issues on national, regional, and international agendas. Questions relating to regional security obviously did not disappear, especially in the wake of the September 11, 2001, attacks on the United States. But those relating to trade and investment, immigration, and the environment rose in importance on regional and international agendas. For instance, one major trend was the formation of arrangements designed to foster integration or, at the least, to manage increased interdependence and globalization. The precursor of many of these attempts was the 1989 free trade agreement between the United States and Canada. Following this treaty, US president George H. W. Bush (1989–1993) began to speak of an arrangement that would encompass all of North

America. In response, Mexican president Carlos Salinas de Gortari (1988–1994) also affirmed that perhaps this proposal was one whose time had come.

Interestingly, for both Canada and Mexico, a movement toward greater economic integration with the United States represented a sharp break from traditional foreign policy orientations. Mexico in particular had taken many measures designed to diminish economic influence from the United States. It nationalized its oil industry in 1938 as well as other industries over the years. Mexico passed legislation in the 1970s protecting its market by limiting the level and sectors of foreign investment. It did not join the major neoliberal trading regime, the General Agreement on Tariffs and Trade (GATT), the precursor to the World Trade Organization, until 1985. But in the early 1990s, all three countries began a round of negotiations that culminated in the December 1993 signing of the North American Free Trade Agreement. Proponents of NAFTA argued that it would accelerate development of the Mexican economy, serve as a basis for a transition from authoritarian to more democratic political processes, and, by providing jobs for Mexicans, staunch the flow of immigration northward to the United States.

In January 1994, however, a group of discontented citizens began staging protests in the southern Mexican state of Chiapas. One of the poorest states in the country, and populated primarily by descendants of the Mayas, Chiapas had not benefited from previous attempts at reform, and some felt NAFTA would only widen the gap between the rich and poor in Mexico and Chiapas. This discontent led to the formation of the Zapatista National Liberation Army (EZLN). As the EZLN gained popular support, the Mexican government's response was to send in the army. The situation developed into a stalemate, with each side accusing the other of human rights abuses and a lack of good faith at the bargaining table. Indeed, it is somewhat ironic that a group critical of globalization has so successfully and adroitly mobilized its instruments (the internet, transportation, and tourism) to marshal support for its cause both within Mexico and throughout the world. This ability of the EZLN to market itself and its ideas has made it difficult for the Mexican government to definitively resolve this conflict.

The challenge of international immigration continued to be an important issue for the United States. During the civil war era in Central America, thousands of refugees fled from Guatemala, El Salvador, and Nicaragua into neighboring countries and northward through Mexico to the United States. Cuban refugees also fled to the sanctuary of the United States due to ongoing economic turmoil and political repression.

Many of these immigrants were returned to the US naval base at Guantanamo Bay, where they languished and occasionally rioted. Haitians seeking economic and political refuge and mobility by entering the United States legally or otherwise were another example of the trend.

The increased importance of immigration as an issue of Latin American international relations can be illustrated by a sensational example: General Augusto Pinochet, the former Chilean head of state who was arrested at the behest of a Spanish judge in October 1998 during a private visit to the United Kingdom. The judge requested that General Pinochet be extradited to Spain to stand trial for human rights abuses against Spanish citizens committed by the military regime that Pinochet headed from 1973 to 1989. The judge based his claim on the allegation that Pinochet had violated international human rights covenants and that these conventions provided the legal basis to prosecute violators even if they were not nationals of the prosecuting countries. The issue raised interesting legal and political questions. For example, if the precedent were set, would it mean that a US president could be tried for human rights violations in the former Yugoslavia, Afghanistan, or Iraq? As one would expect, this episode enflamed passions in Spain, the United Kingdom, and especially in Chile. Ultimately, after a series of judicial and administrative maneuvers, the British and Spanish governments decided to declare General Pinochet medically unfit to stand trial, which permitted him to return to his homeland in March 2000 (Beckett 2002). Upon his return to Chile, Pinochet gave up his life seat in the senate, and until his death in 2006 he was able to avoid prosecution for human rights violations alleged to have occurred during his dictatorship.

Immigration issues are again salient on the United States–Mexico border. Under US president Barack Obama, more migrants were deported than during all prior US administrations combined. He prioritized the "removal," the legal term for deportation, of undocumented aliens who were charged and especially convicted of crimes. Some were removed without being prosecuted, though those who were convicted had to serve out their prison terms (Chishti, Pierce, and Bolter 2017). Under President Trump, immigration policy was radically exclusionary. Refugee resettlements were reduced by about 80 percent, and he became the first US president to prevent anyone from applying for asylum at the US side of the border and to require applicants to first fail to obtain asylum in Mexico or Central America.

Even more unprecedented was the family separation policy to deter further migration. Under Obama, when children, mostly teenagers, came on their own, they were largely fleeing organized crime recruitment and violent intimidation in the "Triangle" countries of Honduras, El Salvador, and Guatemala. During the Trump administration, parents took their much younger children with them to escape the violence and economic deprivation, often traveling in "caravans" to obtain safety in transit. By 2020 it became clear that the administration had not established any reliable tracking procedure and did not know how to locate at least 545 children and connect them with their parents, if that administration even wanted to do so (Dickerson 2020b). Under both administrations, crossings of the US southwest border with Mexico were a fraction, between 15 and 30 percent, of what they had been a decade or two before. Thus, immigration restrictions in the United States reflected reaction to past openness of the border. And the crisis continues. Currently, the Biden administration has faced increasing criticism for its lack of a coherent policy for housing unaccompanied minors and for dealing with historically high numbers of migrants moving north.

Environmental issues, such as those analyzed by Jacquelyn Chase and Susan Place in Chapter 8, have also generated great interest. Perhaps the most striking example of this issue is the concern over the degradation of the rainforest in Brazil, which faces the same dilemma as many countries in the developing world. On the one hand, the Amazon Basin contains vast stores of minerals, some oil, and valuable hardwoods. When cleared, the land provides fertile soil to grow crops or to sustain herds of livestock. This area has resources that can accelerate the process of economic development in Brazil. On the other hand, the "Wild West" atmosphere has led to the disruption of traditional ways of life among the Indigenous peoples living there, violence directed at those opposed to development, and the degradation of the land itself. Between August 2019 and July 2020, approximately 4,300 square miles of Amazonian rainforest were destroyed (*BBC News* 2020). Many varieties of species become extinct annually.

Does Brazil have a duty to protect and conserve a resource that is crucial to the world's atmosphere? Is the rainforest a global human resource even though it is located within the sovereign territory of Brazil? These questions are difficult to resolve. Clearly, the United States itself has had great difficulty controlling fires in California and the Pacific Northwest. As with Brazil, climate change and development have been drivers of these fires in both, even if the United States does not have the largest rainforest in the world. Yet both are also endangered by deforestation and possibly permanent conversion to desert-like conditions without historical precedent if public policy is not responsive. In Brazil, it has been concluded through international human rights monitoring by the United Nations, OAS, and NGOs that the fires come from failing to protect the property rights of Indigenous people.

Nations of the hemisphere, however, did undertake to discuss these issues at an Earth Summit held in Rio de Janeiro in June 1992. The outcome was the Treaty on Preserving Biodiversity. Although hailed as a useful first step toward greater ecological responsibility, the treaty was not ratified initially by the United States. In Kyoto, Japan, in 1997, industrialized nations (except the United States) agreed to cut their emissions of greenhouse gases by an average of 5 percent below 1990 levels during the years 2008–2012. Developing countries adamantly refused any limits on emissions. Participants agreed in principle to create an international emission trading system that would let firms and countries trade emission credits. Such a system could sharply reduce the cost of limiting emissions, but diplomats made slow progress in working out the myriad of rules and procedures that are needed to make the system function.

Other attempts to reach agreement on climate change include the United Nations Climate Change Conference in Copenhagen, Denmark, in December 2009; a follow-on agreement in Cancún, Mexico, in 2010; and the Paris Climate Agreement in 2016. Issues addressed at these conferences are of utmost importance to countries in Latin America and the Caribbean. For example, glaciers in the Andes have been melting at an accelerated pace. Concerns about the preservation of forests, watersheds, and biodiversity are also highly salient to countries in the region. A number of states have undertaken policies to reduce their carbon footprints. Indeed, Costa Rica has made it a goal to become the first carbon-neutral country in the world. Argentina and Mexico have also undertaken measures to promote cleaner sources of energy.

Indigenous organizations have become mobilized in recent decades, but translating international visibility at various United Nations forums, such as the Inter-American Commission of Human Rights, whose resolutions are not legally binding, has found political measures undertaken only in Paraguay, Ecuador, and Bolivia to protect lands from deforestation and acts of violence. The OAS has insisted that governments take preventive measures rather than reacting after the fact. At some point, legally binding cases will be litigated before the Inter-American Court of Human Rights in Costa Rica. Under Article 24 of the Inter-American Declaration of Indigenous Rights of 2016, approved in a resolution of the OAS General Assembly in June 2017, lands are allowed for voluntary isolation from state-sanctioned economic development. So far, strong implementation measures have not been instituted. With respect to investments in the Camisea gas project in Peru and the protection of the Waorani y

Tagaeri-Taromenane peoples in Ecuador, little preventive action has been undertaken. Both the action plan for the UN's Sustainable Development Goals and the 2016 UN Declaration on the Rights of Indigenous Peoples speak to protecting Indigenous communities from exploitation.

A final "environmental" (and security) concern involves the proliferation of nuclear weapons and the issue of technology transfer. Over half a century ago, Latin American nations sought to create a nuclear-free zone. Although the Treaty of Tlatelolco (1967) was hailed as a useful first step, the specter of proliferation threatened the Southern Cone region, as Argentina and Brazil were each assumed to be attempting to acquire a nuclear weapon before the other did. This shadowy arms race was all the more likely because neither country had signed the 1968 Nuclear Non-Proliferation Treaty. In 1990, however, both countries acknowledged the existence of their respective nuclear programs. In 1991, the two countries agreed to establish an Argentine-Brazilian Accounting and Control Commission to verify by mutual inspection the peaceful nature of their nuclear programs. Three years later, Brazil signed the Treaty for the Prohibition of Nuclear Weapons in Latin America and the Caribbean, which called for certification by the UN International Atomic Energy Agency (IAEA) that nuclear facilities were not capable of producing nuclear weapons. The international community expressed some concern that Brazil had balked at permitting IAEA inspectors to tour a uranium enrichment facility under construction in Resende, seventy miles from Rio de Janeiro, in March 2004; in January 2005, inspectors were allowed inside. International observers note that Brazil theoretically could produce highly enriched material for nuclear weapons (Rühle 2010).

Although Brazil has ratified but not signed the Nuclear Non-Proliferation Treaty, it has also committed itself to follow the Missile Technology Control Regime. This has cleared the way for Brazil to undertake commercial development of launchers capable of hurling satellites and other payloads into space. By mid-1997, Brazil became a fourth-tier missile producer. It is also a competitor in the area of civilian space delivery services, an excellent example of accelerating interdependence. Today, Brazil's nuclear capabilities are the most advanced in Latin America; only Argentina has provided serious competition. With Brazil's increasing economic and military power, there are some observers who are concerned that its nuclear submarine program may provide an additional source of material for nuclear weapons (Taylor 2009). The first of five nuclear submarines was launched in 2018. When all its submarines are constructed, Brazil will become only the seventh country (following the United States, the United Kingdom, France, Russia, China, and India) with a nuclear submarine fleet.

International terrorism offers a profoundly different illustration of accelerating interdependence and globalization. A case in point is the tragic September 11, 2001, terrorist attacks on the United States targeting the World Trade Center in New York City and the Pentagon in Washington, D.C. The United States received an outpouring of sympathy from around the globe—including Cuba. In response to the attack, President George W. Bush sent US forces to defeat the Taliban government in Afghanistan. Later, labeling Saddam Hussein as the principal threat to the security of Western civilization, the United States, with the support of the United Kingdom, pressed for a UN resolution authorizing the use of force to disarm (and perhaps to change) the Iraqi regime. The two Latin American representatives on the Security Council, Mexico and Chile voted against the resolution, and both were the focus of an intense lobbying campaign. They tended to be skeptical of the rationale for using force and argued that the resolution would foreclose a successful outcome of the previously approved inspection process.

On March 17, 2003, the United States and the United Kingdom withdrew the resolution for lack of votes and the threat of a veto by France; two days later, the United States, supported by a "coalition of the willing," including Colombia, El Salvador, Nicaragua, Costa Rica, the Dominican Republic, Honduras, and Panama, attacked Iraq, and on April 9, Baghdad fell. However, nation-building in war-torn Iraq proved illusory. A truck-bombing of UN headquarters in Baghdad in August 2003 caused the deaths of twenty-three UN staff members, including Brazil's distinguished representative to the UN, Sérgio Vieira de Mello, who had been charged with creating a working relationship between the occupation authorities and the UN.

The case of Iraq illuminates continuities in Latin America's international orientation. First, it underscores a long-standing predisposition against US interventionism and unilateralism. Although there was much debate in the United States and other parts of the world over the "preemptive unilateralism" of the Bush Doctrine, for many in Latin America there was a certain sense of déjà vu (Prevost and Campos 2007). Second, it illustrates Latin America's differing definitions and perceptions of threats to national security. Political and economic stability and narcoterrorism, rather than the more amorphous war on terror, tend to be higher on the region's agenda. Finally, given the preoccupation of the United States with nation-building in the Middle East and South Asia,

Latin America may have to search for more cooperative regional means for dealing with perceived threats to security.

The Chimera of US Partnership

Latin America has since independence sought to build respectful relations with the United States, hoping to be treated as an equal partner in addressing areas of mutual interest such as immigration, drug trafficking, environmental protection, and hemispheric security.* After all, the United States is bound to Latin America by geography, and Latinos and Latinas are the largest US minority. The restoration and stabilization of democracy in Latin America was expected to improve US–Latin American relations, and economic development gave Latin America the potential to become an important US trade partner. Indeed, NAFTA transformed Mexico into a top trading destination for US goods, and integrated both economies to such an extent that when the Mexican peso was steeply devalued in 1994, it was in the interests of US banks and the US government to assist Mexico in overcoming that crisis. For the United States, a closely linked trade and financial bloc in the Western Hemisphere would have created a huge market capable of negotiating better terms with the European Union and offsetting the rising economic power of China. Yet the envisioned hemispheric trade alliance did not develop, and instead US–Latin American relations have soured.

Second, globalization and diversification of trading partners have decreased Latin America's economic dependence on the United States and made some countries more willing to engage in soft-balancing against US power. In 2005, Latin America rejected a US-initiated plan for the establishment of a Free Trade Area of the Americas (FTAA), in part because the United States was unwilling to relinquish its subsidies for agricultural goods. Latin America's bid for greater economic independence has been driven in part by China's increased demand for resources, which drove up prices on Latin American commodities and generated healthy GDP growth rates even during the 2008 US financial crisis. Between 1995 and 2009, trade between China and Latin America increased dramatically, from about $8 billion to more than $100 billion, with a record year in 2008 at $140 billion even as the US economy took a financial dive (Hearn and León-Manríquez 2011).

---

* This section was written by Shelley McConnell, author of Chapter 4.

Seeking natural resources to fuel its industrial growth, China became the largest trading partner for Chile and Brazil and the second largest for several other countries, and China's trade agreements came with few political strings attached and none of the baggage of a century of US intervention in Latin America's internal affairs. It is worth bearing in mind that Latin America's diversification of its trading partners extended to Europe and the broader Asia Pacific region, and also coincided with homegrown resistance to neoliberalism and public pressure for adoption of heterodox economic policies informed by resource nationalism. These attitudes and market relationships are likely to have lasting effects even as China's growth rate slows. The result is that Latin America is not necessarily less dependent on commodities than in the past, but it is less dependent on the United States.

The region's new willingness to challenge US hegemony was also evident in politics, and was not confined to the countries of the new left. The George W. Bush administration was particularly inept in handling Latin American relations and damaged respect for US leadership (LeoGrande 2007). Since the 1947 signing of the Rio Treaty, a mutual defense pact endorsed by the United States and the countries of Latin America, there has been substantial cooperation between North and South America on security. Latin American countries did not develop nuclear, chemical, or biological weapons, and participated in military training and joint defense exercises with the United States. They collectively condemned Cuba for its importation of Soviet missiles during the 1962 Cuban missile crisis and unanimously denounced the 9/11 attacks on the United States in 2001. The Bush administration squandered that goodwill, however, by abandoning plans for immigration reform and instead closing its borders. Latin America did not fall into line behind the United States in its 2003 invasion of Iraq, and both Mexico and Chile voted against the United States in the UN Security Council vote on that issue. Few Latin American countries joined the "coalition of the willing" to fight alongside the United States in Iraq, and those that did played minor roles.

Given the region's history of state terrorism, it is not surprising that Latin America vehemently rejected the US use of the Guantanamo Bay naval base as an irregular prison and CIA torture center for alleged terrorists (US Senate Select Committee on Intelligence 2012). The Bush administration also demanded that Latin American countries sign agreements providing an exemption such that US citizens could not be sent to face war crime charges at the International Criminal Court (ICC). Although the Bush administration threatened to cut military aid to governments that would not sign the exception, many countries refused, correctly calculating that the United States needed their cooperation on anti-terrorism initiatives more than concessions in relation to the ICC.

The Bush administration soon realized the futility of cutting military aid to its allies and withdrew its demand, but such unilateral strong-arm tactics sent the message that the United States saw Latin America not as a security partner but instead as a subordinate. The Obama and Trump administrations were not interventionist, in terms of troops on the ground in South and Central America—though the United States has almost never placed its troops in any South American country, beyond the role of military advisers. The United States was committed to pressuring the Maduro regime in Venezuela, recognizing the opposition as legitimate, and, under Trump, recognizing the Juan Guaidó shadow government as legitimate. However, a plot by two US citizens to overthrow Maduro in early 2020 was apparently undertaken without any official US support.

In short, an important shift in relations between the countries of the hemisphere is under way in which multilateral and South-South relations are rising in importance and the United States–Latin America relationship is foundering. The signs are evident at the OAS, where several US-endorsed candidates for the post of secretary-general failed to be elected despite that organization's deep dependence on US financial contributions. Rival international organizations that exclude the United States have gained popularity, such as the Community of Latin American and Caribbean States (previously the Rio Group) and the Union of South American Nations (UNASUR) group, established by the left-wing presidents participating in the Bolivarian Alliance for the Americas trade alliance. Latin American countries pushed the Obama administration to permit Cuba's reentry into the OAS, and also threatened to boycott OAS-organized summit meetings of the hemisphere's presidents and prime ministers if Cuba were not invited. Ultimately the United States conceded that issue, and, following tentative improvements in its bilateral relationship with Cuba, in 2015 President Obama shook hands with Cuban president Raul Castro at the Summit of the Americas in Panama.

That rapprochement with Cuba was partly reversed by President Trump, and his proposed wall between the United States and Mexico symbolized a growing United States–Latin America divide. Tightening enforcement against undocumented migrants from Mexico and Central America, separation of children and parents seeking asylum, and termination of temporary protected status for Salvadorans, Hondurans, and Haitians living in the United States have all given the impression that the United States does not appreciate Latin Americans' contributions to the US economy and society. For their part, Latin American leaders criticize the United States for generating the demand for cocaine that drives the drug markets on which armed gangs thrive, and for centering its aid and discourse on anti-terrorism when the main issues hurting Latin Americans are poverty and inequality. To be sure, US–Latin American relations have in the past been episodically characterized by benign neglect, US isolationism, and xenophobia. What is new is that in the twenty-first century, Latin American countries are able to look elsewhere for the partnerships that the United States seems unwilling to provide.

Contemporary Topics

Let us employ our analytic perspectives to better understand salient topics facing Latin American bilateral and multilateral relations in the present— and in the future. From the viewpoint of realism, politico-security issues remain high on the international agenda. One must be mindful, however, that the United States only occasionally considers Latin America to be a central arena in its foreign policy activities; and as discussed earlier, power and influence in the relationship between the United States and Latin America may be changing.

Cast in the light of realism, Cuba, even in its weakened condition, is still perceived as a threat by the United States. The latter continues to maintain an economic embargo it imposed in 1960, passed legislation in the 1990s to make it very difficult for US presidents to lift it, and perennially yo-yoed between relaxing and tightening restrictions for bilateral travel, trade, and diplomatic endeavors. Cast in the light of interdependence and globalization, however, recent events have reflected a change in approach toward this very complex relationship. In January 2011, the Obama administration decided to relax certain restrictions on travel to Cuba. The most notable outcomes of this announcement were that cultural, educational, and religious groups would again be able to visit Cuba after a nearly seven-year hiatus; a number of US airports could be used as points of departure for charter flights for representatives of cultural, student, and religious organizations; and remittances from the United States to Cuba would be expanded to include money sent to non-family members (members of the Cuban government and the Cuban Communist Party were of course excluded). This relaxation was a follow-on to decisions in 2009 that made it easier for those in the United States with family members in Cuba to travel and send money to the island. Seemingly momentous changes were set in motion in 2013 when Cuban president Raul Castro and President Obama shook hands at funeral ceremonies for South African icon Nelson Mandela. Formal recognition and establishment of diplomatic missions took place 2015, and a year later Obama became the first sitting US president to visit the island since Calvin Coolidge in 1928. In the interim, relations have been damaged by mysterious microwave attacks on US and Canadian diplomats in Havana in 2017, and by President Trump's focus on Cuba's ties with Venezuela. Very late in President Trump's tenure, the Department of State relisted Cuba as a state sponsor of terrorism, one of only three other countries (North Korea, Iran, and Syria) so designated.

With respect to combating the production and distribution of illicit drugs, two programs are worthy of mention: Plan Colombia and the Mérida Initiative. The former was a joint venture between Colombia and the United States. Beginning in August 2000 and funded in part with $1.3 billion in US assistance, this ambitious, controversial military and social development program was intended to root out Colombia's drug trade and end its decades-old armed conflict. The program was terminated in 2015, replaced by Peace Colombia, designed to facilitate the implementation of the peace accord signed by the government and the FARC-EP in 2016.

The Mérida Initiative was developed in 2008 to assist governments in Mexico and Central America in eliminating drug and arms smuggling, and in combating an increasingly ferocious and brutal war among Mexican drug cartels primarily located in cities on the Mexico–United States border. More than 50,000 individuals were killed in drug-related violence over a five-year period, and the Mexican government mobilized its military to increase security in border cities such as Ciudad Juárez and Tijuana. One especially troubling aspect of this conflict was that there were indications that the violence began seeping across the border into the United States. A tragic instance of this was the March 15, 2010, murder of a US consular employee and her husband as they crossed from Ciudad Juárez to El Paso, Texas. To critics, who call the initiative "Plan Mexico," the program seemed to mirror the weaknesses of "Plan Colombia," which they argue promoted impunity among the military and paramilitaries with respect to the treatment of suspects and detainees. Of course, critics also point to the necessity of reducing the demand for drugs in the United States as opposed to a constant emphasis on staunching the supply.

A contemporary topic in Latin American relations is a movement toward greater interregional and intraregional trade. With respect to the latter, the rise of Japan, China, and the Pacific Rim, as well as the European Union, has created competitive challenges and opportunities for innovative approaches to development and trade. Many Caribbean states have been participants in the various Lomé conventions and the Cotonou Agreement, intended to provide less developed countries with preferential access to European markets. The European Union has signed economic and commercial agreements with numerous Central and South American states. And momentum toward greater cooperation between the European Union and Latin America and the Caribbean has accelerated as the result of a series of summits. In terms of fostering broader cooperation with Iberian Europe, nineteen Latin American countries, along with Spain and Portugal, have participated in annual Ibero-American summits. One interesting proposal emerging from a recent gathering was to establish an association along the lines of the British Commonwealth.

Obviously, while progress has been made, there have been unintended consequences associated with globalization and accelerating integration. Reactions to these projects have manifested themselves in Latin American domestic and international politics. For example, in a number of countries, electorates chose presidents who tended to be more skeptical and cautious about continuing to pursue the so-called Washington Consensus of freer markets and trade, and these leaders often made significant changes in their countries' foreign policies. In Central America, both the FMLN in El Salvador and the FSLN in Nicaragua gained the presidency through democratic elections. Indeed, Daniel Ortega, the man whom the United States and the Nicaraguan *contras* fought so relentlessly to remove from power during the era of Sandinista rule (1979–1990), was again reelected in 2006. And through a series of electoral and constitutional reforms in 2014, Ortega is now free to run for an unlimited number of five-year terms.

In the Andean region, both Bolivia and Ecuador elected populist presidents who adopted a more leftist, anti-imperialist foreign policy orientation. Each undertook programs designed to empower Indigenous populations in both nations. Evo Morales of Bolivia, elected in 2005, embarked on a world tour to mobilize support for his proposal to "transform" his country. His relationship with Venezuela improved as he questioned the utility of coca eradication programs supported by the United States and alleged that his legitimacy was being undermined by opposition groups tacitly supported by Washington. Reelected in 2009, President Morales took steps to improve bilateral relations with the United States, believing that the election of President Barack Obama in 2008 would result in a positive shift in US foreign policy. However, after 2017, with President Trump in the White House, Morales was no longer welcome in Washington, D.C., and by 2019 he was out of power. In Ecuador, President Rafael Correa (2007–2017) tended to take a more confrontational posture in relations with international lending institutions and the United States. For example, he granted asylum in the Ecuadoran embassy in London to Julian Assange, who as the founder of

WikiLeaks published highly classified material from the US government. Ecuador also moved to strengthen ties with countries associated with the Bolivarian Alliance for the Americas, as well as with Iran.

Venezuela's Hugo Chávez is perhaps the most noteworthy example of an Andean leader who argued that neoliberal economic reforms contributed to more pervasive US influence. He did not support US-led efforts in Afghanistan and Iraq, and he did not forget a 2002 coup attempt against himself, one in which the United States was tacitly involved. He asserted that Latin America, especially given the repercussions of the Great Recession, needed to have greater autonomy from the negative effects of a global economy dominated by the United States and Western Europe. To achieve such autonomy, Chávez proposed the Bolivarian Alliance for the Americas. Members of ALBA, established in 2004, include Venezuela, Cuba, Nicaragua, Bolivia, Dominica, Honduras, Ecuador, Antigua and Barbuda, and Saint Vincent and the Grenadines. It represented an attempt to provide an alternative to the neoliberal projects deemed to be too closely linked to US national interests. Moreover, in 2005 Venezuela established Petrocaribe, a mechanism through which it provided seventeen Caribbean states with low-cost petroleum (Clem and Maingot 2011). Critics maintained that Venezuela's largess, intended to promote leftist policies and pro-Venezuelan foreign policy alliances, has on occasion fostered corrupt practices by recipient governments. The project has languished under the austerity resulting from the country's economic collapse under Venezuela's current president, Nicolás Maduro. Venezuela has looked to extra-hemispheric allies in its quest for regional weight. For example, President Chávez had a warm relationship with Iran, viewing the latter as an ally and a partner in facilitating increased energy production and cooperation in industrial and economic activities. Additionally, both nations have discussed issues of security and arms transfers, and Venezuela has rhetorically supported Iran's development of nuclear technology.

Although nationalist populism has taken a pinkish cast in recent times, historically it has generally arisen as a right-wing phenomenon, as has occurred with the election of Brazilian president Jair Bolsonaro, who in a variety of ways follows in the footsteps of Latin America's predominant military dictatorships during their authoritarian rule from much of 1964–1991. While not as brutally repressive as the conservative populists of the past, Bolsonaro, a former military officer, has taken controversial positions on the Covid-19 pandemic, women's and LGBTQ rights, environmental protection, and political violence. He also had tilted Brazil's foreign policy in directions favoring closer relations with the United States.

International organizations seemingly have been more critical of left-wing governments in the Americas than of right-wing ones, though their factual conclusions are not inaccurate. Both the OAS and the UN Human Rights Council established special investigations of repression of opposition, by the Ortega government in Nicaragua in 2018 and by Maduro's regime in Venezuela in 2020. The UN Human Rights Council established a fact-finding body for Venezuela in 2019 and in September 2020 criticized Venezuela's Maduro government for "crimes against humanity," as well as suppressing political opposition and oppressing freedom of speech and the press since 2014. The mission investigated 223 cases in a 411-page report and an additional 2,891 cases to corroborate that state agents had perpetrated crimes against humanity. "President Maduro and the Ministers of the Interior and of Defense gave orders, coordinated activities and supplied resources for arbitrary killings and systematic torture—[which] amount to crimes against humanity," said Marta Valiñas, chairperson of the mission (United Nations Human Rights Council 2020). At the same time, the council's special rapporteur on unilateral coercive sanctions condemned US sanctions, which were illegally imposed without a UN Security Council resolution and have exacerbated the country's humanitarian crisis. UN calls for peaceful negotiations may not have much impact, but illegal sanctions causing hardship also provide an excuse by a regime for its responsibility for ongoing misery. Additional international meetings of different alliances and organizations have attempted to discuss Latin American regional specificity and cultural relativism concerning human rights claims to nondiscrimination on sexual orientation, gender identity, and sex characteristics. Clearly, such norms are more controversial than the goals of reducing political violence perpetrated by or tolerated by states.

Latin American countries, particularly those in South America, look to such regional institutions as a way to improve cooperation and regional progress. The notion of intertwining aspects of sovereignty to achieve absolute gains is clearly neoliberal in origin. The spillover from regional trading blocs has brought many of these countries together politically as well as economically. Following the controversial presidential elections in Venezuela (2018), Brazil, Costa Rica, Argentina, and Ecuador, among several others, roundly criticized Maduro's supposed victory, choosing instead to support his opponent. As mentioned, while it cannot be said that these countries speak as one on all occasions, the fact that they came together to criticize a nondemocratic process clearly indicates that a substantial norm shift has taken place. Similarly, the OAS's monitoring of the Bolivian election in 2019 concluded that irregularities violated democratic norms of electoral credibility, a conclusion that became even more controversial when the country's military signaled to Evo Morales that he should leave power.

In terms of important state actors, Brazil has emerged a potent regional player. The 2006 discovery of large reserves of petroleum off its east coast has only enhanced Brazil's considerable domestic and external prospects. Brazilian estimates place the number of potential reserves in the neighborhood of 50 billion barrels, which would vault the country into the top ranks of oil producers. As a result, former president Luiz Inácio Lula da Silva (2003–2011) had sought to raise Brazil's foreign policy profile, taking the lead in efforts to move the region toward greater political, economic, and social unity. For example, he viewed his country as a bridge between the United States and members of ALBA. With the election of Jair Bolsonaro, Brazil's foreign policy has tilted to a close relationship with the United States, China, and Israel. Concomitantly, relations with Venezuela and Cuba have cooled.

Bolsonaro's election illustrates another corrosive aspect of the "intermestic" nature of Latin American relations: corruption. Elected in response to widespread perception of corrupt practices in Brazilian administrations, Bolsonaro's attractiveness as a candidate was that he was not tainted by the whiff of scandal, which had resulted in the arrest of one former president and the impeachment of another. The "car wash" money-laundering scandal involving officials of Petrobras, the state-run oil company, and Odebrect, a Brazilian multinational construction firm that payed millions in bribes to government officials in other Latin American countries for favorable bids on government infrastructure contracts, oozed their way across the hemisphere. The aftermath yielded arrests of top governmental officials in countries across the region, with Peru the most affected (Durand 2018). Corruption has had the practical effect of reducing developmental capacity and the governmental legitimacy required for domestic growth and foreign policy latitude.

The influence of extra-hemispheric actors, particularly China and Russia, may increase in the future. One benefit to Latin American states is having counterweights to the political and economic power of the United States and the European Union. With China's rise as a world economic power, Latin America has become a target for investment and trade. Over half of China's approximately $50 billion in external investment is located in Latin America; over the past decade, the dollar value of the Latin America–China trade relationship has topped $150 billion. From China's point of view, Latin America is a source of raw materials and energy to fuel its expanding economy, and a market for a wide array of Chinese goods. From a diplomatic perspective, Latin America is also a means to continue the diplomatic isolation of Taiwan (which China believes is a part of its territory), and to make its presence felt in a region of the world where the United States has traditionally exerted hegemony. Incentives for Latin America include a huge market for export-led growth, investment capital for resource and energy development, and a counterweight to North America (Ellis 2009).

As the United States abandoned various multilateral initiatives under President Trump, many Latin American countries turned to China for support, particularly during the Covid-19 pandemic in 2020. At the second joint forum of the Community of Latin American and Caribbean States (CELAC) and China, held in China in 2018, an agreement on health cooperation to control and prevent disease, which was not considered a highlight of the pact, took on much greater subsequent significance. While the global pandemic disrupted transnational supply chains, China was able to supply countries in the region with which it had diplomatic relations because China is the largest producer of medical supplies in the world. China provided masks and other personal protective equipment, needles, ventilators, ambulances, and oxygen and offered $1 billion in loans for the purchase of vaccines (Sanborn 2020). Brazil, for example, is using a Chinese vaccine to combat the second highest incidence of Covid-19 cases and deaths in the world.

Russia has (re)emerged into the foreign policy calculus of Venezuela, Nicaragua, Cuba, and other Latin American nations. For example, in August 2008 when the post-Soviet state of Georgia began military operations against two breakaway provinces, South Ossetia and Abkhazia, Russia came to the latter's assistance, defeating Georgian troops after a five-day conflict. In the wake of a ceasefire agreement brokered by the European Union, Venezuela and Nicaragua were two of the first countries in the world to recognize the independence of these provinces. Russia has expanded cooperation in military affairs with Venezuela as well as in space exploration with Brazil. It has investments in infrastructural development in Mexico, Argentina, and Chile, and is slowly rebuilding its long-standing relationship with Cuba. The United States has eyed Russia regarding the 2017 directed-microwave attack on US diplomats in the US embassy in Havana, leading to what has become known as the "Havana syndrome," a series of afflictions ranging from hearing loss to memory difficulties (Mackinnon and Gramer 2020). In the realm of public health and responses to the Covid-19 pandemic, Russia's Sputnik V vaccine has become increasingly popular with Latin

American countries to protect their populations against the virus. As the result of bilateral "vaccine diplomacy" between Argentina and Russia, the vaccine has been approved and made available to countries such as Bolivia, Mexico, and Venezuela (McCluskey et al. 2021).

A consideration of significant partners located outside the region comes full circle with a brief mention of Latin American relations with the European Union. The European Union's stance toward Latin America is based on three components: economic cooperation, institutionalized political dialogue, and fostering closer trade linkages. All of these objectives are embodied in biennial European Union–Latin America summits, which alternate between venues in Europe and Latin America. On a more regularized basis, the European Union has focused on deepening dialogues with four Latin American regional organizations. For its dialogue with the Andean states, the European Union links with the Andean Community of Nations (CAN). As one might expect, the Caribbean Community (CARICOM) is the channel for its negotiations with the wider Caribbean. For Central America and the Southern Cone states, the European Union interacts with the Central American Integration System (SICA) and the Southern Common Market (Mercosur), respectively. Chile and Mexico have had more focused contacts with the European Union (Bindi 2010; Mori 2018). Primary points of discussion relate to Latin American concerns over limited access to the European Union market in agricultural products because of the European Union's Common Agricultural Policy. A more recent irritant is a limitation on immigration from the region. The European Union has an interest in continuing to assist developmental and integrative projects proliferating in the region. It does, however, view great disparities in wealth and income and the prevalence of poverty as potential threats to democratic consolidation, regional stability, and growth.

Latin American nations continue to grapple with issues ranging from democratization and development to public health and environmental protection. They have an interest in creating greater bonds with one another in ways that will create incentives for the United States, China, and other members of the global community to approach them as mature partners. It is worth noting that Brazil will play an important role in the region. Neither can Mexico, Argentina, and Chile be ignored. Venezuela will continue to be a reminder of how fragile democratic experiments can be. What is clear is that salient differences of opinion and policy outlooks remain within and between Latin American countries and organizations. Thus the international relations of Latin America will be profoundly affected by the success (or failure) with which the region deals with its problems, opportunities, and challenges.

8

Environmental Challenges

Jacquelyn Chase
and Susan E. Place

In Latin America, as elsewhere, the environment is a
product of interactions between human society and the biophysical
world. These interactions shift over time as a result of technological,
cultural, and demographic change. This chapter provides an overview of
the relationships between society and the environment in Latin America
since pre-Columbian times, passing through the dramatic changes
imposed by European conquerors and the Columbian Exchange, and
considering the contemporary process of globalization and its impacts
on the region's environments, populations, and cities.

The effects of globalization in Latin America filter through inequitable
socioeconomic hierarchies that usually benefit the wealthy few—large
landholders and well-connected entrepreneurs—while the poor majority
suffers most of the negative environmental and social consequences of
articulation with global markets. Foreign debt and dependence on exports
lead Latin American nations to overexploit their natural resources and to
degrade the region's ecosystems. Industrialization and overcrowding in
substandard housing expose people to pollution and other environmental
and biological hazards.

Latin America's environmental challenges are primarily social problems, the result of economic disparities and traditional lack of democratic
political institutions in much of the region. The key to understanding the
relationship between nature and society in Latin America lies in identifying who controls the region's natural resources, especially the land itself.
This, in turn, relates to the quest for economic development that has
engaged the region for almost 200 years. As Shelley McConnell shows

in Chapter 4, competition for access to resources underlies much of the region's legendary political instability. The components of population growth—births, deaths, and migration—have responded to conflicts over resources since the colonial period and should not be considered simply the cause of environmental problems. The drastic slowing of birthrates across most of the region can be traced to urbanization and the rise in consumer society. Infant mortality has responded to vaccination and basic sanitation campaigns throughout the twentieth century with sharp declines, although it was not until several governments focused specifically on the poorest children that these improvements became more just and universal (Scheper-Hughes 2013a, 2013b). Indigenous people and the urban poor are most susceptible to new diseases such as Zika and Covid-19.

Latin America alone represents roughly 40 percent of the world's plant and animal species, is home to six of the world's most biologically diverse countries, and contains within it the single most biologically diverse area in the world, the Amazon rainforest (Bovarnick 2010).

Pre-Columbian Cultures and Latin America's Environments

As Marie Price notes in Chapter 2, humans have occupied the Americas for many millennia. By 1500 C.E., they were living in every ecosystem from the Arctic to Tierra del Fuego, at the southernmost tip of South America, and their population totaled more than that of Europe at the time. Their livelihood strategies ranged from foraging (hunting-gathering) to shifting cultivation in patches of tropical forest to highly intensive farming systems. These systems supported varying population densities, from sparse nomadic populations in the interior deserts of northern Mexico and Patagonia in southern Argentina, to extremely dense populations in Mesoamerica (central and southern Mexico and northern Central America) and the Andes Mountains and adjacent lowlands (Denevan 1992). Awareness of the sophistication and variety of Indigenous agricultural techniques and technology should help to dispel the commonly held stereotype of Latin America as more "natural" and "uncivilized" than Europe and the United States (Mann 2006).

Geographic complexity in the Americas as well as millennia of regional pre-Columbian exchange gave rise to ancient plant domestication and contributed to incredible food diversity (Crosby 1972; Brush 2004). The Mesoamerican and Andean civilizations were supported by intensive agricultural systems and regional trade that moved products across ecological zones. Indigenous agricultural systems were based on the creativity of ancestors who had domesticated many crop plants over several thousand years. The most important food crops were maize, beans, squashes, manioc (cassava), peanuts, tomatoes, potatoes, and several grains, such as quinoa, that grow at high elevations in the Andes. Peru still grows 4,000 types of potatoes, with vibrant colors, different textures, and widely varied flavors.

Over the centuries, Indigenous peoples modified the environment as they devised innovative methods for increasing food production to keep pace with population growth. Methods of agricultural intensification included irrigation systems, terracing, raised fields, sunken fields, drainage systems, and an ingenious system of creating *chinampas* (raised cultivation beds) in the shallow, brackish lakes in the Valley of Mexico. There were an estimated 30,000 acres of these *chinampas* around Tenochtitlán, the Aztec capital. The high productivity of the *chinampas* contributed to the support of Tenochtitlán's pre-Columbian population of perhaps a quarter million. A few remnant *chinampas* can be seen in suburban Mexico City today, where they are marketed for tourists as "The Floating Gardens of Xochimilco." Other evidence of complex environmental modification includes some 1.5 million acres of agricultural terraces in the central Andes and over 1.25 million acres of abandoned raised fields in northern Colombia.

"Simple" village farmers of the tropical lowlands also manipulated nature in ingenious ways. These farmers practiced shifting cultivation, a seminomadic system of farming the tropical forest without destroying it (Roosevelt 1980). They cleared, burned, and planted in scattered patches within the forest. After a few seasons, they abandoned a given field and allowed the forest to regenerate. They planted a wide variety of crops, including many fruit and nut trees, from which they could continue harvesting even after abandoning a given field. They managed the renewal of the forest, selecting for useful species, including trees whose ash provided specific nutrients to the soil when burned. Thus they planned for the future even as they abandoned a given plot. Thousands of years of human management, including long-term mulching and selection of useful wild species, have modified the tropical forests of Latin America. Some scientists believe that such human activities have contributed to the astounding biodiversity of the Amazon Basin. Humans have actually created new soils in the basin, where extensive areas of rich black soils, created by Indigenous agricultural systems and household refuse, have been found amid the infertile red soils that are natural to the region (Hecht and Cockburn 2011).

The Columbian Exchange expanded this diversity. African slaves saw to the expansion of varieties of rice previously unknown to Europeans (Carney and Rosomoff 2009). The global diversity of food also increased through the selection of varieties grown far from the original Latin American "cradles," such as Irish and Russet potatoes. The majority of the world's potato varieties still reside in Peru, where unfortunately climate change is rapidly reducing the land available for their cultivation (Zimmerer and Carter 2002; Food and Agriculture Organization 2008). Similarly, the world can thank Latin America for the domestication of maize (corn), although maize has been "hijacked" by global production networks that threaten the variety of this crop. Subsistence farmers in Mexico have safeguarded many varieties of corn, relied on the crop for food security, and supplied local markets with this ancient staple. The North American Free Trade Agreement maneuvered trade advantages to farmers from the United States and has thus destroyed much of this local system of maize production (Gálvez 2018).

Environmental and Demographic Change in the Colonial Era

European conquest initiated rapid environmental change in Latin America, as noted by Marie Price in Chapter 2. Imposition of European technologies that were ill-suited to Latin America's environmental conditions degraded fragile ecosystems. For example, European farming systems based on the plow caused accelerated soil erosion, especially when used on the hilly or mountainous topography that was prevalent in the areas of Spanish settlement. Another serious ecological consequence of the insertion of Spanish agricultural systems was the introduction of Old World weeds (Parsons 1972). Today, exotic weeds have displaced native species throughout Latin America and constitute a major threat to biodiversity in the region.

European colonialism also introduced into Latin America an economic system based on the export of commodities to Europe. The Spanish colonial system was oriented toward the extraction of mineral wealth, gold and silver, and its importation to Europe. Mining spawned a number of environmental impacts. Forests were quickly decimated to provide timbers for the mines, housing for workers, and charcoal for fuel. Extensive agricultural areas were established to supply the mines and miners with necessities such as food, hides (for ore sacks and pulleys), tallow (to illuminate mines), and grazing for the thousands of mules needed to transport the ore. The desertification created by these activities in the semiarid and mountainous environments in which the mines were located persists today.

The Portuguese, not finding precious metals and large Indigenous populations in Brazil, began extracting brazilwood for the reddish resin used in dyes. However, soon they introduced sugarcane, an Asian crop that was destined to change the face of Latin America. Sugarcane's environmental impacts included deforestation and degradation of the soil. The expansion of sugar plantations, logging, and later coffee into Brazil's Atlantic coastal forest led to the ecosystem's virtual disappearance by the late nineteenth century (Dean 1995).

Sugar is also associated with the invention of a new economic institution, the plantation, which dramatically transformed nature and society in Latin America. The plantation was a commercial agricultural venture designed to specialize in the production of a tropical crop for export to Europe. Its high demand for labor stimulated the African slave trade, forcing at least 10 million Africans into Latin America and the Caribbean. Slave-based plantations caused northeastern Brazil and many Caribbean islands to be populated far beyond their carrying capacities. Haiti, where a desperately poor population struggles to survive in a denuded landscape, exemplifies the end result of centuries of plantation production and slave labor. The devastating earthquake that struck Haiti in 2010 exacerbated these struggles.

As René De La Pedraja explains in Chapter 3, Europeans introduced diseases that decimated the Indigenous population, and Marie Price asserts in Chapter 2 that the most direct and profound impact of the conquest on the Americas was demographic. Whole zones were nearly depopulated and the remaining native inhabitants were relocated, forced to labor for the conquerors, or they fled into the hinterlands. Large areas that were remote from the centers of Spanish and Portuguese settlement reverted to forest, leading to the "pristine myth" that the Americas were unpopulated and ripe for colonization by Europeans. In addition to the destruction of up to 90 percent of the region's preconquest population, displacement, as well as changes in racial and ethnic identities, redefined both the daily life and the course of history and society in the colonies.

High mortality robbed native peoples and enslaved people of future generations, and the reorientation of resource extraction and agriculture in the service of Europeans forced native peoples to leave their homelands and discontinue their traditional livelihoods. Attempts to survive and live ordinary lives in the framework of coerced labor and displacement ranged from resistance through flight to strategic alliances with

Europeans through marriage and reciprocity. Whatever the specific strategy, it often implied mobility, displacement, and resettlement.

In Spanish America, colonial settlers and administrators achieved control over native labor through the land. Native communal lands were converted to Spanish dominion, and Indigenous peoples were often forced onto marginal lands. By the end of the sixteenth century, Spaniards had appropriated most of the good land in the region. They established enormous *haciendas* (estates), some as large as European principalities, relegating the remaining Indigenous populations to serfdom. The Indigenous populations in the uplands of Spanish America eventually returned to growth, even as the colonial economy deprived them of resources. Poverty, rural livelihoods, and the influence of Catholicism conspired to keep fertility relatively high in these areas. They are among the most densely populated regions of Latin America, despite high mortality and persistent out-migration.

In the tropical lowlands of Brazil and the Caribbean islands, the plantation economies' dependence on African slave labor contributed to the racial diversity and complex social hierarchy of Latin America. As with the Indigenous populations of Spanish America, slaves were allowed to practice subsistence farming and their agriculture was pushed to hilly, rocky, or dry areas. This pattern repeated itself in post-slave societies in areas that continued to produce tropical plantation crops. The *morador* (tenant farming) system in northeastern Brazil, for example, thrived until the late twentieth century (Alásia de Heredia 1979). In this arrangement, sugarcane workers lived on designated areas of plantations, tending subsistence crops and working seasonally in the cane harvest and sugar production.

During the colonial period, Portuguese settlers' rising demand for labor, lands, and forest resources led natives to flee to the interior. Hence, evasion became the natives' primary means of resisting forced labor, disease, and disruption of their cultures. Meanwhile, from the southeastern flank of the Portuguese colony, organized bands of *bandeirantes* (pioneer explorers) went as far as the Amazon River in search of native slaves and gold. Intermarriage and trade with Indigenous peoples led to the rise of a mixed *caboclo* (Indigenous and European) culture that has been influential in preserving many aspects of Indigenous life in rural Brazil.

Throughout Spanish and Portuguese America, the quest by the Catholic Church to convert souls also reached far into the interior. The Jesuits formed an extended system of communities among the Guaranís in the Paraguay and Paraná Basins and chains of missions in Baja California and along the Amazon River. In these contexts of contact and exploitation, many native peoples chose to flee upland, inland, and upstream. Legendary accounts of great native migrations in search of the "land without evil" in South America took place even before European contact, driving home the notion that native history has never been static, although the conquest gave new urgency to mobility (Clastres 1995).

Settlements of escaped slaves challenged the authority and security of plantation societies all over the Americas. A group of escaped slaves (known as *quilombos* in Portuguese) formed the Independent Republic of Palmares, which endured for almost a hundred years in a mountainous area in the northeastern region of Portuguese America. It was eventually overcome by military force at the end of the seventeenth century. In Jamaica, maroons (a term referring to escaped slaves that derives from *cimarrones* in Spanish) signed the 1739 treaty with the British, providing them with autonomy that continues symbolically to this day. Also, maroons had occasionally developed trading relationships with plantations and towns, and others are known to have both battled with and cooperated with native peoples (Price 1996). In Brazil, Jamaica, and elsewhere, the descendants of maroons possess unique cultures, but remain among the poorest people of their countries as they continue to struggle for recognition and land rights.

For the seminomadic Indigenous peoples in what later became northwestern Mexico, the colonial frontier yielded opportunities to live largely outside Spanish institutions until the mid-nineteenth century (Radding 1997). Some people turned to nomadic life as a means to flee and resist the conditions of mission life. Interior areas of Latin America—the savannahs and tropical forests of non-Andean South America, and the deserts and scrublands of northern Mexico—were left sparsely populated. Thus, throughout later years, these areas became vulnerable to resource extraction, peasant migration, and commercial agriculture; those who advocated the use and, more often, overuse of these sparsely populated areas declared them "empty."

Independence and the First Neoliberal Era

Latin America's independence from Spain and Portugal did not mark the beginning of democracy and equality but merely opened the region up to investment and intervention by other European powers, especially the British and French, and eventually by North Americans. Latin America continued to export a limited range of commodities. The landed elite retained their power, and a rising entrepreneurial class benefited from its ties to foreign investors. In the second half of the nineteenth century, the first neoliberal era took hold in the region, and foreign investment in export commodities grew rapidly. The export boom was accompanied by an expansion of the agricultural frontier into many of Latin America's hinterlands.

Technological innovations stimulated the production of new commodities for European markets. Just as in the United States, barbed wire, windmills, and railroads contributed to the opening up of the *pampas* (plains) in Argentina and Uruguay and the disappearance of wild grassland ecosystems. As wool and wheat production expanded, an economic boom in the meat industry was made possible by the advent of refrigerated steamships. By the end of the nineteenth century, refrigerated shipping also transformed tropical countries, such as Guatemala, Honduras, Costa Rica, and some of the Caribbean islands. For the first time, perishable tropical crops could be sold in Europe and North America, and a major surge in banana production began. The growing populations of the industrial cities of North America also created demands for tropical commodities, such as coffee and cocoa, which had previously been consumed by only the wealthy.

As large commercial estates formed to produce the new export commodities—coffee, cotton, bananas, and cocoa—they expanded beyond existing farmland and accelerated the process of deforestation that continues today. Expansion of export production during the era of nineteenth-century laissez-faire liberalism was accompanied by changes in land tenure. Much of the region's best farmland, which generally lies in plains and valleys, was concentrated in large commercial farms. At the same time, many Indigenous communities lost their traditional communal land rights and swelled the ranks of the landless rural poor. The landless population sought to survive by clearing plots on marginal land, often hillsides, contributing to deforestation and accelerating erosion.

Globalization and the Environment

As Scott McKinney discusses in Chapter 6, the mid-twentieth century saw many Latin American governments embrace economic nationalism and import substitution industrialization. These policies led to accelerated urbanization and pollution in industrial zones. They also contributed to Latin America's foreign debt crises, along with international events such as the oil crises of the 1970s and 1980s. By the late twentieth century, a neoliberal era had again overtaken Latin America, establishing waves of privatization and heightened foreign investment. The reanimation of export-led economies in the region responded in particular to China's development, with its huge demands for metals, soybeans, petroleum, and other primary goods. Export production expanded into areas previously oriented toward self-sufficient small farms and domestic production as well as into land that was not integrated into the national and global economy, including remote areas of tropical rainforest.

Globalization and neoliberalism were born in crisis in Latin America. During the "lost decade" of the 1980s, Latin America experienced a rash of debt crises that led to the imposition of structural adjustment policies by the World Bank, the International Monetary Fund, and the Inter-American Development Bank. In return for a restructuring of their crushing foreign debts, a number of Latin American countries were made to diversify and expand export production, open their economies to foreign investment, privatize state-owned industries and infrastructure, reduce the size of their government budgets, and raise prices for previously subsidized basic goods and services. These structural adjustments resulted in significant environmental impacts—including expansion of commercial agricultural production, mineral and petroleum extraction, growth of industrial production and concomitant pollution, road and port construction, promotion of international tourism, and a reduction in protection of the environment and public health due to "downsizing" of governments.

The environmental aspects of the debt crisis and the neoliberal response are closely intertwined with social issues. The expansion of agribusiness into previously remote areas has displaced subsistence farming and generated internal migration in three directions, all with environmental consequences. Many displaced peasant farmers have headed for existing urban slums, hoping to find employment. Others have pushed farther into frontier areas, usually to marginal land of low agricultural potential, but highly vulnerable to ecological degradation. In some cases, new urban centers in agricultural regions have become established as a result of rural unemployment and opportunities in agricultural processing, transportation, and services.

Throughout Latin America, the last two decades of the twentieth century also witnessed the resurgence of a fragile democracy. As authoritarian governments were forced out of office and democratic structures became established, civil society began to assert itself. New social movements arose throughout the region. Grassroots organizations focusing on local environmental issues sprang up all over Latin America, sometimes—although not often enough—successfully pressuring governments to reduce environmental hazards. Some of the hundreds of local civil society organizations in Latin America linked up with international organizations to protest globalization in its many manifestations, thus demonstrating connections between the local and the global under economic globalization. They also reveal the uneven nature of globalization. Economic activity has become globalized while social and environmental issues remain primarily local or national—or are perceived as such. Environmental regulation remains confined almost entirely to the national level, limiting its effectiveness in confronting global capital (Roberts and Thanos 2003). In the third decade of the twenty-first century, some countries in Latin America are experiencing a troubling resurgence of authoritarianism and anti-environmentalism, with dire consequences for the region's Indigenous people and remaining protected areas. The following sections illustrate how global processes play out at the local or regional scale in contemporary Latin America.

Resource Extraction: Mining and Petroleum Production
Latin America has supplied valuable minerals to the world since the Spanish discovered gold and silver there in the sixteenth century. As McKinney discusses in Chapter 6, with the advent of the industrial revolution in Europe, markets for industrial minerals began to grow. In the nineteenth century, Chile became the world's leading copper exporter. In turn, other Latin American countries began to export tin, bauxite (aluminum ore), iron, nitrates, and phosphates. The methods of extraction, production, and transport of these commodities in the past were usually controlled by foreign companies that paid little attention to the environmental consequences of their actions. And now, where environmental regulations exist, governments frequently choose not to enforce them in order to maintain a good business climate for foreign investors. This situation continues even though most countries have asserted ownership of their natural resources and, in many cases, of the corresponding corporations that control them.

In the twentieth century, petroleum was discovered in Mexico, Venezuela, and the Ecuadorian Amazon, and most recently along the coast of Brazil. The exploration and extraction of petroleum in Latin America has been associated with environmental damage and disruption of the lives of Indigenous communities in forested areas. First, the roads built by exploration teams opened up previously remote regions to colonization by land-hungry peasants. The resulting deforestation destroyed the livelihoods of Indigenous populations. Second, oil drilling inevitably led to spills that have contaminated land and water. In some areas fires have raged out of control for weeks, causing serious air pollution as well as destruction of any remaining forest near the burning well. In 1979, an enormous blowout of an exploratory well in the southern Gulf of Mexico emitted an estimated 140 million gallons of oil, creating a river of petroleum that flowed for many months. It moved up the Mexican coast, wreaking havoc on both aquatic and coastal ecosystems and even contaminated the coast of Texas before being brought under control. The transport of oil by pipeline and tankers has inevitably entailed leakage that pollutes aquatic and terrestrial ecosystems on a regular, albeit less spectacular, basis.

The Brazilian state of Minas Gerais suffered devastating catastrophes when the retaining dams of two iron ore mines collapsed and released millions of cubic meters of sludge in 2015 and in 2019. In the first event, the hamlet of Bento Rodrigues near the town of Mariana was destroyed and over a dozen workers were killed. The Rio Doce was irreversibly damaged along its 300-mile journey to the Atlantic Ocean. In the second disaster, a worker canteen and surrounding neighborhoods in the municipality of Brumadinho were buried and 272 people killed. The Brazilian conglomerate Vale S.A. was sole owner of the mine involved in the latter disaster and was co-owner with Anglo-Australian BHP in the former (Aleixo and Cequeira 2020). It has yet to answer fully and to the satisfaction of the families of people killed.

Latin American governments, eager for the employment and foreign exchange provided by resource extraction companies, hesitate to impose stringent environmental regulations on them. Foreign corporations may seek to locate companies in Latin America because environmental controls are less rigorous than in the United States or Europe, thus reducing production costs. Nationalized companies, such as Mexico's Petróleos Mexicanos (PEMEX) and Ecuador's Petroecuador, have been notorious for corruption and inefficiency, tendencies that have extended to their environmental policies. All of these factors have conspired to create a dismal record of environmental degradation and public health nightmares in oil- and mineral-rich parts of Latin America.

Deforestation: Causes and Consequences

Despite several decades of worldwide concern over saving the rainforest, Latin America's forests continue to disappear at a rapid rate. The causes are structural: expansion of commercial agricultural production, mineral and petroleum extraction (largely to supply increasing consumer demand in the affluent global North), inequitable domestic economic and social systems, and moderate to high rates of population growth, especially between 1950 and 1980. On the surface, the most obvious threat to forests appears to be the stream of poor migrants following newly built roads into the remaining wild areas in the tropical lowlands of southern Mexico, Central America, and the Amazon Basin (including parts of Brazil, Bolivia, Peru, Ecuador, Colombia, and Venezuela). Large-scale commercial farmers and ranchers often follow closely behind, consolidating the small farms cleared by the pioneers. Although the forests may be cleared by the rural poor, the land often ultimately goes into commercial production, following a decline in soil fertility after the first few years of traditional farming. The poor farmers move on, clearing more forest on the new agricultural frontier while the commercial farms that replace them apply agrochemicals to compensate for the loss of soil fertility. Forest clearance serves the interests of multiple constituencies, including the landless poor; commercial timber, ranching, and agriculture; the politicians who need constituents' votes; and the international lending institutions and commercial interests that demand export production. For these reasons, it is not surprising that environmentalists' warnings about the consequences of deforestation have had such limited effect.

Scientists, environmentalists, and forest dwellers have identified a number of important ecological problems caused by the destruction of tropical rainforests. These include loss of biodiversity, degradation of the soil, climate change, and changes in the local (and possibly regional) water cycle. Studies in the Amazon Basin have shown that precipitation has declined in areas downwind of large deforested areas. Areas that have been denuded also experience increases in flooding during the rainy season and drought stress during the dry season. Deforestation eliminates subsistence resources, including construction materials, firewood, medicinal plants, and protein from wild game upon which people have traditionally depended. Furthermore, previously isolated tribes now find themselves under pressure from development interests, settlers, miners, and oil workers.

Land conflicts between forest people and these groups are escalating. On the Pacific Coast of Colombia, for example, traditional Afro-Colombian populations have been displaced due to conflicts over land and resources. Immediately after they received legal rights to communal landownership in the mid-1990s, armed groups swept in and appropriated their land by force. As a result, entire communities have been moved to refugee settlements while contending groups vie for control over the region and its resources.

In Brazil, Peru, Ecuador, and Colombia, Indigenous groups of the Amazon have succeeded in gaining some legal autonomy and protection of their territories. In Brazil, large expanses of rainforest have been set aside as extractive reserves to protect the resource base of traditional Amazonian populations such as rubber tappers and Brazil nut harvesters. Traditional forest dwellers must sometimes contend with the perception by conservationists that human habitation causes deforestation when in fact human forest dwellers have sustained tropical forests for millennia. However, the more enlightened achievements by forest peoples and their advocates in the Brazilian Amazon have been demeaned and attacked by Brazil's nationalist right-wing president, Jair Bolsonaro, who was elected in 2018 (Rapozo 2021; Surma 2021).

Coastal Development

A special type of forest ecosystem, mangrove swamps, has come under severe pressure in recent decades from global demand for shrimp, lobster, and fish, and from tourist development. Mangroves are specially adapted forests that grow in tropical estuaries and provide many ecological services. They prevent erosion of shorelines and provide protection during hurricanes and tropical storms. They help to break down organic matter deposited by rivers, serving as natural sewage treatment plants. They also provide essential habitat for marine organisms that spawn in estuaries, thus playing an important role in sustaining offshore fisheries.

One of the economically important species that depends on mangrove ecosystems is shrimp, which surpassed tuna to become the number one seafood in the United States in 2001. Shrimp farming emerged as a new industry in the 1980s and 1990s in response to escalating demand from North America and Japan, in conjunction with Latin America's need to diversify and expand exports.

Traditionally, shrimp fishing was a small-scale activity of coastal residents in the American tropics. It was often part of a complex and sustainable livelihood strategy, based on the productivity of natural ecosystems and including other types of fishing and farming on coastal plains. Such livelihood strategies helped preserve the mangrove forests and the health of coastal ecosystems in Latin America.

Industrial shrimp farming requires the destruction of natural mangrove forests, replacing them with artificial ponds and canals. Shrimp farming requires large amounts of artificial nutrients, pesticides, antibiotics, and freshwater, in addition to the natural saltwater. Shrimp excrement joins these substances in the outflow from the shrimp farms. Ponds eventually choke on their own waste and go out of production after a decade or so. They leave behind a devastated environment that is unable to produce wild shrimp. Small-scale traditional fishermen do not fit into this system, which destroys virtually all aspects of their livelihoods. Therefore, many fishing villages have mobilized to oppose the development of shrimp farms. Conflicts with the authorities in Guatemala and Honduras over shrimp farming have been less successful and more violent than in southern Mexico, where small-scale fishermen have kept shrimp farms out of some villages.

Another boom, international tourism, has become a pillar of the coastal economies, most notably in Mexico, Central America, and the Caribbean. In this region, governments strongly encouraged tourism-based development, taking advantage of their tropical climates and spectacular beaches as well as close proximity to the affluent North American market. Creation of tourist enclaves like Cancún and Zihuatanejo in Mexico destroyed mangroves and the fishing villages that depended on them, resulting in substantial displacement of inhabitants and elimination of their systems of livelihood. Over the long run, international tourism generates little employment for local people, other than poorly paid, often seasonal, menial jobs such as chambermaiding and gardening. In addition to its economic impacts on local residents, real estate development for tourism has caused considerable environmental degradation such as deforestation and accelerated erosion due to site development and home construction.

Expansion of Export Agriculture and Industrial Livestock Production

The environmental and social consequences of large-scale commercial agriculture and livestock production include deforestation and accelerated erosion as well as degradation of the soil; pollution of the soil, waterways, and surrounding ecosystems by agricultural chemicals; declining biodiversity of both wild and agroecosystems; the spread of genetically modified organisms (GMOs); and the emergence of new diseases such as swine flu.

The spread of chemical farming has not occurred without controversy and resistance by the people suffering its negative consequences. Chemicals banned from use in the United States are routinely exported and used in Latin American fields. Pesticide poisoning of farm workers has been widely publicized, and a few cases have actually gone to the courts (Wright 2005). For example, dibromochloropropane was banned in the United States because it caused sterility in Dow Chemical workers but continued to be used on bananas in Central America and Ecuador in the 1970s and early 1980s. In 1992 about a thousand Costa Rican workers received monetary settlements, and other workers' cases continued to be litigated throughout the 1990s and beyond. Eventually, 16,000 workers in Latin America who had become sterile (out of an estimated 100,000 worldwide) signed on to a lawsuit that was heard in Texas courts.

By the end of the twentieth century, biotechnology was being applied to crops, in part to reduce the need to use dangerous pesticides. The introduction of GMOs has been controversial for a number of reasons, including their potential contamination of traditional crops. In 2001, GMO-contaminated maize (corn) was discovered in a remote area of Mexico. This region is an important center of biodiversity because it was one of the places where maize was domesticated and is still a zone of traditional peasant farming that is based on the cultivation of a wide range of maize varieties. The large maize gene pool found in this area is considered an ecological treasure, but its future is uncertain. If peasant fields become contaminated with GMOs, traditional varieties may be lost forever and, with them, unique genetic material that humans may need in the future. The GMO controversy has become a worldwide concern and is part of the antiglobalization movement of the early twenty-first century, demonstrating the linkage of local civil society organizations with global movements.

Climate Change

It is difficult to generalize about the effects of climate change in Latin America. Its size and diversity will bring huge variations in the challenges it faces (Mata and Campos 2018). As already noted, deforestation has resulted from the region's economic development strategies. The degradation of the world's largest carbon sink and source of evapotranspiration (water cycle) is both a cause and an effect of climate disruption that will affect the entire planet. The human consequences of climate change are already manifest through displacement, disease, and income declines. Rapid urbanization and globalized extraction and production have driven emissions higher, even though Latin America's contribution to world emissions is only 5 percent. Efforts at reduction of greenhouse gases in Mexico, Brazil, and Argentina are wide of the target set by the Paris Agreement, to which they are signatories.

Droughts have diminished agricultural yields and decreased the amount of productive land. Declining agricultural systems, along with extreme weather, have been linked to increased outmigration from Central America and Puerto Rico. While some areas are experiencing drought, others suffer excessive precipitation, especially in the form of hurricanes, which have devastated many communities in Central America and the Caribbean, with back-to-back events now commonplace.

Rising sea levels have dramatically increased the risk of severe flooding and coastal storms on the Pacific Coast (Dunnell 2018). In the Andes Mountains, glacial melt is causing avalanches and mudslides, which in 2017 displaced over 140,000 in just one city (Casey and Zarate

2017). It is feared that these mudslides will eventually wipe out parts of Lima, a city of over 8 million (Collyns 2017). Water shortages are destined to follow the loss of glaciers.

Deforestation in the Amazon rainforest contributes to warming as burned trees release carbon into the atmosphere. About one-fifth of the area has been deforested. Fires set in Brazil's rainforests, especially in the Amazon region, are both cause and effect of climate change. One estimate was that in 2019, the Brazilian Amazon experienced an 85 percent increase in fires over one year. Farmers and ranchers (small and large) as well as Indigenous people have always practiced seasonal burning, but a convergence of increased deforestation, drought, and warming has made fires exceptionally dangerous in recent years. President Bolsonaro campaigned in Brazil on an anti-environmentalist and "ruralista" platform and has chided the international community for its concerns and ultimately denied that the forest is in danger. Scientists, however, warn that the Amazon forest is about to reach a point when the damage is no longer reversible (McCoy 2019) and may permanently convert to savannah.

Politics and the Environment

Despite the recent nationalist rhetoric of several of Latin America's leaders, transnational movements and organizations in the region continue to advocate on a number of environmental fronts. In September 2020 the UN Human Rights Council urged Colombia to halt some operations at one of the world's largest coal mines because it has seriously damaged the environment and health of the country's largest Indigenous community and is making Indigenous groups more vulnerable to Covid-19 (Boyd 2020).

The region is at the forefront of an international movement begun in 2020 to create "rights of nature" laws in legislatures and courts. At that time, fourteen countries had adopted such laws. Influenced by Indigenous thought, residents can sue on behalf of jungles, rivers, and reefs for harm perpetrated against local ecosystems. The movement is expected to grow over time, though there are strong populist and corporate interests in opposition.

Population: Distribution, Fertility, and Mortality

Intuitively, people often blame environmental and social problems on "overpopulation" rather than on the resource destruction caused by commercial interests and development schemes. Environmental degradation and climate change associated with extraction are more directly related to global markets than to internal demand driven by population

Small family size is the norm; advertisement for a pharmacy in Goiânia, Brazil. Credit: Jacquelyn Chase

growth. For example, only about one-quarter of deforestation in the Brazilian Amazon can be traced to land-hungry peasants clearing land today. Likewise, the pollution of air, water, and land in cities where the majority of Latin Americans live is as much a reflection of unequal development as it is a result of population growth.

Latin America has taken the lead in the developing world by dramatically reversing historically high fertility rates, and this transition toward smaller families strongly correlates with urbanization. On the other hand, urbanization makes manufactured goods and processed foods an integral part of daily life, and it raises the aspirations of people for greater consumption of these commercial products.

Demographic Transition

For the first decades of the twentieth century, a combination of continued high fertility along with mortality declines led to very rapid population growth. Infant mortality and life expectancy have steadily improved for the region. Infant mortality has declined from 126 deaths per 1,000 births in 1950 to 14 in 2019 (United Nations 2020b). Life expectancy has grown from fifty-one to an average of seventy-five years of age for both sexes (United Nations 2020c).

Although population in the region continues to grow, the momentum of that growth has slowed considerably. For example, population doubling time decreased from twenty-five to seventy-five years from 1960 to 2019. Latin American fertility has fallen to a point where the actual rate of natural growth is in decline. The annual growth rate peaked in the 1960s at 2.8 percent. Recent estimates show remarkable convergence: the region as a whole has a growth rate of 0.93 percent a year, and no country has a rate of over 1.9 percent. The growth rates of Cuba, Puerto Rico, Venezuela, and Curaçao are at zero or below zero (World Bank 2020a).

The demographic transition model implies that the interplay between numbers of deaths and births and growth rates roughly follows a predictable path as societies modernize and urbanize. Even though Latin America as a whole appears to be following the model, each country and subregion does so in a unique way and there is no guarantee that present patterns will hold. Under impoverished circumstances, people may choose to have fewer children out of desperation rather than because they have arrived at a new level of well-being. Many of the region's poorest people, in fact, suffer from diseases that are completely preventable, and women still suffer from lack of access to family planning.

Fertility Change

As Susan Tiano and Michael Shea show in Chapter 10, Latin America has experienced enormous declines in fertility in recent decades. The fertility rate is based on the average number of children a woman will bear throughout her lifetime. Fertility in Latin America fell from 6.0 to 2.5 children per woman between 1960 and 2000 and to 2.03 by 2018, which is below replacement fertility.

A combination of factors worked together to make the fertility decline one of the most extreme examples of social change in the past two generations. These included the women's movement, reproductive technologies, urbanization, increased access to higher education, and expectations by ordinary working people for a better life. International organizations such as Zero Population Growth and Planned Parenthood have been active in Latin America, although official policy on population growth is ambiguous, in part because of the enduring influence of the Catholic Church in most countries. Despite opposition from the church, sterilization has become the most sought-after form of birth control by women, to the point where supply of this procedure runs far behind demand in many countries. Abortion, although illegal in every country except Cuba, Guyana, Uruguay, and Argentina, has played an important role in the precipitous decline in Latin American fertility rates. An estimated 6.5 million abortions occurred in Latin America each year between 2010 and 2014 (Guttmacher Institute 2018). This represents about one abortion per three live births and is an indication of unmet need in the region for contraception.

The rise of urban middle-class consumerism, promoted by the mass media, has given Latin Americans the sense that only small families are compatible with wealth. *Telenovelas* (soap operas) typically place small, rich, white families at the center of their plot lines. Having fewer children may give a working family the ability to reach a more humane standard of living. However, rising standards of living also put mounting pressures on resources as people come to expect private vehicles, electronic goods, better housing, and a diet high in meat and processed foods. Most people, however, do not attain middle-class status as a result of lowering their fertility. Rather, as the lives of female breadwinners become a complex mix of part-time, short-term, and irregular employment, having fewer children has become a strategy for women who must work harder and longer to survive.

Health, Morbidity, and Mortality

In Latin America, death rates have declined dramatically with modern urbanization and accompanying advances in water and sewage treatment and vaccination for childhood diseases. Many diseases or conditions that can kill young children, such as diarrhea, can be traced to polluted water. The proportion of people with access to safely managed drinking water is now 74 percent in the region as a whole, with higher rates in cities than in rural areas (82 versus 42 percent).

As cities become megacities, the effects on water supply are contradictory. Population increase, urban sprawl, and industrialization place huge stresses on water supplies and waste treatment. At the same time, because governments concentrate infrastructure in cities, urban dwellers tend to have better access to safe drinking water. These improvements, however, often do not reach the most precarious urban settlements, where extreme population densities contribute to high levels of water contamination. Twenty-four million people living in cities still do not have access to clean water. Construction of sewage treatment facilities lags far behind the delivery of clean water (World Health Organization and UNICEF 2017).

Water shortage and inequities are also a result of climate change, wasteful export-oriented agriculture, and megaprojects that service urban and industrial priorities. Chile is one of the world's top exporters of avocados. In the province of Petorca, each avocado tree uses more water per day than the quota set aside for each resident. The province declared a water emergency in 2019. Water delivered by tanker trucks since 2016 was said to cause diarrhea. Water supplies are also diverted to energy production. In a situation of diminished water supply, projects such as the Alto Maipo Hydroelectric Project in the Andes Mountains exacerbate the situation for rural inhabitants in Chile. The project is set to generate electricity for the capital city of Santiago by diverting the three main tributaries of the Maipo River through some 67 kilometers of tunnels (United Nations 2020a).

Because of these inequities, the decline of many chronic diseases of environmental origin has been inconsistent. Some recent epidemics such as Zika and Covid-19 can be traced to deteriorating conditions in cities together with precarious settlement in frontier areas alongside increased regional, national, and international mobility. The persistence of tropical diseases, like cholera, Chagas, malaria, yellow fever, and dengue, are dependent on environmental conditions close to home such as poor drainage, lack of sewage treatment, polluted water supplies, inadequate trash collection, lack of window screens and mosquito netting, and building materials that harbor insect vectors. Migration into tropical lowland areas and the environmental consequences of settlement in makeshift boomtowns with little medical assistance, public health education, or planning have led to the resurgence of malaria, especially among those without the resources to purchase individual protection (screens, netting, and quinine treatment).

Novel disease outbreaks have had devastating effects on the poor of Latin America as well. In 2009, the emergence of an unusual new form of influenza A in Mexico spawned fear of a global pandemic of the swine flu. The virus incubated in a densely packed, unsanitary, industrial pig farm in the state of Veracruz. The factory farm was a joint venture involving a giant US firm under the provisions of the North American Free Trade Agreement. This joint venture allowed the US firm to raise and slaughter almost a million pigs a year under much less stringent environmental and labor regulations than in the United States. The globalization of agribusiness created the conditions for the emergence of this new variant of swine flu, much like the emergence of the avian flu a few years earlier in factory farms in Southeast Asia.

In 2016, Zika was declared a public emergency (UNDP 2017). Between 60 and 217 million symptomatic and asymptomatic people were infected between 2015 and 2017 in Latin America. The virus is spread through a mosquito vector that thrives in poor neighborhoods. Its association with birth defects (microcephaly) and neurological problems in adults makes the disease a factor in the long-term well-being of people and of the periurban communities where the disease was most prevalent.

Poor young women pregnant with their first child were the most likely to suffer from complications leading to congenital Zika syndrome.

These outbreaks are dwarfed by the novel coronavirus pandemic since 2020. North and South America were the two leading regions in the world for the most cases in the first nine months of the pandemic in 2020. As occurred with many populist leaders like Trump, Putin of Russia, and Orban of Hungary, Brazil's government response to Covid-19 under President Bolsonaro was particularly disorganized. Bolsonaro downplayed the significance of the disease and touted unproven treatments such as the use of hydroxychloroquine as well as phony miracle cures. Personalist regimes in Latin America led by individuals who demanded loyalty above institutional expertise, such as Bolsonaro in Brazil, López in Mexico, Maduro in Venezuela, and Ortega in Nicaragua, responded chaotically to the pandemic.

Early in the pandemic, the Amazon region, particularly the provincial capital of Manaus, saw the highest outbreaks in the country. Given their heightened susceptibility to the disease, Indigenous people are at risk of losing their culture and language as the pandemic rages through their communities (PAHO 2020).

The pandemic's effects on forest people and the urban poor are related to the centuries-old patterns of extraction, urbanization, and unequal development discussed in this chapter. Indigenous people have faced relentless and continued pressure to yield land and resources to settlers, national development projects, and corporations. This has exposed them to disease, cultural erosion, and economic exploitation. The extractive model has supported unequal development whereby a global elite living in capital cities have access to the most sophisticated medical interventions while the poor succumb to the virus while waiting for beds in public hospitals.

Rio de Janeiro's *favelas* (slums) are highly susceptible to the infection. Community transmission in slums results from historical neglect of the public sector, insufficient water supplies, limited resources, dense living conditions, poor access to information, the inability to forgo work, insufficient access to testing and medical care, high comorbidity, and other factors. Nowhere is the city of Rio de Janeiro collecting information by *favela,* even though 24 percent of the city's population lives in some thousand *favela* neighborhoods. In one *favela* it was estimated that an astonishing 25 percent of the community had been infected by the novel coronavirus as of mid-2020 (Reeves 2020). Covid-19 was, at the end of 2020, the leading cause of death in five Latin American countries—Peru, Brazil, Chile, Ecuador, and Panama (Beaubien 2020a).

Violence is another prominent cause of death that varies by where and how people live. Youth homicide deaths rank highest in the world for five Latin American and Caribbean nations, according to the UN Educational, Scientific, and Cultural Organization (UNESCO 2010). Brazil is at the top of this list, with an average annual rate of fifty-five violent deaths per 100,000 people between the ages of fifteen and twenty-four, followed by Colombia, the Virgin Islands, El Salvador, and Venezuela. In Brazil, firearms killed 46 out of 100,000 youth in 2003, a 400 percent increase since 1979. Of the world's top ten nations in deaths by firearms, there were nine Latin American countries (led by Venezuela and Brazil), and the United States. California gangs have appeared among El Salvador's repatriated population, contributing to that country's high rate of youth homicide. Turf wars over the drug trade in urban squatter settlements take a disproportionate share of young lives in all countries. Across the region, young people and their advocates promote alternatives to violence through community-based projects such as the celebrated Afro-Reggae movement in Rio de Janeiro's *favelas,* and national movements that focus on the rights of working children and youth in Peru and Nicaragua.

For Latin America as a whole there is nothing that guarantees that the recent drop in fertility will bring improvements to the environment and society. Alternatively, no one can predict with certainty that a stable population, at 700 million or 900 million, will bring calamity beyond that which many people already suffer in their everyday lives. What we can predict is that most people will experience environmental, social, and economic change from the vantage point of cities, as the region has become overwhelmingly urban. Today 80 percent of the 652 million people across Latin America live in cities and towns. Argentina, Chile, and Uruguay each have more than 90 percent of their population in cities.

Displacement and Immigration

Emigration to the United States has long been an individual response by Latin Americans seeking job opportunities and a better life. This has had substantial impacts on Mexico's own population. By 2005, 10 percent of Mexico's population was living in the United States, and that total was even higher for people of prime working age, thirty to forty-four. By the late 2010s, a number of factors conspired to nearly end net migration from Mexico to the United States, including the economic crisis in the United States, rising incomes in Mexico, the return migration of over a million Mexicans, and tightened border restrictions. By 2011 the numbers of Mexican-born in the United States had stabilized at around 12 million (Passel, Cohn, and Gonzalez-Barrera 2012).

As net migration from Mexico has fallen to zero, economic and political crises in Central America have driven people north. The majority of people awaiting asylum along the Mexican border are from Honduras, Guatemala, and El Salvador. Other regions in the Americas are facing their own crises. The displacement of over 4 million Venezuelans (over 15 percent of the country's population) has made Venezuela the only one in the region with a shrinking population. Since 2014, Peru and Colombia have seen the arrival of millions of displaced Venezuelans and closed their borders to immigrants as the crisis endured into 2020. Haitians are another group who, after the 2010 earthquake, poured into South America and other Caribbean countries looking for opportunities (INURED 2020).

Urbanization in Latin America

Industrialization and accompanying urbanization also carry environmental consequences. Industry never successfully absorbed the majority of new urban residents into the labor force, and the service sector far outnumbers manufacturing as a source of employment. But cities continue to bear the mark of rapid industrialization in their patterns of growth, congestion, and pollution. During the import substitution era (1930s to 1970s), governments promoted heavy industries that created environmental impacts such as air and water pollution. Authoritarian regimes ignored the environmental and public health costs of industrialization, as exemplified by Cubatão, an industrial city near São Paulo, Brazil. It was once dubbed the "Valley of Death" due to the concentration of petrochemical industries there. Toxic emissions from Cubatão's industries have led to elevated incidences of cancer, birth defects, and other health problems among its population. Efforts to vastly reduce pollution levels have succeeded, but it remains one of the most polluted cities in Latin America.

Poorly regulated industries also make residents of industrial cities vulnerable to disasters. For example, in 1984 a large petrochemical plant exploded in the densely populated Mexico City metropolitan area, killing over 2,000, injuring 4,200, and displacing over 200,000 people. Cubatão suffered a fire from a gas leak in the same year that killed hundreds of people in the *favela* Vila Socó. As these two examples demonstrate, the poor are usually the first to be victimized by urban ecological disasters.

Latin America has become one of the most urbanized of all the world's regions, not only due to the pull of jobs, but also because the standard of living in rural areas has lagged significantly behind that of urban areas. Agricultural strategies favoring exports and land monopolies that date back to the colonial period were instrumental in forcing

Central pivot agriculture, Goiás, Brazil.

landless people to leave the countryside from the early twentieth century on. Later, industrialization of agriculture dispossessed large numbers of peasant farmers, and many migrated to urban areas in search of employment. Industrial programs provided a "pull" factor toward the primary cities, which received the most investment.

Although the rate of urbanization varies from country to country, the shift from rural to urban society has been swift and overwhelming. Five decades ago, the majority of Latin Americans lived in the countryside. Today, only about one-fifth of the population is rural. The speed of this transition has made the "urban problem" a key theme in Latin American society. The tendency to perceive rapid urbanization as an invasion by impoverished migrants has deep historical roots dating back to the colonial period.

The fact that most towns were small through most of Latin American history belied their importance as political, military, religious, and economic centers during and after colonialism. With the blessing of their rulers back home, the colonial elite quickly sought to establish towns as bases from which they could obtain resources from their rural hinterlands. In Spanish America, the location of colonial towns was often closely tied to mineral sources and to pre-Columbian settlements. Potosí, founded in 1546 in the Cerro Rico of southern Bolivia, was a notorious example. This city served the excavation and mining site of the world's largest silver deposit. It administered political, ecclesiastical, and economic control of surrounding Indigenous communities, who eventually succumbed to the brutal *mita* system of forced labor. Potosí at one time had 200,000 inhabitants and was the region's largest city.

Coastal settlements supported the plantation economies in Portuguese America and the Caribbean, whereas the deep interior of Portuguese America remained relatively devoid of European settlement for the first century of the conquest. In contrast with the Spanish, Portuguese colonists settled into vast rural dominions, mostly within a few hundred miles of the coast. Along the coast emerged cities such as Rio de Janeiro and Salvador da Bahia that served the trade in minerals, sugar, slaves, and luxury goods. Other towns grew around the need to protect the coastline, such as Fortaleza and Belém. This pattern of coastal urbanization held until the eighteenth century, when the discovery of gold and diamonds gave rise to distant mining towns, such as Vila Rica (Ouro Preto) and Diamantina, both in the state of Minas Gerais. Although this introduced urbanization to the interior of Portuguese America, it also reinforced urbanization along the coast as trade in minerals increased.

As noted earlier, increased urbanization in Latin America was closely associated with governments' efforts to modernize and industrialize in the early to middle twentieth century. Between 1950 and 1960, over 1 million people moved to Mexico City. The following decade, the population rose by 3.5 million, and by 2000 the city was gaining about 6 million more people per decade. By 2004, Mexico City had become one of the world's largest cities. The population of São Paulo almost doubled between 1950 and 1960, growing from 2.3 million to 4.4 million, at a time when wealth generated by coffee in the surrounding region was subsidizing industry and commerce but not supporting small farmers' ability to stay in the countryside. In 2018, São Paulo's population was almost 13 million and the metropolitan area was home to over 20 million.

A signature of urbanization in Latin America and the Caribbean is its "urban primacy," which is the tendency for a large percentage of a country's urban population to live in one or two major cities. For example, over 30 percent of all Chileans, Argentines, and Uruguayans live in their countries' largest metropolitan areas (which also happen to be their capital cities). There has been some redistribution of this urbanization with the rapid growth of smaller cities, but this has not changed the fact that the region's largest cities have become sprawling mega-regions that continue to grow vertiginously.

Migration rates from the 1950s onward overwhelmed housing markets. This, together with people's tenacity for survival and social mobility, has led to squatter settlements, emblematic of the region's rapid urban growth. Zoning, affordable housing, and infrastructure have lagged miserably behind urban growth. As a result, poor people often resort to self-built shelters or doubling-up with relatives. In many Latin American cities, one-third to one-half of the people live in settlements with makeshift housing and substandard services. It is estimated that 60 percent of the population in Mexico City live in some form of substandard or squatter settlement. One of the most famous of these *barrios,* Netzahualcoyotl (Neza), is a veritable city in its own right, home to some 2 million inhabitants. Neza began with squatters occupying the dry lakebed surrounding Mexico City some five decades ago. The residents themselves gradually transformed their shacks into concrete block and stucco homes and successfully fought for basic city services. Squatter settlements not only reflect governments' inability to address urbanization, but also illustrate people's self-reliance and determination to survive. While many people are too poor to pay rent or buy a home, they quickly develop collective and individual strategies for survival. Squatter settlements have been incredibly innovative in devising collective strategies for education, recreation, and job creation. Second- and third-generation squatters have transformed their shantytowns into cities within cities, with a mix of public and private infrastructure, permanent and improved housing, commerce, cultural production, and social differentiation. As these settlements run out of land, they grow skyward as people add new levels onto existing homes.

Urban officials and politicians approached the enormous population influx in different ways. One response was outright slum removal, an approach favored by military dictatorships in the 1960s and 1970s. These forced evictions mostly ended with the return of democracy across Latin America. With such a huge constituency of voting citizens, politicians feared the results of direct confrontation. Self-help housing also subsidized the provision of housing and services in the region's exploding cities through "sweat equity." Because squatter settlements were often on government-owned land, they did not typically set off a confrontation over private property. In the late 1990s and beyond, governments quickened the provision of basic amenities to squatters, but they also have put in place more rigorous environmental zoning. These two tendencies have led to a more restrictive governmental attitude toward urban squatters as well as a limited market for low-income housing. The verticalization of shantytowns has increased the supply of housing and contributed to a rental market in Latin American slums.

Illegal economies, rooted in the international drug trade, quasigovernmental structures, and informal "police" forces, have emerged in the sprawling slums of all Latin American cities. These have become staging grounds for violent rivalries between powerful drug lords and sometimes corrupt government security forces while the majority of the people who live in them attempt to go about their daily lives in peace. Neoliberal economic policies, especially fiscal austerity, have resulted in budget cuts to social programs and to the privatization of water, sanitation, and health services.

Tangled traffic, overburdened sewage systems, noise, and loss of sunlight are some of the outcomes of the spread of the urban core into firsttier suburbs. In search of security and comfort, urban elites have turned to high-rise security towers in the city or to gated communities on the ruralurban fringe. Insufficient environmental oversight has allowed speculators to create notoriously illegal subdivisions that attract rich and middleincome squatters, whose ability to manipulate the judicial systems virtually guarantees the endorsement of their property claims. Their search for security has also produced luxurious shopping centers that have replaced the town plaza as the icon of Latin American leisure and public life.

Unemployment and the struggle for urban livelihoods are associated with many urban environmental problems. Poverty and the informal economy, estimated at 55 percent of jobs by the World Economic Forum of Latin America in 2018, send people into dangerous environments, such as trash heaps and flood zones, that operate below the radar of environmental regulation (International Labour Organization 2018). Lackadaisical waste disposal standards tragically introduced urban trash pickers to the atomic age in the Brazilian city of Goiania in 1987. People who made a living recycling trash took an x-ray cylinder containing cesium-137 from an abandoned hospital and dismantled it at home. Fascinated by its glow, they showed the substance off, passing it around and playing with it. Four people died one month later, many hundreds became ill, and some died years later from cancer. Investigators found waste from the incident over a thousand miles away. On the other hand, grassroots initiatives in major cities have worked to support trash recyclers' access to protective equipment and to fair prices for recycled materials.

In order to reduce environmental and political pressures on the largest cities, government officials and planners have tried to decentralize urban

Trash collector, Goiania, Brazil. Credit: Jacquelyn Chase

growth by encouraging the growth of smaller cities. Other motivations, such as occupation of the interior and political symbolism, have also come into play in these efforts. The construction of Brasília in Brazil and Ciudad Guyana in Venezuela were bold attempts to build cities from the ground up. While these efforts succeeded in creating new pockets of settlement away from the traditional urban cores, this did not slow the galloping growth of cities that were already large when these new towns were constructed, and new towns have become sprawling metropoles. Built in the late 1950s, Brasília has graduated to a metropolitan area with over 4 million people in 2020. Even though the new cities were built with strong planning ideals, they have succumbed to many of the same problems of older cities such as squatters living in shantytowns, chronic pollution, sprawl, violence, and heavy traffic.

Some urban decentralization has occurred as an unintended consequence of regional economic policies, such as export processing zones in the Caribbean Basin, border industrialization in Mexico, frontier occupation in the Amazonian portion of various countries, and rural development based on nontraditional export crops. During the neoliberal era, previously less industrialized countries, such as those of Central America and the Caribbean Basin, became the target of foreign investment in assembly industries such as clothing and electronics. One of the most spectacular sites of this type of industrialization is along the US-Mexican border. In the last two decades of the twentieth century, thousands of *maquiladoras* (assembly plants) were established in this zone to take advantage of its proximity to the United States. The United States represents the largest consumer market in the world while Mexico provides a huge pool of cheap labor and lax environmental regulations. Hundreds of foreign companies were attracted to a region where these factors literally converge.

The *maquiladora* phenomenon stimulated migration to Mexico's border area. By 1990, there were 3.5 million people in eighteen border cities, 6 percent of the country's total urban population that year. By 2019 the population of the two largest border cities (Tijuana and Ciudad Juárez) alone exceeded 3.4 million and the total population for the top ten surpassed 7 million (see Table 8.1). Border enforcement and policy changes in refugee processing in the United States in 2018 left tens of thousands of Central Americans awaiting their fate in camps and shelters in Mexico's border cities, many of them separated from their families.

Urban infrastructure along the border is inadequate to meet the needs of the rapidly growing population where high rates of poverty and the various types of pollution generated by the *maquiladoras* contribute to a host of environmental miseries. Mexico's unaddressed environmental problems are finally receiving attention from people across the border as smog and raw sewage make their way into the United States.

Another facet of urban growth taking place outside countries' primary cities is boomtown growth in frontier regions. The drug trade, peasant migration, mining, and logging have led to the growth of boomtowns throughout the Amazon Basin (Isacson 2020b). With little infrastructure and sudden increases in an impoverished population, these towns have become sites of diseases such as malaria, yellow fever, dengue, and cholera.

Table 8.1   Population of Select Mexican Border Cities, 2005, 2010, and 2019

	2005	2010	2019 Predicted (millions)
Tijuana	1,392,321	1,641,168	2.100
Ciudad Juárez	1,310,302	1,431,072	1.500
Mexicali	854,879	943,326	1.101
Reynosa	520,358	612,711	0.881
Matamoros	463,995	499,767	0.555
Nuevo Laredo	355,832	395,185	0.440
Nogales	192,625	218,948	0.232
San Luis Río Colorado	158,154	165,661	0.192
Piedras Negras	144,393	156,629	0.165
Ciudad Acuña	126,385	137,634	0.216
Total	5,519,244	6,202,101	7.373

Source: Consejo Nacional de Población 2010.

Export-oriented agriculture has expanded into the rural hinterlands in virtually all countries, as noted earlier. Since the 1980s, this expansion has rested on a whole new set of nontraditional export crops such as soybeans, flowers, oranges for frozen concentrate, and forest products for pulp and paper mills. In most cases, profound changes come to regions that are swept into these new activities. In some contexts, this development attracts former peasants to local towns, where some find work in the service sector and agro-processing. But modern agriculture can also be a factor in population loss. The mechanization of cotton and other crops that were essential to rural livelihoods in Argentina's Chaco province eliminated thousands of jobs, leaving people with no alternative but to migrate to Buenos Aires or to other regional centers.

Urban decentralization of the kind described here has not solved the region's urban problems. More often, the same kinds of urban environmental problems spring up in all cities and towns that are growing rapidly, regardless of their size. Smaller towns, in fact, may have a less active and empowered citizenry to address urban pollution and environmental justice. Creative responses to these problems are indeed coming from some of the region's largest cities. Bogotá, Mexico City, São Paulo, and Santiago all have car-free days and other restrictions in place in an attempt to reduce emissions.

Conclusion

Social and environmental problems persist due to a legacy of grossly unequal distribution of land and wealth and the unsustainable consumption and production that have become synonymous with development. Agricultural, forest, and aquatic systems struggle to keep up with demands stemming in part from population growth but perhaps more from increasing globalization and extreme wealth inequalities that drive conspicuous consumption and corruption. The region's colossal size, divergent histories, and unique physical environments make generalizations impossible. Nonetheless, given the finite nature of Earth's air, water, and land resources, Latin Americans will need to find ways to accommodate the needs of the poor and emerging middle classes alongside production systems that have traditionally favored the affluent. Although each country will devise its own solution to this conundrum, reflecting its unique history and physical endowments, solutions will take place in the shared context of urban consolidation, population stabilization, deeply unequal distribution of income, environmental challenges, and ongoing reliance on global markets.

9

Social, Political, and Cultural Identities

Kevin A. Yelvington

By the 2020s, nationalist populism was rising in Europe, the United States, and Latin America. Populist political and social movements and governing regimes were present in varying degrees and forms at different times in Latin America but had been in abeyance since the military dictatorships of 1964–1989. Right-wing populism is a form of authoritarianism that has manifested anti-immigrant nativism, overt and open racism against domestic groups, and populist nationalism. These right-wing movements, varying in each country in Latin America, were partly the result of the emergence of neoliberalism from the 1970s and 1980s to the end of the twentieth century. Neoliberalism was promoted by the United States and the International Monetary Fund in response to the statist regimes that dominated the military and civilian dictatorships and as part of strategies of capitalist accumulation through globalization. Neoliberalism as a structure of governance attempted privatization of state enterprise, set forth austerity budgets to cut social rather than military spending, and emphasized individual responsibility in the economy. One of the main consequences was increasing income inequality in what was already the most unequal region in the world. The retreat of the state from its social welfare responsibilities and the state's strategic intervention on behalf of businesses and ruling groups entailed faster and greater movement of capital and labor across the globe and deregulated financial markets and instruments, and led to an upward redistribution of wealth. In Latin America, the dislocations and crises wrought by neoliberalism, starting in the 1970s and 1980s, paradoxically provided space for various civil society groups to claim rights and resources on the basis of identity. Limited rights were granted to ethnic and multicultural groups by states and ruling groups insofar as they did not seriously threaten established political and economic regimes. As a result, social movements—including culture- and ethnic-based political groups, some seeking a common cause with similar groups beyond their own national borders—began to challenge the social orders of the past and won collective rights to land, education, and jobs. These trends were seemingly compatible with conservative/center-right and liberal/center-left—and even more radical—politics throughout the region.

But the election in October 2018 of Jair Bolsonaro as president of Brazil marked a leap rightward with tremendous implications for social policies having to do with identity and class politics (Atunes 2019). Contrasting with over a century of representations by politicians and academic commentators alike depicting Brazil as a "racial democracy"— an image of Brazil as devoid of US- and European-style racism that captivated imaginations at home and abroad—and making a direct rebuke of more recent attempts enshrined in the country's laws to redress racism and the structural inequalities that were hidden by the "racial democracy" discourse, Bolsonaro, a former captain of the Brazilian army, professed fan of Brazil's military dictatorship (1964–1985), and member of a right-wing political party, on his very first day in office as president, January 1, 2019, made it a point to halt any new registration of lands for Brazil's hundreds of Indigenous groups and for *quilombolas,* Afro-Brazilian residents of *quilombo* settlements that had been established by escaped slaves during the period of slavery. As well, Bolsonaro severely weakened the power of the National Foundation for the Indian, charged with designating Indigenous lands and nature reserves and advocating for Indigenous rights, and instead backed the interests of businesses involved in ranching, logging, mining, and other extractive industries who wanted access to these protected lands.

The land rights of Indigenous people and of the residents of the *quilombos* were supposed to be guaranteed by Brazil's 1988 constitution. At the time of this challenge, the Brazilian Amazon had extraordinary human diversity represented by its 305 distinct groups; there were said to be around a hundred "uncontacted tribes" in Brazil, more than anywhere else on Earth. But Indigenous groups had started to organize and by this time there were more than 200 Indigenous organizations fighting for their land and civil rights. The *quilombolas* faced similar challenges by rural business interests operating outside the law. During his administration (2003–2010), President Luiz Inácio Lula da Silva (most commonly known simply as "Lula") signed more comprehensive legislation to protect *quilombo* land rights, and this was upheld by the Supreme Court in 2018; more than 15 million *quilombolas* live in these areas, and many of them are very poor. Afro-Brazilian civil rights and political organizations extend well beyond them and into urban areas and formal politics; these social movements have a long and influential history.

The implications of these economic, political, and social developments were critical for Latin America's most populous country, at 212 million people in 2019, and the one that arguably had the largest population of people of African descent in the world after Nigeria, and with an Indigenous population approaching a million people. At this historical juncture, globalization, postmodern neoliberal capitalism, and economic, political, and social restructuring produced evolving conceptions of personal and cultural identity accompanied by changing ideological discourses in twenty-first-century Latin America. Consequently, the politics of ethnicity, racism, class, and nationalism underwent significant transformations (Madrid 2012). It is the goal of this chapter to place those processes within a coherent theoretical and historical framework to understand the current scene.

Defining Key Analytic and Theoretical Concepts

The approach this chapter takes, from the perspective of political economy, understands a society's economic system as a central determining force but shows how it develops historically and how it is connected to colonialism, state formation, political power, social institutions, normative values, and forms of subjectivity at many levels. This process is implicated in the production of social and cultural identities. Along with the social relations that underpin ethnicity, manifestations of racism, class, and nationalism, we must consider not only sets of ideas but ideologies. "Ideology" here refers to systematic representations that tend to serve political and economic class interests. These are discursive representations of political positionings. "Ideology" does not comprise merely political opinions, even if those opinions are widely shared and their correctness is widely agreed upon. Ideologies are produced and reside in societal institutions—ultimately social relationships—and arise in historical situations where they are conveyed and combined with, and sometimes opposed to, other forms of knowledge. Ideologies come to have moral and normative force, evoking emotions as evaluative judgments.

Ethnicity is one such ideology. The word *ethnicity* comes from the Greek word *ethnikos,* deriving from the Greek word *ethnos,* meaning "people." It is used here as a broad term to refer to a sense of "peoplehood," as a designation for both oneself and others. Inherent in this concept is the idea of the members of a group being defined as reflecting some set of common characteristics. Ethnicity entails peoples' theories about the nature and origins of the people in question. Ethnic identification for a particular group depends on a contrast set, where an ethnonym, or name for the ethnic group, exists that indicates there are some other people whom the group is not. Ethnicity comes to be understood in relation to some combination of biological or natural; cultural; and even supernatural, other-worldly, sacred, or spiritual factors.

One kind of ethnicity is what becomes known to members of many societies as "race." As anthropologist Conrad Phillip Kottak writes, "When an ethnic group is assumed to have a biological basis (distinctively shared 'blood' or genes), it is called a race. . . . Discrimination against such a group is called racism. . . . However, race, like ethnicity in general, actually is a *cultural* category rather than a biological reality. That is, 'races' are defined through contrasts perceived and perpetuated in particular societies, rather than from scientific classifications based on common genes" (2017: 111, emphasis in original).[1] The history of the production of the ideology of "race" in the West—and it is a particularly Western ideology and set of ideas—is a long and complicated one, and one that unfortunately was often given force by what was taken to be science in various historical periods. It is an ideology that humankind is naturally divided into significant and divergent physical and biological types, that a whole host of abilities, proclivities, and dispositions to act (that is, "culture") follow from these physical natures and are strongly associated with one or another of these types, that these characteristics can be inherited through biological reproduction, and that, furthermore, there is an inherent hierarchy in these types.

The idea of "race" as a kind of ethnicity emerged and was elaborated upon significantly in the context of European voyages of exploration and colonization of Indigenous peoples and in the context of the Atlantic slave trade and New World slavery. Bodies, physical features, and behavior became "racialized"—meaning not the case of already-existing, actual physical features such as skin color or hair texture or eye shape that are simply noticed and then given cultural meaning. It is, rather, the case that certain physical features and their supposed indication of cultural behaviors and intellectual capacities, and those behaviors themselves, become racialized while others do not. While these ideas were orchestrated in the beginning by elites, they came to infiltrate the consciousness of the masses as well. However, many anthropologists and other scientists through the twentieth century and into the twenty-first demonstrated that "race" as is popularly conceived is a mistaken idea. These scientists have shown that, in fact, humankind cannot be neatly or meaningfully categorized into "races."

Therefore, "race," a particular variant of ethnicity, is, like all kinds of ethnicity, a social and cultural construction. That is, it resides not in nature but in social relations (which entail hierarchies of power relations) and cultural meanings. I want to argue here that because "race" does not refer to a biological entity outside of the racialization process, we should refer instead to *racialized groups*—that is, groups who have been racialized as part of a historical process that reifies, or treats as real, the idea of "race." The cause of racialization is *racism*—systematic and systemic processes of exclusion and discrimination connected to material power relationships. Racism itself involves and depends upon wider historical processes generating inequality, but it in a way presents itself as solely about "race"—"disguising collective social practice as inborn individual traits [and] so it entrenches racism in a category to itself, setting it apart from inequality in other guises. Racism and those other forms of inequality are rarely tackled together because they rarely come into view together," consequently "concealing the affiliation between racism and inequality in general. Separate though they may appear to be, they work together and share a central nervous system" (Fields and Fields 2012: 261). These points are key because even when well-meaning people and policies designed for anti-racism and for the redress of historical wrongs separate racism from the historical processes of political economy that generate multiple inequalities, this serves to leave these structures of inequality in place. This is to reify racism, treating it as an autonomous, transhistorical force existing outside of complex, and multiplex, historically specific social relationships. Ironically, this position reproduces central tenets of racist thought informing racist acts.

This means that racism cannot be explained by the idea of "race" alone, nor can ethnocentrism be explained by the idea of "culture" alone. To do so would be to engage in reductionism—that is, reducing complex realities to one cause and, further, given the theoretical thrust of this chapter, locating identity outside of material forces that structure social relationships. Ethnic identity in its many manifestations is determined in the context of power relations, which are derivative and constitutive of social-class relations. The nineteenth-century German journalist, political activist, and theorist Karl Marx (1818–1883) defined *class* as determined by relations to capitalist society's means of production. Either one was a member of the proletarians (workers), who sold its labor to the capitalist, or one was of the capitalist class (bourgeoisie), who bought the labor of the proletarians to make a profit. Class relations are characterized by conflict, and class depends on a complex process of class formation. But Marx also recognized the emergence and existence of middle classes, as well as other forms of stratification such as racism and sexism that modified class composition. Thus, with respect to ethnicity and other significant social identities such as gender, this is where a definition of class begins rather than ends. This is because it is clear there is a relationship between social and cultural criteria such as ethnicity and gender and class position.

To add to and modify Marx's insights we might follow sociologist Pierre Bourdieu (1986) and differentiate between four kinds of resources or "capital": social capital, or membership in groups (including ethnic groups); cultural capital, or lifestyles, aesthetic tastes, educational qualifications, and linguistic styles; economic capital, meaning the productive property and money one possesses; and symbolic capital, the way in which symbols are used to legitimate the possession of a certain configuration of social, cultural, and economic capital. Those groups with relatively higher levels of capital of all kinds dominate those with fewer such resources. But the multidimensional nature of class status, plus the dimension of ethnicity and nationalism, provide avenues for cross-class alliances as well as, conversely, intraclass conflict based on criteria such as education, tastes, and ethnicity.

Nationalism as an idea and ideology can be traced to the late eighteenth century, at the time of the French and American Revolutions. Nationalism shares much with ideologies such as ethnicity and racialized identities. However, there is a crucial difference. Whereas the discourse of ethnicity, especially in the New World, often relates to the ultimate origins of the group in question and how they supposedly have remained unchanged through time and space, nationalism is an ideology that holds that the culture of a geographically defined territory and the political boundaries of that territory conterminous with a state and governance mechanisms are or ought to be congruent in certain essential ways. In the development of ethnicity, the perpetuation of racism, and the elaboration of nationalism in Latin America, the state plays a central role (Loveman 2014). We can define the state as an ensemble of institutions and policies that are relatively autonomous from civil society but able to monopolize public governance and the distribution of public goods on behalf of certain strata and collectivities. Central here is the organization and management of economies. The modern state plays a key role in creating and enforcing a range of laws that have the effect of supporting capital and defining the population through the granting of legal citizenship and many other functions besides. The modern state's authority comes to be hegemonic—a form of power that is enforced by dominant groups so that subordinate groups assent to the dominant group's rule not so much via naked force as through cultural means. But hegemony is never complete and it is therefore contestable. Thus, even if the state has what is basically a monopoly on power and authority, this does not mean that it is always completely successful in its many and often internally contradictory projects. Nor does it mean that the subjectivities it promotes and authorizes are always consonant with its aims, many that they are.

Nationalism is characterized by what Benedict Anderson (1983) called an "imagined community," where this is not "imagined" as in "dreamed up" or "fictitious" but instead a widely used ideology among group leaders or members. And not "community" in the sense of a small face-to-face society, but rather the idea that physically dispersed members of a nation *could* be somehow alike in fundamental ways and could form a community. Nationalism is seen as giving expression to the politically sovereign nation, ideally embodied in a sovereign political state, which is represented as originating out of an ancient past and providing the guidelines for an optimistic future. The nation is imagined to be a "collective individual" (Handler 1988): bounded and apart, unique, and internally homogeneous in some crucial way. This is inculcated and enforced powerfully in religious-like rituals of state (pledges of allegiance, national anthems, tombs of unknown soldiers). Nationalism is no less contested than ethnicity or racialized identities, especially in Latin America, where manifest ethnic pluralism challenges national ideals of homogeneity (Appelbaum, Macpherson, and Rosemblatt 2003).

The approach outlined here does not assume ahead of time the existence of ethnic groups, racialized groups, ethnic identities, or nations in reality. Instead, it is an approach that conceives of these phenomena as coming into being and transforming as part of structured and structuring sociohistorical processes. The materiality of class power is absolutely fundamental to these processes, and has been historically, where ruling groups developed and continue to develop systems creating difference as part of "divide and rule" strategies.

The system of ethnicity, racism, class, and nationalism in Latin America has been somewhat different from those in North America or Europe (although there have been connections and similarities). When North Americans and Europeans encounter this sociocultural system, they are often incredulous and confused. Even though there are similarities between systems, this reaction further shows how these identities reside not in nature and are therefore not cross-cultural universals, but rather are the result of socioeconomic processes in historical social formations.

Sometimes these systems conflict in very public ways. In October 2011, Uruguyan soccer player Luis Suárez, then playing for Liverpool in the English Premier League, caused a furor when during a heated match with bitter rivals Manchester United he repeatedly called United defender Patrice Evra, a Senegal-born Frenchman, *"negro"* ("black-skinned") during a match. The English Football Association (FA) appointed an independent commission to investigate the incident. Suárez claimed he used the term only once and that was to be conciliatory when Evra became angry at what Evra saw as racist abuse. Suárez said the term did not have racist connotations in Uruguyan Spanish. In his defense, Suárez said he was using *"negro"* in the way he did when growing up in Uruguay, as a friendly form of address to people seen as black- or brown-skinned or even just black-haired. The commission found the argument incredible given the acrimonious context, and Suárez was sentenced to an eight-match ban and fined 40,000 pounds. In his book *Cruzando la línea: mi autobiografía* (*Crossing the Line: My Story*), Suárez (2015) argued, "What some people will never want to accept is that the argument took place in Spanish. I did not use the word '*negro*' the way it can be used in English. Negro can refer to anyone with dark hair as well as dark skin, I've been used to the word being used in Spanish in this way all my life. My wife sometimes calls me '*Negro,*' my grandmother used to call my grandfather '*Negrito*' ["little black one"] and she would occasionally call me that too. I'm not trying to pretend it was meant in a friendly way to Evra because clearly we were arguing. But nor was it ever meant as a racist slur."

Another Uruguyan soccer striker playing in England caused contro-versy and pain in late 2020 with his choice of language. Edinson Cavani had just joined Manchester United the previous month from Paris Saint-Germain when, after a match in which he came off the bench and scored two goals to help his team defeat Southampton, he responded to a friend's congratulatory message on his Instagram account with a post saying *"Gracias negrito"* (literally "Thank you, little black one") with an emoji of two hands clasping. When he was made aware of the connotations of his post in English, Cavani deleted it and issued an apology. After the Premier League put Black Lives Matter on the backs of the shirts of all teams at the start of the 2020–2021 season and when players and refer-ees took a knee before every game during the season to affirm an anti-racist stance, and with a long-standing public commitment to kicking the scourge of racism out of soccer made even more pressing as many Black players had recently been the victims of racist abuse on social

Luis Suárez playing for Liverpool. Credit: https://commons.wikimedia.org/wiki/File :Luis_Su%C3%A1rez_D%C3%ADaz_ (cropped).jpg

Patrice Evra playing for Manchester United. Credit: Gordon Flood, https:// commons.wikimedia.org/wiki/File:Patrice _Evra_2008_(cropped).jpeg

media, the FA found that the comment was "insulting, abusive, improper and brought the game into disrepute," and that it constituted "an 'aggravated breach' . . . as it included reference, whether express or implied, to colour and/or race and/or ethnic origin." The FA sentenced Cavani to a three-match ban going into early 2021 and a fine of 100,000 pounds, and mandated sensitivity training. Cavani pleaded guilty to the charge and chose not to contest the case, according to Manchester United, "out of respect for the FA and the fight against racism in football." Cavani wrote on Instagram, "I want to share with you that I accept the disciplinary sanction knowing that I am foreign to English language customs, but I do not share the point of view. . . . I apologise if I offended someone with an expression of affection towards a friend, nothing further in my intention. Those who know me know that my effort always seeks the simplest joy and friendship!"

Shortly afterward, the Uruguayan Academy of Letters, an association of experts on the use of the Spanish language in Uruguay, harshly criticized the FA decision as a "questionable resolution" as a result of its "poverty of cultural and linguistic knowledge." It was joined by the Argentine Academy of Letters, which issued its own statement. But the reaction of the Uruguayan Players Union was even more scathing; it issued a long statement saying that the FA, "far from condemning racism," had "itself committed a discriminatory act against the culture and way of life of the Uruguayan people." It claimed that Cavani's punishment "shows the English FA's biased, dogmatic and ethnocentric vision," and indicates the FA's "ignorance and disdain for a multicultural vision of the world." Cavani, the players' union claimed, "has never committed any conduct that could be interpreted as racist. He merely used a common expression in Latin America to affectionately address a loved one or close friend."

Notably absent from the controversy were Afro-Uruguyan voices. While some older Afro-Uruguayans who commented on the controversy said they understood the term as one of endearment, members of a younger generation were not all in agreement that the term "*negrito*" was harmless. Uruguyan history professor and activist Lucía Martínez said it should be up to Black people to "determine if that term is affectionate or not" and criticized those white Uruguayans and others "who cannot even have the empathy to put themselves in the place of saying 'I, who am white, am determining if the other can be offended or not.'" An activist with the Uruguayan Antiracist Bloc, Mayra da Silva, said that the word "*negrito*" comes from "a quite painful period such as that of the slave trade." She said that while, in her opinion, "Cavani's intention was not racist," we must also think about what the word historically implied—that is, its use during the time of slavery: "Until it is understood that history and the slave period still affect and affect the Afro-descendant population, that there are real consequences to this day, it will be very difficult to give a real debate, work on the issue and deconstruct some expressions." Thus this issue is far from agreed-upon. What a consideration of these incidents shows is that constructs of identity are implicated in larger structures and processes of historical change.

One key area of difference between the Latin American system of ethnogenesis, the process of a people coming into being and thinking of themselves as a distinct kind of people, and those of other societies is the ideology of *mestizaje,* meaning miscegenation or "race"-mixing, as well as a cultural blending. *Mestizaje* has been described as a "foundational theme in the Americas" (Martínez-Echazábal 1998). I do not consider *mestizaje* to be an objective process, independent from social and cultural processes. To do so would assume that "pure races" exist or existed and are or were therefore actually "mixed" in this process. In other words, it would be to assign a false tangibility to *mestizaje*. Yet in the history of ideas pertaining to ethnicity in Latin America, peoples were indeed presumed to be of pure "types" until after the arrival of the *conquistadores* in the New World. European interaction with the Indigenous peoples, and later with enslaved Africans, began this miscegenation process. *Mestizaje* is coupled with the ideology of *blanqueamiento* ("whitening"), where whiteness is valorized and connected to European-derived culture (Jerry 2013). This kind of associative whiteness, where a number of symbols pregnant with meaning are felicitously fused through a process of identification, is hegemonic. Whiteness historically served as the norm for almost all aesthetic and other evaluative standards. So, terms such as *trigueño* do not necessarily denote a person who is *actually* the color of wheat, but they may be applied to avoid affirming that someone is Indigenous or Black, which, given established hierarchies, in many historical circumstances and places has been considered an insult. In fact, such terms as *trigueño* or *mulatto* may be used rather euphemistically to raise a person's social status; conversely, terms such as *negro* may be applied as insults to others. On the other hand, these can be used as terms of self-definition that explicitly go against the grain of the status quo as part of counter-hegemonic politics. *Blanqueamiento* is a way to talk about a society "improving" through mixture, diluting, as it were, Black and Indian elements. Its historical roots are located in European conquest and what the colonizers saw as manifest miscegenation.

At first glance, the ideas of *mestizaje* and *blanqueamiento* stand in stark contrast to the so-called one-drop rule in the United States whereby a person deemed to have any amount of African ancestry—or "one drop" of "Black blood"—is informally and legally reckoned to be "Black." In North America, traditionally at least, the process of constructing racialized groups through the lens of the concept of hypodescent regards the offspring of a Black person and a white person as Black. To the US cultural and legal rule of hypodescent, where one can only fall from the pinnacle of whiteness, there generally exhibits a contrasting informal Latin American rule, that of hyperdescent, in which is held out the possibility of "race mixing" being able to "improve" upon the "race" of the parents in the offspring. By contrast, throughout Latin America a number of identity positions are deduced from an individual's color, ideas about ancestry, and social status in a system typified by ambiguity and negotiation in assigning individuals to ethnic categories, but where nevertheless higher status is accorded to those who approach what is constructed to be a "white/European" ideal. Here color is seen to play a crucial role in modifying a racialized identity. A strategy for those classified as nonwhites might be to marry someone of a lighter skin color to elevate their status as well as the status of any children, whose skin color, it would be assumed, would be of a lighter shade than that of the darker parent. Equally complex are the relative class positions of *campesinos* (as peasants and rural workers are called in Latin America) and their relation to *hacendados,* as well as the economic conditions of urban *trabajadores* (workers), their *sindicatos* (trade unions), the *jefes* (bosses), and *dueños* (business owners).

Every country in Latin America is divided into elites and masses (Gootenberg and Reygadas 2010). The relative distribution of these basic classes, and the interactions with ethnicity and racism, and their effects, varies in different countries (Hooker and Tillery 2016). Class position is based in one's relation to the means of production either as an owner of those means or as one who is forced to sell their labor. But it is also cultural in the sense that, in practice, it is also based on various criteria such as ethnicity, gender, credentials, education, language, membership in certain families, wealth, and status. Certain cultural aspects of class (e.g., a particular way of speaking or an accent) are more highly valued than others. Highly valued cultural aspects of class tend to coincide with and facilitate higher positions in the economic class structure. However, economic and cultural aspects of class do not completely correspond. This allows us to conceive of a society's class structure as having not only cultural differences within classes, but also cross-class alliances based on a number of different criteria. These can and often do include issues of "culture"—the possession of certain linguistic styles and accents, family ties, education, senses of aesthetics, and so forth, that come to be associated with and entailing ethnicity.

Latin American nationalism draws on the European nationalism that began to take its present form at the end of the eighteenth century. As we will now see in this chapter, in colonial Latin America, the process occurred in a context in which ethnic differences were constructed and cultivated to divide and rule. In the postcolonial era, starting in the early nineteenth century, local elites ingeniously crafted discourses of national identity that, while departing somewhat from the colonial discourses they replaced, nevertheless guaranteed the ascendancy of Western and European ethnic identity and cultural forms, which are seen to be embodied in the elite. But while patterns of nationalism remained relatively constant for a number of years, the situation in twenty-first-century Latin America is rapidly changing.

Colonial Social Formations and the Foundations of Identity Politics

The complex chain of events set in motion with Columbus's arrival in the Caribbean in 1492 is touched on here only as it relates to the theme of this chapter. The processes of ethnogenesis in Latin America are intimately connected to the acts of Europeans creating "others." These were initiated at the very beginning of the European colonization of the Caribbean, with Columbus depicting some native groups as "cannibals" to be subjugated, and others as a kind of "noble savage" in need of Christian conversion and colonial tutelage. When Europeans first reached the Caribbean, they encountered a collection of thriving Amerindian societies. The early Spanish settlers' labor needs were met by reducing the native groups in the *encomienda* system, or service grants. The European powers' harsh treatment—reflected in everything from formal policies to everyday cruelties—of the Indigenous Amerindian population and exposing them to European diseases nearly eliminated them. It has been estimated that they numbered as many as 40 million in Mexico and Central and South America before the Europeans arrived. As European colonizers reached the mainland, they encountered, and generally tried to violently subdue, a wide array of societies with diverse cultural traditions in language, social structure, and ways of interacting with the environment—gatherer-hunters, horticulturalists, and agriculturalists. Some were builders of monumental architecture and had developed science, mathematics, and writing systems. Despite this, Columbus's term "*Indios*," that is, "Indians," reflecting his misunderstanding that he had reached India, stuck, as did a kind of reductionism—a process of wrongly reducing complexity to supposed essential elements.

As European colonization continued and European colonists' labor needs were unmet by recalcitrant and resisting Indigenous groups, and unmet by those groups dying from European-borne diseases such as measles and smallpox, the Atlantic slave trade, representing the largest capital investment in the world in its time, was developed to supply plentiful, cheap, and controllable supplies of labor. The massive enslavement and importation of men, women, and children taken from a variety of African societies in West, Central, and even East Africa to perform backbreaking tasks that enriched their overlords occurred in Latin America and the Caribbean from the early 1500s to the mid-1800s. It is estimated that more than 10 million enslaved Africans reached the New World, and another 10 million died en route. Brazil received the largest portion, about 40 percent. The Caribbean as a whole received about 40 percent, Spanish Latin America received about 16 percent, and British North America—including what is now the United States—received about 4 percent of the enslaved Africans.

Enslaved African workers were drawn from varying African ethnic groups, depending on the historical period, and, in the context of mercantilism, different slaving countries imported a different complement of slaves originating from different ports in Africa. New World slavery was quite different from Old World slavery in Europe and in Africa, for example, because of its involvement with capitalism. Some of the nascent ideas and attitudes associated with ethnicity were present in Iberia before the advent of the Atlantic slave trade and can be traced to the development of African slavery in the Islamic world. But in the crucible of the Americas and emerging capitalism, ethnic differences in the Caribbean were constructed and elaborated through the process known as "racial slavery" (Blackburn 1997). This was a process whereby Europeans made Africans and their progeny a racialized group and made the ethnic status "African" or "Black" and the legal status "slave" almost completely overlapping. "Black" and "slave" were so closely associated that even when Blacks were not slaves they had to provide proof of this status.

Despite the Spanish crown's attempts at legal separation, biological and cultural mixing was part of the conquest. Sexual relations of dominance between Spanish men and native women—given the prerogatives of conquest and the male-female imbalance of early colonization—resulted in unions that were characterized by rape, concubinage, and occasionally marriage. Mestizo progeny of whites and native peoples were often defined as "half-breeds" or "mixed-breeds." In Brazil, colonized by the Portuguese, such mixtures were called *mamelucos* as well as *mestiços*. *Mestizaje* under similar conditions of structural and legal inequality continued with the arrival of enslaved Africans. Sexual relations became contested terrain, as white men fanatically tried to prevent white women from marrying or having sexual relationships with non-white men. Women were made to serve as the boundaries of the group, and ideas about women's sexual "purity" were tied to "racial purity." A sexual double standard generally existed, however. White men from all social strata had liaisons with non-white women of lesser status. The men rarely recognized officially any offspring from these unions. Some of these men did informally assist their progeny, who also in some contexts received the benefits accruing to what was seen as an approximation of whiteness.

All "race mixtures" were not deemed to be of the same type. Elaborate systems and nomenclatures emphasizing supposed degrees away from whiteness were established by Spaniards and *criollos* (creoles— people of European descent born in Latin America). *Black, Indian, mestizo, mulatto,* and *pardo* were the commonly used terms for nonwhites. As part and parcel of these processes, there was created the concept of "whiteness." European ethnic identities came to be also seen as "white" racialized identities—showing that classification systems, such as those regarding identities, are themselves the prerogatives of the powerful even if they are sometimes resisted by the disempowered. The Spanish conquest of the Caribbean occurred at the time of the *reconquista,* the reconquering of Spain from the Moors, and at the time of the expulsion of Spain's Jews in 1492. The resultant animating ethos was called *limpieza de sangre,* "purity of blood," and it was transferred to the New World. *Limpieza de sangre,* which had diverse meanings in Spain, in the New World meant institutionalizing whiteness at the top of an ethnic hierarchy that put Blackness and Indianness at the farthest (lowest) end of a continuum. In the Americas, this principle was used to construct racialized groups and determine social and legal status. According to the Spanish (and later others following more or less in kind), so-called race mixtures that occurred between supposed "pure races" and, later, "mixed races" could be charted, and, through such mathematics, they could then be assigned differential rights and entitlements in the colonial society. Of course, "race mixing" was not a free-for-all; it occurred in and through gendered power relations: white men had discretionary power to engage in extralegal affairs with nonwhites, while white women's sexuality was strictly controlled. There was a profusion of categories for racialized groups and concomitant ideas as to their meaning, such as those current in the *sociedad de castas* (caste society) in eighteenth-century New Spain (Mexico), shown in Table 9.1.

Every territory in Latin America had its own system, and only some of the terms overlapped. These ideologies were representations of a rigidly stratified *sociedad de castas.* "Caste" came from the term the

Table 9.1 Ethnogenesis and the Development of Group Categories in Eighteenth-Century New Spain (Mexico)

1. Spaniard and Indian beget mestizo.
2. Mestizo and Spanish woman beget *castizo.*
3. *Castizo* woman and Spaniard beget Spaniard.
4. Spanish woman and black man beget mulatto.
5. Spaniard and mulatto woman beget *morisco.*
6. *Morisco* woman and Spaniard beget albino.
7. Spaniard and albino woman beget *torna atrás* ["turn back," as in "from white"].
8. Indian man and *torna atrás* woman beget lobo.
9. *Lobo* and Indian woman beget *zambaigo.*
10. *Zambaigo* and Indian woman beget *cambujo.*
11. *Cambujo* and mulatto woman beget *albarazado.*
12. *Albarazado* and mulatto woman beget *barcino.*
13. *Barcino* and mulatto woman beget *coyote.*
14. *Coyote* woman and Indian man beget *chamiso.*
15. *Chamiso* woman and mestizo beget *coyote mestizo.*
16. *Coyote mestizo* and mulatto woman beget *ahí te estás* ["there you are"].

Source: Mörner 1967: 58.

Portuguese applied to the complex social structure they encountered in India. *Casta* came to refer to all nonwhites. The *sociedad de castas* was characterized by social and legal discrimination based on ethnicity that was blatant and direct, as well as condescending and patronizing, on the part of the white elites. In traveler Antonio de Ulloa's *Relación Histórica del Viage a la América Meridional* (*Historical Account of a Voyage to South America*) of 1748 there survives a description of the *sociedad de castas* as observed in Cartagena, Lima, Panama, and Santo Domingo and the complex etiquette and rights attached to each designation: "Every person is so jealous of the order of their tribe or caste, that if, through inadvertence, you call them by a degree lower than what they actually are, they are highly offended, never suffering themselves to be deprived of so valuable a gift of fortune." But for those on top, "the conceit of being white alleviates the pressure of every other calamity" (quoted in Maingot 1992: 227). But through the Spanish *cédula de gracias al sacar,* a decree of "thank you for the exception," designed to sew alliances with Spain, high-status and wealthy non-whites were able to buy a dispensation that allowed them to climb the status ladder, even to be considered legally white.

The rigidity of the *sociedad de castas* came to be undermined by the recognition that precise designations were increasingly meaningless, as *mestizaje,* with its ethnic and cultural consequences, was seen to proceed from generation to generation, and the phenomenon of passing from one category to another became common. As the definitional lines blurred, ethnic designations generally became even more vague.

Identity Politics in Independent Latin America

The wars for independence in Latin America in the 1820s started to end the legal discrimination of the *sociedad de castas,* but practices and the ideas surrounding it reflected, even if more loosely, the state of the social structure after independence. Systems of social stratification, based on ethnicity and class, in which skin becomes lighter in color as one goes up the class ladder, were further reinforced despite individual exceptions. The elite culturally absorbed nonwhites who climbed into the upper stratum. By about the 1870s, a common thread was running through the discourse of nationalism in several continental Latin American countries. Elites imagined themselves as part of a European legacy of "civilization." They were influenced by the political, cultural, philosophical, and scientific strains of positivism—a belief in science and progress. Social Darwinism explained the relative economic and political development of countries through deterministic theories—so-called scientific racism. According to these theories, the northern European countries and the United States were relatively prosperous because of the inherent physical and mental superiority of the Anglo-Saxon and Teutonic "races." Latin American elites selected parts of these intellectual movements and applied them to what they saw as the reality of their societies. Brazilian elites, for example—most of whom identified themselves as white—reflected on their "racial" topography: the 1872 census listed only 38 percent as white, 20 percent as Black, and the rest as *pardo* (a designation for a "mixed" group that could refer to mixtures of white and Black, or white and Black and Indigenous backgrounds). African slavery ended only in 1888 in Brazil, the last holdout in the Americas—even later than Cuba (1886) and the United States (1865). In Brazil, free *pardos* had been a large and powerful group during slavery and had often struck a strategic alliance with whites versus Blacks and slaves. As slavery ended, Brazilian elites worried publicly about the "racial" makeup of the country and, thus, about the country's fate. They accepted ideas of white superiority but, contradictorily, denied the immutability and absoluteness of "race." They believed the solution to the country's problems lay in the whitening of the population, "racially" and culturally.

These elites referred to the supposed low fertility among *pardos* and Blacks. They believed miscegenation would gradually whiten and consequently improve the population, ignoring contemporary mainstream "racial" theory, which held that hybrids were degenerate. Toward this end, European immigration was officially encouraged, and immigration laws—although not publicly acknowledged—were structured so that Blacks, Jews, and others were barred from settling in Brazil. Some of these laws, codified from the 1890s until the 1940s, continued to be on the books. By the 1920s, racist thinkers in Brazil and the rest of Latin America even became involved in a "science of racial improvement" called eugenics. As Nancy Leys Stepan (1991) has shown, eugenics provided a supposed scientific legitimation for "whitening."

Brazilian elites were further consoled by nationalist myths generated by an emerging social science and a regional intellectualist tradition. In the 1930s, cultural nationalist Gilberto Freyre (1900–1987) gained prominence for his historical studies of the plantation society in Brazil (Freyre 1986 [1933]). Although Freyre attacked scientific racism, he celebrated miscegenation and cultural diversity. He proclaimed the creation of a new "Luso-tropical" civilization in which "the races" intermingled freely. This was part of the ideological strain that produced the nationalist discourse of *democracia racial* (racial democracy). Critical in Freyre's formulation was his claim that the "Portuguese" element was dominant in this interchange. This ideological discourse—and the political-economic dispensation it was part of—had the effect if not the direct intention of precluding mobilization of disempowered groups based on ethnic identity (and labeled them racist if they did so), allowing the white elite to avoid addressing claims of ethnic discrimination. Elements of this ideological discourse found resonance elsewhere in the region.

Immigration laws have been used throughout the Americas— including by the United States—to sort out the "desirable" and "undesirable" groups that will make up the nation. Latin America as a whole received about 12 million European immigrants between 1850 and 1930. In addition to the arrival of European migrants, there were Middle Easterners, such as the Syrians and Lebanese found in the Caribbean and in Central and South America. There was also significant immigration from Asia. About 200,000 Japanese immigrated to Brazil in the first half of the twentieth century, with another 30,000 locating in Peru. About 300,000 Chinese went, mainly as contract laborers, to Latin America and the Caribbean in the mid-nineteenth century. About 140,000 of the Chinese went to Cuba and 100,000 to Peru, where they were treated so poorly that a series of international incidents occurred, and Chinese officials launched investigations. A further 20,000 Chinese went to various Caribbean islands, and the rest went to Central America and elsewhere. In some places, they maintained ethnically exclusive marriage and mating practices; in other places, they were more apt to assimilate. Often visible and distinct as traders of dry goods and owners of grocery shops, they have occasionally been victimized in nationalist movements. Nearly the entire Chinese community of Sonora, Mexico, for example, was expelled in the 1930s in a particularly fierce moment of post-revolution nationalism.

In Argentina, a country that set up an immigration program and received more than 3 million immigrants from Europe between 1880 and 1930, racist intellectuals viewed the massive immigration of Europeans as further whitening the population. At the end of the nineteenth century, Argentine elites could claim an already white nation with strong European roots and, thus, look down on their Brazilian neighbors. Argentine racist thinkers—foremost among them José Ingenieros (1877–1925)—were convinced of the merits of natural selection, claiming "the white race" would win out in an evolutionary struggle with "colored races," which were incompatible with "superior" white civilization. Argentine elites imagined theirs as a white country, and they pointed to the supposed inevitable disappearance of Indigenous peoples and Blacks. With the influx of European immigrants, the Indigenous proportion of the population declined from 5 percent in 1869 to 0.7 percent of a total of nearly 4 million inhabitants in 1895. Blacks, who in the first third of the nineteenth century had made up 25 percent of the population of Buenos Aires, dropped to 2 percent by 1887. What was not acknowledged were the terror and discrimination behind this supposedly natural process. Native peoples were the victims of continual military campaigns throughout the 1880s: they were killed, forcibly incorporated into the army, or forced to labor in agriculture or domestic service. Sporadic campaigns against them continued until the 1930s. Blacks were confined to a limited number of occupations and to poor living conditions.

The immigration wave of the period 1880–1930 was 43 percent Italian and 34 percent Spanish, and these were given the designation "white"—not always a forgone conclusion in the history of migration to the New World. Once the country was supposedly white, though, the elites' next task was to make it Argentinean. Many immigrants formed their own communities with separate institutions. Italians, Germans, Russian Jews, and others brought with them ideas of trade unionism, anarchism, and socialism that challenged the entrenched social order, and prosperous immigrants were excluded from the elites' inner circles. At the turn of the twentieth century, a revitalization of nationalism entailed glorification of the native Argentine (the *criollo*) and the definition of Argentine culture as characterized by the Spanish language and Hispanic culture, Catholicism, the family, paternalism, and order. This new nationalism had an anti-immigrant component. During the peak immigration years of the early 1900s, Jews represented between 2 percent and 6 percent of total immigration. In the context of anti-immigrant nationalism, they became visible and vulnerable targets as anti-immigrant discourse and activity reached its depths with Catholic Church–inspired anti-Semitism and physical attacks on Jews.

Revolutionary Mexico provides an interesting contrast. In seeking to break with the widespread racist ideas and practices of the long dictatorship of Porfirio Díaz (1876–1911), the emergent thinkers, who gained prominence with the armed revolution beginning in 1910, constructed what became the official ideology of *indigenismo* (indigenism), which had several components and relied on a number of cultural assumptions about "race." Fairly high consensus held that most Mexicans were mestizos. Such attributes as language, religion, dress, family form, and consciousness determined whether one was native or mestizo. And because these attributes were social in origin, they were subject to change.

Indigenismo was not a movement initiated by the Indigenous peoples; it was an elite ideology that advocated the gradual, nonviolent integration of them into Mexican society, especially through education. It venerated Mexico's pre-Hispanic past and attempted to rescue the surviving Indigenous culture from oblivion. The mestizo, as the synthesis of the Indigenous person and the European, was exalted as the true Mexican. Breaking with the scientific racism of the time, philosopher and politician José Vasconcelos referred to mestizos as the *raza cósmica* (cosmic race), "racial" hybrids who were to characterize Mexico and, eventually, the world at large. Those Indigenous peoples who remained were to be absorbed into this "race."

As an ostensibly anti-racist ideology that reached its apogee in the 1930s and has essentially remained dominant since then, *indigenismo* represented a distinct departure from Westernism. Although disputing claims of native and mestizo inferiority, this perspective emphasized innate differences among the white, mestizo, and native racialized groups. *Indigenismo* even led some intellectuals and elites to conclude that mestizos and Amerindians were actually "racially" (their term) and culturally superior to whites. Given all its contradictions, then, official *indigenismo* meant Indigenous peoples as such were marginalized because they were seen to be in the process of becoming what they needed to become to participate in national political life. Images of noble pre-Hispanic native culture with a glorious past were a cornerstone of *indigenismo*. But because it relied on notions of ethnicity, it left the door open for contemporary Indigenous peoples to receive separate and unequal treatment. *Indigenismo* could not legislate social change that would be accompanied by significant socioeconomic transformations. Notions that cultural and biological miscegenation could produce a new kind of human being became common in many Latin American countries, not only Brazil, Venezuela, and Mexico but also countries such as Ecuador, Colombia, and Peru (de la Cadena 2000). *Mestizaje* in its explicitly nationalist mode subordinated claims of ethnic distinctiveness to the ends of the nation. Therefore, those considering themselves Indigenous rejected at times the ideology of *mestizaje*, which also came to be rejected by some Afro-Latinos as they began to be associated with international signs of Blackness.

Late Twentieth-Century Developments

By the late twentieth century the ideological legacy of the *sociedad de castas* was reproduced in the postcolonial political and economic context of Latin American societies. This was seen in academic studies such as the classic ones by anthropologist Marvin Harris (1964, 1970). In one study, a hundred Brazilians in a Bahian fishing village were asked to identify the "race" of three full sisters depicted in photographs. Only six responses identified the three by the same "racial" terms. In fourteen responses, a separate term was used for each of the three sisters, most frequently *blanca* (white) for one and *mulatta* or *morena* (brown) for one or both of the others. A particular Brazilian could be described by as many as thirteen terms by other members of the community. Another hundred people were shown nine portrait drawings meant to depict nine different "racial" types. Around forty "racial" terms were discovered. The highest percentage that agreed on the "race" in any drawing was 70 percent; the lowest was 18 percent. In another study, Harris used a set of seventy-two drawings meant to solicit identification of the "race" of the subject of the drawing on a deck of cards, showing the deck to a hundred native-born Brazilians at five different sites in Brazil: Bahia, Alagoas, Pernambuco, Ceará, Brasília, and São Paulo. The range of designations was bewildering. Harris obtained 492 different categorizations, with 25 percent of the sample responding with fifteen or more categorizations, with the range extending from two to seventy categorizations with the median at nine per respondent. The twelve most commonly employed terms, each of which occurred more than a hundred times, would be incomprehensible to most North Americans or Europeans. They included *moreno, branco, mulatto, preto, negro, alvo, moreno claro, cabo verde, claro, sarard, escurinho,* and *escuro.*

Mauricio Solaún, Eduardo Vélez, and Cynthia Smith (1987) conducted a study in the Caribbean port city of Cartagena, Colombia, that involved interviewing a sample of 120 adults from four social classes: upper, middle, working, and lower. These respondents were shown twenty-two photographs of individuals with varying ethnic identities and styles of dress and were asked to identify the "race" of each. For the twenty-two photographs, there were 128 different designations—an average of seventeen per photo. The authors show how much of the "racial" nomenclature of the *sociedad de castas* has remained, albeit with significant modification: the tendency now is to use descriptive terms. Individuals were perceived, for example, as *blanco aindiado* (white with native features) or *negro fileno* (Black with a straight nose). They were also *claro* (light), *trigueño* (wheat-colored), or *trigueño claro* or *blanco claro.* Many responses, then, included physical characteristics as well as "racial" ones: for example, *rubio* (blond), *acanelado* (cinnamon-colored), *cobrizo* (copper-colored), *blanco no del todo* (white, but not completely so), or *blanco quemado* (burned white).

278   *Kevin A. Yelvington*

Although the nomenclature in Cartagena includes terms and concepts that imply history, for example, *mulatto;* more neutral terms, for example, *claro;* and terms of physical description, for example, *negro por el pelo* (Black because of hair texture), there is—as in the Brazilian studies—evidence that a wide variety of criteria are used to classify individuals. In the Cartagena study, the most frequent use of a term per photograph ranged from 24 percent to 71 percent, with no photo receiving more than 50 percent "racial" (as opposed to color or physically descriptive) terms; 60 percent of the responses were given only twice at the most. In this study, when respondents were asked to describe themselves, only the upper class contained a majority of self-reported *blancos* whereas no *blancos* were found in the lower class. Concomitantly, no *negros* were found in the upper class, where darker individuals referred to themselves as *moreno*. Virtually no respondents positively identified with Blackness. Only a few called themselves *negro,* and terms denoting African ancestry were rarely used. Only twelve respondents called themselves *mulatto*. Collectively, these terms exhibit the effects of *blanqueamiento* and demonstrate the correlation between ethnicity and class, which in turn facilitates or impedes class mobility.

Solaún, Vélez, and Smith's research also showed the extent to which the stain of slavery still existed in Latin America. Thomas Stephens, in his *Dictionary of Latin American Racial and Ethnic Terminology* (1989), listed fifty-nine separate entries of terms that entail *negro* and a modifier. *Negro humo* (smoke black–colored) is a Colombian term that refers to physical description, whereas *negro catedrático* (a Black "chaired professor") is a Cuban term used to refer to Blacks claimed to be feigning education and refinement by misappropriating "white" patterns of speech and upper-class modes of dress. Thus, use of this term is thought to be a way of keeping Blacks "in their place." In many countries in Latin America, the use of the word *negro* for "Black" to identify a person was historically not seen to be polite or politically acceptable, as indicated by the number of mostly pejorative modifiers that accompany its designation. *Prieto* or *moreno* (for "dark" or "brown") were seen as more polite terms than *negro*. Indirection in speech was preferred for such code words as *pelo malo* ("bad" hair) to refer to kinky hair, or *pelo bueno* ("good" hair), meaning straight hair. Some people found themselves described as *de color medio* (of medium color), a distinction that refers to someone who is neither white nor Black. Conversely, *bajo de color* (low in color) referred to skin color, but also to the low social status of Blacks. Often, physical features like an individual's hair were pointed out and used to make value judgments. *Pelo bueno* ("good" hair) referred to straight or wavy hair, for example, whereas *pasa* (raisin) referred to people with kinky hair in a deprecatory way. But direct and hurtful epithets were deployed for those seen to be manifestly of African heritage too. *Negro como una paila* (black as a frying pan) referred to a person with very dark skin, and *morejón* was a derogatory word used for a Black person considered ordinary or ugly.

It is tempting to compare the place of those of African descent with the position of native peoples under late twentieth-century Latin American nationalism. In the 500 years since the conquest, colonial and independent Latin American states' treatment of native peoples has ranged from neglect to attempts at forced integration to genocide. Nowhere in contemporary Latin America was the persecution of native peoples as profound and cruel as in Guatemala. As David Bost, Angélica Lozano-Alonso, and David Marcus detail in Chapter 13, the irony was not lost on world observers when an Indigenous woman from Guatemala, Rigoberta Menchú Tum, was honored with the Nobel Peace Prize in 1992—the quincentennial anniversary of Columbus's first voyage.

As in many Latin American states in which Indigenous peoples were numerous (e.g., they made up more than 60 percent of Guatemala's population by this time), the system of ethnic-class ranking held that the elites were white, followed by *ladinos* (seen as mestizos), and then Indigenous peoples. In many cases, the cultural and ethnic differences between *ladinos* and native peoples were not great. In class terms, however, the differences were stark: *ladinos* were found in a number of occupations and class levels, whereas most native peoples continued to resist proletarianization and incorporation through the late twentieth century. Native peoples throughout the region were a diverse group and, as elsewhere through time, the construct "Indian" obscured significant differences. Indigenous Guatemalans spoke about twenty different Mayan languages. They were organized around the concept of community, and these communities differed from each other culturally in many ways. In the past, native identity had been rooted in the community, although this was changing by the 1990s as some native leaders had started making common cause with other Indigenous groups in Latin America and beyond. Although they were not completely closed and isolated from the influences of the wider society throughout colonial conquest and independence, these communities had still for the most part been able to act as corporate units in political and economic resistance, more or less successfully, against the state and entrenched economic interests.

In elite nationalism, the refrain was familiar. For non-Amerindians, a truly modern and prosperous nation required not only unity but also that the Amerindians give up their separate identity and become integrated—on the oligarchy's terms, of course—into national economic life. Indigenous peoples wanted to retain what they saw as their traditional ways and customs while participating as social and economic equals in a multicultural nation. In Guatemala, integration and class exploitation had always been mediated by the state and its coercive capacities. The system of forced Indigenous plantation labor ended only in 1945 during a period of democratic rule that lasted from 1944 to 1954. As Shelley McConnell explains in Chapter 4, the policies aimed at labor, land, and political reform pursued under the regimes of Juan José Arévalo (1945–1951) and Jacobo Árbenz (1951–1954) were viewed in the context of the Cold War as threatening to US commercial and strategic interests. US efforts to destabilize the Árbenz government, supported by local and international capitalists, culminated in a coup in 1954 that ushered in over three decades of military rule.

In the 1960s, the beginnings of a guerrilla movement in the western highlands of Guatemala—where Indigenous peoples predominated—allowed the United States to manufacture a Cold War–related national security justification to assist the governing elites further in setting up a counterinsurgency military program. Revolutionary groups tried to mobilize Indigenous peoples, who, in an effort to resist cultural and economic exploitation, sometimes joined. In response, beginning in 1975, the military began to use indiscriminate violence against "subversives," who were usually Indigenous people who happened to reside in communities where any form of popular mobilization was taking place. What has been called the "permanent counterinsurgency state" was now in place. The military, composed of *ladinos,* controlled civil society. Entire villages were massacred, rural leaders were tortured, and the crops of Indigenous peoples were destroyed. The military set up permanent bases in the highlands, conscripted around 20 percent of the male inhabitants into the army, and organized "civilian patrols" of Indigenous peoples under direct military command. More than 120,000 people were killed in the over thirty-year rebellion against repressive Guatemalan governments. Human rights agencies report that at least 50,000 Indigenous peoples were killed during the 1980s, about 200,000 were forced into permanent exile, and at some point half of the 2 million highlands residents were displaced from their homes.

Notwithstanding these practices, Guatemalan nationalist discourses depicted itself with Amerindian symbols. The symbolic use of the *traje* (an Indigenous dress) as the Guatemalan "national costume" was used to present an image of Guatemala to international tourists and bolster

Marie Soto and Ixil women celebrate the initial, guilty verdict of former Guatemalan dictator Ríos Montt for genocide in 2013. The verdict was later set aside. Credit: Elena Hermosa, https://commons.wikimedia.org/wiki/File:Guatemala_4,_GHR_16_(9269372204).jpg

the local tourist industry. Profits were imagined to depend on an image of the exotic, cultivated carefully and somewhat intentionally. But as a key component to nationalist ideology, the concept of "Indianness as national essence" went much deeper than any conscious manipulation of symbols for economic gain. Many *ladinos* assumed some sense of identification with "Indianness," taken in an almost spiritual way. This form of Guatemalan nationalism had clear parallels with other forms of nationalism in Latin America, depicting the true soul of the nation as inhering in an Amerindian past.

The Latin American woman who perhaps represented the most strongly contrasting symbol to Rigoberta Menchú, a Quiché Maya, was the blond, blue-eyed, Brazilian, megamarketed superstar Xuxa (pronounced SHOO-sha). Former soft-porn movie actress and *Playboy* model, Xuxa had an incredibly popular children's television show that reached millions in Brazil and elsewhere in Latin America. At the height of her popularity, Xuxa was probably Brazil's best-known celebrity at the time, a larger-than-life media creation who recorded bestselling records, starred in movies that attracted huge audiences, had dolls bearing her likeness, and endorsed a number of products from surfboards to bicycles to soup to cookies. She had her own magazine with a circulation at one time of

700,000. Her concerts were performed in sold-out stadiums, and her live performances garnered the highest pay of any Brazilian entertainer.

The emergence and popularity of Xuxa demonstrated that ideologies of *democracia racial* could coexist with those of exclusivity. In addition to crafting and marketing cultivated images of sexuality and consumerism, Xuxa also played on—and traded in—whiteness. Xuxa was simultaneously the blond ideal of beauty and the ideal of femininity. Young girls would dream of being Xuxa and tried to emulate her and the Paquitas, her blond clone teenage helpers. Xuxa improbably incorporated (and apparently herein was her appeal) a number of contradictory images: at once a sexual, erotic figure and a domestic one, surrounded by adoring children, affirming the aesthetic superiority of whiteness while always assuring Brazilians of her Brazilianness. To this end, her six-year public affair with soccer legend Pelé (Edson Arantes do Nascimento), the most famous Black man in Brazil, served as a legitimation of the veracity of *democracia racial.* Xuxa's blond aesthetic went almost unquestioned in Brazil, yet her own words were revealing. Asked about the "race" issue and her show, Xuxa was quoted as saying, "Some people say that I shouldn't do a show because I am blond. . . . But Brazil is a country of mixed races. You can be blond, brunette, *mulatto;* you can be anything." When asked why all of her cast members were white, she responded with racist assumptions: "Oh! I've already explained; the tests [auditions to be Paquitas] are very difficult." Continuing, she said, "I think blonds have more drive. Besides, we're all blond, but we're all Brazilian!" And when her romance with Pelé ended in 1986, she told the press a story that clearly had insulting racial implications.

The rise of Xuxa, perhaps not coincidentally, came with the relatively recent rise of a Black-consciousness movement in Brazil (building on earlier developments of the 1930s, 1940s, and 1950s) and the growth of a number of organizations whose aims were to empower Blacks politically and economically and to promote a positive Black self-image. Anthropologist John Burdick reported a telling and representative conversation with a Brazilian man in a small bar in a working-class town on the outskirts of Rio de Janeiro: "There is no racism in Brazil! I have the blood of all races in me—white, black, Indian [native]. How could we be racists?" But in a more reflective moment, he said, "There is a saying in Brazil: 'If you're not white you're black.' That's not really true, you know. Here, you can be other things, like me, I'm a *moreno.* But to a white man, I'm a *moreno* only if he likes me; if he doesn't like me, I'm a *mulatto,* or I'm even a *preto* [Black]. They play that game, you know? I guess the real saying should be, 'If you're not white, you lose'" (1992: 40, 44). "Race" as a category was left out of the 1970 census (which was taken during the period of military rule, 1964–1985). "Race" was included in the 1980 census; however, the results of that census were not released until two years later because the director of the census bureau apparently feared they would damage Brazil's image of harmonious ethnic relations. The results were damaging. They showed huge differences in income, with Blacks earning 35 percent as much as whites and *pardos* earning 45 percent of what whites earned. This was part of and, indeed, reflective of a general trend in which the rich got richer and the poor became poorer. In 1960, the wealthiest 10 percent of the population held 40 percent of the national income, while the poorest 50 percent held only 17 percent. By 1990 the portion of the national income held by the poorest 50 percent had declined to just 11 percent, while the wealthiest decile held nearly 51 percent.

In contrast to late twentieth-century nationalist ideologies that emphasized ethnic and cultural mixture, there were other styles of imagining and constructing the nation that depended on exclusivist politics. By the late 1980s, Argentina had emerged from its most recent period of military rule (1976–1983). During this time, thousands of people were kidnapped, tortured, and murdered in the so-called Dirty War. The military leadership that instituted and reigned over the terrorist state justified these measures as to "save Western Christian civilization." With the democratic election of Raúl Alfonsín in 1983 the self-termed "Nationalists" organized to oppose his regime, expressing continuity with the military government's ideological stance. Their influence continued to threaten the elected regime of Carlos Menem (1989–1999) and those of his successors. The Nationalist strain was linked to far-right political groups, and ideologies with its views are expressed by the *carapintadas* (painted faces), the dissident, antidemocratic military faction that sprang up in the late 1980s and protested the trials of those accused of atrocities in the Dirty War, along with Alerta Nacional (National Alert)—a terrorist group that had links to the military and the police.

Nationalist ideology is an almost textbook example of what is called an "invented tradition" in which a mythical past is created and used to serve the needs of the present and the future. The Nationalists called their movement an "authentically Argentine struggle for Catholic truth and Hispanic tradition," a "spiritual" as opposed to a "material" movement, whose aim was to prevent the "breakdown of the country's spiritual unity." They proclaimed that they were "heirs to a millenary civilization grounded on Christian teachings, Greek philosophy, and Roman order." They were on a "crusade" for "moral purification" and the "defense of the national soul." They supported authoritarian rule and were opposed to "liberal philosophy, formal democracy, and ideological colonization." Of course, not every Argentine is a Nationalist (with a capital *N*), but the influence of this movement in education, religion, and political and civil life has been profound.

It is rarely sufficient for the cultural constructions of a nation to proceed solely in a self-referential way. Usually, these constructions are brought about most effectively in contradistinction to some entity or group that the nation is defined against negatively. That is, the nation is not what this group is, and this group is not of the nation. The Nationalists have no trouble finding scapegoats; they were constantly warning of the "subversive" influence of such foreign enemies as Marxism, communism, Freemasonry, and international Zionism.

Internally, anti-Semitism continued to be integral to Argentine nationalism. Similar to those who followed particular ideologies evident at the turn of the twentieth century, Catholic priests, bishops, and others in the 1980s criticized the Alfonsín government for the "many Jews" within it. Alfonsín's Radical Party government, which did include Jewish members, was termed *la sinagoga radical* (the radical synagogue) by right-wing critics. Nationalism often depends on depictions of people within the borders of the nation as not *of* the nation.

The Twenty-First Century: Neoliberal Multiculturalism and the Identity Politics of Recognition

With the worldwide economic crises of the 1970s as a new stage of capitalism, as economist Alfredo Saad-Filho (2005) shows, neoliberal regimes replaced the import substitution industrialization development strategies pursued with some success by Latin American policymakers, state-owned enterprises were privatized, and Latin American finance became more closely integrated into global networks. In this emerging state-backed "neoliberal elite consensus," neoliberal regimes of capital accumulation brought economic policies in the latter decades of the twentieth century, and into the twenty-first, that were designed to promote maximum market exchanges, free trade, private property rights, and individual freedoms, with, on the one hand, the state's role minimized beyond certain key tasks, and on the other, the state intervening in ways to increase the wealth of the already-ruling groups. There were vast changes in state regulation, labor markets, information technology, trade patterns, and resource allocation in order to further deregulate capitalism and strengthen the positions of ruling elites.

Whereas, as we have seen, in previous eras the state and dominant sectors envisioned and desired ethnically and culturally homogeneous nations (von Vacano 2012), the advent of neoliberal political economies now entailed a "neoliberal multiculturalism." With the state receding and ceding many of its social welfare responsibilities and putting its traditional responsibilities back onto the populace, civil society groups forced and took advantage of openings and filled this breach. These included groups devoted to identity politics. While the neoliberal ruling blocs recognized these communities, the identities they were trying to project, and the rights they were claiming in the names of these communities and identities, the recognition came with severe and defined limits. Substantive but limited civil and political rights began to be enjoyed by Indigenous groups and groups of Afro-descendants. Within this project, though, rights were proactively advanced in the name of multiculturalism in order to reconstitute civil society and national culture in new forms of subject-formation formerly the domain of state and elite actors. The effect was to ensure that groups would not engage in a radical politics and one of cross-ethnic, class solidarity to undermine ruling-group hegemony. Under neoliberal governance the activism of *Indios permitidos* ("allowed Indians") (Hale 2004) is restricted to identity politics that help to replace the state's role and responsibility in civil society without seriously threatening the social order. Thus it became a *manageable* multiculturalism. The result was "politics of recognition," where "recognition" refers to a process where certain attributes of groups are signified and positively evaluated, where difference is acknowledged and respected in ways that have political consequences. In this process, too, those doing the recognizing are changed and constructed as much as those being recognized. The conferral of difference in the neoliberal multicultural politics of recognition made the identities of ethnic and racialized groups the idiom through which societal actors would interact in significant ways. Recognition entailed an important political and ideological shift. As a result, space is opened for ethnic and nationalist groups to operate in civil society, changing their public personae at the same time (Yashar 2005).

As sociologist Tianna Paschel (2016) argued, the identity rights activist groups were able to construct themselves and their claims in the language of cultural and ethnic difference. These actors drew upon colonial and postcolonial classificatory systems and ideologies but transformed them in the process. These groups also made common cause with others, creating alliances at national and international levels, and drew upon emerging international agreements and organizations to help pressure their national governments. These included the International Labour Organization's Convention 169 (Indigenous and Tribal Peoples Convention) of 1989; as well, Latin American participation in the

United Nations World Conference Against Racism, Racial Discrimination, Xenophobia, and Related Intolerance, held in 2001 in Durban, South Africa, was key, as was participation in UN forums to promote human rights, such as the 2007 UN Declaration of the Rights of Indigenous Peoples. Protests against the dislocations posed by neoliberal globalization began to be staged in ethnic terms, but, as the result of the increased communication and travel that are concomitant with economic globalization, ethnic groups in Latin America and the Caribbean became aware of the situations of those in North America and elsewhere and now make common cause with them. For instance, Latin American Indigenous groups not only formed coalitions across national borders, but also increasingly united with groups calling themselves Indigenous around the world. And Black groups in Brazil began adopting more international symbols of Blackness, such as Jamaican reggae music and US African American identity ideologies. Many Black movements in Brazil were led by women (Perry 2013).

In many cases, native and disempowered peoples mobilized to protect lands that they considered theirs or to counter environmental threats. In the process, they developed a self-conscious discourse on what they define as distinctive Indigenous culture, constructing identity in the process. A number of Amerindian organizations emerged that captured the attention of those in power. Some began doing so in innovative ways. For example, some Amazonian native groups utilized video and internet technology to press their claims in the court of world opinion and to establish solidarity with Indigenous groups elsewhere. In Brazil, a principal aim of the Black consciousness movement was to convince those Brazilians who identified themselves as *moreno* or *mulatto* to identify themselves as *negro*. In Brazil and elsewhere, as political scientist Juliet Hooker (2009) shows, Afro-Latin Americans formed social movements designed to win collective rights, and throughout parts of Latin America the new neoliberal multicultural regimes have granted (or have been compelled to grant) rights to land, jobs, places in educational institutions, and, overall, cultural recognition. This was often accomplished by affirming links to the African diaspora abroad. The widespread protests in the United States in the summer of 2020 against racism and police brutality and unwarranted police killings of African Americans spread to Latin America with the Black Lives Matter movement, further inspiring Afro-Latin Americans.

These struggles have taken place in the streets, in popular culture, and in the halls of Latin American legislatures, and have even resulted in official changes in Latin American constitutions that acknowledged the countries' multicultural, multiethnic, and pluriethnic makeup. Besides Brazil's 1988 constitution, in Colombia, for example, a 1993 law based on the 1991 constitution outlined territorial and cultural and political rights for Afro-Colombians and laws were enacted that made racism illegal. At the same time, however, Blackness became "ethnicized" and authorized through state processes of recognition (Restrepo 2004). The 1993 Peruvian constitution recognized the "ethnic and cultural plurality of the nation" and the Peruvian state recognized fifty-five Indigenous peoples within its borders. In response to the 1994 neo-Zapatista uprising of native Mayans in the southern state of Chiapas, Mexico included reforms in its constitution to acknowledge the country's ethnic, cultural, and linguistic diversity and recognize, at least in a small way, ongoing discrimination and racism (Trejo 2012). In Guatemala, the decades-long civil war ended with the signing of peace accords in 1996. An Indigenous development fund was established in 1994. Significant was the election of an Indigenous person, Evo Morales, as president of Bolivia. This would have been unthinkable in the past (Postero 2007). Morales, an Indigenous Aymara leader of a coca growers union, became the first Indigenous president of Bolivia, a majority-Indigenous country.

Morales's Movement to Socialism party won a majority in the country's congress in the 2005 elections. He pledged to support Indigenous rights, and a new constitution that would guarantee those rights, and drew the attention of Indigenous leaders from across Latin America and beyond. This occurred after mass protests championed workers, social justice, and Indigenous culture while condemning neoliberalism. The protests aimed at improving the status of Indigenous peoples who have been seen as constituting over 60 percent of Bolivia's population yet were socially, economically, and politically subordinated. In 2009, a new constitution defined Bolivia as a multicultural state recognizing thirty-six Indigenous groups. It guaranteed Indigenous peoples, a number of civil and political rights such as reserved seats in congress and on the Constitutional Court, land, and cultural rights such as respect for their languages, freedom of religion, and permission to practice traditional forms of communal justice. The social exclusions of Indigenous people in Bolivia were very real, but changing an entire society is difficult even when an Indigenous leader like Morales comes to power. His government's social advances included increasing state spending on children from 7.1 percent of the budget in 2005 to 13.6 percent in 2015. Unfortunately, Morales's presidency ended ignominiously in 2019 with allegations of election fraud. (Though Morales was removed via a military coup, his party was elected back into the presidency in an election held a year later).

Other forms of official recognition and associated politics occurred (Bailey 2009). In Brazil, a 2003 law required the teaching of African and Afro-Brazilian history and culture in the country's schools. President Lula took the unprecedented action of naming four Afro-Brazilians as members of his cabinet and appointed an Afro-Brazilian Supreme Court justice. Ethnic holidays also were established. In Brazil there was the Day of the Caboclo, referring to Brazilians identifying of mixed white-Indigenous ancestry; Mixed Race Day, designated for all Brazilians identifying as mixed, including *caboclos;* Indian Day; and Black Awareness Day. In Panama there was the Month of Black Heritage; Afro-Colombian Day, held on May 21 to commemorate the abolition of slavery, was first celebrated in 2001.

One of the demands of these emerging groups was census data and other kinds of research into their situation and living conditions relative to other groups in the societies. They did so in collaboration with international organizations. Many Latin American countries did not require census questions pertaining to ethnic identity, and if they did they had not done so in recent years (see Table 9.2). Investigations into population size and segmentation, and how identity related to relative wealth and poverty, were started by census organizations using sophisticated sampling and statistical analyses. These changes also brought a whole slew of social science research studies conducted by Latin American and overseas social scientists, and often transnational, collaborative groups were formed (Ferrández and Kradolfer 2012). Further, opinion and information surveys were deployed that provided critical information, such as the AmericasBarometer from the Latin American Public Opinion Project at Vanderbilt University, and the Project on Race and Ethnicity in Latin America at Princeton University. Some of this research was consumed in Latin America and it showed the extent to which inequalities existed and persisted. At the same time, the categories, which themselves tended to both reflect and guide consciousness, seemed to shift from the past when Latin American states depicted ethnic differences as a matter of degree rather than as a matter of hard distinction. Ethnic-group boundaries were moving. Indeed, some of the seeming definitional discrepancies in Table 9.2 are reflections of these changes as well as differences in sampling methods (e.g., on the latter, the difference between recent estimates for Bolivia's Indigenous population at over 60 percent and the figure—40.6 percent—given in the Table). In Brazil's 2010 Statute of Racial Equality, the government declared that *pretos* and

Table 9.2   Afro-Descendant and Indigenous Populations (thousands) and
Percentages

	Year	Afro-Descendant Population	%	Indigenous Population	%	Total National Population
Argentina	2010	150	0.4	955	2.4	40,117
Bolivia	2012	24	0.2	4,068	40.6	10,027
Brazil	2010	97,083	50.9	897	0.5	190,733
Chile	2012	97	0.6	1,700	10.2	16,636
Colombia	2005	4,274	10.3	1,393	3.4	41,468
Costa Rica	2011	334	7.8	104	2.4	4,302
Cuba	2012	3,885	34.8	—	—	11,163
Dominican Republic	2010	2,267	24.0	—	—	9,445
Ecuador	2010	1,043	7.2	1,014	7.0	14,484
El Salvador	2007	7	0.1	13	0.2	5,744
Guatemala	2011	5	0.0	4,428	30.1	14,713
Honduras	2011	59	0.7	428	5.1	8,448
Mexico	2010	2,366	2.1	15,700	14.0	112,337
Nicaragua	2005	23	0.4	444	8.6	5,142
Panama	2010	313	9.1	418	12.1	3,454
Paraguay	2012	234	3.5	116	1.7	6,673
Peru	2007	411	1.5	7,600	27.0	28,221
Uruguay	2011	255	7.8	159	4.8	3,286
Venezuela	2011	953	3.5	953	3.5	27,228
Total		113,783	20.6	40,390	7.3	553,661

Source: Telles and Project on Ethnicity and Race in Latin America 2014: 26–27, citing original census reports.

Note: Authors calculate, given differences in how census data are collected, that Afro-descendant population (in thousands) in the Dominican Republic in 2010 is estimated to be 8,046 rather than 2,267; the percentage of Afro-descendants is estimated to be 89.0 rather than 24.0. The Afro-descendant population in Venezuela in 2011 is estimated to be 14,534 rather than 953; the percentage of Afro-descendants is estimated to be 53.4 rather than 3.5. Therefore, the Afro-descendant population in Latin America is estimated to be 136,723 rather than 113,783; the percentage of Afro-descendants in Latin America is estimated to be 24.7 rather than 20.6.

pardos would henceforth form the *população negra* (Black population), meaning the Black population was the country's largest ethnic group, and moving the categorization system closer to the US binary model. While *pretos* and *pardos* both lagged behind whites in terms of educational attainment and income levels, and so the move could be justified in a number of ways, at the same time Brazilians of all kinds often make sharp distinctions between light-skinned *pardos* and dark-skinned *pretos*.

Put in comparative perspective, Latin America has been historically one of the most unequal regions in the world. The crises accompanying neoliberal capitalist restructuring meant increasing foreign debt with structural adjustment policies imposed by international institutions including the International Monetary Fund and the World Bank as conditions for their loans, as well as capital flight, deindustrialization resulting in Brazil in more than a million industrial jobs lost between 1989 and 1997, along with rising unemployment and falling wages. Inequality unsurprisingly rose in this context (Hall and Patrinos 2012). The Gini coefficient is a common measure of inequality. In this index, a score of 0 means that every person has exactly the same income while a score of 1 means that one person has all of the income in a society and everyone else has none. Coming out of Brazil's military dictatorship, Brazil was one of the, if not *the,* most unequal countries in the world, with, according to the World Bank, the highest Gini coefficient ever recorded, of 0.633 in 1989. By the 1990s, most countries in Latin America had Gini coefficients of greater than 0.50. In the same period, the United States, also a very unequal society, had a Gini coefficient of 0.45, meaning even it was more equal than the countries of Latin America. By the 2000s, left-to-popular governments in Argentina, Bolivia, Brazil, Ecuador, Nicaragua, and Venezuela instituted a number of social programs designed to cut down social inequalities. On the other hand, in 2012 Colombia had the seventh-largest Gini score in the world, as it was one of the few countries in Latin America where social spending did not increase.

While the neoliberal project tended to increase the wealth and power of already-established elites, there were counter trends when leftist-to-populist leaders and governments were in power (Blofield 2011). For example, Brazil attempted, under Lula and under the administration of his successor, Dilma Rousseff (2011–2016), until a bloodless coup was staged to remove her, to stave off effects of neoliberalism. After reaching a high of more than 53 percent in 1999, the percentage of national wealth held by the wealthiest 10 percent in Brazil steadily declined to 46.5 percent in 2009. During that same period the poorest 50 percent of the population saw their share of the national income increase from 10.9 percent to 14.1 percent in 2009. The Gini score moved downward toward more equality, from 0.60 in 1995 to 0.52 in 2014. This occurred through investments in education, through various social programs, and through raising the minimum wage. Between 1990 and 2012, the percentage of Brazilians living in extreme poverty decreased from 25 percent to 4 percent.

Some of these programs affected disparities between traditionally dominant and traditionally marginalized ethnic groups, such as in Brazil. In 1990, the average income for households in Brazil headed by whites was 2.4 times greater than that of nonwhites. By 2009 it was 2.0. Differentials in life expectancy between Blacks and whites fell from 6.6 years in 1990 to 3.2 years in 2005, when this gap was less than it was in the United States. The poverty rate for Afro-Brazilians was 22 percent in 2014, which was a reduction of 22.8 percent from 2006, when it was 44.8 percent. Poverty produced predictable negative health outcomes for Afro-Brazilians (Caldwell 2017). Then there were the policies across the region specifically targeting marginalized Indigenous and Afro-descendant ethnic groups. Again, in Brazil, besides setting aside lands for Indigenous and Afro-descendant groups, affirmative-action programs in higher education directly challenged the (self-)image of "racial democracy"—now denounced by activists as a cloak for hidden, insidious racism (Cicalo 2012). In 2001, under political pressure from Black movement groups, the state legislature of Rio de Janeiro state adopted an affirmative-action program. Initially, the movement members intended to use the opportunity of quotas to promote the integration of *pardos* and *pretos* under the *negro* category. However, popular understandings were at odds with adopting the *negro* category. Indeed, a 2010 survey showed that only 6 percent of respondents identified as *negro* on an open-ended question regarding their own "racial" identification. After debate about whether affirmative action should be based on ethnic identity or class or some combination of both, and after elite backlash, the law's legality was affirmed in a 2012 Supreme Court decision; in any event, throughout the 2000s almost all of Brazil's universities had adopted some form of affirmative action. The system received widespread support from the public.

Poverty hit the Indigenous population especially hard. Societal inequality dipped slightly between the 1980s and 1990s but was on the rise again in the 2000s. Bolivia, with its large Indigenous population, had a high inequality index. In Mexico, according to the Indigenous Peoples' Human Development Index, as reported in 2010 by the UN Development Programme, 72 percent of Indigenous Mexicans lived in economic poverty and 38 percent lived in extreme poverty; 93.9 percent of the Indigenous population underperformed in at least one key index dimension, while 64.2 percent failed in at least three of them (United Nations Development Programme 2010). Many Afro-descendant groups across Latin America continued to live in poverty—meaning they did not have access to adequate diets, sanitation systems, or educational opportunities (see Table 9.3).

Neoliberal multiculturalism and recognition did not mean the end of inequalities and of unmet needs for traditionally disempowered groups (Ñopo, Chong, and Moro 2010). Neither did neoliberal multiculturalism and recognition mean an overturning of the status order and racist structures. As Table 9.4 shows, Latin Americans still maintained a system

Table 9.3   Poverty Rates by Ethnic Group in Select Countries (percentages), 2003–2011

| | Blacks and Indigenous | Black-White | | |
		Mulattos	Whites	Differences
Measured by household earnings				
Uruguay (2006)	31.8	50.1	24.4	25.7
Ecuador (2006)	55.8	52.1	31.2[a]	20.9
Brazil (2009)	—	33.8	16.7	17.1
Colombia (2003)	—	61.0	54.1[a]	6.9
Measured by unmet basic needs				
Uruguay (2011)	—	51.3	32.1	19.2
Colombia (2003)	—	34.5	22.7[a]	11.8
Costa Rica (2011)	54.2	34.1	25.5[a]	8.6
Venezuela (2011)	69.7	31.1	22.6	8.5

Source: Andrews 2016: 38.
Note: a. Whites and mestizos.

of cultural understandings of skin color as modifying ethnic categories and further defining racialized groups. Lighter skin tones and "European/white" physical features remain resources in a political economy of identity. Sometimes this occurs in what might seem unexpected ways. In late 2020, a special report to the United Nations Human Rights Council by independent expert Ikponwosa Ero on the treatment and status of people with albinism in Brazil (Ero 2020) documented the many challenges regarding education, employment, health, and stigma and discrimination, including stigma and discrimination emanating from Afro-Brazilian and Indigenous communities from which they come.

Neither did neoliberal multiculturalism and recognition mean sustained political gains for disempowered groups. For example, political scientist Kwame Dixon (2016) shows that even among Afro-Brazilians in Salvador da Bahia—a place that has become internationally associated with Blackness, with stereotyped images of Black cultural production in religion, with the spectacular Afro-Christian Candomblé, and with popular cultural forms associated with Blackness such as music, dance, and Carnival—they have enjoyed only modest gains in occupying political offices at the municipal, state, and federal levels. Further, while they were the majority in the city dubbed "Black Rome," they remained confined to the economic margins.

And neither did neoliberal multiculturalism and recognition mean that ostensibly leftist/progressive political regimes were beyond employing a noxious racist politics. Anthropologist Carmen Martínez Novo

Table 9.4   Inequality by Skin Color Group (percentages)

	Light	Medium	Dark
With university education (excluding students)			
Brazil	22	14	6
Colombia	20	15	13
Mexico	11	4	4
Peru	26	18	15
With primary education (excluding students)			
Brazil	29	31	39
Colombia	20	31	31
Mexico	55	66	73
Peru	14	17	22
In white-collar occupations			
Brazil	30	26	23
Colombia	28	23	26
Mexico	36	28	18
Peru	39	34	31
Domestic worker, farmer, or peasant			
Brazil	13	16	24
Colombia	29	42	35
Mexico	24	36	49
Peru	7	10	12

Source: Telles and Project on Ethnicity and Race in Latin America 2014: 227.

(2018) argues that in the "post-recognition era," when neoliberal regimes have claimed to recognize the rights of Indigenous and Afro-descendant peoples, a renewed racism can be released from the political right or from the political left. She shows how this was accomplished by what she called "ventriloquism," when non-Indians speak for Indigenous people, through the policies of the government of Ecuadorian president Rafael Correa (2007–2017). The notion of *Sumak Kawsay,* a purported ancient Indigenous concept and way of life translated as "Good Living," became central to the 2008 Ecuadorian constitution and all sorts of projects and plans. But *Sumak Kawsay* was really the invention of non-Indigenous and Indigenous elites to justify actions in the ostensible interest of Indigenous peoples. All kinds of projects, including actively pursuing environmentally damaging extractive industries and providing access to Indigenous lands and punishing those who were opposed, were justified under the banner of *Sumak Kawsay.* Parallel developments occurred in a variety of political regimes, including Bolivia, Chile, Colombia, Guatemala, and Mexico. In the process, *Sumak Kawsay,* and similar notions elsewhere, harkens to the colonial past where Indigenous peoples were spoken *for* because it was assumed that they could not speak for themselves. One lesson is that neoliberal

The Pelourinho is a historic neighborhood located in Salvador, Bahia, Brazil. It was the city's center during the Portuguese colonial period, and here is where slaves were punished (pelourinho means "pillory"). It is a testament to the brutal conditions and racism that Afro-Brazilians have endured. Credit: Arian Zwegers, https://commons.wikimedia.org/wiki/File :Salvador,_Largo_do_Pelourinho_(15744 040228).jpg

multiculturalism can deploy new essentialisms and ideological justifications that tend to allow a renewed racism. This way, a "new war on the poor" (Gledhill 2015) could be mounted.

Finally, in Latin America's post-recognition era it has been not just the United States with President Donald Trump's "build the wall" rhetoric and policies where immigration controversies are evident. In the case of Bolivian migrants in Argentina, where a substantial Bolivian community exists, a series of legal measures deemed to be anti-immigrant, including the threat of deportations, raised the ire of Bolivia's President Morales, who criticized Argentinean president Mauricio Macri for the measures, accusing him in 2017 of mimicking Trump's immigration policies, and sent a diplomatic delegation to Buenos Aires to protest.

Conclusion

The cultural constructions and ideologies of ethnicity and nationalism continue to structure reality for the people of Latin America. Class differences, often vast, make sure that these constructed realities matter. And this is even—or especially so—in the context of the region's changing and diverse connections to international economic, political, and cultural forces. The region's peoples are part of an increasingly global popular culture that infiltrates the region via electronic transmissions as well as great migratory flows that circulate from and back to and within the region. For students, the careful analysis of the nature of ethnicity, racism, class, and nationalism is essential for our understanding of contemporary Latin America. This understanding is crucial despite the realization that any discussion of the complexities of ethnicity, racism, class, and nationalism in a region as diverse as Latin America must be based on a perspective that sees general trends combined with marshaling data that are comparative and sensitive to historical differences between societies. What remains true for one context might be quite different for the next. What remains true for one context was not necessarily true always. And what will be true in the future cannot always be gauged from looking at the past. What continues to be certain, however, is that the phenomena of ethnicity, class, and nationalism will continue to affect each other.

But documenting disparities in, say, income by ethnic groups in contemporary times or in the past, while necessary, is not sufficient. These disparities are outcomes of deeper, more profound processes, not explanations in themselves. What we need as a community of scholars, from researchers to undergraduate students studying Latin American societies, are theoretical models that expose and analyze the factors and forces that actually produce these disparities. What I have tried to do in this chapter is to identify causal mechanisms through an approach from a political economy perspective that holds that these outcomes are produced through structured social relationships.

Ethnicity, patterns of racism, class, and nationalism are not "external" to each other in the sense that these constructs are conceived of as real entities "out there" that bump up against each other like billiard balls or beads on a necklace. They are not merely "intersecting" as in street intersections. This relationship is one of mutual constitution. But these constructs, real in their consequences, are mutually constructed and reinforcing of each other from the "inside," where the cultural construction and attendant ideological production related to one phenomenon is accomplished through, and dependent on, the construction of the others as part of underlying, hierarchically structured social relationships—that is, in social relationships of domination and resistance.

When North Americans and Europeans first encounter the ethnic, class, and national arrangements of Latin America either through travel or their studies, they are given pause by the degrees of difference between what they often come to take for granted as fact in their own society and what, for most, becomes a fascinating field of study, even if pursued from afar. Latin American people, whether based in the region or abroad and who have their own agendas, often emphasize for the benefit of North Americans and Europeans themselves the differences between North America and their societies. Here they might tend to emphasize what they depict as "easy" social relations as compared to the United States and Europe and an already-manufactured national consensus. But in the region, like elsewhere, social and cultural arrangements are not as natural as they appear to be and are, therefore, as works of human society and culture, mutable. In Latin America, like elsewhere, identities can and do become vehicles freighted with inequality. And the realities of real differences in income, wealth, status, and influence mean that these differences matter. It is not yet clear where the latest trends will lead, but both the historical structures and these newer processes of change require careful, empathetic analysis for a meaningful understanding of the contemporary scene.

Note

1. However, it should be noted that this way of proceeding is not universally accepted. Established scholars of Latin America and the Caribbean such as Wade (1997) are critical of lumping "race" under ethnicity. However, I hope that my argument for taking a political economy approach and for considering ethnicity as an umbrella term where "race," or, more specifically, racialized populations, is understood as a kind of ethnicity proves fruitful not only for a comparative consideration of the Latin American and Caribbean situation with others (e.g., the United States, the Middle East, Africa), but also for a step toward an explanatory framework.

10

The Roles of Women

Susan Tiano and Michael Shea

Does the paternalistic, *machista* culture embedded within many Latin American societies continue to impede the political and economic advancement of women? The number of female presidents in Latin America decreased from a peak of four in 2014 to none by 2018, with the expiration of Michelle Bachelet's second term in Chile, which followed Cristina Fernández in Argentina and Laura Chinchilla in Costa Rica, plus the impeachment and removal from office of Dilma Rousseff in Brazil. The first female leaders in the region were wives of former leaders, such as Isabel Perón in Argentina and Violeta Chamorro of Nicaragua, who was the first to be directly elected, in 1990. In 2017, women constituted, on average, 30 percent of the legislators in eleven Latin American countries; only Bolivia had a percentage proportionate to the population, with women constituting 53 percent of its legislature (Palomo 2018). Brazilian president Roussef's impeachment and removal by a mostly male, corrupt, and conservative congress has been called, at least partly, an act of misogyny. While women have made some gains, sexism and gender biases continue in many Latin American societies.

The past several decades have brought dramatic change to Latin America, which has boomed economically and, at least until recently, has experienced one of the most significant waves of democratization in modern history. During the 1980s, Ecuador, Peru, Bolivia, Argentina, Uruguay, Brazil, and Chile all replaced military regimes with civilian government that continues to this day, while Mexico shifted from one-party rule toward competitive elections. Such trends have paid off for Latin American democracy (Freedom House 2018; Robinson Country

Violeta Barrios de Chamorro receives the Nicaraguan presidential sash from the previous president Daniel Ortega, April 25, 1990. Credit: Fundación Violeta Chamorro, https:// commons.wikimedia.org/wiki/File:VioletaBcOrtega.jpg

Intelligence Index 2018).[1] It is also the region that ensures the highest degree of political equality for LGBT persons in the developing world (Corrales and Pecheny 2010), extending marriage rights to same-sex couples in Argentina (2010), Brazil (2013), Colombia (2016), and Uruguay (2013) (Pew Research Center 2017), and eroding barriers to LGBT advancement elsewhere in the region. Similarly, despite the persistence of gender discrimination women have made significant strides toward equality and empowerment and have expanded their participation in the political and economic arenas.

Women have been a significant factor in Latin American democratization: they have joined movements for gender inclusion and equality, have agitated for workplace protections, and have mobilized to demand LGBT rights (Safa 1990; Corrales and Pecheny 2010). Their activity is nothing new; Latin American women have catalyzed social change in previous historical epochs. What distinguishes the contemporary period is that women's achievements, and their roles as agents of social change, are more apt to be publicly acknowledged, acclaimed, and rewarded. In previous eras, Latin American women's multiform contributions to public life were obscured by images that defined women exclusively in terms of the private realm of the family and the wife-mother role, thereby concealing their activities outside the home. The current, long-

Mariela Castro addressing the Latin American plenary of the International Conference on LGBT Human Rights in Montreal, July 28, 2006. Credit: Montrealais, https://commons.wikimedia .org/wiki/File:Mariela_Castro.jpg

overdue attention to women's achievements has its intellectual roots in the burgeoning of feminist scholarship since the 1970s, and its practical roots in the dramatic social changes that have transformed gender roles in recent decades. The global media have played a role in bringing information about women's public contributions to international and national awareness, often with far-reaching implications.

Argentina's political history, for example, was irrevocably altered by the globally disseminated images of the Madres de la Plaza de Mayo, the women who helped topple Argentina's repressive military regime by staging weekly demonstrations in one of Buenos Aires's most public plazas to protest the disappearances of their loved ones at the hands of the military government.[2] By framing their protests as expressions of their maternal responsibilities, the *madres* insulated themselves from direct governmental repression until their activities had been too well publicized to be quelled without international protest and their cause had been adopted by international human rights organizations. The resulting political pressure was salient for Argentina's transition to democracy in 1983, showing the world an incontrovertible instance in which women's agency helped shape the course of a nation's history (Schirmer 1993; Bouvard 1994; Chant with Craske 2003: 11).

Another well-known, if less dramatic, example concerns the Mexican women working in multinational *maquiladoras,* who are stimulating industrial development in Mexico by producing goods for global export. *Maquiladora* women are often portrayed as docile, passive, and willing to work for a pittance—the antithesis of the unionized US males whose employment base has eroded due to industrial downsizing and overseas investment (Sklair 1993; Tiano 1994). Nevertheless, women *maquiladora* workers have staged numerous strikes for better wages and working conditions, and this is sparking cross-border organizing and support for *maquiladora* workers from an increasingly broad sector of US labor. As the fates of men and women workers on both sides of the border become increasingly intertwined with the spread of globalization, the scope of *maquiladora* women's contributions is too important to be ignored or occluded by misleading stereotypes (Bandy and Mendez 2003).

Latin American women have always played key productive and political roles, but many have performed them in informal contexts hidden from public view or have had their roles obscured by ideologies that define them exclusively as wives and mothers. The increasing awareness of women's contributions to their communities reflects both a broadening of the scope of their activities and the growing commitment of researchers and the mass media to shed needed light on women's public roles.

Latin American women are a highly diverse group, reflecting the same heterogeneity that characterizes Latin America generally. As Kevin Yelvington illustrates in Chapter 9, women's lives are defined not only by their gender—the social and cultural meanings attributed to biological sex—but also by the complex ways gender interacts with class, race, ethnicity, and sexual orientation or identity to influence women's social roles and relationships. The world of an Indigenous Maya woman in highland Guatemala may seem light-years away from that of an Afro-Latina in a Brazilian *favela* or a third-generation Italian lesbian in Buenos Aires. Yet many features unite women across the region and permit generalizations about their history and contemporary circumstances, some of which are common only to women and some of which are shared with men. Like the lives of their male counterparts, Latin American women's lives have been shaped by the Iberian conquest, which molded their societies after the fashion of their Spanish and Portuguese colonizers and drastically undercut the viability of Indigenous communities. Women also share with men a history of external dependency that has shaped their nations' development and, as Scott McKinney explains in Chapter 6, continues to dictate the terms under which their countries participate in the global economy. This heritage has posed challenges for women and men throughout Latin America, regardless of their specific circumstances. Nevertheless, Latin American women have other experiences in common due to their gender that sharply divide them from the men in their societies.

Production, Reproduction, and Gender Roles and Identities

A useful starting point for exploring the changing roles of Latin American women is the conceptual distinction between production and reproduction and the gender-based division of labor that results from these interlinked activities. Production is the creation of socially useful goods and services. Its continuity requires reproduction—the replenishment of labor and other productive resources. Reproduction involves the day-to-day maintenance and emotional support of family members, some of whom provide the labor for the productive sphere.

Reproduction also includes conceiving, bearing, and caring for children and preparing them for their roles in adulthood. In pre-capitalist societies, both production and reproduction take place within the household and are oriented toward meeting the family's subsistence needs. Under capitalism, a separation exists between the private sphere of household and family, where reproduction occurs, and the public, formal sphere, which is the primary locus of production (Tiano 1984). Between the private and public spheres lies the informal sector, involving activities that often take place within the household, such as preparing and selling food or washing and ironing clothing, that are typically sold commercially (Arizpe 1997).

The gender construction of femininity in Latin America places great emphasis on marriage and motherhood, while women's sexuality is marginalized. Female sexual desire has been viewed as transgressive, with treacherous impacts on the image of the Virgin Mary. Women still often find it difficult to discuss sexual pleasure, and they risk losing their reputations by living with men or having open sexual relations before marriage. Similarly, lesbians continue to confront deeply rooted heterosexist cultural practices and social structures even though Latin American societies are generally becoming more tolerant of sexual relationships among lesbians, gays, bisexuals, and transsexuals. As cultural norms become more open, decriminalization of homosexual practices is likely to occur more quickly than, say, legalization of abortion, which is completely legal in only three countries (Cuba, Uruguay, and Argentina) and is highly restricted in the others. Latin America is not the only region in the world where getting an abortion is very difficult, but it is the only non-Muslim region where this is true.

Historically, in Latin America and elsewhere throughout the world, with the advent of capitalism and the separation between the public and private spheres, the gender division of labor became less reciprocal and less complementary. Women assumed primary responsibility for reproduction and maintaining the domestic sphere, while men were allocated to productive roles in the public sphere. This bifurcated division of labor continues to be supported by patriarchal ideologies that define women in terms of their wife-mother role, whatever their actual marital or childbearing status or their roles in public production (Beechey 1978: 192). In Latin American societies, the dominant ideology of *marianismo,* the cult of the Virgin Mary, glorifies motherhood and cultivates women to be self-sacrificing moral guardians of the family (Stevens 1973: 94; Chant with Craske 2003: 10). According to this belief system, the family is held together spiritually and emotionally through the mother's steadfast devotion. Women's dedication to their families is expected to extend beyond their selfless commitment to childrearing, domestic tasks, caring for the sick and elderly, and other reproductive roles; women must also maintain their purity by remaining within the safe haven of the household (Vaughan 1979: 67). *Marianismo* supports the gender division of labor by deeming public participation to be inconsistent with women's inherent nature and familial responsibilities. Women not only are expected to refrain from undertaking waged employment but also are implored to avoid social or political activities that take them beyond the protective confines of the home. The ideological corollary of *marianismo* is *machismo,* the notion that male sexual identity is bound up in traditional notions of masculinity: in return for serving as the sole source of economic support and decisionmaking authority for the family, a man is entitled to enjoy personal independence, sexual freedom, and unfettered access to public life, as well as the devotion, nurturance, and domestic contributions of his wife or partner.

The dual concepts of *marianismo* and *machismo* and the patriarchal ideology they reflect and support have traditionally limited men's and women's agency by subjecting them to rigid gender role expectations and nonegalitarian relationships. They have reinforced a culture of heteronormativity, the view that society must be arranged around heterosexual institutions, bifurcated gender roles, and rigid norms governing sexual behaviors. Heteronormativity demands that homosexuality, transsexuality, and other nonheterosexual arrangements be eliminated or at least discouraged because they challenge the heterosexual status quo and threaten social order. The association of heterosexuality with stability, procreation, and life itself implies the corollary association between homosexuality and death—of the family, of hallowed traditions, of society as a whole (Feit 2011). In a heteronormative context, the worth of each individual, regardless of sexual orientation, is evaluated according to his or her conformity to heterosexual standards, and this in turn affects the person's social status, legal rights, and employment (Corrales and Pecheny 2010). The heteronormative assumptions of the *marianismo-machismo* ideology reinforce the heterosexual status quo both by demanding conformity to traditional gender roles among heterosexual men and women, and by penalizing LGBT persons in a host of ways that limit their social acceptance and thwart their struggles for equality. Nevertheless, many Latin

American women, LGBT persons, and others wishing to jettison restrictive gender roles have resisted these patriarchal imperatives.

As Table 10.1 demonstrates, sexual desire informs sexual identity in multiform ways. The primary political concern for LGBT persons tends to be the ability to act on their sexual desires and express their sexual identities free from persecution or discrimination (Corrales and Pecheny 2010). The heteronormative assumption that the private sphere is the only legitimate locus of sexual identity and activity is challenged by the LGBT community's very public demand that all private sexual identities be socially and politically recognized as valid (Pecheney 2010).

In Latin America, governments often enact policies that treat homosexuality with varying degrees of illegality despite considerable cultural

Table 10.1 Desire and Sexual Identity

	Desire: Sexual Orientation	Gender Identity: Self-Identity	Gender and Identity Expression
Heterosexual	Predominant or exclusive attraction to the opposite sex	May not be an issue	May or may not deviate from heteronormativity (e.g., macho/effeminate men; effeminate/tomboy women)
Homosexual (men are referred to as gay; women as lesbians)	Predominant or exclusive attraction to the same sex	May or may not identify as LGBT	May or may not deviate from heteronormativity (e.g., macho/effeminate men; effeminate/tomboy women), with one caveat: may display different degrees of "outness" at home, at work, or among friends
Bisexual (men and women)	Attraction to the opposite and the same sex	May or may not identify as LGBT	May or may not deviate from heteronormativity (e.g., macho/effeminate men; effeminate/tomboy women), with one caveat: may display different degrees of "outness" at home, at work, or among friends
Transgender (men and women)	Sexual orientation may or may not be an issue	Rejects gender identity assigned at birth	May or may not deviate from heteronormativity (e.g., macho/effeminate men; effeminate/tomboy women), with one caveat: may display different degrees of "outness" at home, at work, or among friends
Transsexual (men and women)	Sexual orientation may or may not be an issue	Rejects gender identity assigned at birth	Changes appearance, and maybe anatomy

Source: Corrales and Pecheny 2010, adapted from table 1.1: 4.

tolerance among the public, particularly in cities. Gay and lesbian parades in Brazil along Rio's Copacabana Beach have coexisted paradoxically with exaggerated machismo. Homosexuality has been criminalized with selective enforcement, partly based on religious dogma and partly to keep it in the proverbial closet. As elsewhere, less attention has been paid to female homosexuality. In Latin America, "being a man" requires being heterosexual; anything that might be interpreted as homosexual is construed as feminized. The passive fear of being perceived as feminine is said to drive male sexuality. As a result, vibrant gay and bisexual communities continue to coexist with significant public and cultural repression of gay people.

During the 1960s and the 1970s, the demand for LGBT equality was expressed in terms of sexual liberation and willful and public transgression of the laws and norms that result from and reinforce traditional heteronormative sexual mores (Pecheney 2010). As democratization swept across the region in the 1980s, challenges to heteronormativity and movements for sexual equality began to be expressed more in terms of human rights and demands for inclusion and equality (Pecheney 2010). Early lesbian activism was founded upon the philosophical influences of the Latin American Left, mixed gay/lesbian social movements, and the women's liberation movements that characterized feminism in the region (Friedman 2010). In Chile, for example, lesbians joined with feminists and gay men to demand abolishing the law against sodomy, believing it to be an "outdated and paralyzing custom carried over from an oppressive period" and emblematic of the heteronormativity of *machismo/marianismo* (González 2010: 383). Yet in their struggles for sexual liberation and later for acceptance and equality, lesbian women were often left to mobilize on their own behalf, with little or no support from heterosexual women. Because the *machismo/marianismo* dynamic made the notion of female life lived without reference to men as sexual partners unthinkable, lesbians were all but invisible in the women's movement (Friedman 2010).

Women's real-world circumstances have often dramatically contradicted the *marianismo* ideology and the heteronormativity underlying it. Yet it has persisted throughout Latin American history to circumscribe women's activities and define their self-concepts.

Women in Latin American History

At the time of first contact with Europeans, the economic and political circumstances of Indigenous women varied greatly. Most anthropologists posit an inverse relationship between women's status and the degree of class stratification in their societies (Gailey 1987: 51–54). In relatively egalitarian hunting-and-gathering and horticultural societies, where gender divisions of labor were more egalitarian and reciprocal, the complementary productive contributions of both genders offered women considerable economic parity with men (Etienne and Leacock 1980: 6). By contrast, in agricultural societies with elaborate cultivation systems, bureaucratic states, and hierarchically ranked social systems, women's status was below that of the men from their same class. Both the Aztecs, who built a sophisticated empire in what is now central Mexico, and the Incas, who controlled extensive territory in the Andean region, created societies in which women were deemed inferior to men and had more limited access to resources (Nash 1980: 137; Silverblatt 1980: 155).[3] Both empires had grown through a process of conquest in which the subjugated peoples were enslaved and forced to pay tribute to the empire. Similarly, the Carib-speaking people of the West Indies amassed considerable territory by subduing the more peaceful Arawaks, killing the Arawak men and retaining the women in a subordinate status for breeding and labor (Miller 1991: 17). Such dynamics suggest that political conquest stimulated class and gender inequality among Indigenous Latin Americans.

The imposition of colonial rule on the peoples of Latin America produced diverse outcomes, ranging from complete annihilation through disease and warfare to incorporation into radically new social relations intended to produce wealth for the colonial power. The Indigenous populations who were forcefully assimilated into colonial societies were joined by the successive waves of African-born people who were imported to provide labor for the mines and plantations.

Colonization impacted the way Latin American societies reacted to nonheterosexual sexualities, which were tolerated to varying degrees in precolonial times (Tortorici 2012). Scholarly debate surrounds both the extent to which homosexual, bisexual, and transgendered desires were tolerated before the Spanish arrived and the degree to which these desires, when acted upon or expressed as identities, were punished under colonial regimes. The crime of sodomy—whether heterosexual or homosexual—was punished, when it was punished, as a form of religious heresy in Spain and Portugal; but the prosecution of the same acts in their Latin American colonies was often less stringent, because they fell under the jurisdiction of secular authorities (Tortorici 2012). While male homosexual desires were sometimes tolerated by colonizing authorities under certain very limited circumstances, female homosexuality was often ignored altogether—not because it was accepted, but because women were regarded as objects for male sexual desire rather than as autonomous sexual beings with desires of their own. The *marianismo* ideology, and the rigid gender roles it demands and supports, partially allowed for the subjugation of Indigenous peoples, characterized as sodomites in order to justify their repression and often forcible religious conversion (whether or not they ever actually engaged in nonheteronormative sexual activity). This subjugation through the application of criminally enforced heteronormativity would have ramifications for the struggle for LGBT equality in the modern era, and its effects would extend as well to other aspects of political and economic life in the region.

Although each affected group experienced colonialism in its own way, certain commonalities cut across all colonized groups. Regardless of women's circumstances prior to European contact, colonial rule tended to diminish their status (Boserup 1970: 53). Women in horticultural societies, whose productive contributions had given them relative parity with men, found themselves marginalized from socially valued roles and resources. Colonialism also weakened the position of women in stratified agrarian societies because even though precolonial systems had subordinated them to men, these arrangements were more egalitarian than the social and legal systems imposed by the colonizers (Nash 1980).

As colonial administrations implemented the mercantile capitalist economy that was emerging in Europe, Indigenous people were immersed in new relations that exploited their labor and divorced them from productive resources. The Spanish exploited precious metals, agricultural products, and manufactured finery such as hand-woven textiles to enrich Spain's coffers and finance its military exploits. The British and Dutch developed more elaborate global trade networks in which agricultural products from their New World plantations were exchanged for commodities produced elsewhere (Chirot 1977: 22). With the transition from subsistence to market-based production, land originally held in common and farmed cooperatively by both men and women became privately owned. The best land was claimed by the Europeans or awarded to Indigenous elites as compensation for their loyalty. This disadvantaged most Indigenous people, but it was especially harmful to women, whose ability to own and dispose of land was drastically limited under Spanish law. Women were denied title to the land they worked, even after the death or desertion of the legally designated male head of household (Silverblatt 1980: 167).

In some regions, both slave and free women labored along with men to produce agricultural goods for domestic or foreign markets. More typically, women were relegated to subsistence production, often on the most marginal land, or were confined to the domestic sphere, where they engaged in household labor and made items such as woven textiles for family use or market exchange. Such manufacturing often occurred under highly exploitative conditions. In colonial Peru, for example, Indigenous women were often sequestered in locked rooms and forced to weave cloth that colonial administrators appropriated for sale to Europeans. There and elsewhere women were raped or forced into concubinage by the Spanish and their Indigenous allies (Navarro 1999: 32). Women were often sexually victimized by priests, who forced them to prostitute themselves or serve as mistresses as a form of penance for presumed sins (Silverblatt 1980: 169).

Women's responses to the colonial arrangements that limited their legal rights and exploited their labor and sexuality ranged from accommodation to resistance (Navarro 1999: 24). A common accommodative pattern of women during the early colonial period was to become consorts or wives of the colonizers, thereby achieving relatively high status for themselves and their offspring. The Spanish initially encouraged these liaisons to compensate for the scarcity of European women in the colonies, but later saw them as a threat to the Spaniards' racial and cultural homogeneity (Nash 1980: 141). By this time, however, the intermixing of Indigenous, African, and European peoples had laid the basis for complex class- and racially stratified societies in which women at all levels derived their primary status from their roles as reproducers. Elite women were expected to bear children who would perpetuate upper-class privilege, whereas women of the popular classes were expected to breed children to replenish the rapidly dwindling labor force. The policies advanced by the Spanish crown to regulate marriage in the colonies blended with those of the Catholic Church, affecting the lifestyles and values of women across the class spectrum.

Even though colonialism reduced women's access to productive roles and resources, women generated goods for household consumption and products for market exchange. Women's economic roles mirrored their positions in the race-class hierarchy. Upper-class women, whose work was typically confined to the private sphere, managed their households and regulated the care and training of their children. Women in the merchant and artisan classes often played entrepreneurial roles in family enterprises. Most lower-class urban women worked as domestic servants or as laundresses, midwives, *curanderas* (healers), or food vendors. Rural women, in their capacity as subsistence agriculturalists, often not only provisioned their families but also produced a surplus to be traded or sold. The lack of viable economic options in the countryside led many young women to migrate to urban areas, even though their Indigenous origins often exposed them to discrimination and their employment options were typically limited to domestic service and street vending.

During the mid-nineteenth century, Argentina, Brazil, Chile, and Mexico introduced "normal" schools for teacher education and began admitting women to secondary schools and universities (Korrol 1999: 73). Women whose families could afford their educational expenses could now prepare for middle-class careers in healthcare, teaching, and other professions that reflected women's specialization in household tasks. Because women were confined to jobs viewed as extensions of their reproductive roles, their work was undervalued and badly compensated, and their achievements rarely won them much public recognition.

In the twentieth century, Mexico, Argentina, and Brazil developed labor-intensive manufacturing industries to produce basic consumption goods. Women formed the backbone of the labor force in the textile, tobacco, and food-processing industries (Nash 1983: 11; Towner 1979: 49). With the transition to capital-intensive industries during the 1930s and 1940s, however, the preference for male labor reduced women's share of the industrial work force (Tiano 1994: 42; Cravey 1998: 28). In turn-of-the-century Mexico, when textile and tobacco production dominated manufacturing, about 76,000 women held factory jobs; after forty years of industrial diversification, only half as many women held jobs in manufacturing (Vaughan 1979: 78). Similarly, in 1900, over 90 percent of Brazil's industrial labor force was female, but by 1940 women were only 25 percent of the manufacturing work force (Schmink 1986: 137).

Women's expulsion from industry sometimes occurred when men enlisted the state to penalize businesses for hiring women. In Puerto Rico, women constituted such a large share of the manufacturing labor force by the 1930s that the male-dominated unions petitioned the government to help reverse the trend. When the state complied by granting subsidies to industries that hired men, there was a drastic reduction in women's industrial employment (Nash 1983: 8). Similar trends have been documented for Mexico and Brazil (Vaughan 1979; Saffioti 1975). Despite equally discriminatory practices in many other employment sectors, women have continued to maintain a foothold in the formal economy. Yet only in the 1970s did women begin to consolidate their position in the labor force.

Women's contributions to the political life of their societies date from precolonial times, when many Indigenous women were active in the movements that opposed European conquest (Navarro 1999: 37–39). According to documents from the early conquest period, women's boldness on the battlefield terrified Spanish observers, who perceived them as incarnations of the Amazons (Miller 1991: 16). Others resisted colonial incursion by fleeing to remote regions beyond Spanish domination. Some women descendants of the Incas escaped Spanish rule by moving to isolated areas where they reinstated their native religious practices as a form of cultural resistance (Silverblatt 1980: 179).

Women played active roles in the political mobilizations that culminated in the early nineteenth-century independence struggles. Among those immortalized for their heroism are Policarpa Salavarrieta, who was publicly executed by the Spanish for fomenting revolution in Colombia; María Quiteira de Jesús, who distinguished herself in battle in Brazil's independence movement; and Marie Jeanne a-la-Crete-a-Pierrot and Henriette St. Marc, who participated in Haiti's revolts against the French (Korrol 1999: 61).

The increasing political activity of the post-independence era was generally a masculine prerogative within the new postcolonial institutions, which, like their counterparts elsewhere in the Western world, denied women suffrage and other rights to citizenship (Miller 1991). With formal political channels closed to women, those who wished to shape local or national politics did so informally, through their social networks within and outside their families.

The notion that woman can experience sexual pleasure did not gain cultural currency until Vatican II in the early 1960s, but even then, such liberated images sparked resistance. Femicides, the killing of women, are often a reaction to changing norms and practices concerning women's sexuality; while they often occur with impunity, by 2020 they were leading to criminal apprehensions and political scandals in countries like Mexico and Chile. Female sexuality challenges cultural practices of male privilege. Women's lives are more restricted by these gender constructions than men's in ways that go beyond expressions of sexuality to limit their participation in the economic, educational, and political spheres, though substantial improvements have occurred in some countries.

LGBT politics is no exception to this tendency. While Argentina decriminalized homosexual sex in 1886 in emulation of the Napoleonic code, laws remained, as they did in Brazil, Mexico, and Colombia, that could be used to harass, prosecute, and imprison homosexuals on public morality or indecency charges (Encarnación 2016). Argentina cracked down on male prostitution and began enforcing *edictos policiales,* which allowed for the detention and arrest of anyone engaging in "immoral behavior," including public acts of affection by members of the same sex and men dancing together in bars (Encarnación 2016).

Lesbians were less often targets of such repression, not because lesbianism was considered more acceptable, but because the ideology of *machismo* and the greater sexual freedom it allowed men meant they had more opportunities to run afoul of such edicts. Because the patriarchal nature of Latin American societies limited lesbians' political activity, early LGBT movements were often dominated by men (Friedman 2010). When lesbians did organize for themselves, many came from communist, socialist, or anarchist parties and, like their gay male counterparts, struggled not just for acceptance but for sexual liberation (Friedman 2010).

Lesbian, feminist, or not, women's political activity was most apt to flourish in times of political upheaval, when grassroots resistance movements required their support. Just as women had figured centrally in the movements for independence from colonial rule, they also made key contributions to movements against unjust or dictatorial national regimes. During the Mexican Revolution, women fought alongside men on the battlefields, and others accompanied men to battle sites where they cooked, washed clothing, and tended wounds (Macias 1982: 25). In Guatemala, women participated in the strike that helped to depose the autocratic regime of Jorge Ubico in 1944, inaugurating the first free elections in the country's history; in Bolivia, women staged street demonstrations and hunger strikes that helped to bring the National Revolutionary Movement to power in 1952. Cuban women were active in the revolutionary movement that unseated the Batista regime in 1959 and led to a socialist government that formally promoted women's equality (Larguia and Dumoulin 1986).

Movements to transform political regimes were but one form of women's political participation during the pre- and post-independence periods. Much of their political energy was devoted to causes such as female suffrage that directly affected women's well-being. By the late nineteenth century, women in Argentina, Uruguay, Chile, Brazil, Mexico, and Cuba had begun to develop movements that agitated for women's suffrage and other reforms (Korrol 1999: 84). The emergence of feminist political journals gave women a forum for espousing their views on female equality; examples include the Brazilian journal *O Sexo Feminino,* established in the 1870s, and *La Mujer,* which Chilean women published in the 1890s (Miller 1991: 69).

Women also organized conferences such as the International Feminist Congress, which convened in Buenos Aires in 1910, and two feminist congresses held in 1916 in Mérida, Mexico (Korrol 1999: 87). The Mérida conferences illustrated the deep divisions within the Mexican feminist movement. Whereas conservative Catholic women challenged proposals they viewed as threatening to women's traditional roles, the more progressive women advocated platforms that deplored gender inequalities in education and employment and demanded legal reforms to ensure women's equal treatment before the law (Macias 1982: 73–75). Such complexity has contributed to the form of consciousness that has characterized Latin American feminism in the twentieth and twenty-first centuries. Rather than rejecting their feminine roles as wives and mothers, as do many Western feminists, Latin American feminists have sought to eliminate conditions that impede women's ability both to successfully perform those roles and to use them as platforms for critiquing and transforming their societies (Miller 1991: 74).

Contemporary Latin American women have expanded their public participation in both the political and economic spheres. Many have defied social convention by disavowing their reproductive roles, but many—such as Argentina's *madres*—have acted within their capacities as grandmothers, mothers, and wives to make lasting changes in their societies.

Women in the Formal Labor Force

Latin American women's employment patterns have traditionally been shaped by the ideology of *marianismo,* which deems formal labor force participation inappropriate for married women because it interferes with their domestic roles and threatens their families' well-being (Levenson-Estrada 1997: 210). A woman was encouraged to work, if at all, only until she married and had children, at which point she was expected to leave the work force to devote herself to full-time domesticity (Arizpe 1997: 29; Fernandez-Kelly 1983). Partnered women who needed to generate income were expected to do so in the informal sector, where tasks and schedules were more compatible with reproductive duties (Beneria 1992: 92). The cultural injunction against married mothers working for wages led to discriminatory hiring practices that restricted their employment opportunities. This ideology was at the root of protective legislation that circumscribed the range of jobs available to women, preferential hiring practices favoring men, gender-based wage discrimination, men's opposition to their wives' employment, and women's ambivalence about their wage-earning roles (Tiano 1987: 227).

As a result of *marianismo* and the gender division of labor it supports, Latin American women's labor force participation has lagged behind that of women in most of the world (Psacharopoulos and Tzannatos 1992: 49–52). Latin American governments have encouraged this situation to reduce unemployment levels in contexts where demographic growth has exceeded the economy's capacity to provide enough jobs for the working-age population (Gregory 1986: 21). As Table 10.2 suggests, until recently traditional images of women's ideal roles shaped the Latin American work force. In the 1960s, women's labor force participation rarely rose above 25 percent and was less than 20 percent for the bulk of countries for which we have reliable data. While more urbanized countries such as Uruguay (32 percent) and Chile (29 percent) showed higher female employment than rural countries such as Guatemala (13

Table 10.2   Labor Force Participation Rates for Working-Age Women and Men (percentages), 1960–2020

		Male		Female		
		Rate	Change	Rate	Change	Female/Male
Argentina	1960	92.8		24.4		26.3
	1980	90.8	−2.0	33.1	8.7	36.5
	1995	76.2	−14.6	41.3	8.2	54.2
	2000	58.7	−17.5	44.5	3.2	75.8
	2005	61.2	2.5	49.0	4.5	80.1
	2010	74.1	12.9	48.2	−0.8	65.0
	2015	73.2	−0.9	47.3	−0.9	64.6
	2020	72.8	−0.4	49.5	2.2	69.0
Brazil	1960	95.0		18.2		19.2
	1980	92.4	−2.6	33.0	14.8	35.7
	1998	82.0	−10.4	52.8	19.8	64.4
	2000	69.1	−12.9	56.0	3.2	81.0
	2005	69.8	0.7	57.5	1.5	82.4
	2010	76.2	6.4	53.1	−4.4	69.2
	2015	74.7	−1.5	53.2	0.1	71.2
	2020	74.3	−0.4	53.0	−0.2	74.0
Chile	1952	94.5		28.6		30.3
	1982	87.2	−7.3	28.9	0.3	33.1
	1999	74.4	−12.8	36.5	7.6	49.1
	2000	55.8	−18.6	38.0	1.5	68.1
	2005	56.9	1.1	40.6	2.6	71.4
	2010	75.1	18.2	49.2	8.6	65.5
	2015	74.4	−0.7	50.6	1.4	68.0
	2020	73.9	−0.5	49.3	−1.3	73.0
Colombia	1951	97.4		19.0		19.5
	1985	85.4	−12.0	39.4	20.4	46.1
	1999	79.8	−5.6	57.7	18.3	72.3
	2000	68.2	−11.6	54.8	−2.9	80.4
	2005	69.1	0.9	56.6	1.8	81.9
	2010	83.6	14.5	58.5	1.9	69.9
	2015	82.6	−1.0	58.8	0.3	71.2
	2020	80.9	−1.7	57.0	−1.8	74.0

continues

Table 10.2   Continued

		Male		Female		
		Rate	Change	Rate	Change	Female/Male
Costa Rica	1963	97.0		18.6		19.2
	1984	89.7	−7.3	26.4	7.8	29.4
	1999	81.5	−8.2	38.5	12.1	47.2
	2000	59.2	−22.3	38.0	−0.5	64.2
	2005	60.6	1.4	41.1	3.1	67.8
	2010	77.1	16.5	45.9	4.8	59.6
	2015	73.9	−3.1	45.3	−0.6	61.3
	2020	76.5	2.6	46.4	1.1	64.0
Ecuador	1962	97.8		17.7		18.1
	1982	87.7	−10.1	22.6	4.9	25.8
	1998	55.2	−32.5	36.8	14.2	66.7
	2000	64.1	8.9	45.0	8.2	70.2
	2005	65.4	1.3	47.8	2.8	73.1
	2010	79.9	14.5	50.3	2.5	63.0
	2015	81.3	1.5	55.4	5.1	68.2
	2020	81.1	−0.2	54.6	−0.8	70.0
Guatemala	1964	96.2		13.1		13.6
	1981	91.3	−4.9	14.7	1.6	16.1
	1999	87.9	−3.4	45.6	30.9	51.9
	2000	59.3	−28.6	36.5	−9.1	61.6
	2005	61.0	1.7	40.9	4.4	67.0
	2010	88.2	27.2	46.3	5.4	52.5
	2015	85.0	−3.2	40.6	−5.7	47.8
Honduras	1961	52.7		7.7		14.6
	1974	48.8	−3.9	8.9	1.2	18.2
	1999	88.0	39.2	45.8	36.9	52.0
	2000	58.7	−29.3	33.4	−12.4	56.9
	2005	60.5	1.8	37.4	4.0	61.8
	2010	82.8	22.3	40.5	3.1	48.9
	2015	85.8	3.0	50.9	10.4	59.3
	2020	86.0	0.2	50.7	−0.2	61.0
Mexico	1960	96.5		19.1		19.8
	1980	92.4	−4.1	32.7	13.6	35.4
	1999	83.8	−8.6	38.5	5.8	45.9
	2000	58.3	−25.5	37.5	−1.0	64.3
	2005	60.2	1.9	41.0	3.5	68.1
	2010	80.1	19.9	44.6	3.6	55.6
	2015	79.0	−1.1	44.1	−0.4	55.9
	2020	78.6	−0.4	43.5	−0.6	57.0
Panama	1950	97.0		24.9		25.7
	1980	87.3	−9.7	35.7	10.8	40.9
	1999	79.7	−7.6	43.2	7.5	54.2
	2000	61.7	−18.0	42.5	−0.7	68.9
	2005	63.0	1.3	45.5	3.0	72.2
	2010	81.8	18.8	48.4	2.9	59.2
	2015	81.2	−0.6	52.8	4.4	65.0
	2020	80.0	−1.2	51.4	−1.4	67.0

continues

Table 10.2   Continued

		Male		Female		
		Rate	Change	Rate	Change	Female/Male
Peru	1961	96.8		22.7		23.5
	1981	91.3	−5.5	29.0	6.3	31.8
	1999	79.4	−11.9	58.1	29.1	73.2
	2000	68.9	−10.5	57.7	−0.4	83.7
	2005	69.8	0.9	59.2	1.5	84.8
	2010	86.0	16.2	71.1	11.9	82.7
	2015	84.5	−1.6	69.0	−2.2	81.7
	2020	85.0	0.5	69.8	0.8	83.0
Uruguay	1963	93.0		32.0		34.4
	1985	92.4	−0.6	46.0	14.0	49.8
	1998	55.8	−36.6	39.1	−6.9	70.1
	2000	62.8	7.0	50.9	11.8	81.1
	2005	63.1	0.3	51.9	1.0	82.3
	2010	76.0	12.9	55.8	3.9	73.4
	2015	74.4	−1.6	56.1	0.3	75.4
	2020	73.3	−1.1	56.0	−0.1	82.0
Venezuela	1961	96.4		22.1		22.9
	1981	89.0	−7.4	35.0	12.9	39.3
	1997	53.2	−35.8	30.1	−4.9	56.6
	2000	55.3	2.1	37.4	7.3	67.6
	2005	57.0	1.7	40.7	3.3	71.4
	2010	78.2	21.2	50.6	9.9	64.7
	2015	77.4	−0.8	50.2	−0.3	64.9

Sources: Psacharopoulos and Tzannatos 1992; Wilkie 2002; ECLAC 2008; World Bank 2018.
Notes: Honduran participation rates in 1961 and 1974 censuses were calculated differently from those of the other countries, whose rates are the ratio of the economically active population to the working-age (twenty- to sixty-year old) population. Early Honduran rates use the total population (all age categories) as the denominator for calculating male and female participation rates. All data from 2010, 2015, and 2020 based on International Labour Organization modeled estimates.

percent) and Honduras (8 percent),[4] all Latin American nations had relatively low rates of female employment, particularly in contrast with male rates, which were uniformly above 92 percent.[5]

The 1960s and 1970s witnessed considerable growth in women's employment. By the early 1980s, one-third of working-age women in Mexico, Brazil, Argentina, Venezuela, and Panama were in the labor force, as were almost 40 percent of Colombian women and almost half of Uruguayan women. In just twenty years women's economic activity jumped by 20 percent in Colombia and almost 15 percent in Brazil, Uruguay, and Mexico; most other countries saw gains of at least 8 percent. Exceptions include Chile, where the seventeen-year Pinochet regime advocated policies designed to confine women to the home, and Guatemala, where political turmoil stunted both the male and female work force.

Importantly, the rise in women's economic activity was not accompanied by parallel growth in men's employment. In the 1950s and 1960s, upward of 93 percent of Latin American men were economically active— they either held jobs or were unemployed but actively seeking work. This accounted for most men below retirement age who were not in school, producing a "ceiling effect" beyond which rates had little room to rise. With so many men in the work force, it might be reasonable to expect women's employment gains to occur at men's expense. This argument, which often becomes a rationale for maintaining traditional gender roles, envisages men and women as competitors for the same scarce jobs. Feminist social scientists have criticized this "competitive" argument for being inconsistent with the way gender-segregated labor markets operate. Since labor markets channel most working women into "female" occupations like teaching, nursing, and clerical work that men rarely want, rising female employment need not come at men's expense.

The fact that men's economic activity decreased everywhere in Latin America during the 1960s and 1970s, when women's employment was rising throughout the region, could be taken as evidence for the "competitive" scenario. If women had expanded their employment primarily by taking jobs from men, the gains in women's rates would be roughly equivalent to the declines in men's. Yet, except for Costa Rica, where the 7.8 percent increase in women's rates paralleled a 7.3 percent decrease in men's, the trends in women's and men's rates show little correspondence. In some countries, such as Brazil and Uruguay, large increases in women's employment accompanied minimal declines in men's activity. In such cases, even if the entire decline in men's employment was due to women's movement into male jobs, this would account for but a tiny fraction of women's employment growth. Elsewhere the decline in men's economic activity substantially exceeded the rise in women's. In Ecuador, the 5 percent increase in women's employment could not compensate for the 10 percent decrease in men's activity, nor could the 0.3 percent rise in Chilean women's activity make up for the 7 percent drop for Chilean men. In these cases, the fall in male activity was too large to be accounted for by women's increasing participation, even if it did occur at the expense of male employment; clearly other factors played a role in men's worsening employment scenario during the 1960s and 1970s.

The expansion of women's employment continued, and in some countries accelerated, during the last two decades of the twentieth century. By the late 1990s, countries throughout Latin America reported female employment rates of 30 percent or higher.[6] Peru and Colombia, where 58 percent of women were economically active, topped the list, although Brazil was not far behind, with 53 percent female employment. With the exception of Venezuela (30 percent), all the remaining countries reported rates ranging between 37 percent (Chile and Ecuador) and 46 percent (Honduras and Guatemala). The latter two Central American nations showed the largest increase, with Guatemalan women's employment rising by 31 percent and Honduras showing a similar rise. In another group of countries (Peru, Brazil, Colombia, Ecuador, and Costa Rica), women's employment rose by 12 percent or more. With the exception of Colombia, which ranked above most countries in 1980, the countries showing the greatest gains during the period are the ones that had previously lagged behind and thus had the farthest to go. Similarly, of the countries that reported more modest increases or decreases, several, such as Uruguay, Argentina, and Panama, had such high rates during the 1980s that even with small increases they could rank in the middle of the continuum of countries by the late 1990s. By contrast, the slow expansion of women's employment in Mexico and Chile over the period pulled them into the bottom one-third of countries, while Venezuela's 5 percent decrease caused it to plummet from the top one-third in 1980 to dead last in 1999.

During the 1980s and 1990s, men's economic activity declined, in some cases dramatically, throughout the region. By 1999, only a little more than half of working-age men in Uruguay, Venezuela, and Ecuador and three-fourths of men in Argentina and Chile were in the work force. Men fared better in the rest of the region, with rates hovering around 80 percent in six countries (Mexico, Brazil, Costa Rica, Colombia, Panama, and Peru) and rising to 88 percent in Honduras and Guatemala. Unlike the previous period, when there was no clear relationship between men's and women's changing employment patterns, during the late twentieth century the trends in men's and women's rates across countries showed some correlation. Thus, in Guatemala and Honduras, where women's economic activity reveals the largest increases during the period, men's labor force participation declined the least. Conversely, the only two countries in which women's employment actually decreased during the period, Venezuela and Uruguay, were also the ones where male employment declined the most drastically. This suggests that the same factors that contracted employment opportunities for women also restricted them for men, while those that greatly expanded women's employment options also mitigated the negative influences on male employment that were so pervasive in the rest of the region.

These trends continued into the 2000s, when women's employment continued to rise despite slight declines in Peru, Guatemala, Mexico, Costa Rica, and elsewhere. Men's rates also rose in most countries, reversing the downward trend of the 1990s though never reaching the extremely high rates observed in the 1960s and 1970s. The fact that men's employment gains paralleled those for women demonstrates that women's rising economic activity did not occur at the expense of men's. In fact, the growth in women's share of the work force, which had increased so substantially until the 1990s, either stabilized or declined (in Argentina, Brazil, Uruguay, Colombia, Guatemala, and Mexico) during the first two decades of the twentieth century. Only time will tell whether women's employment gains will continue as the twenty-first century proceeds.

Let us explore how Latin American women's typical work histories have changed during the past half century. In the early 1960s, women's economic activity tended to peak early in their life cycle—between the ages of twenty and twenty-five—and to decline steadily with advancing age. This indicates that many women worked prior to marriage and childbearing and then left the work force as they entered their late twenties and early thirties.

By the 1980s, women's economic activity was peaking at a later age. In contrast to the early 1960s, when economic activity was highest among twenty- to twenty-four-year-olds, in the 1980s it was most pronounced among women in their late twenties and early thirties. A related change concerns the age span during which women's employment remained at high levels and the point at which it began to decline steeply. During the 1960s, in every country except Mexico, women's participation dropped steadily after it peaked in their early twenties. By the 1980s, the age span of maximal economic activity had been extended, and women's employment generally did not drop substantially until a later point in their life cycle. By the 1980s, growing numbers of women in their thirties and forties were remaining in the work force. Not only were more women joining the labor force, but more were remaining for a greater portion of their lives or were reentering after leaving to raise their children. These patterns have continued into the present century.

What might account for the rise in economic activity, particularly among women in their thirties and forties, who two or three decades earlier would likely have devoted themselves to full-time domestic roles? One way to explore this question is to use a conceptual distinction made by labor economists between "push" and "pull" factors. Push factors are forces such as economic need that impel women into the work force to support their households. Pull factors are conditions that either attract women into the labor force or expand their employment opportunities. The availability of suitable jobs, the proliferation of schools and adult literacy programs, the weakening of norms that symbolically confine women to the household, and the attraction of noneconomic rewards such as personal autonomy may all operate as pull factors that draw women into the labor force. These two sets of factors need not be mutually exclusive. A woman may be compelled to enter the work force because her household requires her income; at the same time, she may respond to the lure of financial independence, personal fulfillment, or other anticipated benefits of paid employment. The growth in women's economic activity reflected a complex mix of influences that both forced women to take jobs and augmented their incentives and opportunities for paid employment.

Many women joined the work force out of economic need. Throughout the "lost decade" of the 1980s and continuing into the 1990s, Latin American nations were plagued by an economic crisis that dramatically eroded their living standards. As Scott McKinney documents in Chapter 6, the economic crisis ushered in several decades of rampant inflation, rising unemployment, and serial currency devaluations that jeopardized all but the wealthiest households (Cockcroft 1983: 260; Scott 1992: 22). At the same time, the structural adjustment policies most Latin American governments adopted to stabilize their economies led to substantial cuts in state funding for healthcare, education, and other social services and removed price supports for basic commodities (Chuchryk 1991: 152; Lustig 1992: 79). To make matters worse, governments often capped minimum wage levels to counteract inflation, thereby limiting workers' incomes. Rising male unemployment and underemployment often undercut men's traditional roles as family breadwinners (Beneria 1992; Chant 1991). As the data in Table 10.2 demonstrate, the proportion of economically active men in all Latin American countries declined during the period. Even those who were able to hold down jobs often found their wages inadequate to support a household (Fernandez-Kelly 1983: 56; Safa 1995: 24).

These trends were particularly devastating for poorer households, whose already precarious circumstances were further eroded by rising expenses and the elimination of vital government services (Safa 1995: 33). Working- and middle-class households also experienced a drastic decline in their standard of living. Households formulated various strategies to cope with these deteriorating circumstances; most commonly, all working-age members, male and female, had to generate income (Beneria 1992: 92). Daughters and sons often had to discontinue their schooling to take jobs or postpone marriage to help support their parents' households. Many partnered women who had previously devoted themselves to domestic tasks or informal income-generating activities now had to take full-time jobs. Women's wages were especially important for households in which adult men were absent or unemployed (Chant 1991: 158). In some households, men's inability to support their families led to destructive behaviors such as alcohol abuse or caused them to desert their families (Beneria 1992: 91). In others, the lack of local employment options forced men to migrate elsewhere in search of stable wages (Safa 1995: 32). Many women thereby became the sole providers for families without male household heads (Anderson and de la Rosa 1991: 55). In short, economic necessity pushed women from various backgrounds into the work force during the crisis-plagued years of the 1980s and early 1990s.

Yet the upsurge in women's economic activity was not simply a result of economic need and rising male unemployment. Many other trends drew women out of the household, either by expanding their economy's demand for female labor or by increasing the supply of women willing and able to enter the work force. One of the most important pull factors was the growth of women's employment opportunities. During the 1960s and 1970s, when many Latin American nations underwent rapid economic and political development, jobs proliferated for women in both the governmental and market sectors. The locus of women's employment opportunities shifted during the 1980s and 1990s, when the economic crisis brought a halt to the development of previous decades.

As the structural adjustment measures employed to re-stimulate economic growth eroded barriers to foreign trade and investment, multinational corporations, with their well-known preference for female labor in many sectors of their work force, came to account for a growing proportion of jobs in Latin America. Jobs for women proliferated in multinational agribusiness firms, which flocked to Mexico, Chile, and elsewhere to produce fruits and vegetables for export to global consumers (Barrientos et al. 1999; Appendini 2002). Jobs for women also grew in manufacturing, as global firms relocated to Latin America (and elsewhere) to reduce production costs by employing low-wage workers to process products for global export (Fernandez-Kelly 1983; Korrol 1999: 104). Beginning in the 1950s with Puerto Rico's Operation Bootstrap and the 1960s with Mexico's *maquiladora* program, export-led industrialization has become increasingly common throughout Latin America. Women are often preferred for these jobs because they tend to work for lower wages than men and are perceived as more docile, more manually dexterous, and better able to tolerate the monotony of repetitive assembly work (Fuentes and Ehrenreich 1983: 12; Sklair 1993: 171–172).

The expansion of the Mexican *maquiladora* industry illustrates the impact of export-led industrialization on the female labor market. In 1967, two years after the *maquila* program was established, it encompassed seventy-two firms employing 4,000 workers, over 80 percent of whom were women. By 1990, the program had grown to include almost 2,000 firms and over 460,000 workers (Sklair 1993: 54, 68). The stimulus of NAFTA and the booming US economy during the late 1990s greatly accelerated *maquila* investment, augmenting the work force to 1.3 million people by 2000 (Tiano and Ladino 1999) and continuing its expansion into the twenty-first century. In the program's early days, *maquilas* preferred to hire young, single, childless women. As the program grew, the *maquilas* relaxed their employment criteria and hired more older women, partnered women, and women with children, as well as more men (Tiano 1994: 90). The *maquilas'* rapid proliferation and changing recruitment practices had a significant impact on Mexico's female labor market. By providing jobs for women, particularly wives and mothers, who often face employment discrimination, *maquilas* dramatically increased women's employment opportunities in Mexico and in other Latin American countries that have attracted foreign investment in manufacturing (Safa 1995).

The increasing demand for female labor has also reflected the rapid growth of the service sector, much of which involves activities, such as cleaning, food preparation, and personal caretaking, that are viewed as extensions of female roles. Even sectors such as mining and construction, which have traditionally employed men, now include more women. Fortunately for women workers, the crisis-born conditions of the 1980s that forced many women to earn wages also stimulated the demand for female labor. The crisis and its aftermath compelled many businesses to minimize operating costs, which many accomplished by turning to women as a low-cost labor source. Other employers began to recruit women because they viewed them as more reliable than men and less apt to organize workers' unions.

The increased demand for women's labor and the growing acceptance of paid work for partnered women and mothers have augmented women's employment opportunities. But to take advantage of them women must have access to education. Women's educational attainment reflects both objective conditions such as the availability of schools, and subjective factors such as parents' aspirations for their daughters. Since the 1960s, accelerated investment in public education by Latin American governments has led to a proliferation of rural and urban schools. Governments have encouraged parental support for their children's education through mass media campaigns urging parents to enroll and keep their sons and daughters in school (Rothstein 1982: 118).

These efforts led to substantial increases in school enrollments. By 1980, almost all Latin American girls between ages six and eleven were enrolled in primary school (Stromquist 1992: 1), and most adolescent girls in Argentina, Chile, Costa Rica, Ecuador, Panama, Peru, and Uruguay were in secondary school (Chant with Craske 2003: 89). Subsequent decades saw more gains in girls' secondary school enrollments; by 1993, rates approached 70 percent or above in Argentina, Chile, and Colombia, while Guatemala (at 23 percent) was the only country in the region where less than one-third of girls were in secondary school (Chant with Craske 2003: 89). Progress in providing postsecondary education was also considerable. By the mid-1980s, 17 percent of Latin Americans aged twenty to twenty-five were earning a university degree, and in several countries (Argentina, Cuba, Nicaragua, and Panama) women's enrollment exceeded that of men (Stromquist 1992: 2).

Women's advances in public education were uneven. Rural women, particularly those in Indigenous communities, often benefited only minimally from educational reforms. As recently as the 1990s in Guatemala, where Indigenous groups constitute 60 percent of the population, 78 percent of rural women were illiterate; the disparity between comparable rates for rural men (60 percent) and those for urban women (36 percent) suggests that both racism and sexism played a role in limiting Indigenous women's access to education. Indigenous women in Bolivia faced similar obstacles: whereas rural women's illiteracy rates reached 69 percent, only 37 percent of rural men and 23 percent of urban women were unable to read and write (Stromquist 1992: 24). These disparities reflect not only the poorer quality of rural schools but also the cultural and material hurdles Indigenous women have had to overcome to attain an education.

While the economic crisis of the 1980s slowed the progress in educating women in Latin America, it was insufficient to undercut those gains entirely. Even after fifteen years of crisis, women in the 1990s were better prepared to compete for jobs than their counterparts from previous generations. And by the 2010s, women had made such remarkable gains in educational attainment that they had reached parity or near parity with men, as Table 10.3 demonstrates. The regionwide increase in women's educational attainment was another pull factor that augmented women's employment.

Women's rising labor force participation has not simply reflected the accelerating demand for women's labor, their growing educational preparation, and the increasing economic pressures to support their families. Regardless of how much a woman's household may need additional income or how abundant her job opportunities might be, she cannot enter full-time employment if her reproductive responsibilities are too demanding. Most employed women, regardless of their marital status or household composition, receive little help with housework and childcare from male household members (Beneria and Roldan 1987: 123). To avoid being crushed by their double burden, working women must find ways to balance the competing demands of their productive and reproductive roles.

One solution is to have fewer children. Women with small families are better able to make the necessary childcare arrangements to allow

Table 10.3   Female/Male Educational Attainment

Rank	Country	Parity
1	Bahamas	1
1	Barbados	1
1	Brazil	1
1	Cuba	1
1	Jamaica	1
29	Honduras	1
30	Colombia	1
32	Uruguay	1
34	Nicaragua	1
39	Chile	0.999
40	Costa Rica	0.999
44	Argentina	0.998
49	Venezuela	0.997
53	Mexico	0.996
54	Ecuador	0.996
55	Panama	0.995
61	Paraguay	0.994
67	El Salvador	0.992
72	Dominican Republic	0.991
73	Suriname	0.991
82	Peru	0.988
85	Belize	0.988
103	Guatemala	0.962
108	Bolivia	0.956

Source: World Economic Forum 2017.
Note: A value of 1 indicates perfect male/female parity in educational attainment.

them to reenter the labor force, whether as soon after the birth as possible or when the children reach school age or beyond. The spread of family planning throughout much of Latin America during the late twentieth century made it easier for women who wanted smaller families to implement their choices. By the 1990s, most Latin American women in their childbearing years used contraception, with rates ranging from a high of 84 percent in Uruguay to a low of 31 percent in Guatemala (Chant with Craske 2003).[7]

The result was a substantial decline in fertility throughout Latin America. Between 1960 and 1980, the average number of children per woman dropped from 6.0 to 4.6. In 1960, only three countries (Argentina, Cuba, and Uruguay) had fertility rates below 5.0, and thirteen countries had rates above 6.5. Two decades later, only five countries (Bolivia, Ecuador, El Salvador, Honduras, and Nicaragua) had fertility rates above 6.0, and seven countries averaged fewer than 4.5 children per woman. By 2000, thirteen out of nineteen Latin American countries had fertility rates of 3.0 or less (Chant with Craske 2003: 73). Women's declining fertility resulted from various factors, including increased public awareness of the links between overpopulation and economic and ecological difficulties, the growing commitment of Latin American governments to reduce population growth, and the spread of family-planning technologies and information. The expansion of employment opportunities for women also helped lower their fertility, both by augmenting economic incentives to have smaller families and by providing an alternative to motherhood as a way of enhancing social status (Blumberg 1991: 110). Lowered fertility was thus both a cause and a result of women's rising labor force participation. The dramatic drop in fertility throughout Latin America was another pull factor that increased women's employment.

Another stimulus to women's economic activity reflects a change in the prevailing cultural ideology that defines appropriate roles for women. When women are regarded exclusively as wives and mothers, and when work outside the home is considered detrimental to their domestic roles, women face extreme obstacles to formal employment. No matter how great her economic need, a woman will not be able to enter the work force if no employer will hire her or if her partner will not allow her to leave the house. If taking a job would make her worry about neglecting her children, emasculating her husband, or risking her feminine purity, a woman is unlikely to seek or long remain in paid employment. For Indigenous women, these social realities are often exacerbated by pervasive racism and discrimination against Indigenous people. And even though LGBT women are less apt to be burdened by childrearing responsibilities than their heterosexual counterparts, heteronormative images that define all women in terms of the wife-mother role can limit their employment options as well.

One of the most important incentives to women's rising economic activity has thus been the relaxation of cultural norms against their paid employment, particularly for partnered women and mothers (Beneria and Roldan 1987: 49). This normative change has reflected a shift in the *marianismo-machismo* ideology and a reformulation of role expectations that consider men to be ineffectual or unmasculine if they cannot support their households without female assistance. As these rigid gender roles have weakened, women's aspirations have changed accordingly, leading many to acquire the motivation and training to prepare for careers, to remain single or select partners who will not interfere with their jobs, and to plan their childbearing for increased compatibility with wage-earning activities. At the same time, the change in male role definitions has diminished men's resistance to their wives' and daughters' employment and has increased employers' willingness to hire partnered women without fear of spousal reprisals (Tiano 1994: 93–96).

This gender role transformation is both a cause and a result of women's rising educational attainment. With advancing education, women tend to expand their occupational horizons and to question the validity of conventional gender roles for themselves and their daughters. Conversely, parents are more apt to make the necessary sacrifices to keep their daughters in school if they have abandoned conventional gender roles and believe education will foster their daughters' economic security in later life. In addition to promoting women's education, the erosion of traditional gender roles has expanded their job opportunities. Employers are more willing to hire women if they do not anticipate spousal resistance and if they don't expect women to be so committed to their families that they neglect their jobs. In turn, employers' increasing demand for female labor has helped to erode cultural norms proscribing women's employment. The desire to lower costs and achieve other benefits by hiring women has led many employers to reformulate their images of appropriate roles for women to justify their hiring practices. Similarly, governments hoping to attract corporate investment in industries that recruit women have ensured the availability of female labor through media campaigns and other strategies designed to weaken ideological constraints to female employment (Ruiz 1988).

Another expression of this ideological shift in gender roles is the growing embrace of emancipative values and self-expressive values. As economic development and increased levels of education have improved living conditions in much of Latin America, self-expressive and emancipative values have begun to replace survival values. Self-expressive values generally indicate a growing tolerance of foreigners, and gays and lesbians, as well as a desire for greater gender equality (Inglehart and Welzel 2014). Emancipative values, reflecting the universal desire for life free from domination, prioritize freedom of choice and equality of opportunity (Welzel 2017). Table 10.4 shows that, over time, men and women in six Latin American countries have come to value self-expressive and emancipative values over survival values (Inglehart and Welzel 2014). As emancipative values have increasingly guided people's actions, this has stimulated social movements advocating for feminism, equality, and human rights (Welzel 2017). Heterosexual women, lesbians, and the LGBT community generally have benefited from this trend.

While these shifts in values, norms, and ideologies may help to reconcile the cultural contradiction between *marianismo* and women's

Table 10.4   Changing Values in Latin America

Country	World Value Survey Dimension	1981– 1984	1989– 1993	1994– 1999	1999– 2004	2005– 2007	2011– 2014
Argentina	Survival vs. self-expressive	−0.32	0.03	0.67	0.55	0.52	0.40
	Traditional vs. secular	0.14	−0.36	−0.53	−0.99	−0.78	−0.45
Brazil	Survival vs. self-expressive	n.a.	−0.39	0.02	n.a.	0.34	0.23
	Traditional vs. secular	n.a.	−0.89	−1.25	n.a.	−0.98	−0.84
Chile	Survival vs. self-expressive	n.a.	−0.14	−0.07	0.26	−0.01	0.32
	Traditional vs. secular	n.a.	−0.98	−0.69	−0.81	−0.78	−0.38
Mexico	Survival vs. self-expressive	−0.18	0.08	0.26	0.71	1.13	1.23
	Traditional vs. secular	−1.07	−0.20	−0.52	−1.48	−1.50	−1.66
Peru	Survival vs. self-expressive	n.a.	n.a.	−0.13	0.09	n.a.	0.00
	Traditional vs. secular	n.a.	n.a.	−1.21	−1.31	n.a.	−1.10
Uruguay	Survival vs. self-expressive	n.a.	n.a.	0.49	n.a.	1.01	0.70
	Traditional vs. secular	n.a.	n.a.	−0.15	n.a.	−0.34	−0.31

Source: Inglehart and Welzel 2014.

growing need for paid employment, they do not resolve the dilemmas that the rapid flux in female roles is posing for Latin American women. Many women who find themselves forced to take jobs were raised to aspire to full-time motherhood and to view paid work and family duties as incompatible. Many resent their jobs for forcing them to neglect their families. Many others who are committed to their jobs feel guilty about deriving personal satisfaction from work that takes them away from their children (Tiano 1994: 118; Tiano and Ladino 1999). And those who have resolved the conflicting emotions that surround their dual roles nevertheless struggle to balance the competing demands of their "double day" in contexts where governmental and private services for working mothers are sorely lacking (Safa 1990). Many women view this challenge as more than a personal struggle and are organizing to demand institutional changes, such as childcare and workplace reforms, to facilitate their ability to perform their domestic and wage-earning roles simultaneously. Issues such as these are only a few of the many catalysts for the growing political mobilization of women.

Women in Latin American Politics

Although women have always taken part in Latin American social and political movements, the past five decades have witnessed a dramatic upsurge in their participation (Jaquette 1991b: 1). Women have mobilized in unprecedented numbers to support or protest political regimes, agitate for better working conditions, make demands on the state for improved services and affordable commodities, and transform legal and social barriers to gender equality. Much of their activity has avoided formal political channels—both because it has often occurred within authoritarian climates where political parties, trade unions, and mass demonstrations were illegal (Perelli 1991: 101), and because many women have considered institutionalized politics to be futile, corrupt, or inconsistent with their feminine roles (Pires de Rio Caldeira 1990: 72). Instead, Latin American women have developed their own form of politics that stems from their reproductive roles and blurs the boundaries between the public world of politics and the private realm of the family (Safa 1990: 355). The apolitical connotation of the wife-mother role has given women some immunity to protest despotic regimes that have brutally repressed political resistance (Perelli 1991: 107).

The diversity of women's political objectives, agendas, and strategies precludes ready categorization. Most analysts distinguish between political activities in which women join with men to pursue goals that transcend gender differences, and those that unite women around issues specific to them as women. The latter encompass both "feminist" movements, which explicitly aim to achieve gender equality, and nonfeminist "women's" movements, which are organized to satisfy needs or make demands that stem from women's reproductive roles and familial responsibilities (Chinchilla 1993).

Feminist Movements

For most of the twentieth century, feminist movements were confined to a small segment of middle-class women whose goals were alien to most Latin American women (Miller 1991). Lower-class and Indigenous women often saw feminist discourse as at best irrelevant and at worst threatening to their daily lives, in which survival depended upon cooperation with men. Many middle-class women felt little resonance with feminist demands for employment parity, family-planning programs, or divorce reform because they viewed these objectives as inconsistent with their roles as wives and mothers.

Not until the 1970s did the feminist movement gain momentum in Latin America. Mexico City's selection to host the first United Nations International Women's Year Conference in 1975 increased the visibility of Latin American feminism regionally and internationally (Chinchilla 1993: 46). The conference inaugurated a decade-long international effort to address women's issues—many of which were exacerbated by the economic crisis of the 1980s—and bring them to the forefront of public discourse. The United Nations Decade for Women stimulated conferences throughout the region that brought women together to dialogue about issues and strategies. The debates among the various branches of the feminist movement, each with its own agenda and objectives, and the often-heated discourse between feminist and nonfeminist women helped to raise consciousness on all sides (Miller 1991: 201).

Some of the most potent critiques have come from Indigenous women, who have raised concerns that the feminist focus on "gender" obscures important differences between Indigenous and non-Indigenous women (and men). Many Indigenous scholars and activists have argued that gender inequality and oppression are products of colonialism, which eroded what was originally a reciprocal division of labor in which men and women had complementary and equally valued social roles. For example, Mapuche activists deplore the feminist focus on women's rights, which embody Western notions of individual autonomy that drive a wedge between the genders. They argue that a return to role complementarity would restore the lost equilibrium that previously existed between men and women in Indigenous communities (Richards 2005). LBTQ women have offered analogous critiques reflecting their views of the links between gender and capitalism, patriarchy, and heteronormativity. The focus of these critiques is that feminists have tended to place gender relations and gender inequality foremost in their advocacy, while ignoring issues of racism and heteronormativity (Duarte 2012).

In the wake of these critiques, feminist movements have expanded their agendas to incorporate issues of race, class, sexuality, and ethnic diversity. These movements have attempted both to make feminist agendas more relevant to the lives of Indigenous, minority, and LBTQ women, and to increase their appeal to women who support conventional gender roles (Barrig 1991; Duarte 2012). In so doing, Latin American feminists have diversified while continuing the pattern set by their twentieth-century forebears. Even though they might embrace feminine roles as a source of personal power and as platforms from which to agitate for social change, they have also been willing to challenge the heteronormative assumptions behind men's and women's traditional gender roles in order to achieve a greater degree of liberation (Korrol 1999: 84; Duarte 2012). Their contributions illustrate the diversity of perspectives that have given Latin American feminists an important voice within global feminist discourse that portends growing influence in the coming decades.

Mixed-Gender Movements

Latin American women have often joined men in political actions, ranging from short-lived spontaneous protests to long-term organized movements, that have operated both within and outside established political channels (Chinchilla 1993; Jaquette 1991a). Such activities have reflected the nature of the state and its responsiveness to popular demands; the availability of parties, unions, and other formal channels; and the social circumstances and class-based interests of the participants. In many Latin American nations elites have maintained class and racial hierarchies through authoritarian governments that have limited popular participation. Whereas upper-class women have sometimes mobilized to support these regimes, many nonelite women from diverse racial, ethnic, and cultural backgrounds have participated in revolutionary struggles for democratization and social reform.

Early in the twentieth century, women typically supported revolutionary activities indirectly by preparing food, nursing the wounded, gathering intelligence, and providing other types of support for male combatants. The Cuban Revolution, in which women joined in the guerrilla activities, marked a turning point in women's revolutionary activity. The revolution's success in 1959 inspired women to participate, often as armed combatants, in the grassroots resistance movements that arose in Argentina, Brazil, El Salvador, Guatemala, Nicaragua, Peru, and Uruguay (Chinchilla 1993: 41). In only one of those countries, Nicaragua, did the revolutionary forces succeed in changing the political system; in the others, resistance movements provoked repressive government measures to regain "order," many of which led to authoritarian regimes that brutally repressed all forms of political opposition.

While many women participated in regime-challenging movements on the political left, others took part in right-wing movements aimed at maintaining the elite-dominated status quo. In Chile, for example, the "pots and pans" demonstrations of upper-middle- and upper-class women, who took to the streets to protest the rising cost of food, were instrumental in bringing down the socialist government of President Salvador Allende, which fell through a military coup that initiated the authoritarian regime of Augusto Pinochet (Miller 1991: 182; Korrol 1999: 99).

Many of the movements in which women have joined forces with men have not involved direct challenges to regimes. As women have entered the work force in growing numbers, they have come to play more important roles in strikes, work stoppages, and other forms of resistance against poor working conditions (Chinchilla 1993: 43; Levenson-Estrada 1997). Urban labor struggles have involved both working-class women, who have channeled their protests through unions, and middle-class women, who have expressed their grievances through professional organizations. Women have also participated in various student protest movements. In 1968, when the Mexican government responded to a strident student demonstration by shooting at the unarmed protesters, many of the students who were killed were young women (Miller 1991: 6).

Similarly, Indigenous and peasant women have joined with men to demand land reform, improved working conditions on plantations and mines, and other remedies to perceived injustices. In Bolivia, Indigenous Aymará and Quechua women have struggled to resist continual threats to their autonomy and the steady usurpation of their land (Cusicanqui 1990). In Chile, Mapuche women have played an active role in resisting the Chilean state and advocating for the recognition of Mapuche rights (Richards 2005). In Guatemala, a movement has grown up around Rigoberta Menchú, a K'iché Maya Nobel Peace Prize recipient who has won international acclaim for her efforts to draw attention to the plight of Indigenous Guatemalans. Other examples of Indigenous women's struggles include the activities of the Bolivian Housewives

Committee, who worked alongside men to protest labor conditions in the tin mines, and those of the Chiapan peasant women who organized to protest the Mexican government's involvement in free trade initiatives that threatened to impoverish the countryside (Barrios de Chungara with Viezzer 1978; Klubock 1997).

Yet, except for the Central American revolutionary struggles of the 1970s and 1980s, these resistance movements have incorporated only a small proportion of Latin American women. Most women, despite their support for the political activists' ideals, have remained aloof from politics (Pires de Rio Caldeira 1990: 50). Women face a host of barriers to political activity, including opposition from male partners who demand their wives' constant presence in the household; burdensome domestic and childcare responsibilities that limit their time, energy, and physical mobility; internalized images of politics as dangerous, useless, or simply inappropriate for women; and submissive self-conceptions that limit political agency. Indigenous women face additional obstacles that reflect their racial and cultural subordination. Given the pervasiveness of these obstacles to formal political activity, it is not surprising that women's participation has more commonly taken other forms that are more consistent with their reproductive roles and their position within the gender division of labor (Jelin 1990: 186).

Women's Movements

Grassroots movements in which women have been the primary or sole participants have multiplied in recent decades. These movements react to conditions that threaten household survival or hamper women's ability to perform their reproductive roles as wives and mothers. Their primary objective is to demand that the government rectify these conditions by providing needed services, transforming economic conditions, or abandoning oppressive political policies (Safa 1990: 356).

Women's movements typically arise when formal political channels are inoperative or are perceived as ineffective. Their creation signifies women's demands for incorporation into the political arena in a way that reaffirms their identity as women, particularly in their roles as custodians of family welfare (Schirmer 1993: 32). In politicizing issues such as high food prices, unsafe drinking water, lack of sewerage and electricity, inadequate schools, or government cutbacks in healthcare services, these movements erode the traditional division between the private and public spheres (Jaquette 1991a: 188). The boundary weakens when family concerns, traditionally viewed as beyond the scope of "normal" political debate, are defined as public issues and when women use their private roles as wives and mothers to legitimate their entry into the public world of politics (Chuchryk 1991: 156).

Women's movements often emerge when women who share a common concern about a community issue work through their social networks to publicize and gain support for their activities or to organize collective demonstrations. Grounded in neighborhoods where women share common experiences that transcend ethnic, class, or religious differences, they typically involve issues such as cutbacks in basic government services that affect the whole community. This is one reason why poor women, whose economic disadvantage has traditionally muted their political voice, figure so prominently in many women's movements. Yet the primary basis around which poor women organize women's movements is their gender rather than their class position: while acutely conscious of the economic hardships that pervade their lives, they express their concerns as wives and mothers rather than as members of an impoverished class (Safa 1990: 356).

Women's movements have taken various forms, depending on their objectives, participants' circumstances, and the degree of involvement of sponsoring bodies such as churches and nongovernmental organizations. Most fall within two broadly defined categories: economic movements that demand government responses to material deprivation, inadequate infrastructure, or other threats to economic survival; and human rights organizations that challenge repressive government policies. The former, which proliferated in the late twentieth century due to the economic crisis and continue in today's era of privatization and globalization, address survival needs and demand essential government services. The latter, which have emerged in countries suffering under authoritarian regimes, address basic civil rights and demand political democratization. The crisis-born nature of both types of movements may explain their rapid explosion on the Latin American scene; it also helps account for the widespread participation of women, particularly those from the lower classes, who ordinarily would not enter the political arena (Safa 1990: 357).

Women's economic movements stem from diverse sources. Some are rooted in the squatter movements of the 1960s, in which women often organized the overnight "invasions" of empty land by homeless urban dwellers, whose makeshift settlements often evolved into stable urban communities (Jelin 1990: 189). Others owe their existence to the liberation theology wing of the Catholic Church, which offered safe space for women to hold meetings and helped secure food, clothing, and other items for collective distribution (Miller 1991: 196). Some movements arose when spontaneous demonstrations protesting rising food costs, inadequate infrastructure, or the elimination of state-sponsored services forged networks of women who had similar concerns and a shared commitment to addressing them.

Regardless of their source, these movements have aimed to challenge conditions that impair women's domestic role performance. Some movements' strategies have been geared toward helping members survive economic downturns by offering them new ways to generate income or to reduce the rising costs of basic commodities. The communal kitchens organized in Peru, Uruguay, and elsewhere, through which households join to purchase and prepare food, represent one collective strategy for reducing consumption costs (Chuchryk 1991: 154). Another approach has been to organize protest demonstrations and pressure groups to demand basic urban services such as running water, sewerage, and electricity (Bennett 1995; Safa 1990: 361). Women's organizations have protested government cutbacks to healthcare, education, and other public services. Although these movements have met with varying degrees of success and have sometimes evoked heavy-handed treatment by governments aiming to silence women's protests, they continue be a valuable venue for translating women's "private" concerns into public discourse.

Women's human rights movements were galvanized by authoritarian regimes that sought to stamp out opposition by outlawing institutionalized political activities and brutally repressing dissent. These regimes singled out trade union leaders, politicians, academicians, journalists, student activists, and anyone else considered subversive to the regime for imprisonment, torture, or murder. In Argentina, Chile, Guatemala, Uruguay, and elsewhere, many people were kidnapped by government agents who later denied any knowledge of their whereabouts. Public protest of these human rights violations was dangerous and often led to similar treatment for those brash enough to attempt it. Not surprisingly, those best able to form resistance organizations were those with the least political visibility; because women were viewed as apolitical guardians of family welfare, their activities were often immune to government scrutiny (Chuchryk 1993: 87). Mothers' clubs and women's self-help organizations could operate in situations where men's organizations—even those with similar objectives—would have been brutally repressed. In Chile, women's groups won international recognition by making *arpilleras,* or tapestries, that depicted the Pinochet regime's violence, and distributing them surreptitiously to global markets (Agosín 1993: 20). In Guatemala, women's organizations have engaged in a decades-long struggle to account for the 38,000 people who have disappeared since the late 1970s (Schirmer 1993:

40–44). In Argentina, as previously noted, the Madres de la Plaza de Mayo risked and sometimes lost their lives through their courageous efforts to expose their government's widespread human rights violations (Bouvard 1994). In daring to resist a near-totalitarian regime, these women were instrumental to Argentina's re-democratization, particularly with respect to memorializing victims and holding perpetrators to account (Carey 2012).

Women's economic and political movements have achieved varying degrees of success. In some cases, their issues and platforms have been adopted by governments or political parties seeking women's support; in others, women's demands have been largely ignored or have been addressed symbolically by token gestures intended to mollify them without eliminating the root causes of their problems. Even when they have fallen short of their intended objectives, however, women's movements have profoundly affected their members' lives. In giving women a socially legitimate venue for entering public life, these movements have expanded women's horizons and provided them with a sense of personal agency (Chuchryk 1991: 163). Women's participation has enabled them to acquire organizational skills and to forge social networks that decrease their isolation and augment their household decisionmaking power. Although most women have retained their basic commitment to their roles as wives and mothers, many have abandoned the submissive, self-sacrificing trappings of *marianismo* and now see themselves as empowered champions of family welfare. Such changes portend a transformation in gender roles and relationships that will ensure greater autonomy and growing political leadership for subsequent generations of Latin American women.

Women's contributions to the LGBT movements that have proliferated across Latin America have typically been of the "feminist" or "mixed gender" variety. In the early stages of LGBT advocacy, when emphasis was placed on sexual liberation and an outright rejection by both men and women of the rigid gender roles dictated by the *machismo/marianismo* ideology, women struggled alongside men (Corrales and Pecheny 2010; Friedman 2010; Encarnación 2016). Lesbians participated with gay men, bisexuals, and transgendered and transsexual persons to create a "queer public sphere." Through "queer worldmaking," LGBT identity is created via the process of "coming out"—itself a political act—and is reinforced by organizing publications, community centers, websites, and other aspects of LGBT urban life that give and create meaning for LGBT persons, as well as by participating in Pride parades and demonstrations that offer them much-needed visibility

(Friedman 2010; Josephson and Marques 2017: 241). However, at various times in the Latin American LGBT movement, women have found it necessary to advocate for themselves, either because of the unique limitations placed upon them by *marianismo* or because of residual misogyny among the gay men who have tended to take leadership roles in the movement.

Of particular importance for Latin American lesbians was the increased availability of the internet, which allowed them to meet, converse, advocate, and build communities in relative anonymity and across great distances (Friedman 2010). The ability to do these things online shielded lesbian women from the public scorn, persecution, and violence to which life in *machismo/marianismo*-dominated societies often subjects them, and they made full use of this opportunity to publish newsletters and websites dedicated to lesbian issues, LGBT advocacy, and the challenges Latin American lesbians face in coming out (Friedman 2010). Moreover, it allowed lesbian feminists to challenge traditional feminism and to add LGBT concerns to the feminist dialogue in a way that might not have been possible through in-person meetings or conference attendance, particularly during the early waves of liberalization in the region (Friedman 2010; Duarte 2012). The creation of these communities was foundational for lesbians to gain the support networks needed to empower themselves to come out more publicly and

President Michelle Bachelet of Chile in 2009. Credit: Alex Proimos, https:// commons.wikimedia.org/wiki/File:Michele _Bachelet_(2009).jpg

advocate more forcefully not just for LGBT equality within heterosexual societies but for equality within the LGBT movement as well.

In Chapter 4, Shelley McConnell details the achievements of women heads of state in Latin America, even though female power has not diffused to the rest of society through decentralized governance. Especially impressive among these leaders is Michelle Bachelet, who since 2018 has served as the United Nations High Commissioner on Human Rights, after being elected to two terms as Chilean president as a social democrat, having previously suffered torture and arbitrary detention under the dictator Augusto Pinochet. Among her duties have been to investigate alleged torture and political imprisonment, and the absence of healthcare and food in Venezuela; political torture and imprisonment in Nicaragua; and arbitrary migrant detention and family separation in the United States.

Conclusion

The past fifty-plus years have brought dramatic changes for Latin American women. Once symbolically confined to the household and the wife-mother role, women of all backgrounds are increasingly entering the public world of paid employment and political action. Their growing political and labor force participation has resulted from educational advances, cultural changes, declining fertility, and economic and political crises that have threatened the welfare of their families. This participation also both reflects and further stimulates the erosion of cultural ideologies that deem public participation to be inconsistent with women's reproductive roles and prevent the recognition of same-sex desire and nonheterosexual identities as equally valid and deserving of respect and protection. Women's public activities have often been legitimated by cultural discourse and by women themselves as necessary adjuncts to the successful performance of their domestic roles. In defining wage work and political participation as effective means not simply for self-fulfillment or needed social change, but also for caring for their families more effectively, Latin American women are developing their own unique role definitions that erode the rigid boundary between private and public life. In taking advantage of new technologies and new means of communication, women are opening new dialogues across geographical spaces that allow them to challenge long-held assumptions and ideologies about gender roles. In forging these new bases for their identities, Latin American women offer inspiring models for women around the world.

336 Susan Tiano and Michael Shea

Notes

1. The Robinson Country Intelligence Index is a holistic, customizable data visualization tool that incorporates 436 variables across 102 subdimensions for 199 countries and 13 years of data (see https://rcii.gsu.edu). The governance subdimension, which is derived from data from the World Bank's Worldwide Governance Indicators, measures the openness, effectiveness, legitimacy, and responsiveness of a state's governing institutions. In 2018, despite setbacks in Venezuela, Nicaragua, and Honduras, Latin America was considered to be the freest and best-governed region in the global South.

2. For an analysis of Argentina's "Dirty War," in which thousands of Argentines were imprisoned, tortured, and killed at the hands of the military, see Chapter 3 of this book.

3. Some recent writings suggest that gender roles among the Aztecs may have involved more complementarity and parallelism than previous interpretations would suggest. For a discussion of these contrasting perspectives, see Navarro 1999: 10.

4. Reported rates for Honduras in 1961 and 1974 were calculated in a way that underestimates the actual rate of Honduran women's labor force participation. Rather than comparing the number of wage-earning women to the number of women between the ages of twenty and sixty, as did the other Latin American countries, the Honduran census compared employed women to the whole female population. This produces a misleading rate, because the relevant comparison should be confined to women of employment age; had the Honduran census excluded youth and the elderly, its rate would have risen by several percentage points, making it more similar to the rate of its neighbor, Guatemala. By 1999, the Honduran census had changed its procedure to make it conform to the rest of Latin America.

5. Honduras once again provides an exception to this trend, in part because of the way employment rates were calculated, leading to underestimates of men's as well as women's employment.

6. Countries excluded from Table 10.2 because 1960 data were unavailable showed similarly high rates of women's labor force participation during the late 1990s. These include Bolivia (40.5 percent), Cuba (31.7 percent), the Dominican Republic (28.3 percent), El Salvador (44.7 percent), and Paraguay (26.1 percent).

7. Latin American censuses typically measure contraceptive usage only among married women (Chant with Craske 2003), although "marriage" is often defined in a way that includes women cohabitating with male partners, regardless of the official status of their union. If sexually active single women were included in these census surveys, the reported use of contraception would likely be much higher.

11

Education

Fernando M. Reimers

The history of education in Latin America is defined by four waves of globalization—the process of flows of people, products, capital, technology, and ideas, contributing to an integrated and interdependent transnational economy—over the past five centuries and punctuated by contestation over the cultural and political identity of this region and over the goals of empowering all persons to become architects of their own lives and capable of collaborating with others to advance democracy.

The first wave corresponds to the period of colonization, a project designed to extend the territorial, economic, military, and cultural reach of the Spanish and Portuguese empires and to spread the Catholic faith.[1] The second wave began with the period of independence and consolidation of the newly independent republics, which sought to replace the medieval values of the colonizing empires with the humanistic values of the Enlightenment of self-improvement and self-governance. The third wave began after World War II, shaped by the creation of the global international architecture anchored on the Universal Declaration of Human Rights and the creation of the United Nations. The last wave began in the 1990s with the rapid development of technology accelerating the process of global economic integration, and in the case of Latin America corresponds also to the most recent wave of democratization. Each of these waves was accompanied by a set of ideas about the role of educational institutions and a set of priorities that shaped a distinct educational order. This chapter examines the educational consequences of these four waves of globalization.

The process that shaped the educational institutions in Latin America was, from the outset, local as well as global. It engaged local interest groups and ideas, but also drew on support from outside the region. In turn, the ideas and institutions developed as part of the efforts in Latin America to define how education would contribute to define the cultural and political character of the region influenced educational discourse and practices elsewhere. It is in this sense that educational development in the region was part of the process of globalization, the result of ideas flowing in to shape educational institutions and also flowing out to the rest of the world.

The global-local nature of the contested efforts to shape educational institutions in this region can be recognized in four milestones, each corresponding to one of the four waves of globalization: (1) the formulation of the idea of universal human rights at the time of the conquest; (2) the recognition of the role education can play in advancing the political project of self-rule that begins with independence from the empires; (3) the recognition of education as a universal human right as a result of the global education movement as shaped by the Universal Declaration of Human Rights after World War II; and (4) the acceleration of educational inclusion and improvement in the quality and relevance of education beginning in the 1990s, following the "lost decade" caused by the debt crisis of the 1980s, the wave of democratization, and the recent challenges to education caused by the populist backlash and the Covid-19 pandemic.

The First Wave of Globalization: Colonization

A mere nineteen years after the arrival of Christopher Columbus in the Dominican Republic, in 1511, Dominican friar Anton de Montesinos gave the sermon "I Am a Voice Crying in the Wilderness," in which he denounced the enslavement of the Indigenous populations, arguing that the Indigenous had the same souls as the Spanish colonizers, and therefore the same "natural rights." Montesinos advanced this idea in the tail end of the Middle Ages at a time when the Spanish Empire had not yet fully embraced the emerging Renaissance and its humanistic values. The idea was subversive in a social order based on the notion that rulers and religious leaders derived their authority from the proximity to deity, and in an order that subjected most people to a life of servitude, a status to which the newly arrived colonizers attempted to force the Indigenous inhabitants of the Americas. The idea that Indigenous people had souls, and the advocacy of Father Montesinos and his student Bartolomé de las Casas, resulted in the New Laws of the Indies censoring and punishing the abuse, enslavement, and murder of Indigenous people (Fajardo 2013; Jay 2002). De las Casas, who witnessed Montesinos's sermon and was influenced by him, challenged the institution of slavery and the violence against Indigenous people and argued that all mankind was one (Hanke 1994; Huerga 1998). This notion of "natural rights" of different people and the idea that all humanity is one, advanced in the early sixteenth century, are cornerstones of the idea of human rights, which is in turn foundational to the project of educating all.

Such a project of education for all, however, would not have immediate consequences in the educational institutions of the Spanish colonies, which were very much set up to maintain the dependent relationship of these colonies from the Spanish and Portuguese Empires. Universities were set up to educate local administrators, and education was reserved to a small elite group, excluding the majority of the population and, in particular, the Indigenous population and those who were brought in by the colonizers as slaves from Africa.

However, the idea of human rights would eventually influence education as it fed into a set of beliefs that would in time challenge the very nature of the relationship of the colonies to the empires. Ideas such as these, which originated from the encounter of the European colonizers with the Indigenous people of the Americas, and the questions they raised about how the two groups should relate, stimulated philosophers of the Enlightenment such as Jean Jacques Rousseau to advance the notion of the innate goodness of people, uncorrupted by the institutions of Western civilization. This idea was foundational to the notion that social contracts were a construction and therefore perfectible. From his notion followed the even more revolutionary notion that the legitimacy of social contracts depended on the consent of the governed. It was this idea, and others advanced by the philosophers of the Enlightenment, that would in time give rise to the age of revolutions, which would mark the second milestone in the educational journey of Latin America. It was that second wave of globalization that led to the establishment of the first public education systems in the region.

The Second Wave of Globalization: The Age of Revolutions

A second milestone illustrating the global-local dialectic in the development of education in Latin America is the role the powerful theses of the Enlightenment played in shaping a set of political, and educational, aspirations of the region at the time of independence. The origins of that particular milestone are found in three Venezuelans—Francisco de Miranda, Simón Bolívar, and Andrés Bello—and the support they received from ideas and friends in the United States and Europe— underscoring the global-local nature of these developments. Francisco de Miranda, one of the earlier architects of the idea of an independent Latin America, became captivated by the revolutionary notion that ordinary people are capable of self-rule and self-improvement; this idea was more aligned with his temperament and social experiences than the idea that social origin was meant to be destiny.

Miranda grew up in a Caracas governed by the highly stratified, still medieval, norms and customs of the Spanish Empire, which provided experiences against which these revolutionary ideas found resonance. Miranda's father, Sebastian, a successful self-made businessman, was appointed by the governor as captain of the White Canary Islanders, a regiment he led for five years. In spite of the evident business success that led to such an appointment, the local white aristocracy in Caracas (the *mantuanos*) rejected him because of his original social status and challenged his right to be a captain, suggesting he had African ancestors (because he proceeded from the Canary Islands, a Spanish region off the coast of Africa originally settled by Berbers). Captain Miranda requested honorable discharge and began a process to certify his family lineage and demonstrate that he had no African ancestors. After his court victory, Sebastian de Miranda decided to send his son Francisco to Spain to complete his studies, as Francisco had not enjoyed social acceptance by the local aristocracy. In Spain, Francisco purchased a commission as captain of a regiment and joined the Spanish army. This journey brought Francisco de Miranda closer to the intellectual and political ferment that was transforming Europe and North America. In Spain, Miranda studied a range of disciplines and became fascinated by the books of philosophers banned by the Inquisition, such as John Locke. These readings would cause Miranda to question the cultural norms of those in Caracas who had discriminated against his father because he was a self-made man and because they thought he had African roots, and who had greater interest in his lineage than in his achievements. Eventually the Tribunal of the Holy Office of the Inquisition initiated an investigation into Captain Miranda's reading habits, which included a number of texts banned by the Inquisition. He participated in combat in Morocco, and in the siege of Pensacola in the American Revolution. He then left for Cuba where he participated in several battles against the British, and in 1783 he left for the United States, where he met several of the founding fathers (George Washington, Thomas Paine, Samuel Adams, Thomas Jefferson, and Alexander Hamilton) and became especially interested in the role of legislation and of the various colleges in the newly independent nation, visiting Princeton, Yale, and Harvard. He spent a few days with the reverend Ezra Stiles, president of Yale College, who wrote admiringly of the wide-ranging intellectual interests of the young Venezuelan (Racine 2003: 54).

After his travels in North America, Miranda settled in London, and traveled throughout Europe, participating in the French Revolution. In 1810, he hosted a delegation of fellow Venezuelans including Simón Bolívar, Andrés Bello, and Luis López Méndez, who arrived to request support from the British against Napoleon, who had conquered Spain in 1808. During that visit, Miranda introduced the delegation to Joseph Lancaster, an English Quaker educator who had developed a method to educate large numbers of children, based on organizing students in grades, taught by more advanced students, under the supervision of a teacher. Lancaster established a free elementary school based on this method, and eventually a society to extend this method to other countries, the Lancasterian Society for the Promotion of the Education of the Poor. Bolívar was captivated by the idea of a method that allowed extending education to all and sent teachers from Venezuela to train under Lancaster, eventually inviting Lancaster to come to Caracas and see the school those teachers had opened, an invitation Lancaster accepted; he lived in Caracas between 1825 and 1827. The creation of that school, and the transatlantic collaboration that made it possible, epitomize how the expansion of educational opportunities came to be understood as central to the project of self-rule on which the nascent independent republics in Latin America were based. Between the years 1823 and 1886, all nations in Latin America would create legal frameworks that enshrined universal public education as a right of all (Reimers 2006).

Traveling with Bolívar on that visit to London in 1810 was Andrés Bello, a humanist and educator who had been Bolívar's tutor during their youth. Bello had deep interest in the humanistic and scientific ideas emerging in his time. He had met Alexander Humboldt, the German explorer, during Humboldt's visit to Caracas and served as his guide in his explorations. Bello remained in London nineteen years, and in 1829 accepted an invitation of the government of Chile to move to that country, where he eventually helped found the first university, in the spirit of the university that Humboldt's brother, Wilhelm, had established in Germany in 1810—a university that would advance truth, through research, promote critical thinking, and educate the larger public to enable self-governance. Bello worked diligently to create other institutions that would allow self-rule: he led the creation of a civil code, developed a grammar that recognized common use of the language in the Americas, and thus severed the authority of a distant set of canons developed in Spain. As president of the University of Chile, he encouraged faculty to engage in issues of public interest, and he also participated in public debates with Domingo Faustino Sarmiento, which helped to disseminate and consolidate Sarmiento's vision for the role of public education in the newly independent republic. In this way, Andrés Bello laid the corner-stone of the educational institutions of an order inspired by humanism, guided by human reason, and aspiring to social progress.

Domingo Faustino Sarmiento articulated the role that public educa-tion was to play in shaping a mindset that would make self-rule possible. An exiled Argentine professor at the university of which Bello was pres-ident in Chile, he played an important role in shaping legal institutions in that country. The Chilean government sponsored Sarmiento's trip to Europe to study educational systems; on that voyage he happened upon a copy of *The Common School,* the journal Horace Mann was editing in Massachusetts as secretary of education and in which he examined the opportunities and challenges of building an institution that would bring people from all walks of life together, to learn to work together for the sake of progress. Sarmiento embarked to Boston, where he met Mann and his wife, Mary Peabody. Sarmiento returned to Chile no doubt inspired by what he had learned from those conversations about the early experiment in public education in Massachusetts, the first in the United States, and published a monograph articulating his views on the role public education could contribute to advance Chile's liberal aspi-rations. Sarmiento's monograph "Popular Education" became the intel-lectual blueprint for the establishment of public education in Latin America. Sarmiento sustained twelve years of rich correspondence with Mary Peabody Mann, in which she generously offered many ideas and assistance as he became minister of education and eventually president of Argentina—a vivid example of the kind of global partnership that helped shape educational institutions in Latin America (Mann 2001). She persuaded him to establish an astronomical observatory, staffed by several Bostonians who moved to Argentina for that purpose, and shipped a contingent of teachers from Boston to Argentina to create the first English-language textbooks in that country (Peard 2016). Sarmiento's work and writings exemplified the struggle to create institutions that would enable social progress, what he called "civilization," away from the conservative social order in which origin is destiny, which Sarmiento called "barbarism."

    The construction of public education systems in Latin America was thus the result of these early efforts to translate the aspirations of self-rule and cooperation for social progress of the Enlightenment into institutions such as public schools and universities that cultivated the agency and capabilities of ordinary people to rule their lives. The result of these efforts was remarkable; they created in schooling a shared experience for all people and contributed to create societies ruled by law where new social institutions enabled self-improvement and social progress. No longer would self-made men such as Sebástian de Miranda be treated as outcasts; now their social ascent would become a virtue in the new order. Table 11.1 shows that whereas in 1870 only 14 percent of the population in Latin America had some schooling, today most do. These levels of access exceed those of most world regions, with the exception of Western Europe. Such efforts transformed the levels of education of the population and continue to do so. Today, Latin American teenagers have two more years of schooling than their parents. A recent report of educational inclusion in Latin America concludes that the legal frameworks that support education for all in the region are relatively advanced relative to other regions of the world (UNESCO 2021).

    Such expansion of schooling happened as part of larger political projects, often projects of liberals advancing the institutions of modernization

Table 11.1 **Population Who Completed Some Basic Education, Various World Regions (percentages), 1870–2010**

	World	Western Europe	Latin America and Caribbean	East Asia	South and Southeast Asia	Middle East and North Africa	Sub-Saharan Africa
1870	24	60	14	24	2	4	2
1880	27	69	16	26	2	5	2
1890	30	75	20	28	3	5	2
1900	33	81	23	30	5	6	3
1910	36	83	27	33	6	7	4
1920	39	87	32	36	9	8	4
1930	41	87	36	38	12	9	6
1940	46	91	43	42	15	11	10
1950	49	91	54	46	20	14	13
1960	54	94	56	56	26	21	20
1970	61	96	65	72	34	29	25
1980	63	99	72	72	41	39	32
1990	71	100	83	80	54	55	45
2000	79	100	90	87	66	66	58
2010	82	100	94	90	70	74	65

Source: Roser and Ortiz-Ospina 2013.

in competition with conservatives (Reimers 2006). In Mexico, for example, José Vasconcelos became the first secretary of education, in 1921, after serving as president of the National University, advancing a three-pronged project of establishing public schools, promoting libraries, and promoting art, in an effort to develop a sense of cultural identity uniquely Mexican, the *raza cósmica,* and to create institutions that would support modernity.

As was the case with similar efforts in other newly independent republics such as the United States, while relatively progressive for their time those early efforts of educational expansion as part of the consolidation of independent republics did not include Indigenous children and Afro-descendants, who were either systematically denied the opportunity to access school, or included in schools advancing a project of cultural assimilation (UNESCO 2021).

The Third Wave of Globalization: A World Order Based on Human Rights

The third milestone illustrative of the global-local dialectic in the development of education in Latin America is the role the region played and continues to play in shaping the global education movement to educate all children, which began with the inclusion of education as one of the rights included in the declaration adopted at the General Assembly of the newly created United Nations in December 1948.

Exemplar among such contributors was Jaime Torres Bodet. A Mexican humanist intellectual and writer, Torres Bodet advanced numerous innovations during the two terms he served as secretary of education (1943–1946 and 1958–1964). He created the national program of free school textbooks, an idea that inspired many similar initiatives around the world. As one of the founders of the United Nations Educational, Science, and Cultural Organization (UNESCO), Torres Bodet steered the organization toward the promotion of fundamental education for all, an example of how educational ideas from Latin America found global resonance and had significant global implications. Under Torres Bodet's leadership, UNESCO would begin to steer a global education movement to educate all children that significantly transformed the shared experience of humanity, providing most of the world's children the opportunity to access basic schooling (Reimers 2015).

This global movement to educate all children would draw on some of the educational developments in Latin America, as well as feedback ideas that supported further development in the region. The movement that began with the inclusion of education as one of the universal rights in the declaration adopted by the United Nations in 1947 had, as was the case with the Latin American project to educate all, roots in the liberal values of the Enlightenment: the recognition of the fundamental equality of all people, of their same rights and dignity, and of their potential to improve themselves and their communities. Education was a necessary condition to enable such a project of self-improvement. And just as the creation of public education followed the independence of the new Latin American republics as a result of transnational solidarity, so too would the global education movement represent a major effort of global solidarity across national borders to educate all children.

An example of how UNESCO advanced those values and ideas is provided by the work of Mexican American Alberto Báez, who led UNESCO's efforts to promote teaching of science around the world. Born in Puebla, Mexico, Báez moved with his parents to the United States when he was five years old, and eventually studied mathematics in college and physics at Stanford. In 1961 he joined UNESCO to "establish the Division of Science Education, where he advocated for teaching science in secondary schools using a high-quality curriculum supported by low-cost science kits and educational technologies. Báez's chief intellectual contributions to the field of science education centered on the development and dissemination of the ideas that it was necessary to democratize access to high-quality education in developing countries, that science education should focus on developing the capabilities needed to solve practical problems, and on the role of interdisciplinarity and social responsibility as core foundations of science education. He also articulated why high-quality science and technology education to improve living conditions in developing nations would contribute to addressing common global challenges faced by humanity, particularly achieving sustainable forms of human environmental interaction, reducing poverty and uncontrolled demographic expansion, and promoting peace" (Reimers 2007: 369).

It was thus as a result of the local-global dynamics described earlier that the twentieth century marked a period of dramatic educational transformation in Latin America, expanding access in ways that outpaced the significant growth in the population. This was largely the result of government-sponsored efforts, as the state funded, created, and staffed schools. This expansion turned education systems into the largest organizations in most countries, the most visible face of the state in the everyday lives of citizens. This visibility, and the large number of people these systems employed, made the education sector an attractive target for capture to advance partisan political interests, and this politicization of education undermined educational opportunity in three ways: challenging attempts to professionalize education; diverting resources away from educationally sound investments to activities with high partisan payoffs; and undermining the long-term continuity of education strategies, as political changes in administration typically were followed by shifts in education priorities.

However, this dramatic expansion in educational access was also conducive to significant innovation where the local-global dynamics augmented and sustained educational developments. A number of regional initiatives in Latin America provided the mechanisms for cross-border exchange of experiences and support. For instance, as UNESCO was established, it organized a series of regional convenings of ministers of education designed to work with governments in achieving universal primary education. These conferences were followed by technical missions to exchange good practices that would help achieve such targets. One such innovation included the creation of "double shift" schools, the utilization of the same physical school facilities to host two different shifts of students, as a way to double the capacity of existing infrastructure. The double shift school would become critical to the rapid expansion of educational access.

Similarly, innovative approaches to expand access to school in low-density rural areas were developed in Latin America and subsequently spread to other regions. One of them was the "new school" approach. In the 1950s, a young rural Argentinean teacher named Luis Fortunato Iglesias published a book in which he described an approach to personalized instruction in rural multigraded schools: *La Escuela Rural Unitaria* (Ryan 2016). Four years later, at a global conference of ministers of education organized by UNESCO, the organization launched the unitary school as a way to promote active learning in low-density rural areas. UNESCO sponsored the adoption of this project in several countries, including Colombia, where Oscar Mogollón, a gifted rural teacher, adopted it in Pamplona, in the north of Santander. Once he had extended the approach to 150 schools, he met Beryl Levinger, a Peace Corps volunteer who was fascinated by this innovative way to organize schools to personalize instruction. Beryl would eventually write her doctoral dissertation at the University of Alabama on this approach. A few years later, Beryl joined the US Agency for International Development (USAID) and was posted to Colombia. At that time, Vicky Colbert had just been asked to direct the national unitary school project. With funding from USAID, together Mogollón, Colbert, and Levinger transformed the unitary school approach into a scalable model to increase the reach of the principles of personalized and active learning through new protocols and instruments.

Several mechanisms of regional cooperation, such as those created by UNESCO, the Organization of Iberoamerican States, the Alliance for Progress, the Organization of American States, and the Inter-American Development Bank, facilitated the diffusion and adoption of educational innovation throughout Latin America. For example, in 1972, Peru advanced an ambitious education reform, part of a series of economic and social reforms advanced by the military government of Velasco Alvarado. A core element of this reform was an ambitious modality of community participation in schools facilitated by the creation of "educational nuclei." This form of educational decentralization built on an earlier communal approach adopted in Peru in 1946. The Peruvian education reform of Velasco Alvarado received wide attention at the time, as well as support from numerous international organizations. This experiment in community participation would be widely disseminated by UNESCO and other agencies and inform many subsequent efforts at educational decentralization in the region and beyond.

The regional spread of innovation extended to innovations generated by civil society organizations. Fe y Alegria, for instance, an approach to educate children in low-income communities initiated by a Jesuit professor in Caracas in 1955, eventually became a movement of popular education extending to nineteen countries. What was initially one primary school in a low-income community across from the Catholic University of Andrés Bello in Caracas became a network of educational institutions focused on providing education to low-income children that would empower them to take charge of their own destiny and become contributing members of their communities, the very values of the Enlightenment advanced in this case by the religious order founded by Ignatius of Loyola in 1534.

The Fourth Wave of Globalization: The 1990s to the Present

The most recent wave of globalization initially affected educational institutions negatively, stalling the momentum generated during the expansionary period of the 1960s and 1970s, when the region was hit by an external debt crisis that negatively impacted education spending. It is in response to the "lost decade" in education resulting from the programs of economic adjustment implemented during the 1980s that the new wave of democratization and economic strategies placed renewed educational efforts, to advance and focus on including all students, with greater and growing attention to the quality and relevance of education.

Renewed Priority for Education Under Democratization

The wave of democratization in Latin America that began in the 1990s brought renewed attention to education, and with it an intentional focus on the role of education as an avenue of social and economic development. A 1992 report on the basic pillars for changing production patterns with social equity (United Nations Economic Commission for Latin America1992), prepared by Fernando Fajnzylber and a team at the UN Economic Commission for Latin America in Chile, marked an inflexion point in bringing greater attention to education, which had been neglected as the region curbed social spending as part of economic adjustment programs in response to the debt crisis during the 1980s. The document maintained that the abandonment of import substitution as a strategy of economic development in favor of open market competition, and the return of democratic rule to Latin America, required investment in the skills of the population that would allow the region to compete on the basis of knowledge-intensive industries and that would help reduce inequality, as a foundation for democratic stability. These ideas were advanced with the full support of the global institutions created in the wake of World War II to promote the global education movement. Again, as was the case at the time of the formation of the independent nations of Latin America, global-local dynamics provided powerful impetus to educational institutions.

As a result of this emerging consensus on the importance of education to the economic and political future of Latin America over the past quarter century, education became and has remained a significant priority for governments and societies in the region. Latin America invests more on education, as a share of government expenditure and as a share of GDP, than any other region of the world, and education spending has increased over time (UNESCO 2021: fig. 21.1).

Not only has Latin America increased the level of education spending, but it has also increased spending on poorer students through a variety of innovative targeting mechanisms. These include the Fund for the Maintenance and Development of Basic Education and Valorization of Education Professionals, in Brazil, a formula-based allocation established in 2007 and designed to close gaps in per pupil spending across municipalities, which decreased such inequality by 12 percent in five years (UNESCO 2021). Another formula-based allocation targeting financing innovation is Chile's Preferential Education Subsidy, which provides higher transfers per pupil to schools serving the poorest students and includes a specific amount per child plus an additional amount that is proportional to the percentage of children in poverty in the school; these resources are used by schools to fund school improvement strategies (UNESCO 2021). Last, cash transfers to families of low-income children have been used as income support, with contingencies that incentivize school attendance (Reimers, DeShano, and Trevino 2006).

Capitalizing on such growing societal commitment to education, many governments in the region have undertaken reforms aimed at elevating education standards (increasing the years of mandatory instruction and increasing the level of the curriculum), improving teacher preparation, increasing school autonomy, and improving educational management and accountability. Efforts to achieve those goals have included not only governments at the federal, state, and municipal levels, but many different actors of civil society as well. Ambitious efforts to overhaul the curriculum in recent years include reforms in Brazil and Mexico, for example (Reimers 2020).

As a result of these efforts advanced during the fourth wave of globalization, mandatory instruction now covers nine to ten years of schooling, including primary education, which is compulsory in all countries in the region, and lower secondary education, which is compulsory in all countries except Nicaragua. Upper secondary education is now also compulsory in twelve of the nineteen countries in Latin America. These changes have increased the levels of educational attainment of the population as seen in Figure 11.1. Latin America has achieved almost universal attendance to elementary and lower secondary school, while the number of children out of school has declined from 15 million in 2000 to 12 million in 2018 (UNESCO 2021). The greatest levels of exclusion are in upper secondary school. Among the children out of school in 2018, 16 percent were of elementary school age, 22 percent of lower secondary school age, and 62 percent of upper secondary education age. Attendance to upper secondary school increased from 70 percent in 2000 to 83 percent in 2018. During this period, the percentage of children completing primary school increased from 79 to 95 percent; completing lower secondary school from 59 to 81 percent; and completing upper secondary school from 42 to 63 percent. These numbers place Latin America above the global averages of 85 percent, 73 percent, and 49 percent, respectively (UNESCO and Inter-American Development Bank 2020).

As a result of such progress in attendance to school, most children in the region attend school at the elementary level in most countries in

Figure 11.1   Increase in Attendance and Completion Rates in School, 2000–2018

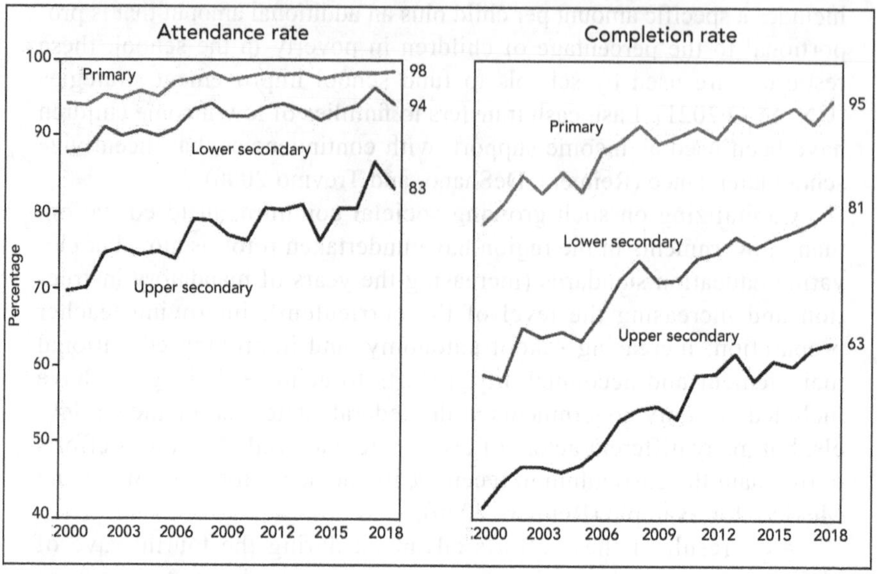

Source: UNESCO 2021: fig 1.2.

the region except Guatemala, Haiti, Honduras, and Nicaragua. At the lower secondary level, most students attend in most countries except Ecuador, El Salvador, Guatemala, and Honduras. At the upper secondary level, the lowest levels of access are in El Salvador, Guatemala, and Honduras, as seen in Figure 11.2.

A number of countries in the region, such as Brazil and Mexico, have adopted ambitious and broad-ranging curricula; most countries have adopted systems to periodically assess student knowledge and skills, and to make such information available to the public; and school autonomy has increased. To protect the independence of assessments of student knowledge, several countries, such as Brazil, Colombia, and Mexico, created quasi-autonomous institutes for the evaluation of education, although the Mexican institute of evaluation was abolished in 2019.

These efforts to improve education have produced almost universal access to school for those between the ages of six to fourteen, and access to four in five of those between the ages of four and five and between the ages of fifteen and seventeen. There have also been significant increases in primary and secondary school completion. Of those who begin primary school, 78 percent complete it, 60 percent complete lower secondary, and 42 percent complete upper secondary (Arias and Martinez

Figure 11.2 Attendance Rate by Education Level (primary, lower secondary, upper secondary), 2018

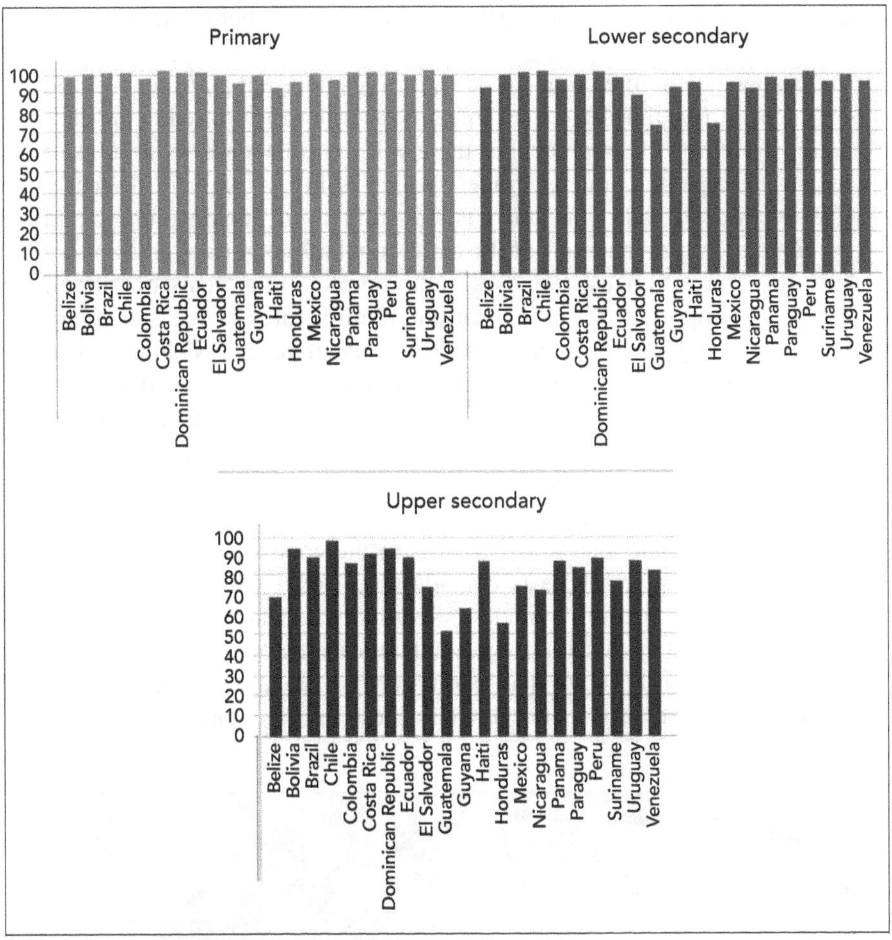

Source: UNESCO and IADB 2020.

2017). A combined index of education and health outcomes created by the World Bank (2021a) shows that over the past decade most countries in Latin America have improved on these measures.

Despite these evident signs of progress, the task of ensuring a universal right to education in Latin America is still in the making. Despite the considerable progress in school attendance and completion of the past two decades, a recent UNESCO report on inclusion concludes that "disadvantaged social groups continue to be excluded from education.

Barriers against access to education of good quality are still too high for people with disabilities, migrants and refugees, indigenous peoples and Afro-descendants, and particularly affect girls belonging to these groups" (2021: vi).

Today, one in three four- to five-year-olds does not go to school, and only four in five thirteen- to seventeen-year-olds are enrolled in the education system, with 14 percent of them still in primary school as a result of having repeated several grades, which is fairly likely in the early grades. Educational opportunity is stratified along socioeconomic and ethnic lines. More than half of the children who live in rural areas or are from low-income backgrounds do not complete nine years of school. There are important variations in completion rates at the secondary level; they are lower in countries such as Guatemala and Nicaragua than in Argentina, Chile, Colombia, and Mexico. While these differences reflect in part differences in the social circumstances children from different backgrounds experience outside of schools, which are considerable in this the region with the highest income inequality in the world, these differences in educational outcomes for students from various social origins relate also to differences in the conditions present in the schools they attend. There is considerable social segregation of students, with low-income students streamed to schools that have less resources. A survey of schools and student learning outcomes conducted by UNESCO (2021) shows that school libraries are underresourced, with students in elementary school having access to three books per student

Public-private partnerships, such as the Alianza Educativa in Colombia, have supported educational innovation in Latin America. Credit: Alianza Educativa

on average; these averages are only one book per student for the poorer students, compared to eight books per student for those of higher socio-economic status. These educational gaps for children from different socioeconomic backgrounds are most visible in completion of second-ary school, as seen in Figure 11.3.

Figure 11.3 Large Gaps in Upper Secondary Education Completion by Wealth, 2014–2018

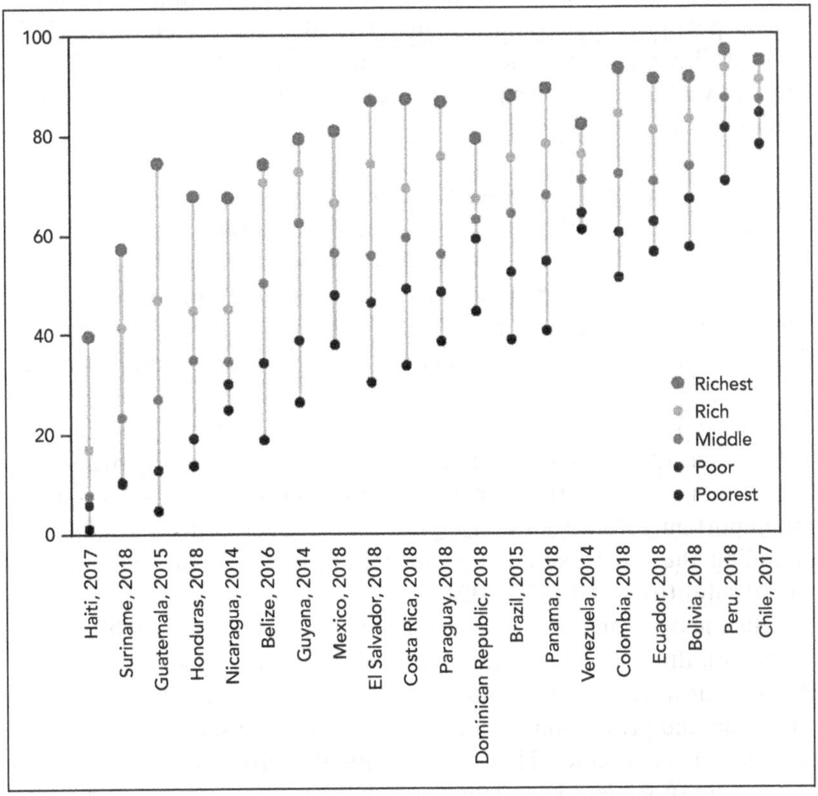

Note: Figure 11.3 indicates that there are large gaps in the rates of upper secondary level education completion by wealth in Central America and South America. Using UNESCO data from 2021, the figure differentiates upper secondary education completion in each country through the use of five wealth categories. The five categories include richest, rich, middle class, poor, and poorest. The highest levels of upper secondary completion and, simultane-ously, smallest wealth gaps, are found in Chile (2017); the lowest levels of upper secondary completion are found in Haiti (2017). The largest gaps in upper secondary level education by wealth are found in Guatemala (2015). Overall, it is apparent that the completion rates of upper secondary level education in Latin American countries vastly differ between the richest and poorest population groups.

Expansion in attendance, completion, and average schooling attained has not translated into high levels of learning for all. Many countries in the region evaluate student knowledge and skills with curriculum-based assessments, and a few participate in international comparative assessments such as those conducted by the International Association for the Evaluation of Educational Achievement (the IEA studies), or the Organization for Economic Cooperation and Development (the PISA studies). Overall, the results of such assessments indicate that students achieve at low levels, relative to the intended goals of the curriculum and relative to their peers in other countries, and show that student knowledge and skills are higher for the more socioeconomically advantaged children. One in two Latin American fifteen-year-olds do not achieve minimum proficiency levels in reading.

An Empowered Civil Society Engages with the State

Unlike the remarkable educational expansion produced by state-led policies during the nineteenth century and most of the twentieth, the progress of the past quarter century has been the result of productive collaborations between governments and civil society, with global collaborations now including also collaborations with civil society organizations. As part of the process of democratization, governments became more open not only to community participation in education but also to more engagement of civil society organizations in educational innovation. A recent report on educational inclusion credits civil society organizations for important reforms in curriculum and teacher education aimed at including the most excluded groups: Indigenous, poor, and students with disabilities (UNESCO 2021).

Business alliances to promote education have been established in many countries in Latin America, such as Colombia, Mexico, and Brazil, that have set out to mobilize citizens to demand higher-quality education and professionalization of education and served to hold governments accountable. This, along with the creation of systems of assessment of student knowledge and skills, has created counterbalancing forces to the risks of state capture of education to advance narrow partisan interests, and in some cases has supported the continuity of sound education policies.

These renewed efforts and partnerships to improve education have created conditions for significant educational innovation in the region. In Chile, for instance, as part of the democratic transition, education became a significant government priority, which resulted in programs to provide support to high-poverty schools, programs to build partnerships

Rural schools in Mexico are part of an expansion of education in Latin America, the result of the creation of the modern nation-states. Social inequality is often reflected in unequal schools and learning opportunities. Credit: Encima de Mexico

between universities and education organizations and schools, programs to overhaul initial teacher education, and a complete revamping of the curriculum. One of Chile's most ambitious programs was a program to use technology to transform education at scale.

Colombia has pioneered approaches to assess democratic citizenship skills, and innovative programs to foster the development of democratic capacities. Mexico has adopted ambitious reforms that include extending three years of preschool education to all children, programs to integrate technology in instruction, and programs of locally led school improvement.

Latin America has pioneered integrated education-health-nutrition programs to support low-income children using conditional cash-transfer programs to incentivize school attendance, health checkups, and good nutrition. These programs are considered a global best practice and have been extended to other regions (UNESCO 2021: tab. 3.1).

Transformations in Higher Education

The modern university is one of the three sister institutions created to advance the project of the Enlightenment, along with public education and democracy. Unlike public education, however, which filled an institutional void in creating a new institution, the universities to advance the humanist project of rational progress had to replace a much older institution, the medieval university created to transmit religious dogma. It is no accident that in the United States, the founding fathers turned their attention to higher education. Benjamin Franklin founded the first scientific society, the American Philosophical Society, and John Adams established the second, the American Academy of Arts and Sciences, tasking it with using the power of the arts and sciences for societal improvement, and to educate the public. Adams also devoted the first several articles of the Massachusetts constitution to higher education, defining what it should teach so that it would contribute to social progress. Franklin also chartered a university, with much emphasis on practical knowledge. And Thomas Jefferson designed the University of Virginia to allow students the experience of a democratic academic community, and to cultivate the capacities for scientific reasoning and civic engagement. The first five articles of the Massachusetts constitution, which John wrote in 1780, all devoted to higher education, articulate a vision of an education for social improvement:

> Wisdom, and knowledge, as well as virtue, diffused generally among the body of the people, being necessary for the preservation of their rights and liberties; and as these depend on spreading the opportunities and advantages of education in the various parts of the country, and among the different orders of the people, it shall be the duty of legislators and magistrates, in all future periods of this Commonwealth, to cherish the interests of literature and the sciences, and all seminaries of them; especially the university at Cambridge, public schools, and grammar schools in the towns; to encourage private societies and public institutions, rewards and immunities, for the promotion of agriculture, arts, sciences, commerce, trades, manufactures, and a natural history of the country; to countenance and inculcate the principles of humanity and general benevolence, public and private charity, industry and frugality, honesty and punctuality in their dealings; sincerity, good humor, and all social affections, and generous sentiments among the people. (Massachusetts Constitution of 1780)

Medieval universities existed in Latin America well before independence; they had been established by religious authorities for the purpose of preparing religious leaders and local administrators loyal to the crown. By design, these institutions were meant to sustain the status quo, not to change it, as were the first medieval universities of Bologna, founded in 1088, and Oxford, founded in 1167.

The notion that social progress was possible was the great invention of the Enlightenment. The founding fathers in Latin America understood that an independent political order would require a different kind of institution than those the crown and the pope had established.

The University of Santo Domingo was established by a papal bull in 1538, and the University of San Marcos received the first royal charter in 1551, the same year the Royal and Pontifical University of Mexico was established; all existed to prepare local administrators who would sustain the authority of crown and church. They were most definitely not meant to promote critical thinking or questioning of revealed truth. This is the reason Francisco de Miranda was so curious about the colleges in the United States during his extended visit. It is also the reason Simón Bolívar sent his son to study at the university that Jefferson had founded. Bolívar raised as his son his nephew Fernando, whose father, Bolívar's brother, died in the war of independence when the child was one year old. Bolívar sent Fernando to study at a boarding school in Philadelphia, and then to the University of Virginia, having corresponded with Jefferson about the creation of the university while he was chartering it. In a letter to the faculty at the University of Virginia, Bolívar outlined his expectations for how a higher education should prepare a person for freedom.

Bolívar's letter, written in 1825, fifteen years after Wilhelm Humboldt chartered the University of Berlin, the first modern research university, expresses hopes that go well beyond the established ideas of what a liberal arts education should be. To the Romans, the liberal arts were the trivium and the quadrivium (grammar, logic, rhetoric, arithmetic, geometry, music, astronomy), and the purpose of such an education was to prepare people to participate in public debate, defend themselves in court, and serve on juries and in the military.

These ideas about the goals of higher education changed little until the Renaissance, when the goals expanded to schooling elites for political administration, the clergy, and now the professions of law and medicine. To the trivium and the quadrivium, the university of the Renaissance added the emerging natural and social sciences: arts (fine arts, music, performing arts, literature); mathematics; natural science (biology, chemistry, physics, astronomy, earth science); philosophy; religious studies; and social science (anthropology, economics, geography, political science, psychology, sociology, linguistics, history).

But in this letter to the faculty at the University of Virginia written in 1825, Bolívar expanded these purposes to include educating for life—morality, taking care of one's health, dance; for trades such as engineering; for modern languages; for relating to others; for social habits, respect for others, and a taste for culture and the arts:

Method to be followed in educating
my nephew Fernando Bolívar

The education of children should always be appropriate to their age, inclinations, genius and temperament.

Once my nephew is older than twelve years old, he should apply himself to learn modern languages, without neglecting his own. Dead languages must be studied after the living are mastered.

Geography and cosmography must be the first knowledge to be gained by a young person.

History, like languages, must be studied learning first contemporary history, to then go back to the darker times.

It is never too early to learn the exact sciences, because they teach analysis in everything, how to proceed from the known to the unknown, and in this way, we learn to think and reason logically.

But the student's ability to calculate must be kept in mind, since not all are equally suited for mathematics.

In general, everyone can learn geometry and understand it; but this is not the case with algebra and integral and differential calculus.

Having a good memory from early on can be a brilliant faculty; but it can also be detrimental to understanding; so, a child who can easily remember the lessons by heart should be taught to learn by heart and to recite the compositions of the great poets. Memory as well as calculus should be developed through exercising them.

Memory should be exercised when possible; but never to the point of exhaustion as this weakens it.

Statistics are essential in the times in which we live, and I want my nephew to learn it.

He will preferably be instructed in mechanics and engineering sciences, but not against his will, if he has no inclination to such studies.

Music is not essential learning, unless he has a passion for this art; but he should gain at least rudimentary knowledge of line drawing, astronomy, chemistry and botany, deepening his knowledge in some of these sciences according to his inclination or taste for some of them.

The teaching of good habits or social habits is as essential as instruction; so, he must be careful to learn in Lord Chesterfield's letters to his son the principles and manners of a gentleman.

Teaching morality in religious maxims and teaching health and life habits is something that no teacher should neglect.

All must study Roman law, as the basis of universal legislation.

Since it is rather difficult to appreciate where art ends and science begins, I would welcome if he were so inclined that he should learn some art or trade, as there are many doctors and lawyers, but we lack good mechanics and farmers who are what the country needs to advance in prosperity and well-being.

If he so chooses, he should practice the dance, which is the poetry of the movement and provides grace and agility to the person, while it is a hygienic exercise in temperate climates.

Above all, I encourage you to inspire in him a taste for the cultured society where the beautiful sex exerts its beneficial influence; and to learn respect for men of age, knowledge and social standing, which makes the young charming, associating it with our hopes for the future.

It would fall on Andrés Bello to establish the first university of the Enlightenment in South America with the University of Chile in 1842. About twenty-five institutions of higher education existed in Latin America at the time of the wars of independence. Afterward, as was the case with public education, the state would take on a significant role in promoting the creation of higher education institutions. During the nineteenth century, strong French influence resulted in many universities following a Napoleonic model of the Grandes Ecoles, with universities following professional curricula. During the twentieth century, as US universities replaced the supremacy of European universities, exchanges with the United States increased, and a number of the most recent developments, such as the development of graduate studies, and the creation of a common undergraduate curriculum in a number of universities in the region reflect North American influences.

Universities in Latin America are highly valued social institutions, which is expressed in the growing demand for access to the university; in the growth of enrollment and in the number of institutions; and in the growing public financing to the university, which has resulted in an increase in real terms of public investment of 53 percent between 2010 and 2017 (UNESCO 2020). Furthermore, society has more confidence in the university than in other social institutions: 70 percent of the population trusts universities (UNESCO 2020). Most research takes place in universities, and universities have taken on a variety of outreach activities aimed at improving the communities of which they are a part. The emphasis on outreach as an important mission of the university dates to the 1918 university reform in Córdoba, which inspired other university reforms in the region. Various national processes deepened this aspiration of the university to contribute to economic and social development. In the case of Mexico, for example, the student movements of 1968, and the response of the federal government to them, motivated a series of reforms to the organic laws that govern the operation of state universities. By the early 1970s, these new laws established the autonomy of state universities (academic, governance, and budgetary) along with a greater emphasis on outreach activities.

In the case of Brazil, the university reform of 1968 modernized the university, creating a network of graduate programs that had an enormous economic, social, and political impact. The creation of social science programs in Brazil established the basis for the democratization of Brazil, even though, paradoxically, such modernization occurred during authoritarian military regimes. It was from the university, in Brazil, where the concern for the creation of democratic institutions and the concern for inequality and social justice arose as priorities that had to be addressed in a democratic framework. It is these reforms that initiated a growing interest in university outreach, leading to various institutional innovations. For example, in 1997, the Ministry of Education established the Educational Support Program, whose mission was to support university research groups to carry out evaluation and research in support of public schools. Five universities created education outreach centers with public schools as part of this program: the University of Juiz de Fora, the University of Belo Horizonte, the University of Brasilia, the Pontifical Catholic University of Rio, and the Federal University of Rio de Janeiro.

Without question universities in Latin America have prepared the leadership of the region; they therefore deserve credit for much of the social progress such leadership has made possible, as well as for the shortcomings of the same. If Latin America has become more democratic over time, it is because universities prepared a democratic political leadership. If industries have developed in Latin America, it is because universities prepared the talent that established those industries. If health conditions of the population have improved, it is because universities educated those who created and maintained such health systems. If science and technology have developed, it took place in universities. If culture and the arts have flourished, it is because universities contributed to preparing those who led such creative processes.

There has been considerable expansion in access to higher education over the past decades in part because globalization has increased demand for university graduates, in part because the success of expansion at lower levels of education has produced more high school graduates, and in part because the middle class has grown. On average, gross enrollment in higher education in Latin America increased from 20 percent in 2000 to 40 percent ten years later. While this is still below the average for the Organization for Economic Cooperation and Development, at 67 percent (OECD 2015: 23), Latin America has achieved higher levels of access to higher education than all world regions, except North America and western, eastern, and central Europe. Furthermore, increases in access to education in Latin America over the past two decades have been proportionately higher than in any other region of the world (Ferreyra et al. 2017: 7). This recent increase in access had disproportionately benefited the poorer students. While the poorest 50 percent of the population accounted for only 16 percent of higher education enrollment in 2000, they accounted for 24 percent of enrollments in 2012 (Ferreyra et al. 2017: 8). Despite such dramatic expansion in access, it is still highly stratified by socioeconomic origin of students, with the most disadvantaged students having less opportunity to access college and, when they access it, less opportunity to access the institutions of higher quality. "The poorest quintile rarely shows an enrolment rate above 20%, and even below 10% for many countries in the region. Meanwhile, the richest quintile generally shows an enrolment rate well above 40%, and even above 50% for many countries" (OECD 2015: 26). There are high rates of college dropout. Half of those between the ages of twenty-five and twenty-nine who have ever started higher education have not completed it. The completion rates seem to have declined over time, as for those aged sixty to sixty-five, 73 percent of those who had started higher education had completed their degrees (Ferreyra et al. 2017: 12). Poorer students are also more likely to drop out from college.

Much of that dramatic expansion in access to higher education was met by new private institutions, which contributed to greater diversity in the type of institutions of higher education. With such diversity the opportunities for innovation in higher education also increased, resulting in greater diversification and differentiation. New areas of study and greater emphasis on graduate studies, for instance, are recent developments. This growth and diversification have caused governments to undertake efforts in accreditation and quality assurance to stimulate improvement and protect the public, as there are concerns that such drastic expansion took place at the expense of quality.

A World Bank study of higher education in Latin America and the Caribbean shows that at present the sector includes about 20 million students, 10,000 institutions, and 60,000 programs (Ferreyra et al. 2017: 2). The largest systems are in Argentina, Brazil, and Mexico. Brazil is an exception to the region in that it prioritized the development of higher education during much of the twentieth century, investing in research and development in ways most other countries did not. In contrast, as a result of the insufficient priority such activities receive, in most countries in the region research and development are underfunded. Consequently, in existing rankings of higher education institutions, five Brazilian universities are among the top ten universities in Latin America. Globally, however, Latin American universities are not among the top in the world; only the University of São Paulo is among the top 300 universities (Ferreyra et al. 2017). Brazilian universities outpace other universities in the region in research productivity, production of patents, and spending on research and development, at 1.15 percent of GDP, compared to 0.43 percent in Mexico and 0.36 percent in Chile (Ferreyra et al. 2017).

There is, however, significant institutional innovation in higher education in Latin America, as is the case for elementary and secondary education. The Institute for the Study of Higher Technology in Monterrey, northern Mexico, for example, has developed unique and novel ways to contribute to the economic and social development of the communities of which it is a part. From a single campus inspired by the Massachusetts Institute of Technology, the institute has evolved into a

Twenty-fifth anniversary of the founding of the University of Guadalajara. Higher education has expanded considerably in Latin America, providing many students the opportunity to be the first in their families to go to college. Credit: Universidad de Guadalajara

multicampus institution in multiple states in Mexico, each of them with governing boards that include representatives from the business commu-nity as a way to seize opportunities to contribute to regional economic development. The institute has also developed novel forms to extend edu-cational opportunities to disadvantaged groups, including online learning and community learning centers.

Progress in expansion in access to higher education notwithstanding, there are concerns with the extent to which universities are producing the graduates whom the labor market needs: "around 36% of the region's firms point to the difficulty of hiring adequately trained employees as a major obstacle. . . . They struggle to find: i) soft skills, such as critical thinking, teamwork or problem-solving capacities; and ii) technical and technological capacities and the competencies needed for new-economy jobs" (OECD 2015: 32).

Higher education, as is the case with basic education, has grown rapidly in Latin America, creating a differentiated and diverse offering that is serving a growing percentage of the population. As a result, the percentage of the population with college education in Latin America is greater than ever, and many college graduates are the first in their families to have gone to college. But there is still unmet demand for access to college, and there are concerns over the quality of some of the programs and institutions. Governments are increasingly playing a key role establishing mechanisms to increase quality and protect the public.

New Challenges to Education in Latin America: Populism and Covid-19

The history of education in Latin America is central to the history of the region itself. Educational institutions have reflected and contributed to the larger political struggles of the societies of Latin America, reflecting the four waves of globalization that have shaped Latin American societies. A powerful impetus for educational development resulted from the second wave of globalization, which supported the aspiration to build a social order ruled by human reason, and enhanced by science, wherein the rights of all were recognized, wherein ordinary people could improve their circumstances and join others in improving society. These ideas of the Enlightenment shaped the efforts of one set of education modernizers in Latin America. Their interests converged with the interests of those who sought to advance modern universities, just as public education and democracy itself are all products of the same project of the Enlightenment. These efforts were further reinforced by initiatives of a second wave of globalization, which were local as well as global, resulting from the construction of the post–World War II global order based on the idea of human rights, and this dialectic between the global and the local shaped the development of education in Latin America, and contributed to shape the global education movement. A more recent fourth wave of globalization, beginning in the last decade of the twentieth century, pushed educational inclusion even further and advanced efforts to make education more relevant to a rapidly changing world. A distinctive trait of this fourth wave was growing participation of civil society in shaping education institutions.

But this education project was also contested at various points in the history of Latin America by conservatives and national populists who did not partake in the view that human reason, science, and freedom would advance collective well-being and that global actors should partake in national affairs. Conservatives and populists placed instead strong bets on *caudillos,* or strongmen, who would advance the interest of the people, unobstructed by the challenges of expert knowledge, deliberation, democratic dissent, or the rule of law, and increasingly rejected globalization and global institutions. A new wave of populism runs through Latin America, reflected in the presidencies of Hugo Chávez and Nicolás Maduro in Venezuela, Nestor Kirchner in Argentina, Evo Morales in Bolivia, Jair Bolsonaro in Brazil, and Andrés Manuel López Obrador in Mexico, among others. To populists, the institutions that the modernizers labored to construct, including those educational institutions designed to prepare people to think for themselves, are an obstacle, for they would much rather communicate directly with the masses, unobstructed by institutions, the rule of law, or other checks and balances. The recent ambitious curriculum reforms in Brazil and Mexico, aimed at developing twenty-first-century skills, were stalled by Bolsonaro and López Obrador (Reimers 2020). Chávez and Maduro instituted a variety of political controls on the education system and universities to force allegiance to the ruling party and leaders. More than two centuries after Francisco de Miranda, Simón Bolívar, Andrés Bello, Domingo Faustino Sarmiento, and others tried to imagine a set of educational institutions that would equip a free people for self-rule, assisted by reason, science, and expertise, the struggle to build those institutions continues.

In March 2020 the region was confronted by a new global challenge, the novel coronavirus causing Covid-19, which would rapidly upend life in all domains. The direct impact of the virus, its toll on human lives, and the indirect impact in economic activity exacerbated inequalities in what was already the most unequal region in the world. Social inequality and vulnerability, and weak health infrastructure, resulted in a disproportionate impact of the pandemic in the region, which was the epicenter for the larger part of 2020, as it was home to six of the top twenty-five death-producing countries in the world. As a result, the economy went into a recession, with GDP contracting 6.9 percent in 2020, the largest contraction in any world region (World Bank 2021a).

Governments ordered the suspension of in-person instruction as part of the efforts to contain the spread of the virus. With the exception of Nicaragua, all countries in the region suspended in-person instruction. The suspension of in-person educational activities in Latin America has been longer than the suspension in any other world region, averaging 159 missed days of classes during 2020 alone (World Bank 2021a). Governments and private educational institutions created a variety of alternative modalities to deliver instruction remotely. Given the limited access to internet connectivity and online devices (only 77 percent of fifteen-year-olds in Latin America have internet at home, and only 45 percent of the students in the poorest quintile do [World Bank 2021a]), many of these alternative modalities involved the use of radio, television, technologies such as WhatsApp, and distribution of textbooks and printed packages. The limited available evidence of the efficacy of those contingency plans to date suggests that access to these alternative modalities has mirrored the large socioeconomic divides that characterize Latin America. As access to opportunities to learn was mediated even more directly than it ordinarily is by supports at home—a place to study, access to connectivity and resources, the freedom to devote time to study, support from educated parents—the already large gaps in opportunity to learn that children experience when schools are in session were augmented. As a result of deficient opportunities to continue learning, many students failed to learn or disengaged from learning, and others altogether stopped attending planned activities (Reimers et al. 2021).

The World Bank estimates that the percentage of children unable to read at the basic level will increase 20 percent, adding an additional 7.6 million children to the "learning poor" (World Bank 2021a). Learning losses for the region, which will disproportionately impact the poorer students, are estimated at 1.3 to 1.7 years of schooling on average, amounting to an economic cost over the lifetimes of the current generation of learners of $1.7 trillion (World Bank 2021a).

The pandemic caused a number of universities in the region to step up as engines of technological and social innovation to mitigate the impact of the crisis. For example, the EAFIT University in Colombia collaborated with the Ministry of Education, developing the platform for digital teaching that supported the national remote teaching strategy during the pandemic. Chile's president invited the presidents of the two main universities in the country, the University of Chile and the Pontifical Catholic University of Chile, to form a social roundtable to collaborate with the government in developing responses to the pandemic. In Mexico, the University of Guadalajara integrated the multiple campuses of the university with the many high schools governed by the university in professional development activities for staff to help them teach remotely. In Brazil, the Getúlio Vargas Foundation collaborated with municipal secretaries of education, supporting the development of strategies to sustain teaching during the pandemic.

There were numerous university-led initiatives to mitigate the health impact of the Covid-19 pandemic, including the development of a molecular test to diagnose Covid-19 by the universities of San Martín and Quilmes in Argentina; the design of low-cost pulmonary ventilators by the Pontificia Universidad Católica del Perú; the design of protective masks for medical personnel by the University of San Carlos de Guatemala; the sequencing of the genome of a strain of Covid-19 by the University of San Francisco de Quito in Ecuador to monitor the virus; the development of a biosensor to detect virus cases in a cost-effective way at the National Autonomous University of Mexico; diagnostic testing at the University of La Plata in Argentina; the development of a sanitizing cabin at the University of Chile; the development of a noninvasive ventilation system at the Autonomous University of Manizales in Colombia; the development of a mechanical ventilation device at the

University of Concepción in Chile; the development of a rapid test to diagnose asymptomatic cases at the Pontificia Universidad Católica de Chile; the development of a disinfectant that eliminates the virus from surfaces at the Universidad de los Andes in Colombia; the development of an edible vaccine against the virus at the Autonomous University of Nuevo León; the development of high-flow oxygen cannulas to treat extreme cases of infection by the University of Piura in Peru; a nasal spray vaccine developed by the University of São Paulo in Brazil; a low-cost test for mass diagnosis developed by Austral University of Chile; the evaluation of existing drugs to attack the disease at the National Autonomous University of Mexico; the development of a molecular diagnostic kit at the Universidad Mayor de San Simón in Bolivia; the development of a mechanical ventilator at the Simón Bolívar University of Venezuela. In Uruguay, the Center for Innovation in Epidemiology Surveillance was established (UNESCO 2020).

In all likelihood the pandemic will undo much of the progress made in closing gaps in access and learning in the past decade, if not more. This could well bring to the region another lost decade for human development, as did the programs of economic adjustment of the 1980s. If it does, the growing education gaps will compound other social challenges, those of poverty, inequality, exclusion, political polarization, mistrust in government and institutions, social violence, and democratic governance. In that context, the urgency of providing all with the opportunities to gain skills to become self-authoring individuals and to collaborate with others in improving their communities, the very aspirations that have driven much progress in education since independence, will become painfully clear, at least to those who hope for a democratic future.

Note

1. While there were distinct and well-developed educational institutions during pre-Columbian times, which I have analyzed elsewhere (Reimers 2006), they are beyond the scope of this book.

12

Religion

Hannah Stewart-Gambino

Religion has been a driving force in Latin America since pre-Columbian times. As illustrated in Chapter 3, Europeans who came to the New World with crosses and swords found religion and politics intertwined in the Indigenous civilizations. Since then, religious beliefs have been influenced by multifaceted encounters between divergent cultures. As stated in the introduction to this book, these interactions shaped enduring legacies that have been modified over time. European *conquistadores* (conquerors) established the Catholic Church as an official institution of the Spanish and Portuguese colonies and suppressed Indigenous religions—many of which were grounded in highly sophisticated civilizations. The significant role of the church continued into the twentieth century.

Beginning in the mid-twentieth century, US and European scholars predicted that the influence of Catholicism and religion in general would decline in Latin America—despite the widespread cultural religiosity of the people—as modernization associated with urban, industrial economic growth transformed the society. Based on the US and European experiences, the so-called modernization school argued that economic growth leads to greater role differentiation and specialization—in the economy and political and social spheres (Peterson, Vásquez, and Williams 2001). According to this view, greater social differentiation and specialization give rise to new, modern institutions—political parties, trade unions, governmental bureaucracies, and myriad social institutions—necessary for the rational functioning of individuals and societies in an increasingly complex world. With modernization, religion will be relegated over time to the private sphere as other, secular institutions assume many functions of the traditional or premodern authority structures in which political, social, and religious authority were interrelated.

As shown in Chapter 6, the twentieth century—albeit with significant boom and bust cycles—was one of significant economic modernizations throughout the region. The religious landscape in Latin America has hardly disappeared or faded into the margins of societies. Rather, the religious monopoly of the Catholic Church has given way to an increasingly vibrant religious marketplace. Religious belief is more volatile and conversions from Catholicism to other forms of Christianity have increased, as have rates of return to new forms of Catholicism. Increased competition between religious institutions fuels changes in the role of churches in local, regional, and national politics. As shown in Chapter 4, church and state authorities have worked with and against one another to inform and control their common subjects.

There was never a monolithic Latin American Catholic Church; Catholic churches must be understood as national (even regional) institutions through which the ecclesial concerns and priorities of the Vatican intersect with the local hierarchies' struggles to make Catholicism and the church meaningful in the concrete reality of believers' lives (Cleary and Stewart-Gambino 1992). Alternative forms of Christianity, syncretic religions, and spiritism compete for relevance in the lives of citizens.

The Colonial Role of the Catholic Church

The historical image of Latin America—the Catholic continent—was one of *conquistadores* with a "sword in one hand and a cross in the other." The role of the Catholic Church in the conquest and subsequent colonial experience is best understood as a partnership between the church and the Spanish crown. Throughout the fifteenth century, the church partnered with the crown in a bloody campaign to reconquer the Iberian Peninsula from the Moors and to expel Jews who did not convert to Catholicism. Because of the church's clear political support for the century-long struggle, it became another arm of the Spanish state. This religiopolitical partnership was carried to the New World. *Conquistadores* and Catholic missionaries traveled together to conquer the Indigenous peoples and take their wealth for the Spanish crown while converting their souls for the Catholic Church. Given the shortage of Spanish personnel and the intersection of church and state, many prelates assumed government posts in the viceroyalties of the New World.

Early missionaries taught Indigenous people the Spanish and Portuguese languages, as well as the Catholic faith in hopes of creating an Amerindian priesthood. During the early conquest, local customs viewed as consistent with Catholicism were tolerated. The Indigenous people's tendency toward syncretism—blending Catholicism with Indigenous beliefs and customs—led subsequent missionaries to take an increasingly intolerant view of all Amerindian religiosity, resulting in a new wave of repression to eliminate local religious icons, worship sites, authorities, and belief structures.

From the beginning of the conquest, the colonial state combined Catholicism and military, political, economic, and social power. Politically, Spanish America was governed by four viceroyalties. The Spanish governors compensated the *conquistadores* with rights to demand tribute and labor from Indigenous peoples, creating a highly stratified class system in which the Spanish and their descendants who were born in the New World lived off the Indigenous populations' labor. The resulting oppression of the Indigenous populations undermined claims that a central purpose of the colonial state was to win souls for Catholicism. At least one voice from within the church denounced the treatment of the Indigenous peoples. Bishop Bartolomé de las Casas, angered by the flagrant abuses of Indigenous peoples, wrote to the Spanish crown begging for new regulations to ameliorate their treatment and called for the importation of African slaves, resulting in the New Laws (1542) governing the treatment of the Indigenous peoples. Prohibitions against the enslavement of Indigenous peoples as well as regulations to prevent other abuses were never successfully enforced and were rescinded when Spanish landowners revolted. De las Casas regretted his support for the importation of slaves after witnessing their wretched conditions and inhuman treatment. The colonial system with its hierarchical oppression of the Indigenous populations cannot be understood simply as the result of abuses associated with military and political subjugation; the colonial system was built in partnership with the Catholic Church, which gave the social order its justification and moral imperative.

The Role of the Catholic Church in Liberal-Conservative Battles

By the early nineteenth century, power was shifting on the European continent—most notably with the rise of British and French military and commercial power. Napoleon's invasion of Spain in 1808 weakened the Spanish crown's ability to enforce its rule in the colonies, giving the *criollos* (Europeans born in the Americas) the opportunity to mount successful independence movements. By the 1820s, Central and South America were home to newly independent states—all ruled by the *criollo* classes who wanted to be free of the crown's demands. These new states were built on the colonial foundations of intertwined religious and political hierarchy in which Catholicism was the official, established state religion. The governments of the newly independent Latin American states were relatively weak and faced formidable challenges by powerful *criollo* elites who wanted to use the power of the new states to advance their economic and political agendas.

Inspired by the Enlightenment ideals of equality, liberty, and justice and in the shadow of the new United States, liberals throughout Latin America revolted against the old order. As noted in Chapter 3, nineteenth-century liberal political parties were anti-clerical parties, and their platforms included a focus on secularization of the state—most notably in public education and state control of rites of passage. Inspired by the democratic developments in Europe and North America, Latin American liberal parties believed in abolishing aristocratic political control and promoting greater decentralization of state power. In opposition were the pro-clerical conservative parties, made up of elites who defended the traditional power of the Catholic Church and the political, economic, and social power of the colonial state's descendants. Conservatives believed in consolidating the power of a centralized state, supported by an established Catholic Church, with the social order organized around clear class lines.

The fundamental divisions in postcolonial Latin American nations gave rise to political and social conflicts throughout the region, often erupting in violence with winner-take-all political consequences that deepened the ideological rift between opposing forces. These conflicts were between opposing *criollos,* not class wars between the rich and poor, but competition for political control of the newly independent states and the associated social and economic power. Opposing philosophical views regarding the role of the Catholic Church in the state became intertwined in the fundamental question of political, economic, and social control of the state.

By the early twentieth century, many of the Catholic Church's powers —control over education and civil authority over birth registries, marriage, and burial—had been won by the states. In most countries, the church had been disestablished, although the circumstances of the separation varied widely. Chile separated the church and state in its 1921 constitution through a negotiation between church and state officials, while the 1917 constitution of post-revolutionary Mexico contained harsh provisions that allowed persecution of the church and its personnel. In many Latin American countries, divisions between liberals and conservatives were based on philosophical grounds regarding the role of the church in modern society as well as economic, urban-rural, and class interests. The Colombian period known as *La Violencia* (1948–1958) left hundreds of thousands killed, and millions displaced, representing the inability of the political system to overcome the deep and radicalized divisions between clerical and anti-clerical camps. Similarly, Mexico's Cristero Rebellion (1927–1929) arose in response to the brutal repression of the church under President Plutarco Elías Calles's government—a particularly virulent anti-clerical regime.

In the twentieth century, political systems rooted in the previous battles between clerical and anti-clerical parties clashed with the rise of new classes whose demands required a more modern, secular state. New parties on the left—notably those associated with Marxism—challenged church authority and the Catholic worldview. The economic modernization of Latin America brought influences from the United States, including evangelical Protestant missionary outreach. By the mid-twentieth century, the Catholic Church faced challenges from secularization, rival religions, and leftist (often Marxist) movements and parties—all offering alternative worldviews to traditional Catholicism. Although one cannot speak of formal "national churches" until the creation of national bishops' conferences in the mid-twentieth century, it is clear that both the form and content of the challenges to the church to maintain its influence among the faithful were largely determined by national boundaries. The church remained powerful in the region through the mid-twentieth century—partly because over 90 percent of the population still considered itself Catholic.

The Catholic Church generally continues to enjoy preferential treatment in various forms. It remains a significant landowner in many countries, and continues to count on special subsidies or tax benefits, and its opposition to divorce, abortion, and homosexuality influences attitudes, although progressive movements recently have won notable legislative and legal victories. The majority of Latin Americans self-identify as Catholics, at least nominally. Right-wing parties often have close ties to their national Catholic church and serve as protectors of church interests in national politics; explicit alliances with Protestants in Brazil and Mexico suggest change is likely. In much of the region, the Catholic Church still provides the only viable alternative to underfunded and inadequate public education.

The Modern Catholic Church

By the second half of the twentieth century, the Catholic Church was at a new crossroads. In countries such as Peru, Chile, and Brazil, progressive Catholics argued that Catholicism could compete for the souls of the masses by addressing the concerns of Marxist political movements. Inspired by Pope Leo XIII's 1891 encyclical *Rerum Novarum* (Rights and Duties of Capital and Labor), Catholic trade unions, self-help organizations, and political parties ranging from center-right to center-left arose across the region to address "the misery and wretchedness pressing so unjustly on the working class" and to compete with the radical and atheistic claims of the Marxist left. Progressive clerics argued that massive urbanization spawned by the migration of the rural poor to cities in search of jobs and survival made uprooted families more vulnerable to recruitment from radical political movements or rival religious beliefs. The Catholic Church remained institutionally and politically aligned with the right, including an increasingly anticommunist political right supported by US intervention.

Pope John XXII announced the second Vatican Council, Vatican II (1960–1963), to respond to the challenges of midcentury global secularization and decline in Catholic church adherence. Vatican II changes were designed to awaken a Catholic spiritual renewal by making the church more relevant to the lives of believers. Beyond such reforms as translating mass from Latin to national languages, Vatican II encouraged more openness to the world, a call for sociopolitical action and analysis, and greater lay participation in the activities and leadership of parishes and dioceses. Vatican II inspired new forms of Catholic sociopolitical engagement when Latin American countries faced deep divisions among the poor and middle classes. Particularly in Brazil, Chile, and Peru, progressive priests, bishops, and nuns began to publicly condemn social and economic injustice, using "liberation theology" to denounce the "structural sins" of dependent capitalism. Liberationists argued that in Latin America, where the population was overwhelmingly poor, Christianity required solidarity with the dispossessed and their hopes for freedom from economic, political, and social oppression.

These progressive forces in the Catholic Church came to a head in the 1968 meeting of the Latin American Episcopal Conference (CELAM) in Medellín, Colombia. CELAM pronounced the Latin American Catholic Church's "preferential option for the poor" and adopted a pastoral strategy based on small parish groups that combined worship, Bible study in light of their daily lives, and a commitment to living out the gospel to serve the community. These groups were called *comunidades eclesiales de base* (ecclesial base communities) and they flourished—particularly in poor neighborhoods—across the region despite differences in their relationship to parish or diocesan authorities.

The communities became important during the wave of military coups in the 1960s and 1970s. Social mobilization became viewed as an unhealthy symptom of the disease (often characterized as a "cancer") of politics. Rather than employing the brutally repressive tactics of the past to destroy political challenges to oligarchic power, these military leaders were inspired by a vision of neoliberal economic development that they believed would fundamentally "depoliticize" society and cause the destruction of the political left and center.

During the 1970s and 1980s, liberation theology and the ecclesial base communities took on particular significance. Because many of the military juntas wrapped themselves in the mantle of religious self-glorification for saving their countries from "godless Marxism," traditional and right-wing elements of the Catholic Church (as well as some Protestant and Pentecostal churches) rushed to align themselves with the brutal dictatorships, lending their tactics to the appearance of moral justification. Progressive Catholics who condemned human rights violations and the economic injustice borne by the poor and middle classes found moral refuge in the liberationist wing of the Catholic Church. For liberationists, sin is not only an individual condition; it should also be understood structurally. Political, economic, and social structures that systematically oppress the poor are sinful; for many Latin American liberationists, the kind of capitalism thrust on the region by the global North and the imperialist United States created endemic poverty, vast gaps between the very rich and the chronically poor, and the politically weak and unstable regimes dominated by powerful economic elites backed by US-armed military forces. For most liberationists, Christians are called to individual repentance and acts of charity and solidarity with the poor and a commitment to engaged social justice. "Radicals" saw an option for the poor in the Marxist notion that class conflict is the engine of history; accommodationist or reformist political strategies that fail to fundamentally change existing power arrangements only preserve the sinful status quo. Christians must join with other political forces to fight (potentially with violence) for real political and economic transformation. For most progressives of the era, the struggle against oppression was understood as better channeled through outreach to the poor and oppressed. The majority of ecclesial base communities primarily focused on facilitating change rather than explicit partisan activity through grassroots, religious self-help and educational groups.

Brazil, with the world's largest Catholic population, was home to the most progressive, liberationist faction in the region. During the 1964–1985 military dictatorship, the Brazilian Catholic Church provided services and protection to the poor and oppressed under constant threat of persecution. During Chile's military dictatorship, the church served as the only channel through which opposition could be voiced. Chilean church leaders welcomed the armed forces for restoring order in 1973 after months under the democratically elected Salvador Allende (1970–1973), and then issued stronger and more pointed criticisms of the regime's human rights violations and economic policies. As in Brazil, scores of new church or church-affiliated local, academic, and workers' organizations were created to protect individuals involved in struggles against the military. In some countries, the role of the church as the "voice of the voiceless" had profound meaning for pro-democracy movements and those suffering from the dislocation of failed neoliberal economic policies and state-sponsored human rights violations. In countries already suffering under long-standing repressive regimes, liberation theology inspired many to join revolutionary movements such as the Sandinista National Liberation Front (FSLN) in its fight to topple Nicaragua's Somoza regime.

The progressive and radical wings of Latin America's Catholic Church were never as extensive as many claimed during the 1960s to 1980s. The commitment of prominent national Catholic bishops' conferences to the protection of human rights and the moral superiority of political democracy over authoritarianism was their most important rule during the brutal years of the region's dictatorships. By the 1980s, many national churches noteworthy in their support of democracy and human rights were eager to withdraw from the political fray and return to a more explicit distinction between public life and personal salvation. In countries where the church had been valiant in condemning human rights violations or supporting pro-democracy forces, ecclesial authorities were keenly aware they had alienated their traditional allies among elites and the political right.

Pope John Paul II (1978–2005) was an advocate for Latin American church leaders who wanted to withdraw to a more universal appeal to personal salvation, regardless of class or ideological suasion. Karol Wojtyla was known as a staunch anticommunist in his native Poland who had been critical of the Vatican II definition of the Catholic Church as "people of God." He long argued for a traditionally hierarchical definition of the institutional church—a church whose authority is made manifest through the pope, cardinals, archbishops, bishops, and priests, with the lay population living in faithful obedience. Pope John Paul II was energetic and charismatic. Penny Lernoux warned in the 1970s that "John Paul, who thinks in terms of peoples—not nation states—is deeply supportive of the populism that enables a people to express political, economic, or social aspirations through religious gestures and symbols." At the same time, "John Paul's Catholicism has a clear set of rules and it is the responsibility of priests to make sure they are obeyed. The civilization he envisions is essentially integralist—a throwback to a Christendom when the church was both the mediating force in secular society and the only source of spiritual salvation" (quoted in Cleary and Stewart-Gambino 1992: 4).

Pope John Paul II launched an offensive against the elements of the progressive, liberationist Latin American church that he viewed as aligned with the Marxist elements that he opposed in the European context or, at best, inappropriately engaged in the worldly sphere of politics in which the laity were granted authority as "people of God." Many mistakenly attributed John Paul's consistent rejection of the liberationist wing of the Latin American church as evidence of conservative political beliefs; rather, John Paul was a charismatic and populist defender of the poor who helped solidify the church's support for democracy. He is best understood as seeking to impose, through his consistently traditionalist appointments of bishops and cardinals, a return to a strictly hierarchical church that adheres to a mission of personal salvation from sin and calls individuals to acts of charity on behalf of the poor. His successor, Pope Benedict XVI (2005–2013), introduced a more muscular defense of traditional Catholic social doctrine, opposing what he viewed as failures of modernity such as secularization and moral relativism. He emphasized strict adherence to traditional Catholic doctrine regarding abortion, homosexuality, and individual sin. The Latin American Catholic progressive movement, whose heyday was during the 1960s–1980s, was weakened, but its legacy can still be found in many parishes even today.

By the 1990s, much of the Latin American church had retreated from the political and social activism of the 1960s–1980s, partly due to the Vatican's influence and partly out of national prelates' desire to withdraw the church from the front lines of the highly charged, often violent, ideological clashes between right and left during the dictatorships and democratic transitions. Even the most progressive national bishops' conferences in the region sought to reconsolidate the church's traditional role in democratic societies where political institutions such as political parties or trade unions could function as the channels for the population's temporal demands and aspirations.

The urge to withdraw from the partisan fray created difficulties for many who had forged their religious identities during the previous period of liberationist activism. During the dictatorships, many poor women had been forced to adopt new roles to support their families, despite their traditional roles in service to the all-male priesthood and religious identities forged in light of the Catholic cult of Mary that glorifies the suffering of motherhood. Poor women organized neighborhood soup kitchens, self-help organizations, and entrepreneurial activities based on crafts such as sewing and cooking. In many countries, help from diocesan or national church organizations provided these women additional training or access to national or international aid. As discussed in Chapter 10, women who emerged as local leaders became involved in networks of church-sponsored organizations, which took them from their traditionally subservient roles in the exclusively private sphere. Poor men also bore the brunt of the state's repression of "political" activity. In an environment where men's ability to be protagonists in their families' survival was repressed, poor women turned to the church, their traditional source of personal refuge.

In countries such as Chile and Brazil, the Catholic Church's retreat from its perceived political stances during the dictatorships (pro-democracy, defense of human rights, and voice of the voiceless) distressed many on the left; this period also saw a reinvigorated conservative Catholicism. Catholic lay elites, the business class, and cultural conservatives found refuge in Catholic movements such as Opus Dei, the Mexican Legionnaires for Christ, and Shoenstat, which are politically anti-leftist, theologically Papist and Marian, and economically aligned with neoliberalism. Pope Benedict XVI (2005–2013) shared these organizations' pre–Vatican II focus on traditional sacraments and distrust of post–Vatican II emphasis on making the liturgy more accessible to laity. Conservative Catholics share a theological understanding of business and wealth creation as a lay vocation. God-given stewardship over the earth, according to conservative Catholics, blesses business activity as a means of benefiting others. Here, the businessman—the job creator—is an instrument of God, a view offering the wealthy a social and charitable role better serving the poor than reformist, leftist, or liberationist Catholic movements. Conservative Catholic movements are mostly associated with private, elite schools and universities founded on conservative Catholic doctrine, and often appeal to conservatives' desire to shield their children from progressive Catholicism.

The withdrawal of the church from progressive engagement resulted in the return to the parishes of many alienated by its stances during the dictatorships—among the traditional elites and the poor. Most Latin American churches refocused on issues of personal salvation, morality (sexuality, divorce, abortion), and traditional charity. The turn from broad political issues perceived as political ideology on a left-right spectrum may have appealed to weary Catholics who wished to remain in the Catholic Church rather than convert to the individualism of Protestant Pentecostalism.

Pope Francis: First Latin American, Jesuit, and Non-European Since the Eighth Century

Jorge Mario Bergoglio, born in Argentina and former archbishop and then cardinal of Buenos Aires (1998–2013), became the first Latin American pope in 2013. Choosing the name "Francis" for St. Francis of Assisi, the new pope signaled to the world that he brought a decidedly more pastoral, less ideologically conservative, vision to the papacy—choosing to eschew many of the formal papal trappings enjoyed by his predecessors, welcoming dialogue regarding the place of the LGBTQ community and women in the Catholic Church and church leadership, aligning with the critique of unbridled capitalism and support for the lives of the poor first espoused by Pope Leo VIII (1878–1903), engaging in interfaith dialogue, and issuing an unusually extensive and detailed theological encyclical calling on all Catholics to combat climate change. Pope Francis remains traditionalist, with traditional Catholic views on abortion, celibacy of the priesthood, and ordination of women. Throughout the region, which he visited seven times before the global pandemic, he is broadly popular for his commitment to the poor and opposition to social inequality. Pope Francis's popularity, particularly among Latin American elites, has made him effective in diplomatic efforts—playing a role in the normalization of US-Cuban relations and US-Venezuelan tensions. His pastoral approach raises the distrust of political conservatives in Latin America, and elsewhere. Argentina is a notable exception to Pope Francis's regional popularity, where many remain deeply critical of his perceived failure to speak out against the junta during Argentina's "Dirty War," in which as many as 30,000 people disappeared and many more were tortured by the state. The Argentine Catholic Church, in contrast to those of Chile and Brazil, was less publicly committed to opposing Argentine human rights violations and supporting pro-democracy movements; the Argentine church never adopted the stance of "voice of the voiceless" or "preferential option for the poor" as did its Southern Cone counterparts. The Argentine church enjoys less public trust and observance as a consequence of the enduring legacy of accusations that church leaders were complicit in the dictatorships. Pope Francis continues to face accusations that, as provincial superior of the Society of Jesus in Argentina between 1973 an 1976, he failed to protect two Jesuit priests who were arrested by the navy and subjected to intense torture. These accusations, coupled with accusations that Pope Francis has failed to deal effectively with Latin American prelates accused of sexual abuse, undercut his general appeal in the region.

The Rise of Evangelical Protestantism

Latin America in the past century has experienced significant increases in the number of individuals identifying as adherents of some form of Protestantism. The term "evangelical" is typically used interchangeably with "Protestantism," yet it encompasses a wide range of mainline traditions that grew out of the global North and into a distinctly Latin American Protestantism, and into Pentecostalism and neo-Pentecostalism. A recent Pew Research Center survey (2017) finds that Catholic identity has declined in every country to varying degrees, and that regionally the share of the population identifying as Catholic has declined to 69 percent (from 90 percent in the mid-twentieth century). Almost 20 percent of Latin Americans now identify as Protestant, 90 percent of whom identify as some form of Pentecostal. Protestants, called "evangelicos" or evangelicals, are typically more observant, going to church and reporting that they pray more often and more consistently than self-identified Catholics. The Protestant or Pentecostal subculture is visible to global observers when political candidates, parties, and movements are publicly associated with their evangelical base. Guatemalan dictator Efrain Rios Montt, one of the region's first evangelical leaders, was installed after a 1982 coup. Leaders throughout the region (Guatemala, Honduras, Chile, Brazil, Venezuela, Colombia, and Costa Rica) that either are themselves evangelical or are publicly supported by evangelical voters are increasingly common. The most visible recent example is Brazil's President Jair Bolsonaro, who was elected with a coalition of Protestant-Evangelical movements. Since their right-wing roots in the 1980s, evangelical political candidates and movements have spanned the political spectrum from left to right, depending on the political opportunities and constraints peculiar to specific countries at given historical moments. Evangelical social theology (both Protestant and Pentecostal) remains broadly culturally conservative, supporting neoliberalism and traditional gender roles and opposing gender identity rights, marriage equality, abortion, LGBTQ rights, and other personal morality issues.

Protestants have long been present in Latin America. In the early twentieth century, the small number of Protestants came almost entirely from mainline Protestant traditions (Lutherans, Baptists, Anglicans, Methodists, Presbyterians) of the European and US immigrants or economic elites associated with economic dominance of the global North. Indigenous conversions to these traditions were rare, and the populations professing these faiths remained relatively stable.

The extraordinary growth of adherents to Protestantism began in Latin America in the 1950s–1960s. By the 1990s, it was widely believed that over 50 million Latin Americans, or approximately 11 percent of the region's population, claimed to be Protestant (Lewis 2004). The question "Is Latin America turning Protestant?" provided a revealing title for a groundbreaking book by David Stoll (1990). If the conversion rates were to continue, Protestants would soon constitute a majority in some countries.

Unlike those Protestants associated with economic elites from the United States and Europe, latter twentieth-century conversions overwhelmingly occurred among the poor and lower middle classes, and the new converts typically join evangelical Protestant (especially Pentecostal) churches and sects. Some of the strength of non-Catholic religious identification can be attributed to renewed mission work funded from the United States. For example, the Mormon Church and Jehovah's Witnesses, and some ideologically conservative evangelical wings of mainstream US churches, funded politically inspired missionary work to compete with liberationist Catholics who sympathized with reformist or revolutionary movements during the civil wars of the 1970s–1980s. Latin American Pentecostalism is not a foreign phenomenon; over 90 percent of the new conversions were and continue to be distinctly Latin American forms of Pentecostalism.

A variety of factors explain conversion to evangelical Protestantism. Pentecostalism fills a religious need for many in poor neighborhoods whose families fled the economic deprivation of the countryside in search of urban economic opportunities. Latin American Catholic churches, despite strong liberationist elements whose "preferential option for the poor" during the 1960s–1980s resulted in unprecedented outreach to poor neighborhoods, never had the resources to develop sufficient religious infrastructure to respond adequately to the religious needs of the poor, or the populations dislocated by rapid urbanization. Additionally, no national Catholic church ever had a strong, institutional presence among the poor and lower middle classes, who always have contained the majority of Latin Americans.

The urban poor's needs create an open terrain for religious competition that is conducive to the growth of Indigenous Pentecostalism.

Pentecostal institutions' operating costs are remarkably low and their religious authority is earned through charismatic preaching—on the streets or in small, storefront locations in poor neighborhoods—rather than through seminary training. Pentecostal churches can be created anywhere. Aspiring Pentecostal pastors freely incorporate Indigenous music, art forms, or cultural references into their services. The service itself is grounded in biblical text and centers on the ability of the pastor to "bring it alive." Some better-established, larger Pentecostal churches are investing in pastoral and seminary training; the Pentecostal Theological Seminary in Ecuador is funded by the Assemblies of God.

Moreover, Pentecostals, like the fundamentalists with whom they are often mistaken, root their belief structures in literal interpretations of biblical text, particularly the descriptions of the experiences of the early Christians as told in the New Testament's Acts of the Apostles. The Pentecost, the moment in which the crucified Christ returns to the apostles, resulting in extraordinary "blessings of the Holy Spirit" such as speaking in tongues, is a cornerstone of Pentecostals' emphasis on the lived experience of the Holy Spirit. Rather than orthodoxy, as interpreted by priests, Pentecostals—like other Protestants—seek individual and direct experience of God through Christ. Pentecostals believe in the individual call to perfection, and the path to perfection is through seizure by the Holy Spirit as manifest by extraordinary gifts. Pentecostals believe that the kinds of miraculous events and personal gifts chronicled in the Acts of the Apostles remain possible for all Christians, and evidence of the gifts of the Holy Spirit is the measure of one's faith. Pentecostals criticize their non-Pentecostal, mainline Christian brethren for emphasizing doctrinal orthodoxy rather than the individual and demonstrable personal experience of the Holy Spirit.

Consistent with Pentecostalism's emphasis on the personal experience of the Holy Spirit, pastors' authority rests on their leadership of the faithful in their quest for a personal, emotionally intense experience of the Holy Spirit. This emphasis is particularly well suited for poor neighborhoods, where financial resources are scarce, access to quality public education is limited, and the reach of the Catholic and traditional Protestant churches is constrained. Pentecostalism's strength is its ability to respond to local needs, traditions, and constraints depending on the charismatic and entrepreneurial skills of local pastors.

Latin American Pentecostalism is committed to grassroots social service. Many Pentecostal churches, particularly those more established, either create or collaborate with grassroots social outreach related to such issues as addiction, unwed pregnancy, domestic violence, religious education of the young, and teen delinquency. At the center of Pentecostals' church membership is a shared experience of the Holy Spirit, not a shared vision for society at large. Most Pentecostals view themselves as apolitical in that their lives and social networks are committed to and built around their religious faith. Additionally, Pentecostals' involvement in social service agencies tends to be part of their commitment to proselytizing potential converts rather than a commitment to a political agenda to change economic or social structures. Pentecostals are typically viewed as inherently "conservative" for their emphasis on personal conversion and repentance of individual sin, contrasting with their more liberal religious counterparts in other denominations whose faith propels them to address the societal causes of social ills.

The greatest growth in recent decades has been in neo-Pentecostal churches. Unlike traditional Pentecostals, for whom conversion often is seen as a spiritual retreat from "worldly" affairs, neo-Pentecostalism—or "health and wealth" or "prosperity gospel" teachings—views prosperity as a measure of Christian self-realization. Social mobility and improvements in personal health often caused by the lifestyle changes made by Pentecostal converts is God's blessing for conversion, a metaphysical worldview bridging Pentecostals' focus on individuals' relationship with the Holy Spirit and the needs and aspirations of socially mobile and more educated believers. Neo-Pentecostal growth is most notable in the wealthier sectors of Latin American society rather than among the poor and dislocated. Neo-Pentecostalism is more open to political and economic associations and modern consumerism. Worship services have high production value and lend themselves to the mass media strategies of so-called mega-churches. Some mega-churches have become well-known and highly visible international organizations, such as Brazil's Universal Church of the Kingdom of God.

Despite predictions of the 1990s that Latin America was "turning Protestant," growth rates have stabilized in most of the region. Socioeconomic and political changes have challenged traditional belief systems and given rise to the appeal of a variety of alternatives.

Secularization

Although the Latin American religious landscape is commonly seen in terms of the competition between Catholicism and other (mostly evangelical) strains of Christianity, secularization—or the rise in numbers who self-identify as having "no religion" and the resulting decline of the relevance of religious belief of any kind—is as threatening to institutional religion as any competing religious worldview or belief. About 4 percent of Latin Americans report that they were raised in a household with no religious identity, yet 8 percent self-identify as having "no religion"—suggesting that religious nonaffiliation is on the rise. Historically, scholars argued that advances in Enlightenment rationality and scientific positivism would result in religious decline and secularization's rise. In European thought, the rapid advances of science, medicine, and technology, along with advancements in the social sciences, validated the view that the decline in religious identification may be attributed to the rise in modern knowledge. Observers have long assumed that Latin America's economic modernization (or that of other less developed regions) would increase higher educational attainment and secularization as greater numbers of people turn from religious identification to a more "modern" worldview.

The recent rise in the percentage of citizens self-identifying as having "no religion" may suggest an increase in secularization. But rather than representing increased modernization, self-identification of "no religion" may arise from the complexity of greater religious pluralism. For individuals who convert, it is often difficult to maintain the same degree of fervor and religious commitment. As the conversion experience fades, individuals can "backslide" into a space between their previous Catholic identity and an at least temporarily waning enthusiasm for their new identity. "Lapsed Catholics," who report occasional church attendance or dalliance with Protestant conversion, can identify themselves as having no religion, yet not necessarily reflect a rejection of religious identity. Whatever explanation for the rise of those professing no religion, both Catholic and Protestant officials view secularization as one of the greatest threats of the modern age.

The threat of secularization has two sides, the loss of souls who will not know the grace of salvation, and the erosion of fundamental values in the public sphere that religious authorities view as preventing the decline of human society. Both Catholics and Protestants share a vision of traditional family roles, and both decry what they perceive to be symptoms of the relegation of faith to churches and the private sphere—divorce, abortion, greater sexual freedom, and contraception. Given the Catholic Church's historical role in Latin America, the fight against secularization and its symptoms is waged in both the political and individual spheres—in public policies, such as support for Catholic schools, legal bans on divorce and abortion, and subsidies for Catholic agencies, as well as individual morality as evidenced by attendance at mass, adherence to traditional morality and social doctrine, and Christian charity.

Historically, Pentecostals and evangelical Protestants have not focused on influencing public policies to combat secularization, mostly because their ranks have been a mosaic of small, pastor-centric groups considered competitors of the Catholic Church and toward whom most Latin American states have been hostile, or neglectful. Evangelical and Pentecostal evangelization emphasizes individual rebirth in Christ, not public policy. Wealthier neo-Pentecostals who express greater openness to nontraditional values are more comfortable with political participation.

Evangelical and Pentecostal mass appeal has social implications, as do the countless local social services for the poor, particularly in combating substance abuse, domestic violence, teen delinquency, and other social ills that are commonplace throughout Latin American *barrios*. Many credit evangelical conversion with changes in particularly male behavior—abstinence from alcohol, faithfulness to wives, taking pride in being an honorable father and head of the family, tangibly improving the lives of women and children. Such religious values, while often dismissed as "traditional" or "conservative," are at the heart of the rejection of secularization by Protestants and Catholics.

If the nineteenth and early twentieth centuries were characterized by a series of conflicts about the role of the Catholic Church in Latin American states, the late twentieth and early twenty-first centuries have witnessed the church's struggle to retain its dominance in the face of rapidly increasing religious pluralism. The church views the trend in citizens claiming that they have no religion as one result of the dramatic rise in the number of evangelical Protestants and evidence of the church's weakening power. Perhaps the clearest statement of the Vatican's traditional perspective on the dangers of evangelical Protestantism is Pope John Paul II's address to Latin American bishops in Santo Domingo in 1992: "We should not underestimate a particular strategy aimed at weakening the bonds that unite Latin American countries and so to undermine the kinds of strength provided by unity. To that end, significant amounts of money are offered to subsidize proselytizing campaigns that try to shatter such Catholic unity" (quoted in Cleary and Stewart-Gambino 1997: 10). Describing non-Catholic religions as "sects" and "rapacious wolves," John Paul II demonstrates the degree of the perceived threat posed by religious competitors throughout Latin America. Pope Benedict XVI, during his 2007 trip to Brazil, repeatedly warned of the dangers of rising Protestantism amid his condemnation of contraception and abortion and the dangerous modern forces of both capitalism and Marxism.

Latin American bishops' conferences supported by John Paul II and Benedict XVI pursued a dual strategy in combating religious pluralism and secularization. National churches used their political muscle to ensure that governments maintained the church's preferential treatment in public policy in areas such as Catholic dominance in public and private education, direct and indirect subsidies, and exclusive reach into the ranks of the military. At the 1992 conference of Latin American bishops, Pope John Paul II called Latin American Catholics to a "new evangelization," or a renewed grassroots vigor to energize the church's ability to meet the religious aspirations of the faithful who turn to alternative faiths. This strategy was composed of several tactics including a greater emphasis on increasing the number of religious personnel and an attempt to adopt popular aspects of Pentecostalism, notably an explicitly charismatic approach to mass and Bible study.

Pope Francis has called Latin American bishops' conferences to greater emphasis on pastoral outreach, while signaling a greater appreciation for ecumenical cooperation. In 2017, Pope Francis invited 300 Pentecostal and evangelical leaders to Rome to join an estimated 30,000 Catholic charismatics in celebrating Pentecost and marking the fiftieth anniversary of the Catholic charismatic renewal. His preferential attention to the poor and issues of inequality, call for a welcoming Catholic Church rather than strict doctrinal adherence, and stylistic simplicity all attest to Pope Francis's publicly stated appreciation for the work of other Christians, even while emphasizing the role of the universal Catholic Church as the only true Christian faith.

Charismatic Catholics

The Catholic charismatic renewal movement has found resonance in Latin America since being introduced by Catholic missionaries in the early 1970s. Popes John Paul II and Benedict XVI strongly endorsed the movement's focus on the Holy Spirit's gifts (hearkening to the same biblical story of the Pentecost that inspires Pentecostalism in all of its forms) and the focus on the power of biblical texts to illuminate contemporary experience. Like their evangelical Protestant counterparts, charismatic Catholics embrace the mass media's ability to reach the faithful. Father Marcelo Rossi, perhaps the best-known Latin American charismatic, is a Brazilian whose 1999 CD of upbeat religious music outsold all other recording artists in the country. Rossi's daily radio show, two weekly television shows, and significant internet presence host regular concerts attracting thousands of young fans. Today, the Catholic charismatic movement is the largest and most vibrant lay movement in the region. Charismatics make up significant percentages of Catholics in Brazil,

Mexico, Colombia, and the Dominican Republic, followed by single-digit proportions in Chile, Argentina, Venezuela, Peru, and Ecuador.

Latin American prelates have been generally supportive of the rejuvenating potential of the charismatic movement, particularly its ability to compete with evangelical Protestants and Pentecostals. Yet Chesnutt (2003) has characterized the Latin American bishops' support as a "yellow light" because of the fear that emphasis on the Holy Spirit's individual experience could undermine the authority of the Catholic hierarchy. While lamenting the appeal of the "sects"—particularly Pentecostals, Seventh Day Adventists, Assemblies of God, Jehovah's Witness, the Foursquare Gospel Church, and the Mormons—Latin American bishops quickly insist that the successful and vibrant Catholic charismatics must defer to the official Catholic Church's authority. The danger presented by non-Catholic charismatics, according to bishops and the Vatican, is their erroneous belief that the direct experience of the Holy Spirit, particularly experienced as rebirth in the Spirit, is the foundational Christian experience. For the Catholic Church, the ecstatic experience of the Holy Spirit is simply one of the experiences of God and is not a necessary precondition to the sanctity or enjoyment of the sacraments. Priests and bishops quickly position the church as the only authority for interpretation of God's will; salvation can be achieved only through the mediation of priests, not through direct experience of God through the personal experience of the Holy Spirit.

Consistent with his greater openness to ecumenism and concern for the poor, at the fiftieth anniversary of the worldwide Catholic charismatic renewal movement in 2016, Pope Francis emphasized that baptism in the Holy Spirit, joyful praise, and social action on behalf of the society are all "inseparably linked." His words were heralded for ecumenical outreach and regarded as clarifying that Catholic charismatics must commit to Catholic pastoral care rather than an inward focus on personal morality at the expense of social concern. The pope's relationship with the Catholic charismatic renewal movement is complicated. His pastoral and social understanding of Catholic social doctrine recognizes some shared values with Latin American evangelicals, unlike Popes John Paul II and Benedict XVI, who supported charismatic Catholics as alternatives to evangelical appeal. Pope Francis supports the Catholic charismatic renewal movement's potential worldwide to respond to the post-pandemic devastation, calling on the movement to recognize that evangelization without attention to the poor and rising inequalities will ring hollow and implicitly critiquing some charismatics' inward focus and doctrinal conservatism.

Major Spiritist Religions

Before the sixteenth-century Spanish and Portuguese conquest, the population of Latin America varied immensely. The largest societies, such as the Andean Incas and the Maya, Olmec, and Aztec of Central America and Mexico, developed highly sophisticated religious institutions with established priesthoods. Elsewhere, less developed Indigenous populations had religious practices that were more tribal. Common to all Indigenous cultures was the forcible imposition of Catholicism after the conquest. Throughout the colonies of the Americas, the European victors prohibited native religions. Indigenous religious practices were either eradicated or merged with Catholicism or other religious beliefs. The imposition of Catholicism on the Indigenous peoples generated revolts using Indigenous religious symbols or figures to build cohesion. Most Indigenous cultures yielded to the official culture of the victorious conquerors—with elements of the original beliefs morphing into their closest Catholic counterpart. A distinct difference between "official Catholicism" and "folk religion" practiced by the majority of the people resulted. These syncretic religions differed across the preexisting, Indigenous cultures. The tension between the Vatican and folk religion as practiced by most people has been a dynamic one historically, with the church occasionally tolerating local practices within Catholicism and reaffirming the official church's authority to determine the boundaries of orthodoxy. Despite the destruction of preconquest civilizations, many of their religious practices continued to survive in some form.

The importation of Black slaves in the first half of the sixteenth century brought a second wave of new religious traditions and cults, this time of the exploited, not of the conquerors. African religious practices were strictly prohibited in the Spanish colonies. They did not disappear, but syncretized with both Catholicism and the Indigenous traditions and—later—with other religions that were transplanted to Latin America. Candomblé de Caboclo, for example, combined African and Indigenous practices, and Umbanda combined African, Indigenous, and other traditions.

Candomblé, particularly popular in northeastern Brazil with over 2 million believers, derives from the West African Yoruba traditions brought by slaves in the eighteenth century. Around the central deity, Oludumare, are *orixas* (spirits) who control individuals' destinies. *Orixas* represent deified ancestors who connect believers with the spiritual world. The word *candomblé* means "dance in honor of the gods," and dance and music are central elements of religious practice. Typical Candomblé followers are poor and racially more "Black" than followers of other Afro-Brazilian cults. Candomblé's popularity among Afro-Brazilians as a symbol of religious belief, and cultural identity, has risen sharply since the end of active state persecution in the 1970s. Many Latin Americans of African descent travel to the Bahia region of Brazil to learn more about their cultural heritage. There is a movement to purge contemporary Candomblé of Catholic elements to reclaim its African roots.

Umbanda combines Christianity's belief in one supreme god and African *orixas* who are paired with Christian saints. Umbanda derives from African Bantu religions, and its Brazilian origins were centered in Rio de Janeiro with a Kardecist wing located in São Paulo. Today, over 20 million followers of Umbanda can be found throughout Brazil and in neighboring countries. Umbanda appeals mostly to poor and middle-class Blacks, whites, and mulattos who seek advice regarding issues such as health, work-related problems, and personal relationships. Worship is organized around a leader called a *pai-de-santo* or *mãe-de-santo,* depending on gender, and mediums (psychics who can act as a medium between the physical world and the spiritual world) who can be possessed by the spirits. Spirits are both Brazilian (deceased native Brazilians called *caboclos*) and African (deceased slaves who died at the hands of abusive owners called *pretos velhos,* or "old blacks"), among several other subgroups of ancestors. Spirits are known for particular strengths such as knowledge of Indigenous herbal remedies, sympathy

Offerings for Iemanjá, goddess of the ocean, Rio Vermelho, Salvador, Brazil. The culture of the city of Salvador is heavily influenced by African elements, including food, dress, religion, and music, originally brought to Brazil by enslaved peoples. Credit: https://commons .wikimedia.org/wiki/File:Offerings _for_Lemanj%C3%A1.jpg

for the oppressed, or particular knowledge of Indigenous ways. During worship, the spirits communicate their advice to supplicants through mediums who have reached the spirits through trances.

Other descendants of West African religions include Vodou (commonly called voodoo and found primarily in Haiti) and Santería (found in Cuba and elsewhere in the Caribbean). Vodou and Santería are spiritist religious practices in which African spirits are associated with Christian saints. In Vodou, *houngans* (charismatic priests) help individuals contact the spirits, typically for health or personal help. Spirits also can be invoked to ward off danger or to attack other harmful spirits. Vodou has a particularly politicized history; it has been severely persecuted sporadically since Haitian independence—usually at the behest of the white, Catholic bishops. Historically, Vodou temples became important centers of Black identity and resistance. In the 1950s, François Duvalier curtailed the persecution of Vodou and mobilized its organizations into militias (known as the Tonton Macoutes) to win the 1957 presidential election. The Tonton Macoutes became a formidable force that intimidated political enemies for the next thirty years.

Cuban-based Santería has similar historical origins to those of Haitian Vodou; Santería beliefs trace back to West Africa and were brought to Cuba by slaves. The word *santería* was a Spanish pejorative term to describe the preoccupation with Christian saints rather than gods among African converts to Catholicism. Like spiritists from West Africa, Cuban slaves shrouded their belief in their own gods, *orishas,* by identifying them as Christian saints. After Cuban independence in 1898, some Santería leaders realized the possibility for personal gain of peddling their ties to the spiritual world as black magic or sorcery. Santería, like the darker side of Vodou, became associated with criminal acts, evil intent, and the ability to harm others with magic spells. In the United States, the popular image of Vodou and Santería as sinister and violent stems from the manipulation of the original spiritist descendants of West African religions.

Venezuela also illustrates syncretism. Although the majority of the population is ostensibly Catholic, many people throughout society believe in varying syntheses of African, Indigenous, and Christian religions. Followers of María Lionsa worship a goddess of nature similar to the Arawak water deity, West African mythical figures, and the Virgin Mary. And *curanderos* (healers) found in Indigenous villages are consulted by Venezuelans from all walks of life. In many countries, social tensions led to tensions or negotiations between idealized versions of the Virgin Mother and the Scarlet Woman, although this dichotomous view has been exaggerated in Latin America.

An orisha in concrete used for ritual purposes. Credit: https://commons .wikimedia.org/wiki/File:Eleggua2005.jpg

Conclusion

The religious landscape of twenty-first-century Latin America continues to be a competitive marketplace, and both Catholicism and evangelicalism will adapt to compete for followers. The Catholic Church is unlikely to regain its religious monopoly. Vatican-backed national hierarchies have redoubled their efforts to meet the peoples' religious aspirations. The church has strengthened its reach into society through renewed focus on meeting the population's spiritual needs and embracing the more charismatic styles of worship characteristic of Pentecostalism, disappointing those inspired by its 1960s–1980s political agenda, including its "preferential option for the poor." Under Pope Francis, the Catholic Church is traditional, rooted in Catholic social doctrine and hierarchical authority, and has redoubled its commitment to saving individual souls through the sacraments and Christian charity *and* a pastoral church concerned with social inequality, poverty, and concern for the environment.

Various forms of evangelical Protestantism continue to provide an important alternative. Sharp evangelical growth has leveled off, while forms of neo-Pentecostalism have increased. Scholarly observers no longer predict that Latin America is "becoming Protestant." Particularly for Pentecostals, the lack of widespread institutional orthodoxy, the flexible path to becoming a pastor, and the tendency of new groups to form when existing churches become too big provide opportunities to adjust worship styles and adapt religious commitments to changing local and national contexts. Evangelical embrace of the media coupled with a charismatic outreach focus guarantees national prominence for media-savvy pastors and their followers. As these national churches become institutionalized, their missions and religiopolitical identities will provide opportunities for new alternatives under the guidance of new pastors. Subsequent generations will challenge evangelical churches to inspire their belief. Scandals similar to those that have plagued more established churches will probably complicate these processes.

Religion's continued relevance in Latin American societies and individuals' lives does not mean that social changes similar to other regions of the world can be, or will be, kept at bay. Despite vigorous Catholic and evangelical opposition, social movements dedicated to the rights of women, LGBTQ communities, Indigenous peoples, and environmental movements have won important victories across the region. Although Latin American divorce rates are relatively lower than in the global North, divorce is now legal in some form throughout the region; Chile was the last country to legalize divorce, in 2004. Although still largely prohibited in much of the region, abortion was legalized in Argentina in 2020. Drawing on Latin America's historical struggles with repressive regimes, many social activists have made significant gains in both public opinion and legal victories by framing their demands as a struggle for human rights, democracy, and citizenship. Faith traditions, while they remain vibrant in Latin America's pluralist religious marketplace, will continue to grapple with broad social changes in the region.

13

The Arts

*David H. Bost, Angélica Lozano-Alonso,
and David Marcus*

This chapter explores the perceptions of writers and
artists who have contributed novels, music, films, and other creative
works to enhance our understanding of Latin American culture.

The Colonial Heritage
Native American Literature
As Chapter 3 reports, the Spanish explorers and *conquistadores* of the
early 1500s were astonished to find New World civilizations that in
some ways rivaled those in Europe. The Mayas, Aztecs, and Incas were
accomplished architects, artists, musicians, sculptors, and dancers. Most
pre-Columbian literature was oral and quickly forgotten after the conquest. Spanish clerics and educated Indians transcribed a few Native
American texts in the sixteenth century. Today these texts are evidence
of a rich literary tradition that flourished in the centuries before the discovery of America.

The Mayas were the only Native American civilization that had
written texts, in hieroglyphic form, almost all of which were destroyed
by the conquerors in the chaotic years after the conquest. A few of these
books survive as Spanish translations. For example, *Popul-Vuh* (the
Mayan "Bible") is a collection of myths, history, philosophy, and legends. *Chilam Balam* is a compilation of history, religion, astronomy,
and medicine, written in Mayan a few years after the conquest by an
anonymous author who used the Spanish alphabet. Some fragments of
Mayan codices and stone inscriptions remain.

The Codex Mendoza is a beautifully preserved Aztec codex. It contains the history of the Aztec rulers and conquests. It is believed to have been made in 1541. Credit: Bodleian Libraries, https:// commons.wikimedia.org/wiki/File:Codex Mendoza01.jpg

The Incas and Aztecs had no actual written language but had an active oral literary culture. The Aztecs used some pictorial representations, called *codices,* whereas the Incas kept accounts on colored, knotted strings called *quipus.* Many performances—often a combination of theater, song, and dance—were ceremonial and ritualistic. The Incan *taqui* was a ritual dance representing the Incan calendar and principal mythological characters. The Aztecs had highly developed theater that was performed in the large open spaces of Tenochtitlán (most of which now lies under the foundations of Mexico City). Drama in the Aztec and Incan empires often constituted an official ceremony performed at the royal court and events reenacted from their historical or mythological past. The Aztecs and Incas also composed lyric and epic poetry that was performed at public ceremonies.

Native American culture survived long after the New World's conquest. The most important native-born chronicler of Incan society was Garcilaso de la Vega. Son of a Spanish captain and an Incan princess, Garcilaso spent his childhood in Peru and his adult years in Spain serving as an officer in the military. Garcilaso was truly bicultural; he spoke fluent Quechua, Peru's Indigenous language, and Spanish and spent his later years writing his monumental *Comentarios Reales del Perú* (Royal Commentaries of Peru, 1609), a history and analysis of Incan culture and the Spanish conquest of Peru. The commentaries repeat many of the stories and legends Garcilaso heard as a child growing up among his Incan family. Spanish historians, in his opinion, had misrepresented the history and culture of his maternal ancestors, which he wanted to correct. Today, his work is one of the most important historical, anthropological, and literary sources for scholars studying ancient Peruvian culture. Garcilaso is perhaps better known in the United States for his detailed history of the ill-fated 1539 De Soto expedition, *La Florida* (1605).

A contemporary of Garcilaso was Guamán Poma de Ayala. His *El Primer Nueva Crónica y Buen Gobierno* (First New Chronicle and Good Government, 1615) is an illustrated history of Peru that challenged the legitimacy of the Spanish conquest of the New World and called for an end to Spain's colonial domination.

Chronicles of the Conquest and Colonization

Virtually every literary form was cultivated during the early colonial period except the novel. Historical writing was mostly testimonial; soldiers, explorers, and missionaries felt compelled to give their version of events in which they had taken part. Columbus's diary of his first voyage (1492) is considered by many literary historians to be the earliest text in Latin American literature. As a writer, Columbus faced a monumental challenge: to communicate an image of the New World in ways that were understandable and compelling to his European audience. Columbus justified further exploration and ultimate conquest by tempting his readers with exaggerated reports of gold and tales of a generous and trusting people who lived in an idyllic paradise.

Active members of the expeditionary forces who defeated native rulers Montezuma and Atahuallpa recorded the conquests of Mexico and Peru. Hernán Cortés, the Spanish captain who led the overthrow of the Aztec Empire, kept Emperor Charles I abreast of events as Spaniards marched on Tenochtitlán. His letters to the monarch are among the most valuable sources of information on one of history's most remarkable military victories. These records were written in part as an attempt to seek monetary or political reward for service to the crown. Cortés wanted to be named ruler of the lands he conquered, a wish the emperor ultimately fulfilled.

Bernal Díaz del Castillo wrote an account of the fall of Mexico, narrated from the point of view of an ordinary soldier. His book, *Historia Verdadera de la Conquista de la Nueva España* (True History of the Conquest of Mexico, 1557), is based primarily on his observations and recollections. Bernal Díaz had an incredible eye for detail: he remembered such things as the number of steps on different Aztec sacrificial temples, the names of horses, and the identities of common soldiers other historians had ignored or forgotten. His work is one of the best colonial Latin American examples of a literary treatment of a historical event. Bernal Díaz, lacking a professional historian's formal academic training, relied on novelistic language and devices to tell his story more eloquently. Hence, many portions of his text sound like a popular tale from a novel of chivalry.

Most colonial-period historical accounts, professional or otherwise, were strongly influenced by literary language and models. Popular historians, such as Bernal Díaz, incorporated elements from popular literature. Learned historians, those commissioned by the crown to write the official story of the conquest and colonization, were well versed in classical historiography and often used ancient Latin masters as their ideals. Gonzalo Fernández de Oviedo wrote his *Historia General y Natural de las Indias* (General and Natural History of the Indies, 1557) using such classical historians as Pliny as his model. Oviedo, nurtured on classical literature through his immersion in Italian Renaissance culture, wrote in extraordinary detail about virtually everything he witnessed during his long residence in the New World.

Perhaps the most important characteristic of Oviedo's work and that of other official chroniclers is their passionate defense of Spain's conquest of America. Oviedo and others felt it was Spain's imperial destiny to dominate and Christianize the New World, even if it meant nearly annihilating Indian culture. There were a few opponents to this position. Dominican priest Bartolomé de las Casas was history's most articulate defender of the Indians; his many historical works feature strongly favorable characterizations of Indians. Conversely, Oviedo and others depicted the Indians in an extraordinarily negative fashion.

Oviedo was succeeded by generations of official chroniclers who were charged with writing general histories of the colonies and censoring other histories to protect Spain's image in the international community. Spain suffered for many years from the Black Legend, the belief in many European countries that Spain had committed numerous atrocities in the New World in the name of religious conversion. The debate over the Indian—helpless victim or godless savage—is one of the most pervasive themes in the colonial as well as contemporary eras. Indianist novels of the nineteenth and twentieth centuries examined the prejudices toward the Indian that still exist hundreds of years after the conquest. Latin American and US Latinx writers who gained fame in the twentieth century, such as Mario Vargas Llosa, Carlos Fuentes, Octavio Paz, Rigoberta Menchú Tum, Gloria Anzaldúa, and Rudolfo Anaya—among many others—continue to explore the presence of Indian culture in contemporary Latin American life.

Not every official in the Spanish army was contemptuous of Indians. In 1542, Alvar Núñez Cabeza de Vaca wrote an extraordinary account of his eight-year journey through the North American southwest, living among the Indians first as a captive and later as their leader; his book was translated as *Castaways* (Naufragios, 1993). Cabeza de Vaca, one of the few who survived a shipwreck off the Texas coast, felt great sympathy for the Indians he befriended during his long trek toward Mexico City. His account of his travels is a veritable treasure of ethnographic and historical information on tribes that have long since vanished. *Castaways* is fairly typical of many Latin American historical works of the colonial period in its reliance upon literary themes and motifs: there are prophecies told and revealed; suspense; betrayals; the supernatural; and a fascination with an immense, exotic, and virtually unknown world ready for exploration, conquest, and eventual settlement.

Captivity among the Indians was a popular topic for colonial historians. In several cases, prisoners returned to their former countries with fascinating stories. The captives were sought out by Spanish authorities because of their valuable information regarding the Indians. The returning captives were not always entirely sympathetic to the conquest and its methods of subjugating the Native Americans.

One of the most remarkable characteristics of certain captive narratives is that the authors reported their assimilation into the foreign culture. Francisco Núñez de Pineda y Bascuñán wrote *Cautiverio Feliz* (The Happy Captive, 1673) as a record of his seven-month captivity among the Araucanian Indians in southern Chile. His story is one of adventure, action, and intrigue. A young captain stationed on the frontier, Bascuñán was captured by the fierce Araucanians during a raid on the outpost. His extended residence among the tribe gave him considerable insights into people generally regarded as savages. His story is unusual for the time: he individualized his descriptions of the Indians and avoided generalizations that were common with earlier historians. Bascuñán did not deny that his captors could behave in a savage fashion, but he also revealed that they were capable of extraordinary generosity and benevolence.

Spanish captivity and residence among the Indians also fascinates contemporary novelists. Argentinean writer Abel Posse published a novel based on Cabeza de Vaca's experiences titled *El Largo Atardecer del Caminante* (The Long Afternoon of the Walker, 1992). Mexican novelist Eugenio Aguirre (1980) wrote about Gonzalo Guerrero, the first Spaniard captured by Native Americans, who apparently led his Mayan captors in a revolt against the Spanish invaders.

The Imaginative Construction of History

By the mid-seventeenth century, many testimonial accounts of the New World's colonization gave way to histories that were more literary in nature. One of the most imaginative accounts of Colombian history is Juan Rodríguez Freyle's *El Carnero y Conquista y Descubrimiento de Nuevo Reino de Granada* (The Conquest of New Granada, 1636). Rodríguez Freyle wrote a traditional history of the founding and settlement of his native Santa Fe de Bogotá, but it also contains tales of sorcery, adultery, lurid accounts of criminal activity in the colony, and myths and legends about Native Americans. Rodríguez Freyle was one of the colonial period's most innovative and expressive writers; his text reveals a dimension of life in the colony that other historians either ignored or understated.

It was fairly common for historical writers during the Latin American colonial era to rely on literary models to invest their stories with a more expressive language. In the sixteenth and seventeenth centuries, often there was no clear distinction between historical and fictional writing regarding truth or reliability. It was not uncommon for historians such as Rodríguez Freyle, Garcilaso de la Vega, or Oviedo to depict individuals, situations, or events with little or no textual evidence. Historians often speculated freely about events and their significance. Some of Rodríguez Freyle's stories were justified as examples of what the author viewed as moral decay within the colony.

One of the best examples of a literary treatment of history in the later colonial period is Mexican intellectual Carlos de Sigüenza y Góngora's *Infortunios de Alonso Ramírez* (The Misadventures of Alonso Ramírez, 1690). Much like a novel, the work recounts Ramírez's extraordinary journey around the world. Alonso Ramírez was a sailor who, through a series of mishaps, shipwrecks, and captivity, circumnavigated the planet—a remarkable feat for his day. He told his story to Sigüenza y Góngora, who constructed an entertaining tale of Alonso's life.

Sigüenza y Góngora's book is very similar to a picaresque novel. Alonso left his native Puerto Rico for Mexico City, where he held a succession of jobs. He went to the Spanish Philippines, where he briefly had a prosperous career as a sailor, traveling and trading widely throughout Asia Pacific. His most dramatic misfortune occurred when he was captured by English pirates who abused and humiliated their prisoners and treated them as slaves. Alonso's crew quickly perished under captivity. Of the original twenty-five who were captured, only eight survived. The pirates finally gave Alonso and his crew the opportunity for freedom, placing them in a small boat with minimal provisions and arms.

Sailing west from Madagascar, Alonso's boat wrecked on the Yucatán shore, and the men eventually wandered back to civilization. Once back in Mexico City, Alonso reported his story to Sigüenza y Góngora. Despite the historical foundations of this story, many novelistic elements give Sigüenza's narrative its strong literary quality: its sense of adventure, humor and irony, political intrigue, first-person narration, and episodic structure.

Sigüenza y Góngora was intensely interested in the American experience and wrote many other works of scientific, anthropological, and historical value. In many of his works, one can detect a nascent American consciousness. Sigüenza bristled with anger, for example, whenever Europeans made disparaging references to the so-called inferiority of the creoles who populated the New World.

Poetry and Drama

Epic poets were among the first to compose literary homages to the individuals who had orchestrated the principal events of the discovery and conquest of the New World. The greatest epic poem written in colonial Latin America is Alonso de Ercilla's "La Araucana" (The Araucanian, 1569–1589), depicting the prolonged wars with fierce Araucanian Indians of Chile. Ercilla's poem is both testimonial—based on his experiences in fighting the tribe—and epic. Perhaps the poem's most distinctive quality is that Ercilla did not avoid showing profound admiration for the honor and valor of these warriors who, year after year, effectively thwarted the best efforts of the Spanish army to defeat them. Ercilla depicted the Araucanians as a highly organized, well-disciplined army. In many regards, the poem is more the story of Caupolicán, the head of the Araucanian forces, than of Pedro de Valdivia, the Spanish leader. "The Araucanian" was extraordinarily popular during its day and for many years afterward, spawning numerous imitations.

The epic tradition was continued into the seventeenth century by Mexican poet Bernardo de Balbuena, whose poem "Grandeza Mexicana" (Mexican Greatness, 1604) is an exuberant tribute to Mexico. Balbuena's careful examination of the Mexican reality is a precursor to the nineteenth-century literary movement of *costumbrismo,* in which writers recorded in minute detail virtually all aspects of daily life. Because of his passionate interest in describing Mexico's complexity, some literary historians regard Balbuena as the first genuinely American poet.

Not all poetry written during the colonial era was an epic tribute to the great events that shaped Spain's American empire. Satirists, such as

Juan del Valle y Caviedes (c. 1645–1697), were bitter critics of many members of colonial society, particularly those who sought to better themselves at the expense of others. Few escaped Caviedes's wrath: aristocrats, religious officials, women, and doctors were among those ridiculed in his poetic compositions. His disregard for doctors was legendary. One of his most widely read poems is "Coloquio que Tuvo Con la Muerte un Médico Moribundo" (Conversation That a Dying Doctor Had with Death, c. 1680), a savage attack on the practice of medicine in colonial Peru.

Like most satirists, Caviedes hated hypocrisy and deceit. In the sonnet "Para Hallar en Palacio Estimaciones" (How to Succeed at Court, c. 1690), Caviedes depicts the "perfect" courtier, one who is certain to get the attention of the viceroy: he is a liar, a clown, a deceiver, a gossip, and, above all, a yes-man. Honesty and integrity have no place in the colonial court. Like Juan Rodríguez Freyle, Caviedes was interested in exploring the dark underside of colonial life in an effort to portray an increasingly complex society many years past the conquest.

Caviedes was one of many in the late seventeenth century who openly admired the Mexican nun Sor Juana Inés de la Cruz, generally regarded as colonial Latin America's greatest writer. Poet, dramatist, essayist, and scholar, Sor Juana's intellectual reputation was unusual for a woman in the seventeenth century. Unable to attend university, Sor Juana was almost entirely self-taught. Before entering the convent she was a well-known figure at the viceregal court, where she often dazzled onlookers with her amazing intelligence and learning.

Sor Juana often found it necessary to defend her life of learning and erudition. One such instance is seen in her famous correspondence with the bishop of Puebla, who had criticized her for spending too much time in her intellectual pursuits to the detriment of her religious duties. Sor Juana's response is the *Respuesta de la Poetisa a la Muy Ilustre Sor Filotea de la Cruz* (Reply to Sor Filotea de la Cruz, 1691), an autobiographical statement that, among other things, defends her right to a life of study and reflection—an inclination that, she argued, God had given her. Sor Juana finally succumbed to the ecclesiastical authorities in 1694, when she sold her impressive library for charity and dedicated herself fully to her religious calling.

Sor Juana was a gifted and prolific poet. Her poems dealt with religion, morality, love, jealousy, death, and other literary topics common during the baroque period. Feminist literary critics recently read with great interest her compositions that criticize men for their unbridled arrogance toward women. One of Sor Juana's best-known poems is "Hombres Necios" (Foolish Men, c. 1690), a work that asks sarcastically why men expect women to be good when it is men who so often lead women astray. Her love poetry, known for its passionate language, is unusual considering the restrictions of her religious order. Her most ambitious poetic attempt is "Primero Sueño" (First Dream, 1692), a long, complex poem that is a philosophical meditation on her search for knowledge and the elusive nature of reality.

Sor Juana was also an accomplished dramatist. Writing during the last years of Spanish theater's golden age, Sor Juana was heavily influenced by Calderón de la Barca, generally regarded as Spain's premier playwright. Sor Juana wrote both secular and religious drama and utilized all of the major styles of her era.

Much of the dramatic literature that preceded Sor Juana was religious in nature. Many of the plays in the sixteenth and seventeenth centuries were written by missionaries interested in using drama to convert the Indians to Christianity. Missionaries often mixed Spanish with native languages and incorporated elements of Indian theater. Following some of the practices of Aztec and Incan theater, missionaries staged many of their plays in outside settings, frequently utilizing costumes and scenery of the Indigenous tribes. The best-known playwright of the sixteenth century was Gonzalo de Eslava, a Mexican priest who wrote primarily religious plays. Eslava, not unlike Bernardo de Balbuena, infused his literature with many references to Mexico.

Seventeenth-century playwrights include two Peruvians, Juan del Valle y Caviedes, who wrote satirical plays on the folly of love, as well as satirical poetry as mentioned earlier, and Juan de Espinosa Medrano, whose principal work was based on the Bible. The greatest name associated with theater in the Latin American colonial period is Mexican-born Juan Ruiz de Alarcón, a writer who emigrated to Spain at an early age. Alarcón, more properly affiliated with Spanish Golden Age theater, was an extremely popular and respected writer of comedies of manners and honor.

The Nineteenth and Twentieth Centuries
The First Novel and Short Story

Critics generally agree that the first novel published in Spanish America was José Joaquín Fernández de Lizardi's *El Periquillo Sarniento* (The Itching Parrot, 1816). In some ways, Lizardi's novel owes more to the eighteenth-century Age of Reason than to the Age of Revolution: it is didactic in tone, containing long, moralizing passages on education and the proper upbringing of young people. The story is about Pedro, an orphan who, like a typical character from Spanish picaresque literature, serves a series of masters while observing and remarking ironically on virtually every aspect of Mexican society. Much like his literary predecessor, Alonso Ramírez, Pedro also sails for the Philippines, is shipwrecked on a desert island, and eventually returns to Mexico, where his life is finally put into some moral order. Lizardi was a well-known social critic in pre-revolutionary Mexico, often writing newspaper articles under the pen name "The Thinker." Once imprisoned for speaking against the colonial viceroy, Lizardi used *The Itching Parrot* as a vehicle for satirical commentary on the need for radical social reform.

Political and social commentary are also the thematic bases for Latin America's first short story, Esteban Echeverría's "El Matadero" (The Slaughterhouse, 1838), published in Argentina. Set during the tyrannical reign of Juan Manuel Rosas, the story tells in graphic detail how a young man from the opposition Unitarian Party is captured by a mob and brutalized. Echeverría's political and social messages were clear: if Argentina was to prosper in the era of independence and self-rule, it needed a centralized, representative government with an educated populace acting responsibly.

One of the lasting legacies of such foundational works as *The Itching Parrot* and "The Slaughterhouse" is the use of literature to bring about social and political change. Much of nineteenth- and twentieth-century literature—novels, short stories, poetry, and drama—protests some situation or condition brought about by the abuse of power and privilege.

Toward an American Identity

Much of the literature written during the decades following independence was a celebration of the diversity of the new nations that emerged from colonialism and conflict. Following the European literary models of romanticism and realism, Latin American authors invested their literature with references to the uniqueness of their newly formed republics. Poets were especially effusive in their depiction of the shifting American reality. Ecuadorian poet José Joaquín Olmedo is credited with being the first Spanish American poet to commemorate in verse America's independence from Spanish rule. His ode "La Victoria de Junín" (The Victory of Junín, 1826), is an elegy to Simón Bolívar and his leadership during the revolutionary period. Similarly, Venezuelan Andrés Bello, one of Bolívar's former teachers, urged his fellow writers to search for inspiration in authentic American topics rather than copying European models.

The poetic elaboration of the American experience perhaps peaked in nineteenth-century literature with the publication of José Hernández's narrative poem "Martín Fierro" (1872), which laments the gradual disappearance of the *gaucho* (cowboy), long a symbol of the Argentine pampas. The poem is the story of a *gaucho* who is forced to serve in the military, where he is mercilessly abused and exploited. Fierro eventually deserts the army and joins the Indians, embittered over the loss of his freedom and autonomy. "Martín Fierro" is the literary predecessor of *Don Segundo Sombra* (1926), Ricardo Güiraldes's famous novelistic rendition of the *gaucho* and his importance to Argentine cultural identity.

A central concern of Domingo Faustino Sarmiento, one of the nineteenth century's greatest essayists and intellectuals, was describing the Argentine consciousness. Sarmiento wrote a classic essay delineating Argentina into two opposing camps, the urban and the rural. Unlike Hernández, Sarmiento perceived the urban mentality as offering education, enlightenment, progress, democracy, and industrial development. An unabashed admirer of Europe, he felt the ignorance, superstition, tyranny, and isolation of rural Argentina—characterized by the *pampas* (grass plains) and *gaucho*—symbolized all that kept his country from emerging from its barbaric past.

Sarmiento's essay "Civilización y Barbarie o vida de Juan Facundo Quiroga" (Civilization and Barbarism, 1845) is ostensibly a psychological study of Juan Facundo Quiroga, a prototypical rural tyrant who supported the *caudillo* Juan Manuel Rosas. In this work, Sarmiento examined what he felt was the root cause of many of Argentina's political problems during the early years of the republic. Surrounded by and containing vast *pampas,* Argentina suffered from extreme isolation, which made effective governance virtually impossible. Sarmiento argued that Argentina's future salvation would occur through dramatic improvement of the educational system and effective centralized government.

Political and social realities of Latin American countries were fully represented in the nineteenth-century novel. One of the most prominent political novelists of the period was José Mármol, whose *Amalia* (1855) depicts Argentina suffering under the regime of Juan Manuel Rosas, thematically similar to Echeverría's "El Matadero." *Amalia,* typical of romantic-school literature, includes conspiracies, political intrigues, hidden identities, and the tragic death of two lovers, the main characters, shortly after their wedding. As with many novelists who are committed primarily to writing about social and political circumstances, Mármol's work contains commentary on contemporary issues of national concern. Critics argued that such political literature—which was more commonplace during the twentieth century—was too severely compromised to constitute an effective work of literary art. Virtually all of Latin America's major contemporary writers, including its Nobel laureates, have at some time written literature that carries an obvious political or social message.

A noteworthy novel with a political message is Gertrudis Gómez de Avellaneda's *Sab* (written 1841, published 1914). During her lifetime, Cuban author Gómez de Avellaneda (1814–1873) was recognized for her romantic poetry expressing the pain of exile and love. More recently, her nation-building novel *Sab* has been studied as an example of feminist liberation and nascent abolitionary sympathies. Gómez de Avellaneda wrote the text in 1841, ten years before *Uncle Tom's Cabin* (1852), although it remained unpublished until 1914. Despite being a slave, Gómez de Avellaneda portrays Sab as a romantic hero who loves Carlota, his master's daughter, but he never acts on those feelings because he respects their racial differences. Because Gómez de Avellaneda presents Sab as a slave who shows more nobility and dignity than the ruling elite, *Sab* is noteworthy for the way it indirectly criticizes the institution of slavery and ties the slave's rights to women's rights.

In the era's romantic poetry and novels, nature often reflects the character's emotions. Additionally, the theme of the struggle with nature was developed by several authors, including Jorge Isaacs of Colombia in his romantic novel *María* (1867), and later writers, such as José Eustacio Rivera, who described the Colombian jungle in *La Vorágine* (The Whirlpool, 1924); Martín Luis Guzmán, who portrayed the Mexican Revolution in *El Águila y la Serpiente* (The Eagle and the Serpent, 1928); and Rómulo Gallegos of Venezuela in *Doña Bárbara* (1929), a work contrasting civilization and barbarism.

The novel was an effective vehicle during the nineteenth century for examining and presenting qualities that reflected a nation's particular identity. Ignacio Manuel Altamirano used the nineteenth-century Mexican novel in the same way Bernardo de Balbuena used epic poetry centuries earlier to defend all that was uniquely Mexican. Altamirano joined Andrés Bello in his fervent desire to incorporate American themes into a national literature. *Clemencia* (1869) was written against the historical backdrop of France's 1863 intervention. In *La Navidad en las Montañas* (Christmas in the Mountains, 1871), Altamirano romanticized life in rural, mountainous Mexico, exposing the beauty and serenity of life far from the capital city.

Although Altamirano had a somewhat romantic, perhaps even idyllic view of rural life, he was an astute observer of the customs and traditions of regional Mexico. His novels incorporated as many traits of Mexican life as possible, showing that Latin Americans had ample subject matter for their literature in their own history and traditions. By the late nineteenth and early twentieth centuries, it was commonplace for authors to write in great detail about subjects that seemed particularly appropriate for their specific countries. Peruvians and Ecuadorians wrote about the plight of the Indian and of Andean culture in general. Chilean novelists, heavily influenced by European naturalism, began to examine the economic and social effects of copper mining on daily life. Argentineans followed José Hernández's example and continued to explore the life of the *gaucho* in a rapidly changing world.

Peruvian Ricardo Palma best exemplified a nineteenth-century writer who found inspiration in his country's mythological and historical records. Palma wrote short sketches, anecdotes, and characterizations based on people and incidents from old Peru. His short folkloric compositions, "Tradiciones Peruanas" (Peruvian Traditions, 1872–1883), are humorous, ironic, satiric narratives that deeply mine Peru's rich colonial and Indigenous heritage, cleverly mixing fact with fiction. As the national library's director, he had easy access to a wealth of original documents that provided source material for his creations. Many of his stories fairly accurately reproduce speech patterns, customs, popular sayings, and common beliefs of the time. Scholars have noted that Palma is one of the most important precursors of the contemporary Spanish American short story.

Modernism

The first major literary movement that took root in Spanish America and was passed to Spain, modernism was heavily influenced by French symbolist poets and late nineteenth-century philosophical currents. Modernists—attempting to renovate literary language, style, themes, and techniques—significantly departed from subject matters that were characteristic of realism and naturalism. Instead of detailed descriptions of regions and local traditions, they opted to write about exotic, often imaginary lands that captivated the poetic sensibilities of this new generation of writers. Captivated by ideas of beauty, elegance, sensuality, and refinement, modernists infused their literary language with references to ancient Greece, the Far East, and the medieval world.

Whereas their realist counterparts were interested in portraying an accurate image of the industrialized world, a world that was often squalid and dangerous, modernist writers depicted realms that were creations of fantasy—places inhabited by princesses and knights, swans and nightingales. Modernists' battle cry was "Art for art's sake." At times they sought to divorce literature from the sordid economic and social realities that characterized their world. Above all, modernism was a movement that attempted to create a new Hispanic literary language, one essentially poetic in nature and reflecting the new aesthetics of cosmopolitan refinement and literary renovation.

Many names are associated with modernism: Cuba's José Martí, Manuel Gutiérrez Nájera of Mexico, Colombia's José Asunción Silva, Cuba's Julián del Casal, and Argentina's Leopoldo Lugones. No one embodies the spirit of modernist thought and practice better than Rubén Darío, a Nicaraguan poet whose work spans the entire movement and defines its basic tenets. Critics often mark the beginning and end, respectively, of modernism with the publication of Darío's *Azul* (Blue, 1888) and his death in 1916. Darío was unquestionably the best-known and most widely imitated Hispanic poet of his generation. His poetry exemplified grace, cultural refinement, extraordinary literary depth, and stylistic elegance. Elevating Hispanic poetry to unprecedented heights in his efforts to revolutionize concepts about literature, Darío showed that it was possible to break from the realist and romantic schools. He wrote about Wagnerian swans, ancient Persian cities, medieval Spanish poets, classical deities, and mythological characters. Darío's greatest contribution to Latin American literature may have been his extraordinary renewal of poetic language.

Of Darío's poems that embody the modernist spirit of innovation and originality, "Sonatina" (1893) perhaps best captures the mood of exoticism and elegance. It describes a beautiful young princess whose melancholy mood contrasts sharply with her opulent home. She lives a life of unparalleled luxury, yet is limited by her excessive wealth. Her fairy godmother reassures her that she will soon be rescued from her "prison" by a knight "who [will] arrive from afar, conqueror of Death." The poem is filled with arcane references to figures from classical mythology, exotic locations, and unusual plants and wildlife. While women were often inspired modernist poets, literary critics note that this representation of women is problematic in its extreme idealization of them. Women inspire but rarely, if ever, have a voice. Women are an object of beauty and desire but nothing more. It is noteworthy that although some women writers were inspired by the movement, such as Delmira Agustini and Alfonsina Storni, they are categorized more often as postmodernist writers.

A common misconception is to regard modernism as a literary movement that completely broke from many Latin American writers' concern with social and political issues. Modernists were concerned primarily with the renovation of literary language, yet they never abandoned some issues that had preoccupied earlier generations of writers, such as how Latin America differed fundamentally from North America. A number of

Darío's poems—including "A Roosevelt" (To Roosevelt, 1905), which takes issue with Theodore Roosevelt's militant nature—openly accuse the United States of being overly aggressive toward its Latin American neighbors, suggesting that its foreign policy was imperialistic.

Criticism of the United States was common among writers of Darío's era. Uruguayan José Enrique Rodó, the greatest essayist of the modernist generation, published *Ariel* (1900), a philosophical treatise on the essential distinctions between Latin America and the United States. Although openly admiring US economic and political power, Rodó was deeply opposed to what he viewed as a US obsession with materialism. Rodó considered Latin Americans to be far more spiritually inclined than North Americans and urged his readers to weigh the benefits of material progress against the advantages of spiritual and cultural achievements.

Darío and Rodó initiated a trend among Latin American writers in the twentieth century to use the United States as a point of reference in their analyses of their own culture and society. Octavio Paz, Mexico's Nobel laureate, for example, wrote *El Laberinto de la Soledad* (The Labyrinth of Solitude, 1950), a book that incisively compares popular Mexican culture with that in the United States, searching the history of each nation for root causes of the vast distinctions between them. Similarly, Carlos Fuentes's *El Espejo Enterrado* (The Buried Mirror, 1992) is a critique of Latin American cultural history.

The impact of modernism on Latin American literature was profound and enduring. Writers nurtured on realist modes of exposition discovered that their stories could be far more expressive and effective if they focused on the eloquent possibilities of language. The long, cumbersome, detailed passages that were common in documentary realism gave way to shorter, more poetic narratives that were highly metaphorical in construction.

Darío was a masterful prose writer as well as poet, and his work provided models and inspiration for countless others—even writers whose subject matter was largely social and political. Mariano Azuela, whose *Los de Abajo* (The Underdogs, 1915) is considered the classic novel of the Mexican Revolution, incorporated modernist literary techniques in his vivid descriptions of the Mexican countryside. Regionalist and Indianist novelists—who continued the struggle for justice on behalf of the Indian well into the twentieth century—were strongly influenced by modernist innovations in language and literature. Modernism, for example, helped to teach regionalist writer Horacio Quiroga how to condense his stories—generally set in the Latin American wilderness—into brief exposés on the tragic nature of human existence.

Literature of the Vanguard

A period that invited an enormous variety of literary styles, techniques, and concerns succeeded modernism. Realist fiction's documentary tendency continued to flourish, and most poetry became an intimate, personal expression. Women writers had far greater visibility, notably poets Delmira Agustini, Alfonsina Storni, Juana de Ibarbourou, and Gabriela Mistral—the latter Latin America's first Nobel laureate in literature. Mistral is difficult to characterize because she falls between the modernists and postmodernists. The postmodernist era's most dramatic development was unquestionably the eruption of the literature of the vanguard.

While Agustini and Storni wrote about women's capacity for love and passion, and reflected a proto-feminist recognition of a lack of female empowerment, Mistral seemed more interested in exploring spiritual themes and maternal love. Some of Mistral's poetry also explored the Latin American landscape, perhaps anticipating fellow Chilean Pablo Neruda's meditations on South America's varied geography.

The vanguard was to literature what cubism was to painting: a complete upheaval of traditional expectations regarding the fundamental premises of artistic expression. By the 1920s, art had witnessed a revolutionary plunge away from realism and into abstraction, and literature soon followed. Literature of the vanguard attempted to push verbal expression away from the rational into the irrational, away from conventional forms of literature in favor of newly created forms, away from old themes toward a new registry of poetic topics reflecting the sensibilities of a new age of technology. The modernists had their swans; the vanguard had airplanes, trains, factories, and cities. Spanish philosopher José Ortega y Gasset wrote about the "dehumanization" of art that occurred during the

Chilean poet and educator Gabriela Mistral (1889–1957) was the first Latin American to be awarded the Nobel Prize in Literature, in 1945. Credit: Rodrio22, https://commons.wikimedia.org/wiki/File: Gabriela_mistral_.jpg

period following World War I, a reference to what he felt was an absence in art of elements reflecting the human experience.

The poetic manifestations of vanguard literature include a total disregard for formal grammatical and stylistic conventions; punctuation is often random and arbitrary. Poets would often avoid a logical exposition of themes and subjects; their poems often appear to be chaotic jumbles of images and incoherent metaphors.

Perhaps the most vivid example of a Latin American poet of the vanguard is Chilean Vicente Huidobro, whose long, rambling poetic meditation "Altazor" (1919) was an invitation to literary anarchy: the only rule was that there were no rules. Huidobro was especially fond of creating words simply for the sound they represented or the rhyme scheme they momentarily fulfilled. "Altazor" has segments that are a collection of invented words that seemingly exist only for the sound they create within the poem. The poem ends with letters, as if erasing the meaning of all words. Huidobro called his poetic efforts "creationism." His thesis, typical of the vanguard generation, was that the poet was exclusively responsible for the burden of inspiration and creativity.

The period of the vanguard had its day, yet its legacy was enduring. Literature was imbued with an experimental verve that has lasted to the present. Novels and short stories of the famous "boom" of the 1960s are indebted to the vanguard for opening the door to literary experimentation, which characterized Latin American literature for most of the twentieth century.

Magical Realism and the Boom

Cuban author Alejo Carpentier first made extensive use of the term "magical realism" (*lo real maravilloso, la maravillosa realidad,* or *el realismo mágico*), after a 1943 trip to Haiti during which he was greatly impressed by the influence of African culture. These influences included myth and music; language and perception; and unexpected alternations of reality, metamorphosis, and magic. They involved a cultural ability or tendency to perceive or emphasize mysterious and magical elements found in everyday reality, in common activities, thus mixing reality and fantasy in a way that is unsurprising for the characters in the narrative world. Numerous examples of this literary technique are found in Carpentier's novel *El Reino de Este Mundo* (The Kingdom of This World, 1949).

Characteristics of magical realism can be traced back to the earliest cultural encounters between Europeans and the Indigenous peoples of the Americas. Columbus, Cortés, and other early explorers of the 1500s were unprepared for the New World they encountered. There was initial confusion about whether they had arrived in some part of Asia (China or India). Their languages lacked words for many of the new things they found; they had to borrow from the Indigenous languages. They were often amazed by the peoples, plants, animals, locales, and customs they experienced. Their reactions thus combined their own wonder with the obvious reality of their surroundings. In some cases, they embellished their "discoveries" to impress their rulers or supporters back in the old country. We can understand why some literary critics argue that more than historical texts, these texts are examples of literary creation.

As the explorers began to learn about Indigenous myths and religious practices, the blending of magic and reality continued, albeit subconsciously. As the Europeans attempted to impose many of their beliefs on the Indigenous peoples, an almost inevitable syncretic evolution of hybrid cultural forms occurred. The introduction of African cultural elements, predominantly in the Caribbean, added substantially to the mix. Chapters 4, 9, and 12 show how this process of amalgamation occurred in politics, ethnic relations, and religious practices, respectively.

The process continued despite participants not having a specific name for it. Known as "El Inca," Garcilaso de la Vega of Peru tried to present the Indigenous perspective and reaction to the encounter by explaining some of the myths and practices of his people. Mexican author Fernández de Lizardi later combined some elements of Indigenous language and belief in his nineteenth-century descriptions of colonial life. As mentioned previously, the most profound and effective blending of these early tendencies to combine history and fiction (reality and myth) occurred in the works of Ricardo Palma. His "Tradiciones Peruanas" (Peruvian Traditions, 1872–1883) combined researched historical fact with local legends and personal commentary, often in an ironic or satirical tone. Jorge Luis Borges, the twentieth-century Argentine author, also successfully used this technique, giving a veneer of historical reality to his creative fantasies in works such as *Ficciones* (Fictions, 1944) and *El Aleph* (1949). Borges is universally renowned for his use of the basic elements of magical realism, including time shifts, dream sequences, and multicultural references.

Authors of the modern Latin American literary "boom" (c. 1960–1970) raised magical realism to the exalted level of a renowned, worldwide literary movement—gaining international stature, recognition, and respect for the previously all-too-often neglected realm of Latin American literature. This boom was exemplified by the unprecedented explosion of Latin American writing on the international literary scene. Many of the works achieved universal appeal, critical acclaim, and financial success.

Interests and characteristics of the boom authors include magical realism, native cultures, myths, combinations of history and fiction, circular time, dreams, the other or the double, creative language, multiple viewpoints, and literary experimentation. The reader becomes an active participant rather than passive observer, because the reader has to untangle the varied literary threads. An excellent example is seen in Julio Cortázar's novel *Rayuela* (Hopscotch, 1963), which the reader can read in chronological order or select chapters in a varied order, thus offering multiple interpretations of the text and altering the plot development. Several of the boom authors were also fond of intellectual games and occasionally referred to other authors, works, and characters, or addressed their readers directly in their writings, thus blurring the boundaries between fiction and reality.

Additionally, the ideals of the boom include some allegiance to certain tenets of the Cuban Revolution—such as greater rights for the poor, individual liberty with group social consciousness, a fairer distribution of wealth, and an improvement in general living standards. The institution Casa de las Américas fostered the interest in Latin American literature with wider publication of both classic and recent texts.

Among the most notable book authors are Cuba's Alejo Carpentier; Mexico's Carlos Fuentes (*La Muerte de Artemio Cruz* [The Death of Artemio Cruz, 1962]); Peru's Mario Vargas Llosa (*La Ciudad y los Perros* [The City and the Dogs, 1962]); Argentina's Julio Cortázar; Colombia's Gabriel García Márquez (*Cien Años de Soledad* [One Hundred Years of Solitude, 1967]); Guatemala's Miguel Ángel Asturias (*El Señor Presidente* [Mr. President, 1946]); and Mexico's Juan Rulfo (*Pedro Páramo,* 1955).

By 1970, several disagreements had developed among the various boom authors. There were political and ideological differences, especially when the Cuban Revolution failed to live up to its promise. There were also social and creative differences, with some desiring greater liberty in literary subject matter and style. Another criticism of the boom is that it was a movement that was entirely made up of men. Though there were well-recognized women authors such as Mexican Elena Poniatowska writing at the time, the movement was in part defined by its masculinity. The authors gave voice to varied segments of society by featuring characters of different ethnic and economic origins, but the movement itself was made up of elite male intellectuals. Although the boom declined, many of its members continued to write and evolve within this genre, even as new authors appeared on the scene.

The techniques of magical realism had become well established and were continued in later works by several authors. Interestingly, of the five

Latin Americans who won the Nobel Prize for Literature, at least three were from the boom, demonstrating the impact this movement had on the world stage. The Nobel laureates include Gabriela Mistral of Chile (1945, poetry); Miguel Ángel Asturias of Guatemala (1967, novels/stories); Pablo Neruda of Chile (1971, poetry); Gabriel García Márquez of Colombia (1982, novels/stories); and Octavio Paz of Mexico (1990, poetry and essays).

Beyond the Boom

Although interest in magical realism continued after the boom, some writers reacted unfavorably to certain techniques employed during that movement. Some opposed the intellectual games played out in a few texts. Differences occurred on many levels—political, social, stylistic, ideological, and creative. Although many of the boom authors continued to work and maintained their literary success, they evolved with changing times.

Literature from the second half of the twentieth century made room for more varied voices, including more women authors. Some who achieved wide recognition are Rosario Castellanos of Mexico (*Balún Canán*, 1957); Elena Poniatowska of Mexico (*La Noche de Tlatelolco* [The Night at Tlatelolco, 1971]); Luisa Valenzuela of Argentina (*El Gato Eficaz* [The Clever Cat, 1972]); and Isabel Allende of Chile (*La Casa de los Espíritus* [The House of the Spirits, 1982]). Gioconda Belli of Nicaragua, Edwidge Danticat of Haiti, and Anacristina Rossi of Costa Rica achieved literary recognition in recent years. Like the authors that proceeded them, their works are often critical of political developments in their countries. It is worth noting that several authors of Latinx/Hispanic descent are writing in the United States in both English and Spanish, including Luis Rafael Sánchez, Miguel Méndez, Oscar Hijuelos, Julia Alvarez, Sandra Cisneros, and Rolando Hinojosa-Smith.

Interest has continued in the multicultural nature of Latin American society. Peruvian José María Arguedas wrote of the Indigenous influences in *Los Ríos Profundos* (Deep Rivers, 1958). The African cultural heritage has been vividly described in the poetry of Nicolás Guillén of Cuba and Luis Palés Matos of Puerto Rico. Peruvian poets defended the poor (César Vallejo) and the Jewish heritage (Isaac Goldemberg). Both Ariel Dorfman and Antonio Skármeta of Chile wrote powerfully on the theme of exile.

One of the most popular forms of Latin American literature in the years following the boom of the 1960s has been the historical novel. The contemporary history novel inherited many of the literary techniques and thematic concerns of magical realism, such as multiple narrators, fluid depiction of time and space, Native American mythology and culture, and fantasy. Contemporary novelists are fascinated with the colonial era because it provides a basis for understanding many of the historical issues of concern today throughout Latin America: the discovery and its political, social, and economic consequences; the plight of the Indian during the conquest; the inception of a nationalistic consciousness; and the movement toward independence. Recently there has been a growth of historical novels written by a new generation of authors who imagine how women have participated in Latin American history. Many of these novels become bestsellers. According to critics, although boom authors are celebrated for their publishing success, critics often disregard other bestselling authors because of their public appeal, regardless of their literary achievements. Some of these novels are Angeles Mastretta's *Arráncame la Vida* (Tear This Heart Out, 1988), Tomás Eloy Martínez's *Santa Evita* (1995), and Isabel Allende's *Hija de la Fortuna* (Daughter of Fortune, 1999). Another trend in current historical novels is to situate them outside of a Latin American context, such as Ignacio Padilla's *Amphitrion* (Shadow Without a Name: A Novel, 2000) and Jorge Volpi's *En Busca de Klingsor* (In Search of Klingsor, 1998), both of which take place in Europe. Globalization impacts literature as it does the world and we can see this in the settings of contemporary novels and in the characters' world knowledge and use of technology.

In what is sometimes an obvious parody of the great figures of early Latin American history—Columbus, Cortés, and the *conquistadores*—a number of writers have presented highly imaginative visions of the past that challenge, distort, and contradict standard accounts of history. In Alejandro Paternain's *Crónica del Descubrimiento* (Chronicle of the Discovery, 1980), for example, a tribe of Indians crosses the Atlantic and "discovers" Europe, a land they consider to be highly uncivilized. Cuban writer Alejo Carpentier, in many ways the father of magical realism, wrote several novels that completely disregard conventional distinctions of time. His *Concierto Barroco* (Baroque Concerto, 1974) juxtaposes elements from modern music—jazz, electric guitars, and Louis Armstrong—with the musical culture of eighteenth-century Venice.

Carpentier was one of many writers who incorporated primary historical documents into their literary treatments of the colonial period, making virtually no distinction between historical and fictional language. Antonio Benítez Rojo's *El Mar de las Lentejas* (Sea of Lentils, 1979), a book about Latin America's first hundred years, uses historical accounts from the era to underpin his fictional story about Columbus's second voyage to America. Virtually all of Latin America's most noted novelists have contributed to this literary genre, including Gabriel

García Márquez (*El General en su Laberinto* [The General in His Labyrinth, 1989]); Carlos Fuentes (*La Campaña* [The Campaign, 1990]); and Mario Vargas Llosa (*La Guerra del Fin del Mundo* [The War of the End of the World, 1981]).

The world learned about Indian rights activist Rigoberta Menchú with the publication of her 1983 testimonial, *I, Rigoberta Menchú: An Indian Woman in Guatemala,* which eventually appeared in eleven languages. The testimonial as a genre gained popularity in the 1980s, when it was used primarily to recount the injustices committed by Latin America's military governments. In the testimonial genre, a person who often has been silenced by their community (often because of his or her race, class, gender, and language) tells their story.

Some testimonials are written by the person who experienced the injustice. Augusto Pinochet's seventeen-year dictatorship in Chile (1973–1990) created the circumstances for political prisoners to tell their stories of captivity and torture. Manuel Guerrero Ceballos wrote *Desde el Túnel* (From the Tunnel, 1976) as a memoir of his 1976 abduction and imprisonment during the height of Pinochet's political repression.

In other cases, such as with Menchú, the story is told to an educated person, who then organizes and publishes it. Menchú's testimony of Quiché Mayan life and culture in the northwest highlands, hardships growing up helping her parents tend their tiny plot and traveling with them to work on coffee and sugar plantations, and state terror directed against her people earned her the Nobel Peace Prize in 1992. Menchú vividly recounts the torture and death of her parents and brother at the hands of the Guatemalan military. Rather than happily mark the 500th anniversary of Columbus in the New World in October 1992, she was quoted as defiantly insisting that "the celebration of Columbus is for us an insult." Some critics, such as anthropologist David Stoll, have questioned the accuracy of certain historical and interpretive aspects of Menchú's text. Her defense of her experience was documented in *Crossing Borders* (1998). The testimonial, valuable because it gives voice to the silenced, is a story often told to a community outsider with a political purpose and must be studied with the benefits and downfalls of these objectives in mind.

From Macondo to McOndo

In 1996, Chilean writers Alberto Fuget and Sergio Gómez published *McOndo,* a collection of stories written by seventeen Latin American male authors. The title is a play on García Márquez's Macondo, the invented town in which *One Hundred Years of Solitude* and many of his magical fictions occur. The idea for the collection arose when one of the authors had a story rejected for publication in the United States because it did not represent Latin America. Although the boom gave Latin American literature worldwide recognition and critical acclaim, it also created expectations of what Latin American literature would be.

This anthology was not meant to be a literary manifesto or to define a new generation of writers, although it was interpreted as such; they are often referred to as the McOndo writers. These authors were born in the late 1960s, and when the anthology appeared, they had published at least one book in Spanish. They reject the stereotype of Latin America as a rural, magical realist place and instead describe it as an urban world of McDonald's, Macintosh computers, malls, and condominiums. This generation plays computer games, watches US films, and listens to rock music. It promotes a virtual reality that is sometimes full of technology, sex, and drugs. Many of the authors in this collection have now rejected their association with this group, but since the publication of *McOndo* they have become some of the most successful contemporary Latin American writers. Moreover, boom authors such as Carlos Fuentes and Mario Vargas Llosa embraced the group and its new vision of Latin America.

McOndo works reflect the realities of Latin America following the creation of NAFTA in 1994, the internet, and a globalized world that is more influenced by pop culture than by a pre-Columbian one. The most critically acclaimed and award-winning authors in this anthology are Chilean Alberto Fuget, Bolivian Edmundo Paz Soldán, Mexican Jordi Soler, and Argentian Juan Form. As is fitting of the computer-age generation, several of these authors are active on social media, and use their personal websites for promotion and for publishing some of their work online. The term *McOndo* has since been used to define works that reflect the effects of globalization in Latin America at the turn of the twenty-first century. Some of the authors not included in the anthology but sharing some of the same characteristics are Mexican Cristina Rivera Garza, Chilean Laura Restrepo, Argentinean Alan Pauls, and Chilean Roberto Bolaño.

In 1996, the same year *McOndo* was published, a group of young Mexican writers declared themselves to be part of "El Crack." They intended to invigorate Mexican literature by returning to the boom's serious and textually challenging literature. They strove to be recognized within Western literary tradition. Like the McOndo authors, this group was accused of being audacious for self-naming their movement. Created in response to difficulties getting published, the self-promotion of both El Crack and McOndo generations worked. As a result of declaring these movements, the authors found publishers for their works. Jorge Volpi's *En Busca de Klingsor* (1999) and Ignacio Padilla's *Amphitryon* (2000) were the award-winning historical novels of the group. Like the *McOndo* movement, the El Crack writers distance themselves from a Latin American literary landscape, often creating characters who are not Latin American. While one movement rejects the boom and another one embraces it, they both no longer feel the need to situate their novels in Latin America but instead turn to a global landscape for inspiration. As technology, free trade, and immigration continue to transcend national borders as the twenty-first century begins, Latin American writers will continue to reflect these changes through their literature.

Latinx Writers

Since the social, political, and ethnic movements of the 1960s in the United States, a group of Latinx writing in English has emerged. Different terms have been used to define this group of US citizens, with "Latinx" being the gender-neutral, politically conscious term currently used to describe people of Latin American descent. Depending on their country of origin, each group has different political, social, and economic reasons for emigrating to the United States.

In his epic poem "I Am Joaquin" (1967), Rodolfo "Corky" Gonzalez imagined a return in the southwest of the mythical Aztlán, homeland of the Aztecs. Tomas Rivera's . . . *Y No Se lo Tragó la Tierra* (. . . And the Earth Did Not Devour Him, 1971) recounts the migrant farm worker's experience; Rivera's bilingual short stories describe economic difficulties and social injustices. Luis Valdez's theater *El Teatro Campesino* (1965–present) served the United Farm Workers by mobilizing and teaching them about their rights.

Through education, the protagonists in Latinx coming-of-age novels find their identity. Characters face the challenge of living between two cultures. Revealing a synthesis of their origins and experiences, they often no longer identify with their country of origin and struggle to find their place in the United States. In *Bless Me, Ultima* (1972), Mexican American author Rodolfo Anaya follows the spiritual awakening of its protagonist, celebrating the power of writing, education, and the Indigenous pre-Hispanic values of the southwest. In Sandra Cisneros's *The House on Mango Street* (1984), a poor Mexican American girl narrates her dream of owning her own home. In *Borderlands* (1987), Gloria Anzaldúa, a leader among the women of color feminist movement, creates a literary *mestizaje* (miscegenation) by mixing a variety of genres and language to reflect on the Chicana experience. Michele Serros's

How to Be a Chicana Role Model (2000) plays with the idea of the Chicana coming-of-age novel by instead highlighting the author's love of hegemonic popular culture. Reyna Grande's memoir *The Distance Between Us* (2013) gives voice to the immigrant experiences of undocumented migrants. Her memoir is noteworthy for documenting the experiences of children who are separated from their parents when they travel north in search of job opportunities, and how that separation impacts their relationship when they are reunited. A common theme among early Latinx authors is their search for an understanding of their identity and place in the United States.

The 1898 Spanish-American War left Cuba and Puerto Rico under US domination. In 1917 the Jones Act extended citizenship to Puerto Ricans, giving them a unique status. Throughout history, as with all immigrants, Puerto Rican immigration peaked when there were economic difficulties in Puerto Rico. Unfortunately, many Puerto Ricans come to the United States only to find a new sort of poverty. While most Chicano/Chicana authors wrote in English, Puerto Rican immigrants preferred to write in Spanish. Initially, works such as René Marques's play *La Carreta* (1953) argued that the only solution for Puerto Rican migrants to redeem themselves from moral and cultural corruption that occurs while living in the United States is to return to the island. Tato Laveira's *La Carreta Made a U Turn* (1979) rejected this view and describes the impossibility of returning to Puerto Rico after immigration. His work celebrates the cultural value of the Puerto Rican immigrant experience. As the title indicates, Laveira combines English and Spanish to create new images reflecting their new reality. Jesús

Oscar Hijuelos (1951–2013) was a Latinx writer of Cuban descent. He was the first Hispanic to win a Pulitzer Prize, for his novel The Mambo Kings Play Songs of Love. *Credit: https://hispanicheritage .org, https://commons.wikimedia.org /wiki/File:Hijuelos.jpg*

Colón became an important voice in the militant literature of the 1960s and 1970s, which embraces its working-class origins and fights for the rights of Nuyoricans—Puerto Ricans living in the United States. Contemporary Puerto Rican authors continue to struggle with their unique citizenship status. Authors such as Luis Rafael Sánchez and Rosario Ferré lived in both countries and have written in either English or Spanish depending on the content and the mood of their works. Both authors translated their own works and considered the choices they made in the language to be an essential part of their storytelling.

Prior to the Cuban Revolution of 1959, Cubans emigrated for economic opportunities. Pulitzer Prize–winning Oscar Hijuelos's *The Mambo Kings Play Songs of Love* (1989) is the story of two brothers who arrive in New York in the late 1940s, to work by day and play music by night. It captures the music of the Caribbean, which defined the era. The Cuban Revolution resulted in a growth of political exiles whose experience is unique, as their immigration was not based on economic needs. Cristina Garcia's *Dreaming in Cuban* (1992) tells the story of a family divided by geography and ideology. It is celebrated for being one of the first novels that presents the experience of Cubans in the United States and on the island.

Unstable political and economic conditions led to immigration from the Caribbean, and Central America. (Caribbean literature and film are discussed in greater depth in the third edition of *Understanding the Contemporary Caribbean*). Dominican American Junot Diaz's *Drown* (1996), a collection of short stories, takes place in the Dominican Republic and the United States. His male protagonists face poverty, hardworking mothers, and absentee fathers. *Drown*'s protagonist, Junior, is a reoccurring character in Diaz's subsequent works. In Julia Alvarez's *How the Garcia Girls Lost Their Accents* (1991), her characters have fled from the Trujillo regime of the Dominican Republic. Unlike their parents, who dream of returning home, the girls search to find a place for themselves.

Several of the aforementioned writers use the historical novel to teach their readers about their countries of origin. Julia Alvarez's *In the Time of Butterflies* (1994) recounts the story of the revolutionary Mirabal sisters, who challenged Trujillo's dictatorship. Sandra Cisneros's *Caramelo* (2000) retells her family's history while incorporating significant events of Mexican and Mexican American history. Junot Díaz's *The Brief Wondrous Life of Oscar Wao* (2007) critiques the Trujillo dictatorship through the story of Oscar Wao. By using popular culture and footnoting, Cisneros and Pulitzer Prize winner (2007) Díaz challenge traditional history-writing.

Literary awards and recognitions granted to many of these authors, both in the United States and abroad, reveal their important contributions to world literature. Once on the fringes of US literature, these authors are now regularly taught in US English classes and in Spanish departments. The idea of *latinidad* is constantly renovated as more established Latinx communities interact with more recent immigrants. Twenty-first-century writers such as Maya Chinchilla, Roberto José Tejada, Rodrigo Toscano, José Rivera, Edwin Torres, Justin Torres, Salvador Plascencia, Giannina Braschi, Oscar Casres, Nina Marie Martínez, and Susana Chávez-Silverman have moved to post-racial representational processes. Latinx authors and performance artists such as La Pocha Nostra and Cybrids use the internet, which allows them freedom and another space to communicate their messages. By taking the best from both literary worlds and from the fields of Latin American studies and American studies, Latinx authors are gaining international acclaim for their works.

Brazil and the Wider Caribbean

Brazil followed a pattern similar to that of the other Latin American nations, though with Portuguese language and culture. Some of the best-known Brazilian writers lived during the nineteenth century: Machado de Assis, Joaquim Nabuco, José de Alencar, Gonçalves Dias, and Castro Alves. The twentieth century also produced important authors in Brazil, including Mário de Andrade, Oswald de Andrade, Carlos Drummond de Andrade, Cecília Meireles, Raquel de Queirós, Jackson de Figueiredo, Graça Aranha, Coelho Neto, and Jorge de Lima.

João Guimarães Rosa published one of his major works, *Grande Sertão, Veredas* (Big Country, Footpaths), in 1956. Jorge Amado treated social themes in such works as *Mar Morto* (Dead Sea, 1936) and *Capitães de Areia* (Captains of Sand, 1937). Other notable writers from the Brazilian republic include regionalists and social realists such as Gilberto Freyre and José Lins do Rêgo; stylist Graciliano Ramos; experimental novelists with innovative narrative techniques such as Erico Veríssimo; and writers who employ powerful, poetic, and magical language such as Clarice Lispector and Nélida Piñón.

Other non-Spanish-speaking nations of the wider Caribbean have produced writers whose works should be included in the discussion of Latin American literature. Orlando Patterson of Jamaica wrote *The Children of Sisyphus* in 1964, which reveals the struggle for survival in Kingston's shantytown society. Jamaican novelist John Hearne wrote

Faces of Love (1957) and *Autumn Equinox* (1959), which study the nation's complex social and psychological relationships. From Dominica in the West Indies, Jean Rhys published her novel *Wide Sargasso Sea* in 1966, which deals with the representation of the creole Caribbean woman. From French-speaking Guadeloupe, Simone Schwarz-Bart wrote two novels, *Pluie et Vent sur Télumée Miracle* (The Bridge of Beyond, 1972) and *Ti Jean l'Horizon* (Between Two Worlds, 1979), which depict the cultural interconnections of the region. These and works by Trinidadian writer V. S. Naipaul (*Guerrillas,* 1975); Antiguan author Jamaica Kincaid (*At the Bottom of the River,* 1983); and St. Lucian epic poet Derek Walcott (*Omeros,* 1990) provide additional perspectives on the wider Caribbean.

Popular Culture

Popular culture strongly influenced literature and society of Latin American nations. Street theaters throughout the region have served as models of social reform, political protest, and artistic creativity. As discussed in Chapter 10, the 1970s protest movement of the mothers of the Plaza de Mayo helped bring down the Argentine dictatorship responsible for the disappearances of many citizens. Nonfiction writing in essays and newspapers also played an important role in the development of Latin American society.

Film became a powerful cultural medium in the twentieth century. Argentina's Manuel Puig wrote *La Traición de Rita Hayworth* (Betrayed by Rita Hayworth, 1968); his *El Beso de la Mujer Araña* (1976) became the important film, play, and Broadway musical *Kiss of the Spider Woman,* which condemned dictatorial excess and prison cruelty. The award-winning film *The Official Story* (1985), directed by Luis Puenzo, grew out of the protests against the Argentine military dictatorship.

As cinema became a dominant artistic form, attempts were gradually made to transfer literary magical realism to film, presenting interesting challenges. Flashback can be used successfully to convey the interplay of past, present, and future that is so important to magical realism's sense of the circularity of time. The use of ancestral or legendary spirits (even ghosts) that appear in works of magical realism can be portrayed through various split-screen and related cinematic techniques. Magical realism should not be confused with horror films or science fiction; it has a lighter, subtler touch than those popular genres.

Perhaps the best-known work of magical realism is García Márquez's aforementioned *Cien Años de Soledad* (One Hundred Years of Solitude,

1967). One episode from the novel was developed into another story by the author, which became the film *Eréndira* (1983). Several of García Márquez's stories were developed for the film series *Love in the Time of Cholera* (named after his novel with this title published in 1988) and the book was made into an English-language film in 2007.

Recently, memoirs have become increasingly popular with Latin American and Latinx authors. Marjorie Agosín described her childhood as a Jewish girl growing up in Chile in *A Cross and a Star* (1997). Another Chilean writer, Isabel Allende, told the very personal tale of the fatal illness of her daughter in *Paula* (1994). Gioconda Belli wrote vividly about her life in Nicaragua in *El País Bajo mi Piel* (2001, translated into English as *The Country Under My Skin* in 2002). Cuban author Reinaldo Arenas offered his life story in *Antes que Anochezca* (published posthumously in 1992), which has been translated into English and produced as a film as *Before Night Falls* (2000). Esmeralda Santiago's *When I Was Puerto Rican* (2006) is one example of how the memoir is used to recount the Latinx experience of immigration to the United States.

Chilean author Isabel Allende's novel *La Casa de los Espíritus* (The House of the Spirits, 1982) was also brought to the screen in English. Mexican author Juan Rulfo's novel *Pedro Páramo* (1955) appeared in a 1970s Mexican film. Rulfo's story of the life of a local *patrón* involved a considerable amount magical realism through flashbacks to different time periods in his life and references to characters, living and dead, who appeared in the work. Angeles Mastretta's novel *Arráncame la Vida* (Tear This Heart Out) was also converted into a film in 2008 and re-creates the political and personal realities of post-revolutionary Mexico.

The 1983 independent film *El Norte* (The North) was a joint US–Latin American production directed by Gregory Nava. Although not directly based on a novel, it beautifully evoked on film the spirit of magical realism. It follows the lives of two young refugees from Guatemala's violence—a brother and sister who escape through Mexico and finally into the United States. One of the most successful attempts to bring magical realism to film was the screen adaptation of Mexican scriptwriter Laura Esquivel's imaginative novel *Como Agua para Chocolate* (Like Water for Chocolate, 1992). The author deftly combined the popular themes of food preparation and romance in a work that portrayed some of the most memorable scenes in the novel. Several auspicious forces must be brought into play with skilled treatment if literary magical realism is to be successfully transferred to film within the sphere of popular culture. Perhaps the reader of a literary work has developed imaginary mental pictures of the elements of magical realism in the piece. He or she expects those but it is difficult to film them in a way that is both magical and realistic.

The importance of family and history are also recurrent themes in Latin American popular culture. Gregory Nava of *El Norte* fame also directed *My Family/Mi Familia* (1995), a film that depicts Latin American history and culture through several generations of a Mexican American family. Significant historical figures from Latin America are being portrayed on film to great critical success. *Frida* (2002) portrays the life story of surrealist artist Frida Kahlo and also successfully portrays many of the artists and political figures of post-revolutionary Mexico. Che Guevaras's *Motorcycle Diaries* (1952) was adapted to film in 2004. In the film, a youthful pre–Cuban Revolution Che discovers his socialist vocation while traveling with his friend on a motorcycle through beautiful Latin American landscapes. As the new millennium continues to unfold, this medium of popular culture in Latin America can be more fully explored.

Mexican visual artists made their mark in the twentieth century thanks largely to the muralists—most notably José Clemente Orozco (1883–1949), Diego Rivera (1886–1957), and David Alfaro Siqueiros (1896–1974). Mexican novelists—most notably Carlos Fuentes (1928–2012), Octavio Paz (1914–1998), Juan Rulfo (1917–1986), and Luis Spota (1925–1985)—matched those contributions in the letters and influenced writers across the world. Neither a muralist nor a novelist, Frida Kahlo (1907–1954) looms large in the US cultural horizon despite her short life, and today her work is a fixture in US art exhibits. Like Kahlo, Mexican directors, cinematographers, and set designers, among others, are influencing the arts in the United States.

Mexican cinema reached its first apogee between 1930 and 1960, with such iconic stars as Cantinflas (1911–1993, whom Charlie Chaplin thought was the best comedian he had ever seen), Maria Félix (1914–2002, a stunning beauty with a personality to match), and Dolores del Río (1904–1983), among others. With the exception of del Río, the first Latin American female actress to cross over to Hollywood with some success, the majority of these stars worked mostly in the Mexican domestic film industry.

Mexico's impact on cinema waned during the 1960s to emerge again in the late twentieth century and into the early twenty-first. This reemergence hinges mostly on Alfonso Arau (1932–present, who directed *Like Water for Chocolate* and served as the father's voice in *Coco*), Alfonso Cuarón (1961–present, whose *Gravity* and *Roma* won seven Oscars and three Oscars, respectively), Alejandro González Iñárritu (1963–present, whose *Birdman, or The Unexpected Virtue of Ignorance* won three Oscars and *The Revenant* won one Oscar), and Guillermo del Toro (1964–present, whose *The Shape of Water* won two Oscars).

Guillermo del Toro directed *Cronos, Pan's Labyrinth,* the *Hellboy* series, *Pacific Rim,* and *Crimson Peak,* all fantasy film genre standouts. A bit tamer than del Toro, Alfonso Cuarón has directed fantasy-oriented films such as *A Little Princess, Harry Potter and the Prisoner of Azkaban,* and *Children of Men.* Alejandro González Iñárritu, although harder to pin down to a specific genre, introduced Mexican actor Gael García Bernal to the big screen in *Amores Perros.*

Additionally, Mexico has provided the industry with such stalwarts as cinematographer Emmanuel Lubezki (1964–present, noted for *A Little Princess, The Birdcage, Meet Joe Black, Sleepy Hollow, Lemony Snicket's A Series of Unfortunate Events, Gravity, Birdman,* and *The Revenant,* among others). He won cinematography Oscars for each of the last three films listed. Rodrigo Prieto (1965–present), another Mexican cimematographer, has sixty-five cinematography credits to his name including *Brokeback Mountain, Argo, The Wolf of Wall Street,* and *The Irishman.* Prieto has been nominated for three Oscars and won four Silver Ariel awards from Mexico's film industry. Eugenio Caballero (1972–present) is a Mexican film set designer with a long list of credits, including *Pan's Labyrinth* and *Roma,* for the latter of which he won an Oscar with Mexican set designer Bárbara Enríquez (1977–present).

Music

Originating from the countries of the Americas and the Caribbean, the music of Latin America is generally sung in Spanish, Portuguese, French, or a number of Indigenous American or African languages.[1] These highly syncretic (hybrid) varieties of music include *rumba, son, cumbia, mariachi, tango, canto lucumí,* among other genres, whose musical sources include African, European, and Indigenous peoples. A musical stew born in the Americas, nowhere else in the world has musical syncretism been sustained so deeply over centuries, with such varied and popular results. This hybridization occurred between music in North America, the Caribbean, the coastal regions of Venezuela and Colombia, Brazil, and elsewhere. Indigenous and Spanish music mixed especially in Mexico, Central America, the Andean region (Ecuador, Peru, Bolivia, Chile, and the Amazon jungle), and the Southern Cone of South America (Uruguay, Paraguay, and Agentina). Indigenous tribes, African slaves, and European colonizers and immigrants initially coexisted and mixed in varying patterns of integration and domination, producing these unique musical hybrids.[2] This musical *mestizaje* reflected deeper and easier cultural mixing than was allowed in society as a whole. White Bolivians who would never live in an Aymara (Indigenous) village would politely applaud for an ensemble performing their music. The *conga* drum, which was once associated exclusively with Black culture in Cuba, was adopted by big bands in the segregated Cuba of the 1930s, eliciting some brief controversy. Music often led to contact between cultures, but rarely to social integration.

Similar musical mixing gave birth in the United States to jazz, rock, and other styles, which subsequently influenced music in Latin America during the twentieth century, giving rise to Latin pop, *rock en español,* Spanish rap, Brazilian reggae, and Puerto Rican *reggaetón,* all having spread throughout much of Latin America.

Four distinct sources, over hundreds of years and across the Americas, created the music of Latin America: Indigenous music (especially in Mexico, Venezuela, the Andean countries, and the Southern Cone); African rhythms brought by Black slaves (especially in Brazil, Colombia, Venezuela, the Guyanas, Panama, the Caribbean, and the United States); European popular music styles; and Europe's classical music traditions. Today, the entire world is familiar with such genres as samba, tango, salsa, and *música andina* (Andean music). This common syncretic process is sometimes obscured by the immensely varied local conditions that gave rise to such different types of music.

Thus, while American jazz in the 1920s and modern Afro-Brazilian *samba* may both combine the same musical roots, they actually sound nothing alike. To understand either one, we must closely examine the particular local environment that birthed it. For example, how did early jazz in the United States reflect Protestant American hymnody, the improvisatory traditions of the brass bands, the rhythmic innovations of ragtime music, and rural blues—all genres distinct to the United States, which fed into the creation of jazz? The differing histories of each region in the Americas, and the different admixture of Black, Indigenous, and European traditions, result in the immensely varied universe of Latin American (and North American) music. Each of these sources of music was itself an agglomeration of multiple nations, languages, and cultures. The African music cultures that were brought to the Americas through the slave trade included those of the Yoruba, the Dahomey, the Congolese, and the Angolan people, whose primary destinations were North America, the Caribbean, and Brazil. These varied music cultures survived differently in each region, depending on the colonial regime. Thus, although both the United States and Brazil depended heavily on African slavery, the actual musical traditions in Brazil and the United States sound very different from each other.

Countries with a greater Indigenous population, such as Bolivia, developed music indebted more to this tradition. Bolivian music is more rooted in Quechua and Aymara (Indigenous) instrumentation, rhythms, and forms of communal music-making than is the music in neighboring Chile. Furthermore, despite genocide and exclusion, all of Latin America, from the *pampas* of Argentina to the *playas* of Puerto Rico, has acknowledged, supported, and incorporated its Indigenous cultures to a much greater extent than has the United States.

These parallel forces created Latin American music, and they resulted in Latin America's immensely varied music genres. Further complicating the musical picture, at the same time as these new vernacular forms developed throughout the Americas, the European tradition of concert music was taking root throughout Latin America—and these composers took part in every major classical music trend and "ism" of the twentieth century, albeit paying more attention to the rhythms and instruments of the Americas, both Indigenous and African, than was the case with the concert repertoire of the United States and Europe. Eventually, the Latin American debt to European classical music was repaid by such Latin American composers as Heitor Villa-Lobos (Brazil), Carlos Chávez (Mexico), and Astor Piazolla (Argentina). Finally, there was great variety in the colonizers' music, as Spain, Portugal, France, Holland, and England brought their distinct vernacular musical traditions to their colonies. Many great writers on Latin American music have commented on these particular sources of the continents' incredible richness (Béhague 1979; Brill 2018; Dratch and Rosow 1984; Goia 2011; Jones 1999; Link and Wendland 2016; Madrid 2012; Manuel and Largey 2016; Murphy 2006; Olsen and Sheehy 2014; Omari-Tunkara 2006; Sublette 2007; Turino 2007).

Indigenous Musical Traditions

When Christopher Columbus arrived in the New World, he encountered a continent with its own ancient traditions of native instruments, music, and dance. The Aztecs in Mexico, the Mayas in Guatemala and the Yucatán Peninsula, and the Incas in modern-day Bolivia and Peru had their own wood and stone flutes, a variety of drums, and, shortly after the European arrival, stringed instruments imitating the Spanish vihuela and guitar. (The armadillo-shell, guitar-like charango seems to have developed in this manner, after the Spanish conquests of the Andean region in the sixteenth century.) For the first few centuries after the *conquista,* the three distinct strands of music in the Americas (Indigenous, European, and African) remained separate, reflecting the violently enforced racial demarcations of the sixteenth through eighteenth centuries. Incas played their flutes and drums, and eventually created guitar-like instruments. Church choirs and choirmasters performed European masses and choral music. African slaves maintained their music within their communities, often as part of African religious ceremonies, in such far-flung locations as the United States, Cuba, the coasts of Venezuela and Colombia, and Brazil. Except for the Andean adoption of guitar-like instruments, there was little documented musical syncretism until the late nineteenth century.

During the twentieth century, Indigenous music increased in quality and in its mainstream acceptance and reception. Arrangements and recordings became more professional, and beginning in the 1950s, Indigenous music groups in the Andes, Venezuela, Mexico, and elsewhere performed for non-Indigenous audiences, often for the first time. Meanwhile folksingers such as Venezuela's Simón Díaz and Argentina's Atahualpa Yupanqui became international stars, singing in Spanish. (Yupanqui was actually born Héctor Chaveru in the Buenos Aires region—Hispanic—but took this stage name to honor legendary Incan kings.) Some of their rhythms were European, but many—for instance, Simón's *joropos* and Yupanqui's *milongas* and *zambas*—were unique American hybrids, often with three-against-two guitar and cuatro strums (more on this metric concept later). By the 1950s, some Latin American governments had created bureaucracies to document and disseminate "folklore," meaning the culture of the Indigenous tribes of these countries. The Bolivian Ministry of Education began to broadcast in Aymara and Quechua in the 1950s.

The second half of the twentieth century witnessed an explosive growth of this "native" music, especially in the Andean region, with such groups as Los Jairas and Las Kjarkas in Bolivia performing formerly religious music for outsiders, in styles such as *Carnavalito, Huayno,* and *San Juanito.* They added the Spanish guitar (and often bass and percussion) to the traditional ensemble, along with formal arrangements to a repertoire that had been less formal in its original environment. Although native music and culture were sometimes squelched in Latin America, they were given a greater presence in society than they had in the United States, especially in areas of South America where the Indigenous people formed the majority of the population, such as Bolivia.

Nueva Canción and Political Music

Nueva canción was the musical genre of Hispanic singer-songwriters who focused on poetic social protest in the 1960s and 1970s, but its arrangements tended to have some elements of Indigenous music. Prominent *nueva canción* artists and groups included Violeta Parra, Victor Jara, Inti-Illimani, and Quilapayún in Chile; Mercedes Sosa, Victor Heredia, and Leon Gieco in Argentina; Daniel Viglietti in Uruguay; Soledad Bravo in Venezuela; Silvio Rodriguez and Pablo Milanés in Cuba; Amparo Ochoa in Mexico; and many others. While it sometimes experimented with rock music and electronics, the *nueva canción* genre focused on the songwriter's lyrics accompanied only by guitar, and many of its performers also sang folk songs, perhaps with some Indigenous instruments such as the pan flute. Although *nueva canción* generally has been associated with progressive or leftist politics in Latin America, many of these artists' original songs were more "poetic" than political, and this poetic aspect distinguishes *nueva canción* from parallel contemporaneous political music in the United States and Europe. Chilean Violeta Parra's famous ballad "Gracias a la Vida" (Here's to Life, 1966) is a poetic list of things to be grateful for in life, while Argentinean Ariel Ramirez's "Alfonsina y el Mar" (Alfonsina and the Ocean, 1969) vividly depicts the suicide of the Argentinian poet Alfonsina Storni. Although both of these *nueva canción* songs featured prominently in the repertoire of singer Mercedes Sosa of Argentina, neither song overtly addresses social issues in Latin America.

Many albums by the artists mentioned here also feature Indigenous instruments—the quena (wood flute), the charango (armadillo-shell guitar), the zampoña (pan flute), and the bombo (Argentinian folkloric drum). This combination of haunting poetry, guitar, and Andean instruments sonically symbolized *nueva canción*'s commitment to the working classes of Latin America throughout the 1960s and 1970s.

The repressive Latin American political context of the time also politicized this music, as it strove to represent daily life more honestly than popular music, with its clichéd tropes of romantic love (as heard, for instance, in the repertoire of the groups Los Panchos or Los Tres Aces). The increasingly repressive context of Latin America in the 1970s included General Augusto Pinochet's September 11, 1973, coup against Chile's elected socialist president, Salvador Allende, with US support, which led to the public torture and execution of *nueva canción* star Victor Jara; the military junta that took over Argentina in January 1976, which led to temporary exile for Mercedes Sosa; and to the events that led to revolution and civil war in Nicaragua and El Salvador at the end of the decade (especially following the assassination of Archbishop Romero in 1980).

The rubric *nueva canción* also applies to socially progressive Christian music. Carlos Mejía Godoy's "Misa Campesina Nicaragüense"

(Nicaraguan Peasant Mass, 1975) reimagines Christ as a humble peasant. In the context of the revolutionary waves present in Latin America at the time, and particularly liberation theology,[3] which was extolled by some in the Catholic Church, Godoy's music belongs firmly to the *nueva canción* movement. When in 1984 songwriter Rubén Blades released his evocative salsa song on Monseñor Romero's assassination,[4] he was following a tradition of depicting Latin America's tough reality first established by *nueva canción* artists such as Victor Jara of Chile in the 1960s—in sharp contrast to the romantic, "rose without thorns" world of Latin American pop music.

Classical Concert Music of Latin America

Apart from the Indigenous music of the Americas, and the progressive political music of the *nueva canción* performers, a classical music tradition that descended directly from Europe's classical music gradually took hold in all of the capital cities of Latin America, beginning in the early colonial era of the sixteenth century. Originally housed in the chapels of major cathedrals, and emphasizing choral singing over instrumental music, this tradition expanded in the late nineteenth century with the founding of musical conservatories in all the major capital cities of Latin America, from the Conservatorio Nacional de México (1866, followed by the founding of the Orquesta Sinfónica de México in 1881) to the Conservatorio Nacional Superior de Música in Buenos Aires (1924). This led to new compositional work in Latin America, touched on only briefly here.

Brazil's most prominent classical composer, and perhaps the most prominent in all of Latin America, is Heitor Villa-Lobos (1887–1959), whose "Bachianas Brasileiras no. 5" has entered the world's standard concert repertoire. Although he had some exposure to classical music, and learned as a child to play guitar, cello, and clarinet, around 1905 he turned toward the vernacular music of Brazil's "dark interior" as his inspiration. He played with street bands and improvised. This combination of European classical influences and vernacular music can be seen in the development of many of the great classical composers of Latin America. In 1917 and 1918, Villa-Lobos met the French composer Darius Milhaud in Brazil, who introduced him to the music of Debussy and Satie. (Villa-Lobos also introduced Milhaud to Brazil's popular music.) After a warm reception in Paris in 1923, Villa-Lobos went on to enjoy a long career as a composer, and late in life received so many international commissions that he experienced a negative backlash, especially in Brazil.

Heitor Villa-Lobos, Brazil's most prominent classical composer, circa 1922. Credit: Public domain, https:// commons.wikimedia.org/wiki/File :Heitor_Vila-Lobos_(c._1922)part.jpg

Mexico's two best-known twentieth-century classical composers are Silvestre Revueltas (1899–1940) and Carlos Chávez (1899–1978). Chávez in particular represents musical "nationalism," a term that denotes in Latin America the musical use of a country's own history and culture, and is commonly applied to many of the region's classical composers. After the Mexican Revolution (1910–1920), Chávez wrote ballet music highlighting Aztec themes, and he used percussion instruments from the native Yaqui people of Mexico in his most popular work, "Sinfonía India" (Second Symphony, 1936). In Argentina, the composer Alberto Ginastera (1916–1983) also incorporated folkloric elements into his concert music, referring to this as "objective nationalism" and "Gauchesco"—that is, utilizing elements that evoked the Argentinian *gaucho,* or the landless cowboy of the *llanos,* the plains. As a young man, Ginastera studied with Aaron Copland at Tanglewood in the 1940s, and spent his final years in Europe and the United States, where his music was often performed.

The most internationally prominent Latin American composer of the past six decades is the *bandoneón* master Astor Piazolla (Argentina, 1921–1992), who began in tango music but also studied in Paris with Nadia Boulanger, the prominent teacher of composers Aaron Copland and Quincy Jones. She reportedly convinced Piazolla to fully embrace

428 David H. Bost, Angélica Lozano-Alonso, and David Marcus

his native *tango* music as a composer, echoing what the composer Ravel had said to Gershwin in the 1920s: "Why become a second-rate Ravel when you are already a first-rate Gershwin?" Among Piazolla's well-known compositions are the instrumental piece "Libertango" and the song "Adiós Nonino." Argentina's active rock scene is also notable, especially as it often incorporates folk instruments. The Argentinan composer Gustavo Santaolalla began in rock music but moved to Hollywood, and later won an Academy Award for the score to the film *Brokeback Mountain.*

Also notable is Venezuela's innovative classical music education program, *El Sistema,* founded in 1975 by José Abreu, which trains impoverished children to play classical instruments. The United States, the United Kingdom, Holland, and other countries have based their own programs on the Venezuelan model. Gustavo Dudamel, the dynamic conductor of the Los Angeles Philharmonic Orchestra, is a product of *El Sistema.*

Vernacular and Popular Music

The sheer quantity of Latin America's vernacular, folkloric, and commercial music makes any summary seem inadequate. The omnipresence of the Spanish guitar in almost every genre of Latin American folkloric music testifies to the importance of Spanish and Portuguese influence across the American continents. What unites many of the folkloric genres of the Americas is this combination of the strummed guitar (with new strum patterns unique to Latin America), Spanish lyrics, and a particular metric phenomenon: the three-against-two meter used in much of Latin folkloric music.[5]

As mentioned, African musical traditions also took root in Latin America during the nineteenth and twentieth centuries, especially in those regions with large Black populations, such as Brazil, the Caribbean, and North America. They have had the most profound influence on Caribbean music, but they also exist, for example, in jazz and rock from the United States, and in Brazilian Capoeira,[6] an Afro-Brazilian cultural manifestation combining martial arts traditions, music, and dance. Most of these neo-African musical practices in the Americas, from Capoeira to Rumba Guaguancó, are now taught and disseminated around the globe. (See Omari-Tunkara 2006 for an in-depth examination of Yoruba culture, which continues to exist in the Americas, especially in Cuba.)

One example of the presence of African culture in Latin America is the Afro-Brazilian genre known as Capoeira, which has been described as music, dance, sport, play, and culture. Capoeira was developed by African slaves in Brazil, dating back to at least the seventeenth century.

Depending on the practitioner, Capoeira can be described as anything from an exercise class to a way of life. In the traditional form, Capoeira games occur in a circle, which is headed by musicians playing one of five traditional Capoeira instruments. One person leads the singing while everyone else responds with a chorus. Two people play Capoeira together in the middle of the circle, responding to the corporal questions posed by their partner with an array of kicks, jumps, spins, and twists. Capoeira is about social interaction, communication, and cooperation. This is reflected in the language used; it is a game between comrades rather than a fight against an opponent. UNESCO declared the *roda* of Capoeira as an intangible cultural heritage of humanity in 2014.

Capoeira is practiced all around the world, though most Capoeira groups still maintain strong ties to Brazil. Those learning Capoeira also learn and practice Samba de Roda, Maculelê, Puxada de Rede, the Portuguese language, and a few traditional instruments, and sing. Through this cooperative hybrid of dance, music, and martial arts, participants learn the history of the art, as well as the fundamentals of movement (rhythm, levels, partnering, self-expression) and the basics of the art's traditional music (instrumentation, songs in Portuguese). This will culminate in the traditional *roda,* where two participants at a time will use the steps they have learned to create a partnered, cooperatively improvisational "game," accompanied by other students playing and singing

*Mestre Ferradura conducting Capoeira de Rua. Credit: https://commons.wikimedia.org/w
/index.php?search=Capoeira&title=Special:MediaSearch&go=Go&type=image*

the music they have studied. In addition to the artistic benefits, Capoeira also enables students to develop strength, endurance, flexibility, focus, and coordination. Today, Capoeira is one of the greatest symbols of Brazilian identity and is present throughout the national territory and in more than 160 countries, on all continents.

To return to guitar-based Spanish music and its three-against-two metric trick, there are many variations—different accents, embellishments, and tempos—but this meter recurs throughout the Americas, in the Argentinian *chacarera* and *zamba*,[7] in the Chilean *cueca*, in the Venezuelan *joropo* (played usually on a cuatro, not a guitar),[8] and in the Mexican *huapango* and *son jarocho*.[9] Although music in Spain sometimes used the three-against-two rhythm, in the Americas it arose independently from multiple sources, including African ones.

Other Latin styles are based on a simple duple meter (two-two or four-four time), rather than the folkloric three-against-two. These folkloric and commercial forms in duple meter occur in various tempos, syncopations, and instrumentations, and include the *bolero*, the *danzón*, the Dominican *merengue* and *bachata*, Mexico's *banda* and *música norteña*, Brazil's *quick forró* (with its unique accordion-and-triangle sound), Argentina's *milonga* and *tango*, and the popular dance crazes of the United States in the 1940s and 1950s—the *mambo* and the *cha-cha-cha*. The same two-two meter is also the basis of the Cuban forms *son montuno*, *salsa*, and *timba*, albeit with much more syncopation in the anticipated bass (the *tumbao*) and in the piano line (the *montuno*), as well as the Puerto Rican folkloric genres *bomba y plena*.

To truly understand these metric categories, one must listen to actual songs. For the triple meter, which often has a three-against-two emphasis in Latin America, recommended songs include "Alma Llanera," the *trío romántico* "Ódiame," and the *nueva canción* song "Cuartetas por Diversion." The duple meter, often with quadruple subdivision, can actually be heard in most other Latin music, regardless of genre or period, from Daniel Santos's old *bolero* "Perdón" to Daddy Yanqui's *reggaetón* "Son Las 12," from Perez Prado's "Mambo no. 5" to Los Van Van's *salsa/timba* "Soy Todo."

The lyrics of Latin American songs include universal themes, such as love ballads and break-up ballads, but certain lyrical aspects are unique to Latin America. First, many folkloric forms assimilate the Spanish poetic genre known as the *décima*, a ten-line poem that can be improvised (for example, in a Cuban *controversia*, a kind of mutual insult contest). The *décima* commonly arises in genres as unrelated as a Chilean *cueca*, a Venezuelan *joropo*, and a *salsa* song from Cuba.

Additionally, there are many beautiful songs of nostalgia and longing for a lost or distant homeland, such as Atahualpa Yupanqui's "Tu que Puedes, Vuélvete," Mercedes Sosa's touching "Cambia, Todo Cambia," and Rubén Blades's salsa version of the *vals peruano* "Todos Vuelven."

Nueva canción opened the door to all manner of previously forbidden social and political topics. Gabino Palomares's powerful song "La Maldicción de la Malinche" imagines Hernán Cortés being cursed by his Aztec lover after conquering Mexico, while criticizing the racism that has been internalized by Indigenous people in Latin America. Victor Jara's closely observed song "Te Recuerdo, Amanda" reimagines love for the working classes of Chile. However, the extent to which Latin American music criticizes social reality depends largely on the observer. The great bulk of commercial music does not comment on race, slavery, or injustice, while Latin American intellectuals, historians, and artists tend to valorize the music that does so, in the *nueva canción* lineage. *Reggaetón* brazenly crosses boundaries of sexual vulgarity in Spanish, but seldom critiques the social or racial order of Latin America. In general, Latin American music at least acknowledges the slavery and racial injustice of the region more than music in the United States does (see, for instance, the songs "Moliendo Café" or "Plantación Adentro").

The *danzón* orchestras, which originally played for the private social clubs of Caribbean landowners in Cuba, Venezuela, and elsewhere in the late 1800s, grew larger. During the first half of the twentieth century, timbales replaced the timpani, pianos invented the montuno-oriented "Latin piano style" in imitation of syncopated guitar arpeggiation, large string sections were added, and the characteristic anticipated bass rhythm was invented. (This tumbao rhythm, unique to Latin music, is usually attributed to "Cachao" Lopez of Cuba.) Recording quality improved as radio flourished throughout Latin America beginning in the 1920s.

Thus, the ensembles that performed Latin music gradually increased in size, instrumentation, and professionalism throughout the twentieth century, adding bass and piano in the 1930s, replacing the guitar's syncopated arpeggiation patterns. Later the bands acquired horn sections, background vocals, full string sections, additional percussion, and a drumset, for which a new technique had to be developed. By the 1950s, a basic five-person "Latin rhythm section" had become standardized to include bass, piano, timbales, congas, and bongo or guira, with additional small percussion played by the vocalists.

By the 1950s, Argentinians were developing larger *tango* orchestras as well, while in Mexico, the craze for *mariachi* music led to larger orchestras, with their own "typical" (albeit invented) costumes and public relations budgets. The *trios* of the 1950s developed their own sound, based on male close-harmony vocals, maracas, guitar, and requinto (the smaller guitar that played the lead melody). "Latin music" was a huge success even in the United States, and New York City became as important a Latin music hub as Buenos Aires, Caracas, or Mexico City. The Caribbean was the rhythmic source of much of this so-called Latin music, but its professional creation and dissemination in New York led to its appreciation all over South America. Many genres of music from the North became as popular in South America as their own music was. Thus, 1970s *salsa,* with its roots in Cuba, Puerto Rico, and New York, became so popular in Latin America that some of its biggest stars are actually from South and Central America. The *salsa* bassist and bandleader Oscar de León is from Venezuela, while the singer, songwriter, and actor Rubén Blades is from Panama. Similarly, *cumbia,* a loping rhythm that originated among the African slave population on the coast of Colombia, gained such popularity in Mexico that many Latinos are unaware of its Colombian origin.

Beginning in the 1940s, the jostling together of Latino and non-Latino musicians in New York City was an explosively creative musical force, giving rise to new musical genres popular throughout the Americas. These new genres include Latin jazz in the 1950s (Tito Puente and Cal Tjader); salsa in the 1970s, which has been called "Cuban music with a New York accent" (Hector Lavóe, Willie Colón, and the Fania All Stars); and reggaetón in the 1990s (Daddy Yanqui and DJ Playero). Reggaetón, drawing on rap and Jamaican dance-hall and developed mainly by Puerto Ricans, has long outstripped salsa or other Latin genres in commercial sales, with the 2017 worldwide phenomenon "Despacito" leading the way.

Finally, classic rock stars who sing in English have always had great popularity in Latin America, with huge touring successes in Brazil, Chile, and Mexico for such bands as the Rolling Stones, Queen, Rod Stewart, and Sting. Many young Latin Americans who do not speak much English have memorized entire classic rock songs in English and sing along at concerts.[10] Without the success and clout of these Anglo rock acts, there may never have been such modern *rock en español* bands as Mexico's Maná and Colombia's Juanes and Aterciopelados. A Nicaraguan immigrant to the United States, Carlos Santana epitomizes the fusion of Latin rhythms with rock music, playing guitar with the dexterity of Eric Clapton or Duane Allman. He first came into international fame at the Woodstock rock concert, in August 1969, which was made into a well-known movie.

Carlos Santana performing at the Cow Palace, San Francisco, December 8, 2006. Credit: https://commons.wikimedia .org/wiki/File:Carlos_Santana_123176.jpg

A Cavalcade of Styles

This brief survey of Latin American literature, film, and music shows us how thoroughly Latin America has syncretized the various cultural strands mentioned above (its Indigenous, European, and African sources), how it has faced the tensions between cultures and social classes, and how it has been buffeted by the world's other cultural tendencies, especially those emanating from North America—sometimes in resistance to them, sometimes in assimilation of them. It shows us that both literature and music existed in Latin America before the arrival of European colonializers but that both were completely remade by the event.

The music of Latin America permeates our culture so deeply that we may not be conscious of its presence. Latin music, in both Spanish and English, creates hit records every few years even in the United States.[11] Whether rootsy or slick, folkloric or modern, political or apolitical, music in the myriad forms described here remains one of Latin America's primary contributions to world culture.

Literature and artistic expression through music, film, dance, and sculpture contribute to Latin America's cultural richness. Genres that are beyond the scope of this chapter, such as graphic arts, also help us to understand Latin American perceptions of reality. Academics who study Latin America are expanding their notion of what texts and artifacts are worthy of study. Television shows, protest music lyrics, and street art are now considered important examples of art production that help us to further understand Latin American culture and identity. In some ways it is as if the field of Latin American literature has come full circle. If we remember that pre-Columbian communities expressed themselves through music, dance, and illustrations, we can see the connections between those art forms and contemporary music, graphic novels, and murals. To fully understand the cultural wealth of Latin America we must study a variety of visual, musical, and textual elements and continue to expand our notions of art.

Notes

1. David Marcus wrote the section on music in this chapter. The third edition of *Understanding the Contemporary Caribbean* deals specifically with the Caribbean region; here we focus on the rest of Latin America, but do discuss common characteristics concerning African roots of the music of both regions.

2. European colonization in India, Asia, Africa, and even Australia also led to interesting musical hybrids, but only in the Americas was it this deep and enduring, only in the Americas did it include Black, Indigenous, and European roots, and only in the Americas did it eventually create the styles of music that dominate the planet today—pop, rock, rap, salsa, and so on.

3. The term *liberation theology* was coined by the Christian socialist Brazilian priest Paolo Freire (1921–1977), author of the influential book *Pedagogy of the Oppressed* (first published in 1968).

4. "El Padre Antonio y su Monaguillo Andrés," from his album *Buscando América*.

5. The technical terms *meter* and *metric* in music refer to the constantly repeated background pattern of stress, of stronger and weaker beats, grouped usually into two-, three-, or four-beat units, as well as the subdivision of each beat into quicker pulses. Triple meter, whether slow or fast, is counted "*one* two three, *one* two three." The Mexican folk song "Cielito Lindo" employs a quick triple meter with little subdivision of the beat, and could be written out in three-four time. One can hear duple or quadruple meter (they amount to the same thing) in Miami Sound Machine's 1985 hit song "Conga," which is in a slower duple meter (two-two time), but with a syncopated, fast quadruple subdivision of the beat (1 e & u 2 e & u 3 e & u 4 e & u). Actually, almost all rock and roll is in quadruple meter (four-four time), but with a "backbeat" (one *two* three *four*) and duple subdivision of each beat: one and *two* and three and *four* and . . . (for instance, the Beatles songs "I Saw Her Standing There" or "Get Back"). Much early rock and doo-wop music, however, is in four-four time, but has a triple subdivision of the beat. Listen, for example, to Fats Domino's "Blueberry Hill" or the Five Satins' "In the Still of the Night," both released in 1956, for a quadruple meter with a triple subdivision of the beat (1 & u 2 & u 3 & u 4 & u).

6. This section on Capoeira was written by Dani da Silva.

7. Not to be confused with the Brazilian *samba*.

8. Venezuela's unofficial national anthem, "Alma Llanera" (Soul of the Plains), is a famous *joropo*.

9. However, the song "La Bamba," the most famous *son jarocho*, is in a fast duple meter, not in three-against-two.

10. This odd phenomenon is referenced in the mid-1980s' song "Los Rolling Stones Nos Culparían" (The Rolling Stones Would Make Us Feel Guilty) by the Mexican duo Roberto y Jaime.

11. A short sampling of these crossover successes would include 1984's "Conga," 1987's "Bamboleo," 1993's "Macarena," 1999's "Livin' la Vida Loca," 2014's "Bailando," and 2017's "Despacito."

14

Looking Forward

Henry (Chip) Carey and
Kathleen Barrett

Latin America is facing a variety of daunting challenges
as it enters the post-pandemic world. Many of these challenges existed
prior to the pandemic but have been exacerbated by policies, or lack
thereof, to stop the spread of Covid-19. Furthermore, it quickly becomes
apparent that these challenges interact with and compound each other.
For example, the historical legacy of civil war affects politics, crime,
inequality, and even the environment today. Similarly, politics, crime, and
inequality could result in a resurgence of civil war.

Typically, people think that political systems reflect the leaders who
shape them. However, the types of leaders that come to power to a great
extent reflect the political institutions and processes that shape them, as
well as historical and cultural factors. Latin America is what might be
called "democracy with adjectives." That is, these democracies are not
yet fully functional since the transitions began over three decades ago.
They lack fully formed checks and balances and inclusive political
processes based on free and fair elections and the rule of law. It does not
seem today like the movement away from democracy is via coups, but
rather by institutional erosion, especially of courts, but also the legislature. Political freedoms, including freedom of speech, press, and association, are under threat in Mexico (United Nations Human Rights Council
2018), Belize, Bolivia, Brazil, Colombia, Ecuador, Guatemala, Honduras,
Nicaragua, Panama, Paraguay, and Peru (Freedom House 2020). Frequently, the judiciary is either not independent or corrupt, which inhibits
its ability to protect rights and fosters government impunity.

In most of Latin America, the trend is toward a primary system for candidate selection, with candidates that win primaries becoming battle-hardened and tending to win the multiparty elections (Carey and Polga-Hecimovich 2006). This reinforces the personalism and populism that also accrue from the region's presidential democracies, with a single leader elected for a fixed term. In Latin America, unlike the English Commonwealth Caribbean, which has parliamentary systems, the presidential cabinets serve at the pleasure of the single leader. Finally, in such presidential systems, in which it is difficult to remove a president through impeachment, the system is more fragile when there are political crises and the leaders cannot be removed until the next election.

Corruption and impunity interact with each other in politics; often one step forward results in two steps back. Electoral corruption, including rigged elections, occurs across Latin America. Recent, extensive protests about the electoral integrity of the 2012 presidential election in Mexico are well known. It is concerning that problems with elections continue to occur throughout Latin America. The 2018 snap elections in Venezuela and the 2019 elections in Bolivia were not viewed as legitimate by election observers. Allegations of fraud were also associated with the elections in Honduras in 2017, Paraguay in 2018, and Panama in 2019.

Corruption and severe inequality demonstrate the weakness of many countries in Latin America. One example of this is the increased role of the military in politics. While citizens perceive other government institutions as weak and ineffectual, the increased presence of the military in political situations portrays them as strong, protective, and popular. Opinion polls in Latin America indicate significantly higher approval ratings for the military than for the police or even the justice system. Unfortunately, citizens are more comfortable with the military than the political institutions, which they see as corrupt and present only to serve and protect the politicians (Isacson 2020d).

Reforms are hindered by the legacy of Latin America's corruption and violence. Latin America's historical violence changed the demographics of areas, reducing the likelihood of improving conditions. As people migrate away from an area to escape the violence, others who are attracted to the opportunities in the area and tend to support, and benefit from, existing local governments move in, thus minimizing the opportunities for change. This allows local political elites to maintain power with less opposition and violence. Even those who remain tend to support the local political elites who instigated the violence. Because those in the area support the local government, the area will appear less violent, and the federal government will not see a need to intervene to force change (Isacson 2020d). Without change, impunity for crime, violence, and corruption will continue, and citizens, particularly minorities, will continue to suffer.

Another historical legacy of migration and internal displacement will likely impact Latin America for years to come. Colombia is second only to Syria in the number of displaced persons (Isacson 2020d). Until Covid-19, record numbers of people were migrating out of Venezuela and the countries of the Northern Triangle (Honduras, Guatemala, and El Salvador). Migration continued during Covid-19 restrictions, and increased with the lifting of those restrictions. Governments are attempting to help those migrating, including Colombia offering a way for undocumented Venezuelan migrants to become citizens (National Public Radio 2021). Additionally, some Latin American countries are attempting to work with the sending countries to resolve underlying issues. Reducing migration depends on both the willingness and the ability of sending governments to make significant changes and of other governments to fund those changes.

Another demonstration of state weakness is the role of nonstate actors in security and provision of public services. Historical violence altered Latin American lives, culture, and environment, most notably for minorities and the Indigenous. Indigenous regions throughout Latin America were, and continue to be, taken over by armed resistance and criminal groups who perpetrate violence against the Indigenous people, occupy and harm their land and environment, deny them self-determination (Isacson 2020c), and force their migration. Landmines continue to destroy lives and property.

The legacy of civil war involves the reformation and remilitarization of former rebels, and new recruiting efforts that even target children. Many of the remilitarized were mid- and high-level participants in illicit activities and have more to gain from continuing those activities than demobilizing. Remilitarized groups are also responsible for violence among themselves, against those who demobilized, and against those they perceive to be socially unacceptable, such as addicts and prostitutes (WOLA 2020b). Until and unless governments can provide effective options to, for example, former FARC members, continued remilitarization will fuel crime and conflict, particularly in Colombia and Venezuela.

In Latin America, crime and economics are entwined. Many Latin Americans depend on criminal activities to survive, and governments depend on the economy, support, and public services provided by criminal organizations. To facilitate their activities, organized crime provides infrastructure that the government is unable or unwilling to provide. For example, organized crime in Colombia and Brazil has paved roads. In Brazil, organized crime controls the *favelas* because the government is not meeting the citizens' needs (Isacson 2020b). In Venezuela, government officials collaborate with organized crime, particularly in illegal extraction of resources, to the benefit of the national economy (Smilde and Ramsey 2020).

Latin American poverty levels vary greatly. In some countries, like Argentina, Chile, and Costa Rica, only about 5 percent of the population lives in extreme poverty, and these countries may continue to grow their economies to eliminate even these poverty levels. A middle group of countries, such as Colombia, Peru, the Dominican Republic, El Salvador, Guatemala, and Ecuador, have absolute poverty levels of from 5 to 35 percent of the population, but these might make some headway in reducing those levels. Finally, countries including Mexico, Nicaragua, and Cuba have little prospect of reducing levels of absolute poverty of about half the population. A particular challenge is Venezuela, where extreme poverty impacts 79 percent of households and the overall poverty rate is 96 percent (Muñoz-Pogossian 2021).

Internally, there is heavy dependence on informal and illegal economies to survive. Latin America is plagued with both inequality of opportunity and inequality of outcome, making illegal activities an important source of primary or supplemental income. For the poor Indigenous, coca production provides basic income that allows them to survive (Isacson 2020c). However, the policies of forced eradication of coca to decrease illegal drug production and violence increase poverty (Isacson, Youngers, and Castro 2020).

Despite helping those with limited economic opportunities, drug trafficking of course has a negative effect on the population, including the Indigenous, because traffickers must operate on the fringes of law. Participating in the drug economy puts people at risk of police action as well as exposing them to the violence of remilitarized guerrillas, organized crime, and gangs (Isacson, Youngers, and Castro 2020). Additionally, drug trafficking in Indigenous areas increases the cost of living, which results in a never-ending struggle against poverty (Cultural Survival 2020).

Impunity is as prevalent for criminal groups as it is for politicians, and some government institutions, such as the judiciary, military, and police, are protecting the criminal groups (Isacson 2020b). The national police and security forces are little help, either because they do not have an effective presence in the area, because they are collaborating with the criminal groups, or because their actions are similar to the criminals' and thus they are a threat to citizens.

Unfortunately, reversing these trends will require difficult and extensive changes to the administration of justice throughout Latin America. The widespread impunity and corruption disincentivizes political elites to enact the needed reforms. Restoring the legitimacy and public perception of the police and judicial systems requires significant institutional and cultural changes as well as a change in political will (Isacson 2020b). Because impunity benefits the political and local elites, and because those who fight to end impunity are punished, elected officials benefit from the status quo. Voter demand for change and intolerance of impunity must increase the cost of refusing to reform the system.

Inequalities in Latin America have been further complicated by Covid-19. Because poor, Indigenous, and minorities such as Afro-Colombians and Afro-Brazilians work in the informal economy, the quarantine forced them to find alternative means to survive. Organized crime continued to operate during quarantine, providing little relief from the violence and offering illegal opportunities for those without work to survive (Isacson 2020b).

The Covid Pandemic

The full impact of Covid-19 on the economies of Latin America has yet to be seen. Argentina defaulted on its international debt for the ninth time in 2020 and faces significant inflation (Dube and Pérez 2020), although its credit rating was raised after the $65 billion debt was restructured (Squires 2020). The Center for Strategic and International Studies estimated that the Latin American economy would shrink 8.1 percent in 2020 and projected only 3.6 percent growth in 2021 (Cottani 2020). Standard and Poor is estimating that Latin American countries will lose between 6 and 7 percent of GDP (Oliveros-Rosen 2020). Meanwhile, inflation across the region is increasing, and was at 5.9 percent in June 2020 (Focus Economics 2020). Sales and employment across Latin America fell dramatically between April and July 2020, in some cases to below 40 percent (Werner 2020). Although fall 2020 saw some improvement, there are concerns that inflation, unemployment, and lack of government subsidies will negatively impact economic recovery (*Xinhuanet* 2020).

Consequently, Latin America is facing significant economic challenges internally, regionally, and internationally. How the countries recover from the Covid-related downturn will depend on their policies and the ability of the international system, particularly China and the United States, to recover. Latin America must also address the income inequality that is facilitating illegal activities. The full impact on Latin America of Covid-19 and associated government actions has yet to be felt. In May 2020, 40 percent of the daily deaths worldwide were in Latin America, and the disease remained on the rise in many of these countries (Nugent 2020). The year 2021 is seeing an increase in cases and a disparity in the distribution of vaccines (Pozzebon 2021). Unfortunately, the disease exacerbates and is exacerbated by the underlying problems throughout Latin America.

Latin American countries responded to Covid-19 in a variety of ways with a variety of results. Peru, despite being one of the earliest in the world to implement strict bans (Nugent 2020), has the largest number of cases per capita in Latin America (UNDP Peru 2020) and experienced a resurgence in April 2021 driven by new variants, resulting in its deadliest week yet (Brook 2021). At that time, Peru had the highest percentage of deaths from all causes in the region that exceeded the number expected during a noncrisis period, the best measure of Covid's real impact because of high variation in testing rates across countries (Giattino et al. 2021). Chile implemented strict lockdown and testing after seeing its first cases, but by July 2020 had the highest per capita infection rate of major countries worldwide (Beaubien 2020b). El Salvador implemented a national emergency and increased the capacity of hospitals to respond to Covid before confirmation of the first case (UNDP El Salvador 2020) and enforced tough measures (Renteria 2020b), but had to postpone reopening plans due to the continued increase in the number of cases (Renteria 2020b). Paraguay, which also imposed a strict lockdown, had experienced only 4,827 deaths as of April 2021. Brazil and Mexico, both of which resisted and continue to resist lockdowns, also experienced a high number of cases (Nugent 2020). The consistent factors are underfunded healthcare systems and the large percentage of people working in the informal economy (Nugent 2020). Although several countries took measures to improve, and even build, medical equipment facilities as a response to the outbreak, many of the healthcare systems throughout the region are collapsing or are near collapse (UNDP 2020b). For example, Peru's health system is regarded as the worst in Latin America and has collapsed under the weight of the outbreak (UNDP Peru 2020). In Chile, the spread of the infection despite lockdown is blamed in part on the inadequate public healthcare on which the poor depend, although the wealthy can afford private, higher-quality healthcare (Beaubien 2020b). In Ecuador, streets were littered with corpses when the health system broke down (Dube and de Córdoba 2020).

As mentioned, the informal, and illegal, economies continued to operate despite quarantines and lockdowns. Rates of people working in the informal economy vary in Latin America from 25 to 70 percent of the work force. In Colombia, 50 percent of the informal work force is composed of Venezuelan refugees (Dowling 2020), making them doubly vulnerable. Informal workers frequently lack access to healthcare and economic protections, and therefore are forced to risk exposure to provide for their families (UNDP 2020b). For example, one of the reasons for the spread of the virus in Chile is that people working in the informal sector, such as gardeners and housekeepers, were exposed to the wealthy, who brought the virus into the country (Beaubien 2020b). Not only are those in the informal economy being forced to violate the protective measures implemented by governments, but they are also being negatively impacted by those same protective measures. Although there are economic backstops in place for workers in the formal sector, this is not the case for informal sector workers. Some governments in Latin America, such as those of Colombia, Brazil, and El Salvador, are taking measures to protect informal workers, but others, such as Guatemala and Honduras, are not (UNDP 2020b).

Both the underfunded, and disparate, healthcare systems and the population working in the informal sector illustrate how the high inequality pervasive throughout Latin America affects, and is affected by, Covid-19. However, corruption is also a significant issue with Covid. Corruption is prevalent in the misreporting of Covid cases. For example, the number of actual deaths as a result of Covid in Ecuador may be as much as fifteen times higher than reported (León and Kurmanaev 2020). Measures enacted by the various governments throughout Latin America were implemented quickly with little oversight, thus providing opportunities for corruption. As this outbreak continues to unfold, the full extent of corruption will become more apparent.

One particular concern is the effect of Covid-19 policies on migrants, particularly those trying to escape Venezuela and the Northern Triangle. At the Mexican-US border, where asylum seekers from the Northern Triangle were awaiting their fate, conditions put migrants, refugees, and asylum seekers at increased risk of contracting Covid. Because of the negative impact of the virus on the Colombian economy, approximately 70,000 of those who fled from Venezuela returned (Dowling 2020) when they lost their Colombian jobs, only to be forced into quarantine in crowded facilities with poor sanitation (Grattan 2020). Additionally, refugees and asylum seekers face increased violence in their travels since police are diverted to enforcing lockdowns (Dowling 2020). As lockdowns ease, Venezuelans are once again feeding into Colombia despite continued closure of official routes, people being unwilling to help due to fear of contagion, and increasing control of the informal routes by armed groups (Palau and Rueda 2020).

The lines between the topics discussed here are blurred and the prospect for the future of Latin America lies at the intersection of these topics. Latin American countries are not dealing with individual problems; they are dealing with a combination of problems that feed one another. Nowhere is this better seen than with the impact of Covid-19. Although dealing with Covid puts pressure on the healthcare system, people, economies, and government, several Latin American countries started 2020 with significant problems that worsened as a result of the pandemic. Paraguay was in the middle of a dengue outbreak when Covid hit, which allowed it to react quickly, but compounded the stress on the healthcare system and increased Covid risks for individuals (UNDP Paraguay 2020). Argentina, Costa Rica, and Ecuador were already in the middle of economic crises. Venezuela is dealing with social, economic, political, and migration crises at the same time as the virus.

Environmental Disruption

Latin America's people, economies, and future health are heavily influenced, both positively and negatively, by its geography. The area experiences frequent earthquakes and hurricanes, while climate change and the destruction of the Amazon rainforest are causing droughts and flooding. These natural disasters impact the most vulnerable, and, with high economic inequality, and inequality of public services including healthcare, a large portion of Latin America's population are at risk.

Latin America also has an abundance of natural resources including oil, gold, lithium, salt flats, and the Amazon rainforest. Legal and illegal extraction of these resources, which increases during financial crises, supports Latin America's economy while destroying the environment. Latin American property laws facilitate resource extraction and the resulting damage to the environment. In many Latin American countries, personal or Indigenous ownership applies only to the top layer of land; the governments retain ownership of the subsoil (Pressly 2019) and all rights to any resources therein. Furthermore, many Latin Americans lack formal ownership of the property on which they live, which limits access to credit, insurance, and other benefits that require proof of property ownership. This is a significant issue when natural disasters occur, because people cannot prove that they own the property, so they cannot obtain financial help to recover.

Many borders between Latin American countries are remote, unguarded, and porous. Communities living on one side of a border interact with those on the other side daily and may have dual citizenship. Many communities depend on the rivers that mark borders for transportation, because they have few if any roads (Isacson 2020c). Porous borders also facilitate migration, both humanitarian and illegal, and transportation of illegal goods, benefiting local elites, organized crime, and even countries (Smilde and Ramsey 2020). As Latin American governments, frequently upon the insistence or with the support of the United States, try to stop illegal trafficking, they threaten the security, culture, life, and livelihoods of the traditional border communities.

The destruction of the Amazon due to fires was at a ten-year high in August 2020, and the fires are spreading beyond the deforested areas and destroying virgin forest, indicating that the burning is uncontrolled. Additionally, the area experienced a more severe drought in 2020 than in 2019, and a more sustained fire peak than in previous years. Destruction of the rainforest decreases rainfall. Both the fires and the drought are contributing, at least in part, to the warming of the North Atlantic, as are Bolsonaro's policies allowing development in the Amazon region (Spring 2020). Consequently, 40 percent of the Amazon rainforest is nearing the tilting point of becoming a savannah rather than a rainforest, a change that will be nearly impossible to reverse (Harvey 2020). Destruction of the Amazon destroys self-isolating Indigenous cultures, and an unknown number of species of flora and fauna, and negatively impacts Earth's atmosphere.

Latin America's high urbanization facilitates the spread of disease. For example, one-third of the population of Peru lives in Lima, which had 70 percent of the Covid-19 cases in Peru (Nugent 2020). There is also a rural-urban disparity of public services. The number of wealthy people and density of population in urban centers ensure better access to all public services, including healthcare and education, than in rural populations, although this does not mean that everyone in the urban centers has access to quality public services. Conversely, urban centers are more likely to experience social unrest and protests.

It is imperative that Latin American governments find a way to protect both the rural and urban environments and prioritize environmental protection over perceived negative economic consequences. Climate change, which increases the frequency and strength of natural disasters, and the lack of formal property rights, will increase economic and social inequalities.

Racial and Ethnic Conflict

Latin America is very diverse, with various Indigenous groups and groups descendent from various African immigrants, such as Afro-Latins or, more specifically, Afro-Colombians. Minorities are among the poorest and most discriminated against, with little prospect for improvement. Both women and LGBTQ people face significant discrimination in Latin America despite efforts to improve their situation. When gender is mixed with another factor, such as being a minority or a coca grower, the discrimination is exacerbated.

Being Afro-Latin or Indigenous significantly increases the likelihood for lifelong poverty because of the lack of access to opportunities for education and employment. Afro-Latins are disproportionately victims of violence throughout Latin America. For example, Afro-Latins are 54 percent of the population of Brazil but are among the poorest, and are likely to live in a *favela* where they will fall victim to violence before their thirtieth birthday. These groups also face violence from the security forces, which prevents them from obtaining protection and justice (Isacson 2020b).

Both Indigenous and Afro-Latin groups live in rural and urban communities that lack government services, including roads, education, healthcare, and security. Therefore, these communities are also prime areas for armed groups. Government presence is usually undertaken to fight the armed groups, which brings additional violence. If the Indigenous leaders take a stand against the violence or illegal activities to protect their communities, the armed groups retaliate with violence (Casserly and Parrado 2020) or the government accuses them of hindering development (Specter 2019). Therefore, Indigenous and Afro-Latins have little trust or faith in the government (Isacson 2020d). Rather than rely on the state for security in their remote areas, the unarmed Indigenous guards provide security for the community as well as Indigenous leaders (Isacson 2020c). Despite their lack of arms, these groups provide functions similar to armed police.

Gender Issues

Throughout Latin America, LGBTQ people are more concerned about their safety than their rights. Both private individuals and the security forces kill LGBTQ people with impunity. This is worse for women and transgender women who work in the sex industry. The lack of statistics about violence against LGBTQ people facilitates impunity (Isacson 2020b). Without accurate data on this violence, there is little pressure to increase protections for the LGBTQ community.

Women who are victims of domestic violence receive little help because police may not respond to a call and because of frequent impunity for perpetrators (Isacson 2020b). Additionally, since most domestic violence occurs at night, there are few services available to help women when they need it the most. Femicide, like violence against LGBTQ people, suffers from lack of data despite increasing occurrences, particularly in Mexico. Although fewer women are killed than men, there are significant differences in the crimes that need to be recognized to solve the underlying problems. Women are more likely to be killed at home by someone they know, although that is changing (Zissis 2020).

Covid created hardships for migrant women and children, particularly those attempting to flee Venezuela. Unable to earn a living in either the formal or the informal economy during lockdowns, women turned to, or were sold into, sex work. As police focused on enforcing the lockdown, gender-based violence increased, children became rape victims, and armed groups forcibly recruited boys and girls into human trafficking. Sex workers who once had access to shelter and medical care were forced into the streets and their medical services were stopped (Dowling 2020).

There is currently an evangelical movement throughout Latin America and it is impacting the rights of women, minorities, Indigenous, and LGBTQ people. As women, minorities, and particularly LGBTQ people gain rights, evangelical movements are creating a backlash that is undermining, even reversing, the gains made. The backlash gains strength with the election of populist presidents aligned with this movement, as has occurred with Bolsonaro in Brazil and Áñez in Bolivia (Isacson 2020a, 2020b).

Because of their vulnerability, minorities face inequalities of opportunity, violence, and underlying discrimination. Improving the situation for minorities involves fighting crime, extending services to currently underserved areas, creating opportunities that effectively replace illegal income, and addressing the underlying social and systemic problems while preventing an evangelically imposed backsliding. Facilitating existing advocacy efforts by women and LGBTQ people, usually at the grassroots level, may be the most effective way to effect change.

Corruption

The problems faced daily by the Latin American countries interact with each other. Corruption weakens the legitimacy of the governments, puts the environment at risk, and facilitates impunity for crimes, which further exacerbates discrimination and inequality. Working in the informal and illegal sectors increases the likelihood of violence and decreases access to social protections, which sustains inequality. International pressure provides opportunities for governments to bow to the wishes of the powerful countries, or those willing to turn their backs on important national issues such as human rights violations and the environment. However, Latin America's history of social movements, combined with current advocacy efforts, offers hope for improvement in the future. One promising sign is that the countries of Latin America are offering protections to the most vulnerable during lockdowns (UNDP 2020b).

As of this writing, the two areas with the poorest prospects for the future are Venezuela and the countries of the Northern Triangle. The consequences of corruption and high inequality are driving high levels of migration from these countries. Improving their situation depends on the willingness of the international community to negotiate with all parties and support governments willing to reconcile and reform their countries. This will require a change in attitude and focus of the international, and particularly regional, communities. However, unless the issues are resolved in these two areas, the spillover effects, including migration, crime, and economic impacts, will continue and could escalate.

It is useful to consider two ways to statistically analyze the Latin American region. One is the Robinson Country Intelligence Index, a holistic, customizable data visualization tool that incorporates 436 variables across 102 subdimensions for 199 countries and thirteen years of data (see http://www.rcii.gsu.edu). The governance subdimension, which is derived from data from the World Bank's Worldwide Governance Indicators, measures the openness, effectiveness, legitimacy, and responsiveness of a state's governing institutions (see Brown, Cavusgil, and Lord 2015). In this index, countries are ranked and scored according to their performance in each variable, with a low rank (1) and a high score (1,000) denoting the best performance. The governance subdimension is further divided into variables: voice and accountability; political stability and absence of violence; government effectiveness; regulatory quality; rule of law; and control of corruption.

Voice and accountability captures perceptions of the extent to which a country's citizens are able to participate in selecting their government, as well as freedom of expression, association, and the press. Political stability and absence of violence measures the perceptions of the likelihood that the government will be destabilized or overthrown by unconstitutional or violent means, including domestic violence and terrorism. Countries that are functioning democracies, but are marred by politically motivated violence, may not score well on this indicator. Government effectiveness captures perceptions of the quality of public services, the quality of the civil service and the degree of its independence from political pressures, the quality of policy formulation and implementation, and the credibility of government commitment to such policies. Regulatory quality captures perceptions of the ability of the government to formulate and implement sound policies and regulations that permit and promote private sector development. Rule of law captures perceptions of the extent to which agents have confidence in and abide by the rules of society. This variable includes the quality of contract enforcement, the quality of police and the courts, the risk of crime and violence, and the protection of property rights (including intellectual property rights). And finally, control of corruption captures perceptions of the extent to which public power is exercised for private gain, including both petty and grand forms of corruption, as well as "capture" of the state by elites and private interests. As the data reveal, Latin American countries perform relatively well in governance indicators when compared to other developing countries in the global South.

In Table 14.1, one can see the variation within the region and worldwide rankings. All of the seven variables are measures of democracy, with lower scores indicating lower levels of democracy, and higher scores indicating higher levels of democracy. Generally speaking, and not coming as a surprise, the best scores on these various measures are recorded by Uruguay, Chile, Costa Rica, and Brazil. For example, when one examines voice and accountability, which represents the ability of the public to voice their opposition against their government and hold it accountable for its misdeeds, in countries like Venezuela, Ecuador, Cuba, Bolivia, Nicaragua, Guatemala, and Honduras the comparatively lower scores for these countries represent the harsher stance their respective governments have taken in recent times toward protesters, the media, human rights groups, and anyone who challenges the ruling status quo. A similar observation applies to political stability and absence of violence.

Looking at the data, one can also clearly distinguish between the consolidation of democracy in many of the former British colonies in the Caribbean and the former colonies of Spain, France, and Portugal throughout Latin America—for example, Haiti versus Jamaica, Grenada, and St. Lucia. Although these countries are essentially considered "developing" by most economic measures, they differ substantially in terms of their democratic progress, with Haiti scoring very low relative to the former British colonies of Jamaica, Grenada, and St. Lucia. The information included throughout this book further corroborates these findings.

Table 14.1   Governance Indicators (by score), 2019

Country	Voice and Accountability	Control of Corruption	Rule of Law	Regulatory Quality	Government Effectiveness	Absence of Violence
Argentina	66.50	53.37	37.02	33.65	49.04	43.33
Bolivia	42.36	25.96	11.06	12.50	24.52	23.33
Brazil	56.62	42.31	47.60	48.08	43.75	24.76
Chile	81.28	83.17	82.69	84.13	81.73	54.76
Colombia	55.17	48.08	38.46	66.35	55.77	15.71
Costa Rica	85.71	75.96	70.19	68.75	67.79	60.48
Ecuador	48.77	34.62	29.81	19.71	37.02	40.95
El Salvador	51.72	32.69	23.56	56.25	35.58	42.86
Guatemala	35.47	18.75	13.94	44.23	26.44	25.24
Honduras	31.03	23.08	15.39	34.13	30.29	27.14
Mexico	45.32	22.60	27.40	59.62	45.67	29.95
Nicaragua	19.21	12.50	9.62	25.00	21.63	13.33
Panama	67.00	30.77	50.48	64.90	55.29	58.10
Paraguay	49.75	22.12	31.25	46.63	33.17	47.14
Peru	57.14	36.54	33.17	71.63	49.52	42.38
Uruguay	89.66	87.98	74.52	70.19	74.52	86.19
Venezuela	10.34	4.33	0.48	0.48	4.33	9.05

Source: Kaufmann and Kraay 2019.

Table 14.2 shows Latin American countries' ranking on the UN Development Programme's Human Development Index (HDI). The HDI index combines dozens of measures of quality of life, knowledge, and standard of living. Chile has the highest ranking in human development in the region, ranking 43rd best in the world out of 189 countries. Not too far behind are Argentina (46th), Uruguay (55th), Costa Rica (62nd), Mexico (74th), and Peru (79th). Bolivia (107th), Venezuela (113th), El Salvador (124th), Guatemala (127th), Nicaragua (128th), and Honduras (132nd) show the lowest ratings in Central and South America in the HDI composite ratings for 2019, as reported in the UN Development Programme's 2020 annual report.

Breaking this down into topics covered in this chapter, we can see a numerical illustration of the issues. On human inequality, the Latin American region is below the world average although well above sub-Saharan Africa. Life expectancy and health expenditures need to be considered together and put into context. Latin America is second only to the OECD states for life expectancy. It has the highest percent of GDP spent on healthcare. However, money does not always translate into a sustainable healthcare system. Latin America's unemployment rate in 2019 was second highest among regions in the world the year before Covid-19 emerged in March 2020. The intersection of these indicators is sometimes paradoxical. Guatemala has the highest inequality in the

Table 14.2   Ranking and Score on Human Development Index and Select
Indicators, 2019

	HDI Rank, 2019	Human Inequality, 2019	Life Expectancy, 2019	Health Expenditure, 2017	Income Index, 2019	Unemployment (%), 2019
Argentina	46	13.2	0.872	9.1	0.809	9.8
Bolivia	107	23.7	0.792	6.4	0.672	3.5
Brazil	84	24.4	0.86	9.5	0.749	12.1
Chile	43	15.9	0.926	9	0.823	7.1
Colombia	83	21.6	0.881	7.2	0.749	9.7
Costa Rica	62	17.5	0.927	7.3	0.788	11.9
Ecuador	86	18.4	0.877	8.3	0.711	4
El Salvador	124	21.1	0.82	7.2	0.669	4.1
Guatemala	127	26.9	0.835	5.8	0.671	2.5
Honduras	132	24.8	0.85	7.9	0.6	5.4
Mexico	74	20.8	0.847	5.5	0.794	3.4
Nicaragua	128	23.2	0.838	8.6	0.599	6.8
Panama	57	20.1	0.9	7.3	0.859	3.9
Paraguay	103	22.8	0.835	6.7	0.726	4.8
Peru	79	18.8	0.873	5	0.726	3.3
Uruguay	55	12.6	0.891	9.3	0.801	8.7
Venezuela	113	17	0.801	1.2	0.643	8.8
Very high human development		10.7	0.917	12	0.921	5.5
High human development		17.6	0.851	5.7	0.749	6
Medium human development		25.9	0.758	3.7	0.622	5.2
Low human development		31.3	0.638	4.6	0.5	5.8
Developing countries		22.3	0.789	5.4	0.704	5.8
Regions						
Arab states		24.3	0.801	4.9	0.754	10.9
East Asia and the Pacific		16.5	0.853	4.9	0.754	3.9
Europe and Central Asia		11.7	0.837	4.9	0.784	9.9
Latin America and the Caribbean		21.5	0.855	8	0.755	8.1
South Asia		25.4	0.768	4.1	0.631	5.5
Sub-Saharan Africa		30.5	0.639	5.1	0.545	6.4
Least-developed countries		28.4	0.698	4.1	0.51	4.8
Small island developing states		24.2	0.8	5.9	0.764	5.7
Organization for Economic Cooperation and Development states		11.8	0.929		0.923	5.5
World		20.2	0.812		0.773	5.6

Sources: Calculated from data in UNDP 2020a; UNDESA 2019a; UNESCO Institute for Statistics 2020; United Nations Statistics Division 2020b; World Bank 2020b; Barro and Lee 2018; International Monetary Fund 2020; ILO 2020.

region, but the lowest unemployment rate. Argentina and Colombia rank best in the region on the HDI, yet have the third and fourth highest unemployment rates. In other words, Latin American countries are often in the middle on average, but have varying weak links and strengths. Addressing these issues will require building on strengths, ensuring that money is spent effectively, and creatively addressing weaknesses.

Largest Challenges

The top three challenges facing Latin America today are the same as the top issues for voters within each of the countries: crime, inequality, and migration. Latin America has the highest murder and inequality rates in the world, both of which are driving migration.

Although addressing the root causes of both crime and inequality is the obvious solution to solving all three problems, this is not easily accomplished. Aid given directly to the countries may not benefit those most in need, due to corruption. International efforts to end impunity for corruption threaten the political elites, and therefore are thwarted by national governments. Providing aid to help eradicate coca plants to stop illegal drugs results in increased violence and poverty as well as harm to the Indigenous communities and the environment. The illegal activities supporting armed groups also provide necessary income for both ordinary citizens and some governments (Isacson 2020c). Armed groups provide public services that the government is unable, or unwilling, to provide (Isacson 2020b).

In other words, a common problem underlying crime, inequality, and migration is what amounts to a crisis of governance. Widespread corruption at the highest levels of government delegitimizes its rule, leading to frequent calls for the impeachment or resignation of the president. The inability of governments to provide services leads to inequality, protests, armed resistance, destruction of Indigenous areas, and migration. Efforts to increase development result in destruction of the environment and criminal control of extractive industries, which in turn leads to migration and inequality.

Latin America can rely on a strong history for human protections. In the 1980s, Latin Americans used international human rights norms to fight dictatorships. Latin America led the world in creating a regional convention against corruption, establishing a treaty to protect the human rights of older persons, and incorporating Indigenous rights into national constitutions. This belief in progressive human rights, and willingness to demand their protection by governments, will help Latin America move past current problems into a better future.

However, the ability of Latin American governments to reduce inequality and poverty depends on the effectiveness of their economies. The neoliberal reforms of the 1990s ended the hyperinflation and generally high unemployment of the dictatorships of the 1980s, but also increased inequality, with uneven effects on macroeconomic growth in many Latin American countries. The paradox of increasing middle-class size and increased poverty and homelessness remains a common feature of the continent. Some countries, like Argentina, face new economic crises seemingly every decade. Covid-19's impact on the economies of Latin America remains unknown, although indications are that recovery will be slow.

So, what are the prospects for Latin America in the next five or even ten years? It depends. Latin America's economic recovery from Covid will not be easy and will depend on the recovery of its international partners. The protection of Latin America's environment will depend on the willingness of national governments to prioritize environment over economics, crime, and corruption, which will be difficult because of the region's economic status. Environmental protection will also depend on the willingness of countries and transnational corporations to listen to the Indigenous groups and respect their opinions. Increased security will depend on the political will and ability of Latin American governments to end impunity and rebuild the legitimacy of and confidence in the justice system, and end inequality and discrimination.

Acronyms

ALBA	Bolivarian Alliance for the Americas
APEC	Asia-Pacific Economic Cooperation
CAN	Andean Community of Nations
CARICOM	Caribbean Community
CELAC	Community of Latin American and Caribbean States
CELAM	Latin American Episcopal Conference
CIA	Central Intelligence Agency (United States)
CVRD	Companhía do Vale do Río Doce (Brazil)
ECLAC	Economic Commission for Latin America and the Caribbean (United Nations)
ELN	National Liberation Army (Colombia)
EZLN	Zapatista National Liberation Army (Mexico)
FARC	Revolutionary Armed Forces of Colombia
FARC-EP	Revolutionary Armed Forces of Colombia–People's Army
FDI	foreign direct investment
FMLN	Farabundo Martí National Liberation Front (El Salvador)
FSLN	Sandinista National Liberation Front (Nicaragua)
FTA	free trade agreement
FTAA	Free Trade Area of the Americas
GATT	General Agreement on Tariffs and Trade

GDP	gross domestic product
GMO	genetically modified organism
GNI	gross national income
HDI	Human Development Index
IACHR	Inter-American Court of Human Rights
IAEA	International Atomic Energy Agency
ICC	International Criminal Court
ILO	International Labour Organization
IMF	International Monetary Fund
Mercosur	Southern Common Market
MNC	multinational corporation
NAFTA	North American Free Trade Agreement
NGO	nongovernmental organization
OAS	Organization of American States
OECD	Organization for Economic Cooperation and Development
OPEC	Organization of Petroleum Exporting Countries
PAHO	Pan American Health Organization
PAN	National Action Party (Mexico)
PDVSA	Petróleos de Venezuela Sociedad Anónima
PEMEX	Petróleos Mexicanos
PRI	Institutional Revolutionary Party (Mexico)
SICA	Central American Integration System
UNASUR	Union of South American Nations
UNDP	United Nations Development Programme
UNESCO	United Nations Educational, Scientific, and Cultural Organization
UNHCR	United Nations High Commissioner for Refugees
USAID	US Agency for International Development
USMCA	United States–Mexico–Canada Agreement
WHO	World Health Organization
WTO	World Trade Organization

Basic Political Data

This Basic Political Data section was compiled by Thomas J. D'Agostino. Data for capital city, independence date, population, current leadership, and elections categories were obtained from the CIA *World Factbook* (available at https://www.cia.gov/library/publications /the-world-factbook), which was current as of October 2021. The Human Development Index (HDI) scores cited below were drawn from the Human Development Reports (UNDP 2020a). The HDI ratings range from 0.0 (lowest) to 1.0 (highest) as a representation of the general state of affairs for each nation's citizenry. More specifically, the HDI reflects a combination of average literacy, life expectancy, and per capita income levels.

Antigua and Barbuda
Capital City   Saint John's
Date of Independence from Great Britain   November 1, 1981
Population   99,175
HDI Score   0.778
Current Leader   Prime Minister Gaston Browne (since June 2014)
Type of Government   Parliamentary democracy
Elections   Last held in March 2018. Next elections by March 2023.

Argentina
Capital City   Buenos Aires
Date of Independence from Spain   July 9, 1816
Population   45,864,941
HDI Score   0.845

Current Leader   President Alberto Angel Fernandez
(since December 2019)
Type of Government   Republic
Elections   Last held in October 2019. Next elections in October 2023.

Bahamas, The
Capital City   Nassau
Independence from Great Britain   July 10, 1973
Population   352,655
HDI Score   0.814
Current Leader   Prime Minister Philip Davis (since September 2021)
Type of Government   Parliamentary democracy
Elections   Last held in May 2017. Next elections by May 2022.

Barbados
Capital City   Bridgetown
Date of Independence from Great Britain   November 30, 1966
Population   301,865
HDI Score   0.814
Current Leader   Prime Minister Mia Mottley (since May 2018)
Type of Government   Parliamentary democracy
Elections   Last held in June 2018. Next elections by 2023.

Belize
Capital City   Belmopan
Date of Independence from Great Britain   September 21, 1981
Population   405,633
HDI Score   0.716
Current Leader   Prime Minister Juan Antonio Briceno
(since February 2020)
Type of Government   Parliamentary democracy
Elections   Last held in February November 2020.
Next elections by November 2025.

Bolivia
Capital City   La Paz
Date of Independence from Spain   August 6, 1825
Population   11,758,869
HDI Score   0.718
Current Leader   President Luis Alberto Arce Catacora
(since November 2020)
Type of Government   Presidential Republic
Elections   Last held in October 2020. Next elections in October 2025.

Brazil
Capital City   Brasília
Date of Independence from Portugal   September 7, 1822
Population   213,445,417
HDI Score   0.765
Current Leader   President Jair Bolsonaro (since January 2019)
Type of Government   Federal presidential republic
Elections   Last held in October 2018. Next elections in October 2022.

Chile
Capital City   Santiago
Date of Independence from Spain   September 18, 1810
Population   18,307,925
HDI Score   0.851
Current Leader   President Sebastián Piñera Echenique
   (since March 2018)
Type of Government   Presidential republic
Elections   Last held in December 2017. Next elections in
   November/December 2021.

Colombia
Capital City   Bogotá
Date of Independence from Spain   July 20, 1810
Population   50,355,650
HDI Score   0.767
Current Leader   President Ivan Duque Marquez (since August 2018)
Type of Government   Presidential republic
Elections   Last held in May 2018. Next elections in May 2022.

Costa Rica
Capital City   San José
Date of Independence from Spain   September 15, 1821
Population   5,151,140
HDI Score   0.810
Current Leader   President Carlos Alvarado Quesada (since May 2018)
Type of Government   Republic
Elections   Last held in February 2018. Next elections in February 2022.

Cuba
Capital City   Havana
Date of Independence from Spain   December 10, 1898
Date of Independence from United States   May 20, 1902
Population   11,032,343

HDI Score   0.783
Current Leader   President Miguel Diaz-Canel (since October 2019)
Type of Government   Communist state
Elections   Last held in February 2019. Next elections in February 2024.

Dominica

Capital City   Roseau
Date of Independence from Great Britain   November 3, 1978
Population   74,584
HDI Score   0.742
Current Leader   Prime Minister Roosevelt Skerrit (since January 2004)
Type of Government   Parliamentary republic
Elections   Last held in December 2019. Next elections by October 2023.

Dominican Republic

Capital City   Santo Domingo
Date of Independence from Haiti   February 27, 1844
Population   10,597,348
HDI Score   0.756
Current Leader   President Luis Rodolfo Abinader Corona
  (since August 2020)
Type of Government   Presidential republic
Elections   Last held in July 2020. Next elections in May 2024.

Ecuador

Capital City   Quito
Date of Independence from Spain   May 24, 1822
Population   17,093,159
HDI Score   0.759
Current Leader   President Guillermo Lasso Mendoza (since May 2021)
Type of Government   Presidential republic
Elections   Last held in April 2021. Next elections in February 2025.

El Salvador

Capital City   San Salvador
Date of Independence from Spain   September 15, 1821
Population   6,528,135
HDI Score   0.673
Current Leader   President Nayib Armando Bukele Ortez
  (since June 2019)
Type of Government   Presidential republic
Elections   Last held in February 2019. Next elections in February
  2019.

Grenada
Capital City   Saint George's
Date of Independence from Great Britain   February 7, 1974
Population   113,570
HDI Score   0.779
Current Leader   Prime Minister Keith Mitchell (since February 2013)
Type of Government   Parliamentary democracy
Elections   Last held in April 2018. Next elections by 2023.

Guatemala
Capital City   Guatemala City
Date of Independence from Spain   September 15, 1821
Population   17,422,821
HDI Score   0.663
Current Leader   President Alejandro Giammattei (since January 2020)
Type of Government   Presidential republic
Elections   Last held in August 2019. Next elections in June 2023.

Guyana
Capital City   Georgetown
Date of Independence from Great Britain   May 26, 1966
Population   787,971
HDI Score   0.682
Current Leader   President Mohammed Irfaan Ali (since August 2020)
Type of Government   Parliamentary republic
Elections   Last held in March 2020. Next elections in March 2025.

Haiti
Capital City   Port-au-Prince
Date of Independence from France   January 1, 1804
Population   11,198,240
HDI Score   0.510
Current Leader   Prime Minister Ariel Henry (since July 2021)
Type of Government   Semi-presidential republic
Elections   Last held in November 2016. Next elections in 2022.

Honduras
Capital City   Tegucigalpa
Date of Independence from Spain   September 15, 1821
Population   9,346,277
HDI Score   0.634
Current Leader   President Juan Orlando Hernández Alvarado
   (since January 2014)

Type of Government   Presidential republic
Elections   Last held in November 2021. Next elections in
   November 2025.

Jamaica
Capital City   Kingston
Date of Independence from Great Britain   August 6, 1962
Population   2,816,602
HDI Score   0.734
Current Leader   Prime Minister Andrew Holness (since March 2016)
Type of Government   Parliamentary democracy
Elections   Last held in September 2020. Next elections by
   September 2025.

Mexico
Capital City   Mexico City (Federal District)
Date of Independence from Spain   September 16, 1810
Population   130,207,372
HDI Score   0.779
Current Leader   President Andres Manuel Lopez Obrador
   (since December 2018)
Type of Government   Federal presidential republic
Elections   Last held in July 2018. Next elections in July 2024.

Nicaragua
Capital City   Managua
Date of Independence from Spain   September 15, 1821
Population   6,243,931
HDI Score   0.660
Current Leader   President Jose Daniel Ortega (since January 2007)
Type of Government   Presidential republic
Elections   Last held in November 2021. Next elections in
   November 2026.

Panama
Capital City   Ciudad de Panamá
Date of Independence from Spain   November 28, 1821
Date of Independence from Colombia   November 3, 1903
Population   3,928,646
HDI Score   0.815
Current Leader   President Laurentino "Nito" Cortizo Cohen
   (since July 2019)

Type of Government   Presidential republic
Elections   Last held in May 2019. Next elections in May 2024.

Paraguay
Capital City   Asunción
Date of Independence from Spain   May 14, 1811
Population   7,272,639
HDI Score   0.728
Current Leader   President Mario Abdo Benitez (since August 2018)
Type of Government   Presidential republic
Elections   Last held in April 2018. Next elections in April 2023.

Peru
Capital City   Lima
Date of Independence from Spain   July 28, 1821
Population   32,201,224
HDI Score   0.777
Current Leader   President Jose Pedro Castillo (since July 2021)
Type of Government   Presidential republic
Elections   Last held in April 2021. Next elections in April 2026.

Saint Kitts and Nevis
Capital City   Basseterre
Date of Independence from Great Britain   September 19, 1983
Population   54,149
HDI Score   0.779
Current Leader   Prime Minister Timothy Harris (since February 2015)
Type of Government   Federal parliamentary democracy
Elections   Last held in June 2020. Next elections by January 2025.

Saint Lucia
Capital City   Castries
Date of Independence from Great Britain   February 22, 1979
Population   184,863
HDI Score   0.759
Current Leader   Prime Minister Philip J. Pierre (since July 2021)
Type of Government   Parliamentary democracy
Elections   Last held in July 2021. Next elections by 2026.

Saint Vincent and the Grenadines
Capital City   Kingstown
Date of Independence from Great Britain   October 27, 1979

Population   101,145
HDI Score   0.738
Current Leader   Prime Minister Ralph E. Gonsalves (since March 2001)
Type of Government   Parliamentary democracy
Elections   Last held in November 2020. Next elections by 2025.

Suriname
Capital City   Paramaribo
Date of Independence from the Netherlands   November 25, 1975
Population   614,749
HDI Score   0.738
Current Leader   President Chandrikapersad Santokhi (since July 2020)
Type of Government   Presidential republic
Elections   Last held in July 2020. Next elections in May 2025.

Trinidad and Tobago
Capital City   Port-of-Spain
Date of Independence from Great Britain   August 31, 1962
Population   1,221,047
HDI Score   0.796
Current Leader   Prime Minister Paula-Mae Weekes (since March 2018)
Type of Government   Parliamentary republic
Elections   Last held in January 2018. Next elections by February 2023.

Uruguay
Capital City   Montevideo
Date of Independence from Brazil   August 25, 1825
Population   3,398,239
HDI Score   0.817
Current Leader   President Luis Alberto Lacalle Pou (since March 2020)
Type of Government   Presidential republic
Elections   Last held in October 2019. Next elections in October 2024.

Venezuela
Capital City   Caracas
Date of Independence from Spain   July 5, 1811
Population   29,069,153
HDI Score   0.711
Current Leader   President Nicolás Maduro Moros (since April 2013)
Type of Government   Federal presidential republic
Elections   Last held in May 2018. Next elections in 2024.

List of Nonindependent Territories

The list of nonindependent territories is based, with minor adjustments, on the Nonindependent Territories list published in the second edition of *Understanding the Contemporary Caribbean* (Lynne Rienner, 2009). Although the Falkland (Malvinas) Islands, as well as the South Georgia and South Sandwich Islands under British control, are technically in the South Atlantic Ocean, they were included for geopolitical reasons. First, they are located on the eastern edge of the Scotia Sea, which is a maritime extension of the South American continent. Second, these territories' political past and present are very much a part of colonial history in South America—with particular reference to the Falkland Islands War between Great Britain and Argentina.

South America
French Guiana   Overseas Department of France (1946)
Falkland Islands   Under British administration since 1908. Briefly occupied by Argentina in 1982. Currently listed as being administered by Great Britain while claimed by Argentina.
South Georgia and the South Sandwich Islands   Under British administration since 1908. Briefly occupied by Argentina in 1982. Currently listed as being administered by Great Britain while claimed by Argentina.

Central America and the Caribbean
Anguilla   British Overseas Territory (1980)
Aruba   Member of the Kingdom of the Netherlands (1986)

Bonaire   Special Municipality of the Netherlands (2010)
British Virgin Islands   British Overseas Territory (1967)
Cayman Islands   British Overseas Territory (1962)
Curaçao   Member of the Kingdom of the Netherlands (2010)
Guadeloupe   Overseas Department of France (1946)
Martinique   Overseas Department of France (1946)
Montserrat   British Overseas Territory (1966)
Puerto Rico   Commonwealth ("free associated state") associated with
   the United States (1952)
Saba   Special Municipality of the Netherlands (2010)
St. Barthélemy   Overseas Collectivity of France (2007)
St. Eustatius   Special Municipality of the Netherlands (2010)
St. Maarten   Member of the Kingdom of the Netherlands (2010)
St. Martin   Overseas Collectivity of France (2007)
Turks and Caicos   British Overseas Territory (1962)
US Virgin Islands   US territory with local self-government (1968)

References

Abadinsky, Howard. 2010. *Organized Crime.* Belmont, CA: Wadsworth.

Agosín, Marjorie. 1993. "Introduction." In *Surviving Beyond Fear,* Marjorie Agosín, ed. New York: White Pines, 15–28.

Aguirre Azócar, Daniel, and Matthias Erlandsen. 2018. "Digital Public Diplomacy in Latin America: Challenges and Opportunities." *Revista Mexicana de Política Exterior* 113 (May–August): 119–139.

———. 2001. *Handbook of Research on the International Relations of Latin America and the Caribbean.* Boulder: Westview.

Ahmed, Azam. 2019. "Where the Police Wear Masks, and the Bodies Pile Up Fast." *New York Times,* December 21. https://www.nytimes.com/2019/12/20/world/americas/brazil-police-shootings-murder.html.

Alásia de Heredia, Beatriz Maria. 1979. *A Morada da Vida: Trabalho Familiar de Pequenos Productores no Nordeste do Brasil.* Rio de Janeiro: Editora Paz e Terra.

Alatorre, José Eduardo, Álvaro Calderón, Wilson Peres, Miguel Pérez Ludeña, and Carlos Razo. 2009. *Foreign Direct Investment in Latin America and the Caribbean.* Santiago: United Nations Economic Commission on Latin America and the Caribbean. http://www.eclac.org.

Aleixo, Leticia, and Daniel Cerqueira. 2020. "Brumadinho Disaster, Year 1: Corporate Impunity and European Justice." https://tinyurl.com/ydytdsvh.

Allen, William R. 1987. "Mercantilism." In *The New Palgrave: A Dictionary of Economics,* vol. 3, John Eatwell, Murray Milgate, and Peter Newman, eds. London: Macmillan, 445–449.

Alonso, Carlos J. 1990. *The Spanish American Regional Novel.* New York: Cambridge University Press.

Álvarez Herrera, Bernardo. 2008. "Revolutionary Road? Debating Venezuela's Progress." *Foreign Affairs* 87, no. 4: 158–160.

Amnesty International. 2018. *Gun Violence: Key Facts.* https://www.amnesty.org/en/what-we-do/arms-control/gun-violence/.

———. 2020. "Nicaragua: Ortega Government Appears to Be Preparing for a New Phase of Repression." September 30. https://www.amnesty.org/en/latest/news/2020/09/nicaragua-gobierno-pareciera-preparar-nueva-fase-represion.

Anderson, Benedict. 1983. *Imagined Communities: Reflections on the Origin and Spread of Nationalism*. London: Verso.

Anderson, Joan, and Martin de la Rosa. 1991. "Economic Survival Strategies of Poor Families on the Mexican Border." *Journal of Borderlands Studies* 6: 51–68.

Anderson, Jon Lee. 2020. "Letter from Bolivia: The Burnt Palace—Was Evo Morales Deposed, or Did He Flee Justice?" *New Yorker,* March 23.

Andolina, Robert. 2003. "The Sovereign and Its Shadow: Constituent Assembly and Indigenous Movement in Ecuador." *Journal of Latin American Studies* 35, no. 4: 721–750.

Andrews, George Reid. 2016. *Afro-Latin America: Black Lives, 1600–2000.* Cambridge: Harvard University Press.

Appelbaum, Nancy P., Anne S. Macpherson, and Karin Alejandra Rosemblatt, eds. 2003. *Race and Nation in Modern Latin America*. Chapel Hill: University of North Carolina Press.

Appendini, Kirsten. 2002. "'From Where Have All the Flowers Come?' Women Workers in Mexico's Nontraditional Markets." In *Shifting Burdens: Gender and Agrarian Change Under Neoliberalism,* Shahra Razavi, ed. Bloomfield, CT: Kumarian, 93–108.

Ardao, Arturo. 1980. *Génesis de la Idea y el Nombre de América Latina.* Caracas: Centro de Estudios Latinoamericanos Rómulo Gallegos.

Arias Ortiz, Elena, and Valentina Martinez. 2017. "5 Key Achievements in Education for Latin America and the Caribbean." March 16. https://blogs.iadb.org /educacion/2017/03/16/cima-5-key-achievements-in-education-for-latin-america -and-the-caribbean.

Arizpe, Lourdes. 1993. "An Overview of Women's Education in Latin America and the Caribbean." In *The Politics of Women's Education,* Jill Conway and Susan Bourgue, eds. Ann Arbor: University of Michigan Press, 171–182.

———. 1997. "Women in the Informal Labor Sector." In *Women and National Development,* Wellesley Editorial Committee, ed. Chicago: University of Chicago Press, 25–37.

Armendáriz, Beatriz, and Felipe Larraín B. 2017. *The Economics of Contemporary Latin America.* Cambridge: Massachusetts Institute of Technology Press.

Arocena, Felipe, and Kirk S. Bowman. 2014. *Lessons from Latin America: Innovations in Politics, Culture, and Development.* Toronto: University of Toronto Press.

Atkins, G. Pope. 1999. *Latin America and the Caribbean in the International System.* Boulder: Westview.

Atunes, Ricardo. 2019. "The Preemptive Counterrevolution and the Rise of the Far Right in Brazil." Translated by Lisa B. Santana. *Monthly Review* 71, no. 3: 89–103.

Augenbraum, Harold, and Margarite Fernández Olmos, eds. 1997. *The Latino Reader: An American Literary Tradition from 1542 to the Present.* Boston: Houghton Mifflin.

Baddeley, Oriana, and Valerie Fraser. 1989. *Drawing the Line: Art and Cultural Identity in Latin America.* New York: Routledge, Chapman, and Hall.

Baer, Werner. 2008. *The Brazilian Economy: Growth and Development.* 6th ed. Boulder: Lynne Rienner.

Bailey, Stanley R. 2009. *Legacies of Race: Identities, Attitudes, and Politics in Brazil.* Stanford: Stanford University Press.

Bakewell, Peter. 1996. "Potosí." In *Encyclopedia of Latin American History and Culture,* vol. 4, Barbara A. Tenenbaum, ed. New York: Scribner's, 461–463.

Bakewell, Peter, and Kendall W. Brown. 1996. "Mining." In *Encyclopedia of Latin American History and Culture,* vol. 4, Barbara A. Tenenbaum, ed. New York: Scribner's, 58–64.

Bandy, Joe, and Bickham Mendez. 2003. "'A Place of Their Own': Women Organizers in the *Maquilas* of Nicaragua and Mexico." *Mobilization: An International Journal* 8, no. 2: 173–188.

Barbosa, David. 2010. "China Passes Japan as Second Largest Economy." *New York Times,* August 15.

Barrientos, Stephanie, Anna Bee, Ann Matear, and Isabel Vogel. 1999. *Women and Agribusiness: Working Miracles in the Chilean Fruit Export Sector.* London: Macmillan.

Barrig, Maruja. 1991. "The Difficult Equilibrium Between Bread and Roses: Women's Organizations and the Transition from Dictatorship to Democracy in Peru." In *The Women's Movement in Latin America,* Jane Jaquette, ed. Boulder: Westview, 114–148.

Barrios de Chungara, Domitila, with Moema Viezzer. 1978. *Let Me Speak!* New York: Monthly Review.

Bartilow, Horace A. 2019. *Drug War Pathologies: Embedded Corporatism and U.S. Drug Enforcement in the Americas.* Chapel Hill: University of North Carolina Press.

BBC News. 2018. "Costa Rica Election: Carlos Alvarado Set to Be President." April 2. https://www.bbc.com/news/world-latin-america-43614744.

———. 2020. "Brazil's Amazon: Deforestation 'Surges to a 12-year High.'" November 30. https://www.bbc.com/news/world-latin-america-55130304.

Beaubien, Jason. 2020a. "Chart: COVID-19 Is Now Leading Killer in 5 Latin American Nations." National Public Radio, December 18. https://tinyurl.com/ybrquqp7.

———. 2020b. "How Chile Ended Up with One of the Highest COVID-19 Rates." National Public Radio, July 2. https://www.npr.org/sections/goatsandsoda/2020/07/02/885207834/covid-19-exploits-cracks-in-chilean-society.

Bebbington, Anthony, and Jeffrey Bury. 2014. *Subterranean Struggles: New Dynamics of Mining, Oil, and Gas in Latin America.* Austin: University of Texas Press.

Beckerman, Paul. 2002. "Longer-Term Origins of Ecuador's 'Predollarization' Crisis." In *Crisis and Dollarization in Ecuador: Stability, Growth, and Social Equity,* Paul Beckerman and Andrés Solimano, eds. Washington, DC: World Bank, 17–80.

Beckett, Andy. 2002. *Pinochet in Piccadilly.* London: Faber and Faber.

Beechey, Veronica. 1978. "Women and Production: A Critical Analysis of Some Sociological Theories of Women's Work." In *Feminism and Materialism,* Annette Kuhn and AnnMarie Wolpe, eds. London: Routledge, 155–197.

Beezley, William, and Judith Ewell. 1987. *The Human Tradition in Latin America: The Twentieth Century.* Wilmington, DE: Scholarly Resources.

Béhague, Gerard H. 1979. *Music in Latin America: An Introduction.* Englewood Cliffs, NJ: Prentice Hall.

Beneria, Lourdes. 1992. "The Mexican Debt Crisis: Restructuring the Economy and the Household." In *Unequal Burden: Economic Crises, Persistent Poverty, and Women's Work,* Lourdes Beneria and Shelly Feldman, eds. Boulder: Westview, 83–104.

Beneria, Lourdes, and Martha Roldan. 1987. *The Crossroads of Class and Gender.* Chicago: University of Chicago Press.

Bennett, Vivienne. 1995. "Gender, Class, and Water: Women and the Politics of Water Service in Monterrey, Mexico." *Latin American Perspectives* 22, no. 2: 76–99.

Berg, Ryan C., and Thiago de Aragao. 2020. "For Brazil's Bolsonaro, U.S.-China Tensions Are a Challenge and an Opportunity." *World Politics Review*, September 24. https://www.worldpoliticsreview.com/articles/29083/for-brazil-s-bolsonaro-china-u-s-rivalry-is-a-challenge-and-an-opportunity.

Bergman, Marcelo. 2018. *More Money, More Crime*. Oxford: Oxford University Press.

Bethell, Leslie, ed. 2008. *Cambridge History of Latin America*. Vol. 11. Cambridge: Cambridge University Press.

Beverley, John, and Marc Zimmerman. 1990. *Literature and Politics in the Central American Revolutions*. Austin: University of Texas Press.

Bindi, Federiga, ed. 2010. *The Foreign Policy of the European Union: Assessing Europe's Role in the World*. Washington, DC: Brookings Institution.

Blackburn, Robin. 1997. *The Making of New World Slavery: From the Baroque to the Modern, 1492–1800*. London: Verso.

Blofield, Merike, ed. 2011. *The Great Gap: Inequality and the Politics of Redistribution in Latin America*. University Park: Pennsylvania State University Press.

Blumberg, Rae Lesser. 1991. "Income Under Female Versus Male Control." In *Gender, Family, and Economy: The Triple Overlap*, Rae Lesser Blumberg, ed. Newbury Park, CA: Sage, 97–127.

Borgen Project. 2019. "Seven Facts About Overpopulation in Brazil." August 25. https://borgenproject.org/facts-about-overpopulation-in-brazil/.

Borsdorf, Axel, and Christoph Stadel. 2015. *The Andes: A Geographical Portrait*. Basel, Cham: Springer.

Boserup, Ester. 1970. *Women's Role in Economic Development*. New York: St. Martin's.

Bourdieu, Pierre. 1986. "The Forms of Capital." In *Handbook of Theory and Research for the Sociology of Education*, John G. Richardson, ed. Westport: Greenwood, 241–258.

Bouvard, Marguerite Guzman. 1994. *Revolutionizing Motherhood: The Mothers of the Plaza de Mayo*. Wilmington, DE: Scholarly Resources.

Bouvier, Virginia M., ed. 2002. *The Globalization of U.S.–Latin American Relations: Democracy, Intervention, and Human Rights*. Westport: Praeger.

Bovarnick, Andrew. 2010. "Importance of Biodiversity and Ecosystems in Economic Growth and Equity in Latin America and the Caribbean: An Economic Valuation of Ecosystems." New York: United Nations Development Programme. https://www.undp.org/40653391-c855-4098-81e0-a45e0c9e5a45.

Boyd, Stephanie. 2020. "You've Done Nothing!" *The New Internationalist*. https://newint.org/features/2020/10/06/feature-peru-amazon-indigenous-covid.

Boyer, Richard, and Geoffrey Spurling. 1999. *Colonial Lives: Documents on Latin American History*. New York: Oxford University Press.

Brill, Mark. 2018. *Music of Latin America and the Caribbean*. 2nd ed. Oxfordshire, UK: Taylor and Francis.

Brook, Benedict. 2021. "Amid Election and COVID Crisis, Some Citizens of Peru Have to Choose Between Voting and Breathing." News.com.au, April 12. https://www.news.com.au/lifestyle/health/health-problems/amid-election-and-covid-crisis-some-citizens-of-peru-have-to-choose-between-voting-and-breathing/news-story/74d3d8ff7b9bc0255a6a594c687511cd.

Brown, Christopher L., S. Tamir Cavusgil, and A. Wayne Lord. 2015. "Country-Risk Measurement and Analysis: A New Conceptualization and Managerial Tool." *International Business Review* 24: 246–265.

Brown, David. 2003. *Santeria Enthroned: Art, Ritual, and Innovation in an Afro-Cuban Religion*. Chicago: University of Chicago Press.

Brown, Jonathan C. 2004. *Latin America: A Social History of the Colonial Period.* 2nd ed. Orlando, FL: Harcourt.

———. 2011. *A Brief History of Argentina.* New York: Facts on File.

Brown, Kendall W. 1996a. "Peru: Conquest Through Independence." In *Encyclopedia of Latin American History and Culture,* vol. 4, Barbara A. Tenenbaum, ed. New York: Scribner's, 356–364.

———. 1996b. "Quinto Real." In *Encyclopedia of Latin American History and Culture,* vol. 4, Barbara A. Tenenbaum, ed. New York: Scribner's, 512–513.

Brush, Stephen B. 2004. *Farmers' Bounty: Locating Crop Diversity in the Contemporary World.* New Haven: Yale University Press.

Buchanan, Michael. 2020. "Colombia's New Cocaine War." January 30. https://www.bbc.co.uk/sounds/play/p081tbxy.

Buenaventura-Posso, Elisa, and Susan E. Brown. 1980. "Forced Transition from Egalitarianism to Male Dominance: The Bari of Colombia." In *Women and Colonization: Anthropological Perspectives,* Mona Etienne and Eleanor Leacock, eds. New York: Praeger, 109–133.

Bulmer-Thomas, Victor. 1994. *The Economic History of Latin America Since Independence.* Cambridge: Cambridge University Press.

Bunson, Matthew E., ed. 2008. *Catholic Almanac 2008.* Huntington, IN: Our Sunday Visitor.

Burdick, John. 1992. "The Myth of Racial Democracy." *NACLA Report on the Americas* 25, no. 4: 40–44.

———. 2004. *Legacies of Liberation: The Progressive Catholic Church in Brazil at the Start of a New Millennium.* Burlington, VT: Ashgate.

Burkholder, Mark A., and Lyman L. Johnson. 2018. *Colonial Latin America.* 10th ed. New York: Oxford University Press.

Burns, E. Bradford. 1993. *A History of Brazil.* 3rd ed. New York: Columbia University Press.

Burton, Julianne, ed. 1986. *Cinema and Social Change in Latin America.* Austin: University of Texas Press.

Bushnell, David. 1993. *The Making of Modern Colombia: A Nation in Spite of Itself.* Berkeley: University of California Press.

Bushnell, David, and Neill Macaulay. 1994. *The Emergence of Latin America in the Nineteenth Century.* 2nd ed. New York: Oxford University Press.

Butt, Nathalie, et al. 2019. "The Supply Chain of Violence." *Nature Sustainability* 2 (August): 742–747.

Caldwell, Kia Lilly. 2017. *Health Equity in Brazil: Intersections of Gender, Race, and Policy.* Urbana: University of Illinois Press.

Cardoso, Eliana, and Ann Helwege. 1992. *Latin America's Economy: Diversity, Trends, and Conflicts.* Cambridge: Massachusetts Institute of Technology Press.

Cardoso, Fernando Henrique, and Enzo Faletto. 1979. *Dependency and Development in Latin America.* Berkeley: University of California Press.

Carey, Henry F. 2012. *Reaping What You Sow: A Comparative Examination of Torture Reform in the United States, France, Argentina, and Israel.* Santa Barbara, CA: Praeger.

———. 2019. "Urban Unrest Propels Global Wave of Protests." November 14. https://theconversation.com/urban-unrest-propels-global-wave-of-protests-126306.

———, ed. 2021. *Peacebuilding Paradigms: The Impact of Theoretical Diversity on Implementing Sustainable Peace.* New York: Cambridge University Press.

Carey, John M., and John Polga-Hecimovich. 2006. "Primary Elections and Candidate Strength in Latin America." *Journal of Politics* 68, no. 3: 530–543.

Carney, Judith, and Richard Nicholas Rosomoff. 2009. *In the Shadow of Slavery: Africa's Botanical Legacy in the Atlantic World.* Los Angeles: University of California Press.

Casey, Nicholas, and Andrea Zarate. 2017. "Mud Erased a Village in Peru, a Sign of Larger Perils in South America." *New York Times,* April 6. https://www.nytimes.com/2017/04/06/world/americas/peru-floods-mudslides-south-america.html.

Casserly, J., and A. G. Parrado. 2020. "Colombia's New Cocaine War." *BBC: The Documentary Podcast,* January. https://www.bbc.co.uk/sounds/play/p081tbxy.

CEPAL (Comisión Económica para América Latina). 2005. "Comercio Exterior: Exportaciones e Importaciones Según Destino y Origen por Principales Zonas Económicas, 1980, 1985, 1990, 1995–2002." *Cuadernos Estadísticos de la CEPAL,* no. 31 (December): 59. https://www.cepal.org/es/publicaciones/4309-comercio-exterior-exportaciones-importaciones-segun-destino-origen-principales.

———. 2019. "ECLAC: The Region Has Underestimated Inequality." November 28. Press release. https://www.cepal.org/en/pressreleases/eclac-region-has-underestimated-inequality.

———. "2020 Economic Survey of Latin America and the Caribbean." https://www.cepal.org/en/publications/type/economic-survey-latin-america-and-caribbean.

Cerrutti, Marcela, and Rodolfo Bertoncello. 2003. "Urbanization and Internal Migration Patterns in Latin America." Paper prepared for the Conference on African Migration in Comparative Perspective, Johannesburg.

Chanaday, Amaryll, ed. 1994. *Latin American Identity and Constructions of Difference.* Minneapolis: University of Minnesota Press.

Chant, Sylvia. 1991. *Women and Survival in Mexican Cities: Perspectives on Gender, Labour Markets, and Low Income Households.* Manchester: Manchester University Press.

Chant, Sylvia, with Nikki Craske. 2003. *Gender in Latin America.* New Brunswick, NJ: Rutgers University Press.

Chase, Jacquelyn, ed. 2002. *The Spaces of Neoliberalism: Land, Place, and Family in Latin America.* Bloomfield, CT: Kumarian.

Chesnutt, R. Andrew. 2003. *Competitive Spirits: Latin America's New Religious Economy.* New York: Oxford University Press.

Chiappari, Christopher L. 2007. "Culture, Power, and Identity: Negotiating Between Catholic Orthodoxy and Popular Practice." *Latin American Research Review* 42, no. 3: 282–296.

Chicoine, Luke. 2017. Homicides in Mexico and the Expiration of the U.S. Federal Assault Weapons Ban." *Journal of Economic Geography* 17, no. 4: 825–856.

Chinchilla, Norma Stoltz. 1993. "Gender and National Politics: Issues and Trends in Women's Participation in Latin American Movements." In *Researching Women in Latin America and the Caribbean,* Edna Acosta-Belén and Christine E. Bose, eds. Boulder: Westview, 37–54.

Chirot, Daniel. 1977. *Social Change in the Twentieth Century.* New York: Harcourt Brace Jovanovich.

Chishti, Muzaffar, Sarah Pierce, and Jessica Bolter. 2017. "The Obama Record on Deportations: Deporter in Chief or Not?" January 26. https://www.migrationpolicy.org/article/obama-record-deportations-deporter-chief-or-not.

Christen, Catherine, Selene Herculano, Kathryn Hochstetler, Renae Prell, Marie Price, and J. Timmons Roberts. 1998. "Latin American Environmentalism:

Comparative Views." *Studies in Comparative International Development* 33, no. 2: 58–87.

Chuchryk, Patricia. 1991. "Feminist Anti-Authoritarian Politics: The Role of Women's Organizations in the Chilean Transition to Democracy." In *The Women's Movement in Latin America,* Jane Jaquette, ed. Boulder: Westview, 149–184.

———. 1993. "Subversive Mothers: The Women's Opposition to the Military Regime in Chile." In *Surviving Beyond Fear,* Marjorie Agosín, ed. New York: White Pine, 86–97.

Cicalo, André. 2012. *Urban Encounters: Affirmative Action and Black Identities in Brazil.* New York: Palgrave Macmillan.

Clastres, Hélène. 1995. *The Land Without Evil: Tupi-Guarani Prophetism.* Urbana: University of Illinois Press.

Cleary, Edward L. 2004. "Shopping Around: Questions About Latin American Conversions." *International Bulletin of Missionary Research* 28, no. 2: 50–54.

———. 2007. *Mobilizing for Human Rights in Latin America.* Bloomfield, CT: Kumarian Press.

Cleary, Edward L., and Timothy Steigenga. 2004. *Resurgent Voices in Latin America: Indigenous Peoples, Political Mobilization, and Religious Change.* New Brunswick, NJ: Rutgers University Press.

Cleary, Edward L., and Hannah Stewart-Gambino, eds. 1992. *Conflict and Competition: The Latin American Church in a Changing Environment.* Boulder: Lynne Rienner.

———, eds. 1997. *Power, Politics, and Pentecostals in Latin America.* Boulder: Westview.

Clem, Ralph S., and Anthony P. Maingot, eds. 2011. *Venezuela's Petro-Diplomacy: Hugo Chávez's Foreign Policy.* Gainesville: University of Florida Press.

Cockroft, James. 1983. *Mexico: Class Formation, Capital Accumulation, and the State.* New York: Monthly Review.

Cockcroft, James D., Andre Gunder Frank, and Dale L. Johnson. 1972. *Dependence and Underdevelopment: Latin America's Political Economy.* New York: Doubleday.

Coe, Michael D., and Rex Koontz. 2008. *Mexico: From the Olmecs to the Aztecs.* 6th ed. New York: Thames and Hudson.

Coleman, Nancy. 2020. "Why We're Capitalizing Black." *New York Times,* July 5. https://www.nytimes.com/2020/07/05/insider/capitalized-black.html.

Collier, Simon, and William F. Sater. 2010. *A History of Chile, 1808–2002.* Cambridge: Cambridge University Press.

Collyns, Dan. 2017. "Lima's Time Bomb: How Mudslides Threaten the World's Great 'Self-Built' City." *The Guardian,* June 20. https://www.theguardian.com /cities/2017/jun/20/living-time-bomb-lima-flash-floods-peru-mudslides.

CONADEP. 1984. "Nunca Más—Informe Conadep." The National Commission on the Disappeared (CONADEP—Argentina). http://www.desaparecidos.org /nuncamas/web/investig/articulo/nuncamas/nmas0001.htm.

Consejo Nacional de Población. 2010. "Población Total de los Municipios a Mitad de Año, 2005–2030." http://www.conapo.gob.mx/work/models/CONAPO /Resource/05274c9d-157f-4dd4-9110-d0a0f864d96a/municipales.html.

Convention on Enforced Disappearances (CED). 2019. "Initial Report of Chile." United Nations Document CED/C/SR.279. April 17. https://tbinternet.ohchr.org /layouts/15/treatybodyexternal/Download.aspx?symbolno=CED%2FC%2FSR .279&Lang=en.

Corden, W. M. 1984. "Booming Sector and Dutch Disease Economics: Survey and Consolidation." *Oxford Economic Papers* 36: 359–380.

Córdova, Efrén. 1996. "The Situation of Cuban Workers During the 'Special Period in Peacetime.'" *Cuba in Transition* 6: 358–368.

Corporación Latinbarómetro. 2017. *Informe 2017.* https://www.latinobarometro.org /latNewsShowMore.jsp?evYEAR=2018&evMONTH=1&evYEAR=2018&ev MONTH=1.

Corrales, Javier, and Mario Pecheny. 2010. "The Comparative Politics of Sexuality in Latin America." In *The Politics of Sexuality in Latin America: A Reader on Lesbian, Gay, Bisexual, and Transgendered Rights,* Javier Corrales and Mario Pecheny, eds. Pittsburg: University of Pittsburg Press.

Cottani, Joaquín. 2020. "The Effects of Covid-19 on Latin America's Economy." November 18. https://www.csis.org/analysis/effects-covid-19-latin-americas -economy.

Council on Foreign Relations. 2021. "Criminal Violence in Mexico." https://www .cfr.org/global-conflict-tracker/conflict/criminal-violence-mexico.

Crandall, Russell C. 2008. *The United States and Latin America: After the Cold War.* New York: Cambridge University Press.

Cravey, Altha J. 1998. *Women and Work in Mexico's Maquiladoras.* Lanham: Rowman and Littlefield.

Crosby, Alfred W., Jr. 1972. *The Columbian Exchange: Biological and Cultural Consequences of 1492.* Westport: Greenwood.

Cull, Nicholas J. 2019. *Public Diplomacy: Foundations for Global Engagement in the Digital Age.* Medford, MA: Polity.

Cultural Survival. 2020. "Coca and Cocaine in Bolivia: Death Lies in Between." *Cultural Survival.* https://www.culturalsurvival.org/news/coca-and-cocaine -bolivia-death-lies-between.

Curtin, Philip D. 1969. *The Atlantic Slave Trade: A Census.* Madison: University of Wisconsin Press.

Cusicanqui, Silvia Rivera. 1990. "Indigenous Women and Community Resistance: History and Memory." In *Women and Change in Latin America,* Elizabeth Jelin, ed. London: Zed, 151–183.

Dahrendorf, Ralf. 1987. "Liberalism." In *The New Palgrave: A Dictionary of Economics,* vol. 3, John Eatwell, Murray Milgate, and Peter Newman, eds. London: Macmillan, 173–175.

Dammert, Lucía. 2005. "Mano Inteligente Contra la Delincuencia." *El Mercurio,* October 16.

de la Cadena, Marisol. 2000. *Indigenous Mestizos: The Politics of Race and Culture in Cuzco, Peru, 1919–1991.* Durham, NC: Duke University Press.

De La Pedraja, René. 2006–2013. *Wars of Latin America, 1899–2013.* 3 vols. Jefferson, NC: McFarland.

de los Santos, Nancy. 2002. *The Bronze Screen: One Hundred Years of the Latino Image in Hollywood.* Questar video.

de Paula, Luciana Araujo. 2015. "The 'Grey Zones' of Democracy in Brazil: The 'Militia' Phenomenon and Contemporary Security Issues in Rio de Janeiro." *Spatial Justice,* no. 8.

de Theije, Marjo, and Cecília Loreto Mariz. 2008. "Localizing and Globalizing Processes in Brazilian Catholicism: Comparing Inculturation in Liberationist and Charismatic Catholic Cultures." *Latin American Research Review* 43, no. 1: 33–54.

Dean, Warren. 1995. *With Broadax and Firebrand: The Destruction of the Brazilian Atlantic Forest.* Berkeley: University of California Press.

Deeds, Susan M., Michael C. Meyer, and William L. Sherman. 2017. *The Course of Mexican History.* 11th ed. New York: Oxford University Press.

Denevan, William. 1992. *The Native Population of the Americas in 1492.* 2nd ed. Madison: University of Wisconsin Press.

Dent, David W. 2009. *Hot Spot Latin America.* Westport: Greenwood.

Diamond, Larry Jay. 2008. *The Spirit of Democracy: The Struggle to Build Free Societies Throughout the World.* New York: Times Books and Holt.

———. 2018. "El Salvador's Rising Political Star." *The Economist,* March 10. https://www.economist.com/the-americas/2018/03/10/el-salvadors-rising -political-star.

Dickerson, Caitlin. 2020a. "Migrant Children from Other Countries Are Being Expelled into Mexico." *New York Times,* October 30. https://www.nytimes .com/2020/10/30/us/migrant-children-expulsions-mexico.html?action=click &module=Top%20Stories&pgtype=Homepage.

———. 2020b. "Parents of 545 Children Separated at the Border Cannot Be Found." *New York Times,* October 21. https://www.nytimes.com/2020/10/21/us/migrant -children-separated.html?searchResultPosition=1.

Dixon, Kwame. 2016. *Afro-Politics and Civil Society in Salvador da Bahia, Brazil.* Gainesville: University of Florida Press.

Dobbs, Michael. 2009. *One Minute to Midnight: Kenney, Khrushchev, and Castro on the Brink of Nuclear War.* New York: Vintage.

Domínguez, Jorge, with David Mares, Manuel Orozco, David Scott Palmer, Francisco Rojas Aravena, and Andrés Serbin. 2003. *Boundary Disputes in Latin America,* no. 50. Washington, DC: US Institute of Peace.

Dorfman, Ariel. 1991. *Some Write to the Future: Essays on Contemporary Latin American Fiction.* Durham, NC: Duke University Press.

———. 2018. "Chile: Now More Than Ever." *New York Review of Books,* August 16.

Dornbusch, Rudiger, and Sebastian Edwards. 1991. "The Macroeconomics of Populism." In *The Macroeconomics of Populism in Latin America,* Rudiger Dornbusch and Sebastian Edwards, eds. Chicago: University of Chicago Press, 7–13.

dos Santos, Theotonio. 1970. "The Structure of Dependence." *American Economic Review* 60, no. 2 (May): 231–236.

Dowling, Paddy. 2020. "A Dollar for Sex: Venezuela's Women Tricked and Trafficked." *The Guardian,* July 30. https://www.theguardian.com/global-development/2020 /jul/30/a-dollar-for-sex-venezuelas-women-tricked-and-trafficked.

Dratch, Howard, and Eugene Rosow, directors. 1984. *The Roots of Rhythm.* Three-part video series, narrated by Harry Belafonte. PBS.

Drogus, Carol Ann, and Hannah Stewart-Gambino. 2005. *Activist Faith: Grassroots Women in Democratic Brazil and Chile.* University Park: Pennsylvania State University Press.

Duarte, Ángela Ixkic Bastian. 2012. "From the Margins of Latin American Feminism: Indigenous and Lesbian Feminisms." *Signs* 38, no. 1 (September): 153–178.

Dube, Ryan, and José de Córdoba. 2020. "Ecuador City Beat One of World's Worst Outbreaks of Covid-19." *Wall Street Journal,* June 30. https://www.wsj .com/articles/ecuador-city-beat-one-of-worlds-worst-outbreaks-of-covid-19 -11593532974.

Dube, Ryan, and Santiago Pérez. 2020. "Argentina Defaults on Sovereign Debt amid Coronavirus Crisis." *Wall Street Journal,* May 22. https://www.wsj.com /articles/argentina-moves-closer-to-sovereign-debt-default-amid-coronavirus -crisis-11590160035.

Dunnell, Tony. 2018. "The Effects of Climate Change in Peru: Problems and Solutions." http://www.newperuvian.com/effects-of-climate-change-in-peru.

Durand, Francisco. 2018. *Odebrecht: La Empresa que Capturaba Gobiernos.* Lima: Pontifica Universidad Catholica del Peru and Oxfam.

Eatwell, John. 1987. "Import Substitution and Export-Led Growth." In *The New Palgrave: A Dictionary of Economics,* vol. 3, John Eatwell, Murray Milgate, and Peter Newman, eds. London: Macmillan, 737–738.

ECLAC (Economic Commission for Latin America and the Caribbean). 1998. *The Decade for Women in Latin America and the Caribbean: Background and Prospects.* Santiago: United Nations.

———. 2008. *Statistical Yearbook for Latin America and the Caribbean: Economic Participation Rate by Sex.* Santiago. http://websie.eclac.cl/anuario_estadistico /anuario_2008/eng/index.asp.

———. 2019. "ECLAC: The Region Has Underestimated Inequality." November 28. https://www.cepal.org/en/pressreleases/eclac-region-has-underestimated -inequality.

The Economist. 2018. "El Salvador's Rising Political Star." March 10. https:// www.economist.com/the-americas/2018/03/10/el-salvadors-rising-political -star.

Edwards, Sebastian. 1995. *Crisis and Reform in Latin America: From Despair to Hope.* Oxford: Oxford University Press.

Edwards, Sebastian, and Alejandra Cox Edwards. *Monetarism and Liberalization: The Chilean Experiment.* 2nd ed. Chicago: University of Chicago Press. 1991.

Ellis, R. Evan. 2009. *China in Latin America: The Whats and Wherefores.* Boulder: Lynne Rienner.

Enamorado, Ted, Luis-Felipe López-Calva, Carlos Rodríguez-Castelán, and Hernán Winkler. 2014. "Income Inequality and Violent Crime." Washington, DC: World Bank.

Encarnación, Omar G. 2002. "Venezuela's 'Civil Society Coup.'" *World Policy Journal* 19, no. 2: 38.

———. 2016. *Out in the Periphery: Latin America's Gay Rights Revolution.* New York: Oxford University Press.

Endoh, Toake. 2009. *Exporting Japan: Politics of Emigration to Latin America.* Urbana: University of Illinois Press.

Erikson, Daniel. 2005. "Cuba, China, and Venezuela: New Developments." *Cuba in Transition* 15: 410–418.

Ero, Ikponwosa. 2020. *Report of the Independent Expert on the Enjoyment of Human Rights by Persons with Albinism.* New York: United Nations Human Rights Council. https://documents-dds-ny.un.org/doc/UNDOC/GEN/G20/337 /18/pdf/G2033718.pdf?OpenElement.

Esberg, Jane. 2020. "More Than Cartels: Counting Mexico's Crime Rings." May 8. https://www.crisisgroup.org/latin-america-caribbean/mexico/more-cartels -counting-mexicos-crime-rings.

Etienne, Mona, and Eleanor Leacock. 1980. "Introduction." In *Women and Colonization: Anthropological Perspectives,* Mona Etienne and Eleanor Leacock, eds. New York: Praeger, 1–24.

Europa Publications, ed. 2021. *South America, Central America, and the Caribbean 2010.* 18th ed. London: Routledge.

European Union. 2019. "EU Announces €18.5 Million Humanitarian Aid Package for Latin America and the Caribbean." July 23. https://ec.europa.eu/echo /news/eu-announces-185-million-humanitarian-aid-package-latin-america-and -caribbean_en.

Evans, Peter. 1979. *Dependent Development: The Alliance of Multinational, State, and Local Capital in Brazil.* Princeton: Princeton University Press.

Ezcurra, Exequiel, Marisa Mazari-Hiriart, Irene Pisanty, and Adrián Guillermo Aguilar. 1999. *The Basin of Mexico: Critical Environmental Issues and Sustainability.* New York: United Nations University Press.

Fajardo, Luis. 2013. "Fray Antón de Montesinos: Su Narrativa y los Derechos de los Pueblos Indígenas en las Constituciones de Nuestra América." *Hallazgos,* January 1.

Falcoff, Mark. 1996. "Argentina: The Twentieth Century." In *Encyclopedia of Latin American History and Culture,* vol. 1, Barbara A. Tenenbaum, ed. New York: Scribner's, 152–160.

Fausto, Boris, and Sergio Fausto. 2014. *A Concise History of Brazil.* 2nd ed. Cambridge: Cambridge University Press.

Feit, Mario. 2011. *Democratic Anxieties: Same-Sex Marriage, Death, and Citizenship.* Lanham, MD: Lexington Books.

Fernandez-Kelly, Maria Patricia. 1983. *For We Are Sold: I and My People.* Albany: State University of New York Press.

Ferrández, Luis Fernando Angosto, and Sabine Kradolfer, eds. 2012. *Everlasting Countdowns: Race, Ethnicity, and National Censuses in Latin American States.* Newcastle-upon-Tyne: Cambridge Scholars.

Ferreyra, María Marta, Ciro Avitabile, Javier Botero Álvarez, Francisco Haimovich Paz, and Sergio Urzúa. 2017. *At a Crossroads: Higher Education in Latin America and the Caribbean.* Washington, DC: World Bank. https://openknowledge .worldbank.org/handle/10986/26489.

Fields, Karen E., and Barbara J. Fields. 2012. *Racecraft: The Soul of Inequality in American Life.* London: Verso.

Focus Economics. 2020. "Economic Snapshot for Latin America." https://www .focus-economics.com/regions/latin-america.

Folkerts-Landau, David, and Takatoshi Ito. 1995. *International Capital Markets: Developments, Prospects, and Policy Issues.* Washington, DC: International Monetary Fund, August.

Food and Agriculture Organization. 2008. "Potato and Biodiversity: International Year of the Potato." http://www.fao.org/potato-2008/en/potato/biodiversity .html.

Forsyth, Peter J., and Stephen J. Nicholas. 1983. "The Decline of Spanish Industry and the Price Revolution: A Neoclassical Analysis." *Journal of European Economic History* 12, no. 3: 601–610.

Foy, Felician A., ed. 1974. *Catholic Almanac 1975.* Huntington, IN: Our Sunday Visitor.

Fraga, Arminio. 2004. "Latin America Since the 1990s: Rising from the Sickbed?" *Journal of Economic Perspectives* 18, no. 2 (Spring): 89–106.

Franko, Patrice. 2007. *The Puzzle of Latin American Economic Development.* 3rd ed. Lanham: Rowman and Littlefield.

Franz, Tobias. 2020. "COVID-19 and Economic Development in Latin America." London: University of London, School of Oriental and African Studies. https://www.soas.ac.uk/economics/events/22apr2020-covid-19-and-economic -development-in-latin-america-webinar.html.

Fraser, B. J. 2018. "Latin American Bishops Call for 'Ecological Conversion.'" *Catholic News Service,* March 23. https://www.ncronline.org/news/earthbeat /latin-american-bishops-call-ecological-conversion.

Freedom House. 2018. *Freedom in the World 2018.* https://freedomhouse.org /report/freedom-world/freedom-world-2018.

———. 2020. *Freedom in the World 2020.* https://freedomhouse.org/report/freedom -world/2020.

Freire, Paolo. 2000 [1968]. *Pedagogy of the Oppressed.* New York: Continuum.

French-Davis, Ricardo. 2010. *Economic Reforms in Chile: From Dictatorship to Democracy.* 2nd ed. New York: Palgrave Macmillan.

Freston, Paul. 2004. *Protestant Political Parties: A Global Survey.* Burlington, VT: Ashgate.

Freyre, Gilberto. 1986 [1933]. *The Masters and the Slaves: A Study in the Development of Brazilian Civilization.* Translated by Samuel Putnam. Berkeley: University of California Press.

Friedman, Elisabeth Jay. 2010. "Lesbians in (Cyber)Space." In *The Politics of Sexuality in Latin America: A Reader on Lesbian, Gay, Bisexual, and Transgendered Rights,* Javier Corrales and Mario Pecheny, eds. Pittsburg: University of Pittsburg Press, 312–333.

Fuentes, Annette, and Barbara Ehrenreich. 1983. *Women in the Global Factory.* New York: South End.

Fuget, Alberto, ed. 1986. *McOndo.* Barcelona: Mondadori.

Fund for Peace. 2020. "Fragile States Index." https://fragilestatesindex.org/country-data.

Gailey, Christina Ward. 1987. "Evolutionary Perspectives on Gender Hierarchy." In *Analyzing Gender: A Handbook of Social Science Research,* Beth Hess and Myra Marx Ferree, eds. Newbury Park, CA: Sage, 22–67.

Galeano, Eduardo. 1973. *Open Veins of Latin America.* New York: Monthly Review.

Gálvez, Alyshia. 2018. *Eating NAFTA: Trade, Food Policies, and the Destruction of Mexico.* Oakland: University of California Press.

García Luna, Genaro. 2011. *El Nuevo Modelo de Seguridad.* Mexico City: Nostra Ediciones.

García-Pinto, Magdalena, and Trudy Balch. 1991. *Women Writers of Latin America: Intimate Histories.* Austin: University of Texas Press.

Gardiner, C. H. 2020. "In Brazil's Prisons, Inequality Isn't Just a Condition, It's the Law." *Christian Science Monitor Weekly,* September 28.

Garner, William R. 1966. *The Chaco Dispute: A Study in Prestige Diplomacy.* Washington, DC: PublicAffairs.

Garrard-Burnett, Virginia, ed. 2000. *On Earth as It Is in Heaven: Religion in Modern Latin America.* Wilmington, DE: Scholarly Resources.

Gautier, Mari-Lise Gazarian. 1989. *Interviews with Latin American Writers.* Elmwood Park, IL: Dalkey Archive.

Gentleman, Judith. 1996. "Mexico Since 1910." In *Encyclopedia of Latin American History and Culture,* vol. 4, Barbara A. Tenenbaum, ed. New York: Scribner's, 14–23.

Giattino, Charlie, Hannah Ritchie, Max Roser, Esteban Ortiz-Ospina, and Joe Hasell. 2021. "Excess Mortality During the Coronavirus Pandemic (COVID-19)." *Our World in Data.* August 18. https://ourworldindata.org/excess-mortality-covid.

Gledhill, John. 2015. *The New War on the Poor: The Production of Insecurity in Latin America.* London: Zed.

Global Alliance for the Rights of Nature. 2020. "What Is Rights of Nature." https://therightsofnature.org/what-is-rights-of-nature.

Goia, Ted. 2011. *The History of Jazz.* New York: Oxford University Press/OSO.

Goldman, Francisco. 2019. "Trump Enabled an 'Act of Organized Crime' in Guatemala." *New York Times,* June 18. https://www.nytimes.com/2019/06/18/opinion/guatemala-election.html.

Gonzáles, Elizabeth, et al. 2021. "The Coronavirus in Latin America." February 10. https://www.as-coa.org/articles/coronavirus-latin-america.

González, Héctor Núñez. 2010. "Political Practices and Alliance Strategies." In *The Politics of Sexuality in Latin America: A Reader on Lesbian, Gay, Bisexual, and Transgendered Rights,* Javier Corrales and Mario Pecheny, eds. Pittsburg: University of Pittsburg Press, 381–386.

González Echeverría, Roberto. 2012. *Modern Latin American Literature: A Very Short Introduction.* Oxford: Oxford University Press.

González-Echevarría, Roberto, and Enrique Pupo-Walker, eds. 1996. *Cambridge History of Latin American Literature.* 3 vols. New York: Cambridge University Press.

Goodman, Joshua. 2018. "Trump Pressed Aides on Venezuela Invasion." Associated Press, July 4. https://apnews.com/a3309c4990ac4581834d4a654f7746ef/US -official:-Trump-pressed-aides-about-Venezuela-invasion.

Goodrich, Diana Sorensen. 1986. *The Reader and the Text: Interpretive Strategies for Latin American Literatures.* Purdue University Monographs in Romance Languages no. 18. Erdenheim, PA: John Benjamins.

Gootenberg, Paul, and Luis Reygadas, eds. 2010. *Indelible Inequalities in Latin America: Insights from History, Politics, and Culture.* Durham, NC: Duke University Press.

Government of Peru. 2019. Presentation to the United Nations Committee on Enforced Disappearances, 281st meeting, "Consideration of Reports of States Parties to the Convention." April. https://documents-dds-ny.un.org/doc/UNDOC /GEN/G19/104/48/pdf/G1910448.pdf?OpenElement.

Gracia, Jorge J. E., and Mireya Camurati. 1989. *Philosophy and Literature in Latin America: A Critical Assessment of the Current Situation.* Albany: State University of New York Press.

Grattan, Steven. 2020. "Returning Venezuelans in Squalid Quarantine Face Uncertain Future," *The Guardian,* April 16. https://www.theguardian.com/global -development/2020/apr/16/venezuelans-returning-squalid-quarantine -migrants.

Green, Duncan, and Sue Branford. 2013. *Faces of Latin America.* 4th ed. New York: Monthly Review.

Gregory, Peter. 1986. *The Myth of Market Failure.* Baltimore: Johns Hopkins University Press.

Griffin, Paul. 2017. "The Carbon Majors Database: CDP Carbon Majors Report 2017." *CDP.* https://b8f65cb373b1b7b15feb-c70d8ead6ced550b4d987d7c03 fcdd1d.ssl.cf3.rackcdn.com/cms/reports/documents/000/002/327/original /Carbon-Majors-Report-2017.pdf?1499691240.

Grow, Michael. 2008. *US Presidents and Latin American Interventions: Pursuing Regime Change in the Cold War.* Lawrence: University of Kansas Press.

Gunder Frank, Andre. 1967. *Capitalism and Underdevelopment in Latin America: Historical Studies of Chile and Brazil.* New York: Monthly Review.

Guttmacher Institute. 2018. "Fact Sheet: Abortion in Latin America and the Caribbean." https://www.guttmacher.org/sites/default/files/factsheet/ib_aww -latin-america.pdf.

Guzmán, José Miguel, Susheela Singh, Germán Rodríguez, and Edith A. Pantelides, eds. 1996. *The Fertility Transition in Latin America.* Oxford: Clarendon. https://tinyurl.com/yyspxcup.

Hale, Charles R. 2004. "Rethinking Indigenous Politics in the Era of the 'Indio Permitido.'" *Report on the Americas* 38, no. 2: 16–21.

Hall, Gillette H., and Harry Anthony Patrinos. 2012. "Latin America." In *Indigenous Peoples, Poverty, and Development,* Gillette H. Hall and Harry Anthony Patrinos, eds. Cambridge: Cambridge University Press, 344–358.

Handler, Richard. 1988. *Nationalism and the Politics of Culture in Quebec.* Madison: University of Wisconsin Press.

Hanke, Lewis. 1994. *All Mankind Is One: A Study of the Disputation Between Bartolomé de las Casas and Juan Ginés de Sepúlveda in 1550 on the Intellectual and Religious Capacity of the American Indians.* DeKalb, IL: Northern Illinois University Press.

Hardoy, Jorge E., and David Satterthwaite. 1995. *Squatter Citizen.* London: Earthscan.

Haring, Clarence C. 1985. *The Spanish Empire in America.* New York: Harcourt Brace.

Harris, Marvin. 1964. "Racial Identity in Brazil." *Luso-Brazilian Review* 1, no. 6: 21–28.

———. 1970. "Referential Ambiguity in the Calculus of Brazilian Racial Identity." *Southwestern Journal of Anthropology* 26, no. 1: 1–14.

Harris, Richard L. 2007. *Death of a Revolutionary: Che Guevara's Last Mission.* New York: Norton.

Harrison, Lawrence E. 1997. *The Pan-American Dream.* New York: Routledge.

Hart, Stephen. 2007. *Companion to Spanish American Literature.* London: Tamesis.

Hart, Stephen, and Richard Young, eds. 2003. *Contemporary Latin American Cultural Studies.* London: Arnold.

Harvey, Fiona. 2020. "Amazon Near Tipping Point of Switching from Rainforest to Savannah—Study." *The Guardian,* October 5. https://www.theguardian.com/environment/2020/oct/05/amazon-near-tipping-point-of-switching-from-rainforest-to-savannah-study.

Hastings, Max, and Simon Jenkins. 1984. *The Battle for the Falklands.* New York: Norton.

Hayner, Priscilla B. 2011. *Unspeakable Truths: Transitional Justice and the Challenge of Truth Commissions.* New York: Routledge.

Hearn, Adrian H., and José Luís León-Maríquez. 2011. *China Engages Latin America: Tracing the Trajectory.* Boulder: Lynne Rienner.

Hecht, Susanna. 2005. "Soybeans, Development, and Conservation on the Amazon Frontier." *Development and Change* 36, no. 2: 375–404.

Hecht, Susanna, and Alexander Cockburn. 1989, 2011 (updated). *The Fate of the Forest: Developers, Destroyers, and Defenders of the Amazon.* London: Verso.

Hedges, Jill. 2011. *Argentina: A Modern History.* London: Tauris.

Hemming, John. 1978. *Red Gold: The Conquest of the Brazilian Indians, 1500–1760.* Cambridge: Harvard University Press.

Herlihy, Peter, and Taylor A. Tappan. 2019. "Recognizing Indigenous Miskitu Territory in Honduras." *Geographical Review* 109, no. 1: 67–86.

Herrero, Ana Vanessa, Anthony Falola, and Alex Horton. 2020. "Venezuela's Maduro Says Two Americans Captured in Failed Invasion Attempt." *Washington Post,* May 4. https://www.washingtonpost.com/world/the_americas/venezuelas-maduro-says-two-americans-captured-in-failed-invasion-attempt/2020/05/04/11630f82-8e6b-11ea-9322-a29e75effc93_story.html.

Hill, David. 2018. "The War Goes On: One Tribe Caught Up in Colombia's Armed Conflict." *The Guardian,* June 27. https://www.theguardian.com/environment/andes-to-the-amazon/2018/jun/27/the-war-goes-on-one-tribe-caught-up-in-colombias-armed-conflict.

Hillman, Richard S. 1994. *Democracy for the Privileged: Crisis and Transition in Venezuela.* Boulder: Lynne Rienner.

Hillman, Richard S., and Margaret V. Ekstrom. 1990. "Political Cynicism in Contemporary Caribbean Fiction." *Secolas Annals* 21 (March): 71–78.

Holden, Robert H., and Eric Zolov, eds. 2000. *Latin America and the United States: A Documentary History.* New York: Oxford University Press.

Hooker, Juliet. 2009. *Race and the Politics of Solidarity.* New York: Oxford University Press.

Hooker, Juliet, and Alvin B. Tillery Jr., eds. 2016. *The Double Bind: The Politics of Racial and Class Inequalities in the Americas.* Washington, DC: American Political Science Association.

Huerga, Alvaro. 1998. *Fray Bartolomé de las Casas, Vida y Obras.* Madrid: Alianza.

Human Rights Watch. 2019. "Nicaragua: Events of 2018." https://www.hrw.org/world-report/2019/country-chapters/nicaragua.

———. 2021. "Nicaragua: Trumped Up Charges Against Critics: Hazardous Detention Conditions, No Due Process, Arbitrary Prosecutions." September 20. https://www.hrw.org/news/2021/09/20/nicaragua-trumped-charges-against-critics#.

Huntington, Samuel P. 1968. *Political Order in Changing Societies.* New Haven: Yale University Press.

———. 1991. *The Third Wave: Democratization in the Late Twentieth Century.* Norman: University of Oklahoma Press.

Inglehart, Ronald, and Christian Welzel. 2014. "World Values Survey: Findings and Insights." http://www.worldvaluessurvey.org/WVSContents.jsp?CMSID=Findings.

International Crisis Group. 2007. *Venezuela: Political Reform or Regime Demise.* https://www.crisisgroup.org/latin-america-caribbean/andes/venezuela/venezuela-political-reform-or-regime-demise.

———. 2020. Report No. 80 Latin America and the Caribbean. *Mexico's Everyday War: Guerrero and the Trials of Peace.* May 4. https://www.crisisgroup.org/latin-america-caribbean/mexico/80-mexicos-everyday-war-guerrero-and-trials-peace.

International Labour Organization (ILO). 2018. *Panorama Laboral: América Latina y el Caribe.* Lima: OIT. https://www.ilo.org/wcmsp5/groups/public/---americas/---ro-lima/documents/publication/wcms_654969.pdf.

———. 2020. ILOSTAT database, https://ilostat.ilo.org/data.

International Monetary Fund. 2010–2019. "Brazil." https://www.imf.org/en/Publications/WEO/Brazil.

———. 2020. "Outlook for Latin America and the Caribbean: An Intensifying Pandemic." *IMF Blog,* June 26. https://blogs.imf.org/2020/06/26/outlook-for-latin-america-and-the-caribbean-an-intensifying-pandemic.

INURED (Inter-University Institute for Research and Development). 2020. "Post-Earthquake Haitian Migration to Latin America." Working paper.

IPCC (Intergovernmental Panel on Climate Change). 2014. *Climate Change 2014: Impacts, Adaptation and Vulnerability—Part B: Regional Aspects.* New York: Cambridge University Press.

Isacson, Adam. 2019. "Bolivia's Post-Evo Meltdown." November 14. https://www.wola.org/analysis/bolivias-post-evo-meltdown.

———. 2020a. "Challenges and Tools for Latin America's Struggle for Equality." June 23. https://www.wola.org/analysis/challenges-and-tools-for-latin-americas-struggle-for-equality.

———. 2020b. "Demining Sacred Space in Colombia's Amazon Basin." June 25. https://wolapodcast.libsyn.com/demining-sacred-space-in-colombias-amazon-basin.

———. 2020c. "Democracy, Displacement, and 'Political Cleansing' in Colombia's Armed Conflict." April 16. https://www.wola.org/analysis/democracy-displacement-and-political-cleansing-in-colombias-armed-conflict.

————. 2020d. "Soldiers and Civilians in Latin America Today." March 30. https://www.wola.org/analysis/soldiers-and-civilians-in-latin-america-today.

Isacson, Adam, and Gimena Sánchez-Garzoli. 2019. "Protest and Politics in Post-Conflict Colombia." December 17. https://www.wola.org/analysis/protest-and-politics-in-post-conflict-colombia.

Isacson, Adam, Coletta Youngers, and Terésa García Castro. 2020. "Women Coca and Poppy Growers Mobilizing for Social Change." March 17. https://www.wola.org/analysis/women-coca-and-poppy-growers-mobilizing-for-social-change.

Ituasso, Arthur. 2019. "Digital Media and Public Opinion in Brazil After Trump 2016." December 26. https://www.opendemocracy.net/en/democraciaabierta/public-opinion-in-brazil-after-the-campaigns-of-trump-and-bolsonaro.

Jackiewicz, Edward L., and Fernando J. Bosco. 2016. *Placing Latin America: Contemporary Themes in Human Geography.* 3rd ed. Lanham: Rowman and Littlefield.

Jaquette, Jane. 1991a. "Conclusion: Women and the New Democratic Politics." In *The Women's Movement in Latin America,* Jane Jaquette, ed. Boulder: Westview, 185–208.

————. 1991b. "Introduction." In *The Women's Movement in Latin America,* Jane Jaquette, ed. Boulder: Westview, 1–17.

Jaquette, Jane S., and Sharon L. Wolchik. 1998. *Women and Democracy: Latin America and Central and Eastern Europe.* Baltimore: Johns Hopkins University Press.

Jay, Feliz. 2002. *Three Dominican Pioneers in the New World: Antonio de Montesinos, Domingo de Betanzos, Gonzalo Lucero.* Lewiston, NY: Edward Mellen.

Jelin, Elizabeth, ed. 1990. *Women and Change in Latin America.* London: Zed.

————. 2003. *State Repression and the Labors of Memory.* Minneapolis: University of Minnesota Press.

Jerry, Anthony. 2013. "Talking About Mestizaje: History, Value, and the Racial Present." *Journal of Pan African Studies* 6, no. 1 (July): 110–124. http://www.jpanafrican.org/docs/vol6no1/6.1-7Talking.pdf.

Jessup, Philip C. 1931. "The Estrada Doctrine." *American Journal of International Law* 25, no. 4: 719–723.

Johnson, Paul C. 2002. *Secrets, Gossip, and God: The Transformation of Brazilian Candomblé.* New York: Oxford University Press.

Jones, Leroi. 1999. *Blues People: Negro Music in White America.* New York: Harper Perennial.

Josephson, Jyl, and Thais Marques. 2017. "How Queer Feminist Political Theory Could Transform Political Science." *LGBTQ Politics: A Critical Reader.* New York: New York University Press.

Kaminsky, Amy K. 1993. *Reading the Body Politic: A Feminist Criticism of Latin America.* Minneapolis: University of Minnesota Press.

Kanellos, Nicolás, ed. 2002. *Herencia: The Anthology of Hispanic Literature of the United States.* New York: Oxford University Press.

Karl, Terry Lynn. 2003. "The Vicious Cycle of Inequality in Latin America." In *What Justice? Whose Justice? Fighting for Fairness in Latin America,* S. E. Eckstein and T. Crowley, eds. Berkeley: University of California Press, 133–157.

Kaufmann, D., and A. Kraay. 2019. "Worldwide Governance Indicators." World Bank. https://info.worldbank.org/governance/wgi/Home/Reports.

Keen, Benjamin. 1986. *Latin American Civilization and History.* Boulder: Westview.

Keen, Benjamin, and Keith Hayes. 2013. *A History of Latin America.* 9th ed. Boston: Houghton Mifflin.

Kehoe, Alice Beck. 2017. *North America Before the European Invasions.* London: Routledge.

Kennon, Isabel. 2020. "Costa Rica Legalized Same Sex Marriage: Where Does the Rest of Latin America Stand on Marriage Equality?" June 2. https://www .atlanticcouncil.org/blogs/new-atlanticist/costa-rica-legalized-same-sex -marriage-where-does-the-rest-of-latin-america-stand-on-marriage-equality.

Kent, Robert. 2006. *Latin America: Regions and People.* New York: Guilford.

Keohane, Robert O., and Joseph S. Nye. 1977. *Power and Interdependence: World Politics in Transition.* Boston: Little, Brown.

Kerr, Lucille. 1992. *Reclaiming the Author: Figures and Fictions from Spanish America.* Durham, NC: Duke University Press.

Khater, Akram. 2017. "Phoenician or Arab, Lebanese or Syrian: Who Were the Early Immigrants to America?" https://lebanesestudies.news.chass.ncsu.edu/2017 /09/20/phoenician-or-arab.

King, John. 1990. *Magical Reels: A History of Cinema in Latin America.* London: Routledge, Chapman, and Hall.

Klein, Herbert S. 1992. *Bolivia: The Evolution of a Multi-Ethnic Society.* 2nd ed. New York: Oxford University Press.

———. 2011. *A Concise History of Bolivia.* 2nd ed. Cambridge: Cambridge University Press.

Klubock, Thomas Miller. 1997. "Morality and Good Habits: The Construction of Gender and Class in the Chilean Copper Mines, 1904–1951." In *The Gendered Worlds of Latin American Women Workers,* John D. French and Daniel James, eds. Durham, NC: Duke University Press, 232–263.

Knight, Allan. 2002. *Mexico: The Colonial Era.* New York: Cambridge University Press.

Knight, Franklin W. 2012. *The Caribbean: The Genesis of a Fragmented Nationalism.* 3rd ed. New York: Oxford University Press.

Kolbe, Laura. 2020. "Mysterious and Infinitely Solitary." *New York Review of Books,* April 23.

Kolinski, Charles J. 1965. *Independence or Death! The Story of the Paraguayan War.* Gainesville: University of Florida Press.

Korrol, Virginia Sánchez. 1999. "Women in Nineteenth- and Twentieth-Century Latin America and the Caribbean." In *Women in Latin America and the Caribbean: Restoring Women to History,* Marysa Navarro and Virginia Sánchez Korrol, eds. Bloomington: Indiana University Press, 59–106.

Kottak, Conrad Phillip. 2017. *Cultural Anthropology: Appreciating Cultural Diversity.* 17th ed. New York: McGraw-Hill.

Krause, Enrique. 2020. "Mexico Has Few Reasons to Celebrate the USMCA as Violence Flares in Alarming Way." *Washington Post,* July 1. https://www .washingtonpost.com/opinions/2020/07/01/mexico-has-few-reasons-celebrate -usmca-violence-flares-alarming-ways.

Lapper, Richard. 2021. *Beef, Bible, and Bullets: Brazil in the Age of Bolsonaro.* Manchester: Manchester University Press.

Larguia, Isabel, and John Dumoulin. 1986. "Women's Equality and the Cuban Revolution." In *Women and Change in Latin America,* June Nash and Helen Safa, eds. South Hadley, MA: Bergin and Garvey, 344–368.

Larrain, Felipe, and Patricio Meller. 1991. "The Socialist-Populist Chilean Experience, 1970–1973." In *The Macroeconomics of Populism in Latin America,* Rudiger

Dornbusch and Sebastian Edwards, eds. Chicago: University of Chicago Press, 175–214.

Lederer, Edith M. 2020. "UN: Global Tourism Lost $320B Due to the Pandemic." Associated Press, August 25. https://abcnews.go.com/Health/wireStory/global-tourism-lost-320-billion-months-virus-72589342.

LeoGrande, William M. 2007. "The Poverty of Imagination: George W. Bush's Policy in Latin America." *Journal of Latin American Studies* 39, no. 2 (May): 355–385.

León, José María Cabrera, and Anatoly Kurmanaev. 2020. "Ecuador's Death Toll During Outbreak Is Among the Worst in the World." *New York Times,* April 23. https://www.nytimes.com/2020/04/23/world/americas/ecuador-deaths-coronavirus.html?auth=login-email&login=email.

León-Portilla, Miguel. 1986. *Pre-Columbian Literatures of Mexico.* Norman: University of Oklahoma Press.

Levenson-Estrada, Deborah. 1997. "The Loneliness of Working-Class Feminism: Women in the 'Male World' of Labor Unions, Guatemala City, 1970s." In *The Gendered Worlds of Latin American Women Workers,* John D. French and Daniel James, eds. Durham, NC: Duke University Press, 208–231.

Levitsky, Steven, and Kenneth M. Roberts, eds. 2011. *The Resurgence of the Latin American Left.* Baltimore: Johns Hopkins University Press.

Levitt, Barry S. 2012. *Power in the Balance: Presidents, Parties, and Legislatures in Peru and Beyond.* Notre Dame, IN: University of Notre Dame Press.

Lewis, Donald M., ed. 2004. *Christianity Reborn: The Global Expansion of Evangelicalism in the Twentieth Century.* Grand Rapids, MI: Eerdmans.

Lindstrom, Naomi. 1994. *Twentieth-Century Spanish American Fiction.* Austin: University of Texas Press.

Link, Kacey, and Kristin Wendland. 2016. *Tracing Tangueros: Argentine Tango Instrumental Music.* New York: Oxford University Press.

Liss, Sheldon B. 1996. "Cuba." In *Encyclopedia of Latin American History and Culture,* vol. 2, Barbara A. Tenenbaum, ed. New York: Scribner's, 314–317.

Llanos, Marianos, and Leiv Marsteintredet, eds. 2010. *Presidential Breakdowns in Latin America: Causes and Outcomes of Executive Instability in Developing Democracies.* New York: Palgrave Macmillan.

Lockhart, James. 1994. *The Nahuas After the Conquest: A Social and Cultural History of the Indians of Central Mexico, Sixteenth Through Eighteenth Centuries.* Stanford: University of California Press.

Lombardi, John V. 1982. *Venezuela: The Search for Order—the Dream of Progress.* New York: Oxford University Press.

Londoño, Ernesto, Manuela Andreoni, and Leticia Casado. 2020. "A Family Business: A Corruption Inquiry Threatens Brazil's Bolsonaro." *New York Times,* August 29.

Long, Ciara. 2017. "Big Data Firm Cambridge Analytica to Target Brazil's Dissatisfied Middle Class." *Brazilian Report,* December 18. https://brazilian.report/power/2017/12/18/big-data-cambridge-analytica-brazil.

Long, Tom. 2020. "Historical Antecedents and Post–World War II Regionalism in the Americas." *World Politics* 7 (April): 214–253.

Loveman, Brian. 1998. *Chile: The Legacy of Hispanic Capitalism.* 2nd ed. New York: Oxford University Press.

Loveman, Mara. 2014. *National Colors: Racial Classification and the State in Latin America.* New York: Oxford University Press.

Lowy, Michael. 1996. *The War of Gods: Religion and Politics in Latin America.* London: Verso.

Lustig, Nora. 1992. *Mexico: The Remaking of an Economy.* Washington, DC: Brookings Institution.

Mac Adam, Alfred J. 1987. *Textual Confrontations: Comparative Readings in Latin American Literature.* Chicago: University of Chicago Press.

Mace, Gordan, Jean-Philippe Thérien, and Paul A. Haslam, eds. 2007. *Governing the Americas: Assessing Multilateral Institutions.* Boulder: Lynne Rienner.

Macias, Anna. 1982. *Against All Odds: The Feminist Movement in Mexico to 1940.* Westport: Greenwood.

Mackinnon, Amy, and Robbie Gramer. 2020. "U.S. Diplomats and Spies Likely Targeted by Radio Frequency Energy, Long-Withheld Report Determines." *Foreign Policy,* May 5. https://foreignpolicy.com/2020/12/05/us-diplomats -havana-syndrome-cuba-china-russia-radio-frequency.

MacLachlan, Colin. 1996. "Mexico: The Colonial Period." In *Encyclopedia of Latin American History and Culture,* vol. 4, Barbara A. Tenenbaum, ed. New York: Scribner's, 1–6.

Madrid, Alejandro. 2012. *Music in Mexico: Experiencing Music, Expressing Culture.* Oxford, England: Oxford University Press.

Madrid, Raúl L. 2012. *The Rise of Ethnic Politics in Latin America.* Cambridge: Cambridge University Press.

Maingot, Anthony P. 1992. "Race, Color, and Class in the Caribbean." In *The Americas: Interpretive Essays,* Alfred Stepan, ed. New York: Oxford University Press, 220–247.

Mann, Charles C. 2000. "Earthmovers of the Amazon." *Science,* February 4. https://science.sciencemag.org/content/287/5454/786.full.

———. 2006. *1491: New Revelations of the Americas Before Columbus.* New York: Vintage.

———. 2008. "Ancient Earthmovers of the Amazon." *Science,* August 28. https:// science.sciencemag.org/content/321/5893/1148.

Mann, Mary Tyler Peabody. 2001. *My Dear Sir: Mary Mann's Letters to Sarmiento, 1865–1881.* Belgrano, Argentina: Instituto Cultural Argentino Norteamericano.

Manuel, Peter, and Michael Largey. 2016. *Caribbean Currents: Caribbean Music from Rumba to Reggae.* 3rd ed. Philadelphia: Temple University Press.

Marklund, Carl. 2020. "Double Loyalties? Small-State Solidarity and the Debates on New International Economic Order in Sweden During the Long 1970s." *Scandinavian Journal of History* 45 (July): 384–406.

Martin, David. 1990. *Tongues of Fire: The Explosion of Protestantism in Latin America.* Oxford: Blackwell.

Martin, Gerald. 1989. *Journeys Through the Labyrinth: Latin American Fiction of the Twentieth Century.* New York: Routledge, Chapman, and Hall.

Martínez-Echazábal, Lourdes. 1998. "*Mestizaje* and the Discourse of National/Cultural Identity in Latin America, 1845–1959." *Latin American Perspectives* 25, no. 3: 21–42.

Martínez Novo, Carmen. 2018. "Ventriloquism, Racism, and the Politics of Decoloniality in Ecuador." *Cultural Studies* 32, no. 3: 389–413.

Mata, Luis Jose, and Max Campos. 2018. "Latin America: Chapter 14 of the IPCC Report on Climate Change." https://www.ipcc.ch/site/assets/uploads/2018/03 /wg2TARchap14.pdf.

McCluskey, Mitchell, Stefano Pozzebon, Tatiana Arias, and Time Lister. 2021. "Russia's Sputnik V Vaccine Expands Its Reach in Latin America." March 3. https://www.cnn.com/2021/03/03/americas/sputnik-latin-america-spreads-intl -latam/index.html.

McConnell, Shelley A. 2010. "The Return of *Continuismo?*" *Current History* 109, no. 724: 74–80.

McCoy, Terrence. 2019. "The Amazon Is Burning: Bolsonaro Says His Critics Are Setting the Fires, to Make Him Look Bad." *Washington Post,* August 22. https://tinyurl.com/y2topmwv.

McSherry, J. Patrice. 2005. *Predatory States: Operation Condor and Covert War in Latin America.* Lanham: Rowman and Littlefield.

Menton, Seymour. 1993. *Latin America's New Historical Novel.* Austin: University of Texas Press.

Messer, Ellen. 2010. "II.B.3. Potatoes (White)." In *The Cambridge World History of Food,* Kenneth F. Kiple and Kreimhild Conee Ornelas, eds. http://www.Cambridge.org/us/books/kiple/potatoes.htm.

Meyer, Michael C., William L. Sherman, and Susan M. Deeds. 2017. *The Course of Mexican History.* 11th ed. New York: Oxford University Press.

Miller, Francesca. 1991. *Latin American Women and the Search for Social Justice.* Hanover, NH: University Press of New England.

Miller, Shawn William. 2007. *An Environmental History of Latin America.* New York: Cambridge University Press.

Mills, Kenneth, William B. Taylor, and Sandra Lauderdale Graham. 2002. *Colonial Latin America: A Documentary History.* Wilmington, DE: Scholarly Resources.

Mithen, Steven. 2004. *After the Ice: A Global Human History, 20,000–5,000 BC.* Cambridge: Harvard University Press.

Mora, Frank D., and Jeanne A. K. Hey. 2003. *Latin American and Caribbean Foreign Policy.* New York: Rowman and Littlefield.

Morán González, John. 2016. *The Cambridge Companion to Latina/o American Literature.* Cambridge: Cambridge University Press.

Moravcsik, Andrew. 1997. "Taking Preferences Seriously: A Liberal Theory of International Politics." *International Organization* 51: 513–553.

Morgenthau, Hans J., and Kenneth R. Thompson. 1985. *Politics Among Nations: The Struggle for Power and Peace.* 6th ed. New York: Knopf.

Mörner, Magnus. 1967. *Race Mixture in the History of Latin America.* Boston: Little, Brown.

Mori, Antonella, ed. 2018. *EU and Latin America: A Stronger Partnership?* Milan: Ledizioni.

Moseley, Michael E. 2001. *The Incas and Their Ancestors: The Archaeology of Peru.* New York: Thames and Hudson.

Muñoz-Pogossian, Betilde. 2021. "Venezuela's Migrant Crisis Is Made of Desperate Women." *Caracas Chronicles,* March 26. https://www.caracaschronicles.com/2021/03/26/venezuelas-migrant-crisis-is-made-of-desperate-women.

Murphy, John. 2006. *Music in Brazil: Experiencing Music, Expressing Culture.* Oxford, England: Oxford University Press.

Murphy, Joseph M. 1993. *Santería: African Spirits in America.* Boston: Beacon.

Nash, June. 1980. "Aztec Women: The Transition from Status to Class in Empire and Colony." In *Women and Colonization: Anthropological Perspectives,* Mona Etienne and Eleanor Leacock, eds. New York: Praeger, 134–148.

———. 1983. "The Impact of the Changing International Division of Labor on Different Sectors of the Labor Force." In *Women, Men, and the International Division of Labor,* June Nash and Maria Patricia Fernandez-Kelly, eds. Albany: State University of New York Press, 3–38.

National Public Radio. 2021. "'A Huge Opportunity': Venezuelan Migrants Welcome Colombia's New Open-Door Policy." February 26. https://www.npr.org

/2021/02/26/971776007/a-huge-opportunity-venezuelan-migrants-welcome-colombias-new-open-door-policy.

Navarro, Marysa. 1999. "Women in Pre-Columbian and Colonial Latin America and the Caribbean." In *Women in Latin America and the Caribbean: Restoring Women to History,* Marysa Navarro and Virginia Sánchez Korrol, eds. Bloomington: Indiana University Press, 5–57.

Ñopo, Hugo, Alberto Chong, and Andrea Moro, eds. 2010. *Discrimination in Latin America: An Economic Perspective.* Washington, DC: Inter-American Development Bank and World Bank.

Nugent, Ciara. 2020. "Peru Locked Down Hard and Early: Why Is Its Coronavirus Outbreak So Bad?" *Time,* June. https://time.com/5844768/peru-coronavirus.

Nye, Joseph. 2004. *Soft Power: The Means to Success in World Politics.* Cambridge, MA: PublicAffairs and Perseus.

Oakes, James. 2017. "Our Wicked War." *New York Review of Books,* November 23.

O'Brien, Thomas F. 2007. *Making the Americas: The United States and Latin America from the Age of Revolutions to the Era of Globalization.* Albuquerque: University of New Mexico Press.

O'Donnell, Guillermo. 1979. "Tensions in the Bureaucratic-Authoritarian State and the Question of Democracy." In *The New Authoritarianism in Latin America,* David Collier, ed. Princeton: Princeton University Press, 285–318.

———. 1993. "On the State, Democratization, and Some Conceptual Problems." Working Paper no. 192. Notre Dame: Helen Kellogg Institute for International Studies.

———. 1994. "Delegative Democracy." *Journal of Democracy* 5, no. 1: 55–69.

———. 1998. "Horizontal Accountability in New Democracies." *Journal of Democracy* 9, no. 3: 112–126.

O'Donnell, Guillermo A., Philippe C. Schmitter, and Laurence L. Whitehead, eds. 1986. *Transitions from Authoritarian Rule: Comparative Perspectives.* Baltimore: Johns Hopkins University Press.

OECD (Organization for Economic Cooperation and Development). 2015. "E-Learning in Higher Education in Latin America." http://www.oecd-ilibrary.org/education/e-learning-in-higher-education-in-latin-america_9789264209992-en.

Oliver, Luís. 2011. Author interview with the director, Consejo Nacional de Seguridad Privada, Mexico City.

Oliveros-Rosen, Elijah. 2020. "Economic Research: Latin American Economies Are Last In and Last Out of the Pandemic." https://www.spglobal.com/ratings/en/research/articles/200630-economic-research-latin-american-economies-are-last-in-and-last-out-of-the-pandemic-11555443.

Olsen, Dale A., and Daniel A. Sheehy. 2014. *The Garland Handbook of Latin American Music.* 2nd ed. Abingdon, England: Routledge, Taylor & Francis Group, 2014.

Omari-Tunkara, M. S. 2006. *Manipulating the Sacred: Yoruba Art, Resistance, and Ritual in Brazilian Candomblé.* Detroit: Wayne State University Press.

O'Neil, Patrick H., Karl Fields, and Don Share. 2015. *Cases in Comparative Politics.* 5th ed. New York: Norton.

Oroxom, Roxanne, and Amanda Glassman. 2018. "Call a Spade a Spade: Venezuela Is a Public-Health Emergency." September 21. https://www.cgdev.org/blog/call-spade-spade-venezuela-public-health-emergency.

Ortega, Julio. 1984. *Poetics of Change: The New Spanish-American Narrative.* Austin: University of Texas Press.

Oslender, Ulrich. 2007. "Violence in Development: The Logic of Forced Displacement on Colombia's Pacific Coast." *Development in Practice* 17, no. 6: 752–764.

Oxhorn, Philip D. 1995. *Organizing Civil Society: The Popular Sectors and the Struggle for Democracy in Chile*. University Park: Pennsylvania State University Press.

Pagden, Anthony. 1993. *European Encounters with the New World*. New Haven: Yale University Press.

PAHO (Pan American Health Organization). 2020. "Indigenous and Afro-Descendant Voices Must Be Front and Center of COVID-19 Response in the Americas, Says PAHO." October 30. https://tinyurl.com/y8zd8ekj.

Palau, Mariana, and Manuela Rueda. 2020. "Venezuelans Once Again Fleeing on Foot as Troubles Mount." Associated Press, October 9. https://apnews.com/article/virus-outbreak-transportation-medellin-immigration-colombia-98d010ec0c97c02ec7682250b14a50e0.

Palma, José Gabriel. 1987. "Dependency." In *The New Palgrave: A Dictionary of Economics,* vol. 1, John Eatwell, Murray Milgate, and Peter Newman, eds. London: Macmillan, 802–805.

Palomo, Elvira. 2018. "From Four to Zero: Latin America Loses Its Female Presidents." *El Pais,* March 14. https://english.elpais.com/elpais/2018/03/14/inenglish/1521019893_528904.html.

Parsons, James. 1972. "Spread of African Pasture Grasses to the American Tropics." *Journal of Range Management* 25, no. 1: 12–17.

Paschel, Tianna S. 2016. *Becoming Black Political Subjects: Movements and Ethno-Racial Rights in Colombia and Brazil*. Princeton: Princeton University Press.

Passel, Jeffrey, D'Vera Cohn, and Ana Gonzalez-Barrera. 2012. "Migration Between the U.S. and Mexico." https://www.pewresearch.org/hispanic/2012/04/23/ii-migration-between-the-u-s-and-mexico/#mexican-migration-history-u-s-perspective.

Pastor, Robert A., ed. 1989. *Democracy in the Americas: Stopping the Pendulum*. New York: Holmes and Meier.

Payne, Judith, and Earl Fitz. 1993. *Ambiguity and Gender in the New Novel of Spanish America*. Iowa City: University of Iowa Press.

Peard, Julyan. 2016. *An American Teacher in Argentina: Mary Gorman's Nineteenth-Century Odyssey from New Mexico to the Pampas*. Lewisburg, PA: Bucknell University Press.

Pecheney, Mario. 2010. "Sociability, Secrets, and Identities: Key Issues in Sexual Politics in Latin America." In *The Politics of Sexuality in Latin America: A Reader on Lesbian, Gay, Bisexual, and Transgendered Rights,* Javier Corrales and Mario Pecheny, eds. Pittsburgh: University of Pittsburgh Press, 102–121.

Peloso, Vincent. 1996. "Peru Since Independence." In *Encyclopedia of Latin American History and Culture,* vol. 4, Barbara A. Tenenbaum, ed. New York: Scribner's, 364–374.

Perelli, Carina. 1991. "Putting Conservatism to Good Use: Women and Unorthodox Politics in Uruguay, from Breakdown to Transition." In *The Women's Movement in Latin America,* Jane Jaquette, ed. Boulder: Westview, 95–113.

Pérez, Louis A., Jr. 2014. *Cuba: Between Reform and Revolution*. 5th ed. New York: Oxford University Press.

Pérez-Firmat, Gustavo, ed. 1990. *Do the Americas Have a Common Literature?* Durham, NC: Duke University Press.

Pérez-Liñán, Aníbal, and Andrea Castagnola. 2009. "Presidential Control of High Courts in Latin America: A Long-Term View (1904–2006)." *Journal of Politics in Latin America* 1, no. 2: 87–114.

Perry, Keisha-Khan Y. 2013. *Black Women Against the Land Grab: The Fight for Racial Justice in Brazil*. Minneapolis: University of Minnesota Press.

Peterson, Anna L., and Manuel A. Vásquez, eds. 2008. *Latin American Religions: Histories and Documents in Context.* New York: New York University Press.

Peterson, Anna L., Manuel A. Vásquez, and Philip J. Williams, eds. 2001. *Christianity, Social Change, and Globalization in the Americas.* New Brunswick, NJ: Rutgers University Press.

Pew Research Center. 2013. "Brazil's Changing Religious Landscape." July 18. http://www.pewforum.org/2013/07/18/brazils-changing-religious-landscape.

———. 2017. "Gay Marriage Around the World." http://www.pewforum.org/2017/08/08/gay-marriage-around-the-world-2013.

Pierce, Sarah, and Jessica Bolter. 2020. "Dismantling and Reconstructing the U.S. Immigration System: A Catalog of Changes Under the Trump Presidency." July. https://www.migrationpolicy.org/research/us-immigration-system-changes-trump-presidency.

Pires de Rio Caldeira, Teresa. 1990. "Women, Daily Life, and Politics." In *Women and Change in Latin America,* Elizabeth Jelin, ed. London: Zed, 47–78.

Place, Susan E., ed. 2001. *Tropical Rainforests: Latin American Nature and Society in Transition.* Wilmington, DE: Scholarly Resources.

Plokhy, Serhii. 2021. *Nuclear Folly: A History of the Cuban Missile Crisis.* New York: Norton.

Policía Nacional de Ecuador. 2006. *Saludo a cargo del señor comandante general.* Quito: Policía Nacional de Ecuador.

Population Reference Bureau. 2020. *World Population Data Sheet.* Washington, DC.

Postero, Nancy Grey. 2007. *Now We Are Citizens: Indigenous Politics in Postmulticultural Bolivia.* Stanford: Stanford University Press.

Pozzebon, Stefano. 2021. "Latin America's Grueling Battle with COVID-19 Isn't Letting Up." April 5. https://www.cnn.com/2021/04/05/americas/latin-america-covid-19-intl-latam/index.html.

Prada, P. 2016. "As Brazil Veers Right, Evangelical Bishop Elected Rio Mayor." Reuters, October 30. http://www.reuters.com/article/us-brazil-election-idUSKBN12U0UZ.

Pressly, L. 2019. "Argentina's 'White Gold' Rush." October 17. https://www.bbc.co.uk/programmes/p07r8t2f.

Prevost, Gary, and Carlos Oliva Campos, eds. 2007. *The Bush Doctrine and Latin America.* New York: Palgrave Macmillan.

Price, Marie, and Catherine Cooper. 2007. "Competing Visions, Shifting Boundaries: The Construction of Latin America as a World Region." *Journal of Geography* 106: 113–122.

Price, Richard, ed. 1996. *Maroon Society: Rebel Slave Communities in the Americas.* 3rd ed. Baltimore: Johns Hopkins University Press.

Przeworski, Adam, Michael E. Alvarez, José Antonio Cheibub, and Fernando Limongi. 2000. *Democracy and Development: Political Institutions and Well-Being in the World, 1950–1990.* Cambridge: Cambridge University Press.

Psacharopoulos, George, and Zafiris Tzannatos. 1992. *Case Studies on Women's Employment and Pay in Latin America: Overview and Methodology.* Washington, DC: World Bank.

Racine, Karen. 2003. *Francisco de Miranda: A Transatlantic Life in the Age of Revolution.* Wilmington, DE: Scholarly Resources.

Radding, Cynthia. 1997. *Wandering Peoples: Colonialism, Ethnic Spaces, and Ecological Frontiers in Northwestern Mexico, 1700–1850.* Durham, NC: Duke University Press.

Rapozo, Pedro. 2021. "Necropolitics, State of Exception, and Violence Against Indigenous People in the Amazon Region During the Bolsonaro Administration."

Brazilian Political Science Review 15, no. 2. https://orcid.org/0000-0003-3843-5811.

Reeves, Philip. 2020. "COVID-19 Infection Rate in Rio's Favelas Far Exceeds Official Count, a New Study Says." National Public Radio, June 25. https://tinyurl.com/y4fr88nf.

Reimers, Fernando M. 2006. "Social Progress in Latin America." In *Cambridge Economic History of Latin America,* vol. 2, Victor Bulmer-Thomas and John Coatsworth, eds. Cambridge: Cambridge University Press, 427–480.

———. 2007. "Alberto Vinicio Baez and the Promotion of Science Education in the Developing World." *Prospects* 37, no. 3 (September): 369–381.

———. 2015. "Educating the Children of the Poor: A Paradoxical Global Movement." In *Rethinking Education and Poverty,* William G. Tierney, ed. Baltimore: Johns Hopkins University Press, 18–37.

———, ed. 2020. *Audacious Education Purposes.* Cham, Switzerland: Springer.

Reimers, Fernando, Uche Amaechi, Alysha Banerji, and Margaret Wang, eds. 2021. "An Educational Calamity: Learning and Teaching During the Covid-19 Pandemic." Independently published.

Reimers, Fernando, Carol DeShano, and Ernesto Trevino. 2006. "Where Is the 'Education' in the Conditional Transfers for Education?" Montreal: UNESCO Institute for Statistics.

Remmer, Karen L. 1992. "The Process of Democratization in Latin America." *Studies in Comparative International Development* 27: 3–24.

Renteria, Nelson. 2020a. "El Salvador Delays Next Steps in Reopening Economy as COVID-19 Cases Rise." Reuters, July 5. https://www.reuters.com/article/us-health-coronavirus-el-salvador/el-salvador-delays-next-steps-in-reopening-economy-as-covid-19-cases-rise-idUSKBN2460NE.

———. 2020b. "El Salvador's President Extends Lockdown, Crimping Law Allowing Restart of Economy." Reuters, May 19. https://www.reuters.com/article/us-health-coronavirus-el-salvador/el-salvadors-president-extends-lockdown-crimping-law-allowing-restart-of-economy-idUSKBN22V2XS.

Restrepo, Eduardo. 2004. "Ethnicization of Blackness in Colombia: Toward De-Racializing Theoretical and Political Imagination." *Cultural Studies* 18, no. 5: 698–753.

Reuters. 2020. "U.N. Water Rights Expert Questions Chile's Avocado and Energy Priorities." August 20. https://tinyurl.com/y3cnnv2z.

Richards, Patricia. 2005. "The Politics of Gender, Human Rights, and Being Indigenous in Chile." *Gender and Society* 19, no. 2: 199–220.

Roberts, J. Timmons, and Nikki Demetria Thanos. 2003. *Trouble in Paradise: Globalization and Environmental Crisis in Latin America.* New York: Routledge.

Roberts, Kenneth M. 2007. "Latin America's Populist Revival." *SAIS Review of International Affairs* 27, no. 1: 3–15.

Rock, David. 1987. *Argentina, 1516–1987: From Spanish Colonization to Alfonsín.* Berkeley: University of California Press.

Rodríguez, Francisco. 2008. "An Empty Revolution: The Unfulfilled Promises of Hugo Chávez." *Foreign Affairs* 87, no. 2: 249–254.

Roett, Riordan, and Guadalupe Paz, eds. 2003. *Latin America in a Changing Global Environment.* Boulder: Lynne Rienner.

Roosevelt, Anna Curtenius. 1980. *Parmana: Prehistoric Maize and Manioc Subsistence Along the Amazon and Orinoco.* Studies in Archaeology. New York: Academic Press.

Roser, Max, and Esteban Ortiz-Ospina. 2013. "Primary and Secondary Education." Our World in Data. https://ourworldindata.org/primary-and-secondary-education.

Rotberg, Robert I., ed. 2018. *Corruption in Latin America*. Cham, Switzerland: Springer.

Rothenberg, Daniel, ed. 2012. *Comisión para el Esclarecimiento Histórico*. New York: Palgrave Macmillan.

Rothstein, Frances. 1982. *Three Different Worlds: Women, Men, and Children in an Industrializing Community*. Westport: Greenwood.

Rühle, Hans. 2010. "Is Brazil Developing the Bomb?" *Der Spiegel*, May 7. https://www.spiegel.de/international/world/nuclear-proliferation-in-latin -america-is-brazil-developing-the-bomb-a-693336.html.

Ruiz, Vicki. 1988. "Mexican Women and the Multinationals: The Packaging of the Border Industrialization Program." Presentation for the Historical Perspectives on American Labor Conference, Ithaca.

Russell-Wood, A. J. R. 1996. "Brazil: The Colonial Era, 1500–1808." In *Encyclopedia of Latin American History and Culture*, vol. 1, Barbara A. Tenenbaum, ed. New York: Scribner's, 410–420.

Ryan, Alex. 2016. "Scaling Innovation: The Escuela Nueva Story." August 2. https://medium.com/the-overlap/scaling-innovation-the-escuela-nueva-story -d324a3d07797.

Saad-Filho, Alfredo. 2005. "The Political Economy of Neoliberalism in Latin America." In *Neoliberalism: A Critical Reader*, Alfredo Saad-Filho and Deborah Johnston, eds. London: Pluto, 222–229.

Sabet, Daniel. 2012. *Police Reform in Mexico*. Stanford: Stanford University Press.

Safa, Helen. 1990. "Women's Social Movements in Latin America." *Gender and Society* 4, no. 3: 354–369.

———. 1995. *The Myth of the Male Breadwinner: Women and Industrialization in the Caribbean*. Boulder: Westview.

Saffioti, Heleieth. 1975. "Female Labor and Capitalism in the United States and Brazil." In *Women Cross-Culturally: Change and Challenge*, Ruby Rohrlich-Leavitt, ed. The Hague: Mouton, 59–94.

Sanborn, Cynthia A. 2020. "Latin America and China in Times of COVID-19." https://www.wilsoncenter.org/sites/default/files/media/uploads/documents/FINAL %20Updated%20Sanborn%20Article.pdf.

Sánchez-Albornoz, Nicolás. 1974. *The Population of Latin America: A History*. Berkeley: University of California Press.

Sater, William F. 2009. *Andean Tragedy: Fighting the War of the Pacific*. Lincoln: University of Nebraska Press.

Satterthwaite, David. 2003. "The Links Between Poverty and the Environment in Urban Areas of Africa, Asia, and Latin America." *Annals: American Academy of Political and Social Science* 590, no. 1: 73–92.

Scheper-Hughes, Nancy. 2013a. "No More Angel Babies on the Alto Do Cruzeiro: A Dispatch from Brazil's Revolution in Child Survival." https://tinyurl.com/y7 kuxacl.

———. 2013b. "No More Angel Babies on the Alto Do Cruzeiro: A Dispatch from Brazil's Revolution in Child Survival." *Natural History Magazine*. June. https:// tinyurl.com/2pv536su.

Schirmer, Jennifer. 1993. "'Those Who Die for Life Cannot Be Called Dead': Women and Human Rights Protest in Latin America." In *Surviving Beyond Fear*, Marjorie Agosín, ed. New York: White Pine, 31–57.

Schmink, Marianne. 1986. "Women and Urban Industrial Development in Brazil." In *Women and Change in Latin America*, June Nash and Helen Safa, eds. South Hadley, MA: Bergin and Garvey, 136–164.

Schneider, Ben Ross. 2009. "Big Business in Brazil: Leveraging Natural Endowments and State Support for International Expansion." In *Brazil as an Economic Superpower: Understanding Brazil's Changing Role in the Global Economy,* Lael Brainard and Leonardo Martinez-Diaz eds. Washington, DC: Brookings Institution, 159–185.

Schodt, David W. 1987. *Ecuador: An Andean Enigma.* Boulder: Westview.

Schroeder, Shannin. 2004. *Rediscovering Magical Realism in the Americas.* Westport: Praeger.

Scott, Katherine. 1992. "Women in the Labor Force in Bolivia: Participation and Earnings." In *Case Studies on Women's Employment and Pay in Latin America,* George Psacharopoulos and Zafiris Tzannatos, eds. Washington, DC: World Bank, 21–38.

Shaw, Carolyn M. 2004. *Cooperation, Conflict, and Consensus in the Organization of American States.* New York: Palgrave Macmillan.

Shaw, Donald L. 1998. *The Post-Boom in Spanish American Fiction.* Albany: State University of New York Press.

Sheahan, John. 1987. *Patterns of Development in Latin America: Poverty, Repression, and Economic Strategy.* Princeton: Princeton University Press.

Silverblatt, Irene. 1980. "'The Universe Has Turned Inside Out . . . There Is No Justice for Us Here': Andean Women Under Spanish Rule." In *Women and Colonization: Anthropological Perspectives,* Mona Etienne and Eleanor Leacock, eds. New York: Praeger, 149–185.

Skidmore, Thomas E., and Peter H. Smith. 2018. *Modern Latin America.* 9th ed. New York: Oxford University Press.

Sklair, Leslie. 1993. *Assembling for Development: The Maquila Industry in Mexico and the United States.* San Diego, CA: Center for US-Mexican Studies.

Smilde, David, and Geoff Ramsey. 2020. "Beyond the 'Narcostate' Narrative: Addressing Organized Crime and Corruption in Venezuela." March 23. https://www.wola.org/analysis/beyond-the-narcostate-narrative-addressing-organized-crime-and-corruption-in-venezuela.

Smith, C. R. 2009. "Monte Verde." Address to Cabrillo Anthropology Department, Cabrillo College, Aptos, CA, September 2.

Smith, Christian, and Joshua Prokopy, eds. 1999. *Latin American Religion in Motion.* New York: Routledge.

Smith, Paul Julian. 1992. *Representing the Other: "Race," Text, and Gender in Spanish and Spanish American Narrative.* New York: Oxford University Press.

Solaún, Mauricio, Eduardo Vélez, and Cynthia Smith. 1987. "*Claro, Trigueño, Moreno:* Testing for Race in Cartagena." *Caribbean Review* 15, no. 3: 18–19.

Solé, Carlos A., ed. 1989. *Latin American Writers.* 3 vols. New York: Macmillan.

Spanier, John, and Eric Uslaner. 1978. *How American Foreign Policy Is Made.* New York: Holt, Rinehart, and Winston.

Specter, E. 2019. "These Indigenous Activists Are Fighting for the Future of a Ravaged Amazon." *Vogue.* October 14. https://www.vogue.com/article/indigenous-activists-amazon.

Spring, Jake. 2020. "Brazil's Amazon Fires Worsen in September, Threaten Virgin Forests." Reuters, September 9. https://www.usnews.com/news/world/articles/2020-09-09/brazils-amazon-fires-worsen-in-september-threaten-virgin-forests.

Squires, Scott. 2020. "Argentina Exits Ninth Default After $65 Billion Debt Deal." September 7. https://www.bloomberg.com/news/articles/2020-09-07/argentina-lifted-from-default-after-65-billion-restructuring.

Statistical Yearbook of the Church 1994. 1996. Vatican City: Central Statistics Office of the Church.

Stavig, Ward. 1999. *The World of Túpac Amaru: Conflict, Community, and Identity in Colonial Peru.* Lincoln: University of Nebraska Press.

Stepan, Nancy Leys. 1991. *"The Hour of Eugenics": Race, Gender, and Nation in Latin America.* Ithaca: Cornell University Press.

Stephens, Thomas M. 1989. *Dictionary of Latin American Racial and Ethnic Terminology.* Gainesville: University of Florida Press.

Stevens, Donald F., ed. 1997. *Based on a True Story: Latin American History at the Movies.* Wilmington, DE: Scholarly Resources.

Stevens, Evelyn. 1973. "Marianismo: The Other Face of Machismo in Latin America." In *Female and Male in Latin America,* Ann Pescatello, ed. Pittsburgh: University of Pittsburgh Press, 89–102.

Stiglitz, Joseph E. 2002. *Globalization and Its Discontents.* New York: Norton.

Stoll, David. 1990. *Is Latin America Turning Protestant? The Politics of Evangelical Growth.* Berkeley: University of California Press.

Stromquist, Nelly. 1992. *Women and Education in Latin America.* Boulder: Lynne Rienner.

Suárez, Luis, with Peter Jeson and Sid Lowe. 2015. *Cruzando la línea: mi autobiografía* [Crossing the Line: My Story]. Madrid: Pàmies.

Sublette, Ned. 2007. *Cuba and Its Music.* Chicago: Chicago Review Press.

Surma, Kati. 2021. "Are Bolsonaro's Attacks on the Amazon and Indigenous Tribes International Crimes?" https://insideclimatenews.org/news/11082021/amazon -indigenous-tribes-jair-bolsonaro-international-criminal-court/.

Swanson, Philip. 1990. *Landmarks in Modern Latin American Fiction.* New York: Routledge, Chapman, and Hall.

———. 1995. *The New Novel in Latin America.* Manchester: Manchester University Press.

———, ed. 2003. *The Companion to Latin American Studies.* London: Arnold.

Tacconi, Luca, ed. 2007. *Illegal Logging.* London: Earthscan.

Taffet, Jeffrey. 2007. *Foreign Aid as Foreign Policy: The Alliance for Progress in Latin America.* New York: Routledge.

Taylor, Diana. 1991. *Theatre of Crisis: Drama and Politics in Latin America.* Lexington: University of Kentucky Press.

Taylor, Paul D. 2009. "Why Does Brazil Need Nuclear Submarines?" *Proceedings Magazine* 135 (June): 1276.

Telles, Edward E., and Project on Ethnicity and Race in Latin America. 2014. *Pigmentocracies: Ethnicity, Race, and Color in Latin America.* Chapel Hill: University of North Carolina Press.

Tenenbaum, Barbara. 1996. "Mexico 1810–1910." In *Encyclopedia of Latin American History and Culture,* vol. 4, Barbara A. Tenenbaum, ed. New York: Scribner's, 6–14.

Thaler, Kai M. 2018. "Nicaragua: A Return to Caudillismo." *Journal of Democracy* 28, no. 2: 157–169.

Thorp, Rosemary. 1991. *Economic Management and Economic Development in Peru and Colombia.* Pittsburgh: University of Pittsburgh Press.

———. 1998. *Progress, Poverty, and Exclusion: An Economic History of Latin America in the 20th Century.* Washington, DC: Inter-American Development Bank.

Tiano, Susan. 1984. "The Public-Private Dichotomy: Theoretical Perspectives on Women in Development." *Social Science Journal* 21: 13–28.

———. 1987. "Gender, Work, and World Capitalism: Third World Women's Role in Development." In *Analyzing Gender: A Handbook of Social Science Research,* Beth Hess and Myra Marx Ferree, eds. Newbury Park, CA: Sage, 216–243.

———. 1994. *Patriarchy on the Line: Labor, Gender, and Ideology in the Mexican Maquila Industry.* Philadelphia: Temple University Press.

———. 2006. "The Changing Gender Composition of the Maquiladora Work Force Along the U.S.-Mexico Border." In *Women and Change at the U.S.-Mexico Border: Mobility, Labor, and Activism,* Doreen J. Mattingly and Ellen R. Hansen, eds. Tucson: University of Arizona Press, 73–90.

Tiano, Susan, and Carolina Ladino. 1999. "Dating, Mating, and Motherhood: Identity Construction Among Mexican Maquila Workers." *Environment and Planning* 31, no. 2: 305–325.

Topik, Steven, Carlos Marichal, and Frank Zephyr, eds. 2006. *From Silver to Cocaine: Latin American Commodity Chains and the Building of the World Economy, 1500–2000.* Durham, NC: Duke University Press.

Torres, A. 2020. "Brazilian Cop Is Seen Standing on Black Woman's Neck." *Daily Mail,* July 13. https://www.dailymail.co.uk/news/article-8518979/Brazilian-cop -seen-STANDING-black-womans-neck.html.

Tortorici, Zeb. 2012. "Against Nature: Sodomy and Homosexuality in Colonial Latin America." *History Compass* 10, no. 2: 161–178.

Towner, Margaret. 1979. "Monopoly Capitalism and Women's Work During the Porfiriato." In *Women in Latin America,* William Bollinger et al., eds. Riverside, CA: Latin American Perspectives, 47–62.

Transparency International. 2017. "Corruption Perceptions Index." https://www .transparency.org/news/feature/corruption_perceptions_index_2017.

Trejo, Guillermo. 2012. *Popular Movements in Autocracies: Religion, Repression, and Indigenous Collective Action in Mexico.* Cambridge: Cambridge University Press.

Tulchin, Joseph S., and Ralph S. Espach, eds. 2000. *Latin America in the New International System.* Boulder: Lynne Rienner.

Turino, Thomas. 2007. *Music in the Andes: Experiencing Music, Expressing Culture.* New York: Oxford University Press.

UNDP (United Nations Development Programme). 2010. *Informe sobre desarrollo humano de los pueblos indígenas en Mexico 2010: El reto de la desigualdad de oportunidades* [Human development report on Mexican indigenous peoples, 2010: The challenge of opportunity inequality]. Mexico City: Programa de las Naciones Unidas para el Desarrollo.

———. 2017. "A Socio-Economic Impact Assessment of the Zika Virus in Latin America and the Caribbean: With a Focus on Brazil, Colombia, and Suriname." https://tinyurl.com/yxls82pg.

———. 2020a. "Human Development Reports: Latest Human Development Index Ranking." http://hdr.undp.org/en/content/latest-human-development-index-ranking.

———. 2020b. "UNDP COVID-19 Response by Country." https://www.latinamerica .undp.org/content/rblac/en/home/coronavirus/undp-response-by-country.html.

———. El Salvador. 2020. "Support to the National Response and Recovery to Contain the Impact of COVID-19." May 29. https://www.latinamerica.undp.org/content /dam/rblac/docs/COVID-19-Country-Programme/LATEST/UNDP-RBLAC -SLV%20CV19%20Respond%20Fiche_v29May2020.pdf.

———. Paraguay. 2020. "Support to the National Response and Recovery to Contain the Impact of COVID-19." June 8. https://www.latinamerica.undp.org/content/dam /rblac/docs/COVID-19-Country-Programme/LATEST/UNDP-RBLAC-PRY %20CV19%20Respond%20Fiche_v8Jun2020.pdf.

———. Peru. 2020. "Support to the National Response and Recovery to Contain the Impact of COVID-19." June 7. https://www.latinamerica.undp.org/content/dam /rblac/docs/COVID-19-Country-Programme/LATEST/UNDP-RBLAC-PER %20CV19%20Respond%20Fiche_v7Jun2020.pdf.

UNESCO (United Nations Educational, Scientific, and Cultural Organization). 2010. "Education, Youth, and Development." August 30. Document prepared for the World Youth Conference, Leon, Guanajuato, Mexico. http://www .unesco.org/new/en/media-services/single-view/news/education_youth_and _development_unesco_in_latin_america_an.

———. 2020. "Investigación y vínculo con la sociedad en universidades de América Latina." Paris: UNESCO.

———. 2021. "Global Education Monitoring Report 2020: Latin America and the Caribbean—Inclusion and Education, All Means All." Paris. https://en.unesco.org /gem-report/LAC2020inclusion.

UNESCO and IADB (Inter-American Development Bank). 2020. "Reopening Schools in Latin America and the Caribbean." Santiago: UNESCO Regional Office for Education in Latin America and the Caribbean.

Ungar, Mark. 2011. *Policing Democracy*. Baltimore: Johns Hopkins University Press.

United Nations. 1991. *The World's Women 1970–1990: Trends and Statistics*. New York.

———. 2019. "Income Equality Trends." https://www.un.org/development/desa/dspd /wp-content/uploads/sites/22/2020/01/World-Social-Report-2020-FullReport.pdf.

———. 2020a. "Chile Must Prioritise Water and Health Rights over Economic Interests, Says UN Expert." August 20. https://tinyurl.com/y3w3vm72.

———. 2020b. "Infant Mortality Rate, for Both Sexes Combined (Infant Deaths per 1,000 Live Births)." https://tinyurl.com/y5ddwob2.

———. 2020c. "Latin America and the Caribbean Life Expectancy, 1950–2021." https://tinyurl.com/y4ujtxsm.

———. 2020d. "UN Expert Calls for Halt to Mining at Controversial Colombia Site." September 28. https://www.ohchr.org/EN/NewsEvents/Pages/DisplayNews.aspx ?NewsID=26306&LangID=E.

United Nations Economic Commission for Latin America. 1992. *Education and Knowledge: Basic Pillars of Changing Production Patterns with Social Equity.* Santiago: Libros de la CEPAL.

United Nations Human Rights Council. 2018. "Report of the Independent Expert on the Promotion of a Democratic and Equitable International Order on His Mission to the Bolivarian Republic of Venezuela and Ecuador." https://documents-dds -ny.un.org/doc/UNDOC/GEN/G18/239/31/pdf/G1823931.pdf?OpenElement.

———. 2020. "Venezuela: UN Report Urges Accountability for Crimes Against Humanity." September 16. https://www.ohchr.org/EN/HRBodies/HRC/Pages/News-Detail.aspx?NewsID=26247&LangID=E.

UNODC. 2020. *Estudio mundial sobre tráfico de armas de fuego 2020*. Oficina de las Naciones Unidas contra la Droga y el Delito, New York. https://www .unodc.org/documents/data-and-analysis/Firearms/Global_Study_Ex_Summary _es.pdf.

US Customs and Border Patrol. 2019. Statistics, https://www.cbp.gov/newsroom /stats/sw-border-migration/fy-2019.

US Energy Information Administration. 1998. "25th Anniversary of the 1973 Oil Embargo." Washington, DC: US Department of Energy, July.

———. 2010. "Table 5.18: Crude Oil Domestic First Purchase Prices, Selected Years, 1949–2009." In *Annual Energy Review 2009*. Washington, DC: US Department of Energy, August.

US Senate Select Committee on Intelligence. 2012. "Committee Study of the Central Intelligence Agency's Detention and Interrogation Program." December 13. https://fas.org/irp/congress/2014_rpt/ssci-rdi.pdf.

van Cott, Donna Lee. 2004. "Broadening Democracy: Latin America's Indigenous Peoples' Movements." *Current History* 103, no. 670 (February): 80–85.

Vanden, Harry E., and Gary Prevost. 2002. *Politics of Latin America: The Power Game.* New York: Oxford University Press.

Vásquez, Manuel A., and Marie Friedmann Marquardt, eds. 2003. *Globalizing the Sacred: Religion Across the Americas.* New Brunswick, NJ: Rutgers University Press.

Vaughan, Mary. 1979. "Women, Class, and Education in Mexico, 1880–1928." In *Women in Latin America,* William Bollinger et al., eds. Riverside, CA: Latin American Perspectives, 63–80.

Veccia, Theresa R. 1997. "'My Duty as a Woman': Gender Ideology, Work, and Working-Class Women's Lives in São Paulo, Brazil, 1900–1950." In *The Gendered Worlds of Latin American Women Workers,* John D. French and Daniel James, eds. Durham, NC: Duke University Press, 100–146.

von Vacano, Diego A. 2012. *The Color of Citizenship: Race, Modernity, and Latin American/Hispanic Political Thought.* Oxford: Oxford University Press.

Wade, Peter. 1997. *Race and Ethnicity in Latin America.* London: Pluto.

Waltz, Kenneth. 1979. *Theory of International Politics.* New York: McGraw-Hill.

Weatherford, Jack. 1988. *Indian Givers: How the Indians of the Americas Transformed the World.* New York: Fawcett Columbine.

Weisbrot, Mark, and Jeffrey Sachs. 2019. "Punishing Civilians: U.S. Sanctions on Venezuela." *Challenge* 62, no. 5: 299–321.

Weiss, Rachel, ed. 1991. *Being America: Essays on Art, Literature of Latin America.* Fredonia, NY: White Pine.

Weitzman, Hal. 2012. *Latin Lessons: How South America Stopped Listening to the United States and Started Prospering.* Hoboken, NJ: Wiley.

Welti, Carlos. 2002. "Adolescents in Latin America: Facing the Future with Skepticism." In *The World's Youth: Adolescence in Eight Regions of the Globe,* B. Bradford Brown, Reed Larson, and T. S. Saraswathi, eds. New York: Cambridge University Press, 276–306.

Welzel, Christian. 2017. *Freedom Rising: Human Empowerment and the Quest for Emancipation.* New York: Cambridge University Press.

Wendt, Alexander. 1999. *Social Theory of International Politics.* New York: Cambridge University Press.

Werner, Alejandro. 2020. "Outlook for Latin America and the Caribbean: An Intensifying Pandemic." June 26. https://blogs.imf.org/2020/06/26/outlook-for-latin-america-and-the-caribbean-an-intensifying-pandemic.

Werner, Alejandro, Takuji Komatsuzaki, and Carlo Pizzinelli. 2021. "Short-Term Shot and Long-Term Healing for Latin America and the Caribbean." *IMF blog.* April 15. https://blogs.imf.org/2021/04/15/short-term-shot-and-long-term-healing-for-latin-america-and-the-caribbean/

Whalen, Christopher. 2007. "Venezuela's Oil Trap." *International Economy* 21, no. 2: 58–61.

Wiarda, Howard J., and Harvey F. Kline. 1985. *Latin American Politics and Development.* Boulder: Westview.

Wilkie, James, ed. 2000. *Statistical Abstract of Latin America.* Vol. 38. Los Angeles: UCLA Latin American Center.

Wilkie, Richard, ed. 1997. *Statistical Abstract of Latin America.* Vol. 35. Los Angeles: University of California Press.

Williams, Mark Eric. 2012. *Understanding U.S.–Latin American Relations.* New York: Routledge.

Williams, Raymond L. 1995. *The Postmodern Novel in Latin America.* New York: St. Martin's.

Winkler Prins, Antoinette M. G. A., and Kent Mathewson, eds. 2021. *Forest, Field, and Fallow: Selections by William Denevan.* Cham, Switzerland: Springer.

Witte, G., M. B. Sheridan, J. Slater, and L. Sly. 2020. "Global Surge in Corona Virus Cases Is Being Fed by the Developing World—and the US." *Washington Post,* July 14. https://www.washingtonpost.com/national/global-surge-in-coronavirus-cases-is-being-fed-by-the-developing-world—and-the-us/2020/07/14/1e9ca48e-c605-11ea-8ffe-372be8d82298_story.html.

WOLA (Washington Office on Latin America). 2020a. "A Crucial Fight in Guatemala's Fight Against Impunity." June 10. https://www.wola.org/analysis/a-crucial-moment-for-guatemalas-fight-against-impunity.

———. 2020b. "FARC Dissident Groups." https://colombiapeace.org/farc-dissident-groups.

———. 2020c. "Unless the United States Adopts These 5 Immigration Strategies, COVID-19 Could Portend Another Humanitarian Crisis on Our Border." June 30. https://www.wola.org/analysis/5-regional-migration-strategies-covid-19-united-states.

Woodward, Ralph Lee, Jr. 2001. *Central America: A Nation Divided.* 3rd ed. New York: Oxford University Press.

World Bank. 2009. *World Development Indicators 2009.* Washington, DC: International Bank for Reconstruction and Development.

———. 2014a. *Inequality in a Lower Growth Latin America.* Washington, DC: Office of the Chief Economist for Latin America and the Caribbean.

———. 2014b. *The Labor Market Story Behind Latin America's Transformation.* Washington, DC.

———. 2018. *World Development Indicators 2018.* Washington, DC: International Bank for Reconstruction and Development.

———. 2020a. "Population Growth (Annual %), Latin America and the Caribbean." https://data.worldbank.org/indicator/SP.POP.GROW?locations=ZJ&most_recent_value_desc=true.

———. 2020b. World Development Indicators database. Washington, DC. http://data.worldbank.org.

———. 2021a. "Acting Now to Protect the Human Capital of Our Children: The Costs of and Response to COVID-19 Pandemic's Impact on the Education Sector in Latin America and the Caribbean." https://openknowledge.worldbank.org/handle/10986/35276?locale-attribute=en.

———. 2021b. *World Development Indicators 2010–2021.* Washington, DC: International Bank for Reconstruction and Development.

World Economic Forum. 2017. *Global Gender Gap Report 2017.* http://reports.weforum.org/global-gender-gap-report-2017/dataexplorer.

World Economic Forum for Latin America. 2018. "It's Time to Tackle the Informal Economy Problem in Latin America." https://www.weforum.org/agenda/2018/03/it-s-time-to-tackle-informal-economy-problem-latin-america/.

World Health Organization and UNICEF (United Nations Children's Fund). 2017. "Water Supply, Sanitation, and Hygiene." https://www.unicef.org/wash.

Worldometer. "Countries Where COVID-19 Has Spread." https://www.worldometers.info/coronavirus/countries-where-coronavirus-has-spread/. Accessed September 30, 2021.

Wright, Angus. 2005. *The Death of Ramon Gonzalez: The Modern Agricultural Dilemma.* Updated ed. Austin: University of Texas.

Wright, Thomas C. 2007. *State Terrorism in Latin America: Chile, Argentina, and International Human Rights.* Lanham: Rowman and Littlefield.

———. 2018. *Latin America in the Era of the Cuban Revolution.* 3rd ed. Santa Barbara, CA: Praeger.

Xinhuanet. 2020. "Brazil's Vehicle Output Falls Eleven Percent Year on Year in September." October 8. http://www.xinhuanet.com/english/2020–10/08/c_1394 24749.htm.

Yashar, Deborah J. 2005. *Contesting Citizenship in Latin America: The Rise of Indigenous Movements and the Postliberal Challenge.* Cambridge: Cambridge University Press.

Young, Kenneth R. 1996. "Threats to Biological Diversity Caused by Coca/Cocaine Deforestation in Peru." *Environmental Conservation* 23, no. 1: 7–15.

Zamora, Lois Parkinson. 1989. *Writing the Apocalypse: Historical Vision in US and Latin American Fiction.* New York: Cambridge University Press.

Zimmerer, Karl S., and Eric P. Carter. 2002. *Conservation and Sustainability in Latin America and the Caribbean: Latin America in the 21st Century.* 27th Yearbook of the Conference of Latin Americanist Geographers. Austin: University of Texas Press.

Zissis, Carin. 2020. "LatAm in Focus: Mexico's Fight Against Femicide Reaches a Boiling Point." Americas Society/Council of the Americas. March 3. https://soundcloud.com/ascoa/mexicos-fight-against-femicide-reaches-a -boiling-point.

The Contributors

Kathleen Barrett is assistant professor of civic engagement and public service at the University of West Georgia

David H. Bost is professor emeritus of modern languages and literatures at Furman University.

Henry (Chip) Carey is associate professor of political science at Georgia State University. He is author and editor of a dozen books, most recently, *Peacebuilding Paradigms* (2021).

Jacquelyn Chase is professor of geography and planning at California State University at Chico, where she is also a faculty associate of the Center for Water and the Environment

René De La Pedraja, who was born in Cuba, is professor of history at Canisius College.

Cleveland Fraser is professor of politics and international affairs at Furman University.
Angélica Lozano-Alonso is professor of Spanish at Furman University and faculty director of the Office for Innovation and Entrepreneurship.

David Marcus, an Arabic-language instructor at the Georgia Institute of Technology, has performed with fifteen Latin bands since 1978, from salsa to mariachi ensembles. His PhD dissertation from the University of Georgia is on the orchestral work, *La Mer*, by Debussy.

Shelley A. McConnell is associate professor of government at St. Lawrence University, specializing in Latin American politics, and was previously the book review editor for *Latin American Research Review*.

Scott McKinney is professor emeritus of economics and Latin American studies at Hobart and William Smith Colleges.

Stacey Mitchell is assistant professor of political science at Georgia State University's Dunwoody Campus.

Susan E. Place is professor emerita of geography at California State University at Chico.

Marie Price is professor of geography and international affairs at the George Washington University and is president of the American Geographical Society.

Fernando M. Reimers is Ford Foundation Professor of International Education at the Harvard Graduate School of Education, where his research and teaching focus on educating students to improve the world.

Michael Shea is a PhD candidate in political science at Georgia State University in Atlanta.

Hannah W. Stewart-Gambino holds a joint appointment in international affairs and government and law at Lafayette College.

Susan Tiano is professor emerita, in the Department of Sociology at the University of New Mexico.

Mark Ungar, professor of political science and criminal justice at the Graduate Center of the City University of New York, has written five books and about numerous articles on citizen security and political violence and is a police reform adviser with several international organizations and national governments.

Kevin A. Yelvington is professor of anthropology at the University of South Florida in Tampa.

Index

abortion, 244–245
Abreu, José, 428
Adams, John, 356
affirmative action, 36
African culture: influencing magical
realism in literature, 408;
multicultural literature, 410; popular
and vernacular music, 428–429;
religious practices, 36; spiritist
religions, 386–387; syncretic music,
421–423
Afro-Latin Americans: access to
education, 352; Afro-Descendant and
Indigenous Populations, 289(table);
Brazil's economic, political and
social rights, 258–259; neoliberal
multiculturalism, 285–286, 288;
racial conflict, 444; racial inequality,
36; racial mixing, 30–32; racist
soccer incidents, 266; the role of
marginalization in crime, 122–123;
slave trade, 269; spiritist religions,
386–388
Agosín, Marjorie, 419
agriculture: Andean region geology,
15–16, 15(fig.); boom and bust
cycles, 153–154; Brazil's physical
geography, 17; Caribbean plantation
agriculture, 48; colonial legacy of
racism, 6; Columbian Exchange,
29–30; commodity lottery, 150–151;

contribution to urbanization,
249–250; deforestation, 22–23;
droughts and hurricanes, 21; effect of
colonization on women's status,
306–307; emigration, 33;
environmental degradation, 230–233,
240–241; European
commercialization, 233–234;
industrial revolution, 66–68; non-
traditional exports, 25; pre-
Columbian economic life, 144–146,
228–230; water resource use,
245–246; women in the labor force,
319–320
agropastoral life: livestock production,
30, 240–241, 246; pre-Columbian
economic life, 144–145
Aguirre, Eugenio, 395
Agustini, Delmira, 406
Alfonsín, Raúl, 88, 283
Allende, Isabel, 410–411, 419
Allende, Salvador, 84–85, 88–89, 95,
163–164, 204, 374, 425
Altamirano, Ignacio Manuel, 402
"Altazor" (Huidobro), 407
Alto Maipo Hydroelectric Project, 246
Alvarado Muñoz, Fabricio, 189
Alvarado Quesada, Carlos, 189
Alvarez, Julia, 416
Amado, Jorge, 417
Amalia (Mármol), 401–402

Amazon Rainforest, 151, 228, 242, 442–443
Amazon River, geology of, 17
Anaya, Rodolfo, 414
Andean Pact (1969), 171
Andes mountains, geography of, 14–16
animism, 36
anti-clerical violence, 371
anticommunist policy, US, 94–95
antiglobalization movement, 241
anti-Semitism, Argentine nationalism and, 284
Anzaldúa, Gloria, 414
appropriateness, the logic of, 192
Arau, Alfonso, 420–421
Árbenz, Jacobo, 82, 95, 280
Arce, Luis, 108
Arenas, Reinaldo, 419
Arévalo, Juan José, 82
Argentina: Afro-Descendant and Indigenous Populations, 289(table); British attacks on, 53; bureaucratic-authoritarian regime, 87–88; capital flows, 173–175; changing gender values, 325(table); classical music, 427–428; collapse of military authority, 99; community-oriented policing, 141–142; convertibility, 175; Covid-19 pandemic, 439; *danzón* music, 431–432; Dirty War, 377–378; emigration, 33; European commercialization of, 234; geography, 15–16; governance indicators, 448(table); human development indicators, 449(table); import substitution industrialization, 158; industrialization, 66; *Madres de la Plaza de Mayo,* 299, 333; metric variations in music, 430; military campaign against the Indians, 76–77; missing persons, 99–100; nationalist ideology, 283–284; nuclear proliferation, 214; poetic depictions of an Argentine consciousness, 400–401; political reforms, 71–72; Pope Francis, 377–378; population figures, 26; prison conditions, 134; racist anti-immigration policies, 294; resource extraction, 24; river basins, 17; Spanish conquest, 41; urban growth, 68; War of the Triple Alliance, 73, 197–198; wars against Spain, 57; whitening the population through immigration, 274–275; women's labor force participation, 312(table); women's political participation, 109–110; working with at-risk youth, 140
Arguedas, José María, 410
Ariel (Rodó), 405
arts: dance, 392, 428–429, 431–432; music, 421–432; poetry and drama, 397–399; popular culture, 418–421; theater, 392, 397–399, 418. *See also* literature
Asian immigrants, 32, 274
Assange, Julian, 221–222
Asturias, Miguel Ángel, 409
attendance rates in education, 349–351
attorneys general, 132
audiencia, 45, 51–52
Austral Plan, 173
authoritarian rule: alternating with democracy, 93–94; Argentinian Church failure during, 377–378; citizens' political mobilization, 111; democratic failure, 105–109; democratic transition, 98–102; galvanizing women's rights movements, 332–333; Hispanic transformation, 44; liberation theology, 374; Mexico under Díaz, 72; military coups, 96–98; right-wing populism, 257–258; role of the Church in, 373; shifting from democracy, 112; US military intervention in Latin America, 94–96; Venezuela's democratic decline, 106
automobile production, 156–157
Aztec civilization: economic life, 145–146; gender roles, 336(n3); Iberian expansion, 27–28; Latinx writings, 414; literary culture, 392; population decline, 27–28; Spanish conquest, 40; women's status, 305
Azuela, Mariano, 405

Bachelet, Michelle, 117, 334(fig.), 335
Baez, Alberto, 345
Balboa, Vasco Núñez de, 40
Balbuena, Bernardo de, 397, 402
Balmaceda, José Manuel, 71

bandeiras, 48–49
Bay of Pigs, 95, 204
Belaúnde Terry, Fernando, 162–163
Belli, Gioconda, 419
Bello, Andrés, 340–342, 358–359, 400, 402–403
Belo Monte Dam, 17
Benedict XVI, 375, 383–385
Benítez Rojo, Antonio, 411–412
Bergoglio, Jorge Mario. *See* Francis I
biological diversity, 228
Black Lives Matter movement, 5, 127, 264–265, 286
Black-consciousness movements, 5, 127, 264–265, 282–283, 286
Blades, Rubén, 432
blanqueamiento (whitening), 267
Bless Me, Ultima (Anaya), 414
Bolaño, Roberto, 413
Bolívar, Fernando, 357–358
Bolívar, Simón: Gran Colombia, 60–61; higher education methods, 357–358; history of Latin American education, 340–341; poetic depictions, 400; the wars against Spain, 54, 57
Bolivarian Alliance for the Americas (ALBA), 106, 222
Bolivia: Afro-Descendant and Indigenous Populations, 289(table); Chaco War, 74; colonial urbanization, 251; declining democracy, 106–108; early colonial revolts, 51–52; electoral integrity, 436; foreign investment, 179; governance indicators, 448(table); human development indicators, 449(table); Indigenous music, 424; Indigenous politicians, 111; neoliberal multiculturalism, 287; populist government, 221–222; prison conditions, 133–134; racial discrimination, 37; rise of nationalist leftists, 102; syncretic music, 423; tensions with Chile, 185; term limits, 117; vigilantism, 125; women's political participation, 329–330
Bolivian Housewives Committee, 329–330
Bolsa Familia, 108, 178
Bolsonaro, Jair: anti-environmentalist policies, 239, 242, 443; Brazil as a

racial democracy, 258; China policy, 180; corruption allegations, 114; Covid-19 response, 115, 184, 247; education controls, 364; foreign policy, 224; gender issues, 445; ideology, 108; political stance, 222; political theology, 378; regional rise of populism, 3–4
boom, literary, 408–409, 413
boom-bust, economic: commodity-led development, 153–154, 180–181; export revenues, 153; global recession, 206; production and consumption effects, 148–149
boomtown growth, 255
border disputes, 45, 72–75
Borderlands (Anzaldúa), 414
boundaries of Latin America, 11; border wars, 42, 72–75
Bourbons, 50–51, 149
Bourdieu, Pierre, 262
Brazil: African slaves, 269–270; Afro-Descendant and Indigenous Populations, 289(table); Asian immigrants, 32; Black-consciousness movement, 286; bureaucratic-authoritarian regime, 86–87; Capoeira, 428–430; cash transfer programs, 108; changing gender values, 325(table); classical music, 426–427; coffee production, 152; corruption, 114; Covid-19 pandemic, 4, 115, 440; criminal justice system, 133; defaulting on debt, 97; democratic status, 98–99, 114, 206–207; destruction of the Indian nations, 75–77; economic crisis, 175–176; economic structures, 143; environmental degradation through mining, 236–237; ethnic identity, 281–283; export earnings, 24; falling poverty rates, 103; gender and sexuality, 304; gold rush economy, 148; governance indicators, 448(table); higher education development, 361; human development indicators, 449(table); import substitution industrialization, 158–160; increased spending on education, 348–349; independence from Portugal, 58–59; inequality by

skin color group, 293(table); liberal-conservative tensions, 69; liberation theology, 374; literary development, 417–418; military coup, 162; nuclear proliferation, 214–215; oil reserves, 224; organized crime, 438; political reforms, 71–72; politics of recognition, 288–289; popular and vernacular music, 428–429; population figures, 1, 26; populism, 108; postcolonial ethnic categorizations, 277–278; pre-Columbian economic life, 144; prison conditions, 134; progressive governance, 104; as racial democracy, 258; racial discrimination, 36–37; racial injustice, 5; racial mixing, 270; rainforest protections, 238–239; religious practices, 36; response to Covid-19, 247; river basins, 17; slave economy, 65–66, 232; spiritist religions, 386–388; staving off neoliberalism, 290–291; steamship service, 67; 21st-century economy, 177–178; university reform, 359–360; urban growth, 68; urbanization and crime, 123; Uruguayan revolt, 61–62; Vatican II, 372; War of the Triple Alliance, 73, 198; women's labor force participation, 312(table), 316; Xuxa's popularity, 281–282. *See also* Bolsonaro, Jair; Portuguese rule in Brazil
Britain: aggression against Spanish America, 50, 52–54, 62–63; Brazilian independence from Portugal, 58–59; emerging Latin American governments, 62; Latin American industrialization, 66; neocolonial control of Latin America, 92–93; post-independence intervention in Latin America, 233–234; war debt, 65–66. *See also* United Kingdom
"broken windows" theory of police reform, 128–130
Bucaram, Abdalá, 116
Bukele, Nayib, 131–132
bureaucratic-authoritarian regimes, 81, 86–90

Bush, George H.W., 210
Bush, George W., 217–218

Cabeza de Vaca, Alvar Núñez de, 395
cacao production, 154
Calderón, Felipe, 128, 130
Cambridge Analytica, 115
Canada. *See* North American Free Trade Agreement
Candomblé de Caboclo, 292, 386
Cantinflas, 420
capital flows, 167(table), 174, 176–177
capitalism: Marx defining class, 261–262; neoliberal multiculturalism replacing import substitution industrialization, 284–285; production, reproduction, and gender roles, 301; production and income distribution, 151–152
Capoeira, 428–429
captive narratives, 395, 412
Cardoso, Fernando Henrique, 172, 194
Caribbean Basin: British attacks on, 53; construction of ethnic differences, 270; European Union links, 226; global warming, 21; Hispanic transformation, 44; hurricanes, 20–21; Iberian expansion, 28; indentured labor, 32–33; influencing magical realism in literature, 408; language, 35; Latinx writers, 416; literary development, 417–418; physical geology, 16; plantation economies, 232; pre-conquest women's status, 305; religious practices, 36; sources of Latin music, 432; Spanish conquest, 40, 47; US Monroe Doctrine, 92; Vodou and Santería, 388. *See also specific countries*
Carpentier, Alejo, 407, 409, 411
cash transfer programs, 108, 349
caste system, 271–272
Castrim Narueka, 299(fig.)
Castro, Fidel, 95, 160
Castro, Raul, 219
Catholic Church: charismatic renewal movement, 384–385; colonial establishment and contemporary presence, 367–369; conquest as Spanish imperial destiny, 394;

declining fertility rates, 244–245; effects of post-independence liberalism, 150; forced conversion of Indigenous populations, 386; gender construction of femininity, 301; growing religious pluralism, 383; liberal-conservative divide, 369–371; Mexico curtailing privileges of, 78; modern role, 372–377; Pope Francis, 377–378; postwar collapse of democracies, 94–95; secularization and, 383; Spanish authority, 45–46; Spanish conquest, 39–40; support of military regimes, 96; transnational political influence, 196. *See also* conversion, religious

caudillos (strongmen), 70, 91–92, 116, 363, 401

Cavallo, Domingo, 173

Cavani, Edinson, 264, 266

Caviedes, Juan del Valle y, 398–399

census data, 273, 283, 288, 289(table), 314(table), 336(n4)

Central America: authoritarian rule, 94; deforestation, 22; democratic transition, 98–99; emigration, 33; geology, 16; hurricanes during Covid-19, 20; independence form Spain, 58; Latinx writers, 416; Mexico's hegemonic aspirations, 197; native-language speakers, 35; non-traditional exports, 25; police power, 129; post-independence political fragmentation, 60; tropical climates, 19; US anticommunist intervention, 96. *See also individual countries*

Central Intelligence Agency (CIA), 82, 84–86, 95, 209, 217–218

cesium-137, 253

cha-cha-cha, 430

Chaco War, 74, 74(fig.)

Chamorro, Violeta Barrios de, 297, 298(fig.)

charismatic renewal movement, 384–385

Chávez, Carlos, 427

Chávez, Hugo: border disputes, 45; challenging education policy, 363–364; dismantling democratic institutions, 106; personality cult, 104; resistance to neoliberalism, 102,

222; social spending, 176. *See also* Venezuela

Chicago Boys, 169–170, 205

Chilam Balam (Mayan text), 391

Chile: Afro-Descendant and Indigenous Populations, 289(table); bureaucratic-authoritarian regime, 88–89; changing gender values, 325(table); church-state separation, 370–371; community-oriented policing, 141; conservative Catholicism, 376; Covid-19 pandemic, 365, 440; debt crisis, 169–170; democratic experiment, 84–85; democratic opening, 207; democratic transition, 98–99; economic development models, 163–165; education, 342, 355, 361, 365; foreign investment increases, 179; geography, 15–16; governance indicators, 448(table); human development indicators, 449(table); import substitution industrialization, 80–81; invasion of Peru, 61; liberation theology, 372, 374; literary realism, 407; military campaign against the Indians, 76–77; natural resources, 25; neoliberalism, 204–205; post-independence political development, 70–72; pre-Columbian economic life, 144–145; progressive governance, 104; steamship service, 67; tensions with Bolivia, 185; term limits, 117; US-supported coup, 95, 204; the wars against Spain, 57–58; women's human rights movements, 332–333; women's labor force participation, 312(table), 316; women's protest movements, 329

China: commodity-led development, 180–181; Cuba's trading partners, 161; Latin American trade with, 102–103; political and economic rise, 224–225; trade agreements, 217

chinampas (cultivation beds), 229

Christianity. *See* Catholic Church; Protestantism

church-state separation, 370–371

Cienfuegos, Salvador, 130–131

Cisneros, Sandra, 414, 416

citizen inclusion, 109–111

citizenship: Latinx writers, 415–416

civil conflict: inhibiting institutional
reform, 127–128; maroons, 31–32;
militarizing drug control, 130–131
civil law systems, 91–92
civil society: civil society-state
engagement in education, 354–355;
community-oriented policing,
125–126; neoliberal multiculturalism,
285
civil society organizations, 111–112
class relations, 261–262; changing
fertility rates and, 245; distribution
and interactions, 267–268;
Guatemala's ethnic class ranking,
279–280; industrialization, 80;
inequalities, 37; Marx defining,
261–262; pre-conquest Indigenous
women's status, 304–305; under
Spanish rule, 44–45; women's status
under colonial rule, 306–308
class rock, 432
classical music, 426–428
climate: river basins, 17–21; tropical
zones, 18–20
climate change, 241–242
coastal development, 239–240, 251
coca production, 107, 438
Codex Mendoza, 392(fig.)
coffee production, 32, 152–154, 159,
231, 234, 412
Colbert, Vicky, 346–347
Cold War: Chile's democratic
experiment, 84–85; international
relations, 201–204; Nicaragua's
revolution, 85–86; US anticommunist
policy, 94–95; US intervention in
Guatemala, 82
Colombia, 56; Afro-Descendant and
Indigenous Populations, 289(table);
coffee production, 152; community-
oriented policing, 140–141; coups
and conspiracies, 69; Covid-19
pandemic, 441–442; displaced
persons, 437; early colonial revolts,
52; election of Uribe, 104;
governance indicators, 448(table);
human development indicators,
449(table); impunity rate, 125;
inequality by skin color group,
293(table); intermestic politics,
187–188; neoliberal multiculturalism,

287; organized crime, 438; political
role of guerrilla groups, 94;
population figures, 26; postcolonial
ethnic categorizations, 277–278;
religious divide, 371; rural
multigraded schools, 346; Spanish
conquest, 41; tensions with Ecuador
and Venezuela, 185; US-Colombian
drug initiatives, 220; the wars against
Spain, 57; women's labor force
participation, 313(table), 316
Colón, Jesús, 416
colonial legacy: environmental and
demographic change, 230–233;
history of education, 337–339;
international relations, 197–198;
language development, 34–35;
literary chronicles of the conquest,
393–395; Native American literature,
391–393; poetry and drama,
397–399; political culture, 91–92;
post-independence economies,
64–66; racial mixing and
immigration, 30–33; racializing
identity, 260–261; social formations
and identity politics, 268–272
colonial rule: causal factors in
democratic variation, 5–6;
deforestation, 22; democratic
development, 7; development of
education, 337; diversity and
abundance of natural resources, 24;
economic life, 146–150; expansion of
colonial powers, 2–3; historical
context, 42–47; human geography,
11–13; imaginative accounts of
Columbian history, 396–397; role of
the Catholic Church, 368–369;
urbanization, 250–251; view of
nonheterosexual individuals,
305–306; women's status, 306–308.
See also conquest; Portuguese rule in
Brazil; Spanish rule
Color de Mello, Fernando, 116
Columbian Exchange, 13, 29–30,
146–147, 230
Columbus, Christopher, 269, 393
Comentarios Reales del Perú
(Garcilaso), 392–393
commodity exports, 24, 153–155
commodity lottery, 150–151, 153

commodity-led development, 179–181, 181(table)
The Common School, 342
communist threat, 202–204, 207
community justice committees, 125
Community of Latin American and Caribbean States (CELAC) forum, 225
community-oriented policing, 125–126, 140–142
concentration camps, Chile's, 89
concertación (Peru's economic policy), 172
Concierto Barroca (Carpentier), 411
conflict, racial and ethnic, 444
conquest, Spanish, 39–42; Aztec alliance, 146; historical novels challenging the accounts of, 411; history of education, 337–339; Indigenous decline, 13; Indigenous musical traditions, 423–424; Indigenous women's opposition movements, 308–309; influencing magical realism in literature, 407–408; legacy of the transformation, 91–92; literary chronicles, 393–395; in *nuevo canción,* 431; population growth and urbanization, 26–27; racial mixing, 266–267; religious influences, 367; role of the Catholic Church, 368–369; shaping women's lives, 300. *See also* colonial rule
consciousness, Argentine, 400–401
consequences, the logic of, 192
constructivism: international relations analysis, 193–194
consumption: changing family size, 245; Cuba's economic model, 161; economic development and income distribution, 152–153; urbanization increasing, 243
consumption effect of economic booms, 148–149
continuismo, 116–117
contras (counterrevolutionaries), 95–96, 207
conversion, religious, 75–76, 232–233, 379, 381–382, 386, 394
convertibility system, 174–175
core-periphery theory, 194

Correa, Rafael, 221–222
corruption: Brazil's Bolsonaro, 224; Chávez's oppression of the opposition and media groups, 106; Covid-19 reporting, 441; crisis of governance, 450–451; of democratic institutions, 435–436; of drug control operations, 130–131; early colonial revolts, 51–52; environmental crime, 137–138; Honduran police and state institutional reform, 139–140; impunity, 124–125; inadequate police capacity, 126–127; leaders and politicians, 114–115; nationalized petroleum companies, 237; Peru's transitional justice, 101; police, 126–127, 130; prisons, 133–134; Rousseff's ouster, 108; Spanish colonial government, 44–45; state legitimacy, 445–446
Cortázar, Julio, 409
Cortés, Hernán, 40, 393
Costa Rica: Afro-Descendant and Indigenous Populations, 289(table); governance indicators, 448(table); human development indicators, 449(table); intermestic political activities, 188–189; liberal democracy, 94; pesticide poisoning, 240; women's labor force participation, 313(table)
counterinsurgency: Mexico, 55–56; US intervention in Guatemala, 280–281
counterrevolutionary war, 95–96
coups and coup attempts: Argentina's bureaucratic-authoritarian regime, 87–88; Brazil's military regime, 87, 162; Chile, 70–71, 85, 88–89; democratic opening in Paraguay, 206–207; international effect of Honduran politics, 188; interrupting democratic consolidation, 94; Mexico, 69; OAS norms, 101–102; Peru's leftist military regime, 162–163; social mobilization through the Church, 373; suppressing socialist guerrilla movements, 96; US intervention in Guatemala, 82
Covid-19 pandemic, 185, 435; effect on education, 364–366; effect on migration, 183–184; effects of

globalization on disease, 3–5; El
Salvador's prison policy, 131–132;
environmental factors, 246–247;
exposing and increasing inequalities,
114–115, 439; global
interdependence, 196; globalization
and education, 8–9; hurricanes
during, 20; impact on women and
children, 445; international challenge,
187; prison conditions, 134; Russia's
vaccine, 225–226
"craft" crimes, 134–135
crime: criminal justice system failure,
132–134; current policy responses,
138–142; economics intertwining
with, 437–438; environmental,
137–138; evolving nature of
criminality, 134–136; firearms
fueling violence, 136–137; impact
and targets, 7; impact of state
reforms, 125–136; militarizing drug
control, 130; penal reforms, 128–129;
social causes, 122–125
criminal justice system: delays and
impunity, 124–125; improving police
training, 138–139; worsening crime,
132–134
criollo class, 44–45, 50, 52–54, 57–58,
270–271, 275, 370
crisis of governance, 450–451
Cristero Rebellion (Mexico), 371
Crossing Borders (Menchú), 412
Cuarón, Alfonso, 2, 420–421
Cuba: Afro-Descendant and Indigenous
Populations, 289(table); Bay of Pigs,
95, 204; Cold War-era politics and
ideology, 202–204; contemporary US
relations, 219–220; early colonial
revolts, 54; economic and social
change, 160; industrialization, 66;
Latin music roots, 432; Latinx
writers, 415–416; magical realism in
literature, 407; multicultural
literature, 410; Russian connections,
225; Santería, 388; slave economy,
65–66; Spanish conquest, 40;
syncretic religions, 36; US
acquisition, 199; US control of, 92;
US rapprochement, 218–219;
women's political mobilization, 310
Cuban Missile Crisis, 95, 217

Cuban Revolution, 81–83, 96, 161–162,
328–329, 409
cuisine, global influences on, 2–3
cultural capital, 262
culture and cultural influences: Hispanic
transformation, 42–44; historical
novels, 410–411; identity in Latinx
literature, 414; Indigenous
perspective in magical realism, 408;
maroon societies, 31; popular
perceptions, 1–2; spiritist religions,
386–388; syncretic music, 421–422;
syncretic religion, 37–38. *See also*
Indigenous culture; literature; music
currency board, Argentina's, 173
curriculum reform, 288, 349, 364

da Silva, Mayra, 266
dance: Capoeira, 428–429; *danzón*
orchestras, 431–432; Native
American, 392
Darío, Ruben, 404–405
data-mining, 115
de las Casas, Bartolemé, 42, 338–339,
369, 394
de León, Oscar, 432
death squads, 99–100
debt, national: covering oil shocks, 205;
defaulting, 155; military regimes
incurring, 97–98; newly independent
countries, 150; post-independence
governments, 65
debt crisis: economic dynamics,
166–172; effect on education,
347–362; globalization,
neoliberalism, and environmental
impacts, 234–235; heterodox
economic policy, 170–172; impacts
on economic indicators, 169(table);
as a "lost decade," 97–98
decentralization: of education, 347; of
security, 131–132; urban zones,
254–256
declining terms of trade, 156
deforestation: biodiversity destruction,
22–23; causes and environmental
consequences, 237–239; climate
change, 242; crime involved in,
137–138; mobilizing Indigenous
organizations, 213–214; oil industry,
236–237; population growth, 243

del Río, Dolores, 420
del Toro, Guillermo, 2, 421
delegative democracy, 117
democracy: alternating with authoritarian rule, 93–98; challenges to, 112–119; Chile's democratic experiment, 84–85; colonial legacy, 7; disenchantment with, 104–105; divide between left and right regimes, 108–109; fragile democracy and environmental policies, 235–236; Latin America's democratic opening, 90; Mexico's decline, 112–113; presidential power threatening, 127–128; racial democracy, 258, 273–274, 282, 291; Robinson Country Intelligence Index, 447; US military intervention in Latin America, 94–96; variations in, 5; "with adjectives," 435; women's politicization, 109–110
democratic consolidation: obstacles to, 105; Robinson Country Intelligence Index, 447–448
democratic failure, role of police in, 127–128
democratic institutions, weakness and failure of, 93–94, 116, 118–119
democratic transition, 98–102, 116–117
democratization: challenging heteronormativity, 304; international involvement, 188–199, 206–209; prioritizing education, 348–354; women's political representation, 297–299
demographic transition, 243–244
dependency theory, 156, 160, 194–196
dependent development, 159
deregulation of banking, 170
desacato (contempt) laws, 115
Desde el Túnel (Guerrero Ceballos), 412
desert climates, 19
development, economic. *See* economic development
Díaz, Junot, 416
Díaz, Porfirio, 72, 76, 154, 275–276
Díaz, Simón, 424
Díaz del Castillo, Bernal, 393–394
Dictionary of Latin American Racial and Ethnic Terminology (Stephens), 278
Dirty War (Argentina), 283, 377–378

disappeared individuals: advocacy groups, 111; statistics on, 99–101; women's political participation, 109–110, 332–333
disease: Columbian Exchange, 29–30; commercial agriculture and livestock production, 240–241, 246; decimating Indigenous populations, 28, 147–148; effects of globalization, 3–5; environmental origins, 246; health, morbidity, and mortality, 245–248; Spanish conquest, 40–41; spread through urbanization, 443
displaced persons, 248–249, 437
The Distance Between Us (Grande), 415
dollar diplomacy, 199
domestic labor, 322–323, 331–332
domestic violence, 445
Dominican Republic, 63; Afro-Descendant and Indigenous Populations, 289(table); democratic transition, 98–99; history of education, 338; Latinx writers, 416; penitentiary system reform, 139; US intervention, 95, 199, 204
Dorfman, Ariel, 410
double-shift schools, 346
drama, 392, 397–399, 418
drought, 21, 241, 245–246
drug trafficking: Bolivia's institutional reforms, 128; cartel involvement in politics, 188; effect on poorer populations, 253; effects on Indigenous populations, 438; Honduran policy response to crime, 139; influencing foreign policy, 209; militarizing drug control, 130–131; US initiatives, 220; US responsibility for, 218–219
due process protections, 124–125, 133
Dutch colonialism, 48
Dutch Disease, 148–149
Duvalier, François, 388

Earth Summit (1992), 213
earthquakes, 15–16, 105, 231
ecclesial base communities, 372–373
economic capital, 262
economic crisis: debt crisis, 166–172; global economy and capital flows, 173–175; intermestic politics, 190;

northward migration, 249;
prioritizing education, 348; shaping
international relations, 187; structural
adjustment measures, 98, 206,
289–290, 319–320; Venezuela's
falling oil revenue, 106; women in
the work force, 318
economic development: Chile's two
models, 163–165; coastal areas,
239–240; commodity-led, 180–181;
diversity in, 12–13; Ecuador's
national development plan, 153;
environmental challenges relating
nature and society, 227–228; factors
affecting, 151; Peru's ore and metal
exports, 162–163. *See also* import
substitution industrialization;
industrialization
economic growth: during the Cold War,
202; effect on religious institutions,
367–368; peso crisis, 175; rising
commodity prices and, 181(table)
economic indicators, effect of the debt
crisis on, 169(table)
economic nationalism: environmental
impacts, 234–235
economic reforms: Spanish Bourbons,
50
economic women's movements,
331–333
economies: border wars, 72–75; Brazil's
military regime, 87; Chávez's oil
diplomacy, 106; Chile under
Pinochet, 89; colonial period,
146–150; Covid-19 pandemic effects,
183–184, 439–442; Cuba's
communist model, 160–162; the debt
crisis, 166–172; dependency theory
analysis of Latin America, 194–195;
diverse policy development,
182–185; early 20th century, 79–81;
emergence and expansion of
neoliberalism, 204–205; of emerging
states, 64–68; falling poverty and
inequality under leftist governments,
102–104; global interdependence,
196; import substitution
industrialization, 79–80, 156–160;
international politics of the 19802,
206–209; Latin America as an
emerging market, 173–177; military

governments, 97, 162; moving
towards global integration, 209–210;
newly independent countries,
150–156; Portuguese Brazil, 47–50;
pre-Columbian economic life,
144–146; social, cultural, and
economic identity, 262–263; Spanish
colonial rule, 47; 21st-century Latin
America, 177–182
Ecuador: Afro-Descendant and
Indigenous Populations, 289(table);
border wars, 74–75; Covid-19
pandemic, 3, 440–441; democratic
transition, 98–99; economic crisis,
175; export revenues, 153;
governance indicators, 448(table);
human development indicators,
449(table); Indigenous political
mobilization, 110–111; literary
identity, 403; populist government,
221–222; pre-Columbian economic
life, 144–145; tensions with
Colombia, 185; trust in the military,
113–114; twenty-first-century
socialism, 102; women's labor force
participation, 313(table), 316
education: access to, 8–9, 119, 320–321,
343–346, 349–353, 360–366;
attendance and completion rates,
349–351; civil society-state
engagement, 354–355; classical
music, 428; completion rates by
country, 343(table); female/male
educational attainment, 322(table);
impact of Covid-19 on, 364–366;
Lizardi's novels, 399–400; Mexico's
indigenismo, 276; police training,
138–139; populists challenging
current education policy, 363–364;
Portuguese reforms in Brazil, 59;
prioritization under democratization,
348–354; rights-based policies,
344–347; transformations in higher
education, 355–362; women's
attainment, 320–322, 324
education, history and development of:
the age of revolutions, 339–344;
colonization, 338–339; teacher
education under colonial rule, 308
education reform: Mexico's higher
education, 359

"El Crack," 413–414
El Mar de las Lentejas (Benítez Rojo), 411–412
El Niño, 20–21
El Norte (film), 419
El Periquillo Sarniento (Lizardi), 399–400
El Salvador: Afro-Descendant and Indigenous Populations, 289(table); Covid-19 pandemic, 4, 440; disenchantment with democracy, 104–105; firearms control, 140; governance indicators, 448(table); human development indicators, 449(table); impunity rate, 125; increasing civilian insecurity, 131–132; US military intervention, 95–96, 207
election fraud: Bolivia, 107–108, 287–288; Mexico, 77; regional response, 223–224
elections: Chile's democratic experiment, 84–85; democratic culture, 93–94; evangelical voter support, 378; increasing manipulation of, 117; information operations, 115; Ortega's manipulation and control of, 105, 112; party underdevelopment, 117–118; primary system of candidate selection, 436; term limits, 105–107, 116–117; twenty-first-century socialism, 102
electoral reform: Argentina, 72; Mexico, 99
emancipative values, 324–326
Embraer aircraft, 178–179
emerging market, Latin America as, 173–177
emigration within Latin America, 33–34
empowerment of citizens, 109–111
encomienda system, 269
energy industry: hydroelectric power, 17–18, 246; urban access, 23–24. *See also* oil production
English Football Association (FA), 264–266
English Premier League, 264
Enlightenment ideals: anti-clerical shift, 370; educational innovation, 347; higher education, 355–357; history of Latin American education, 339–340;

rights-based education policy, 345; secularization, 382
environmental challenges, 21–24; climate change, 241–242; coastal development, 239–240; colonial era environmental and demographic change, 230–233; consequences of deforestation, 237–239; effects of globalization, 234–242; health, morbidity, and mortality, 245–248; the impact of pre-Columbian cultures, 228–230; independence leading to commercial exploitation, 233–234; industrial livestock production, 240–241; international relations, 212–214; politics and, 242; population factors, 242–249; resource allocation, 442–443; socioeconomic connections, 8; support for conservation, 38; tectonic movement, 15; urbanization, 249–256
environmental crime, 137–138
Ercilla, Alonso de, 397
Espinosa Medrano, Juan de, 399
Esquivel, Laura, 419–420
Estrada Doctrine (1930), 200
ethnicity: African slaves, 269–270; Guatemala's ethnic class ranking, 279–280; neoliberal multiculturalism and the politics of recognition, 284–294; postcolonial ethnic categorizations, 276–279; race and, 296(n1); racial and ethnic conflict, 444; racial mixing, 270–271; racial slavery, 270; scientific racism, 272–273; social and cultural identity, 259–261
ethnogenesis, 266, 268–269, 271(table)
ethnographic writings, 395
eugenics, 273
European culture: syncretic music, 421–423
Evra, Patrice, 264, 265(fig.)
executive power: anti-democratic trends, 116; checks and balances, 117; judicial power and, 118–119; over security policy, 127–132
export economy: agriculture expansion, 256; biological legacy, 24; Brazil's military regime, 162; import substitution industrialization, 158;

Indians as obstacles to, 76–77; leveraging commodity exports into development, 179–180; newly independent countries, 150–151; revenues, 153–154; women in the labor force, 319–320

extrajudicial killings: Argentina, 100

Facebook data breach, 115
Falkland Islands, 88, 186, 207–208
family size, 243–245
fantasy, literary images, 403–405
favelas, 2, 123, 141, 143, 247–249, 444
Fe y Alegria, 347
federalism versus centralism, 70
Félix, Maria, 420
femicide, 309, 445
femininity, the gender construction of, 301
feminist movements, 101(fig.), 310–311, 326–328
Ferdinand VII of Spain, 53–56
Ferré, Rosario, 416
fertility rates, 243–245, 273, 323
fictional construction of Columbian history, 396–397
film industry, 2, 418–420
firearms: El Salvador's security policy, 140; fueling crime and violence, 136–137; role in crime rate, 124
fishing: environmental impact of coastal development, 239–240; pre-Columbian economic life, 144
Floyd, George, 4–5
folk music, 430–431
Fome Zero (hunger program), 178
Fonseca, Ramón, 138
forced assimilation, 27
foreign direct investment (FDI): Brazil under Lula, 177–178; Chile's growth, 179; impact of capital flows, 173; Mexico under Díaz, 72; mining, 68; during the oil downturn, 205–206; Russia, 225–226
foreign policy. *See* international relations
Fragile States Index, 106
France: capture of Ferdinand VII, 54; etymology of Latin America, 11–12; French Revolution, 52–53, 341; influence on higher education, 359; Mexican monarchy, 70, 198; post-

independence intervention in Latin America, 233–234
Francis I, 9, 36, 377–378, 384–385
Franklin, Benjamin, 356
free trade agreements (FTAs), 171
French Revolution, 52–53, 341
Freyre, Gilberto, 273–274, 417
Fuentes, Carlos, 405, 409, 412
Fuget, Alberto, 412–413
Fujimori, Alberto, 117, 172

gang violence: Mexico, 112–113; urbanization and, 123
García, Alan, 101, 171–172
Garcia, Cristina, 415
García Marquez, Gabriel, 409, 411–413, 418–419
Garcilaso de la Vega, 392, 408
gauchos (cowboys), 401; musical nationalism, 427
gender roles: *machismo,* 302–304, 310, 324, 333–335; *marianismo,* 301–304, 311–313, 324–326, 333–334; reproduction, 300–304, 322–324, 326–327; violence associated with, 444–445; women's movements challenging, 331–332
General Agreement on Tariffs and Trade (GATT), 210
genetically modified organisms (GMOs), 240–241
geography, 442–443; colonial legacy of human geography, 11–13; diversity, 6–7; natural resource diversity and wealth, 24–25; physical settings, 14–17; plant domestication and diversity, 228–229
geology, 14–15; economic development, 151
Ginastera, Alberto, 427
Gini coefficient, 103, 122, 182, 290
glaciers, 21
global warming, 21; climate change, 241–242. *See also* environmental challenges
globalization: dependency theory, 195–196; education, 8–9, 337–338, 360–361; environmental impacts of, 227, 234–242; expansion of colonial powers, 2–3; literary impact, 411; McOndo literature, 413; movement

of disease, 3–5; rights-based education policy, 344–347; transnational networks, 33–34
gold rush economy, Brazil's, 48–49, 148
Gómez, Sergio, 412–413
Gómez de Avellaneda, Gertrudis, 402
Gonzalez, Rodolfo "Corky," 414
González Iñárritu, Alejandro, 420–421
Gonzalo de Eslava, Fernán, 399
Good Neighbor Policy, 200
Goulart, João, 87, 162
governance indicators, 447, 448(table)
Gran Colombia, 60–61, 74, 197
Grande, Reyna, 415
"Grandeza Mexicana" (Balbuena), 397
grassroots movements, women's, 330–335
Great Depression, 79, 155
group identities, 8. *See also* identity
Guadalupe-Hidalgo, Treaty of (1848), 64
Guamán Poma de Ayala, Felipe, 393
Guatemala: Afro-Descendant and Indigenous Populations, 289(table); anticrime forces, 130; arms trafficking, 136–137; CIA overthrow of the government, 95; corruption, 114; elite nationalism, 280–281; ethnic class ranking, 279–280; governance indicators, 448(table); human development indicators, 449(table); Indigenous political participation, 111; Maya civilization, 28(fig.); neoliberal multiculturalism, 287; private security sector, 134; revolutionary regimes, 82; rise of evangelical Protestantism, 378; US military support to authoritarian governments, 95–96; women's labor force participation, 313(table), 316; women's political participation, 310, 329
Guerrero, Gonzalo, 395
Guerrero Ceballos, Manuel, 412
guerrilla movements: border wars, 73; bureaucratic-authoritarian regimes, 86–87; Central America, 6; Colombia, 94, 104, 136, 187–189; Cuba, 83, 160; drug economy, 438; Ecuador, 185; Guatemala, 82, 280; Mexico's liberal-conservative struggles, 70; military suppression,

96; Nicaragua, 207; Peru, 84, 100, 209; the wars against Spain, 54–58
Guevara, Che, 161, 420
Guillén, Nicolás, 410
Guyana: election monitoring, 118(fig.)
Guzmán, Joaquín "El Chapo," 130

Haiti: deforestation, 23; democratic failure, 105; environmental degradation, 23, 231; immigration to the United States, 211; influencing magical realism in literature, 407; invasion of Santo Domingo, 62; language, 35; slave rebellions, 53; US occupation, 199; Vodou, 388; women in independence movements, 309
Harris, Marvin, 277
health: Cuba's communist policies, 161; education-health integration programs, 355; environmental pressures, 245–248; urbanization and, 249–256. *See also* Covid-19 pandemic
Hearne, John, 417–418
hegemonic authority, 119, 193, 197, 201, 217, 263, 267
Hernández, José, 400–401
heterodoxy, economic, 171–173
heteronormativity, 302–304, 306, 324, 328
Hidalgo, Miguel, 54–56
higher education: affirmative-action programs, 291; impact of Covid-19 on education, 365; transformations in, 355–362
Hijuelos, Oscar, 415(fig.), 416
historical novels, 410–411, 414
historical political economy, 8
"Hombres Necios" (Sor Juana), 398–399
homicide, 121, 123(table), 124, 248
Honduras: Afro-Descendant and Indigenous Populations, 289(table); governance indicators, 448(table); human development indicators, 449(table); impunity rate, 125; intermestic politics, 188; policy response to crime, 139–140; women's labor force participation, 313(table), 316, 336(n4)
The House on Mango Street (Cisneros), 414

How to Be a Chicana Role Model (Serros), 414–415
Huidobro, Vicente, 407
human development indicators, 449(table)
human geography: colonial history and legacy, 11–13; emigration and transnational networks, 33–34; geography of the possible, 37–38; language, 34–35; race and inequality, 36–37; religion, 35–36
human rights movements: state reform, 125; women's movements, 331–333
human rights norms, 450–451
human rights violations: Chile under Pinochet, 89–90; IACHR cases, 189–190; by military and police, 96; outgoing military governments, 99–100; Progressive Catholics and, 373
Humboldt, Alexander, 341, 357
Humboldt Current, 151
hurricanes, 20–21
hydroelectric power, 17–18, 246
hyper-presidential constitutions, 116
hypodescent, 267

"I Am Joaquin" (Gonzalez), 414
Ibarbourou, Juana de, 406
Iberian colonization. *See* conquest; Portuguese rule in Brazil; Spanish rule
identity: Brazilian Capoeira, 430; colonial social formations, 268–272; constructing and assigning racial identity, 270–272; defining class, 261–262; defining ethnic identity, 261–262; desire and sexual identity, 303(table); effects of neoliberalism on, 257–259; elite nationalism and integrated identity, 279–281; emergence of an American literary identity, 400–403; gender roles and identities, 300–304; identity politics in independent Latin America, 272–276; Indigenous Guatemalans, 279–280; *latinidad* in Latinx writings, 415–417; Latinx literature, 414; LGBT, 333–334; marketing Brazil's Xuxa, 281–282; *mestizaje* and *blanqueamiento*, 266–267;

Mexico's *indigenismo*, 275–276; nationalist ideologies, 283–284; neoliberal multiculturalism, 284–294; political role of educational expansion, 343–344; politics of recognition, 285–294; popular perceptions of Latin America, 2; postcolonial ethnic categorizations, 276–279; racial mixing, 30–31; religion and secularism, 381–382; religious identities of poor women, 376; shift from Catholic to Protestant, 378–379; socioeconomic processes forming, 261–264
ideology: defining nationalism, 262–263; Mexico's *indigenismo*, 275–276; social and cultural identity, 259–261
Iglesias, Luis Fortunato, 346
illegal economies, 253
imagined community, 263
immigration: colonial Brazil, 48; effect of the Covid-19 pandemic, 183–184, 441–442; emigration within Latin America, 33–34; foreign policy impacts, 198; Indigenous decline, 13; as international relations issue, 210–212; labor for Spanish mining, 148; Latinx writers, 415–416; magical realism in film, 418–421; memoirs, 419; Middle Easterners, 3; population effects, 248–249; racial mixing and racial purity, 273–275; racial mixing during colonial rule, 30–33; racist anti-immigration policies, 294; steamship service, 67; US relations, 218–219; widespread displacement, 437
impeachment, 108, 116, 119, 224, 297, 436, 450
import substitution industrialization, 79–81; Cold War economic growth, 202; dependency theory analysis, 156–160; environmental impacts, 234–235; neoliberal multiculturalism replacing, 284–285; prioritizing education, 348. *See also* economic development; industrialization
Inca civilization: cultural expansion, 145; oral literary culture, 392; Spanish conquest, 40–41

income distribution: Chile's economic populism, 163–165; export production linkages, 151–153; Peru's development plan, 163; Venezuela's economic restructuring, 176

indentured labor, 33

independence: Brazilian, 58–59; development of education, 337; development through immigration, 32; Dominican Republic, 63; emerging governments, 60–68; identity politics in independent Latin America, 272–276; Napoleon's invasion of Spain, 369–370; political and cultural legacy, 91–92

independence movements: colonial economic legacy, 149–150; external influences on, 52–54; history of Latin American education, 339–344; the wars against Spain, 54–58; women's roles in, 309

Indigenous culture: American literary identity, 403; Hispanic transformation, 42–44; influencing magical realism in literature, 407–408; multicultural literature, 410; musical traditions, 423–424; Native American literature, 391–393; native language persistence, 35; neoliberal multiculturalism, 285; origins of *nueva canción* and political music, 424–426; rainforest protection, 238–239; religious intolerance of missionaries, 369; rise of evangelical Pentecostalism, 379–380; spiritist religions, 386–388; syncretic music, 421–423; transformation through conquest, 91. *See also* pre-Columbian era

Indigenous populations: access to education, 352; armed resistance, 437; attempts at racial "whitening," 275; colonial-era demographic change, 230–233; Columbus's depiction of, 269; conquest and enslavement of, 39–42, 91; conversion to Catholicism, 46; decline under European colonialism, 13; the drug economy, 438; early colonial revolts, 51–52; effects of environmental degradation, 443;

ethnic categorization, 279; ethnic-class ranking systems, 279–280; European disease decimating, 147–148; feminist movements, 327–328; fighting for land rights in Brazil, 258–259; forced assimilation, 27; Guatemala's ethnic class ranking, 279–280; inequality and poverty under neoliberalism, 291–292; international relations, 213–214; low socioeconomic indicators, 37; marginalization leading to crime, 122–123; obstacles to women's formal employment, 323–324; political empowerment, 109–111; population decline, 27–28; post-independence destruction of the Indian nations, 75–77; pre-conquest women's status, 304–306; racial conflict, 444; racial mixing, 30–31, 37–38; women's political participation, 329–330

industrialization: commodity-led development, 180; economic stages of, 66–68; post-independence economies, 64–66; women's labor, 308. *See also* economic development; import substitution industrialization

inequality, 12–13; Brazil's economic gaps, 143; cash transfer programs, 108; colonial legacy of land distribution, 149–150; consequences of deforestation, 237–239; Covid-19 pandemic, 4, 364–366, 439, 441; decline in income inequality, 181–182; defining race, racism, and ethnicity, 261; educational access and completion, 352–354; effect of the Washington Consensus, 98; environmental challenges, 227–228, 443–444; Gini coefficients, 182, 289–291; in globalization, 236; human development indicators, 448–449; impact of Covid-19 on education access, 364–366; impacts on health, 245–248; import substitution industrialization, 156–160; *marianismo* and *machismo* defining gender roles and identities, 302–303; political divisiveness, 118–119; in prison conditions, 134;

progressive leaders addressing, 102–103; in racialized groups, 261; reflection political and institutional weakness, 436; by skin color group, 293(table)

infant mortality, 243–244

informal economy: effects of Covid-19, 440–441; evolving nature of crime, 135–136; poorer populations, 253, 438; women's income, 109

informal sector: gender roles, 301

information collection: Honduran police and state institutional reform, 139–140

information operations, 115

Inquisition, Tribunal of the Holy Office, 46, 340–341

Institute for the Study of Higher Technology, Monterrey, Mexico, 361–362

institutional church, 374–375

institutional reform, 127–128

Institutionalized Revolutionary Party (PRI; Mexico), 99

integration, forced, 278–279

Inter-American Conference (1948), 202

Inter-American Court of Human Rights (IACHR), 188–190

Inter-American Democratic Charter, 101–102

Inter-American Treaty of Reciprocal Assistance (Rio Pact), 202

interdependence, global, 195–196, 209–210

intermestic politics, 187–188, 224

International Criminal Court (ICC), 217–218

International Monetary Fund (IMF), 98, 206

international relations: analytic perspectives of Latin America's role, 190–196; Cold War era, 201–204; democratization and free market economics, 206–209; dependency and debt, 204–206; environmental challenges, 212–214; global events shaping, 187; historical legacies, 197–201; immigration issues, 210–212; intermestic politics, 188–190; mobilizing Indigenous organizations, 213–214; moving

towards global integration, 209–210; nuclear proliferation, 214–215; regional and international response to authoritarian governments, 223–224; resisting US hegemony, 216–219; rise of populism, 221–222; territorial disputes, 185–187; terrorism, 215–216

invented traditions, 283–284

Iota Global, 115

Iraq, US war in, 215–216

The Itching Parrot (Lizardi), 399–400

Iturbide, Agustín de, 58

Japanese immigrants, 32

jazz, 422–423, 432

Jefferson, Thomas, 356

Jesuits, 46

Jiménez de Quesada, Gonzalo, 41

John Paul II, 374–375, 383–385

John XXII, 372

Johnson, Lyndon B., 95

Juárez, Benito, 69–70

judicial systems: during the Bourbon era, 51; colonial legacy, 91–92; IACHR cases, 188–190; political power, 118–119; under Spanish rule, 45

juntas, 54

Kahlo, Frida, 420

Kincaid, Jamaica, 418

Kirchner, Nestor: progressive governance, 104

Kottak, Conrad Phillip, 260

Kuczynski, Pedro Pablo, 101

Kyoto Protocols, 213

"La Araucana" (Ercilla), 397

La Carreta made a U Turn (Laveira), 415–416

La Violencia (Colombia), 371

labor: decline in men's economic activity, 316–317; effect of colonization on women's status, 306–308; gender roles, 300–304; Guatemala's Indigenous exploitation, 280; import substitution industrialization, 80, 158–159; labor unions, 80; Marx defining class, 261–262; Mexico's *maquiladora* women, 299–300; Spanish mining,

147–148; women in the formal labor force, 336(n4); women's obstacles to formal employment, 323–324; women's political involvement, 329–330

labor, division of: *marianismo* defining women's roles, 301–302

labor strikes, 154–155

ladinos (color category), 279–281

Lagos, Ricardo, 104

Lancaster, Joseph: history of Latin American education, 341

land and land rights: Brazil's economic inequalities, 143; Catholic Church holdings, 46, 150, 371; colonial legacy of distribution, 149–150; environmental disruption, 443; Indigenous struggles in Brazil, 258–259; Indigenous survival, 29; land conflicts and resource control, 238–239; maroon societies' claims, 31–32; Mexico's distribution programs, 78; redistribution of Church and Indigenous lands, 150

Landless Workers Movement (Brazil), 111

language: colonial legacy, 11; conversion of Indigenous populations, 46, 369; cultural rights, 287; effect of Covid-19 on culture and, 247; Hispanic expansion and transformation, 27, 31, 43; history of Latin American education, 341–342; human geography, 34–35, 37; Incas and Aztecs, 392; Indigenous diversity, 279; Latin American literature, 394, 396, 399, 403–412, 414–417; Latin American music, 421–422, 429; 19th-century education, 357–358; racist soccer incident, 264–266; social stratification, 268–269, 275; under Spanish rule, 42–43; Vatican II, 372

lapsed Catholics, 382

Latin America, etymology of, 11–12

Latin American Episcopal Conference (CELAM), 372–373

Latin music, 431–432

Latinx writers, 414–417, 419

Laveira, Tato, 415–416

League of Nations, 200

leftist movements and governments, 102–109; decreasing inequality, 290–291; early lesbian activism, 304; falling poverty and inequality, 102–104; international organizations' view of, 223; mixed-gender movements, 329; Peru's military coup, 162–163; racist politics of neoliberal regimes, 292–293

legislatures: executive oversight, 117

Leo VIII, 377

Leo XIII, 372

Lernoux, Penny, 375

Levinger, Beryl, 346–347

LGBTQ community: effect of colonization, 305–306; effects of democratization, 297–298; feminist critique, 328; *marianismo* and *machismo* defining gender roles and identities, 302–304; obstacles to women's formal employment, 323–324; Pope Francis's stance, 377–378; security and rights, 444–445; women's political history, 309–310; women's political participation, 333–335

liberalism: analyzing international relations, 192; benefits to democratization, 6; failure of, 153–154; post-independence philosophy, 150

liberation theology, 331–332, 372–377, 379, 426, 434(n3)

life expectancy figures, 26, 243–244, 448

Like Water for Chocolate (Esquivel), 419–420

limpieza de sangre (purity of blood), 271

linkages, production, 151–152, 156–157

Lins do Rêgo, José, 417

literature: Brazil and the Caribbean Basin, 417–418; conquest chronicles, 393–395; early novels and short stories, 399–400; emergence of an American identity, 400–403; imaginative accounts of Columbian history, 396–397; Latinx writers, 414–417; the literary boom, 408–409; Macondo to McOndo, 412–414; magical realism, 407–410; modernism, 403–405; Native

American, 391–393; post-boom evolution, 410–412; realist fiction, 406–407
lithium mining, 25
livestock management, 30, 240–241, 246
Lizardi, José Joaquín Fernández de, 399–400, 408
llanos, 17–18, 18(fig.)
Local Works program (USAID), 194
López, Francisco, 73
López Méndez, Luis: history of Latin American education, 341
López Obrador, Andres Manuel, 363–364
"lost decade": economic impacts, 97–98, 172; education, 347–348; effect on impoverished populations, 168; environmental impacts, 235; structural adjustment, 206; women in the work force, 318
low-income communities: educational innovation, 347; educational segregation, 352–353; education-health integration programs, 355; impact of Covid-19 on education, 364–366; increased spending on education, 348–349. *See also* poverty
Lubezki, Emmanuel, 421
Lula da Silva, Luiz Ignácio: economic policy, 177–178; foreign policy, 224; Indigenous land rights, 258–259; poverty relief, 36–37; progressive governance, 104; staving off neoliberalism, 290

machismo (masculinity), 302–304, 310, 324, 333–335
Madero, Francisco, 77, 154–155
Madres de la Plaza de Mayo, 299, 333
Maduro, Nicolas, 106, 183, 218, 223
Magellan, Ferdinand, 40
magical realism, 407–410, 418–420
mambo, 430
The Mambo Kings Play Songs of Love (Hijuelos), 416
Manchester United, 264
mandatory education, 349
Mann, Horace, 342
Mann, Mary Peabody, 342
mano dura ("iron fist") policies, 129

manufacturing: China's trade, 180; import substitution industrialization, 79–81, 156–160; women's labor, 308; WWII-era growth, 155(table)
maquiladoras, 254–255, 299–300, 319–320
maras (gangs), 131, 134, 136–137, 139
María Lionza, 388–389
mariachi music, 431–432
marianismo (cult of the Virgin Mary), 301–304, 311–313, 324–326, 333–334
Marie Jeanne a-la-Crete-a-Pierrot, 309
"market" crimes, 134–135
Mármol, José, 401–402
maroons (runaway slaves), 31, 233
Marques, René, 415
marriage equality, 189
Marx, Karl: defining class, 261–262
mass transportation, 23–24
Mastretta, Angeles, 419
Maya civilization, 28(fig.); economic life, 145; language, 35; literature, 391
McOndo (Fuget and Gómez), 412–413
media: Chávez's oppression of the opposition, 106; El Salvador's oppression of, 131–132; Guatemalan monopoly control, 114; political violence threatening, 115
Mejía Godoy, Carlos, 425–426
memoir, 419
Menchú, Rigoberta, 278–280, 329, 412
Menem, Carlos, 117, 172–173, 283
mercantilism, 147–149, 269–270, 306–308
Mérida Initiative, 220
Mesa Central (Mexico), 16
mestizaje (race-mixing), 266–267, 270–271, 271(table), 272, 276
mestizos (mixed race people), 7, 30–32, 37, 49–52, 75, 270–271, 275–276, 279
meter in vernacular music, 430–431, 434(n5)
Mexican Revolution, 77–79; literary modernism, 405; musical nationalism, 427; women's role in, 310
Mexican War, 63–64
Mexico: Afro-Descendant and Indigenous Populations, 289(table);

Alonso's captive narrative, 396–397; Aztec theater, 392; centralization of police, 132; changing gender values, 325(table); church-state separation, 371; cinema industry, 420–421; conquest chronicles, 393–394; coups and conspiracies, 69; Covid-19 pandemic, 4, 365, 440; *danzón* music, 431–432; debt crisis, 97, 167; deforestation, 22; democratic transition, 99; early colonial revolts, 54; education, 361–362, 365; electoral integrity, 436; emigration, 33; environmental degradation through petroleum, 236–237; femicide, 445; firearms and homicide, 124; foreign direct investment, 179; French monarchy in, 70, 198; gang negotiation, 132; GMO contamination, 241; governance indicators, 448(table); hegemonic aspirations, 197; human development indicators, 449(table); Iberian expansion, 28; immigration to the United States, 33–34; import substitution industrialization, 80–81; impunity rate, 124–125; independence struggles, 54–55; *indigenismo* ideology, 275–276; industrialization, 66; inequality by skin color group, 293(table); intermestic politics, 188; liberal programs during the *Porfiriato,* 154; limiting US economic influence, 210; literary identity, 402–403; Middle East migration, 3; migration to the United States, 248–249; militarizing drug control, 130; nationalization of oil production, 67, 78, 200; neoliberal multiculturalism, 287; North-South economic dialogue, 205–206; peso crisis, 174–175; physical geology, 16; poetry, 397; political revolution, 200; population figures, 1, 26; post-independence political fragmentation, 60, 72; pre-Columbian economic life, 145–146; racial discrimination, 37; rebellion against Bourbon rule, 149; religious practices, 36; resource extraction, 24–25; security system reform, 128; Spain's attempted reconquest, 63; Spanish conquest, 40; Spanish Inquisition, 46; UN International Women's Year Conference, 327; university reform, 359; urbanization, 251; US drug initiatives, 220; vigilantism, 125; violence challenging democracy, 112–113; war debt, 65; the wars against Spain, 58; women's labor force participation, 299–300, 313(table), 319–320

migration, declining democracy driving, 119

military, Latin American: citizens' political mobilization, 111; crimefighting role, 121; demilitarizing the police, 125; democratic transitions, 99; increasing political role, 436; Uribe's anti-rebel military campaign, 104. *See also* coups and coup attempts

military, Spanish: Bourbon rule, 51; defense against the British, 53; transporting goods, 149

military, US and British: neocolonialism in Latin America, 92–93; US anticommunist policy in Latin America, 94–96. *See also* coups and coup attempts

military regimes: Bolivia, 107–108; Chile, 88–89; Cuban model, 161–162; election of Brazil's Bolsonaro, 114; Peru, 83–84; US anticommunist intervention in Central America, 96; women's politicization under, 109–110

mining and mineral wealth: Brazil, 149, 178–179; Chile's nationalization, 84–85; Chile's trade deficit, 165; environmental impacts, 230–231, 236–237; extraction and export, 151; falling prices, 25; foreign investment, 67–68; industrial revolution, 66–68; Peru's economic development plan, 162–163; Spanish control of, 147–148; War of the Pacific, 73

Miranda, Francisco de, 340–341, 357

Miranda, Sebastian de, 340, 343

missionaries: Black Legend, 42; charismatic renewal movement, 384; colonial-era contact and exploitation,

232–233; dramatic literature, 399;
  religious intolerance, 369
Mistral, Gabriela, 406, 406(fig.)
mixed-gender movements, 328–330
modernism, literary influences on,
  403–405
modernization: demographic changes,
  244; expansion of schooling,
  343–344
Mogollón, Oscar, 346–347
monetarism, 170
Monroe Doctrine, 92, 198–199
Montesinos: history of education,
  338–339
Morales, Evo, 107(fig.); election of,
  287–288; eliminating term limits,
  106–107, 117; foreign policy, 221;
  Indigenous inclusion, 37; regional
  hostility, 185; twenty-first-century
  socialism, 102
Morelos, José María, 54–55
Morillo, Pablo, 56–57
Mossack, Jürgen, 138
Movement to Socialism party (Bolivia),
  287
MS-19 crime syndicate, 131–132
multiculturalism, neoliberal, 284–294
multinational corporations (MNCs), 158,
  169, 178–179, 195, 206
Murillo, Rosario, 112
music: Carpentier's historical novel, 411;
  charismatic renewal movement,
  384–385; classical, 426–428;
  Indigenous traditions, 423–424; jazz,
  422–423, 432; Latinx writers, 415;
  meter, 430–431, 434(n5); *nueva
  canción* and political music,
  424–426; popular perceptions, 1–2;
  vernacular and popular, 428–432

Naipaul, V.S., 418
National Action Party (PAN; Mexico),
  99
national churches, 371, 374, 376, 384,
  390
national parks, 21–22
nationalism: Cuban Revolution, 81–83;
  defining, 262–263; environmental
  impacts of economic nationalism,
  234–235; European roots of, 268;
  Guatemala's elites, 279–281; musical,

427; nationalist ideology, 283–284;
  race, ethnicity, and class, 272–273;
  requiring an integrated identity,
  279–280
nationalization: Chile's copper mines,
  84–85; Mexico's oil industry, 67, 78,
  200; Peru's banking, 172
natural disasters: climate change,
  241–242; desert climates, 19;
  environmental disruption, 442–443;
  Haiti, 105; hurricanes, 20–21; rural
  agriculture, 23; tectonic movement,
  16. *See also* oil production
natural resources: Amazon extraction,
  18; British designs on, 52–54;
  competition for, 227–228, 231–232;
  diversity and abundance, 13, 24–25;
  Portuguese Brazil, 47–50; regional
  environmental challenges, 22;
  regional geology, 15; Spanish
  conquest, 41; support for
  conservation, 38. *See also* mining and
  mineral wealth
nature, literary depictions of the struggle
  with, 402
Nava, Gregory, 419–420
navy, Spanish, 63
neoliberal economic policies: analyzing
  international relations, 192; Brazil's
  inequalities, 143; the debt crisis and
  the Washington Consensus, 170–171;
  effect on social and political identity,
  257–259; emergence and expansion
  of, 204–205; European intervention
  in Latin America, 233–234;
  globalization and environmental
  impacts, 234–236; heterodox
  economic policy as response,
  171–172; leftist nationalism
  countering, 102–108; the "lost
  decade," 98; volatile capital flows,
  173–176; waning influence, 176–177
neoliberal multiculturalism, 284–294
Neolithic revolution, 144–145
neo-Pentecostals, 381
Neruda, Pablo, 406
new police model (Mexico), 128
"new school" approach, 346
Nicaragua: Afro-Descendant and
  Indigenous Populations, 289(table);
  Covid-19 pandemic, 115; democratic

decline, 105, 112; governance indicators, 448(table); human development indicators, 449(table); impunity rate, 125; international response to the Ortega government, 223; literary modernism, 404; revolution, 85–86; rise of nationalist leftists, 102; Russian connections, 225; Somoza's ouster, 207; US military intervention, 95–96, 199

Nobel Prize, 104, 279, 329, 405–406, 410, 412

Noriega, Manuel, 209

"normal" schools, 308

North American Free Trade Agreement (NAFTA): agribusiness, 246; global integration, 209–210; Indigenous protests, 110–111; McOndo literature, 413; Mexico's capital flows, 174; regional economic integration, 187; threatening maize production, 230; women in the labor force, 319–320

Northern Triangle, 121, 131, 136–137, 437, 441–442, 446

nuclear proliferation, 214

nueva canción, 424–426, 431

Núñez de Pineda y Bascuñán, Francisco, 395

Obama, Barack, 211–212, 218–220

Obeah, 36

Obregón, Álvaro, 78

oil production: Brazil's oil reserves, 224; Brazil's Petrobras, 179; Chávez's oil diplomacy, 106; environmental impacts, 236–237; export production linkages, 151; Indigenous protests, 110–111; Mexico's nationalization, 67, 78, 200; petroleum boom, 153; Venezuela, 25; Venezuela's income redistribution, 176

oil shock, 166–172, 205

Olmec civilization, 145

Olmedo, José Joaquín, 400

One Hundred Years of Solitude (García Marquez), 412–413, 418–419

one-drop rule, 267

Operation Bootstrap, 319–320

Organization of American States (OAS), 101–102, 107, 202, 203(fig.), 223–224

Organization of Petroleum Exporting Countries (OPEC), 166

organized crime, 437–438

Ortega, Daniel, 102, 105, 112

Ortega y Gasset, José, 406–407

oversight: police reforms, 129

Oviedo, Gonzalo Fernández de, 394

oxisols, 23

Pachakutik National Unity Movement, 111

Pacific, War of the, 73

Padilla, Ignacio, 411, 414

Páez, José Antonio, 70

Palés Matos, Luis, 410

Palma, Ricardo, 403, 408

Palmares, Independent Republic of, 233

pampas (grass plains), 17–18, 76–77, 234, 401

Panama, 174(fig.); Afro-Descendant and Indigenous Populations, 289(table); governance indicators, 448(table); Hispanic transformation, 44; human development indicators, 449(table); Spanish conquest, 40; US invasion, 209; women's labor force participation, 313(table)

Panama Papers corruption scandal, 137–138

Pan-Americanism, 199

Paraguay: Afro-Descendant and Indigenous Populations, 289(table); Chaco War, 74; Covid-19 pandemic, 440; governance indicators, 448(table); human development indicators, 449(table); independence from Spain, 61–62; Lugo's impeachment, 116; Spanish conquest, 41; War of the Triple Alliance, 73, 197–198

Parra, Violeta, 425

Paternain, Alejandro, 411

patriarchal ideology: feminist critiques, 328; Iberian origins, 91–92, 94; limiting lesbians' political activity, 309–310; women's roles in the family, 301–303

Patterson, Orlando, 417

Pauls, Alan, 413

Paz, Octavio, 405

Paz Soldán, Edmundo, 413

Pelé, 282
Peña Nieto, Enrique, 132
Pentecostals, 373, 377–381, 383–385, 389
Perón, Isabel, 88
Perón, Juan, 80, 88, 158
personalism, 436
personality cult, Venezuela's, 104
Peru: annexation of Ecuador, 60–61; border wars, 74–75; changing gender values, 325(table); Columbian Exchange, 230; conquest chronicles, 393; Covid-19 response, 440; displaced Venezuelans, 249; early colonial revolts, 51–52; economic development and income distribution, 152–153; educational innovation, 347; European disease, 147–148; governance indicators, 448(table); heterodox economic policy, 171–172; human development indicators, 449(table); independence from Spain, 61; Indigenous politicians, 111; inequality by skin color group, 293(table); insurrection against Spain, 44; Japanese immigrants, 32; leftist military coup, 162; liberation theology, 372; literary identity, 403; magical realism in literature, 408; military regime, 83–84; multicultural literature, 410; natural resources, 25; neoliberal multiculturalism, 287; police training, 138; pre-Columbian economic life, 144; prison conditions, 133–134; prosecuting human rights abuses, 100–101; rebellion against Bourbon rule, 149; Spanish conquest, 40–41, 393; Spanish Inquisition, 46; war debt, 65; women's labor force participation, 314(table), 316; women's status under mercantilism, 306–307
peso crisis (Mexico), 174–176
pesticide poisoning, 240–241
Petrobras, 179, 224
Petróleos de Venezuela Sociedad Anónima (PDVSA), 176
physical geography, 14–24
Piazolla, Astor, 427–428
Pink Tide, 190
Pinochet, Augusto: avoiding prosecution for human rights violations, 211; disappeared individuals and extrajudicial killings, 100; economic policy, 165; military coup, 85, 89; political music, 425; political ouster, 207; testimonial narratives, 412; US military intervention, 95
pirates, 149, 396–397
Pizarro, Francisco, 40–41
Plan Colombia, 220
plantation economies: Brazil's gold rush, 148; environmental degradation, 231–233; racial mixing, 273–274; war debt, 65–66
Plata Basin, 17
plate tectonics, 14–17
Platt Amendment (1901), 199–200
pluralism, religious, 382–383
poetry, 397–401, 404, 410
police: Brazil's racial injustice, 5; community-oriented policing, 125–126, 140–142; criminal involvement, 121; criminal justice system failure, 132–134; demilitarization, 125; eradicating opposition in Nicaragua, 112; government policy control, 127–132; inadequate capacity, 126–127; increased training, 138
police brutality, 127
political culture: authoritarian rule alternating with democracy, 93–98; Iberian origins, 91–92
political music, 424–426
political parties, underdevelopment of, 117–118
political reform: Mexico, 77
political representation, neoliberal multiculturalism and, 292–293
politics: anti-clerical regimes, 371; border wars, 72–75; Brazil's military regime, 87; Catholic Church governance, 368–369; the Church's transnational political influence, 196; citizen inclusion and empowerment, 109–111; conservative Catholicism, 375–377; democratic transition, 98–102; environmental policy, 242; evangelical voters and leaders, 378; expansion of schooling, 343–344; feminist movements, 327–328; fight against secularization, 382–383; Haitian Tonton Macoutes, 388;

Hispanic transformation, 44; identity politics in independent Latin America, 272–276; increasing corruption, 435–437; intermestic politics, 187–188; international relations during the Cold War, 201–204; liberal-conservative tensions, 69–71; literary depictions of the Argentine consciousness, 401; literary modernism, 404–405; Mexican Revolution, 77–79; mixed-gender movements, 328–330; moving towards global integration, 209–210; nationalist leftists, 102–109; Pentecostal social involvement, 380–381; Pope Francis's popularity, 377–378; popular perceptions, 1–2; post-independence fragmentation, 60–62; post-independence philosophy, 150; progressive Catholicism, 372–376; reforms and stability, 1870-1910s, 71; spectrum of political values, 108–109; spread of Covid-19, 3–4; women's movements, 327–328, 330–335; women's representation, 297–299, 308–311, 326–335

Ponte Estratégia, 115
popular culture, 418–421
popular music, 428–432
population, 26; colonial-era environmental degradation and demographic change, 230–233; effects of migration, 248–249; Iberian expansion, 28–29; the nexus of environmental and social problems, 242–249

populism: Bolivia and Ecuador, 221–222; candidate selection reinforcing, 436; challenging education policy, 363–364; economic populism, 163–164; effects of Covid-19, 3; evangelical Protestantism and, 445; information operations influencing elections, 115; populist economy, 176; populist presidents, 108–109; response to Covid-19, 247

Popul-Vuh (Mayan "Bible"), 391
Porfiriato (Mexico), 154
Portales, Diego, 70–71
Portuguese rule in Brazil, 11, 47–50; economic life, 149–150;

environmental degradation, 231; resource extraction and mercantilism, 13. *See also* Brazil; colonial rule
positivism, 272–273
Posse, Abel, 395
post-independence states: economic life and structures, 150–156
post-racial society, Brazil as, 5
poverty and poor populations: colonial origins of, 92; conversions to Protestantism, 379; Covid-19 pandemic, 4, 246–247; economic indicators, 438; effects of the debt crisis, 168; environmental degradation, 8, 23; evangelical Protestants, 383; heterodox economic theory, 171–172; impact and targets of crime, 7; Morales's transformation of Bolivia, 107; Pentecostal belief structures, 380–381; progressive Catholicism addressing, 372–375; progressive leaders addressing, 102–103; racial and ethnic inequalities, 290–291, 444; rates by ethnic group, 292(table); spiritist religions, 386–388; urbanization and the environment, 253. *See also* low-income communities

power relations: determining ethnic identity, 261–262
pre-Columbian era: economic life, 144–146; environmental systems, 228–230; religion and politics, 367; spiritist religions, 386–388
Preserving Biodiversity, Treaty on, 213
presidential removal, 116
presidential systems, 91–92
Prieto, Rodrigo, 421
"Primero Sueño" (Sor Juana), 399
prison: criminal justice process, 133–134; penal reform, 138–139
private security sector, 134
privatization: Brazil, 178–179
production: the basis of class position, 268; effect of colonization on women's status, 306–308; export production linkages, 151–153; import substitution industrialization, 157–158; Marx defining class, 261–262; Spanish mining, 148; women's roles and identities, 300–304

production effect of economic booms, 148–149
Progressive Catholicism, 372
proportional representation rules, 117–118
prosecutorial power, increasing, 132–133
protest: Africans resisting enslavement, 31; Brazil's racial injustice, 5; ethnic protest against neoliberalism, 286; film and literature, 418; *Madres de la Plaza de Mayo,* 299, 333; against NAFTA, 210; *nueva canción* and political music, 424–426
Protestantism: challenging Church authority, 371; charismatic renewal movements, 385; Church support of, 385; growth and self-identification, 381–383, 389–390; increasing presence of, 378–381; jazz music, 422; political stance, 373; secularization and, 383; syncretic religion, 35–36
Puente, Tito, 432
Puenzo, Luis, 418
Puerto Rico: Latin jazz, 432; Latinx writers, 415–416; multicultural literature, 410; US acquisition, 199; women in the labor force, 308, 319–320
Puig, Manuel, 418
Pulitzer Prize, 415(fig.)
pull factors in labor economics, 318, 322
push factors in labor economics, 318

quilombos (runaway slaves), 31, 233, 258–259
quinoa production, 25
quipus (Inca account strings), 392
Quiroga, Horacio, 405
Quiteira de Jesús, Maria, 309

race and racism: Brazil's Black-consciousness movement, 282–283; colonial legacy, 5–6; defining ethnicity and race, 260–261, 296(n1); group identities, 8; regional human geography, 36–37; scientific, 272–273; soccer incidents, 264–266; socially constructing, 266–268. *See also* Afro-Latin Americans; Indigenous populations
rachadinha (financial corruption), 114

racial categorization: Brazil, 282–283; neoliberal multiculturalism and the politics of recognition, 285–294; race as a social construction, 261; racial mixing, 30–31, 267–268, 271; shifting terminology, 277, 288–289, 292
racial democracy, 258, 273–274, 282, 291
racial extermination, 52
racial injustice, 4–5
racial mixing, 30–33, 266–268, 270–275
racial purity, 266–267
racial slavery, 270
railroads, 66, 159
rainforests, 443
Ramirez, Ariel, 425
Ramos, Graciliano, 417
Rayuela (Cortázar), 409
raza cósmica (Mexico), 344
Reagan administration, 95–96, 207
real estate bubble, 175
realism: international relations perspective, 191–192
realist fiction, 406–407
rebellions: against Bourbon rule, 149; early colonial revolts, 51–52; the history of Latin American education, 339–344; Indigenous women's opposition movements, 308–309; ousting Mexico's Díaz, 77; Portuguese Empire in Brazil, 59; the wars against Spain, 54–58
recognition, politics of, 285–294
regulatory quality, 447
religion: colonial imposition of Catholicism, 35–36; colonial legacy, 11; conversion of native populations, 46, 75–76; liberation theology, 331–332, 372–377, 379, 426, 434(n3); maroon spiritism, 31–32; *nueva canción* music, 425–426; Pentecostal belief structures, 380; the role of higher education, 355–356; secularization, 381–384; spiritism, 31–32, 42–43, 386–388; syncretism, 35–36; women's roles in the family, 301–302; the writings of Sor Juana, 398–399. *See also* Catholic Church; Protestantism
remittances, 34, 219
Renaissance ideals: education, 357

reproduction: women in the labor force, 322–324; women's political realms, 326–327; women's roles and identities, 300–304
Rerum Novarum (Rights and Duties of Capital and Labor), 372
resistance movements, women's participation in, 328–329
resource extraction: European mercantilism, 147; impact on maroon societies, 31–32. *See also* mining and mineral wealth; oil production
resource nationalism, 102
resources, human, 262
Restrepo, Laura, 413
revolutionary nationalism: Chile's democratic experiment, 84–85; Cuban Revolution, 81–83; Mexican Revolution, 77–79; Nicaraguan revolution, 85–86; Peru, 83–84; women's support of, 328–329
Revueltas, Silvestre, 427
Rhys, Jean, 418
rights, civil and political: neoliberal multiculturalism, 285
right-wing movements, 257–258
Rio Bravo, 18
Rio Treaty, 217
Rios Montt, Efrain, 378
rising sea levels, 241
river basins, 17–21
Rivera Garza, Cristina, 413
Robinson Country Intelligence Index, 297–298, 336(n1), 446
Roca, Julio, 76
rock music, 432
Rodó, José Enrique, 405
Rodriguez, Robert, 2
Rodríguez Freyle, Juan, 396, 398
Roosevelt, Franklin D., 200
Roosevelt, Theodore, 92, 198–199, 405
Rosa, João Guimarães, 417
Rosas, Juan Manuel, 70, 76, 400–401
Rossi, Marcelo, 384–385
Rousseff, Dilma, 108, 290
Ruiz de Alarcón, Juan, 399
Rulfo, Juan, 409, 419
rural areas: civil society-state engagement in education, 354–355; educational access and completion, 352; expanding access to schools, 346; women's employment, 312–313;

women's status under colonial rule, 307–308
Russia: foreign policy involvement, 225

Sab (Gómez de Avellaneda), 402
Salavarrieta, Policarpa, 309
salsa music, 426, 430, 432
San Martín, José de, 57
Sánchez, Luis Rafael, 416
Sandinista National Liberation Front (FSLN), 85–86, 95–96, 105, 374
Santa Cruz, Andrés, 61, 71
Santana, Carlos, 432, 433(fig.)
Santería, 388
Santiago, Esmeralda, 419
Santo Domingo: Church concerns over religious pluralism, 383; US occupation of Florida, 62. *See also* Dominican Republic
Santos, Juan Manuel, 104
Sarmiento, Domingo Faustino, 342, 401
satirical literature, 397–398
science education, 345, 356, 361–362
scientific racism, 272–273
Sea of Lentils (Beníto Rojo), 411–412
sea-level rise, 21
secondary education: inequality in educational access and completion, 352–354, 353(fig.); mandatory education, 349
secularization, 371–372, 375, 381–384
self-expressive values, 324–326
Sendero Luminoso (Shining Path; Peru), 100, 209
September 11, 2001, 102
Serros, Michele, 414–415
service sector jobs, women in, 320–321
sex industry, 444
sexuality: constrictions on female sexuality, 309–310; marginalization of women's, 301–304; marketing Brazil's Xuxa, 282; racial mixing, 270; victimization of women under colonial rule, 306–307
shields (landforms), 16–17
Sigüenza y Góngora, Carlos, 396
silver mining, 13, 16, 24–25, 65, 67, 147–149, 230, 251. *See also* mining and mineral wealth
single-party politics, Mexico's, 78
slave rebellions, 53

slavery: agricultural expansion, 230;
Brazil, 48–49, 75–76, 143; Catholic
enslavement of Indigenous peoples,
369; colonial legacy of racism, 5–6;
ethnic terms, 278; history of
education in the Caribbean, 338–339;
importation of Africans, 269; labor
for Spanish mining, 148; Mexico, 76;
racial mixing, 31; Spanish conquest,
39–42; spiritist religion, 386; sugar
production, 30; war debt, 65–66; war
over US expansion, 63–64
slum removal, 252–253
smuggling, 47, 130–131
snowballing, democratic, 98–99
soccer, 264–266
social capital, 262
social change, the role of literature in,
400
Social Darwinism, 272–273
social development, education as an
avenue towards, 348
social embeddedness of crime, 135
social issues: literary modernism,
404–405
social media, divisiveness of, 115
social movements: antiviolence
awareness, 248; environmental
protection, 22; against Mexico's
Porfiriato, 154–155; Pentecostalism,
380–381
social reforms: educational innovation,
347
social spending, 102–103
social stratification: ethnicity and class,
272–273
socialist movements, 95–96; nationalist
leftists, 102; twenty-first-century
socialism, 102
sociedad de castas (caste system),
271–272, 276–277
Somoza regimes, 85, 207, 374
"Sonatina" (Darío), 404
Sor Juana Inés de la Cruz, 398–399
Soviet Union: Cuba's economy, 161;
intervention in El Salvador, 207;
transitions to democracy, 98. See also
Cold War
soybean production, 18, 24
Spanish rule: Bourbons, 50–51;
Columbian Exchange, 29–30;

conquest and enslavement, 39–42;
conquest as imperial destiny, 394;
human geography, 11–12; Napoleon's
threat to, 369–370; resource
extraction and mercantilism, 13,
147–149; the wars against Spain,
54–58. See also conquest
Spanish Succession, War of, 50–51
Spanish-American War, 415
spiritism, 31–32, 42–43, 386–388
squatter movements and settlements, 24,
252–253, 331
St. Marc, Henriette, 309
state agencies and institutions: church-
state separation, 370–371; civil
society-state engagement in
education, 354–355; crime policy
responses, 138–142; criminals
infiltrating, 135; educational
transformation, 345–346; export
revenues, 153; firearms control, 137;
Robinson Country Intelligence Index,
446; role in ethnicity and
nationalism, 262–263
state capture, 447
state failure: failing democracies, 105
state weakness, 436–438
steel production, 159
Stephens, Thomas, 278
Stoll, David, 379, 412
Storni, Alfonsina, 406, 425
street theaters, 418
Stroessner, Alfredo, 206–207
structural adjustment measures, 98, 206,
289–290, 319–320
student movements, 329, 359
Suárez, Luis, 264, 265(fig.)
suffrage, women's, 309–310
sugar production, 30, 33, 48–49, 68, 149,
160, 231
Sumak Kawsay ("Good Living"
concept), 293–294
swine flu, 246
symbolic capital, 262
syncretic music, 421–422, 433
syncretic religion, 36–38, 386, 388–389

Tactical Analysis System (Chile), 141
Taiwan, diplomatic isolation of, 225
tango music, 421–422, 427–428,
430–431

taqui (Incan dance), 392
technology transfer, 214
telenovelas (soap operas), 245
Tenochtitlán: Aztec theater, 392; conquest, 40, 393; decline, 27–28; economic life, 229; population, 146
tequila effect, 174–175
term limits, presidential: *continuismo,* 116–117; Morales's outlawing of Bolivia's, 106–107; Nicaragua's Ortega eliminating, 105
territorial disputes: Andean region, 185–187; border wars, 72–75; Falkland Islands, 88, 207–208; post-independence claims, 45; War of the Triple Alliance, 197–198
terrorism: international relations, 215–216; Latin America's global integration, 187; US use of Guantanamo Bay, 217–218
testimonial narratives, 412
theater culture, 392, 397–399, 418
tierra fria (colder lands), 20
tierra templata (temperate lands), 19–20
Tjader, Cal, 432
Toledo, Alejandro, 37
Tonton Macoutes, 388
topography, economic development and, 151
Tordesillas, Treaty of, 27
Torres Bodet, Jaime, 344
tourism, 38, 229, 240
trade: British incursions into Latin America, 59, 63; Chile's deficit, 165; China's role in, 217, 224–225; commodity lottery, 150–151; Cuba, 161; the debt crisis and the Washington Consensus, 170–171; dependency theory analysis, 194–195; Dutch Disease, 148–149; expansion of colonial powers, 2–3; increasing regional economic integration, 187; industrial revolution, 66–68; natural resource extraction, 13; oil shock, 166–172; political reforms, 71–72; pre-Columbian economic life, 145; war debt, 65
trade embargoes: US embargo in Cuba, 83; US embargo in Nicaragua, 95
trade liberalization, 170–171
trade unions, Church support of, 372

"Tradiciones Peruanas" (Palma), 408
transitional justice: legacy of military repression, 99–100
translatinas (transnational firms), 177–179, 183
transnational networks, 33–34
transnationalization: of cuisine, 3; diffusion of Latino culture, 13
trash recycling, 253
trigueño (color categorization), 267, 277
Trinidad: Caribbean literature, 418
Triple Alliance, War of (1864–1870), 73, 197–198
tropical zones, climate of, 19
Trump, Donald, 115, 211–212, 218
truth commissions, 99–100
Túpac Amaru II, 52
Tupac Amaru Revolutionary Movement (Peru), 100
"Twelve Apostles," 172

Ubico, Jorge, 82
Umbanda, 36, 386–388
UN Declaration of the Rights of Indigenous Peoples (2007), 286
UN Economic Commission for Latin America in Chile, 348
UN International Women's Year Conference, 327
UN Security Council, 192–193, 193(fig.)
United Fruit Company, 82, 95, 155
United Kingdom: Falkland Islands dispute, 88, 186, 207–208; funding economic development, 198
United Nations: new international economic order, 205–206
United Nations Decade for Women, 327
United Nations Educational, Science, and Cultural Organization (UNESCO), 344–347, 352–353
United Provinces of Central America, 197
United States: aggression against Spanish America, 62; anticommunist policy in Latin America, 94–96; arms trafficking, 136–137; Bolivia's institutional reforms, 128; Brazil's industrialization, 159; Chávez's resistance to, 222; Cold War-era international relations, 201–204; colonial legacy of racism, 5–6;

consolidation of strong Latin governments, 71; constructing race, 267; contemporary Cuban relations, 219–220; Cuba's economic model, 160; dependency theory analysis of Latin America, 195; drug initiatives, 220–221; emerging market economies, 173; free trade agreements, 171; fruit and sugar markets, 68; Gini coefficient, 182, 290; Guatemalan coup, 280; higher education methods and ideals, 356–359; increasing investment in Latin America, 155; independence, 53; Indian refugees, 76; intervention in Nicaragua, 85–86; interventions in Latin America, 94–96, 186–187, 198–200; Latin American immigration, 210–211; Latin American structural adjustment measures, 98; Latin America's educational development, 340–341; Latin music, 432–433; Latinx ties, 33–34; as literary point of reference, 405; Mexican gang violence, 112–113; migration from Mexico, 248–249; Monroe Doctrine, 92; music and film influences, 1–2; neocolonial control of Latin America, 92–93; oil shock, 166–167; population figures, 26; post-boom literary evolution, 410; questioning Bolivia's elections, 107–108; realist perspective of international relations, 191–192; resisting the hegemony of, 216–219; the role of religion in higher education, 355–356; supporting democratic governments, 98–99; syncretic music, 422; using immigration for racial purification, 274; war in Iraq, 215–216; war with Mexico, 63–64

United States–Mexico–Canada Agreement (USMCA), 187
universal human right, education as, 337–339, 344–347, 349–352
urban primacy, 251–252
urban zones: Brazil's inequalities, 143; Colombia's community-oriented policing, 140–141; Covid-19 pandemic, 246–247; environmental issues associated with, 21–24; expanding police forces, 131; Indigenous Pentecostalism, 379–380; population demographics, 38; population figures, 26; spread of disease, 443; women's employment, 312–313; women's labor struggles, 329

urbanization: declining fertility rates, 243; environmental and demographic changes, 249–256; environmental impacts on health, 245–248; industrialization and export expansion, 68; the role in crime, 123–124; watershed degradation, 18
Uribe, Álvaro, 45, 117
Uruguay: Afro-Descendant and Indigenous Populations, 289(table); changing gender values, 325(table); democratic transition, 98–99; European commercialization of, 234; governance indicators, 448(table); human development indicators, 449(table); literary modernism, 405; racist soccer incidents, 264–266; War of the Triple Alliance, 73, 197–198; women's labor force participation, 314(table)
US Agency for International Development (USAID), 194, 346–347

vaccine diplomacy, 225–226
Valdivia, Pedro de, 41
Vargas, Getulio, 80, 159
Vargas Llosa, Mario, 409, 412
Vasconcelos, José, 276
Vatican II, 372
Velasco Alvarado, Juan, 83–84, 162–163, 347
Venezuela: Afro-Descendant and Indigenous Populations, 289(table); centralization of police, 132; classical music, 428; Covid-19 pandemic, 445; Cuba's trading partners, 161; democratic decline, 106; displaced persons, 249; electoral integrity, 436; emigration, 13, 33; expanding police forces, 131; falling poverty rates, 103; foreign investment, 179; governance indicators, 448(table); the

history of Latin American education, 339–341; human development indicators, 449(table); IACHR cases, 189–190; increasing migration from, 437; international response to the Maduro government, 223; liberal democracy, 94; North-South economic dialogue, 205–206; oil shock and debt crisis, 183; organized crime, 438; police reform, 129–130; religious syncretism, 388–389; resistance to neoliberalism, 102; Russian connections, 225; Spanish conquest, 40, 56–57; tensions with Colombia, 185; urban decentralization, 254; urbanization and crime, 123; US intervention, 187; war debt, 65; the wars against Spain, 54, 57; women's labor force participation, 314(table), 316

vernacular music, 428–432

vigilantism, 125

Villa, Francisco "Pancho," 199

Villa-Lobos, Heitor, 426, 427(fig.)

violence: cause of death, 248; domestic, 445; against environmental activists, 138; erosion of citizen security, 121–122; against LGBTQ individuals, 444–445

Vodou, 36, 388

volcanoes, 16

Volpi, Jorge, 411, 414

Walcott, Derek, 418

Washington Consensus, 98, 108–109, 170, 173, 176–177

water resources, 17–21, 245–246

whiteness, 266–267, 270–271, 273–274

women and girls: access to education, 352; Brazil's Xuxa, 281–282; Caribbean literature, 418; changing fertility rates, 243–245; domestic violence, 445; educational attainment, 320–322, 324; feminist movements, 327–328; historical novels, 411; labor force activity during the lost decade, 318–320; in Latin American history, 304–311; Latinx writers, 414–415; *Madres de la Plaza de Mayo,* 299, 333; *maquiladora* industry, 299–300, 319–320; Mexican gang violence, 112–113; mixed-gender movements, 328–330; obstacles to formal employment, 323–324; political empowerment, 109; political representation, 326–335; Pope Francis's stance, 377–378; population figures, 26; post-boom literary evolution, 410; production, reproduction, roles, and identities, 300–304; religious identities of poor women, 376; rise in labor force activity, 315–318; the role of marginalization in crime, 122–123; self-expressive and emancipative values, 324–326; sexual purity and racial purity, 270; writers of realist fiction, 406–407; the writings of Sor Juana, 398–399; Zika virus, 246–247

women's movements, 327–328, 330–335

Workers Party (Brazil), 177–178

World War I, 79, 155

World War II, 94–95, 155, 200–201

Xuxa, 281–282

Yaqui societies, 76

youth: Colombia's community-oriented policing, 140–141; El Salvador's security policy, 140; homicide deaths, 122–123, 248

Yupanqui, Atahualpa, 424

Zapata, Emiliano, 154–155

Zapatista National Liberation Army (EZLN), 188, 210

Zapatista revolt, 174

Zelaya, Manuel, 188

zero tolerance policies, 128–129

Zika virus, 246–247

About the Book

This new edition of *Understanding Contemporary Latin America,* the first under the editorship of Henry (Chip) Carey, reflects the many changes that have occurred in the region in the decade since the previous edition was published. An entirely new chapter on crime and security, along with new treatments of such classic subjects as geography, history, politics, economics, international relations, and more, make for an unparalleled introduction to the complexities of Latin America today.

Henry (Chip) Carey is associate professor of political science at Georgia State University.